C0063 55773

D1142151

A
REVOLUTION
OF
FEELING

Also by Rachel Hewitt

Map of a Nation:
A Biography of the Ordnance Survey

A
REVOLUTION
OF
FEELING

The Decade that Forged
the Modern Mind

RACHEL HEWITT

GRANTA

Granta Publications, 12 Addison Avenue, London W11 4QR

First published in Great Britain by Granta Books 2017

Copyright © Rachel Hewitt 2017

Rachel Hewitt has asserted her moral right
under the Copyright, Designs and Patents Act, 1988,
to be identified as the author of this work.

The illustration credits on pp. 532–533 constitute
an extension of this copyright page.

All rights reserved.
This book is copyright material and must not be copied,
reproduced, transferred, distributed, leased, licensed or publicly
performed or used in any way except as specifically permitted in writing
by the publisher, as allowed under the terms and conditions under
which it was purchased or as strictly permitted by applicable
copyright law. Any unauthorized distribution or use of
this text may be a direct infringement of the author's
and publisher's rights, and those responsible
may be liable in law accordingly.

A CIP catalogue record for this book
is available from the British Library.

1 3 5 7 9 10 8 6 4 2

ISBN 978 1 84708 573 3
eISBN 978 1 84708 575 7

Typeset in Caslon by M Rules

Printed and bound by
CPI Group (UK) Ltd, Croydon, CR0 4YY

*For Molly, Martha and Esme
and for Josie Camus (1979–2014)*

CONTENTS

THE AGE OF DESPAIR

ILLUSTRATIONS

Plate Section

Illustrations in Text

Introduction

THE HISTORY OF EMOTION

On 2 November 1804, a thirty-one-year-old woman, Anna, wrote – somewhat playfully, mostly reproachfully – to a friend of her husband, called Davies. He was suffering from self-professed 'mental or moral lethargy' and threatening to 'rob' his local community of his 'society ... forever'. 'Leave your study, & your bees & come to [us]!' Anna exhorted. 'I am half ready to quarrel with you for being so gloomy[;] if I can but once catch hold of you I'll laugh you out of it,' she promised, with tactless cheer. Then her tone grew more serious. Davies had expressed a desire for 'euthanasia'. 'Tell me,' she insisted, 'how you could possibly wish to be without feeling! I cannot reason you out of this, I would not laugh at you yet certainly I think you wrong.' Once, she had considered him 'morally invulnerable'. But now his professions of desire to be 'without feeling' made her doubt.[1]

The conversation was between two people on either side of a cultural gulf. One chirpily considered 'feeling' – even, perhaps especially, pain – as the basis of moral invincibility. For Anna, feeling was a purifying and educational experience. 'Passionate' emotion stemmed from an internal 'feeling of right' and was reined in through conscious efforts to cultivate 'happiness' in human 'society'. Her correspondent, Davies – gloomy, guilt-wracked, suicidal, sensing his own life's significance to be of an 'evanescent quantity to the universe' – wanted nothing from feeling but its cessation. He turned to pharmaceutical remedies like 'digitalis' in his quest for emotional oblivion.

How could two people, so intimate in all other respects, enter-tain such wildly divergent views about emotion: its pleasurable or painful nature, its purpose, its management? An understand-ing of their differing attitudes can be found in the events of the years leading up to their conversation, events which tipped the emotional climate of communities across the British Isles from happiness into melancholy. This book will explore how the final decade of the eighteenth century saw a revolution of feeling in which the emotional culture of Enlightenment Britain collapsed and was replaced by a new approach to feeling and desire. It will excavate the components of that revolution, how it was brought about, and the impact it has had on us today. During the politically turbulent 1790s, history was not just played out in people's feelings; it changed their *feelings about feeling*. Beliefs about emotion – its purpose, its physiology, its management, its desirability – were dramatically overturned in the space of just a decade.

Like ideas, our emotions have a history. Their history is partly personal and idiosyncratic, glimmers of mostly forgotten child-hood experiences; the result of memories that, for Proust's narrator, yoked sensations of 'all-powerful joy' to 'those short, plump little cakes called "petites madeleines"'.[2] At the opposite extreme, the history of emotion has been thought to extend right back to the earliest stages not just of humanity, but of all mammalian life forms. In 1952 the American neuroscientist Paul MacLean claimed that emotion is produced in one of the most evolutionarily ancient parts of the brain – the 'limbic system' – a complex and contested neurological horseshoe in which the amygdala, emotion's command centre, nestles like an ovary, coiled in readiness to release its missives of anger, sadness, or love.[3] Charles Darwin, too, had identified how the bristling of hair during fear was an ancient 'serviceable associated habit' that once rallied a primate's confidence along with the illusion of size; but he thought that same emotional behaviour, transmitted to mostly hairless humans millennia later, had become a redundant tic.[4] And in the 1950s, the developmental psychologist John Bowlby found in babies' abject wails of terror, frustrated gripes, or caws of relieved recognition of their mothers, relics of primitive and 'instinctive' human behaviour that were once traits designed to ensure survival in 'the environment of evolutionary adaptedness': emotion is the mouthpiece through which the wails and chirrups of the primitive savannah sound in the present day.[5]

Emotion's history is not just a narrative of physiological traits passed on through the ages by evolutionary inheritance. Neither is its history confined to the specific life experiences of the individual. Emotion is also produced at the intersection between each person and the culture they inhabit. Different communities, in different countries, at different historical moments, have entertained wildly divergent ideas about emotion: what it is, what it is for, where it originates and how it functions, which particular emotions exist and which are most important, whether and how the emotions could or should be managed, and the language with which feelings are labelled and depicted. There is no universal consensus, either now or historically, even to the simple question 'What is an emotion?' Ideas about emotion, specific to the culture in which we operate, shape each and every one of us, in both our most mundane and our most dramatically transformative encounters with feeling. And the cultural imperatives shaping emotion are closely linked to political priorities: ideas about women's irrational and incontinent temperament are recruited to excuse and justify their under-representation in public life. The history of emotion – the history of changes in attitudes to emotion – presents a novel and startling way of seeing, or feeling, political change.

How do you feel when you feel nervous? Perhaps you become aware of fluttering hands, a pitching sensation in the stomach, the delicate flowering of sweat on the skin, a heart fast and light as a rotary blade; nightmarish visions whipping past the mind's eye of scornful faces and mocking laughter. Maybe you notice a hypersensitive faculty of hearing, ears straining for the sound of the phone; eyes darting to its screen; irritation prickling at interruptions, at competing demands for attention. Perhaps you begin to berate yourself for 'getting in such a state' and turn to cognitive behavioural therapy or mindfulness methods for managing anxiety; take deep, relaxing breaths; or use visualization techniques. If you disclose your state to another person, or to a private journal or on social media, do you use phrases representing yourself as a 'bundle of nerves', with your 'heart in your mouth', 'butterflies in your stomach' or 'breaking out in a cold sweat'? Today writers on emotion generally consider it to be a phenomenon comprised of physiological changes, combined with conscious and unconscious ideas about the emotion's stimulus, and also with ideas about the emotion itself: about its purpose, treatment and the language available to us to clothe it. Every single one of the constituent elements in the experience of nervousness described above is shaped to greater or lesser degree by the society we inhabit. Our emotions are a principal means by which our culture's imperatives are imprinted onto our innermost, most private nooks of experience.

For example, numerous physiological alterations occur during a state of nervousness – but our attention is drawn to some more than others. Neuroscientists today understand the involvement of neurotransmitters and peptides, such as corticotropin-releasing factor, to be major mediators of symptoms of anxiety disorders. But when describing anxiety's symptoms, most laypeople focus instead on tremors, mental distraction, and effects on breathing and bowels: in his novel *The Kite Runner,* Khaled Hosseini fleshes out 'panic' by describing how 'you order your lungs to draw air, NOW, you need air, need it NOW. But your airways ignore you. They collapse, tighten, squeeze, and suddenly you're breathing through a drinking straw'.[6] The precise body parts onto which attention is focused during an emotion alter across space and time. In the Middle Ages in Britain, when many physicians attributed 'the passions' to 'the humours' – chemical changes within the blood – a medical text called *Liber pantegni* classified emotions according to the movement of a 'vital spirit' to or from the heart.[7] In the seventeenth and eighteenth centuries, French and British physicians and philosophers focused on the nervous system's 'cords' as the principal mechanism through which the soul was tugged into emotional reaction: the basis of our contemporary word 'nervous' and hence the eighteenth-century images of nerves with which each chapter of this book begins. And by the nineteenth century, phrenologists and psychologists were predominantly attending to the role of the brain in emotion. Across historical periods, the 'hydraulic theory' of how emotion operates in the body has encouraged adherents to attribute violent passionate outbursts to an accumulation of pressure when a desire is obstructed from reaching satisfaction, or when bodily fluids (for example, semen) are hindered from ejaculation. Today hydraulic theory still infects the English language: we describe the difficulty of containing 'pent up' anger or desire; rage 'simmering' and 'boiling over' after being 'bottled up', 'exploding' into violence, blood 'boiling', sexual frustration 'building up' and needing a 'release'. It urges us to explain away predominantly male frustration and violence with recourse to physiological changes in male bodily fluids, an example of how mainstream ideas about the physiology of emotion may harbour political priorities.

The *purpose* of an emotion, and its 'solution' or treatment, has also been subject to cultural interpretation. Is an emotion a movement of the soul that can turn to, or away from, God, in the shape of obedience and disobedience, and requires strict regulation, as Saint Augustine suggested? Is it an investment in fundamentally meaningless objects and events, which acts as a 'disobedien[ce] to reason' and requires 'dissent' from its impulses, as Stoics advocated?[8] A poisonous mental state clouding and defiling the mind, resulting in unwholesome actions, as Buddhists maintain? A symptom of frustration and deprivation, necessitating social change, as followers of the philosopher Jean-Jacques Rousseau claimed? An external visitation, as the Greek tragedian Aeschylus depicted it? A naturally occurring expression of desire, whose obstruction causes damage, requiring capitulation, as hydraulic theory proposes? All these explanations of the nature and purpose of emotion have been offered at various points and places in history. And even in the same culture there is rarely consensus. One present-day psychiatrist on the Sharecare website defines 'the purpose of anxiety' as to 'tell you that there is something dangerous in your environment' and to motivate you to 'stay and fight, or to run for your life', while another on the same site disagrees, characterizing anxiety as an 'overwhelming' and 'disruptive' disorder that is predominantly pointless and irritating, which may be erased pharmaceutically.[9]

It is the language in which emotion is clothed that opens the clearest view of how cultural attitudes shape our personal experiences of feeling. The very word 'emotion' originally meant a 'movement, disturbance, perturbation', mostly in the form of 'political agitation, civil unrest; a public commotion or uprising'. In 1562, John Shute's English translation of a play by

Andrea Cambini referred to 'the great tumultes and emotiones that were in Fraunce betwene the king and the nobilitie'.[10] Up until the second half of the eighteenth century, emotion chiefly designated political rebellion, and what we would now call emotion was represented instead by a variety of terms including 'passions', 'appetites', 'affections' and 'sentiments'. These denoted emotional variants whose resonances derived from early Christian theology. 'Appetites' roughly translates to the modern ideas of primitive drives, lusts and desires. 'Affections' and 'sentiments' were largely agreed to be feelings regulated by reason or the will; they were voluntary, and were essential to religious and moral behaviour. 'Passions' were both generic and an earthier, more unruly force – the raw material prior to regulation.[11] When the word 'emotion' came into greater currency at the end of the eighteenth century, it maintained its older connotations of riotous disturbance, and signified a negative 'agitation of mind': emotions were rebels against reason which 'brawl with one another and so cause riots and tumults' and 'aspire to unbounded licence and dominion'.[12] As the historian Thomas Dixon points out, the transition from 'passions' to 'emotions' did not just constitute a shift from a more to a less approving attitude to emotion. In the course of that transition, the old varied, nuanced categories of 'affections' and 'sentiments' were erased in the shadow of the monolithic new term 'emotion'. At the cusp of the nineteenth century the patron, pottery heir, photographer and would-be pedagogue Thomas Wedgwood would designate 'emotion' as 'new nomenclature in treating an old science', which 'seems intended to express only one class of sensations'.[13] The cultural shift in emotion arguably ushered in a less subtle attitude, stripping the 'passions' and 'affections' of their religious connotations.

Linguistic changes regarding emotion are visible not just in general terminology, but in the specific repertoire of individual emotions that particular societies recognize, value or suppress.

Disgust, anger, fear, happiness, sadness, surprise have been called 'primary' or 'basic' emotions, for their apparent ubiquity across countries and historical periods. They translate easily, denoting similar physiological symptoms and cultural resonances wherever they are employed. But many emotions are not so translatable, across either historical or geographical space. When a language provides a label and definition for an emotion, it is because the culture values that emotion enough to encourage its recognition and promote its discussion. English offers a plethora of near-synonyms for embarrassment: discomfiture, awkwardness, mortification, shame, humility, uneasiness, self-consciousness. The linguistic abundance mirrors the significance to British culture of propriety, decorum, politeness and respectability. The Gaelic word *sgriob* denotes 'itchiness on the upper lip before taking a sip of whisky'. Although the same physiological symptom may exist in non-Gaelic-speaking countries, it does not have a distinct label in places where whisky-drinking is not so highly prized or analysed. Welsh *hiraeth* has been defined as 'homesickness tinged with grief or sadness over the lost or departed, and the earnest desire for the Wales of the past'.[14] *Hiraeth* shares some of the same physiological traits that the English language classifies under the term 'homesickness' or French under *nostalgie* – fatigue, nausea, insomnia – but *hiraeth*'s reliance on culturally specific ideas about Welsh history and landscape makes it literally untranslatable into other languages.[15]

The contemporary artist Pei-Ying Lin has created maps of more 'untranslatable emotions', showing how they can only be described in other languages by proximity or distance from existing emotions, but not mapped directly onto those terms. Portuguese *saudade*, 'a somewhat melancholic feeling of incompleteness', can only be approximated to the Anglo-American experience of 'yearning'. Russian *tocka*, an 'ache of soul, a longing with nothing to long for', is triangulated between English 'melancholy', 'depression' and 'longing': it is a highly culturally specific mental mirror of the simultaneously claustrophobic and agoraphobic vastness of the Russian physical expanse.[16] Lin positions Dutch *gezelligheid* – the 'comfort and coziness of being at home, with friends, with loved ones, or general togetherness' – between English 'togetherness', 'joy' and 'satisfaction'. Czech *litost* (torment resulting from the sudden sight of one's own misery), German *Schadenfreude* (pleasure derived from somebody else's misfortune) and Filipino *gigil* (the urge to squeeze something cute), all reflect priorities unique to the country and historical period from which they emerged.[17] The importance of language in valuing or suppressing particular emotions is played out in every single emotional experience we recognize ourselves as having, and, indeed, also in those experiences of which we remain oblivious, or do not have at all. As the German social psychologist Erich Fromm put it, 'an experience rarely comes into awareness for which the language has no word'.[18] Who, among non-Gaelic speakers, has been alert to that faint upper-lip prickle, as the dram of whisky hovers on the cusp of the mouth? Most are not. Is its failure to arise a symptom of physiological difference, or of the lack of the vocabulary necessary to accord the experience a place on the throne of conscious recognition?

Even within the same culture, there is rarely ideological consensus about what emotion is, what it is for, where and how it operates in the body. But similar *questions* do tend to be asked about emotion within a single community, at a precise moment in time. Debates tend to be centred around agreed focal points. In the second half of eighteenth-century Britain, many who thought and wrote about the passions asked questions about the emotional character of 'primitive man': whether humans in the 'state of nature' were either innately 'benevolent' and 'sociable', or fundamentally 'independent' and self-sufficient, or whether they were driven by 'self-interested' and violent, antisocial, acquisitive 'instincts' and 'lusts'. Did 'civilisation' thwart and corrupt natural 'benevolence', or did it impose salutary 'regulations' on violent, self-interested drives? Philosophers and novelists wondered about the relationship between individual passions and 'sociable' behaviour, and how people might be persuaded to reconcile their 'self-love' with the deprivations essential to community: were 'sympathy' and 'benevolence' acquired skills or the results of a 'common sense' or *sensus communis*? Were systems of emotional 'regulation' more effective if the incentive was acquisition of 'religious virtue', or social 'praise', 'fame' and 'reward'? Some philosophers maintained the seventeenth-century habit of listing and categorizing emotions: René Descartes, for example, had defined 'love' as a passion directed towards an object conceived to be personally beneficial, and the French painter and art theorist Charles Le Brun had produced a catalogue of emotive facial expressions in his *Méthode pour apprendre à dessiner les passions [Method for Learning to Draw the Passions]*, four of which appear at the beginning of each section of this book.[19] In the eighteenth century, a similar type of categorization was frequently used to determine which sentiments were especially important to 'sociability', and many wondered how 'sympathy' and 'pity' served to 'transmit' feeling between individuals. Some political writers queried how the passions related to material inequalities. A few paralleled emotional exchanges to economic ones, and advocated systems of emotional 'regulation' in comparable terms to financial controls.

Many of these eighteenth-century debates, questions and the linguistic conventions in which they are couched are entirely alien to those who think about emotion in twenty-first-century Britain and America. Today, we tend to ask questions about whether 'repression' or 'liberation' of 'emotion' – 'letting it all hang out' – is more 'psychologically healthy'. Popular websites encourage us to ask, 'How do I feel?' and, 'How do I know?'; and provide strategies for those who seek to 'manage' their emotions, feelings, mood-swings, desires and libido'.[20] Mainstream approaches to emotion coalesce around particular feelings or moods: stress, tension, anxiety, anger, love, depression, and happiness. We might discuss whether emotional 'management' is aimed at individual 'wellbeing' or 'social harmony'; and talk in terms of 'mental health', and 'therapies' that are provided as solutions to individual 'disorders' and 'problems'. We might debate the efficacy of therapies such as mindfulness, cognitive behavioural therapy, primal scream therapy, psychoanalysis, Gestalt therapy and so on. Many ask questions about the gendered nature of emotion: whether men are 'from Mars', and are more emotionally inarticulate and repressed than women, and whether this leads to worse mental health and more prevalent suicidal ideation? And whether 'women are from Venus', and if their irrational and incontinent emotionality might disqualify them from apparently rational pursuits such as politics and economics. Debates about nature versus nurture are familiar topics within the contemporary discussion of emotion: whether traumatic childhood memories create damaged psyches, or whether maternal attachment can foster secure personalities.

The profound alteration in the vocabulary of emotion that took place between the eighteenth century and the present day is reflected in this book's subtitle: 'the decade that forged the modern mind'. In this context, 'mind' is a shorthand for 'emotional landscape', pointing to forces responsible for constructing temperament that are larger than the individual. Eighteenth-century writers might have deployed 'manners' instead: a term with a capacious meaning, signifying at once 'habitual behaviour or conduct', 'the conditions of society' and 'the moral code of a society'. But in the present day, as emotion has become depoliticized, our usage of 'manners' has shrunk to denote mostly 'outward bearing, deportment; a person's characteristic style of attitude, gesture, or speech,' losing the word's wider allusion to the socioeconomic order.[21] Unlike in the eighteenth century, in twenty-first-century Anglo-American culture our language of emotion has no single word to adequately convey how emotion is produced at the intersection of internal *and* external causes and effects. 'Mind' reflects the focus on the individual, on psychology and on the brain that emerged after the collapse of eighteenth-century attitudes to emotion.

As the starkly different cultural attitudes and conversations about feeling in eighteenth-century and contemporary Britain demonstrate, emotional cultures could change, and fast. New words for emotion in general, and for specific feelings, could come to the fore; new repertoires of emotion could be generated and paradigm shifts could occur in medical theories about the origin and operation of the passions in the body. Precisely such a revolution of feeling took place in the last decade of the eighteenth century. In 1791, the reactionary politician Edmund Burke was attributing the very survival of society to the 'subject[ion]' of 'the inclinations of men' and of 'their passions', whilst also defending the 'complicated mass of human passions' as 'refractions and reflections' of 'primitive' man, and therefore possessed of a 'natural' ability to 'instruct our reason'.[22] Burke reflected a widespread assumption in the eighteenth century that the passions were avowedly political. By the 1790s, many writers had come to conceive of the passions as responses to satisfaction or frustration, eloquent witnesses to deprivation and inequality, stimulants to potentially revolutionary behaviour; they believed that emotional 'regulation' paralleled political methods of policing the populace's behaviour. But by the end of the decade, in 1800, the poet William Wordsworth would describe how 'emotion' was produced by 'recollection in tranquillity' of an earlier 'emotion', which gradually produced a kindred feeling 'by a species of reaction ... in the mind', eroding tranquillity and leading to 'the spontaneous overflow of powerful feelings' in the form of 'poetry'.[23] In Wordsworth's formulation, the origins and expressions of emotion all took place in the individual's mind, memory and imagination, set at a remove from material history. This was a new – and, for many, a strange – emotional landscape.

As Burke's statements indicated, eighteenth-century writers optimistically insisted on the passions' political relevance, their importance to 'sociability' and reform, and the revolutionary motivating force of 'hope'. In place of this emotional culture a new mindset emerged at the beginning of the nineteenth century, designated an 'age of despair' by the poet Percy Bysshe Shelley.[24] Accommodation and adaptation was emphasized instead of political reform or revolution; caution, guilt, sin and 'atonement' in place of hope; emotion was approached as an individual rather than collective phenomenon; and the category of 'passions' was replaced by that of 'emotion', ushering in a depoliticized and frequently negative view of feeling. Attitudes to emotion shine a light onto cultural imperatives, and that revolution of feeling at the end of the Enlightenment was bound up with dramatic shifts in gender relations, political protest, economic theory and theological beliefs.

The revolution of feeling in 1790s Britain was deeply enmeshed with a more tangible revolution: the French Revolution, and the corresponding hopes for imminent radical change that it stimulated across the Channel. In the climate of heady optimism following the fall of the Bastille on 14 July 1789, the 1790s saw political radicals take Enlightenment hopes for the passions' political significance to their apotheosis. In pamphlets, in flourishing popular political societies, and in individual and shared projects, radicals described how utopian communities might eradicate 'unsocial passions', and how schemes for redistributing property and wealth would necessarily entail the redistribution of emotional 'attachments' too (for example, replacing the institution of marriage with polygamous alternatives). But for such radical proponents of the passions' political potential, the decade would prove disappointing in its fullest sense. The French Revolution's unpredicted course, and the British administration's unfavourable response to radicals' and reformers' desires, did not just bring about the collapse of specific hopeful projects; it resulted, for many, in *disappoint-ment* in its earliest meaning of deprivation and dispossession.[25] As the political climate turned increasingly reactionary, many radicals lost everything: they were deprived and dispossessed of employment, liberty, even life. And that disappointment did not just change the way they felt, launching thousands of men and women from hope to despair: it changed the way that they felt about feeling. The collapse of the British reform movement was counterpointed by the erosion of optimistic views about history's direction towards 'perfectibility', the benevolent nature of liberated passion, and emotion's motivating force for change.

Edmund Burke designated 'the most important of all revolu-tions' in the 1790s to be that 'revolution in sentiments'.[26] This book will narrate that cultural revolution in emotion through the lives of five initial optimists in the 1790s: the young poet Samuel Taylor Coleridge, the philosophers William Godwin and Mary Wollstonecraft, the physician Thomas Beddoes and the first photographer, Thomas Wedgwood. At first they sought to reform sex, education, commerce, marriage, politics and medi-cine by focusing on emotional change. But by the decade's end, they were entertaining dramatically different conceptions of feeling: some disowned their former views; others shrugged off their hope for the realization of change.

The transition from hope to fruition – or to disappointment – is rarely clear or swift. Hopes are gambles. They are expressions of optimism about the likelihood of objectives being fulfilled. And the nature of hope wavers between confidence and uncer-tain doubt according to changes in the political and personal environment. So this book is structured around the prevailing confident, hopeful, doubtful or despairing mood of four discrete eras of the 1790s, using phrases coined by the poet William Wordsworth, who himself underwent the same internal shift in response to the French Revolution's progress. The 'spirits strong in hope' that were conjured up by the fall of the Bastille in 1789 lasted until the end of 1792, when massacres in Paris and France's imminent declaration of war against Britain led to 'discouragement' – but not eradication – of hope: hope both that France would succeed in establishing the model of an enlightened state, and that Britain would follow suit. The shift from 'hope discouraged' to suspicion of imminent disappointment took place after the end of 1794, when hopes initially raised by the British government's failure to prosecute key radicals were dashed by the introduction of grossly repressive legislation. The decisive transition from 'disappointment sore' to states of personal and political 'despair' for the book's protagonists occurred between summer 1797 and spring 1798, as a radical uprising was at last attempted, and quashed. Many of the challenges to the prevailing Enlightenment view of emotion that had been quietly gathering momentum for the previous fifty years came to the fore and precipitated a paradigm shift in Britain's emotional culture. That course led directly to our twenty-first-century emotional landscape: the 1790s was the decade that forged the modern mind.

I

Spirits Strong
in Hope

Chapter 1

THE UNLOOKED-FOR DAWN

On 13 November 1791, William Godwin 'dine[d] at Johnson's with Paine, Shovet & Wolstencraft'. He recorded in his diary, in characteristically brisk fashion, that they 'talk[ed] of monarchy, Tooke, Johnson, Voltaire, pursuits and religion'.[1] The evening brought together, in person and as subjects of conversation, some of the most influential individuals in Britain's recent history of radical politics. 'Radical' had only just been coined as a term designating extensive political and social reform that reached all the way 'to the roots'. Radicals advocated more revolutionary forms of change than 'reformers', but in practice many conflated the two groups. And Johnson's dinner-party guests were radicals who sought to live up to the label by reforming society's very foundations.[2]

Godwin's host, Joseph Johnson, was on the eve of his fifty-third birthday. He was a compact man with tightly curled hair, large dark eyes, a taut, mobile expression, and an asthmatic rasp. One of London's most famous – and infamous – literary publishers, he had lived and worked at the heart of the city's book trade, in St Paul's Churchyard, for the last twenty years. A nineteenth-century historian described how the Churchyard arced around the cathedral like a 'bow' around the 'string'.[3] The air resounded with chatter from the numerous coffee houses, inns and bookshops whose circular central counters, intimate nooks and tantalizing window displays were expressly intended to foster conversation about current political events. At number 72, at the tip of the bow – close to where the Churchyard meets Ludgate Hill and Paternoster Row – Johnson had his shop. And in a cosy, irregularly shaped upstairs room, in which guests were a little 'straitened for space', he held regular dinners, serving plain food – boiled cod, vegetables, rice pudding – over which heated argument and equally fervent agreement between members of his wide circle of friends added to the din swelling up from below.[4] The poet and educationalist Anna Laetitia Barbauld, the mathematician John Bonnycastle, the visionary artist William Blake, the Scottish physician George Fordyce, and those at the vanguard of radicalism and reform – Richard Price, John Horne Tooke, Thomas Paine, Thomas Holcroft – were frequent guests at these weekly meetings.

William Godwin was a thirty-five-year-old political writer who had spent his early adulthood in strenuous study of hyper-Calvinist religious doctrines. Calvin had predicted the damnation of 99 per cent of humanity, but Godwin immersed himself in the even dourer writings of Robert Sandeman, who had grimly forecast the condemnation to hell of 'ninety-nine in a hundred of the followers' of Calvin.[5] In 1778, whilst temporarily appointed dissenting minister at Ware in Hertfordshire, Godwin had met the preacher and poet Joseph Fawcett, celebrated later by William Hazlitt as 'the person of the most refined and least contracted taste I ever knew'.[6] Fawcett's open-minded and optimistic conversation had made a great impression on Godwin. Fawcett's favourite writers, the French Enlightenment philosophers Baron d'Holbach, Claude Adrien Helvétius, and Jean-Jacques Rousseau, cast a slant of brilliant daylight into the unremitted bleakness of the young Godwin's outlook, with their emphasis on the forward-looking, transformative potential of political education. Godwin later identified Fawcett as one of his 'four principal instructors' to whom he felt his 'mind indebted for improvement'.[7] It was largely thanks to Fawcett that, in the wake of their meeting, Godwin left the ministry, executed a dramatic political volte-face from Toryism to reform, and embarked upon a career as a writer.

Despite this cheerful early effect on Godwin, Fawcett himself would eventually become an icon of the devastating emotional impact of the disappointments suffered by radicals in the 1790s. In 1814 the poet William Wordsworth would memorialize him in his long poem *The Excursion* as one who found a 'glorious opening, the unlooked-for dawn' in the French Revolution, but later became 'Tormented' and 'inwardly opprest' by its unexpected 'failure'. In Wordsworth's account, Fawcett would become a 'Solitary' hermit, in retreat from the disappointing world, surrounded by the broken remnants of his rational hopes: 'scraps of paper, some/ Scribbled with verse; a broken angling-rod/ And shattered telescope'.[8] Godwin, too, would suffer the same trajectory during the 1790s, describing himself at the end of the decade as having 'fallen into one common grave ... with the cause of liberty'.[9] But at Johnson's dinner in 1791, the future seemed infinitely more hopeful.

In 1784, Godwin had been given the weighty responsibility of writing the British and foreign history section of the *New Annual Register*, an annual reference work that functioned as a 'general repository of history, politics and literature for the year'.[10] Godwin held this position for seven years, until a few months before Johnson's dinner party, when he had left the *New Annual Register* to work on a ground-breaking treatise on radical political theory. In keeping with his new vocation and

his determinedly optimistic outlook, Godwin finally rid himself
of the austere black garb of a dissenting minister by cutting off
his hair and donning a gaudy new blue coat, blue stockings,
yellow breeches and waistcoat.[11] His friends were surprised at
how well this new image suited Godwin's once 'puny' but now
'well-made' physique.[12] He was not a handsome man, but the
geometric lines of his high, straight brow, aquiline nose, and
determined jaw chimed with his self-image as a stoic defender
of emotional self-control.

That day at Johnson's, the conversation likely reached beyond
the intimate gathering to touch upon one subject in particular,
as debates between radicals had done for the previous two years:
the French Revolution. On 18 July 1789, the *London Chronicle*
had printed a hurried 'Postscript' to its Saturday edition,
proclaiming that 'Civil War in France' had broken out. 'The
commotions which have for some time past agitated this kingdom have at length been brought to a crisis,' its correspondent
continued breathlessly:

> No personal safety exists there, all property is unprotected,
> and the lives of the first men in the state [are] in such momen-
> tary danger as to oblige them to fly their country; public
> business of every kind is suspended, the whole system of
> government annihilated, and even the King and Queen are
> impelled to shut themselves up in the palace of Versailles
> with a strong guard for their security. Such is the picture of
> Paris at the present moment, where rebellion has reared her
> standard, and so widely spread her ravages that no one can
> judge where they will end.[13]

The philosopher Mary Wollstonecraft – another of Johnson's
dinner-party guests that evening – would later provide a blow-
by-blow account of how resentment of the French monarchy,

clergy and aristocracy had been escalating over the second half of the eighteenth century. Their 'fangs of despotism' had sunk into the populace via regressive taxes disproportionately burdening the labouring classes, in order to pay enormous debts accrued by the French government during the Seven Years' War (1754–1763) and the American War of Independence (1775–1783). Scandals surrounding Louis XVI and Marie Antoinette, such as the 'diamond necklace affair' – in which the queen was accused of trying to defraud the crown jewellers of the value of a diamond necklace – increased popular 'disappointment' in the 'majestic WILL of the king'.[14] Virulent misogyny poured forth in pornographic representations of Marie Antoinette embroiled in orgies, bestiality, lesbianism and incest, in which her alleged sexual depravity was depicted as a concomitant of a corrupt monarchy.[15] Pamphlets, newspapers and lengthy tomes cascaded from the French printing presses during the eighteenth century, providing the discontented French populace with an ideological framework for their resistance to the old regime. Political writers propagated ideals such as freedom of religion, the monarch's accountability, the principle 'that all authority, which did not originate with [the people], was illegal and despotic', the dismantling of feudal privileges, separation of church and state, and even republicanism.[16] By the end of the century, much of the French populace were well informed of their political rights and aspirations, and acutely aware of the old regime's shortcomings.

Wollstonecraft would recount how, by 1789, the situation had become dangerously volatile. Harvest failures had led to 'apprehension of a famine'. After the Comptroller-General of Finances, Charles Alexandre de Calonne, had failed to effect an 'equalization of taxes', in May 1789 the king announced that the 'Estates-General', a body last called in 1614, would be summoned.[17] His move was widely interpreted as a sign of monarchical weakness: in the past, the Estates-General had provided a medium through which aristocrats might articulate grievances to the king. The Estates-General was composed of three groupings: 303 delegates representing the 'First Estate' of the clergy, 291 advocating for the 'Second' of the nobility, and 610 endorsing the 'Third Estate' of 95 per cent of the French population. Between 10 and 17 June, the Third Estate broke away and declared itself the new 'National Assembly' of France. It pronounced that all taxes enacted by any individuals or bodies other than the people's elected representatives were illegal; that the national debt would potentially be liquidated; and inquiries instigated into the causes of 'scarcity that afflicted the kingdom; and to search for a remedy the most prompt and effectual'.[18]

On 20 June 1789 Louis XVI ordered the closure of the National Assembly's meeting hall. Defiant, the delegates moved to a nearby tennis court where 'they joined hands solemnly, and took God to witness, that they would not separate, till a constitution should be completed'. Wollstonecraft pictured how 'the heroism which excited' these first architects of a new France 'produced an overflow of sensibility that kindled into a blaze of patriotism every social feeling'.[19] It seemed that the country was being born out of the liberation of natural passion. The unfinished canvas of Jacques-Louis David's *The Tennis Court Oath*, painted between 1790 and 1794, showed how raw emotion impelled every member of the National Assembly into free, expansive gestures, illuminated by a brilliant shaft of light – or lightning – and refreshed by a gust of stormy but pure air blowing in from the west: from America, whose own revolution had concluded just six years previously.

The historian Simon Schama has described how such natural, emancipated emotion had acquired cult-like status in late-eighteenth-century France. It was manifested in a new emotional regime in which breastfeeding was promoted; a new literary vocabulary developed, centring around words like *tendresse* (tenderness), *âme* (soul), *amitié* (friendship) and *sensibilité* (sensibility); and responses to death shifted from stoic fortitude to uninhibited grief. The philosopher Jean-Jacques Rousseau was this movement's hero: his writings had traced the passions' origin back to primitive humanity, and he had shown how distressing or violent passions eloquently testified to civilization's corruption. The French Revolution's first architects, Schama claims, constructed an idealized image of a French 'citizen' on the basis of 'this first hot eruption of the Romantic sensibility', in speeches and oratory embracing authentic emotional response, and in iconic imagery such as personifications of Liberty, or the figure of Marianne, dressed in unstructured clothing.[20]

On 11 July 1789, Louis XVI dismissed the popular Jacques Necker as his financial minister, and the Assembly began a continuous session to avoid repeated eviction. As troops gathered in the capital, citizens became convinced that the monarchy was implacably opposed to the people. Riots and looting broke out. Parisians seized caches of arms from the Hôtel des Invalides and from the Hôtel du Garde-meuble, and, on the afternoon of 14 July, descended on the Bastille – 'justly reckoned the strongest and most terrific prison in Europe, or perhaps in the world' – to raid its hoard of weapons. Wollstonecraft recounted how, in 'the madness of despair', the prison governor Marquis Bernard-René de Launay 'is said to have rolled down large masses of stone from the platform on the heads of the people, to have endeavoured to blow up the fortress, and even to kill himself'. But 'resolution, more powerful than all the engines and batteries in the world, made the draw-bridges fall, and the walls give way'.[21] The Bastille fell: decades of discontent solidified into a revolution.

French political theory tended to be less empirical, and more theoretical, utopian and radical than its British equivalent.[22] In French historiography, the revolution is frequently approached as a dramatic and successful transformation of French society, which clearly divided the feudalism of the past from the

incipient democracy of 1789 onwards. But across the Channel
in Britain, few understood the French Revolution's significance
within the context of France's recent history or its tradition of
political theory. Most welcomed it, not as a utopian transformation, but as a natural progression from ideas that had been
kindling slowly since Britain's own 'Glorious Revolution' in
1688. Even the *London Chronicle*, which printed so panicked a
response to the storming of the Bastille, reported approvingly
how the French Revolution was a 'burst[ing] forth' of 'the
flame of liberty', and reminded its readership that the Glorious
Revolution had demonstrated that 'when a whole nation, with an
enlightened mind, asserts their claim to the privileges of men,
experience has told us, that it is not in the power of Monarchs
to withhold their rights'.[23]

In 1688, Britons had ousted their king, James Stuart, who was
feared to be a Catholic sympathizer, tending towards absolut-
ism, and brought over the Dutch Protestant William of Orange
as a replacement. A constitutional monarchy was established,
restricting the monarch's power by checks and balances such
as the Bill of Rights and the Act of Settlement. The new constitution that emerged in 1688 and 1689 was the pride of the
nation, Whigs and Tories alike. The monarchy survived, but its
superstitious, mystical taint was removed and replaced with a
more rational relationship between citizen and state. The Bill
of Rights declared that it was illegal for monarchs or politicians
to suspend laws or levy taxes without parliamentary consent.
It protected the right of subjects to petition the king, and
defended them against excessive bail and 'cruel and unusual
punishments'. And it established the free election of members of
parliament and freedom of speech in parliamentary debates. It
was as important to Britain's national identity in the eighteenth
century as Magna Carta had been in the thirteenth. Many historians considered – and, indeed, still do – that the Bill of Rights
neutralized British citizens' hostility to the state, prevented

the outbreak of a bloody uprising, and secured the monarchy's survival, albeit in an enfeebled form, for the next three hundred years and beyond.

The Glorious Revolution was not a perfect, conclusive end to attempts to reform the British political system. In the late seventeenth and early eighteenth centuries, Irish and English intellectuals – such as the Irish politicians Robert, first Viscount Molesworth, John Toland and William Molyneux, and the British politician and writer Anthony Ashley Cooper, third Earl of Shaftesbury – began to defend rights and liberties that they considered had been neglected by the 1688 political settlement. The resulting reform movement recalled political theories penned during the English Civil War of the seventeenth century and called for shorter parliamentary terms, more frequent elections, rotation of official offices, exclusion of 'placemen' (those given paid roles in exchange for political support), and an extension of voting rights. Even after 1688, suffrage remained heavily restricted according to property. In the counties, ownership of land bringing in an annual rent of forty shillings was a prerequisite to gain voting rights, and groups barred from owning sufficient property, including women and Catholics, were automatically excluded. The campaign to extend voting rights to 'universal suffrage' – a term generally used to signify all men, but not women, children, prisoners and the mentally incapable – was a cornerstone of the eighteenth-century reform movement.

As the eighteenth century progressed, the reform movement garnered political power, partly by seeking support in the City of London. In 1768, the radical journalist John Wilkes was elected Member of Parliament for Middlesex, but was soon imprisoned on the grounds that he had been formally outlawed from Britain in 1764 after publishing a pornographic poem. Wilkes' professional supporters formed a Society for the Supporters of the Bill of Rights. First they sought to raise money for Wilkes'

expenses, but their remit widened under its (probable) founder
Parson John Horne (later John Horne Tooke, one of the topics
of conversation at Johnson's dinner party). After Wilkes was
released from prison and expressed displeasure at the society's
newly broadened manifesto, Horne Tooke set up a breakaway
Constitutional Society. In 1774 and 1775, one of the original
society's most influential members, a Scot in his late fifties
called James Burgh, codified its principles in his three-volume
Political Disquisitions, which condemned financial dependants'
exclusion from suffrage and incited his readers to establish a
national association to generate a radical programme of reform.

By the late 1770s, the reform movement had found aristocratic supporters: the scandal-ridden Whig politician Charles
James Fox; the 'radical Duke', Charles Lennox, third Duke
of Richmond; and Lord Mahon, later to become third Earl
Stanhope, brother-in-law of the future prime minister William
Pitt the Younger.[24] The Yorkshire Association was formed
during a meeting of the county's landed gentlemen in York's
Assembly Rooms on 30 December 1779, and determined to
agitate for electoral reform. When its aims became increasingly
conservative, Major John Cartwright established the Society for
Constitutional Information in 1780. He stated that its objective
was to resurrect 'our ancient constitution' and 'to revive in the
minds of their fellow-citizens, THE COMMONALTY AT LARGE,
a knowledge of their lost Rights'.[25] This evoked the 'Norman
yoke': the influential idea that Anglo-Saxon England had
enjoyed a 'Golden Age' of rights and liberties protected under
King Alfred's Free Constitution, but had subsequently lost those
protections upon the Norman Conquest, which introduced an
era of aristocratic and feudal oppression. Radicals' and reformers' rhetoric in the 1790s would be divided between envisaging
political change tending towards future perfection, and nostalgic
efforts to resurrect lost Golden Ages.

Under the guidance of such influential leaders and societies,

on 2 June 1780 a bill for parliamentary reform – manhood suffrage, annual parliaments and revision of electoral districts – was
presented before the House of Commons. But the anti-Catholic
Gordon Riots broke out the same day, and the reform movement's association with religious tolerance meant that it faced
censure in the immediate reactionary aftermath, and the bill
failed. A further motion was presented to parliament on 7 May
1783 by a relatively new politician, twenty-four-year-old William
Pitt the Younger, who called himself an 'Independent Whig'
but would come to be labelled as a 'new Tory'.[26] This bill was
defeated, as was Pitt's final attempt at passing a parliamentary
reform bill in April 1785, this time as Britain's prime minister.
The eighteenth century had provided much cause for optimism
among political reformers, via the flourishing of political societies and campaigns, and the wide dissemination of progressive
ideas in an expanding marketplace for political pamphlets, trea-
tises and satires. But the repeated failure to enshrine a reform
bill in legislation in the 1780s marked a temporary slide into
anxiety and disappointment.

The French Revolution suddenly and dramatically ushered in
new hope in Britain. It provided a welcome vision of a state in
which 'the rights of men [were] better understood than ever',
demonstrated by 'thirty millions of people, indignant and
resolute, spurning at slavery and demanding liberty with an
irresistible voice'. This, the dissenting minister Richard Price
explained in his soft Glamorgan accent to an enthralled audience in the Old Jewry meeting-house on 4 November 1789, at a
lecture marking the hundredth anniversary of the Bill of Rights,
was the inevitable consequence of God's progressive plan for
civilization. It was a further step on the path to perfectibility.
The 1688 Revolution had set in train a series of political reforms,
Price argued, through which 'the right to liberty of conscience
in religious matters' had been established, alongside citizens'

'right to resist power when abused' and, most crucially 'the right
to chuse our own governors, to cashier them for misconduct, and
to frame a government for ourselves'.[27] The French Revolution
initially won a generally enthusiastic reception across the political spectrum in Britain, injecting reformers and radicals with
hope that their movement's aims would finally come to fruition.

In late 1791 that hopeful energy coalesced in the formation
of popular political societies across Britain, aimed at agitating
for 'a fair and equal representation'. In Sheffield, at first '5 or 6
Mechanicks' began meeting in one another's houses, sharing
grievances about 'the enormous high prices of Provisions' and
the fact that 'when a man works hard for thirteen or fourteen
hours a day, the week through, [he] is [still] not able to maintain
his family'. In November 1791, those 'Mechanicks' grouped
together into a formal society whose intentions were to 'show
the people the reason, the ground of all their complaints and
sufferings'. The culprits, they claimed, were parliamentary
privilege and corruption, 'Monopolists ... of all Ranks', and
'the Mock Representation of the People'; and they planned to
combat such injustices through 'peaceable reform' and accessible political education. By March 1792 membership of the
Sheffield Society for Constitutional Information would mush-
room to nearly 2,000. The society would adopt an organizational
structure splitting it into divisions of between ten and thirty
members, who would meet every fortnight on the same night in
different public houses, and appoint delegates to represent them
at general meetings. The Sheffield Constitutional Society's
popularity mirrored the renewed vitality of the original Society
for Constitutional Information, which had become moribund in
the 1780s after financial scandals, unwillingness to compromise,
diversion from its original aims, and declining membership after
the failure of parliamentary bills for reform. In 1788, on the cen-
tenary of the Glorious Revolution, the Society for Constitutional
Information joined with the London Revolution Society to

renew its inquiry into parliamentary representation. The following year, it adopted 'with pleasure' the London Revolution Society's congratulatory message to the new French National Assembly and looked forward with baited breath to the propagation of a 'pure and equal representation throughout Europe and, eventually, the whole world', holding up the French and American Revolutions as visible evidence that that dissemination was already occurring.[28]

At the same time that the Sheffield Constitutional Society was attracting thousands of new members, a London shoemaker called Thomas Hardy began planning a metropolitan association based on principles that the Duke of Richmond had set out in 1783: that political reform might best be achieved by uniting through correspondence sympathetic individuals and societies throughout the British Isles. On 25 January 1792 Hardy gathered together interested friends at the Bell tavern, near the Strand, and agreed an outline plan for a 'London Corresponding Society' (LCS). Within a few months, the society's membership rose from eight to seventy, and from April onwards Hardy followed the Sheffield society by splitting the LCS into nine divisions, of between thirty and sixty members each. At the beginning of May, the university-educated Maurice Margarot – a true 'citizen of the world', born in Portugal, educated in Geneva, present in Paris during the revolution – was elected the LCS's chair, and Hardy its secretary and treasurer. Weekly membership of the LCS cost one penny, to cover the cost of postage and stationery and to print political pamphlets, and attracted members from 'journeymen, tradesmen and mechanics' to those with 'political experience' and aristocrats; from radicals envisaging revolution to more moderate reformers. Regardless of income, all paid the same membership fee.[29] By 1794, the membership had expanded so greatly that Hardy described how, at the general meeting, 'the multitude who assembled at the tavern in the first floor [were] so heavy that one of the principal beams of the floor broke in the middle and gave way about a foot and threatened destruction to the whole building and also to the large company that were in the house'.[30] The LCS's organizational structure was orderly and democratic, but its meetings were often convivial, raucous affairs in public houses, with toasts, songs and dining: the apotheosis of the eighteenth-century ideal of 'sociability', in which free debate in coffee houses and taverns formed a counterweight to formal political authority.

From almost the moment of their inception, popular political societies were accused of having seditious and riotous intentions. Reactionaries conflated non-violent reformers and ascetic radicals with the most brutal agitators of revolutionary France. Many responded by explicitly repudiating such allegations and emphasizing their commitment to 'peaceable reform'. The Society for Constitutional Information and the London Corresponding Society were deeply invested, not in violent revolution, but in political education, partly through the dissemination of cheap pamphlets. In the nineteenth century the essayist William Hazlitt would suggest that the French Revolution itself was 'a remote but inevitable result of the invention of the art of printing': the consequence of improving political literacy through France, thanks to the enormous upsurge in publication during the Enlightenment.[31] Britain's printing presses were also sparked into frenzied action by the French Revolution, in a 'pamphlet war' that placed reading and writing at the centre of political engagement, and which historians retrospectively call 'the French Revolution debate' or 'controversy'.[32] With some important exceptions – political texts published as multi-volume books costing at least one pound – most pamphlets cost between one penny and three shillings, and were published swiftly, their printers anticipating that they would be perused once before being tossed aside. Participants in the controversy debated whether the French Revolution was a progressive step towards greater liberty and rights, or an ushering in of bloody anarchy.

One of the most important publications in the French Revolution debate reached the reading public on 21 February 1791. Thomas Paine's *Rights of Man* was a trenchant critique of class hierarchy, inequality and 'the base idea of man having property in man', which sold around 250,000 copies before the publication of the second part in 1793, and inspired around eighty replies.[33] Joseph Johnson had originally agreed to publish Paine's text, but he withdrew it shortly after publication for fear of prosecution. Paine denigrated the British royal family's descent from William of Orange – a mere 'man' whom Britons had 'clothe[d] with power, on purpose to put themselves in fear of him ... like bondmen and bondwomen, for ever'.[34] And his book praised the idea of transferring 'Sovereignty' from the king to the nation. This could be read as inciting a republican revolution in Britain and Johnson feared accusations of sedition. The publisher J. S. Jordan stepped into the breach and published *Rights of Man* himself on 16 March 1791. It caused a cataclysm. Reprints were demanded almost immediately and within two months around 50,000 copies were in circulation, being read aloud to enthralled groups in inns, coffee houses and at political gatherings. Paine went to France soon after its publication, where an acquaintance reported in disgust that he was becoming 'drunk with vanity'.[35]

The dinner at Johnson's on 13 November 1791 had largely come about because Godwin was eager to meet the author of *Rights of Man*. He and Paine had first met in person nine days earlier, at an annual feast held by the London Revolution Society. A few days later Godwin wrote to Paine, regretting that 'in the hurry & confusion of a numerous meeting, I had not an opportunity of ... saying some things'. 'I regard you, sir,' he wrote somewhat obsequiously, 'as having been the unalterable champion of liberty in America, in England & in France, from the purest views to the happiness and the virtue of mankind.' 'I,' Godwin continued immodestly, 'have devoted my life to these glorious purposes'. Shouldn't 'men employed in the same great purposes' engage in 'a cordial & unreserved intercourse'?[36] Godwin asked Paine, seeking an invitation to his apartment to discuss politics in person. Instead, it was at Johnson's shop that the two men were finally brought together.

Unfortunately for Godwin, the dinner that night did not live up to his hopes. A few other guests were present: the unidentified 'Shovet', and a woman, 'Wolstencraft', whom Godwin would later describe as bearing the reputation of a 'rude, pedantic, dictatorial virago'.[37] Paine was taciturn, and Godwin himself had an unappealing habit of shutting his mouth decisively after every utterance, 'seem[ing] to close the discussion at the same time'.[38] Mary Wollstonecraft was more than willing to fill the gaps in the conversation. In Godwin's horrified memory of the evening, she criticized his political heroes, articulated what he considered to be tediously conventional opinions on religion, and expressed a pessimistic and 'gloomy' outlook, in contrast both to his own relatively recent 'strong propensity to favourable construction' and to the hopeful atmosphere among reformers in the early 1790s. Although Paine 'threw in occasionally some shrewd and striking remarks, the conversation lay principally between me and Mary', Godwin recounted wearily, and he departed Johnson's house berating himself for having indulged such a shallow, unsubtle, dull thinker.[39]

But Wollstonecraft had more than earned her presence at Johnson's dinner. She had been one of the first to weigh into the French Revolution controversy. William Godwin would later relate how the French Revolution had given 'a shock to the human intellect through every region of the globe,' and that it had produced an especially 'conspicuous effect in the progress of Mary's reflections'. He claimed that her 'respect for establishments' like the Church of England had been 'undermined'. Godwin would summon an image of how, in the revolution's wake, Wollstonecraft 'seized her pen in the first burst of

indignation, an emotion of which she was strongly susceptible' and composed a treatise marked by 'the vehemence and
impetuousness of its eloquence'. Haste – up-to-the-minute relevance – was essential to respond to the fast-moving debate. And,
as was customary when such swift publication was important,
Wollstonecraft's book was sent to the printer in stages, as her
pen flew through each section, before the whole was finished.
Once or twice, she lost her nerve and 'began to repent of her
undertaking'. Joseph Johnson humoured her, reassuring her that
he 'would cheerfully throw aside' the printed sheets 'if it would
contribute to her happiness'.[40] His refusal to provide flattering
reassurance irritated Wollstonecraft into finishing the book and
her *Vindication of the Rights of Men* duly reached booksellers
around Britain on 29 November 1790, priced cheaply at 1s. 6d.

Wollstonecraft's *Vindication of the Rights of Men* was remarkable for identifying that the French Revolution controversy was,
in essence, a debate about the relationship between politics
and 'the passions'. Throughout the eighteenth century, philosophers, theologians, novelists, poets and painters in Britain
had transformed readers' understanding of the passions' role
in society. Seventeenth-century philosophers had echoed their
early Christian predecessors by casting passions as disturbances
to both human nature and communities. Prior to the eighteenth century, religious virtue and social order were considered
dependent on forceful constraint of the passions, and moral philosophers saw their role as instructing 'politicians and teach[ing]
them by governing their passions to govern their kingdoms'.[41]

By the beginning of the eighteenth century, the movement
for wider political representation and more accountable government was mirrored by greater leniency towards the passions.
Many began to see them not as challenges to social order, but as
the very medium through which social order was made possible.
It was in 'benevolent' passions like sympathy, compassion and
pity, that philosophers like Shaftesbury considered that humans'

most virtuous and sociable instincts were revealed. The French
Revolution was widely considered to be the offspring of this
dramatic shift in approach to emotion, in which the passions
were no longer inferior elements of the soul, to be subjugated,
but authentic expressions of man in the state of nature, to be
freely expressed and heard.

The eighteenth century is frequently characterized as the
'Age of Reason', the title of a work published by Paine in the
mid-1790s.[42] But this image of the Enlightenment as an era of
dispassionate, cool, intellectual endeavour tells only one side of
the story. So too does the alternative popular conception of the
eighteenth century as a period of sexual liberation, relatively
permissive of 'transgressive' behaviours involving pornography,
masturbation and homosexuality. Alone, neither story is true.
Arguments about the passions rarely polarized into advocating,
at one extreme, the complete suppression of emotion, and at the
other its liberation: stoicism versus letting it all hang out. The
eighteenth century might be more aptly designated an 'Age of
Regulation'. Writers on emotion were preoccupied by the nature
of what the historian William Reddy has called 'emotional
regimes': the degree to which the passions should be regulated,
how and why, and the level of liberation or authoritarian control
that should be exerted over them.[43] This was considered an
avowedly political matter. As we shall see, the passions were
conceived variously as symptoms of self-interested desire,
expressions of innate sociability, traits of society's 'lowest'
classes, forms of attachment to property, and the currency
through which individuals were knitted together into communities. Many pointed out the close connection between emotional
regulation and negotiations between individuals' competing
desires in the economic marketplace.

In the *Vindication of the Rights of Men*, Wollstonecraft eloquently explored the passions' political role, by diving into a
debate that was raging between two reformers: one radical, one

lapsed. A year earlier, on 4 November 1789, Richard Price's radical lecture 'A Discourse on the Love of our Country' had stressed that the French Revolution required that British residents thoroughly interrogate their commitment to their state. Nationalism, the 'love of our country', was, wrote Price, 'a noble passion, but, like all other passions, it requires regulation and direction. In its most parochial form, nationalism expressed humanity's regrettable tendency to feel 'affection' in proportion to people's 'degree of nearness to us'. Without rigorous training, people's small-minded emotional attachments – to their families, their homes, their own back yards, their countries – could set them *against*, or make them indifferent to, foreigners and overseas states that were equally deserving of rational regard. Price called for British citizens to 'correct and purify this passion' of partiality. The 'blind and narrow principle' of nationalism could be overcome, he claimed, when reason was allowed to firmly control the passions. Reason could divert emotion away from nimbyish concerns, and channel it into 'universal benevolence': a type of rational care towards 'all men, even our enemies'. It was a form of well-wishing stripped of partiality and acquisitiveness, and based on calm assessment of merit. 'In pursuing particularly the interest of our country we ought to carry our views beyond it,' Price argued; 'we ought to consider ourselves as citizens of the world, and take care to maintain a just regard to the rights of other countries' through 'universal benevolence'.[44]

In March 1790, four months later, the sixty-one-year-old Whig politician Edmund Burke began drafting an outraged retort. Until the late 1780s, Burke had joined reformers in supporting the colonists during the American War of Independence of 1775–83, and had alienated his Bristol constituents by supporting the lifting of trade restrictions on the Irish – resulting in greater competition for Bristol merchants – as well as relief of Irish Catholics, relief of insolvent debtors, and the abolition of the slave trade. All were manifestations of the 'spirit of

independence' that he perceived to be spreading in the wake
of the United States' Declaration of Independence on 4 July
1776. As a vocal supporter of many of the key causes of the
eighteenth-century movement for parliamentary reform, it was
widely expected that Burke would demonstrate the same bullish
enthusiasm for the French Revolution as most other Whigs, radicals and reformers in Britain. But he had become hostile to the
campaign to increase toleration of religious dissenters – those
who opposed the doctrines of the Anglican church and thereby
faced exclusion from many aspects of public life in Britain. To
Burke, 'rational dissent' seemed to tend increasingly towards
sedition and in 1789, he even absented himself from a parliamentary debate in which he was expected to argue in favour of
the repeal of the Test and Corporation Acts, the key pieces of
legislation by which dissenters were restricted.[45] To Burke, the
outbreak of the French Revolution, and the British reform movement's support for it, seemed to confirm the disloyal, atheist
tendencies of the reformers, and Burke made his apostasy clear
by coming out in incontrovertible opposition to the revolution.
But it was Price's triumphant claim that the French Revolution
represented the strict regulation of emotion by reason in politics
that spurred Burke into print.

Nationalism, love of one's own country above all other
nations, was natural and desirable, Burke countered, because it
was based on emotional investment. The strongest love felt by
men was for personal *property*, he argued: for wives, families,
and, chiefly, for exclusively owned land. Indeed, men mainly
loved their families, claimed Burke, because it was through
familial inheritance that they had the 'power of perpetuating
our property'. 'Love of our country' was an extension of men's
love for their private land, and the families through which it
was perpetuated. The relationship between men and their
private property gave them a financial and emotional stake –
an 'interest' and 'investment' (words with dual economic and

emotional meanings) – in the future of the country, of which their land was a constituent part. And because 'the characteristic essence of property, formed out of the combined principles of its acquisition and conservation, is to be unequal', further political inequalities – of class, sex, race, religion – were inevitable. Just as those who were not able to invest financially in a business venture had no share in its 'power, authority, and direction', neither should those who did not own land have any power to influence the state. Domestic attachments to property were microcosms of national responsibilities. 'To be attached to the subdivision, to love the little platoon we belong to in society,' Burke wrote in an oft-quoted phrase, 'is the first principle (the germ as it were) of public affections. It is the first link in the series by which we proceed towards a love to our country and to mankind'.[46]

The alternative, Burke feared, was the cold, clinical, dispassionate attitude that he saw embodied in Richard Price; of 'indifference' to 'domestic affections'. If men's attachments to property were dissolved, emotional anarchy would ensue, Burke predicted. Ownership entailed duty towards property, which imposed regulations upon the passions. The chivalric code provided Burke with an example of how emotion was regulated by men's responsibilities towards their private property; in particular, towards their wives. He mourned the recent passing of 'the age of chivalry' in France, and the demise of 'a nation of gallant men . . . of men of honour and of cavaliers', to be replaced by 'sophisters, oeconomists, and calculators' emphasizing equality. A horrific landmark in this demise of chivalry, for Burke, was the revolutionaries' treatment of Marie Antoinette on 6 October 1789, when she was arrested, 'forced to abandon the sanctuary of the most splendid palace in the world, which they left swimming in blood', and led through Paris 'amidst the horrid yells, and shrilling screams'. Burke anticipated that 'licentious[ness]' and 'habitual dissoluteness' would inevitably result from the liberation of men from their responsibilities to property: because, in his view, the passions could not be made to disappear, and disregard for them in favour of cold reason merely freed them to operate without regulation.[47] Burke identified that the two faces of radical attitudes to the passions – stoic indifference and revolutionary violence – were two sides of the same coin. He described how one group of middle- and upper-class intellectual radicals – like Price and Godwin – denigrated the passions as small-minded agents of selfish, antisocial attachments, and adopted postures of cool, classical rationality. But their rejection of regulatory conventions like chivalry, on the basis that it fostered emotion and inequality, and their refusal to adequately deal with emotion, merely liberated the citizenry's passions to be let loose in murderous violence. In lurid tones, Burke prophesied that the new regime of unregulated emotion in France would free the 'swinish multitude' to engage in murderous, bloody acts: to 'rashly ... hack that aged parent in pieces', trampling their nation 'into the mire', cheered on by 'all the unutterable abominations of the furies of hell, in the abused shape of the vilest of women'.[48]

Burke's impassioned retort to Richard Price was published on 1 November 1790, entitled *Reflections on the Revolution in France*. Despite its relatively high price of five shillings, it was an instant success, selling 7,000 copies in its first week, 19,000 in its first year in the British public domain, and a further 13,000 copies in France. It went through nine editions before Burke's death in 1797, by which time 30,000 copies had been sold in Britain. The landed establishment, predictably, were delighted to read Burke's account of the precious role of landowners' sensibility in upholding the emotional virtue of the nation. King George III commissioned specially bound copies to present as gifts, considering that 'it was a book which every gentleman ought to read'.[49] And the vice chancellor of Oxford University was petitioned to bestow an honorary degree on Burke.[50] Burke's lurid prophecies of the revolution's future descent into murderous violence divided readers. It converted some wavering supporters into determined counter-revolutionaries. But his extravagant language repelled others, and some even warned that such 'mischief' would prove Burke's own political downfall.[51]

Wollstonecraft's *Vindication of the Rights of Men* was the first retort – the first of forty-five direct responses to Burke penned between 1 November 1790 and 31 October 1791 – to emerge, crackling with righteous annoyance, from the presses. His reference to the 'swinish multitude' demonstrated, she said, that it was not British reformers who were governed by 'the influence of a ruling passion', but Burke himself, who was clearly writing out of 'pangs of hurt vanity' and 'gall of bitterness'. She accused him of cynically whipping up his readers' passions, to 'excite emotion instead of the calm reciprocation of mutual esteem and unimpassioned respect'. And she denied that any ideology centred on emotion, such as Burke's celebration of chivalry, could maintain the principled consistency he hoped for, but that it would twist and turn with public opinion: 'the conscience that is under the direction of transient ebullitions of feeling, is not very tender or consistent, when the current runs another way'. Burke's politics were the product of a 'chaotic state of mind' verging on 'madness', Wollstonecraft declared. His behaviour had been that of a 'violent revolutionist', not the chivalric ideal of a man whose passions were kept in close check by duty of care to his social inferiors.[52]

But neither did Wollstonecraft entirely agree with the extent to which Price asserted the necessity of 'correct[ing] and purify[ing]' the passions. Wollstonecraft took a different position about the passions' role in politics to Burke and Price. She argued that the passions could not be eradicated from political engagement, but nor should the inequalities of current emotional exchanges and intimate relationships be defended, as Burke had done through his celebration of chivalry. Wollstonecraft insisted that radical political ideals – such as the redistribution of property and the erosion of inequality – were not just top-down structural changes; they would be felt every day, in every single human relationship, in each partner's emotional demands and concessions. The revolutionary 'citizen' was not an abstract concept, but would be born in families and homes through radical alterations to domestic interactions, as well as in popular political societies and the House of Commons through legislative change. 'The character of a master of a family, a husband and a father, forms the citizen imperceptibly, by producing a sober manliness of thought, and orderly behaviour,' she wrote.[53] Progressive political change would begin and end with revolutions of feeling in all human relationships.

Between them, Price, Burke and Wollstonecraft thrust the passions' relevance to political engagement into the limelight. Questions about the emotional character of radicals and loyalists would dominate political debates throughout the rest of the decade. Were 'the people' characterized by the wild, violent passions that Burke had depicted? Was this an inherent trait or the product of deprivation and oppression? Was there a place in the political world for such passion, or did political participation require the tempering of emotion into calm, rational equilibrium? Was emotional investment always built on ownership: was it possible to care for a person, family, or nation, without owning some part of it? What were the consequences of placing reason and emotion in a hierarchical relationship, rather than on an equal footing?

The question of the role that emotion played in politics was, in general, less troubling for the political and religious establishment, who – as Burke, on the right of the Whigs, demonstrated – tended to be comfortable with the emotions embodied in the rituals and symbolism of the British social hierarchy: coronations, weddings, flags, the social and emotive iconography of the Church of England.[54] But the issue was – and still is – agonizing for the political 'left' (the terminology of left and right would emerge during the 1790s). Reformers and radicals were torn between two traditions: in one, emotions like anger, rage, resentment and fury were celebrated as the eloquent, if occasionally violent, retort of oppressed classes against an elitist establishment. The other tradition, from which writers like Price emerged, denigrated unregulated emotion as the basis of an irrational, narrow-minded, nimbyish outlook based on exclusive private ownership, and conceived emotive social institutions like the family and the nation as obstacles to a rational regard for the wellbeing of the world's citizens.

Such confusion about the political (un)desirability of emotion was painfully visible during campaigns on the left for Britain to 'Remain' or 'Leave' the European Union in summer 2016. Many Remain campaigners opposed themselves as rational actors to the 'intellectually ... bankrupt', 'paranoid populism' and 'vitriolic' emotion of the slogans employed by the Leave campaign, such as 'Take back control' and 'We want our country back'. The 'logic of "remain" must triumph over the emotion of "leave",' one journalist wrote. MSN News described how, whilst the Remain campaign focused on 'the economic case', Leave exploited emotions connected to 'uncontrolled immigration'.[55] Examining the words employed most frequently by the two campaigns, the politics lecturer Simon Usherwood concluded that while the Remain campaign made 'a kind of rational economic argument', those behind Leave were more fixated on 'emotional arguments'.[56] But in the wake of Britain's vote to leave the EU, Remainers belatedly invoked emotional attachments to the EU that they had previously eschewed. Demonstrators wielded placards declaring, 'We Love the EU'; social media memes emerged declaring, 'I love EU', and petitions to remain, after all, included comments such as 'I love Europe and all its diversity'; we 'need' Europe; leaving 'hurts' and is 'crazy' 'madness'.

Not all Remainers were on the political left, nor all Leavers

on the right. But on the whole, Brexit campaigns revealed the
left's especial ambivalence about deploying emotional rhetoric and arguments in political debate. Similarly in the 1790s,
emotion was an especially contested subject within the radical
movement, as well as between the 'right' and 'left'. Accusations
of unruly, violent emotional behaviour were levelled at each
side in the French Revolution controversy, and, within radical
circles too, by ascetics like Godwin, at his more openly passionate radical colleagues. Reformers and the establishment, alike,
found themselves denying similarities between their supporters'
behaviour and that of the increasingly violent revolutionaries
in France. Johnson's dinner party on 13 November 1791 had
brought together Godwin and Paine, who may have noted
approvingly that the French National Assembly was characterized by 'none of those mean passions which mark the character
of impertinent governments, founding themselves on their own
authority, or on the absurdity of hereditary succession', and the
pair may have derided, too, the 'frenzy of passion' voiced by
lapsed reformers like Burke and the popular political societies.[57]

That dinner was also a landmark in late-eighteenth-century
politics for having introduced Godwin to Wollstonecraft. Despite
their inauspicious start, they would prove two of the most eloquent analysts of the passions in the 1790s. The eighteenth
century had produced an optimistic vision of the passions' political importance, whereas in the preceding century the passions
had been conceived as enemies of society, not its architects. But
at the very end of the Enlightenment, the French Revolution
drew emotion into greater contestation. This would affect not
just the specific hopes that radicals in Britain entertained for
bringing about political change through emotional reform, but
the nature of hope itself. Godwin and Wollstonecraft's lives
and writings would show how political vicissitudes shaped
their individual temperaments. And they would demonstrate
how such historical changes possessed a legacy in feelings and

relationships, and, moreover, in radically altered attitudes to emotion and hope. In Godwin and Wollstonecraft's lives, such alterations would result from independent reflection, alongside mutual conversation and influence. Radicals like Godwin and Wollstonecraft would find that the political hopes they cherished in 1791 would be battered throughout the course of the 1790s, as mercilessly as the revolutionaries of 14 July 1789 had beaten, stabbed and decapitated the Bastille's governor, whose head was subsequently paraded about Paris on a pike. Many would become wary of hope based on emotional intuition and passionate conviction, and would seek a firmer, more rational footing. Out of the broken, bleeding hopes of the 1790s there would emerge a new approach to historical change, hope, and the 'virtue' of the passions.

Chapter 2

THE DISTRIBUTION OF HUMAN HAPPINESS

Mary Wollstonecraft's fascination with emotion was far from theoretical. Of the political writers who came to prominence in the 1790s, she was one of the most fixated on a particular emotion that would shape the decade: disappointment. She mined her experiences of it, analysing its subjective qualities, its psychological impact, the resilience required to overcome its devastation, and its moral and spiritual purpose. Wollstonecraft's stern, uncompromising demeanour, from which William Godwin recoiled at their first meeting, was partly the result of her somewhat morbid relish of 'pain and disappointment' as salutary, purifying experiences through which personal errors and fatuous hopes might meet with necessary correction, or as necessary earthly trials.[1]

Wollstonecraft initially had faith that the collapse of hope revealed something new, something previously misunderstood, about the universe: 'my philosophy, as well as my religion,' she wrote early in her life, 'will ever teach me to look on misfortunes as blessings, which like a bitter potion is disagreeable to the palate tho' 'tis grateful to the Stomach – I hope mine have not been thrown away on me, but that I am both the wiser, and better for them.'[2] Wollstonecraft had had an Anglican upbringing, but later she came to follow largely self-fashioned religious principles, as did many rational dissenters at the time.[3] The polymath Joseph Priestley – whose investigations into subjects as diverse as history, biography, electricity, theology, language and grammar, political theory, jurisprudence, optics, philosophy and 'pneumatics' illuminated the intellectual landscape of eighteenth-century Britain – had argued that the Creator had a non-interventionist relationship with the natural world. God had set laws in motion – laws whose workings might be discovered through experiment and observation – but would not subsequently intervene. The comparison of God to a 'watchmaker' was inferred throughout the seventeenth and eighteenth centuries by natural philosophers including Johannes Kepler, Isaac Newton, Bernard de Fontenelle and William Paley, who saw in the intricate order of the universe a benevolent divine plan, tending towards happiness.[4] Priestley agreed that humanity was set on a path of continual improvement – that '*whatever is, is right*' – where even disappointments and failures were necessary steps.[5] 'Disappointment' was only 'painful' for 'indulged children' and 'kings', who had failed to acquire 'a habit of patience and forbearance', Priestley wrote disdainfully.[6] William Godwin also described how disappointment was merely the result of 'some unobserved bias' that had 'disappointed [a] prediction'; but that its helpful illumination would prompt 'a fresh investigation' and 'will probably lay open' the truth.[7] Such viewpoints supported a perception of historical progress later called the 'Whig interpretation of history': the idea that, over time, societies inevitably progress

steadily towards greater liberty and enlightenment. This optimistic vision would be severely tested before the decade was
out.

Wollstonecraft's personal disillusionments had been many. Her
father, Edward, a violent, frequently drunken farmer, had moved
his wife and children from one business failure to another; from
Epping, to Walkington and Beverley in Yorkshire's East Riding,
to Hoxton in north-east London, to Laugharne in South Wales,
and to Walworth in south London. Wollstonecraft had tried to
protect her mother, Elizabeth, from his 'ungovernable temper'
by sleeping on the landing outside Elizabeth's bedroom, yet she
never felt she came 'first' in her mother's affections.[8] Each move
wrenched Wollstonecraft away from close friendships and sur-
rogate families: from her friend Jane Arden in Beverley, whose
father, an itinerant lecturer, encouraged Wollstonecraft's education; and from Reverend Clare and his wife in Hoxton, who 'took
some pains to cultivate my understanding'. In 1774, the Clares
had introduced her to a young woman living in Newington
Butts, south of the Thames, called Fanny Blood. Blood was
two years older than Wollstonecraft, who ardently described
how Blood's 'feminine' skills in writing, singing, painting and
sewing combined with her 'agreeable' and 'improving' 'masculine' conversation to inspire devotion. She is 'a friend, whom I
love better than all the world beside', Wollstonecraft wrote to
Arden, confessing that 'To live with this friend is the height
of my ambition'. But she also knew that disappointment was a
likely outcome of this hope. Blood suffered from consumption,
and she was set to marry an Irish merchant, Hugh Skeys, who
promised to take her to a 'neighbouring Kingdom' to 'restore
her health'.[9]

By 1781, when she was twenty-two years old, Wollstonecraft
had been separated from Blood by financial necessity, and was
working as a lady's companion to a formidable Bath resident,

Sarah Dawson. Godwin would later describe how 'Mary was the only person ... in her treatment of whom [Dawson] had felt herself under any restraint'.[10] Wollstonecraft's early life had left her with a severe, heavy-hearted demeanour and a tendency to depressive introspection, which clearly disarmed her older employer. A portrait made of Wollstonecraft ten years later in 1791 shows quizzical, somewhat mocking brows, lips set in resignation, and a direct, accusatory gaze that a marginally paralysed eyelid could occasionally offset into an expression of boredom. She was not an easy or carefree companion. In the autumn of 1781, her mother was diagnosed with dropsy: oedema, or fluid retention. Wollstonecraft immediately left Bath and moved home, where she tended her mother until her death in April 1782. Elizabeth's last words – 'A little patience, and all will be over!' – became an obsessively repeated internal refrain through which Wollstonecraft would self-narrate her own suffering, and even the female condition.[11]

In the aftermath of her mother's death, Wollstonecraft felt principally responsible for her two sisters' upkeep. By the summer of 1784, with characteristic resourcefulness, she had established a school in London, along with her sister Eliza and Fanny Blood. This failed, but a second attempt temporarily succeeded. For nearly two years, Wollstonecraft, Blood, Eliza and her other sister, Everina, managed to scrape together a living by running a school in Newington Green, with two families of lodgers and nearly twenty pupils. The project collapsed after Blood's consumption worsened and she finally married Skeys and departed for Lisbon. Upon hearing that Blood had become pregnant, Wollstonecraft determined to travel to Portugal. She arrived in November 1785 to find Blood grievously ill and in premature labour. A baby boy was born, but Blood herself died a few days later, on 29 November. In the terrible lead-up to her death, Wollstonecraft had struggled to calibrate her hopes to the probability of Blood's survival: 'I *labour* to be resigned,' she wrote to Eliza, 'and by the time I am a little so some *faint* hope sets my thoughts again a float – and for a moment I look forward to days, that will, alas! I fear, never come.'[12]

It was one thing to profess faith that disappointment might beneficially correct erroneous hopes. It was quite another to transform the unbearable pain of a friend's death into the cheerful perception of a rational learning experience. Over ten years later Wollstonecraft would still feel that Blood 'is present with me', even though the 'grave has closed over [her]'.[13] Even before Blood's death, she had occasionally wondered if 'it is best sometimes to be deceived – and to expect what we are never likely to meet with', since, 'deluded by false hopes, the time would seem shorter, while we are hastening to a better world'.[14] Wollstonecraft was coming to feel that delusion and hope, even if it could never be realized, could be more comforting than the cold, hard truth. This was an example of how personal disappointments can change how people view the nature and function of disappointment itself – events don't just alter the way that their participants and victims feel; they can change how they think, and feel, about emotion. Before the century was out, there would be many more examples of how such personal disappointments underpinned shifts in how the world viewed the nature and purpose of failure and feeling. Many would mirror Wollstonecraft's experience: that particularly painful episodes of disappointment could make it impossible to sustain faith in its salutary role, or to keep believing in the optimistic forward motion of the universe.

Wollstonecraft left Portugal around 20 December 1785, and returned home to find that, in her absence, the 'school dwindles to nothing, and we shall soon lose our last boarder'. Once the building had been lost, she spent some time living at the Newington Green house of Rev. John Prior, an under-master at Eton. The school's demise was a severe blow. 'I can only anticipate misery,' Wollstonecraft wrote, worrying about the prospects of her two sisters and Fanny's brother George. But she tried to rally: 'The Will of Heaven be done! – I will labour to be resigned'.[15] Despite its collapse, the school project had not been an unmitigated disaster. It had integrated Wollstonecraft into the dissenting community of Newington Green, where she had attended the square, squat Unitarian Church, with its high, tiled roof and functional plainness that pained her Anglican sensibilities. She had met Richard Price, who was minister there; and had become friendly with the famous radical James Burgh and his wife Hannah Harding, who had given financial and practical support to Wollstonecraft's school.

The school had also opened up opportunities to Wollstonecraft by establishing her as an innovative pedagogical theorist.[16] One had led her to the publisher Joseph Johnson, to whom she was introduced by the Rev. John Hewlett, another Newington Green friend. Johnson was fascinated by the contemporary educational theories of Anna Laetitia Barbauld, who had been running the Palgrave Academy in Suffolk with a curriculum centred on science and modern languages instead of classics. He encouraged Wollstonecraft to write a book on female education, *Thoughts on the Education of Daughters*. The ten guineas she received allowed her to establish the surviving Blood family and her own sisters in relative security.[17] In July 1786, thanks to her friend Prior, another opportunity took Wollstonecraft to Ireland, as a governess to the children of Lady Kingsborough, one of the wealthiest Irish heiresses.

In the Kingsboroughs' family seat of Mitchelstown Castle, in county Cork, the 'melancholy' and 'gloom' that had been gathering over the course of Wollstonecraft's disappointing twenty-seven years descended with full force.[18] Catherine Fitzgerald, Lady Kingsborough – whose initial pronouncements about desiring more than an 'ornamental ... education' for her girls had sounded promising – proved a let-down. Wollstonecraft found herself bored by conversations about 'matrimony and dress', 'tormented to death by dogs', and embroiled in a scandal surrounding Lord Kingsborough's dalliance with the former governess.[19] Unlikely gossip would later circulate that Wollstonecraft had herself wanted 'to discharge the Marriage Duties, with [Lady Kingsborough's] husband'.[20] She suffered financial defeats too: she suspected that her brother had cheated her out of dues from a family lawsuit, and her expectations of assistance from Hugh Skeys were disappointed. Consumption struck the wider Kingsborough family, and Wollstonecraft worried terribly about her favourite ward, the thirteen-year-old Margaret King. In December 1786, she realized that it was a year since her beloved Blood's death. Wollstonecraft's mental distress began to manifest itself physically and 'a disappointment with respect to [Everina's] visit made me almost faint'.[21] She felt abandoned by both sisters. 'I am endeavouring to conquer myself – I am trying to be resigned to my fate,' she wrote feverishly to Blood's brother George, but 'the ghost of my former joys, and vanished hopes, haun[t] me continually.'[22]

By June 1787 Wollstonecraft had returned to Britain. The Kingsboroughs, en route to a Continental tour, took a vacation in the spa development of Bristol Hotwells, where hot springs bubbled up through the rocks of the Avon Gorge. Wollstonecraft did not go further with them. Her fondness for Margaret had made her an antagonist in Lady Kingsborough's eyes, and she was summarily dismissed, without wages, but also without a loan she had been led to expect in order to establish a new school. Wollstonecraft turned to Joseph Johnson: 'You are my only friend,' she wrote pathetically, 'the only person I am *intimate* with. – I never had a father, or a brother – you have been both to me, ever since I knew you'. She confessed to him her 'long[ing] for a little peace and *independence*!' after 'near nine-and-twenty years' of 'many *severe* disappointments'.[23]

Wollstonecraft's faith in Johnson was one of her few hopes that did not meet with failure. He found her a smart new house,

49 George Street, part of a new development by Blackfriars Bridge in Southwark, which was being erected beside open fields that were used as 'tenter grounds', where newly made cloth was dried. He encouraged her to publish a novel she had written in Ireland: *Mary, a Fiction*. The protagonist, Mary, is a neglected, self-taught female genius who, after leaving a husband, Charles, befriends a local girl, Ann, who subsequently becomes consumptive and – like Blood – travels to Lisbon, where she later dies. After Ann's death, Mary enters into a relationship with Henry, who, too, dies of consumption. Charles returns from Europe, and they establish an unsatisfying life together before, the novel implies, Mary dies young. Nakedly autobiographical, *Mary* offers a bleak account of the disappointing nature of human relationships, in which the male surrogates that stand in for Blood prove equally unsatisfying.

After *Mary*, Johnson gave Wollstonecraft reviews to write for his newly founded journal, the *Analytical Review*. And he commissioned translations from her, including *Of the Importance of Religious Opinions* by Jacques Necker, French finance minister under Louis XVI, and the three-volume *Elements of Morality; for the Use of Children* by the German educationalist Christian Gotthilf Salzmann. Wollstonecraft would later describe Necker's text as 'a large book [of] various metaphysical shreds of arguments . . . inflated and confused as the thoughts were far fetched and connected'.[24] But, at the age of twenty-nine, after many years of disappointment and before the promising advent of the French Revolution, Wollstonecraft may have found Necker's celebration of religion as a rational mechanism to regulate hopeful passions and reconcile them to inequality and 'despotism' more fitting to her own experiences.[25] Similarly, Salzmann's manual stressed that morality in children depended on their learning to make hopeful passions conform to rational assessment of 'the real value of every thing'.[26]

The younger Wollstonecraft had immersed herself in the

subjective emotional experience of her early disappointments, reflecting many dissenters' hope that minute analysis of failure and disappointment might reveal truths about Providence. But the thirty-year-old woman who emerged, emotionally bruised but intact and financially independent thanks to her writing, was becoming sterner and more controlled. By the late 1780s, Wollstonecraft was less cavalier about the painful nature of disappointment and the value of psychological distress. She knew how excruciating it could be. She had come to believe how necessary it was to use the faculty of reason to keep 'imagination' and hope within the 'verge of probability'; to avoid disappointment in the first place, not to expressly seek out its revelations. And she started to consider hopeful 'fancy' not as a miraculous tool of personal transformation and forward-driving optimism, but as a potentially dangerous seduction away from clear-eyed 'judgment' of the world, as it is.[27] Wollstonecraft was endeavouring to cultivate calm forbearance and reconciliation to the status quo, in place of the dramatic and often frenzied rebellions of her youth. Gain 'more dominion over your passions', she exhorted Fanny Blood's brother George, as she had recently urged herself.[28] It had been a hard-won lesson.

The optimistic climate ushered in by the French Revolution at the beginning of the 1790s presented a challenge to those who, like Wollstonecraft, were endeavouring to yoke their hopes to the probability that they would be realized. How, exactly, many radicals wondered, were they supposed to assess whether their hopes for political change were likely to bear fruit? Priestley had been convinced 'that there is a *Providence*' that 'superintends the whole system of nature', through which, 'from the beginning of the world [God] has been training men to virtue and happiness'.[29] Priestley was not a fan of 'gaming', believing that it enticed 'modern *unbelievers*' to invest 'faith in that nonentity *fortune*'.[30] But, for many, the often obscure workings of Providence did resemble 'fortune', and the investment of hope in a particular version of historical change could feel precisely like a gamble. Priestley had approached disappointment as a nonchalant gambler might feel on losing a small stake: the 'pressure of trouble or disappointment' might become bearable if seen to clarify the laws of Providence, allowing subsequent bets to be made on a firmer footing.[31] But Wollstonecraft was coming to feel that this was too offhand an approach to the pain of lost hope.

During the 1790s, William Godwin jotted notes in a 'Philosophical Notebook' about what he called the 'judgment of attainableness': the acts of judgement and prediction upon which all hopes are founded.[32] For Godwin, judgement of attainableness required rational analysis of the hospitable or hostile environment in which the hoped-for event was to occur. As human knowledge improved, Godwin hoped that this calculated approach would reduce, and ultimately eliminate, occurrences of disappointment. It placed hope firmly under the cosh of reason. But Godwin's approach also raised the question of whether a person should only desire what he or she is likely to get. Is there worth in continuing to hope for something that may not – perhaps almost certainly will not – come to fruition? Are there objectives whose intrinsic value warrants the continued nurturing of fragile, even impossible, hope, despite the pain of inevitable and repeated disappointment?

In *The Sane Society* (1955), the social psychologist Erich Fromm points out the conservative tendency of many contemporary psychological and psychiatric therapies, which often encourage people to make their hopes conform to the likelihood of materialization – to Godwin's 'judgment of attainableness'. Fromm objects that our hopes and emotions are frequently expressions not of whims that are easily tossed aside or adapted, but of what the French philosopher Simone Weil called 'the needs of the soul'. For Fromm, these needs include 'relatedness', 'rootedness', 'unity'; for Weil, 'order', 'liberty', 'obedience', 'responsibility', 'equality' and 'hierarchy'.[33] Hope is often an expression of desire for the satisfaction of such inalienable human wants. Negative emotions frequently stem from the disappointment of those hopes and are an eloquent testimony to the failure of a society to meets its inhabitants' deepest needs. Therapies encouraging individuals to make their hopes conform to what society is prepared to offer are prioritizing individual 'adjustment' over social change. For example, the therapist Sarah Edelman cites one of the principal aims of cognitive behavioural therapy (CBT) – a hugely popular form of contemporary evidence-based psychotherapy – as reducing episodes of 'disappointment' by reining in our hopes on the basis that 'things do not always work out the way we would like'.[34] An online stress-management course based upon CBT, offered by a British university, encourages its staff to 'change their ways of thinking'. Instead of tackling the stresses of the academic profession – long hours, many young academics on poorly paid temporary contracts – the course advises lecturers to stop expecting that 'I should be treated with respect', and to relinquish hope that 'My work should be appreciated by my boss/peers/staff/significant others'. As a means of allowing the individual to find temporary respite from an oppressive world, or to prioritise certain battles whilst relinquishing others, CBT can be invaluable. But as a universally applied philosophy of resignation, it prompts concerns similar to those levelled by Fromm against conservative psychotherapies in general: 'These [psychological] professions are in the process of becoming a serious danger to the development of man.' Such practices convert the social critique contained in individuals' distressing emotions into criticisms of individuals themselves: 'The specialists in this field tell you what the "normal" person is, and, correspondingly, what is wrong with you; they devise the methods to help you adjust, be happy, be normal.'[35]

Radicals in the 1790s found themselves faced with the

dilemma of whether they should maintain their political and personal hopes, defending their belief in the possibility of a freer, more equal society, in the face of an increasingly inhospitable, reactionary environment. Many considered the passions as expressions of primal needs unmet by society, as would Fromm over 150 years later. The question of whether to make hope conform to what was likely in a progressively more conservative climate, or to cling on to improbable but important radical hopes and face the pain resulting from repeated disappointment, proved to be a highly personal negotiation. It depended on individuals' resilience to living out of kilter with their society's provisions, and the level of their investment in their political objectives. Over the course of the decade, the penalties for pursuing unpopular aims would become more and more intolerable, and many who defended their objectives valiantly at first would find themselves capitulating, conforming, and lowering their expectations. And as radicals' 'judgments of attainableness' changed over the 1790s, so too did the mainstream approach to hope itself. Priestley's vision of hope as a providential gamble fell out of favour, and was replaced by a more serious, measured language of 'probability', 'statistics' and 'normality', stripping hope of emotion and placing it on a securer foundation of rational research and numerical calculation.

Despite her anxieties about disappointment, when Wollstonecraft first met Godwin at Johnson's dinner in 1791, she had no desire to rid her political hopes of the involvement of feeling. Indeed, she was in the midst of a political project whose principal incarnation was emotional reform. Wollstonecraft saw the inequalities of sex, class, race and wealth that debased the public sphere of late-eighteenth-century Britain clearly inscribed in domestic relationships, and especially sexual relations between men and women. Through brave, unconventional and 'scandalous' projects to transform such personal relationships into meetings of equals, she hoped that a wider programme of political reform might be achieved. As the literary historian Andrew Cayton argues, for Wollstonecraft 'successful revolution was the sum total of a mass of individual conversion experiences'.[36] Her relationships were not trivial distractions from her political writings, and biographers' interest in them is not necessarily prurient. She pursued them with zealous and impassioned commitment as urgent political interventions, designed to instigate an ambitious programme of emotional change. She was anticipating by almost two hundred years the rallying cry of second-wave feminism, that 'the personal is political'. And, at the time that she first met Godwin and entered into the French Revolution controversy, she was deeply immersed in the first of these 'daring projects'.[37]

It was via Joseph Johnson that, in 1787, Wollstonecraft had made a significant new acquaintance. Henry Fuseli – a forty-six-year-old Swiss painter, born Johann Heinrich Füssli – was a compact, dapper man, who had his hair powdered and styled each morning by a personal hairdresser. Beseeching blue eyes sat atop rugged features: an aquiline nose, stocky jaw and petulant full lips. Fuseli could be both 'a shy man' and deliberately 'repulsive', and although Wollstonecraft was one of Johnson's closest friends and was fascinated by Fuseli's career as a one-time poet and famous painter, Fuseli's friend John Knowles described how 'it was some time before they became intimately acquainted'.[38] A painting that Fuseli had exhibited in 1782, *The Nightmare*, had made him famous, renowned for his outlandish, 'shockingly mad' imagination, and for his erotic, sensual escapades. The painting depicts a woman opulently sprawled on her back across a bed, sat upon by a dark incubus hunkered down over her pelvis and stomach, all surrounded by dark red velvet curtains through which the terrifying head of a staring, grinning horse – the 'night mare' itself – pokes. It was rumoured to have been inspired by Fuseli's unrequited love for Anna Landolt, the twenty-one-year-old niece of the poet and physiognomist

Johann Caspar Lavater, and some whispered that the squatting incubus bore a remarkable resemblance to Fuseli himself.[39] He deliberately cultivated an image as a 'malevolent' and witty lothario dabbling in bisexuality, and an artistic 'genius', repelling the ascetic Godwin, who sniffed that Fuseli was the most 'conceited man' he'd ever met.[40] In June 1788, Fuseli had married the young model, socialite and artist Sophia Rawlins, and he set about compiling a compendium of frequently erotic portraits and studies of his wife. 'The aim is to astonish,' he declared in a lecture to the Royal Academy.[41]

Fuseli liked to think that, next to his posturing, flirtatious demeanour, Wollstonecraft became painfully self-conscious of her dowdy and serious appearance. Fuseli's friend Knowles mockingly recounted how, when Charles Maurice de Talleyrand-Périgord, the French politician and author of the 'Report on Public Instruction', came to visit Wollstonecraft, she presented him with wine in a teacup. And Knowles laughed at her as a 'philosophical sloven', whose 'habit of coarse cloth, such as is now worn by milk-women, black worsted stockings, and a beaver hat, with her hair hanging lank about her shoulders' were only marginally redeemed by having become modish in the wake of the French Revolution.[42] Then, fripperies such as powdered hair and rigid boning were rejected by radicals in France and Britain as aristocratic emblems and artificial constraints of the natural body. Wollstonecraft certainly saw something in Fuseli to admire and obsess over: 'I always catch something from the rich torrent of his conversation, worth treasuring up in my memory, to exercise my understanding,' she may have professed admiringly.[43] Funded by her increasing fame – which surpassed Fuseli's, no doubt to his annoyance – she seems to have made some changes to her own appearance, investing in new and brighter clothes and, later, furnishing smarter lodgings for herself, alone, on Store Street, near Bedford Square in Bloomsbury.

From a young age, Wollstonecraft had been worried about the

constraints of marriage on women, no doubt traumatized by her father's abuse of her mother. In 1782, at the age of twenty-three, upon hearing about the wedding of her friend Jane Arden's sister, Wollstonecraft had resolutely professed that 'I will not marry'. She knew that single women's earning potential was extremely limited, but still remained convinced that 'it is a happy thing to be a mere blank, and to be able to pursue one's own whims, where they lead, without having a husband and half a hundred children at hand to teaze and controul a poor woman who wishes to be free'.[44] At the beginning of the eighteenth century, among landed families marriage had chiefly been a financial arrangement to cement alliances or acquire property, and most middle-class and aristocratic marriages had been decided by parents. The erosion of authoritarian or absolutist relations in politics was mirrored by the political philosopher John Locke's redefinition, at the end of the seventeenth century, of marriage as a contract between consenting parties, and Bishop Fleetwood also started to stress the 'reciprocal duty obliging each party': wives' duty was to be 'submissive, subject and obedient to their husbands', but husbands were equally obligated to 'love their wives'. Attitudes to marriage were bound up with changing views of the passions. As the passions became increasingly accepted as society's very underpinning, rather than its enemy, marriage began to acquire importance as 'a prime source of pleasure, both emotional and sexual', instead of a property negotiation and necessary curb on male libido.[45] Once marriages were more likely to be arranged by the participants themselves, and men started to focus on amassing enough wealth to sustain wives and children in the name of pleasure, the average marrying age for men increased to their late twenties. But the rise of the 'egalitarian marriage' by the mid-eighteenth century did not ameliorate the principal limitations that it continued to impose on women.[46] On the basis of the fiction that husband and wife were one person, a tract of 1777 described how, in marriage, 'the very being or legal existence of a woman is suspended'.[47] A married woman's moveable goods passed into outright possession of her husband, who also acquired the right to manage any land and its profits that she might own. Wives were unable to enter into economic contracts on their own, and even basic purchases on credit could only be done in their husband's name. Small loopholes existed which allowed wives to stretch their role as their husbands' 'agents' to become enthusiastic consumers in the eighteenth-century marketplace. But there was no escaping the limitations that marriage imposed upon eighteenth-century women, and many women perceived wives to be 'Slaves to their Husbands'.[48]

Wollstonecraft's opposition to marriage had become entrenched in 1783, when her younger sister Eliza, 'Bess', who had married an affluent shipwright from Rotherhithe called Meredith Bishop, gave birth to a baby girl, also called Mary. Eliza became acutely depressed in the months after birth, and Wollstonecraft described in distress how 'Her ideas are all disjointed and a number of wild whims float on her imagination'; 'she seems to think she has been very ill used,' Wollstonecraft reported, linking Eliza's desperately sick mental state to her husband's determination to 'gratify the ruling passion'.[49] Fuelled by anger towards Meredith and what she saw as his domineering sense of sexual entitlement, Wollstonecraft became convinced that 'the only expedient to save Bess' was to engineer her swift escape from the marriage. By January 1784, Eliza had been deftly removed, and Wollstonecraft was left relishing her accomplishment. She was brutally sanguine about the separation of mother and baby: 'The poor brat,' she wrote to her other sister, Everina. 'It had got a little hold on my affections – some time or other I hope we shall get it'. But, she continued, 'the thought of having assisted to bring about so desirable an event' as Eliza and Meredith's separation 'will ever give me pleasure to think of'.[50]

Before Fuseli, Wollstonecraft's encounters with men had

confirmed her suspicions that they were too deeply tainted by power and money to be able to offer partnerships based on equal power and responsibility. At the young age of fourteen or fifteen, she was already writing sadly of how 'romantic notions of friendship' had been 'disappointed' by 'some infidelity in a love affair'.[51] Much later, in the summer of 1790, when Wollstonecraft, at thirty-one, had exceeded the usual marriageable age and was on her way to being famous, she was horrified to receive a marriage proposal from a go-between, on behalf of a man she had briefly encountered at Johnson's. It was clear to Wollstonecraft that the proposal was intended not as a shared endeavour to realize her lofty ideals of domestic affections as a microcosm for the emotional requirements of citizenship, but, at best, as a form of condescending financial patronage or, at worst, as an attempt to exploit her poverty and purchase her body. She received these 'mercenary considerations' as 'an insult' from the 'superficial puppy', 'that I could for a moment think of *prostituting* my person for a maintenance'. Wollstonecraft turned her fury on the go-between, berating him that 'you were rude and *cruel*, to step forward to insult a woman, whose conduct and misfortunes demand respect'.[52]

It is not exactly clear what Wollstonecraft envisaged from her relationship with Fuseli. Her letters to him were subsequently destroyed by her grandson, perhaps hinting at their scandalous content. The principal biographical account of their friendship derives from Fuseli's friend Knowles, who flatters the artist's self-image as an irresistible 'gran[d] soul' of sexual energy, and makes fun of Wollstonecraft's apparently frantic attempts to entice his attention.[53] Perhaps she saw the relationship as a political project: the conversion of a man who openly professed his disdain for women's 'fugitive' genius and agreed with Pope that 'women have no character at all', and whose heart was, in Wollstonecraft's own words, slimed over by 'that reptile Vanity'.[54] The poet Samuel Taylor Coleridge would later optimistically describe how a man's 'fierceness' might be 'transmute[d] . . . into virtuous energy'; what a coup it would be, to pen Fuseli's feral fierceness within a virtuous relationship in which he and she both applied themselves, with equal ardour, to schooling their spirited desires.[55] Marriage stripped a woman of economic and physical power, but Wollstonecraft also disparaged promiscuity and sexual incontinence as threats to the rational regulation of emotion, on which she saw both religious virtue and political power depend. She was likely not directly suggesting a sexual relationship to Fuseli – although the longevity of her efforts, and the destruction of her correspondence, implies that her time spent with the posturing artist was seasoned with enough flirtation to offend conventional sensibilities. Letters 'hop[ing] to inspire' affection arrived by the ream at his house, most of which – Knowles says – Fuseli absent-mindedly placed 'unopened in his pocket' or tossed to one side.[56] Perhaps an intense friendship could provide the rational framework in which a man and woman demonstrated equal emotional control over themselves and one another.

In August 1790, Johnson gently suggested that Wollstonecraft take a country break, to extricate herself temporarily from her infatuation with Fuseli, and visit her friend Henry Dison Gabell, a schoolmaster, in Warminster. Gabell had recently married an Oxfordshire woman called Anne Gage, and the couple were – in Wollstonecraft's eyes – sickeningly happy. She began her stay in determinedly good humour, swearing unconvincingly to Everina that 'I am never disgusted by the frequent *bodily* display' of their affection.[57] But a couple of weeks later, the injustice of the Gabells' mutual satisfaction, beside her own unrequited love, began to rankle and Wollstonecraft was writing of happy couples as 'my inferiors – inferiors because they could find happiness in a world like this'.[58] She had come to see clearly that the unequal distribution of material property, with which reformers were preoccupied, was closely allied to the similarly inequitable 'distribution of human happiness'.[59] This was not just the result of the institution of marriage. Wollstonecraft would soon turn her attention to exposing the degree to which the unequal apportioning of traits, according to gender, was written into the very fabric of eighteenth-century emotional culture.

3

A REVOLUTION IN
FEMALE MANNERS

On 3 January 1792, Mary Wollstonecraft submitted the
final page of a new work to the printer. *A Vindication
of the Rights of Woman* was a sustained, blistering
attack on the material, intellectual and emotional structures
that kept women in a state of infantilization and oppression. An
immediate success, the book later became a classic of feminist
philosophy, claimed by Millicent Garrett Fawcett as the spur
to early-twentieth-century campaigns for female suffrage, but
Wollstonecraft would rebuke herself for having dashed it off
in such a short space of time (probably between six and twelve
weeks). 'I am dissatisfied with myself for not having done justice to the subject,' she wrote in irritation; 'had I allowed myself
more time I could have written a better book'.[1]

In revolutionary France, women were unprecedentedly visible
on the political stage. They had participated in the storming of

the Bastille, and on 4 October 1789 a cohort of thousands, led by
Parisian market women, had marched on Versailles to protest at
the high price and scarcity of bread. Historians agree that many
of the landmark events of the French Revolution 'would [not]
have succeeded without' women's input.[2] But even as early as
1793, it was obvious that women's rights were being deliberately
sidelined by male politicians and that the prescribed republican
female roles were rigidly patriarchal: 'Women! Do you want to
be Républicaines? ... Be simple in your dress, hard-working
in your homes, never go to the popular assemblies wanting to
speak there. But let your occasional presence there encourage
your children.'[3] By the end of 1793 all women's political societies
in France were banned, and the feminist playwright and activ-
ist Olympe de Gouges was executed. She had once demanded
of her sisters, 'O women, women, when will you stop being so
blind? What advantages have you gained from the Revolution?'[4]
The same might have been asked of the predominantly male
eighteenth-century reform movement and the popular societies of the 1790s, which often met in taverns, where women
were excluded. Male reformers invested energy in defending
dissenters' rights, pressing for the abolition of slavery, and
relaxation of Irish trade restrictions, but few acknowledged the
constraints and abuses suffered by women. Priestley's son-in-law
Thomas Cooper was unusual in having 'considered the subject
of the Rights of Women'. He found himself 'perfectly unable to
suggest any Argument in support of the political Superiority so
generally arrogated by the Male Sex', but relegated the 'discovery' to a footnote in his 'Propositions Respecting the Foundation
of Civil Government' (1790).[5]

Effectively excluded from political agitation in the corresponding societies, Wollstonecraft defended 'the rights of
woman' in alternative settings: in her personal relationships, and
in her writing. In *A Vindication of the Rights of Woman* she traced
women's disenfranchisement back to one of the most pervasive

stereotypes about emotion: that 'man was made to reason, women to feel'.[6] The association of men with rationality and women with 'irrational' feeling is as ancient as patriarchy itself, and as old as the concept of a partitioned mind and body, self or soul. From some of the earliest philosophical works on emotion, such as those by St Augustine in the fourth and fifth centuries AD, the 'passions' have been associated with 'the inferior part[s]' of a hierarchically organized soul, aligned with 'animal', sensory, instinctual qualities and, by extension, with subordinate classes, including women.[7] In the fourth and fifth centuries BC, Plato insisted that 'it is fitting for the reasoning part of the soul (*to logistikon*) to rule, since it is wise and takes thought for the whole soul', and that ungoverned passions were dangerously disruptive to the state.[8] Aristotle too pictured the human soul as divided into two aspects: the first, rational and dominant, the second constituted by the appetites, whose subservience was the basis of self-control (*enkrateia*). The hierarchical soul found a kindred framework in the hierarchical lens of gender. Aristotle praised obedience as an ideal quality of the body's passions and of the body politic's women; he encouraged dominance and control in men and their reason.[9] Augustine paralleled the loss of control of the 'superior part' of the soul over forceful, unruly passions, including jealousy, anger, envy and licentiousness, with men's loss of control over women, as evinced by Adam and Eve in Eden.[10] The Fall, implied Augustine, was a descent into a state in which women, and passions, were no longer reliably subjugated to men's reason.

Wollstonecraft's *A Vindication of the Rights of Woman* located this Manichean vision alive and well in the emotional culture of the late eighteenth century, which still attributed superior reason to men and inferior passion to women, and attributed social disorder to women's disobedience. Wollstonecraft hugely admired the historian Catharine Macaulay's *Letters on Education*, which held up women's education as the basis of a successful republic.[11] Education, reflected Wollstonecraft, was one of the principal areas on which male tyranny was stamped: it was one of the causes of women's 'senses [becoming] inflamed, and their understandings neglected'.[12] The type of education currently allowed to women excluded them from rational subjects like philosophy, politics, theology, classical literature and science. By denying women the opportunity to cultivate reason, they were denied the ability to rationally regulate their passions, and therefore debarred from political power, from intellectual or economic endeavour, and even from attaining religious virtue.

Instead, the prevalent emotional culture encouraged women to indulge what was believed to be their innately passionate nature, their susceptibility 'to love or lust': 'gentleness, docility, and a spaniel-like affection are, on this ground, consistently recommended as the cardinal virtues of the sex'. They became 'the prey of their senses' and of men's sexual whims, 'the toy of man, his rattle, and it must jingle in his ears whenever, dismissing reason, he chooses to be amused'.[13] It is 'time', Wollstonecraft wrote, 'to restore to [women] their lost dignity – and make them, as a part of the human species, labour by reforming themselves to reform the world'. She hoped that her book would incite 'a revolution in female manners'.[14] 'Manners' had a much more capacious meaning than in the present day, referring not to a precise system of etiquette, but to behavioural traits and moral codes, strongly linked to a society's material conditions.

Wollstonecraft was certain that women's propensity to behave more emotionally than men was the product not of innate characteristics, but of their subjugation by men within a sexist culture. And she held the 'cult of sensibility' particularly responsible for cementing the association between women and irrational feeling.[15] Philosophers from Aristotle to Descartes had tried to naturalize gendered differences in behaviour by attributing them to distinctions in the physiological construction of souls. Proponents of the cult of sensibility brought this biological distinction up to date, by exploiting contemporary theories of the nervous system to account for women's supposedly exceptional emotional sensitivity and inability to exert rational self-control.

Some of the most influential explanations of the medical basis for emotion in the eighteenth century focused on the nerves. In *The Passions of the Soul* (1649), the French philosopher René Descartes had offered a simple mechanical explanation for sensation. Nerves, consisting of the 'pith or internal substance' of the brain, and extending from the brain to the extremities, were moved like puppet-strings when muscles moved, he thought, which 'makes the part of the brain it comes from move, in the same way in which, when we pull one end of a cord, we make the other move'. 'Passions' were the result of a particular type of this internal movement, affecting the soul alone, which, Descartes concluded, was located in the 'pineal gland': 'the little gland in the middle of the brain, whence it radiates into all the rest of the body by the mediation of spirits, nerves, and even blood'.[16] Descartes thought passions, as physiological phenomena, were 'excitations of the soul', disturbances of the pineal gland caused by movements of the nerves and the animal spirits, whose motions might be explained using the physical laws that described the movement of matter – both solid and fluid – in the physical world.

Similarly, philosophers and medics in the eighteenth century transposed mechanistic laws describing the motion of solid matter, or the dynamics of fluid, onto the nervous system. The French physician and philosopher Julien Offray de La Mettrie was not alone in conceiving of 'man' – including the workings of the mind and temperament – as 'a machine'.[17] The Scottish physician George Cheyne depicted the human body in 1733 as 'a Machine of an infinite Number and Variety of different Channels and Pipes, filled with various and different Liquors and Fluids', in which the nerves ran from the brain to the extremities. Once 'struck on or touch'd' by an external stimulus, the nerves – comprising solid and fluid components – conveyed 'the Sound and Harmony to this sentient Principle, or *Musician*' in the brain, like 'an infinite Number of Hammers' tapping on 'a Bell in a Steeple'.[18] In the next decade, the philosopher David Hartley described how sensations triggered 'vibrations' in the 'medullary substance' of the nerves, while ideas or memories of sensations triggered smaller motions: 'Vibratiuncles and Miniatures'. He compared those motions to when 'in a concert of music the air is agitated by vibrations of a very complex kind'.[19] In 1765, the President of the Royal College of Physicians, Robert Whytt, depicted nerves as a network of 'small cords' extending from the brain to 'every part of the body'.[20] And the physician William Battie suggested in 1758 that, whilst the nerves themselves were solid, they were surrounded by conduits – including blood vessels – which were susceptible to tumours pressing on the nerves and, 'by compressing a sufficient quantity of medullary matter create delusive sensations,' 'ending in Madness'.[21]

These medical theories all connected the passions to sensation. They claimed that sensory perception of the material world was responsible for creating passions via the operation of the nerves; and that, at the other end of the process, these interior feelings were translated into physical expressions of emotion. Physicians such as Whytt, Battie and Cheyne constructed an image of a human body electrically alive to every prick, each velvet caress, every sting, burn and smart that kindled in the nerves upon physical contact with the material world. These ideas were the heart of the 'cult of sensibility', in which novelists, poets, artists and philosophers celebrated the body's sensitive, sympathetic interaction with the material world as the basis of sociable behaviour. The clergyman and novelist Laurence Sterne, author of *Tristram Shandy* and *A Sentimental Journey*, was one of the principal writers who depicted bodies not just as sensitive recipients of minutely variegated sensations, but also as eloquent communicators of the 'sentiments' that were stimulated by them: prostrated in grief, bursting into 'a flood of tears', blushing, trembling, stuttering, faltering. Between 1768 and 1781, the artist Angelica Kauffman painted a tableau inspired by Sterne's *Sentimental Journey*, in which three figures exchange pitying looks and charitable gestures that interweave the trio into a miniature encapsulation of emotional community. It was through such frank emotional displays that sympathy, pity and charity were awakened in observers, Sterne thought, and it was through sympathy that human societies were knitted together through the transmission of passions. Sterne, and other proponents of the schools of sensibility and sociability, imagined human societies as networks of individuals connected through exchanges of feeling via sympathy. Cities were not impersonal systems, but nuclei composed of pullulating passions and sensations, great 'sensori[a] of the world'.[22]

Most subscribers to the cult of sensibility thought that women's distinctive physiology rendered them particularly susceptible to spontaneous emotional displays, and peculiarly unable to exert control over them. Whytt suggested that bodily organs operated in 'sympathy' with one another, just as individual people did; and that women's unique possession of a uterus acted as an echo-chamber, magnifying nervous pain beyond levels experienced by men, resulting in 'delicate women' frequently experiencing 'fainting and convulsions', especially around the time of menstruation.[23] Cheyne went further, attributing the 'Solids, the Firmness, Force, and Strength of the Muscles' necessary to control the nervous system's entreaties solely to 'the *Male*', whereas 'the *Female*', he claimed, was merely a weak, passive and pliable 'Habitation' for sperm ('the seminal Animalcul') and not an independent, rational moral agent.[24]

Wollstonecraft excoriated the cult of sensibility's religious implications, its notion that 'the image of God' dwelt in 'matter' and was perceived through 'sensation'. She nurtured a less sensual form of religion, believing that 'virtue' was instead the result of rigorous 'exercise of reason' to direct the passions towards love of an immaterial God: it required the sacrifice of pleasure, and an effort to make the seductive 'delusions of passion' cooperate with 'the order of creation' and 'the Father of spirits'.[25] In *A Vindication of the Rights of Woman*, she particularly targeted the idea, propagated by the cult of sensibility, that it was women who were naturally prone to irrational – and religiously immoral – sensual behaviour. Wollstonecraft condemned how women were uniquely encouraged to devote themselves to 'cramping their understandings' through lack of education, and 'sharpening their senses' in order to excite 'the sexual attention of men'.[26] Wollstonecraft turned especial fury on her political adversary Edmund Burke, who, in 1757, had penned *A Philosophical Enquiry in the Origin of our Ideas of the Sublime and Beautiful*. Burke had attributed to 'nature' – not culture – the 'notion' that 'Beauty in distress is much the most affecting beauty', and he celebrated 'weakness and imperfection', smallness, 'modesty', even 'sickness' in women as alluring attributes.[27] In *A Vindication of the Rights of Men* Wollstonecraft had held Burke responsible, as one of the chief influences on the cult of sensibility, for persuading women 'not to cultivate the moral virtues that might chance to excite respect', but to 'turn all their attention to their persons, systematically neglecting morals to secure beauty', and fostering a 'laxity of morals in the female world' that rendered women vulnerable to 'a libertine imagination'.[28]

The target of Wollstonecraft's anger – the stereotype of emotional, confused women and cool, rational, powerful men – dominates the present-day approach to emotion. John Gray's *Men are from Mars, Women are from Venus* (1992) is one of the most famous twentieth-century articulations of the claim that men and women 'almost seem to be from different planets, speaking different languages and needing different nourishment'. Men, Gray claims, value 'power, competency, efficiency, and achievement' and are 'interested in "objects" and "things" rather than people and feelings', while women value 'love, communication, beauty, and relationships' and define their self-worth 'through their feelings and the quality of their relationships'.[29] Whereas eighteenth-century doctors attributed this supposed difference to sexed variations in the nervous system's physiology, similar modern-day claims tend to focus on the brain. The relocation of the principal seat of emotion from the nervous system to the brain took place in the nineteenth century, fuelled in part by the emergence of psychiatry and psychology as disciplines most concerned with emotion, but also manifested in the rise of brain 'sciences' like phrenology. Even in the midst of that shift, the claim that female biology renders women peculiarly susceptible to uncontrolled emotion remained constant. The social psychologist Carol Tavris has described how nineteenth-century physicians held the variance in size between male and female brains, particularly in the frontal lobes, responsible for 'women's alleged intellectual failings and emotional weaknesses'.[30] In the twentieth and twenty-first centuries, it is not brain *size* that is generally held responsible for 'innate' differences in male and female emotional behaviour, but a mixture of genes, brain structure and activity, and, increasingly, the role of neurotransmitters and hormones, such as testosterone.

For example, Allan and Barbara Pease, and Susan Pinker independently use neuroimaging studies to show how, when men perceive emotion in people's facial expressions, this involves localized activity in one hemisphere of the brain, whereas women's perceptions of emotion involve activity across both hemispheres; they conclude that women invest more types of activities with emotion than men, who keep its influence strictly limited.[31] The neuroscientist Simon Baron-Cohen has devised the 'empathizing-systematizing theory' to describe five different brain 'types', claiming that 'female brains' score higher on measures of empathy and 'male brains' on measures of systematizing. He links the development of 'male' systematizing brains to exposure to foetal testosterone, and evokes evolutionary psychology, such as prehistorical narratives of women's greater immersion in childrearing and community-formation, to explain the apparent propensity of the female brain to empathize.[32] The neuropsychiatrist Louann Brizendine uses theories, including Baron-Cohen's, about the different ways in which men and women's brains process emotions to claim that, compared to women's apparently greater emotional intuition and gut instinct, men 'don't seem to have the same innate ability to read faces and tone of voice for emotional nuance'.[33]

Such views about the neuroscientific basis for dramatic differences in emotional behaviour between the sexes do not go unchallenged, however. The psychologist Cordelia Fine labels the lazy recruitment of neuroscience's veneer of authority in the service of gendered stereotypes 'neurosexism'.[34] Just as Wollstonecraft had pointed to the pervasive influence of culture, not biology, on women's emotional behaviour, many contemporary neuroscientists admit it is virtually impossible to isolate 'innate' differences in male and female brains. Brain activity alters with repeated behaviour: the brain of a woman encouraged by her culture to engage in habitual emotive behaviour will demonstrate marked differences to the brain of a man culturally dissuaded from emotive behaviour. In a recent article for *Neuroethics* the philosopher Robyn Bluhm argued that 'there is an important difference between knowing that an area of the brain is *involved in* some behavior (or differs in activity between two groups) and knowing how it *contributes to* that behavior or difference'.[35] And it is not by any means a neutral statement to claim that males have an innate propensity for reason, and women for emotion. The types of employment that Baron-Cohen suggests are inherently suited to male 'systematizing' brains – including engineering, science, computer programming, law – are, as the sociolinguist Deborah Cameron points out, 'more varied, more creative, and better rewarded' than the jobs he considers suited to female 'empathizing' brains, such as teaching and nursing.[36] To assert that women are innately precluded from such well-paid jobs by dint of missing out on a foetal testosterone surge is a modern manifestation of eighteenth-century physicians' claims that women's uniquely sensitive nervous system rendered them unable to command the reason apparently essential to any job involving power and status.

It is also debatable whether men are actually as unemotional as we tend to think. Contemporary masculinity denigrates *some* types of emotional expression among men, but not all: fear, but not anger, for example. The notion that women are much more emotionally articulate than men, incontinently spewing out a torrent of confessional and sentimental reflection and gossip, is also 'a myth', argues Cameron. A linguistic study of the use of emotion words among a large sample of speakers found little gendered difference in the frequency of emotive language employed by men and women, and only variations in the type of words: males tend to employ words relating to anger and aggression more frequently than women.[37] Sociologists Clive Seale and Jonathan Charteris-Black have also explored variations in men and women's use of emotional language in relation to serious illness. They discovered that, although women tended to be 'more likely' to talk about crying or 'being upset or fearful', men were 'not averse to speaking about emotions', and used words relating to 'depression', and swear words related to frustration, with higher frequency than women. In many examples, greater variations in emotional language occurred according to socio-economic class than gender.[38]

One popular extrapolation from the stereotype that women are more emotional than men is the claim that men's inability to vocalize their feelings leads to a higher suicide rate, among young men in particular. In 2015 a *Guardian* opinion piece claimed that 'men struggle desperately to express their feelings and this struggle seriously affects the quality of their lives'.[39] In 2013, suicide was the leading cause of death for both men and women in the 20–34 age bracket, but 24 per cent of men, compared to 12 per cent of women, in that bracket died by suicide. This statistic (from the Office for National Statistics in Britain) is frequently invoked by the media to back up the claim that more men suffer fatally from their apparent emotional repression than women. But multiple factors complicate and even contradict this claim. In 2014 a World Health Organization report showed that, in the 15–19 age bracket, suicide is the leading killer of girls in Europe, whereas road-traffic injury kills most men in that demographic.[40] And although more men than women did die by suicide in the 20–34 age bracket in 2013, this is partly explained by men frequently attempting suicide using more violent methods, such as hanging, strangulation, suffocation or firearms, which are more likely to result in death.[41] In 2007 a survey of Adult Psychiatric Morbidity in England found that more women both contemplated suicide (19.2 per cent) and acted on it (6.9 per cent) than men (14 per cent and 4.3 per cent, respectively), but that they were more likely to use 'non-violent' means, such as overdoses, which were less likely to result in death.[42] The number of women suffering mental health disorders is far higher than men – around 20–40 per cent higher – and a recent study by the NHS has discovered that one in eight women aged 16–24 in England screen positive for Post-Traumatic Stress Disorder.[43] This is not to suggest that male suicide should not be taken seriously. But the claim that men are disproportionately vulnerable to suicidal ideation as a result of a culture of masculinity denigrating emotional communication among men is not conclusively supported by evidence, either that men are more suicidal or depressed than women, or that men are significantly less emotional then women.

It is not only doubtful whether men do suffer worse mental health than women, but the axiom that emotional expression is uncomplicatedly beneficial to well-being, and can fend off depression and suicidal ideation, also does not hold up to scrutiny. Freud claimed that repression obstructed emotion's inexorable 'flow' into expression, causing desires and emotions to be perverted into the outlets of 'hysterical symptoms'. Psychoanalytic therapy, he hoped, would release that pent-up pressure and neutralize emotions so that they would no longer manifest in hysterical symptoms.[44] But it is surprisingly difficult to find hard and fast evidence testifying to how simply 'talking about it' improves mental health.

Firstly, well-being is hard to measure. Each individual's state of happiness is composed of multiple factors, traits and variables, including physical health, childhood attachment and experiences, the weather's influence, and sufficient economic wealth. The multiplicity of these contributing factors makes analysis of the contentment of large groups of people very difficult to measure accurately. It is even harder to determine whether contributing factors – such as emotional articulacy – are correlations or causes of happiness. Research by the psychologist Jordi Quoidbach claims that 'emodiversity' – 'the variety and relative abundance of the emotions that humans experience', and the ability to name them – 'is an independent predictor of mental and physical health'.[45] But many studies have shown links between higher levels of education (leading to an expanded vocabulary in all areas, including emotion) and better adult mental health, due to the fact that education generates 'additional economic resources, fewer chronic stressors, healthier lifestyles, more social support'.[46]

Secondly, both Cameron and Tavris independently question the role that communication plays in 'the pursuit of happiness'.[47] Tavris debunks the corresponding assumptions that expressing anger *always* dissipates it, whilst silently harbouring anger can lead to poor mental health. She shows how 'ventilation' of anger can actually lead to a breakdown in relationships, higher blood-pressure, lowered self-esteem, dwelling and rumination, and can exacerbate the initial problem; and she cautiously suggests very specific conditions under which the expression of anger can be effective: 'cathartic experiences do not feel good because they have emptied some physiological energy reservoir, but because they have accomplished a social goal: the redemption of justice, reinforcement of the social order'.[48] A study of 'The Psychology of Suicidal Behaviour' by Rory O'Connor and Matthew Nock in *Lancet Psychiatry* also makes an importantly distinction between 'brooding rumination' and 'reflective pondering'. O'Connor and Nock found that 'a tendency to suppress unwanted thoughts was associated with both suicidal ideation and attempts', but that not all forms of emotional articulation were equally benefi-cial. Reflective pondering might allow a person to contemplate 'the reasons for his or her symptoms and potential solutions'. But brooding rumination – 'repetitive focus on an individual's own symptoms of distress' – has 'been linked with suicidal thoughts and distress'.[49] 'Talking about it', then, is not beneficial because of a physiological need to 'discharge' negative emotion. Confession's therapeutic effects may derive from the attachment and, in eighteenth-century terms, the 'sociability', cemented during the interaction. Ruminating in isolation, dwelling and self-narrating, does not provide this social consolation and sup-port for mental distress. 'Talking about it' is not a cure-all for angry, frustrated emotions.

A Vindication of the Rights of Woman tackled the eighteenth-century predecessors of sexist beliefs about gendered emotions and caused a literary stir. Many female readers recognized their own intellectual frustration in Wollstonecraft's attack on women's exclusion from rational activity. The poet and admirer of Godwin, Rachel Prescott, in Blackburn, recalled that it was Wollstonecraft's book that 'first induced me to think'.[50] The

Scottish writer Anne MacVicar Grant – often known as 'Mrs Anne Grant of Laggan' – reported how it was so in demand that there was barely time to read it, before it was snatched away by the next eager recipient.[51] Predictably, however, some men recoiled at Wollstonecraft's challenge to the orthodoxy. William Godwin privately considered it 'a very unequal performance ... deficient in method and arrangement'. He thought Wollstonecraft's repeated condemnations of Burke in both *Vindications* unseemly and 'too contemptuous and intemperate [a] treatment of the great man', and put her criticisms down to simple disappointment at Burke's abandonment of the reform movement.[52] The *Critical Review* advised Wollstonecraft to become more 'feminine' in order to be 'infinitely happier', and various writers satirized her encouragement of women's adoption of 'masculine' reason.[53] Maria Edgeworth encapsulated her censure of Wollstonecraft in the loud, 'bold, masculine', jocular, but untrustworthy cross-dressing figure of Harriet Freke in her novel *Belinda*.[54]

For Wollstonecraft, the second *Vindication* marked the end of a period of literary aridity. Between the publication of her *Reply to Burke* in November 1790 and the commencement of its follow-up in October 1791, her obsession with Fuseli had diverted her energies away from writing. Knowles described how for 'more than twelve months "she [had written] nothing but criticisms for the Analytical Review," and even these, which required but little exertion of the talents which she possessed, would not have been written but for her daily necessities'.[55] After the second *Vindication*'s publication in January 1792, some of Wollstonecraft's friends thought she would be better off throwing herself into a mooted second volume. But it was still her relationship with Fuseli that occupied the centre of her political imagination. And where better to attempt to challenge the inequalities she had identified in relations between men and women than in revolutionary France? French politicians' commitment to offering alternative models of relationships was becoming evident: the French Legislative Assembly was working towards legalizing divorce, and even allowing women to instigate the proceedings. France certainly promised to offer a welcoming location for the unconventional polygamous set-up she was entertaining. So, in the middle of June 1792, Wollstonecraft, her publisher Johnson, Henry and Sophia Fuseli all discussed the possibility of making a 'summer excursion to Paris'.[56] The other three were likely motivated simply by the desire to witness the progress of the French Revolution, but Wollstonecraft may have privately harboured hopes that the *frisson* of revolutionary Paris would bring the married Fuseli around to the unconventional relationship that she had been suggesting. But, as we shall see, history intervened. The French visit would provide Wollstonecraft with the life-changing emotional and sexual exhilaration she was seeking, but it would take a very different shape to that she originally anticipated.

Chapter 4

THE INHUMANITY OF KINGS

As Mary Wollstonecraft was planning a foray into revolutionary France, a nervous 'little, fat democrat' with heavy-lidded eyes, insignificant chin, apologetic mouth and receding fine hair was entering the ongoing French Revolution controversy.[1] Like Wollstonecraft, he too was pre-occupied with the relationship between politics and emotion. In 1792, Thomas Beddoes was a thirty-two-year-old lecturer in chemistry at the University of Oxford. Although he began the 1790s by articulating conventional Enlightenment views about how the passions operate, by the end of the decade his research would disprove one of the era's most tenacious medical theories of emotion. The fissures caused by the seismic shift in emotional culture would be especially visible in Beddoes' life and work.

His best friend, Davies Giddy – an athletic, handsome, occasionally taciturn Cornishman, seven years younger – had been a student of Beddoes' at Pembroke College, Oxford, and described his lecturer and friend affectionately, as of a

'congenial, muddling disposition'.[2] Beddoes was an uneasy fit
at Oxford. He was a political radical amid the university's ultra-
conservatives, a stammering Shropshire lad terrified of women,
and a lecturer – a 'Chemical Reader' – whose research interests
fell between the disciplines of chemistry and medicine. But the
French Revolution, and the newly galvanized radical movement
in Britain, provided Beddoes with an intellectual and political
environment in which he felt at home.

In the summer of 1791, Beddoes and Giddy had taken a
holiday in the West Country, to visit Giddy's family house.
Discontent was steadily mounting throughout Britain in the
early 1790s, driven on the one hand by a labouring class suffering
tolls, tithes, and rising prices, and inspired to varying degrees
by the model of a successful uprising in France; and, on the
other, by a conservative establishment concerned about a bloody
mob-driven Terror on British soil. Beddoes and Giddy travelled through Bristol, and found the city in a febrile state. The
mayor had received a threat from a local counter-revolutionary
'Church and King' mob – loyalist reactionaries, who frequently
resorted to violence – warning that 'We are coming Near ...
2,000 Good harty hail strong Rufins [ruffians] which will Pull
Down your fine Manchin [Mansion] house' in protest against the
radical movement's support for religious tolerance.[3] In August,
Beddoes learned of riots in Shropshire, near his home town of
Shifnal; colliers at his friend William Reynolds' ironworks at
Ketley, angered by new regulations, plotted to murder their
employer. Reynolds was informed of the conspiracy in advance,
and responded by sending to Birmingham for firearms, clamping
down on the sale of alcohol, and offering to meet personally
with each of the 2,000 workers who gathered outside his gates
to discuss their grievances. 'In a few hours peace was restor'd'
and 'two men and a woman' were arrested.[4]

Despite the upheavals of 1791, Beddoes and Giddy had had
a joyous summer. Filled with heady optimism at the progress of

the French Revolution, they had fearlessly worn revolutionary cockades as they stomped along the paths criss-crossing the Land's End peninsula. Beddoes was invited to a dance at the new house of the Cornish Copper Company's director and, in a moment of recklessness, he pinned a cockade to the bandeau of a young Cornish woman, 'Miss M. J.'.[5] Later that holiday, Beddoes wrote a poem about this 'Rosalind of Cornwall's Bowers', the 'Beauty' whose 'polished brow' was overshadowed by 'Freedom's garland'.[6] The poem acquired a certain degree of fame. One reader sent him 'a most superb cockade' while another commissioned 'a celebrated composer at Liverpool' to set it to music.[7] More bizarrely, Beddoes discovered that his friend William Reynolds had been so 'wonderfully smitten with the account I was able to give of the elegant accomplishments of the lady' that he had commissioned a 'portrait of the lady', complete with cockade, for his own entertainment, 'in the French sense of that term at least': possibly hinting at its use as a masturbatory aid.[8]

The French Revolution galvanized Beddoes into more than sentimental poetry. He began to discuss with Giddy the implications of political reform for medical progress. Since the revolution's outbreak in 1789, especially during holidays in the Scottish Highlands and return visits to Shropshire, Beddoes had witnessed first-hand the effects of illness on country people unable to afford doctors. He was preoccupied by debates about the best way of helping such people, now that there seemed widespread sympathy across the country for progressive social measures. Should the sick be empowered to treat themselves, or medicine professionalized and access to skilled doctors widened, he wondered? Were resources better directed towards preventing, or treating, illness? Was ill health a product of inequality, and should medicine tackle the symptoms or the political and financial causes?[9] In the summer of 1791, Beddoes opposed a scheme to establish a county hospital in Truro, pointing out the

uncertainty of the private philanthropy on which such an institution would have to depend. And in a 'spot in the field' between
Giddy's house in Tredrea and St Erth, Beddoes later claimed
to have experienced an epiphany.[10] It struck him that treatment
of one of the most fatal diseases of the eighteenth century –
consumption – had been overwhelmingly skewed towards the
wealthy, who were encouraged to take expensive recuperative
trips to Britain's spa towns and the warmer climates of Portugal
and the French Riviera. He thought that there was great need for
an institution dedicated to treating poor consumptive patients,
using the most innovative methods available.

As the long summer days of their West Country tour grew
shorter and darker, the political storm clouds began to gather.
Giddy was astounded to hear of his own nomination as sheriff
of Cornwall. It was a privilege, but also a bind – he would have
to leave Oxford, Beddoes and revolutionary politics, and confine
himself to preventing popular violence in Cornwall. At the end
of the summer, Beddoes wrote up his criticisms of privately
funded hospitals in a paper, 'Considerations on Infirmaries',
but his superiors at Oxford noted its radical implications and
'trace[d] a chain of ideas from the French Revolution to doubts
concerning the extensive usefulness of hospitals'.[11] Beddoes
was acquiring a reputation as an 'incurably heterodox' political free-thinker, which was cemented when, at the end of the
year, he proposed establishing a radical provincial newspaper in
Shrewsbury or perhaps around Birmingham to provide unbiased
reporting of the French Revolution and British reform efforts.[12]
Comparing French accounts of the revolution's progress with
those in British papers had made Beddoes very 'aware that our
newspapers . . . select every thing that can bring discredit upon
[the National Assembly] & suppress the rest'.[13] By early 1792, he
had become positive that 'Pitt or his gang [have bought] over the
printers of the country papers to their side'.[14]

This was not necessarily paranoia. Prime Minister William

Pitt, along with his former collaborators in reform, Charles Lennox, the Duke of Richmond, and Edmund Burke, had abandoned his earlier political sympathies for reform. Pitt had championed the cause of the American colonists during the American War of Independence, urging the then prime minister Lord North to make peace with the rebels, and had unsuccessfully promoted numerous reform bills in parliament. But after the outbreak of the French Revolution in 1789, Pitt began to clamp down on the publication of 'seditious' texts, determined to defend Britain against the wild and violent passions that had been unleashed by democratic progress in France. This was just the beginning of a much more dramatic volte-face for Pitt; later in the 1790s, he would be held up as the archetype of political betrayal and apostasy, and would find himself surrounded by angry crowds shouting 'No war, no Pitt, cheap bread' and pelting his carriage windows with stones.[15]

The need to defend the freedom of the press became urgent when the second part of Tom Paine's *Rights of Man* was published in February 1792. As in the first part, Paine attacked monarchy and social hierarchy, emphasized the necessary subordination of the government to its people, and urged that 'nature, reason and experience' must form a 'guide' to a more representative political system. But Part Two was far more radical than its predecessor. Paine described how all systems of government, founded, as Burke described, on the basis of property and 'hereditary succession', were merely forms of 'government through the medium of passions'. Wanting to 'speak an open and disinterested language, dictated by no passion', Paine eschewed all forms of government on the basis that humans possessed a 'natural instinct' that made them sociable: 'The more perfect civilisation is, the less occasion has it for government, because the more does it regulate its own affairs, and govern itself.'[16] To conservatives and reactionaries, it rang out as the voice of anarchy.

Paine hoped that *Rights of Man* would get 'the ear of John Bull'. But shortly after the publication of Part Two, the American statesman Gouverneur Morris, who thought Paine 'inflated to the Eyes', prophetically recorded in his diary: 'He seems Cock Sure of bringing about a Revolution in Great Britain, and I think it quite as likely that he will be promoted to the Pilory [*sic*]'.[17] Part Two of Paine's book did indeed get the attention of British readers. Cheap editions, compiling the most popular and incendiary extracts, were circulated, and Paine's work was discussed in newly established political societies throughout the land. Disconcerted by the books' extraordinary popularity, establishment newspapers accused him of treasonous behaviour and, at the end of May 1792, Paine's publisher, Joseph Johnson, was indicted for sedition. Two weeks later, as Morris had predicted, Paine himself was summoned on a charge of seditious libel, around the same time that a Royal Proclamation against Seditious Writings and Publications was issued.

Beddoes' plan to defy the government's crack-down on radical publications by establishing a radical newspaper was slow to take flight: he knew that it 'will be a losing project at first'.[18] So in 1792, as Wollstonecraft was publishing her attack on the gendered hierarchy of emotion and formulating her Parisian scheme, Beddoes entered the French Revolution controversy and developed the debate about the political relevance of the passions. In a number of works, he claimed to be able to explain the origins of revolutionary violence. Wollstonecraft had shown how changes to individuals' intimate behaviour towards one another might form the nuclei of what Burke had called a general 'revolution in sentiment'. But, in the long run, Beddoes hoped to use his medical expertise to elucidate the physiology of what the philosopher and economist Adam Smith called the 'unsocial passions', and even to find 'cures' that might undergird a more peaceful and contented society.[19]

*

One of Beddoes' first works, printed in 1792, was the long poem *Alexander's Expedition down the Hydaspes & the Indus to the Indian Ocean*, which imitated the poetic style of the natural philosopher, physician and poet Erasmus Darwin, whom Beddoes had first met in the late 1780s. Whereas Darwin's obsession was botany, Beddoes dealt with human tyranny and subjugation. *Alexander's Expedition down the Hydaspes* analysed the relationship between 'the Tyrant's and the Conqueror's shame' and 'Sympathy [that] could melt that feeling breast'.[20] In his *Reflections*, Burke had attributed the popular violence visible in France to the inherently unruly, irrational passions of the 'mob', reflecting the ancient hierarchical view of reason's relation to emotion. Beddoes rejected Burke's explanation. Instead, in letters and poetry in the early 1790s, he argued that there was nothing intrinsically right- or left-wing, upper- or labouring-class, about wild passion and violence. '[A] savage spirit in the people and tyranny in the possessors of power are to one another cause and effect,' Beddoes declared.[21] Violent emotion was not innate to 'the mob', regardless of circumstance. It was a universal response to oppression. And it could be dissolved by a more 'sympathetic' form of government.

Beddoes' conclusions about tyranny's capacity to drum up violent passion in the populace had been formed during two major disturbances the previous year. At 3 p.m. on 14 July 1791, a group of eighty-one supporters of the French Revolution had gathered at Thomas Dadley's Hotel, on Temple Row in Birmingham, 'to commemorate the auspicious day' in 1789 that had 'witnessed the emancipation of twenty-six millions of people from the yoke of despotism' in France. The dinner had been advertised in local newspapers over the preceding days, and graffiti had been spotted across Birmingham, proclaiming 'Church and King for ever' and 'destruction to the Presbyterians'.[22]

The British reform movement was closely connected to campaigns for religious tolerance. Religious dissenters had faced institutionalized discrimination since the Restoration of the British monarchy in the 1660s. In December 1661 King Charles II had passed the Corporation Act, which stipulated that no one could be elected to any office relating to the government of a city or corporation without having received, in the last twelve months, the Holy Communion according to Anglican rites. This was ostensibly a means to restrict the power of Catholics, but in reality it was aimed more at the Presbyterians, who had acquired significant political power during the English Civil War. In 1673 the Corporation Act was followed by the Test Act, which enforced on every person in a civil or military office the obligation of taking certain oaths pledging allegiance to the monarch as Supreme Governor of the Church of England, and of receiving the sacrament within three months of taking office. The Test and Corporation Acts effectively debarred Catholics and dissenters, who refused such oaths and sacraments, from all official jobs.[23]

Despite concessions made by the 1689 Toleration Act, dissenters were, throughout the eighteenth century, excluded from universities as students or lecturers; forbidden from holding municipal or Crown offices; barred from important chartered companies (such as the Bank of England, the East India Company and the South Sea Company); and disqualified from holding significant roles in local hospitals, almshouses and workhouses. British dissenters like Joseph Priestley, Joseph Johnson and Richard Price, and especially women with dissenting connections, were excluded from full participation in the civil and political life of eighteenth-century Britain. As the reform movement made progress, provincial literary and philosophical societies and popular political associations, including the corresponding societies, were dominated by dissenting merchants, industrialists, writers and editors. Many of them saw their own fight for religious liberty mirrored in contemporary campaigns, such as support for the colonists during the American War of

Independence between 1775 and 1783. The polymathic chemist and theologian Joseph Priestley, a Unitarian, was a prime example. In 1780, he came to Birmingham as a senior minister of one of the largest and wealthiest dissenting congregations in England. He became an active member of the Lunar Society, meeting regularly – at each full moon – with local scientists and schemers ('projectors'), including Erasmus Darwin, the steam-engine manufacturers Matthew Boulton and James Watt, the educationalist Richard Lovell Edgeworth, and the Wedgwood family, to discuss projects to improve humanity's living conditions through medicine, engineering, science and education. And he wrote vocally in support of campaigns to repeal the Corporation and Test Acts, in a *Letter to the Rt. Honourable William Pitt* in 1787 and in subsequent sermons.

Priestley had decided not to attend the Birmingham commemorative dinner on 14 July 1791, on the recommendation of friends fearing trouble. These concerns were justified. When the celebrators arrived, they encountered a daunting phalanx of protestors, almost equal in number to themselves, screaming 'No Popery'. By 7 or 8 p.m. the demonstrators had swelled to hundreds. They were chiefly local apprentices and labourers, opportunist looters, and a sober, determined core of 'hired hands' paid by Tory magistrates, who granted them immunity from arrest and prosecution.[24] This rabble hurled stones at the departing reformers, before laying waste to the hotel. The city's Quaker meeting house was next, then Priestley's New Meeting chapel, which was burned to the ground, followed by another dissenting church.

Priestley later described how it was 'remarkably calm, and clear', under bright 'moon-light' that night. News had already reached him of the mob's advance, and he had decamped to the house of friends, William Russell, the merchant and chief vestryman of the New Meeting congregation, and his wife, Martha. Priestley recalled how, as the mob rounded on his own house and laboratory at Fair Hill in Sparkbrook, 'we could see to a considerable distance, and being upon a rising ground, we distinctly heard all that passed at the house, every shout of the mob, and almost every stroke of the instruments they had provided for breaking the doors and the furniture'.[25] Priestley's pupils, Thomas Wright Hill and Thomas Clark, secreted some of his possessions in an adjoining field, barred the doors and secured the shutters; and Hill collared one of the thugs and hauled him before the local jailer, who released him on the grounds that he had orders to take in no prisoners that night. By dawn, Priestley's once magnificent house had been burned to the ground – after much trouble to get a fire started – and his library, scientific instruments, unique manuscripts and domestic possessions lost for ever. A painting entitled *Destruction of Dr. Priestley's House and Laboratory ... After a picture sketched on the spot* shows drunken malcontents hurling furniture, vases and papers from the broken windows of the top floor, whilst dismantling the house's brickwork amid plumes of acrid smoke and flames.

The rioters continued their destruction for another three days, proceeding through a list of dissenters' residences and workplaces. The homes of John Ryland, John Taylor, Joseph Jukes, John Coates, John Hobson, Thomas Hawkes, William Russell and John Harwood were all ransacked and burned, along with local dissenting chapels.[26] The poet William Hutton mourned that, 'on the morning of the 15th I was a rich man; in the evening I was ruined'.[27] Rioters were heard yelling, 'Church and King for ever ... Don't leave them Presbyterian dogs a place standing'.[28] Magistrates turned away army volunteers on the spurious grounds that 'We have our plans'. One magistrate, Joseph Carles, was even said to have assured the rioters that 'I will stand your friend, as far as lies in my power.'[29]

It was only on the afternoon of Sunday, 17 July 1791, three whole days after the riots had begun, that troops arrived from Nottingham after a belated appeal from Birmingham's magistrates to the Home Office; and the riots finally fizzled out as their perpetrators drifted away. Although the government subsequently issued a reward for identification of the ringleaders, the trial, which took place in August 1791, was a charade, and Pitt's ministers obstructed a subsequent government inquiry. In 1792 the Home Secretary, Henry Dundas, assured British citizens that the government had done everything in its power to suppress the violence. This was despite a wealth of evidence that not only had magistrates purposely allowed the riots to continue; they had even instigated them. The 'Priestley Riots', as they became known, confirmed the burgeoning suspicions of activists like Beddoes that the most pronounced episodes of outright violence and underhand plots in the early 1790s derived not from the radical left – with whom such dangerous behaviour was associated by writers like Burke – but from the conservative establishment itself, desperate to fend off a French-style uprising at any cost. The Priestley Riots were also one of the first indications that British reformers' hopes would not reach fruition without a battle.

Birmingham was not the only place to be shattered by riots in July 1791. Thousands of miles away, on the outskirts of the city of Cap François, in the French colony of Saint-Domingue (now Haiti), slaves formed a plan to destroy the plantations, massacre their brutal white governors and take control of the colony. Earlier that year, French soldiers had landed at Saint-Domingue's main port, Port-au-Prince, with the news that the National Assembly had declared all men – including slaves – free and equal.[30] The French Revolution, and the National Assembly's official recognition of the male slaves' full humanity and equality, inspired the slaves to seize power. The plan of July 1791 did not entirely succeed, but it was a stepping stone to a massive revolt a few weeks later, on 21 August 1791, which involved 100,000 slaves, the death of 4,000 plantation owners and workers, and the destruction of 180 sugar plantations.

Finally, in 1804, from the blood and flames of thirteen years of rebellion, a state would emerge that was free from slavery, ruled over by former slaves.

News of the Saint-Domingue revolution was greeted enthusiastically in Britain, where an abolitionist movement had been gathering momentum since the late 1780s. Over the course of the eighteenth century, popular attitudes to slavery had radically shifted from unquestioning acceptance to widespread criticism and revulsion. Anne Stott, biographer of the evangelical abolitionist and educator Hannah More, has called this turnaround 'one of the most remarkable changes in sensibility in human history'.[31] The change was partly fuelled by eighteenth-century theories of emotion. The cult of sensibility's celebration of the acute sensations of the suffering body helped many to accept the slaves' humanity, while moral philosophers, including Adam Smith and David Hume, insisted on the importance of sympathy and charity to social cohesion. (As an economist, Smith was also opposed to slavery as an inefficient system of production, in which unpropertied slaves had no incentive to work.) The change in attitude took sustenance from Jean-Jacques Rousseau's idealization of the 'noble savage' as a figure uncorrupted by the immorality of white civilization. And abolition was also propelled by the Protestant religious movement of evangelicalism, whose early leader John Wesley stressed that salvation relied – not as the Puritans believed, on prolonged moral struggle – but only upon faith in Christ, which could make a believer 'perfect in love' and bring about a heartfelt conversion experience. Evangelicals set great store by the doctrine of spiritual equality which held that slaves, like Europeans, were made in the image of God.[32]

In the wake of the Saint-Domingue revolution, Thomas Beddoes threw himself into efforts in Shropshire to support a parliamentary bill for the abolition of the slave trade, probably campaigning alongside Darwin, Reynolds and Archdeacon

Plymley, the leader of the Society for Effecting an Abolition of the Slave Trade in Shropshire. Beddoes penned a petition calling for the collection of signatures in favour of abolition from across Britain, to show 'the universal voice of the nation'. And he fervently supported a scheme to persuade British consumers to eschew slave-produced West Indian sugar in favour of ethical alternatives such as American maple syrup and Chinese imports, to 'undermine an evil which our legislature has not virtue enough to extirpate'.[33]

The most pronounced effect that the Saint-Domingue revolution and the Priestley Riots had upon Beddoes was to clarify his views about the operation of the passions. He realized that the Priestley Riots had become more vicious upon the militia's arrival, and he compared the Church and King mob's behaviour to the 'mad devastation' and 'promiscuous massacre' perpetrated by the slaves in Saint-Domingue.[34] At around the same time, the trial of Warren Hastings, the de facto Governor-General of India, which lasted from 1788 to 1795, opened Beddoes' eyes to the corruption, criminality and colonial brutality perpetrated by the East India Company in India. Beddoes claimed that 'the inhumanity of kings' was directly responsible for provoking popular violence.[35] Tom Paine had made a similar point, pointing to the Priestley Riots as an example of 'tumults' that 'did not proceed from the want of a government, but that government itself was the generating cause'.[36]

Beddoes explained that the imposition of authoritarian constraints on individuals' freedoms obstructed citizens' natural passions, causing them to erupt in violence, anger, hatred and other unsocial emotions. This was as true an explanation of the murderous behaviour of the Haitian slaves and the *sans-culottes* of revolutionary France – a nebulous urban mobilization of the labouring poor – as it was of the loyalist Church and King mob during the Priestley Riots, he thought. It was, Beddoes claimed, in his first foray into political writing in 1792, a universal fact of human behaviour. The theory behind Beddoes' political explanation of the passions is today often called the 'hydraulic theory' of emotion. It dominated popular understanding of how the passions operated in the eighteenth century and would preoccupy Beddoes for the remainder of the decade. In 1792, he was principally concerned with the political ramifications of hydraulic theory, but over the following years he would become fascinated by its medical basis. But it wasn't until the end of the decade that Beddoes' own experiments would disprove medical justifications for hydraulic theory, while the 1790s' political course would challenge hydraulic explanations of popular violence. Beddoes would be left groping in an unfamiliar landscape for alternative explanations of how the passions operate in the body, and for new justifications for the psychological dangers of authoritarian government.

Today, hydraulic turns of phrase still encourage us to think of the emotions as, in the words of the historian Barbara Rosenwein, 'great liquids within each person, heaving and frothing, eager to be let out'.[37] We talk of emotional 'outbursts', of 'flipping my lid', 'erupting' into obscenities, of passion needing 'to be channelled' or to 'find an outlet' and not to be 'bottled up'. The trope of a man with steam coming out of his ears is instantly legible. This idea was influentially expressed in the Aristotelian poetic idea of 'catharsis' – the purging of excessive emotion – and its later transformation by Sigmund Freud's colleague Josef Breuer into a psychological treatment that sought to lessen the force of trauma by freeing repressed emotions. In his early work, Freud revitalized hydraulic theory's popularity by describing 'repression' as a process whereby 'wishes and desires' are prevented from 'obtaining discharge' from the psyche. 'The libido,' Freud wrote, 'behaves like a stream whose main bed has become blocked. It proceeds to fill up collateral channels which may hitherto have been empty'.[38]

The hydraulic theory of emotion has been part of

Anglo-American culture since the medieval period. Its popularity ebbs and flows, but it never entirely evaporates. At the beginning of the 1790s, hydraulic theory was in the ascendancy. To reformers like Beddoes, it offered an explanation, seemingly based on up-to-the-minute scientific and medical discoveries about fluid pressure, which warned of the dangers of oppression and excessive authoritarian restraint, hindering the populace's free expression of emotion and desire. Those dangers would be played out in the individual body and in the body politic. Liberal keystones like freedom of speech took on a new importance as 'safety valves' allowing the free discharge of emotion, preventing it from accumulating and bursting out in more threatening forms of expression.

To conservative readers, this was a veiled threat. Beddoes' hydraulic argument against oppression was also being made by the radical William Frend in his pamphlet *Peace and Union* (1793). 'If neglected' and suppressed, Frend wrote, disenfranchised classes' resentment at their deprivations and 'abuses' would 'continue to increase, till the ruling powers are in fear for their own safety'.[39] Paine, too, had claimed that there were two types of revolution. One was directed by a serene heart, and utilized the 'weapons' of 'reason and discussion, persuasion and conviction' in the aim of working towards 'some great and positive good'. But a more dangerous type of rebellion, Paine warned, stemmed from the need to 'avoid or get rid of some great calamity', and took place when oppressive regulations led to the 'temper' of deprived classes becoming 'incensed', and turning to 'violent' methods.[40]

After the fall of the old regime, the increasingly violent nature of the French Revolution seemed to bear out Beddoes' theory that oppression is met with explosive, hydraulic outbursts of passion. But in France, authoritarian behaviour was no longer the preserve of that old regime. At the start of February 1792, Beddoes wrote anxiously that a 'conspiracy of Despots' was dominating France's Constituent Assembly, neglecting the workers, and demonstrating 'intolerable' behaviour.[41] The Jacobin Club had initially been formed during the convening of the Estates-General in 1789 as the *Club Breton*, comprised of representatives from Brittany. They were soon joined by deputies from other regions, and the group reformed in November 1789, and met regularly at a Dominican monastery on Rue Saint-Honoré. The Dominicans' first residence in Paris had been on the Rue St Jacques, hence their nickname of 'Jacobins'. The club was, at first, a broad church, widening its membership beyond official deputies, and numbering former aristocrats and peasants among those who attended its stirring, noisy meetings. In February 1790, the club had formally stated its objectives – to prepare for questions raised in the National Assembly; to establish and strengthen the constitution; and to correspond with other like-minded societies – and its members agreed that any participant unsympathetic in thought or action with these aims would be expelled.

By the beginning of 1791, the Jacobins were establishing a network of affiliated clubs throughout France, and the *World* newspaper reported in Britain that they now possessed the 'Sovereign power'.[42] The *St James's Chronicle* recounted how 'the Jacobin club at Paris' was displaying worryingly intolerant behaviour, and attempting 'to prevent, by force, the assembling of any adverse society'.[43] In July 1791, the Jacobins split over discussions about the future of the monarchy in France. Moderates, who supported the plan for a constitutional monarchy and sought to preserve Louis XVI's position, departed to form the short-lived Society of Feuillants, whilst those who pressed for Louis XVI's overthrow remained in a radicalized version of the Jacobin Club. British newspapers considered this latter new manifestation a group of 'malefactors'.[44]

Even the remaining Jacobins were riven by key political rifts.

A group of politicians, initially representatives of the Gironde region of France, clustered around Jacques Pierre Brissot de Warville. Brissot was an impetuous idealist, a skilled orator, an abolitionist, pornographer, journalist and enthusiast for American democracy, who had been elected head of the French government in its new incarnation as the Legislative Assembly. In February 1792 Brissot proposed to extend the principles of the revolution to neighbouring Austria. This provoked a furious response from a Jacobin member whose fame was in the ascendancy. Maximilien Robespierre's unassuming, delicate, feline appearance, almost inaudible speaking voice and verbose oratory belied the impression he made on his audiences. Mirabeau said of Robespierre, known to contemporaries as 'the Incorruptible', that 'he will go far. He believes everything he says.'[45] His veneer of personal purity and irreproachability, his uncompromising moral stance, and his coolly argued, theoretical and extreme approach to the revolution's direction set him apart from contemporaries like Brissot, who seemed mired in worldly, sensual compromises. In response to Brissot's proposition of war, Robespierre argued that the 'most extravagant idea that can arise in a politician's head is to believe that it is enough for a people to invade a foreign country to make it adopt their laws and their constitution'.[46] The prospect of international war – of military violence joining the popular ferocity that punctuated the revolution's progress – coupled with the obvious and heated rifts among some of the most dynamic players in the French Revolution, dismayed Beddoes.

By July 1792 Beddoes was convinced that the 'evil spirits' of the 'Jacobin club' were plotting another revolution.[47] In April, under Brissot's aegis, the Legislative Assembly had declared war on Austria. It marked the beginning of a war that would last twenty-three years. The previous year had seen a bad harvest, and, combined with the decline of the currency in the early years of the revolution, this led to rising food prices and attacks

on grocery stores in the spring. Leaders of the *sans-culottes* began
to demand state regulation of grain and draconian punishments
for those accused of hoarding or speculation.[48] In the wake of the
declaration of war, radical political clubs thrived in France. The
journalist and politician Jean-Paul Marat renewed publication
of his journal *L'Ami du peuple* after several hiatuses the previous
year, and mercilessly attacked the 'Austrian Committee' – a
purported cabal of Austrian sympathizers among the king's
court, supposedly presided over by Marie-Antoinette herself –
for undermining French military efforts. Popular hatred of the
monarchy had been rising since 21 June 1791, when the royal
family had been discovered attempting to flee to the eastern
frontier, and were unceremoniously returned to Paris and confined to the Tuileries Palace, where they had been resident
under surveillance since October 1789. The Girondins – still,
at this point, members of the Jacobin Club – pursued a policy
of intimidation against the king. They demanded the dismissal
of his 6,000 personal bodyguards, the Swiss Guard, who had
acted as personal protectors of the French monarch since 1480
and were thought to harbour royalist sympathies and hostility
towards the revolution. Louis XVI responded by exercising his
constitutional veto: he dismissed the Girondin ministers and
formed a ministry composed of Feuillants.

Riled by this display of monarchic authority and the casual
removal of Girondin ministers, demonstrators gathered in the
Faubourgs Saint-Antoine and Saint-Marcel from 5 a.m. on
20 June 1792. They bore a petition and intended to plant a
liberty tree in the grounds of the Tuileries to commemorate
the anniversary of the Tennis Court Oath and its values. The
Girondins harnessed the electric political energies crackling
through sections of Paris and permitted the demonstration – now
numbering around 30,000 – to march upon the Tuileries. Many
were armed with sabres, pikes and cannon, and were waving
revolutionary banners; strains of the revolutionary chorus *'Ça ira'*

were counterpointed with yells of '*Vive la nation!*' and '*Vivent les sans-culottes!*' The crowd poured into the barely defended palace and found the king, separated from them only by a line of body-guards. He adamantly refused to reinstate the Girondin ministers or to dismiss the Swiss Guard. But he accepted a red hat presented to him on a pike, and a glass of wine, and toasted the health of the people of Paris. The hurriedly convened Assembly sent deputies to calm the crowds, and the mayor, Pétion, urged the demonstrators to retire. They melted away. But it was clear not only that the monarch's authority was close to dissolving, but that popular political energies threatened a sequel. 'I am much more afraid of their machinating than of the abuse of the King[']s constitutional but ill-bestowed veto,' fretted Beddoes.[49]

Shortly after 10 August 1792, Beddoes received news that things had got much worse in Paris. The 'new revolution' or 'civil war' that he had predicted in France seemed – terrifyingly – to be materializing.[50] After the attempted uprising on 20 June 1792, hostility towards Louis XVI had increased. The Girondin Pierre Vergniaud accused the king of coordinating foreign courts to oppose the French Revolutionary Army at war. The Assembly invited provincial members of the National Guard – a French militia, separate from the army and sympathetic to the revolution – to come to Paris, ostensibly for the annual 14 July celebrations. In early August, news reached Paris of a manifesto issued by the Duke of Brunswick, who was in charge of the Prussian forces, threatening 'an exemplary and forever memorable vengeance, by giving up the city of Paris to a military execution, and total destruction' if the French royal family were harmed, and promising to 'restore to the king the security and the liberty of which he is now deprived'.[51] Many interpreted this as a promise of retribution for actions already committed: it seemed that there was nothing left to lose.

In London, the *General Evening Post* quoted from a letter from Paris about the events of 10 August, which Beddoes relayed to Giddy in agitation: 'The tocsin sounded in the night.'[52] Representatives from each section of Paris sat through the night in discussion. After hours of debate, an insurrectional Jacobin Commune – an unofficial alternative to the formal Paris Commune, the city's government, comprised of 144 delegates elected by the forty-eight divisions of the city – declared its independence, and coordinated an attack on the Tuileries. As the National Guard amassed and marched, the king was abandoned by his three principal defenders, including Pétion, Paris's mayor.

The assault began at eight in the morning. The king's Swiss Guard initially put up resistance, for which they earned denunciation as traitors by the *sans-culottes*. But they were soon pushed back into the palace, whereupon Louis XVI ordered them to retire: a command they knew implied almost certain death. The Swiss Guard continued fighting until their ammunition ran low and then they were driven back, some into the palace, some scattering into the gardens and the Parliament House. 'I just heard that the palace is forced & the Swiss guards put to the sword,' Beddoes wrote in agitation. A massacre ensued. Two-thirds of the 900 Swiss Guard were killed, some dragged under the statue of their employer Louis XVI to be put to death. Then 'About 20 Aristocrats were seized, & the heads of 6 of them cut off at 8 o'clock, & carried about the streets. At 9 the King Queen and R[oyal] Family got to the Assembly. At [half past] 10 a decree was passed that the King had forfeited the crown.'[53] Once news reached the Legislative Assembly that the insurrection had been successful, they suspended the king's powers, placing Louis under guard and transporting him to the Temple prison. On 21 September 1792 the First French Republic was proclaimed and, a few months later, after more evidence had been uncovered purportedly revealing Louis' opposition to the revolution, the king was notified of his impending trial for treason. The insurrectional Commune now had the political ascendancy in the Legislative Assembly. They were supported by a newly armed force, comprised of *sans-culottes* from the forty-eight Paris sections who had seized arms from arsenals around Paris in the days leading up to 10 August.

The Commune took the revolution in a very different direction from the Girondins' focus on constitutional reform and liberal democracy. For aristocrats, especially, 10 August marked the decisive fall of the old regime, and a second revolution whose importance arguably exceeded that of 14 July 1789. The Commune turned their attention towards arming the civilian population, agitating for universal suffrage, stripping away all relics of noble privilege, and suppressing counter-revolutionary 'conspiracy' by establishing a Comité de Surveillance (Committee of Vigilance). After 10 August, there was public pressure for a tribunal to isolate and try the royalists arrested during the insurrection, and the Extraordinary Tribunal was established on 17 August. From 15 August, all Paris's monasteries were closed and religious orders dissolved, and members of the clergy, of the royalist press, and servants of Louis and Marie-Antoinette were detained. In the third week of August, a guillotine was set up in the Place du Carrousel, in front of the Tuileries, and over the last two weeks of September, more than 1,000 people were taken into custody on the flimsiest of pretences.

On 2 September, news reached Paris that the Duke of Brunswick's troops had captured the fortress at Verdun, in northeast France. Calls for retribution against counter-revolutionaries who might have assisted Brunswick's army grew louder and then murderous. Groups broke into prisons around Paris, massacring inmates feared to be conspiring with the duke. Hundreds of priests, either in convents or in the process of being transported into prisons, were attacked, mutilated and murdered by alliances of Jacobin supporters and *sans-culottes*. Between 2 and 7 September, Paris prisons hosted trials of around 3,000 prisoners including priests, Swiss guards and aristocrats, among them the

Princesse de Lamballe, Marie-Antoinette's closest friend and favourite, whom she had made Superintendent of the Queen's Household, with a stipend of 150,000 livres per year. Some 1,100 to 1,300 prisoners were executed, their bodies piled high in front of the Grand Châtelet, on the right bank of the Seine.

Beddoes was not alone in reading the events of 10 August, and the September Massacres, as crises that revealed the extent to which, after being released from the constraints of the old regime, the French populace's 'appetite for blood seems to have grown by feeding upon it'.[54] But despite the revolution's obvious imperfections, he pointed to its admirable achievements over the last three years: the abolition of tithes, improvement of agriculture, eradication of poor rates and – by extension – poverty, extinguishing of public debt, and the establishment of 'an honest, cheap and unoppressive government'. And he tried to argue that 'the attack of the Tuileries and the deposition of Louis are justified' by the right of an 'unjustly attacked' and 'infamously betrayed' public 'to rise in self-defence'.[55] Beddoes hoped that once the hydraulic energy of the French people's newly released passions had dissipated, the revolution would continue its methodical progress in a state of calm. A little verse circulated in response, referring to 'BEDDOES, the philosophic Chymist's Guide,/ The Bigot's Scourge, of Democrats the Pride'.[56]

By the end of 1792, Beddoes' political writings had placed him in defiant opposition to the climate of his workplace. At the end of the eighteenth century, Oxford University was a bastion of establishment privilege. All students had to profess the thirty-nine articles of the Church of England's doctrine, and any form of religious deviation was regarded with suspicion. Since the revolution, the University's management had closed ranks. On 14 July 1791, the Rector of Lincoln College, Edward Tatham, had organized a protest to encourage 'the inhabitants of the City and precincts of Oxford' to form 'an Association for preserving Liberty Peace and Property against Republicans and Levellers of every Description'. In December 1792, the university made numerous addresses proclaiming its loyalty to the monarchy, and launched a highly successful collection of subscriptions for émigré clergy fleeing France after the Pope's recent condemnation of the new constitution.[57]

Beddoes was not the only one to feel himself, as a radical, increasingly out of place in the British university environment. In Cambridge, the Unitarian lecturer William Frend was writing his pamphlet, *Peace and Union Recommended to the Associated Bodies of Republicans and Anti-Republicans*, which would be published in 1793. The pamphlet's support for the repeal of the Test Act caused, in Frend's words, 'no small sensation'.[58] He was denounced by the Master and fellows of Jesus College, and put on trial in Cambridge's Senate House for offending against the Cambridge university statute *'De Concionibus* concerning publick Sermons'.[59] After an unsuccessful appeal, on 27 September 1793 Frend found the gates of Jesus College locked and chained against him, and was forced to leave.

In the late summer of 1792, Beddoes had met the vice chancellor of Oxford University to tender his resignation. He explained that it would take some time to move the vast array of his mineralogical specimens that were currently housed in the university's chemical laboratory, and proposed continuing to lecture until their removal could be arranged the following spring. The vice chancellor, a man called John Cooke, who was also President of Corpus Christi College, seems to have interpreted Beddoes' resignation as a professional negotiation and, with an eye to the main chance, he saw an opportunity for securing state funding to make Beddoes' position permanent. Cooke persuaded Beddoes to delay his resignation until he had petitioned the Home Office to transform his post into a Regius Professorship, a university position with royal patronage.

This suggests that Beddoes did not fully explain the political discomfort behind his intended departure; and, indeed, that his discomfort did not outweigh the prospect of a permanent, generously salaried, prestigious post – even one funded by the establishment that he detested.

Beddoes followed Cooke's instructions and petitioned the Home Office. He was initially successful, until Henry Dundas probed further into Beddoes' reputation and received reports that he was a 'most violent *Democrate* and that he takes great pains to seduce Young Men to the same political principles with himself', and that he has 'lately been very active in sowing sedition ... particularly by the distribution of Pamphlets of a very mischievous and inflamatory tendency'.[60] Beddoes' petition was smartly rejected. His name was added to a Home Office list of political dissidents, beside Joseph Priestley's; and he confirmed his decision to leave Oxford in the spring of 1793. This time, the resignation was accepted. In April 1793, Beddoes wrote from Oxford that '[I] feel my residence here very uncomfortable ... [I] find strong marks of aversion in the looks & conduct of the clergy here'. He was 'going through the tedious process of packing up some of my things' and planned to have left by the end of the month.[61] Beddoes knew that he had become 'eminently and much beyond my importance, odious to Pitt and his gang'.[62]

After some deliberation, Beddoes settled on Bristol as his new home. Aged thirty-three, he had determined to set up as a doctor, and the Hotwells spa, just south of Clifton, offered a continual stream of ailing patients. Two men helped Beddoes to establish himself in Bristol. At around the same time as Beddoes' move in spring 1793, a man called John Wedgwood, heir to the Wedgwood pottery business in Etruria, Stoke-on-Trent, extricated himself from the family firm, set up as a London banker, and purchased Cote House in Westbury on Trym, just three miles from Bristol Hotwells. His younger brother Tom was a frequent visitor to his new house, and was soon introduced to Beddoes in Bristol through their mutual friend, the chemist and industrialist James Keir, a member of the Lunar Society.

Tom Wedgwood was a gentle, quiet but unwavering young man in his early twenties, whose health was more fragile than the vases, mugs and bowls produced by his family's factory. Tom and John's father, the master potter Josiah Wedgwood, was also a member of the Lunar Society; a resilient, resourceful man with a fondness for red meat and the dark beer known as porter, his right leg had been amputated without anaesthetic after a severe bout of smallpox, exacerbated by being 'over walk'd and over work'd', in 1768.[63] This was just a year before Josiah opened the factory that would become the longest-running British business to remain in unbroken family succession. In 1791, his sons, Tom, John and the younger brother Josiah ('Jos'), all became partners at Etruria. But Tom Wedgwood wasn't interested in the stuff of potteries: the basalt and jasperware, the intricacies of kiln temperatures, and the tasks of travel and negotiation assigned to him. A year earlier, at the age of eighteen, he had informed his father that he and his friend John Leslie intended to 'cultivate the virtues of the heart in a *temporal* retirement from the *world at large*', paying particular attention to 'moderat[ing] and correct[ing]' the 'passions and affections'.[64] Josiah had refused his permission, staunchly insisting on 'the blessings of society'. So instead Tom squirrelled himself away in Etruria's laboratories, using its equipment for amateur scientific experimentation. He became fascinated by the relationship between heat and light, and published two articles that were read before the Royal Society on 'the production of Light from different bodies by heat and attrition'. He tested Newton's 'corpuscular' theory of light, which postulated that hot bodies throw off light 'corpuscles' at speed, by attempting to rotate sails positioned on a delicate axis using the 'force' of light. Wedgwood sent his work to Priestley, who replied admiringly – and punningly – that the essays would 'throw some new light on a very important subject about which we as yet know very little'.[65]

In April 1792, a few weeks before his twenty-first birthday, Tom Wedgwood collapsed. He started suffering headaches intense enough to make him scream, damaged eyesight, exhaustion and acute depression. A few years earlier, he had been praised for exemplifying 'the spirit of the Stoic', one 'whose passions are subordinate to his reason'.[66] He had penned upbeat, offhand reflections on the 'imaginary evil' of 'disappointment' that stemmed from mere failure of expectation, as opposed to substantial loss.[67] But suddenly Wedgwood was inhabiting a very different emotional landscape. His light-filled early life was clouded over with physical pain, paranoia, 'anticipation ... of disagreeable events' magnified 'ten times more' than reasonable. His passions were no longer subordinate to reason; they terrorized every minute of what he would come to call 'a maimed life'.[68]

In the summer of 1792, Wedgwood's brother Jos sent him to Paris, hoping that participating in the fête to mark the third anniversary of the fall of the Bastille would restore some hope to his spirits. Wedgwood travelled in early July with Gregory Watt, the son of the Lunar Society member and steam-engine manufacturer James Watt. Gregory, Tom wrote to his father Josiah, 'is a furious democrat – detests the King' and was excitedly predicting 'a new revolution' which 'will in all probability be fatal' to Louis XVI. But he himself found no exhilaration in the Parisian ferment, and complained that the 'streets of Paris stink more than the dirtiest hole in London, and you cannot walk even in this dry time, without repeated splashes'.[69] He returned home, resigned his partnership of the Wedgwood pottery firm, and briefly considered emigrating to America; he was dissuaded by his friend Leslie, who assured him that American 'society is neither sufficiently enlightened for you, nor sufficiently refined'. Stay in Britain, Leslie encouraged Wedgwood, where 'we may reasonably hope that the impulse lately given to men's minds will soon triumph over every obstacle, and finally produce a general renovation of things'.[70] So he stayed, and surrendered himself to a chronic decay that his brother Jos, in distress, labelled a 'general wasting away'.[71] Wedgwood would come to act as champion and facilitator of Beddoes' most prized projects, and would also bring together all the chief participants in the 1790s' revolution of feeling – Thomas Beddoes, Mary Wollstonecraft, William Godwin, Samuel Taylor Coleridge and William Wordsworth – in a project seeking to perfect human life by eradicating pain, inspired by his own bodily and psychological suffering.

Another man also made Beddoes feel instantly at home in Bristol. The previous year, James Keir had introduced Beddoes to the polymath Richard Lovell Edgeworth, father of the novelist Maria Edgeworth, who would satirize Mary Wollstonecraft's 'masculine' reason. Beddoes instantly warmed to Richard Lovell Edgeworth as 'in every respect a superior man'.[72] In spring 1793 Edgeworth was nearly fifty years old and in Bristol to seek medical help for his son Lovell, who was suffering from consumption. Edgeworth helped Beddoes to find a house, to meet patients – including his own son – and he offered like-minded companionship. Both he and Beddoes were preoccupied by the subject of education, and this dominated their early conversations. Education was one of the favourite subjects of radicals and reform enthusiasts: the education of a child was thought to directly replicate the way in which individuals become socialized and governed. The state's political government of the individual was widely considered to be immediately related to parents' or tutors' cultivation of the immature mind, so political reform was thought to necessitate new pedagogic theories. As the literary critic James K. Chandler puts it, 'a political utopia is implicit in every theory of education' and 'utopian political schemes' often 'produce fresh thinking about education'.[73] Education was the subject on which many radicals pinned their hopes for political change.

Beddoes saw in strict educational methods a counterpart to the authoritarian political systems he criticized for provoking hydraulic outbursts of violence. He censured tutors who forced students to repeat 'pious ejaculations' and he was certain that no child formed belief 'because they were commanded to believe so and so'.[74] He loathed the elementary primer *Reading-made-easy* (referred to in different dialects as 'ready-may-deazy', 'Readin'-med-aisy' and 'readamadeasy'), which focused on repeated phrases and rote lessons. Such rigid, uncompromising educational systems, Beddoes wrote in a *Letter on Early Instruction*, 'stifle ... benevolent tendencies' and 'so far brutalize the mind and so entirely pervert our sympathy as to make us feel pleasure from the pain of our fellow-creatures'. They were the pedagogical equivalent of the oppressive political measures inflicted on the Priestley rioters and the Haitian slaves. Indeed, Beddoes reflected, the rioters' behaviour was probably the product of a similarly inhumane upbringing and education: 'if a small portion of human kindness had been infused into their bosoms by such a mode of instruction, as I wish to see generally adopted among the poor,' Beddoes wrote, 'they never could have committed excesses so disgraceful to their age and country'.[75] He wanted to see Britain adopt an educational system that would 'prepar[e] the mind for benevolent principles of action' and nurture the 'mechanism of human nature' which 'has made us very early sensible to kindness'.[76] It was through education that hydraulic violence, contained within, and prompted by, the 'inhumanity of kings', might be dissipated: by teaching sympathy to the ruling classes, and by encouraging subordinate groups to channel their angry energy into kindness and benevolence.

Despite this optimistic beginning to his new life in Bristol in spring 1793, Beddoes could not help but be aware that the general mood had shifted. The events of 10 August 1792 and the

September Massacres in Paris had put paid to the unqualified hope for political progress in France and Britain that had buoyed up reformers in the first years of the 1790s. Revolutionary France's descent into violence, coupled with its increasingly authoritarian Jacobin leadership, meant that British radicals were no longer sure of the presence, across the Channel, of a real-life model of the type of progress towards liberal 'perfect-ibility' that many envisaged. France's declaration of war on Austria in spring 1792 made military hostilities between France and Britain a likelihood. British radicals worried that their own nation, which they had hoped to draw into a closer political alliance with France, would now be set against their revolution-ary neighbour. And they feared that the confrontation would result in an entrenchment of conservative, nationalist values in Britain, instead of the longed-for embrace of universal – or at least pan-European – benevolence.

The course that a hope will take – whether the hope of individuals or communities – is never obvious from the outset. In the initial stages, when enough evidence coalesces to make some kind of change a reasonable expectation, hope may be buoyant, confident, consisting of delicious anticipation of its subject's near-certain materialization. Or it may be tentative, propelled into existence through a conviction of its desirabil-ity and rightness, but its vigour tempered by awareness of the obstacles it faces. Before hope solidifies into certain success or definitive disappointment, its constituent parts – its propor-tions of confidence and doubt – frequently shift, like levels of liquid in chemistry flasks. Events in Paris on 10 August and the September Massacres had brought about one of these alterations in the composition of radicals' hopes in the 1790s, tipping the balance from confidence to a much more uncertain and muted state.

Beddoes' letters encapsulate how the optimism he had experienced in the immediate wake of the revolution was changing. He wrote to Davies Giddy in July 1792 that 'I have felt ... the weariness of the eternal disappointment of [my] hopes & opinions' and was left with 'no jot of heart or hope'.[77] He wasn't yet ready to relinquish his aspirations. But he had been protesting since the beginning of the year that 'these untoward circumstances & the constant fluctuation of my own opinion respecting French affairs have contributed to render my feelings very uncomfortable ... I do not like to be thus at the mercy of the last newspaper'.[78] By autumn 1792, British radicals widely acknowledged that they had moved from a period when their collective 'spirit [had been] strong/ In hope' to a new phase of the decade, in which 'hope hath been discouraged' but rallied onwards nevertheless, wounded but not entirely deterred.[79]

II

Hope Discouraged

Chapter 5

THE PURIFYING ALCHEMY
OF EDUCATION

Thomas Beddoes' new friend in Bristol, Richard Lovell Edgeworth, was one of the most famous proponents of the revolutionary potential of education. Earlier in the century he had been involved in one of the most notorious Enlightenment projects to eschew discipline and rote learning and attend instead to the child's passions, in order to 'make a loving and feeling being'.[1] Edgeworth was an inspirational model of Enlightenment optimism – but also represented a dire warning.

Edgeworth had dedicated his twenties and thirties to myriad bizarre innovations: an enormous hamster wheel designed to transport humans at high speed across the ground; a sail affixed to a carriage, whose terrifying velocity spooked him into abandoning the project; a wooden horse with eight legs to clamber over walls – a premonition of modern caterpillar-tracks; an umbrella for keeping haystacks dry; and a machine for cutting turnips, like a giant food processor. With a serious, penetrating stare but otherwise impish features – delicately curved eyebrows, curled hair, a small sensuous mouth – Edgeworth was eternally full of vim: aged sixty, he would still show off his agility by bounding over the dining-room table. He boasted of his life-long immunity to the rush of gambling, reflecting that 'I never felt an inclination for cards, dice, or lotteries'.[2] But this did not stop him, around 1769, wagering the enormous sum of £500 (equivalent to around £35,000 today) on the prediction that he would receive news of the winner of a race at Newmarket long before London bookmakers. Edgeworth set about devising a system of telegraphic communication that would relay this information four hours faster than the swiftest messenger on horseback. He won the bet, but refused to accept the prize money. The episode convinced him of the military and civil utility of telegraphs, but it also undermined his purported indifference to the exhilaration of gambling. Indeed, in the 1760s and 1770s, Edgeworth and his friend Thomas Day had entered into a venture with the highest stake yet: the 'bod[ies] and mind[s]' of three children.[3]

Edgeworth married Anna Maria Elers, his first wife – there would be four in total – in a clandestine ceremony in Scotland in the early 1760s. Within a year the couple had moved to the family estate at Edgeworthstown in County Longford in Ireland. On 29 May 1764, two days before Edgeworth's twentieth birthday, Richard, or 'Dick' – the first of his twenty-two children – was born. In the autumn of the following year, the young family moved back to England, staying first with Anna Maria's relations in Oxfordshire, then moving to Hare Hatch in Berkshire, where Edgeworth waited to be called to the Bar in London. It was during this period, spent idling at home with a young infant, that he 'formed a strong desire', in his words, 'to educate my son according to the system of Rousseau'. 'My wife complied with my wishes,' he continued, 'and the body and mind of my son were to be left as much as possible to the education of nature and *of accident*.'[4]

Jean-Jacques Rousseau's *Émile, ou de l'éducation* had been published, in five sections, in France in 1762, two years before Dick's birth. In response to a controversial section on natural religion in the fourth book, it was promptly banned, and Rousseau fled France for Britain three years later. The first English translation also appeared in 1762, and over the following three decades the book's influence across Europe and America was so profound that the philosopher Immanuel Kant likened it to the French Revolution. Indeed, some directly attributed the revolution to 'the opinions of Rousseau', who was proclaimed by the National Assembly to be 'the first founder of the French constitution'.[5] Much of the celebration of naturalism and untutored emotion in late Enlightenment France was fuelled by reading Rousseau. Edmund Burke described the National Assembly's delegates' efforts to 'resemble' Rousseau as a form of vampirish parasitism: 'His blood they transfuse into their minds and into their manners. Him they study; him they meditate; him they turn over in all the time they can spare from the laborious mischief of the day, or the debauches of the night. Rousseau is their canon of holy writ ... he is their standard figure of perfection'.[6]

Rousseau was central to the eighteenth-century debate about education and the passions which questioned whether humans are innately 'virtuous' – benevolent and sociable – or whether they are naturally self-interested and antisocial. There were radical differences of opinion. Philosophers including Thomas Hobbes, Joseph Butler and Bernard Mandeville declared that, in the 'state of nature', prior to forming into communities, humans were self-interested, driven by selfish desires that released unmeasured carnal and destructive emotions: hate, lust, anger. Samuel von Pufendorf thought people were 'impolitick animals' motivated by 'thirst after things superfluous' and by 'quick

Resentment of injuries, and eager Desire of Revenge'.[7] Hobbes famously described the state of nature as 'war of every one against every one', characterized by 'continual fear and danger of violent death', and primitive human life as 'solitary, poor, nasty, brutish, and short'.[8] The first societies had only come about, Mandeville and Hobbes argued, because communal living satisfied egoistic desires for competition and fame to a greater extent than was possible in the solitary state of nature. Mandeville saw the 'great mart' of eighteenth-century Britain primarily existing to fulfil innate lusts for primitive objects (food, sex) in the guise of luxurious 'Equivalents'. The apparently 'civilised' world was a place of deceit, a ragged veil over cut-throat desires, in which 'the fine Gentleman ... need not practise any greater Self-Denial than the Savage'.[9]

The philosophers Anthony Ashley-Cooper (third Earl of Shaftesbury) and Francis Hutcheson fervently refuted such a pessimistic, bleak outlook on human nature. They claimed instead that humans possessed 'Kind *Instincts*'. They talked 'of natural Affections *to associate*; of *natural Affections*, of *Compassion*, of *Love of Company*, a *Sense of Gratitude*, a *Determination* to honour and love the Authors of any good Offices toward any Part of Mankind'.[10] Shaftesbury described how humans had an innate 'social feeling', an inherent 'publick Spirit', a desire to love and live with others that was as intrinsic as hunger or thirst and which motivated individuals to form into families, clans and states.[11] Benevolence was a 'common sense' (*sensus communis*), and moral failings were infrequent occurrences that arose only when people ignored what Hutcheson described as 'the natural feelings of the heart'.[12]

These opposing viewpoints had very different implications for theories of government and education. Hobbes and Pufendorf argued that a strict sovereign authority was necessary to curb and control humanity's chaotic, destructive instincts: a firm, even an absolute, monarch, mirrored in a severe and uncompromising tutor who urged the stringent subjugation of the passions to reason. But Shaftesbury's and Hutcheson's heirs emphasized the need to free and cultivate innate sociability. Many of their followers considered the constitutional monarchy established in the United Kingdom after 1688 to be the ideal political form to empower and gently regulate benevolent instincts, and stressed the corresponding need for education to develop and guide its young citizens' behaviour in a gentle, respectful manner.

Jean-Jacques Rousseau departed from both Hobbes and Shaftesbury in this debate. He was a favourite among political reformers for being relatively optimistic about humanity's innate nature whilst trenchantly criticizing existing social inequalities. William Godwin proclaimed him to be 'the greatest of all philosophers' for showing how 'the vices of individuals arise out of the vices of government'.[13] Rousseau argued that in the 'state of nature' man was neither violently antisocial nor naturally benevolent, but merely solitary and independent. 'Original man', he wrote, experienced strong, instinctual desires for 'nourishment, a woman and rest', and was able to ensure that 'all his needs are satisfied' independently of other men: 'Whoever does what he wants is happy if he is self-sufficient; this is the case of the man living in the state of nature.'[14]

Rousseau conceived of the passions as expressions of desire, servants in its employment: passions, he wrote, 'take their origin from our needs' and 'incline [us] to provide for those needs'.[15] He described how anger, resentment, irritation, lust and hunger draw attention to, and reinforce, the supplications of desires that had not yet been met. The passions are therefore symptoms of desires left unsatisfied; warning signs of frustration. In the 'state of nature', Rousseau wrote, needs are immediately met and passions therefore rarely exist: they are 'minimally active'.[16] But 'civilisation' was entirely characterized by the ill effects of delayed satisfaction to man's desires. Mandeville had similarly described how society was built upon the 'multiplicity of [man's]

Desires and the continual Opposition he meets with in his Endeavours to gratify them'.[17] 'Fashion' repeatedly promised satisfaction through the acquisition of luxurious items, Mandeville explained, but the continued survival of the commercial economy was predicated on the fundamentally unsatisfying nature of its commodities and the endurance of customers' hunger. Rousseau described how, in the state of nature, man had had 'an unlimited right to everything he wants': access to everything but ownership of nothing. Civilization offered the consolation of private property – man gained 'ownership of all he possesses' – but that gain was paired with loss of access to the full range of satisfactions he had once experienced.[18] The Fall into 'civilisation' was a fall into frustration and, therefore, a fall into emotion; into the passions.

Rousseau compared the transition of 'primitive' man into social man to a child's development into adulthood. Both gave up innocence, freedom, independence, satisfaction and tranquillity for compromise, confinement, frustration and its inevitable outcome in emotional turbulence. 'Everything is good as it leaves the hands of the Author of things; everything degenerates in the hands of man,' Rousseau proclaimed in *Émile*, echoing his famous initial declaration in *The Social Contract* that 'Man is born free, and everywhere he is in chains'.[19] For Rousseau, education should be primarily concerned with helping the child manage the frustrated passions that result from his transition into adult society. This was not a utopian pedagogic vision; it provided a blueprint for protecting childhood self-sufficiency and attaining relative satisfaction in a fundamentally unsatisfying world.

Émile stresses the importance of physical health, exercise and freedom, instructing that babies must not be swaddled, but dressed in 'loose and large diapers which leave all [their] limbs free', and breastfed by their mothers, not wet-nurses.[20] Its eponymous hero, Émile, grows strong by eschewing hats; becoming hardened to the cold; sleeping in uncomfortable beds; feeling at home in 'all the elements', water and air as well as land;

refining his visual faculty to a surveyor's level of precision, his sense of touch to the sensitivity of a blind man, and cultivating a 'natural' appetite for bland, simple flavours. He is allowed to sleep for long periods to recover from his exertions and, with no rules imposed by his tutor on the amount he can eat, he learns to regulate his gluttony naturally. In Émile's early years, his tutor's role is to manage the sensations to which the young boy is exposed: a plethora of 'sounds, figures' and images, from which intellectual ideas are prohibited. Between the ages of twelve and thirteen, 'the goal is less to teach him a truth than to show him how he must always go about discovering the truth'. But it is in puberty that the most important work is done: 'to make a loving and feeling being'.[21] Émile must learn to distinguish between the self-love that serves his deepest instinctual needs (*amour de soi*) and the self-esteem that depends on 'the judgments of others' (*amour propre*). He is helped in nurturing the former, which is 'always good and always in conformity with order', whilst managing the latter's calls. He learns to use reason as a 'law which regulates' the passions, and thus resists becoming a dependent 'slave of [his own] desires'.[22]

Rousseau's educational scheme was criticized for applying both too heavy and too light a hand to child development. Godwin would disparage Rousseau's 'whole system of education' as 'a series of tricks, a puppet-show exhibition, of which the master holds the wires, & the scholar is never to suspect in what manner they are moved'.[23] But the extent to which Rousseau actually intended *Émile* to be a practical manual is questionable. He described it as 'a new system of education the plan of which I present for the study of the wise and *not a method for fathers and mothers*'. And he told a correspondent that 'it is impossible to make an Emile. [It is not] a real educational treatise [but] quite a philosophical work'.[24] Rousseau certainly did not follow its precepts himself. His first five children, born to Thérèse LeVasseur in the 1740s and 1750s, were swiftly 'placed in the Foundling's Hospital'; Rousseau admitted that he 'did not even keep a record of their dates of birth'.[25] Nevertheless, the book spawned a number of attempts to apply its principles in practice. And the experiments of Richard Lovell Edgeworth and his friend Thomas Day were perhaps the most famous historical examples of Rousseauvian education in action.

Edgeworth began by dressing his young son Dick 'without stockings, with his arms bare, in a jacket and trowsers ... which were at that time novel and extraordinary' and 'succeeded in making him remarkably hardy'. Rousseau detested some parents' tendency to mollycoddle their children and aspired that 'my pupil will often have bruises'. A rough-and-tumble upbringing duly 'succeeded in making [Dick] fearless of danger, and, what is more difficult, capable of bearing privation of every sort'.[26] Rousseau recommended that the tutor should not be afraid of confessing his own ignorance. '"I don't know" is a phrase which goes over so well with both of us and which we repeat so often that it no longer costs either of us a thing.' Edgeworth also maintained that 'children should not be discouraged' from proffering 'puzzling questions and observations,' but 'on the contrary, according to the advice of Rousseau, parents should fairly and truly confess their ignorance'.[27]

By pre-adolescence, Dick appeared to have realized his father's hopes. 'He had all the virtues of a child bred in the hut of a savage,' Edgeworth proclaimed proudly. Although 'of books he had less knowledge at four or five years old, than most children have at that age' – an ignorance of which Rousseau emphatically approved – 'of mechanics he had a clearer conception, and ... more invention, than any child I had then seen'. Aged thirteen, Dick even won a medal marking his 'early mechanic genius'. Moreover, his proud parent boasted that 'he was bold, free, fearless, generous; he had a ready and keen use of all his senses, and of his judgment ... He was, by all who saw him, whether of the higher or lower classes, taken notice of; and by all considered

as very clever.' Dick seemed to be realizing Rousseau's promise
that it was possible to sustain innate virtue in a corrupt society.
And all this had been achieved in the face of widespread ridicule
and opposition to Edgeworth's scheme, some even from 'friends
and relations'.[28]

One friend's response to his project was far from contemptuous. Thomas Day, a dishevelled, wealthy eccentric whom
Edgeworth had first met during a university vacation – a
moment Edgeworth subsequently referred to as the beginning
of a 'new era in my life' – enthusiastically encouraged him.[29]
Day was a man who had repeatedly come up against, in his
own words, 'reiterated disappointments in love'; perhaps not
unrelated to his pockmarked skin, heavy-lidded eyes, dumpy
physique, and penchant for washing his 'raven locks' in the
stream.[30] By 1768, the twenty-year-old Day had become 'suspicious of the female sex, and averse to risking his happiness
for their charms or their society'. Like Edgeworth, Day adored
Rousseau, rapturously declaring that 'were all the books in the
world to be destroyed . . . the second book I should wish to save,
after the Bible, would be Rousseau's *Emilius*'.[31] Prompted by
Edgeworth's apparent success with Dick, Day decided to begin
his own project. But where Edgeworth had wanted to transform
his son into an incarnation of primitive man, Day's intention was
more worldly: to create 'the perfect wife'.[32]

Émile's final book makes it clear that, when Rousseau so vividly depicted the characteristics of 'man' in the state of nature,
he was indeed specifically referring to *men*. Reflecting spurious
eighteenth-century medical claims about sex-based differences
in the operation of the passions, Rousseau argued that men
and women experience desire very differently. Delays to men's
satisfaction led to emotional torment and social upheaval. But
women's innate weakness, tendency to acquiescence and insufficiently developed sense of 'injustice' made them, in his view,

naturally designed to absorb male desire, not to experience or express their own. While 'one [sex] must necessarily will and be able; it suffices that the other put up little resistance', he wrote. 'Woman is made specially to please man ... to please and to be subjugated'; 'woman is made to yield to man and to endure even his injustice'.[33]

For Rousseau, women's education should therefore not be aimed at negotiating the satisfaction of their primal desires in a society designed to frustrate them, as his system of male education was set on doing. Women must instead be educated solely to manage and satisfy male desire. A woman who refuses to consent to her husband's sexual and other wishes risks provoking his 'immoderate Passions'. Her too frequent consent might exacerbate male desire beyond its 'natural' limits. Expression of any autonomous sexual desire on her own part, Rousseau warned, would have dire consequences, 'dissolv[ing] the family and break[ing] all the bonds of nature'.[34] Men aspire towards freedom, independence and satisfaction, but women can only hope to attain 'modesty' and 'virtue'. Virtue was typically aligned in the eighteenth century with behaviour promoting the continuation and flourishing of societies. For men, virtue involved the active and politicized practice of sympathy, pity, charity and benevolence in the public sphere, but Rousseau defined female virtue as passive and domestic: 'an enthusiasm which ... keeps all her petty inclinations subjected to so noble a passion' as 'causing the happiness of a decent man'.[35] The historian Mary McAlpin has described how such anxieties about the consequences of women's derogation of their duty to regulate male sexual desire became acute in the 1790s. In that decade, there emerged an 'assumption' that, were complete cultural collapse to occur in the wake of the French Revolution, the 'principal cause' would be 'the premature awakening of sexual desire in young girls'.[36] The aftermath of that decade saw an even stricter policing of all sexual desire, but particularly of women's.

With the intention of finding a young girl to train in Rousseauvian fashion, to manage his home and his whims, Thomas Day and his dissolute friend John Bicknell paid a visit to the Foundling Hospital in Shrewsbury in the winter of 1769. There Day selected an auburn-haired twelve-year-old girl 'of remarkably promising appearance' and took her home, naming her Sabrina Sidney after the republican politician Algernon Sidney.[37] A few days later, Day went to a second Foundling Hospital, on Brunswick Square in London, where he identified another ward, an eleven-year-old girl he renamed Lucretia. He planned to bring up both girls strictly in accordance with Rousseau's principles of female education. The orphan who responded most pleasingly, Day intended to marry.

Before long, both Edgeworth's and Day's projects began to falter. At first, Day expressed nothing but optimism for his scheme's progress. 'I am not disappointed in any one respect,' Day enthused: 'I have made them, in respect to temper, two such girls, as, I may perhaps say without vanity, you have never seen at the same age. They ... are always contented, and think nothing so agreeable as waiting upon me (a moderate convenience for a lazy man).' Sabrina and Lucretia appeared to conform readily to Rousseau's maxim that 'woman is made specially to please man'.[38] But Day's Victorian biographer, John Blackman, tells a very different story. In spring 1770, Day took the two children to Avignon, where he hoped to find respite from the suggestive remarks that passers-by in Britain levelled at a single man in charge of two young girls. Blackman described how these 'children teased and perplexed him continually, they frequently quarrelled, and at length fell ill with the smallpox ... They kept him to their bedside, and would not be left for the space of ten minutes without screaming and making the house ring with their noises.' Lucretia was the first to overtly resist her education in female subjugation. On the trio's return to Britain from Avignon, Day summarily dismissed her, 'finding her ...

not disposed to follow his regimen'.[39] He apprenticed her to a
Ludgate milliner, and provided her with a dowry of £300 that
paved the way for a marriage to a London linen-draper.[40] Day
never contacted her again.

By 1774, Day was testing seventeen-year-old Sabrina's ded-
ication by such horrifyingly abusive acts as firing pistols at her
petticoats and dropping hot sealing wax on her skin. But her
devotion to (or fear of) Day did not seem to waver. Edgeworth
thought that Day 'certainly was never more loved by any woman',
and 'was persuaded, that he would marry her immediately'.[41]
But then, one time, Day 'left Sabrina at the house of a friend
under strict injunctions as to some peculiar fancies of his own;
in particular, some restrictions as to her dress. She neglected,
forgot, or undervalued some thing ... She did, or she did not,
wear certain long sleeves, and some handkerchief, which had
been the subject of his dislike, or of his liking; and he, considering this circumstance as a criterion of her attachment, and as a
proof of her want of strength of mind, quitted her for ever!' The
bewildered girl was sent to live alone with 'a lady in the country'.
Many years later, the debauched and now ailing John Bicknell,
with whom Day had first selected Sabrina from the Foundling
Hospital, began to consider 'that it would be a comfort to secure
a companion for middle life, and a friend, perhaps a nurse, for his
declining years'. He remembered Sabrina, located and married
her, with Day's sulky consent. Within three years, Bicknell had
died, and Edgeworth described how 'poor Sabrina ... was left
unprovided for, with two infant sons'.[42]

At first, Edgeworth's hopes for Dick seemed to be more promising. When his son was eight years old, Edgeworth and Day
travelled to France together with the young boy, where they met
Rousseau himself. The philosopher led the child on a two-hour
walk, and reported back that 'he thought him a boy of abilities,
which had been well cultivated,' but with a tendency to patriotism and 'prejudice'.[43] But Dick's 'patriotism' was the least of his

problems. He became incorrigibly unruly, resentful, distressed, and desperate to please his father, who was so emotionally undemonstrative that Dick's sister Maria – born four years after Dick – wrote, 'my Father will never [express] *Love*'.[44] Even Day warned Edgeworth that there was some cause to 'trouble yourself about Dick's reading and writing'. By the time of the boy's adolescence, Edgeworth was referring to 'the mistaken principles of Rousseau' and Day to 'the warnings he early gave a fond father about his son'.[45] When Dick was around twelve years old, Edgeworth was 'persuaded by [his] friends' to send him away to a boarding school. He later admitted that, 'unfortunately for my eldest son', he had not 'sufficiently prepared him for the change [from] the Rousseau system'.[46]

Poor Dick found it impossible to adjust to the rigid routines of his new institutionalized life. He had been educated in emotional liberty, with a focus on nurturing and gratifying his desires. Clashing with the rigors and deprivations of eighteenth-century boarding-school life, Dick apparently developed a violent temper that one day had fatal consequences: according to one account, he killed a friend in a duel after having 'entice[d]' his twelve-year-old sister into marriage.[47] In the aftermath, Edgeworth expressed 'a wish that Dick should not stay in Ireland' and his son duly 'acquired a vague notion of the happiness of a seafaring life' and 'went to sea'. Edgeworth cut him out of his will and testament and wrote that 'my mind is now relieved from a very heavy care, by Dicks going to sea after behaving as ill as usual'. He consoled himself with the thought that his son's 'hardihood and fearlessness of danger appeared to fit him for a sailor's life'.[48]

Neither Edgeworth nor Day suffered particularly from their projects' failures. Most liberals who encountered the details responded admiringly to the two men's efforts as 'the most distinguished ornament[s]' of Enlightenment Britain.[49] Edgeworth subsequently turned his attention cheerily from education and fatherhood to clock manufacture, and appeared not to give Dick a second thought, even denying that he had ever felt 'partiality ... towards my son'.[50] Day tried to inflict a Rousseauvian training scheme on further prospective wives, until his friend William Small directed his attention to a Chesterfield heiress called Esther Milnes. At first, Day applied strict Rousseauvian criteria, querying if she was 'tall, and strong, and healthy' and declaring an objection to 'her large fortune'. The exasperated Small demanded of Day, 'Can you possibly expect that a woman ... should be formed exactly according to a picture that exists in your imagination?'[51] Day and Milnes were married at Bath on 7 August 1778. Day went on to write one of the most popular educational books for children of the eighteenth century, *The History of Sandford and Merton*, which was published and widely read until the end of the nineteenth century. He personified Rousseauvian ideals in the character of Harry Sandford, a farmer's son, who prefers his life of innocent manual labour and simple pleasures to the unsatisfying luxuries of his bourgeois friend Tommy Merton. But Day's book also rejected important aspects of Rousseau's scheme. Rousseau had allowed Émile to peruse only *Robinson Crusoe*, but Day advocated reading a wide range of childhood literature from a young age. And the book notably failed to tackle the question of female education, replacing the real-life Sabrina and Lucretia with two fictional boys.[52]

The victims of Edgeworth and Day's schemes were not so lucky as their masterminds. In September 1789, Day was killed, thrown from his wild horse. Inspired by a Rousseauvian aversion to discipline, he had refused to break it in. Sabrina was then the thirty-two-year-old widow of John Bicknell, who had died two years earlier. Edgeworth's daughter Maria related how she 'put herself into deep mourning' for Day. Her bereft state prompted his widow, Esther Milne, to reflect upon Day's treatment of Sabrina, and she considered the poor woman 'doubly entitled to *my* pity and assistance'. Esther settled on Sabrina 'an annuity, not less than thirty, or more than fifty p[oun]ds a year'.[53] Much later, Sabrina would beg Edgeworth's daughter Maria to 'say *as little as possible* respecting' the 'repugnant & distressing' 'romantick fancies' of Thomas Day, in a biography of Richard Lovell Edgeworth on which Maria was working.[54]

By his own admission, Edgeworth had not been an attentive father. He had withheld affection, gone beyond Rousseau's recommendations in neglecting Dick's formal education, and had been quick to reject both his son and his Rousseauvian enthusiasm when Dick's behaviour began to reflect embarrassingly on Edgeworth himself. But, against the odds, Dick appeared to turn his life around and partially restore Edgeworth's hopes. Dick arrived in Virginia in the late 1780s. By the end of the decade he had managed to purchase land in Cheraw District, South Carolina and Anson County, North Carolina. The latter land he subsequently renamed Sneydsborough, after his stepmother Honora Sneyd, whom Edgeworth had married after his first wife died in 1773, shortly after giving birth to Anna Edgeworth, her third daughter. Honora was very close to Dick's own age and he had formed an intimate bond with her. He obtained work as a tutor in the household of a Huguenot colonist called Claudius Pegues, and married a Methodist, Elizabeth Knight, with whom he had three boys, Nathaniel Lovell, Achilles Sneyd and Richard.

In November 1791, aged twenty-seven, after at least half a decade's separation from his father, Dick attempted a reconciliation from across the Atlantic. At the top of a letter to his sister, Edgeworth scribbled a hasty, excited note: 'I have this moment heard from ... S[outh] Carolina – Dick is alive, married, & has made me a Grandfather! & will probably be here or with you soon'. Edgeworth evidently wrote back encouragingly to his son, as Dick replied on 28 February 1792 that 'the more I think of your letter, your kindness, and your desire of establishing me in this country the stronger is my desire to see you ... I find my affections are too strong and that I shall never be happy till I see you.' Edgeworth responded to his 'dear son' that his letter 'gave me inexpressible pleasure – I now not only give you my permission but I earnestly request that you will come to see me as soon as possible'. He signed off 'your affectionate father'.[55]

When Thomas Beddoes and Richard Lovell Edgeworth first met in Bristol in the spring of 1793, Dick had only relatively recently departed from Bristol. He had been there with his family throughout the summer of 1792, and when he came to leave, Maria wrote that 'we could not part with him without great pain and regret for he made us all extremely fond of him'. Edgeworth gave his son £1,000 'with which [Dick] says He shall do better than any Body in the part of America where he is set-tled', and Maria commented proudly that 'My Father seems to have no doubt of his success'. The family speculated excitedly whether Dick would use the money to clear 'land for a plantation either of rice or indian corn or for planting peach orchards for peach brandy' or 'to farm cattle'. Dick promised to visit Britain again in four years' time, and he announced his intention – with no trace of irony – to 'send over to [his father], who has promised to educate him his eldest son Lovell, who is between three & four years old & as he says a very sprightly fine child'.[56] In July 1793, shortly after Beddoes' arrival in Bristol, Dick wrote to reas-sure his family that he had returned safely to America, that he had used his father's money to purchase cattle, and 'his farm is going on bonnily . . . and that his Lady improves & pleases him'. 'I wish we had a telescope that could reach to the Backwoods of America,' Maria wrote wistfully.[57]

Despite Dick's apparent desire to bestow a similar type of education on his own children, by 1793 Rousseauvian pedagog-ical theory was falling out of favour. The increasing violence of the French Revolution was starting to prompt many political commentators to question philosophies centred on liberation, instead of regulation, of the passions. The incontrovertible failure of Day's project, and the uncertain outcome of Edgeworth's, also reflected a general trend in which attempts to excavate the character of 'man in the state of nature' were fading in popularity. This was visible in changing attitudes to 'wild children': children who had been abandoned at a young age, growing up in isolation or cohabiting with animals. Early in the eighteenth century, educational theorists had seized enthusiastically on wild children, hoping to find in them the characteristics of natural man, so that – in the words of the French naturalist Georges-Louis Leclerc, Comte de Buffon – 'the state of pure nature' could be translated into 'a known state'.[58] Peter of Hanover was found in a forest near Hamelin in Germany in 1724, in his early teens, wearing the remnants of a shirt and living on berries. He was sent to London to be observed by Dr John Arbuthnot, where he was idealized as an innocent alternative to the decadence of the English court. Marie-Angélique Leblanc was first sighted in an orchard near the village of Songi in the Champagne region of north-east France in September 1731. She seemed to demonstrate the physical agility and strength of a 'savage', killing a bulldog with one blow, scaling trees, swinging through the woods, skinning a rabbit and eating it raw.

By the time that Beddoes met Edgeworth, optimism about what feral children might reveal was on the wane. It had been hoped that Peter of Hanover would demonstrate a primitive sexual virility, but he disappointed researchers by appearing generally indifferent to women. And Marie-Angélique's behaviour gave the lie to Rousseau's account of women's natural weakness. In her study of *The Wild Girl, Natural Man, and the Monster*, the historian Julia V. Douthwaite describes how Marie-Angélique was treated in a way designed not to illuminate her primitive nature, but to coerce her to conform to social mores. She was placed in a convent, and subjected to a life of 'silence, immobility, physical constraint and social surveillance'.[59] But the discovery of Victor of Aveyron, perhaps the most famous wild child, in forests surrounding the village of Lacaune in southern France, in 1798, demonstrated how the hopes once invested in feral children had dissolved. Victor was obsessed by food and indifferent to human affection. Whereas observers at the beginning of the century might have extrapolated these traits as glimpses of primitive humanity, at the end of the century, as Europe was coming out of the Enlightenment, Victor's doctors thought that his behavioural 'impairments' were symptoms of profound damage.[60] By the second decade of the nineteenth century, this was the prevailing attitude to wild children. The surgeon William Lawrence would write in the 1810s how such children 'are merely instances of defective organization; malformed animals, incapable of speech, and exhibiting few and imperfect mental phenomena; pathological specimens, therefore, rather than examples of human perfection. Nothing can be conceived as more widely removed from the natural condition of man, than these half-witted beings'.[61]

Attitudes to education and the child were radically affected by the failure of optimism about humanity's innately 'free' and 'good' nature in the 1790s. Growing scepticism about the liberation of emotion – a scepticism that was also damaging reformers' hopes in that decade – made many readers look askance on educational theories that emphasised freedom over constraint.[62] Changing attitudes to 'wild children', and the failure of Edgeworth and Day's Rousseauvian educational schemes, were both symptoms of and contributing factors to that revolution of feeling from optimism to pessimism, hope to disappointment, confidence in human virtue to caution. Edgeworth and Beddoes would not yet relinquish education as a mechanism to construct an ideal citizen, a 'loving and feeling being'. Although Edgeworth abandoned specifically Rousseauvian theory after Dick's birth, and did not inflict his experimental imagination so zealously on his later children, he did remain fascinated by contemporary pedagogical ideas. But Edgeworth and Beddoes' uncertainty about the propriety of Rousseauvian educational ideas, and their rooting around for alternative theories, reflected growing caution about the desirability of preserving children's 'primitive' characteristics in their transition into adulthood.

For Beddoes and Edgeworth, when they first became acquainted in spring 1793, however, the future was not entirely gloomy. In May that year, in the first month of his new life in Bristol, Thomas Beddoes wrote to Davies Giddy that he had 'become intimately acquainted with a girl whose character began by pleasing me & has almost succeeded in astonishing & overawing me'.[63] He was talking about Anna Edgeworth, Richard Lovell Edgeworth's third daughter. Anna had accompanied her father to Bristol to help care for her half-brother Lovell, during his treatment for consumption. She was twenty years old, startlingly bright – showing an 'extraordinary proficiency in mathematics' – playful and 'extremely gay where she is acquainted'.[64] Her stepmother, Honora Sneyd, had taken the opposite approach to Edgeworth's upbringing of Dick, disciplining Anna strictly. By the age of three, Anna was forced to dress herself and make her own bed, with the punishment of a forfeited breakfast if she failed.[65]

By his own admission, Thomas Beddoes was at first blustering, nervous, 'uninteresting', and 'kn[e]w not well what to say', but Anna kindly and confidently took charge of the conversation though he was thirteen years older than herself. They discovered a great deal in common, crucially in their political opinions and their unconventional expectations of marriage. In his first letter about Anna Edgeworth, Thomas Beddoes described how 'she had never been so romantic as to imagine that only one woman in the world w[oul]d suit a particular man'.[66] Many years later, Anna would find that the maxim was equally true in reverse: that one man might not be sufficient to suit an individual woman either.

Beddoes quickly became a cherished fixture in the

Edgeworth family residence, describing with glee how Anna's younger siblings – there were nine by the time that Beddoes first met her – 'jump about me, entreat me to go to Ireland, and consider my occasional absence from dinner a serious calamity'. He repaid their devotion, coming up with practical toys – small gardening tools, a pulley, printing blocks – that delighted the children and provided opportunity for Beddoes to discuss theories of child development with the family.[67]

Richard Edgeworth and his eldest daughter Maria were working on a treatise on 'practical education' that would recommend careful attention to, and manipulation of, 'the first impressions which infants receive'.[68] Having jettisoned Rousseau, Edgeworth had now become entranced by a very different philosopher, who was adored by Beddoes: David Hartley. In his *Observations on Man* (1749), Hartley had built on reflections made by the philosopher John Locke. In the seventeenth century, it was common to believe that infants came into the world riddled with original sin. But at the end of that century, Locke described the infant mind as like 'white paper, void of all characters'. He was not the first to come up with the *tabula rasa* theory, but Locke's *Essay Concerning Human Understanding* (1689) was the most influential expression of the theory that all ideas and knowledge – though not the mind's faculties or instincts – are formed through experience alone, through contact with the world's sensory qualities, and imprinted onto the 'blank slate' of the child's mind.[69] Locke had also traced the process by which simple sensations might become associated – often by occurring simultaneously or in quick succession – to form more complex ideas in the constantly developing infant mind. This was a decisive retort to proponents of original sin, and to those claiming humanity to be innately virtuous, or, in fact, to anyone who thought that they could identify any 'primitive' human characteristics at all. Locke's followers were more cautious than Rousseauvians. They saw education as a process of moulding children's early ideas and sensations in order to form the basis of virtuous behaviour, rather than defending desires and interests that were relics of 'man in the state of nature'.

Sixty years after the publication of Locke's theory, David Hartley claimed that it was during an emotion that ideas became associated in particularly interesting and important ways. He described how the particles of the nervous system vibrated each time an idea occurred in the individual's body and mind; and explained that sensations generated larger vibrations than intellectual ideas. When enough ideas became associated in order to generate the level or strength of vibration usually garnered during a sensation, then an 'affection' or 'passion' was produced: 'our passions or affections can be no more than aggregates of simple ideas united by association'.[70] Specific passions were the result of varying combinations of ideas, sensations of pleasure and pain, and levels of involvement of the imagination. 'Ambition' or desire (for example, the desire for a hot bath) was created when a sensation (feeling shivery) occurred at the same time as pain or discomfort that motivated the individual to seek change from the present moment, and as the imagination raised the possibility of immersing oneself in pleasantly hot water.[71]

Hartley was particularly interested in how the distinctive nature of each person's sexual desire was formed from the ideas, memories, sensations and emotions to which they had been exposed from the moment of birth. Libido and sexual fantasy were formed, Hartley thought, from a combination of memories of pleasure or pain that had been gained in early childhood through touching and playing with the genitals. These memories combined with socially derived ideas about shame and 'virtue'; and ideas about a specific object of desire: 'the apprehended beauty of the person, or perfection of [their] mind'.[72] Hartley was interested in how what we might today call sexual and emotional 'disorders' might be managed using his theory of the association of ideas, or 'associationism'. The association of ideas did not just form emotional behaviour in the first place, he emphasized: manipulation of the ideas and beliefs behind the passions could subsequently change them. 'It is of the utmost consequence to morality and religion, that the affections and passions should be analysed into their simple compounding parts,' Hartley wrote. 'For thus we may learn how to cherish and improve good ones, check and root out such as are mischievous and immoral', and make our passions conform to 'our intellectual and religious wants'. Exposing a sex addict to the horrifying physical effects of venereal disease, by taking them to visit a VD hospital, would cause them to associate intercourse with 'hatred and abhorrence' and instil the desire to regulate an 'excessive' libido. For Hartley, what Coleridge would call the 'purifying alchemy of Education' was the principal means by which such emotional change, via the correction of a person's association of ideas, might occur.[73]

Associationism shares some similarities with the contemporary pseudoscience Neuro-Linguistic Programming, and with cognitive behavioural therapy (CBT), which claims that 'our *cognitions* – thoughts and beliefs about a situation – largely determine how we feel and behave' and that 'while we may not be able to change other people or our life circumstances, we can change the way we think about them'.[74] Like CBT, associationism could be optimistic or pessimistic. Utopian theorists hoped that associationist educational methods might give rise to ideas and emotions in the child that could form the basis of a reformed, healthier society. Those who were more circumspect approached associationism as a means to ameliorate the most antisocial behaviours of an imperfect world, or, even more conservatively, to help individuals adapt to the status quo. The psychotherapist and philosopher R. T. Fancher has criticized how 'the basic norm of cognitive therapy is this: except for how the patient thinks, everything is okay'.[75] (Cognitive behavioural therapists retort that the method's aims are not to encourage

the individual to acquiesce to situations of abuse and deprivation, but to enable them to see the world's inequalities and
unfairnesses clearly, and to adjust their expectations of change
accordingly.)

Beddoes saw in associationism the potential to channel the
passions' hydraulic force into sociable behaviour. Probably
inspired by Hartley, Coleridge would later describe how education could 'transmute the fierceness of an ignorant man into
virtuous energy'.[76] By altering the ideas and beliefs underpinning each passion, education might weaken the violent force
of emotion and provide new channels through which it might
be expressed. The evangelical Hannah More conceived of
education's purpose as to 'rectify' the 'corrupt nature and evil
dispositions' that children 'bring into the world', by means of a
'disposition' in the tutor that was 'strong' enough to 'counteract
it'.[77] But reading Hartley showed Beddoes how education could
gently and benevolently channel children's energy into virtuous
behaviour, rather than seeking to suppress it through an authoritarian attitude. Hartley was greatly admired by Joseph Priestley,
who declared associationism to be 'itself a form of mental
chemistry', whose effects on education were comparable to the
chemical revolution's significance in the history of scientific progress.[78] Priestley had published an abridged edition of Hartley's
Observations of Man in 1775, hoping to popularise it, and he
had compared the process by which ideas became associated
in the mind to the coalescing of simple chemical elements. For
Beddoes, associationism was attractive not just for its similarities
to his specialism of chemistry. More importantly, it appealed to
his radical political hopes. Associationism demonstrated that the
hydraulic operation of the passions did not sentence humanity
to involuntary, destructive reactions to oppression. 'Unless the
mass of the people *be trained to humanity*, no place or person
can be fully secure from the effects of popular fury,' he wrote at
the end of 1792, but he was confident that, 'thanks, however, to

Locke and his followers, a better prospect seems to be opening before us'.[79]

In late May 1793, Beddoes described to his friend Davies Giddy how Richard Lovell Edgeworth 'perceived more clearly the turn his daughter's inclinations were taking than I had'.[80] In truth, despite their enthusiasm for establishing a close connection, all three parties – Edgeworth, Anna and Beddoes – harboured anxieties about the match. Beddoes fretted that 'I am taken for one insensible to women'. Although he was adamant that a misleading 'exterior roughness' belied his 'susceptibility of impression', his apparent indifference to sex would cause problems for the marriage in the future.[81] Anna worried about the constraints of monogamous marriage and was anxious that 'all married men ... shall grow tired of a woman, of whom they must see a great deal'.[82] And Edgeworth reported to friends in Ireland that 'the object of Anna's affections is a little fat democrat of considerable abilities'. He recognized that Beddoes was 'a man of honour and virtue, enthusiastic and sanguine and very fond of Anna' and that his medical projects were likely to 'succeed and make a fortune'. But he was anxious that Beddoes's subversive political views, and his lack of tactical shrewdness, would scupper his ambitions and financial future: 'if he bloweth the trumpet of sedition the aristocracy will rather go to hell with Satan than with any democratic Devil'.[83]

Nevertheless, the three put aside their doubts and drew up a financial settlement. Edgeworth required Beddoes to add an extra £100 per year to his own capital to secure the marriage, and Davies Giddy willingly offered the sum. Anna herself imposed a requirement that, before committing to marriage, she and Beddoes would test their relationship by enforcing a separation 'to try whether the sentiment is durable'. She wanted to 'improve herself in the useful art of housekeeping', and asked her father to 'put her in the way of Irish Lords, Squires, Captains &c. &c.' to trial her commitment to monogamy. Beddoes was unconcerned, writing that he had 'no wish to extend any thing like a promise; such a bond ought never to keep people together'.[84] By the end of the year, the Edgeworth entourage had returned to their estate in Ireland, and Beddoes was left in Bristol, building up his medical practice.

In September 1793, Beddoes' intention to discover the root causes and cures of hydraulic violence became urgent when riots began on the bridge in the centre of Bristol. In 1768, the city corporation had had the bridge rebuilt, passing the cost onto citizens through taxes and tolls. Bristolians were initially assured that the bridge tolls would end once £2,000 had been raised, probably in September 1793. But when that date came, the corporation informed Bristolians that the tolls would continue into 1794. The corporation had form for making unpopular moves to extend its own authority (for example, via powers to suppress 'nuisances', combined with upgraded lighting and paving) and passing on the bill to citizens. In 1790, proposals for a new jail – the costs of which would be met through taxes – were defeated after residents protested. Two years later, citizens were appalled when the corporation presented a parliamentary bill with the same aim, in an underhand manner. Continuing the bridge tolls was received in the same light. It was a devastating blow in a year that also saw failed spring harvests and a financial crash linked to country bankers' over-extension of credit. Trade centres like Bristol bore the brunt, and by summer 1793, in the words of Samuel Seyer, who was writing a history of Bristol at the time, 'there was scarcely a tradesman in the city who did not feel the common calamity in his own circumstances'.[85]

An old bridge statute stipulated that, if there was a nine-day hiatus in toll payments, reintroduction required an Act of Parliament, so on 19 September 1793, protestors removed and burned the bridge's gates. When, nine days later, the corporation simply reinstated the gates and tolls, within a few hours a 'very considerable number of persons' completely destroyed them again. The corporation summoned the Herefordshire militia, who opened fire, killing one person and wounding two or three. Over the following days, growing crowds gathered on the bridge and, on 30 September, they set fire to the toll houses. This time troops from the national army were called in and started shooting: ten died and over fifty were wounded. On 1 October, an eyewitness described how 'revenge, alone, dwelt in the breast of the people', who smashed the windows of key municipal buildings, including the Guildhall and the Council House. The Herefordshire militia slunk away, but were replaced by regiments from Monmouthshire and Brecon and a party of dragoons. When four individuals offered to raise the outstanding costs of repairing the bridge from private subscriptions rather than taxes and tolls, the corporation grudgingly agreed, tolls were removed, and the riots ended.[86] Shortly afterwards, Beddoes wrote to Giddy describing how the Bristol rioters' successful protest made 'the triumph of despotism see[m] at present scarce so sure as it lately did'. But he also thought that despotism's 'opposite' – popular fury – 'can hardly be said to be desirable' either. 'The present generation in every country of Europe has much evil & very little good to look forward to' if a solution could not be found to authoritarian governments provoking the populace's passions, he reflected sadly.[87]

Chapter 6

NECK OR NOTHING

For Mary Wollstonecraft, popular violence in the form of the attack on the Tuileries Palace 10 August and the September Massacres of 1792 also shaped her emotional projects. It put a temporary kibosh on her plans to travel to France with the Fuselis and Johnson. Instead, Johnson suggested that she accompany him to Berkshire, to visit a friend. On their return in mid-September 1792, she was amused to realize that they had become the subject of gossip: that 'the world, to talk big, married m[e] to [Johnson] whilst we were away'.[1] But her sights were still set on France. It seemed to promise a welcoming home for those – like Wollstonecraft – who hoped to effect widespread political change through reforms to domestic relations, and her affection for Fuseli seems to have remained undiminished.

On 20 September 1792, France allowed divorce under three conditions: mutual consent; an appeal from one spouse regarding incompatibility; or an accusation levelled by one spouse against the other about violence or abuse, abandonment, emigration, absence, criminal behaviour or mental breakdown. This revolutionized marriage in France. Under the old regime, marriages could only be dissolved upon annulment by the Catholic Church or a legal separation. But the revolution severed marriage from the church, and approached it as a civil phenomenon, a microcosm of the political contract between individual and state. The Revolution itself had resulted from citizens asserting their liberty to reject the monarchy and form a new relationship with authority. The divorce laws transformed marriage into a similar civil contract into which no one individual should be locked without continuing consent.[2]

When the legislation permitting divorce was passed, Wollstonecraft joked that in 'Paris, indeed, I might take a husband for the time being, and get divorced when my truant heart longed again to nestle with its old friends'.[3] She was not alone in seeing the utopian optimism, combined with the terrifying ubiquity of death, that characterized France in the revolution's early years, as a heady context for sexual experimentation. Johnson's co-editor at the *Analytical Review*, Thomas Christie, a Scottish banker who had abandoned commerce to pursue medicine, had recently returned to London from Paris. He was buoyant about a new relationship with a married woman he had met in France, who had become pregnant with his child.[4] Similarly, the twenty-one-year-old writer and poet William Wordsworth arrived in Orléans, south of Paris, on 6 December 1791; within three months he had entered into a relationship with Marie Anne 'Annette' Vallon, four years older than himself, who swiftly became pregnant and gave birth to their child, Anne-Caroline Wordsworth, on 15 December 1792.[5]

Some British radicals looked to France as a model of how the liberation of desire from strict regulatory constraints like marriage might be part of wide-reaching political reforms. Some hoped that liberated desire would result in greater 'productivity' of states like happiness and sexual fulfilment – but also in the reproduction of children. The writer James Henry Lawrence predicted that freeing women from social mores hindering their sensuality would stimulate their application to sexual labour with an unprecedented diligence that could only work in men's favour.[6] Lawrence compared the emancipation of women's sexuality to the disintegration of feudalism. 'When bondage was abolished,' he wrote, 'the land-holders conceived themselves ruined; but their estates were cultivated by freemen, and they found themselves richer than before. In like manner men would profit by the liberty of women'. And as women's liberated desires drove up the sexual and domestic productivity to which they were 'naturally' suited, men's freed energies would be able to reach full potential in the public sphere: 'What a race of politicians, generals, and philosophers, might be expected from a nation, where every lofty [male] soul were unimpeded, by the care of providing for its offspring,' he wondered. A 'nation of bachelors would be the sovereign of the world!'.[7]

Lawrence foresaw that the liberation of desire – letting libido off the leash of regulatory conventions like marriage and monogamy – would have very different consequences for men and women. Christie left the French mother of his child when the baby was a few weeks old, for Rebecca Thomson, granddaughter of the wealthy proprietor of the London carpet manufacturing company Moore & Co., a firm with whom he entered into commercial partnership. Wordsworth returned to Britain alone in December 1792, leaving Annette behind, still entertaining hopes of marriage. He did not see her, or his daughter, again until 1802, when, accompanied by his sister, Dorothy, Wordsworth arranged a meeting with Annette and Caroline in Calais, to prepare them for his forthcoming marriage to Mary Hutchinson.[8] The drastically different consequences of sexual liberation for men and women would give some sexual radicals – especially women – pause for thought. Many concluded

that such extreme defiance of social mores was best confined
to separatist utopian settlements, to avoid exposing the women
to censure by the wider community. And some grew sceptical
about the propriety of sexual liberation, in terms that anticipated
later critiques of free-market economics: that lack of regulation
allows existing inequalities to be reinforced.

Eighteenth-century discussions about the propriety of liber-
ating desire overtly or implicitly treated the subject of emotion
in the language of economics. This is a largely alien concept
to us now: we tend to analyse our own emotions in terms of
how they feel to us as individuals: the subjective transformations they offer, the upheavals they present in our day-to-day
mental life. The NHS website deals with 'anger', for example,
almost entirely as a phenomenon that creates difficulties for the
individual in whom it erupts: rapid heartbeat, tense shoulders,
clenched fists, which can be dealt with through swimming,
yoga and meditation.[9] But eighteenth-century writers did not
approach the 'passions', 'sentiments', 'affections' or 'appetites'
as subjective states occurring *within* an individual, but rather as
motivations for sympathetic exchanges *between* people, knitting
them together into an economy of 'fellow feeling'. This was not
just metaphor. Economics can be viewed as 'the study of human
wants', the 'science of craving'.[10] Economic theories accounting
for patterns in the desire for, and provision of, material commodities might therefore facilitate analysis of how individuals
pursued the desire for material and immaterial satisfactions – for
sex, affection, fame, approval, love – through their passions. It
was the collapse of this view of the passions in the 1790s – due
to heightened anxiety about philosophies of liberation and
to the detachment of emotion from politics – that would lay
the groundwork for our contemporary, solipsistic emotional
landscape.

The economist and philosopher Adam Smith is most famous
today for *An Inquiry into the Nature and Causes of the Wealth of*

Nations (1776), a foundational text of classical economics, which claimed that commercial regulation was counterproductive, and that a nation's wealth was maximized when its capacity to produce goods and services was set free. Smith had also written a treatise entitled *The Theory of Moral Sentiments* (1759), which was one of the most important publications on the passions in the eighteenth century. In that treatise, he conceived the passions to be commodities that, like other products, were subject to the same human 'propensity to truck, barter, and exchange one thing for another' that he would describe so influentially in the *Wealth of Nations*.[11] This emotional trade took place principally through the action of 'sympathy', in which a witness to another's display of feeling might agree to share in that passion, in return for a warm 'fellow-feeling'.[12] Like the vision of a self-regulating financial economy that he would develop, Smith proposed that the emotional economy was self-regulating, through the concept of 'propriety'. Propriety was a form of value – set by social mores, individual priorities and, to a limited extent, religious standards – that placed an onus on everybody to temper their emotional displays to a reasonable and appropriate degree; a degree that was *sympathetic*. When this self-control had been exerted, propriety then required the witness to offer sympathy in return. If either party failed to live up to these ethical standards – through which 'passions' were reined in to become 'moral sentiments' – the emotional transaction collapsed and the possibility of sociability disappeared: 'We become intolerable to one another. I can neither support your company, nor you mine. You are confounded at my violence and passion, and I am enraged at your cold insensibility and want of feeling'.[13] But when the transaction was successful, and the emotional economy flourished, an 'invisible hand' would ensure the whole community benefited from increased sociability resulting from the encouragement of self-interest.[14]

Across much of Europe from the sixteenth century onwards,

the economic theory of 'mercantilism' had dominated. Many of its proponents advocated economic regulation and controls as a means of bolstering state power. Britain's Navigation Acts, for example, encouraged exports and discouraged imports to contain the benefits of colonial trade within the empire. In France, Louis XIV defined the goal of economic policies as bolstering the state according to the king's diktats. So, for many, mercantilism was allied to absolute monarchy, and to the fiscal-military state, which generated revenue to support its armed forces.[15] Mercantilists had stressed the necessity of maintaining the working population in a state of economic oppression at the 'margins of subsistence' – denied education or leisure that might prove distracting from productive work – whilst focusing on the accumulation of the ruler's wealth (often in the form of bullion) as a gauge of success.

In the second half of the eighteenth century, virulent opposition to mercantilism was voiced by adherents of the French economic theory of 'physiocracy'. Physiocrats like François Quesnay argued that the source of a nation's wealth was its productive (agricultural) labour, and they defended the freedom of individuals – particularly the labouring classes, on whose oppression the ruler's wealth depended – to determine the nature and quantity of their own work. Physiocrats maintained that economic systems work best when individuals' self-interested desire to engage in productive work complements other citizens' self-interested desire to consume certain commodities, unfettered by any regulation.

Today Adam Smith is generally seen as the father of the free market, an icon of libertarianism and neoliberalism. To many on the left, he is synonymous with the market's reinforcement of social and economic inequality. But in the latter half of the eighteenth century, in the context of its economic history of mercantilism and physiocracy, Smith's theories of a liberated economy of desire, freed from service to a despotic ruler, provided some liberal reformers with a progressive vision of how the poor might escape economic oppression, whilst the overall production of happiness and wealth might be increased. Smith's wariness of government derived in part from his understanding of how it might be co-opted by private interests. 'People of the same trade seldom meet together ... but the conversation ends in a conspiracy against the publick, or in some contrivance to raise prices,' he wrote in *Wealth of Nations*, whilst pointing out that 'we have no acts of parliament against combining to lower the price of work; but many against combining to raise it'.[16] The literary historian Philip Connell has described how 'an association of revolutionary ideology with the physiocratic doctrine of free trade was in fact a recurrent element of British political discourse in the years after 1789'.[17] And efforts have been made by historians in the last twenty years to reclaim Smith as a 'radical and egalitarian'; both Iain McLean and Emma Rothschild argue that Smith's reputation was first yoked to conservatism in an effort to defend his legacy during the reactionary backlash that took place after the French Revolution.[18] But in the early 1790s, before that backlash materialized, the most radical of sexual liberals adopted economic theories like Smith's to support the freeing of libido from the stifling control of marriage.

Wollstonecraft was not an advocate of liberated sexuality, considering it sensual and 'a passion which may have a mixture of dross in it'. But she renewed her efforts to persuade Fuseli to play his part in the innovative relationship she seems to have planned for them. According to Fuseli's friend Knowles, she protested that her 'passion' was not the result of a 'criminal' pursuit of 'pleasure', but a 'rational desire' to 'rise superior' above her 'earthly habitation'.[19] One autumn day in 1792, it seems that Wollstonecraft rallied all her 'temerity' and turned up on Fuseli's doorstep. Encountering his wife Sophia, she explained pragmatically that 'she wished to become an inmate in her family'. She confessed that she had long felt that 'although Mrs Fuseli had a right to the person of her husband, she, Mrs. Wollstonecraft, might claim, and, for congeniality of sentiments and talents, hold a place in his heart', for she hoped 'to unite herself to his mind'.[20] This proposition, Wollstonecraft clarified – and one can only imagine the look on Sophia's face – 'arises from the sincere affection which I have for your husband, for I find that I cannot live without the satisfaction of seeing and conversing with him daily'.[21] Within a matter of seconds, Wollstonecraft's hopes were dashed. Sophia instantly showed her the door. After Fuseli, presumably, made no effort to offer sympathy or hope, Wollstonecraft retreated, her pride having taken a substantial knock. Subdued, she apologized to him, for 'having disturbed the quiet tenour of his life'.[22]

London now held out no hope. Wollstonecraft determined 'to set out for Paris in the course of a fortnight or three weeks', she wrote to her friend, the historian and patron William Roscoe. 'I go alone[:] neck or nothing is the word'.[23] She had given up on the immediate prospect of establishing a domestic microcosm of a reformed society. But, with no new book in the pipeline and no alternative candidate to replace Fuseli, she decided to witness the 'revolution of sentiments' taking place in revolutionary Paris at first hand. Wollstonecraft arranged to stay with the daughter of her sister Eliza's former employer. Aline Fillietaz had married a wealthy Frenchman, and owned an 'immense' impersonal house on the rue Meslée (now Meslay), a house containing 'one folding door opening after another'.[24] Wollstonecraft borrowed £30 from her sisters and, despite 'vapourish fears' about the likelihood of war breaking out between France and Britain, she set off in early December 1792.[25]

Wollstonecraft arrived in Paris to find a city on tenterhooks, poised between the murderous violence of the September Massacres and the impending trial of the king. It was this dreadful suspense, with its simmering undercurrent of ferocity, that

Wordsworth had fled. Wollstonecraft's apartments were within sight of the triumphal arch of the Porte Saint-Martin, commissioned in the 1670s by Louis XIV to commemorate his military victories, and a reminder of the high point of monarchic power. Now, over two hundred years later, *sans-culottes* wielding pikes and clubs ambled around its base. Wollstonecraft was also just minutes away from the Temple prison, where the royal family were being held. The top-floor attic of 22 rue Meslée offered a panoramic view of Paris and of the hubristic rise and fall of the French monarchy.

At first, the city exhausted her: 'the striking contrasts of riches and poverty, elegance and slovenliness, urbanity and deceit, every where caught my eye, and saddened my soul'.[26] Wollstonecraft was suffering from a chesty cough and wrote, weakly, to Everina that 'I apply so closely to the language, and labour so continually to understand what I hear that I never go to bed without a head ache – and my spirits are fatigued with endeavouring to form a just opinion of public affairs'.[27] Soon, though, she found friends. A month or so before her arrival, the British Club of Jacobins, also known as the Society of the Friends of the Rights of Man, had hosted its inaugural meeting. This took place at White's 'English' Hotel, on the Passage des Petits Pères, not far from the Tuileries, right next to the Hôtel des États-Unis. Its fifty inaugural committee members and their fifty guests had toasted the French army's successes and drafted a congratulatory address to the National Convention. Despite the burgeoning force of political reaction in Britain, they optimistically looked forward to the revolution crossing the Channel – to the 'speedy abolition of hereditary titles and feudal distinctions in England' – and raised glasses to the 'English patriots' and the 'lady defenders of the Revolution'.[28] They continued to meet every Thursday and Sunday throughout November and December.

White's became a hub for emigrants from England, Scotland

and Ireland. Formal members of the club and hangers-on included the radical printer John Hurford Stone, the lawyer John Frost, the Irish aristocrat and radical Lord Edward Fitzgerald, the Scottish pamphleteer John Oswald, newspaper editor Sampson Perry, and former MP Sir Robert Smith.[29] Most were associates of the Girondins, a political grouping cemented as much by friendship as by professional links.[30] White's Hotel brought together revolutionary tourists wanting to witness the political action, and opportunists looking for openings that would allow new fortunes to be made. Among the latter was Joel Barlow, a swaggering, apparently rather humourless American, who had left a career in law to become a land agent and radical pamphleteer. Wollstonecraft knew him from London, from Johnson's dinners. Although she was disconcerted by his enthusiasm for revolutionary violence, he and his wife Ruth had been kind, attempting to further her brother Charles' prospects. Joel travelled to Paris in November 1792 to deliver a congratulatory address to the new National Convention, which replaced the Legislative Assembly after the September Massacres and held its meetings in the newly vacated Tuileries Palace. He subsequently threw himself into French politics, campaigning for election to the Convention himself, and trying to persuade residents of the Italian region of Piedmont to welcome the revolutionary troops. Joel remained an entrepreneur at heart, sniffing out business opportunities through the tremors of the revolution, meeting American land agents, and finding ways to defy the English naval blockade, which restricted imports and exports.[31]

Joel Barlow introduced Wollstonecraft, as a 'lady defender of the revolution' herself, to Tom Paine, whom she had already met at Johnson's. In Britain Paine had been summoned on a charge of seditious libel in May 1792, but his trial had been postponed until December that year. Having been granted honorary French citizenship, he arrived in Paris just days after the September Massacres. Despite speaking minimal French, Paine was elected a deputy to the new National Convention. In December 1792, he was found guilty of seditious libel for Part Two of the *Rights of Man* and was outlawed from Britain *in absentia*, hence his continued residence in France.[32] Wollstonecraft also met the 'odd philanthropist' Count Gustav von Schlabrendorf, who was caught up in a short-lived but passionate engagement to Thomas Christie's sister. And she encountered the British writer Helen Maria Williams, who had stayed intermittently in Paris since the summer of 1790, and had published anonymously two volumes of *Letters from France*. Six more volumes would follow, and it became one of the most famous eyewitness accounts of the revolution, tracing its 'great change' from 'the triumph of human kind' at the storming of the Bastille to the 'wrecking' of 'Liberty' on the 'rocks' of the September Massacres. In 1792, Williams was still hopeful that the revolution would 'spread fragrance over a regenerated land', and Wollstonecraft '*rather* like[d] her' and the glamorous gatherings she arranged of 'the majority of the leaders in the French revolution'.[33]

In the evening of 26 December 1792, Wollstonecraft sat down to write, somewhat tremulously, to Johnson: 'About nine o'clock this morning, the king passed by my window, moving silently along (excepting now and then a few strokes on the drum, which rendered the stillness more awful) through empty streets'.[34] It was the day of the second part of the trial of Louis XVI: the defence of 'Louis Capet', as he had been designated. He faced charges of supporting counter-revolutionary rebellions, undermining the military defence of France, protecting internal enemies of the revolution, and causing 'the blood of Frenchmen to flow'.[35] Wollstonecraft had expected outbreaks of violence after the trial, but she described proudly, and with relief, how 'this day was not stained with blood' and that the citizens 'are returning home with composed countenances'. 'For the first time since I entered France,' she reflected, 'I bowed to the majesty of the people, and respected the propriety of behaviour so perfectly in unison with my own feelings.' But an 'association of ideas made the tears flow', she admitted, when the sight of Louis 'in a hackney coach, going to meet death' conjured up historical memories of his predecessor, the 'Sun King', Louis XIV, 'entering the capital with all his pomp ... only to see the sunshine of prosperity overshadowed by the sublime gloom of misery'.[36] The French monarchy's fate made Wollstonecraft think of her own past disillusionments, when she had been seduced by 'that wanton, the Imagination, with her artful coquetry, who lures us forward, and makes us run over a rough road, pushing aside every obstacle merely to catch to a disappointment'.[37]

Less than a month later, at 10.22 a.m. on 21 January 1793, Louis Capet was guillotined at the Place de la Révolution. Wollstonecraft was surrounded by men bullish about the execution. Barlow crowed that King George's head should be next, and Paine had supported France's shift to republicanism since 1791.[38] But Wollstonecraft was haunted by the disorder and violence of revolutionary Paris. 'I want to see something alive,' she had pleaded prior to the execution in a letter to Johnson; 'death in so many frightful shapes has taken hold of my fancy'. She was plagued by visions of 'eyes glar[ing] through a glass-door opposite my chair, and bloody hands shook at me'.[39] Her sisters were surprised by the gloomy tone of her letters home, and Eliza confided to Everina that 'I am *convinced* that M. has met with some great disappointment lately,' conspiratorially pondering whether there might be 'a Cause' beyond being 'rather *disgusted* with the French in general'.[40]

Wollstonecraft's nightmares increased over the following months. After Louis' execution, Britain had expelled the French Ambassador, and on 1 February 1793 France declared war. Many in Britain initially hoped the war could be brought to a swift conclusion, but it would last for another twenty-two years, until 1815. In the spring of 1793, the National Convention established the Committee of Public Safety and an extraordinary criminal

tribunal to identify and bring to trial enemies of the revolution.
This signalled a shift in political power from the Girondins
to the more radical Jacobins: the 'Montagnards' – the occupi-
ers of the 'mountain', the highest benches in the Legislative
Assembly – led by Robespierre. Fearing themselves personally
at risk, the Girondins created the 'Commission of Twelve' to
wrest back authority over the arrest of conspirators. But in late
May 1793 the Montagnards removed the Commission of Twelve,
and on 1 June a petition demanding the arrest of the Girondins
themselves was referred to the Committee of Public Safety.
Girondin newspapers were shut down, and Jacques Pierre
Brissot, along with twenty-eight supporters, was arrested. He
escaped, was recaptured and tried for being an 'agent of the
counter-revolution and of the foreign powers, especially Britain',
for having opposed the execution of Louis XVI, and calling
for the reinstatement of the constitutional monarchy that had
been established in 1791. Brissot was executed by guillotine on
31 October 1793. Wollstonecraft felt a 'sort of indefinite terror'
when the news spread around Paris, later describing the fear
and grief as 'one of the most intolerable sensations she had ever
experienced'.[41]

The guillotine claimed more heads over the summer, and
death stalked Paris in other guises too. The journalist Jean-
Paul Marat, who had helped to engineer the Girondins' fall, was
murdered in his bathtub on 13 July by a young woman called
Charlotte Corday. The British Club at White's Hotel dissolved,
and many returned to Britain. During the period known as the
Terror, over 16,000 were executed in Paris alone, and a further
25,000 across France. Wollstonecraft tried to leave France, contemplating a move to Switzerland. She applied for a passport,
but it had not arrived by the time she concluded that 'I could not
think of staying any longer at Madame F's'.[42] So, in June 1793,
Wollstonecraft quit Paris for the outlying village of Neuilly-sur-
Seine, going to a house tended by the Fillietaz family's 'old

Gardener'. Despite the blood and horror of Paris, Wollstonecraft felt herself to be 'in better health and spirits than I have ever enjoyed since I came to France'.[43] The transformation was palpable to her correspondents, and Eliza wrote to her younger sister, 'What say you Everina now to the *Continental air.* – Or is it *A Love?* ... That has wrought the Miracle?'[44] She was on the mark. Godwin later described how, in June 1793, Wollstonecraft had 'arrived at the situation, which, for two or three preceding years, her reason had pointed out to her as affording the most substantial prospect of happiness'.[45] 'I have a plan in my head', she wrote excitedly; and 'I will venture to *promise* that brighter days are in store'.[46]

In early spring 1793, as the frosts had begun to thaw in the new French republic, Mary Wollstonecraft had made the acquaintance of an American recently arrived in Paris: a novelist, land-agent and enthusiastic Girondist called Gilbert Imlay. After serving as a lieutenant during the American War of Independence of 1775–83, Imlay had embraced the opportunities that opened up in the newly autonomous United States. America held a special place in the imagination of British reformers and radicals. It offered a vision of more egalitarian access to property. In Britain, political power was linked to property ownership, through the 'forty-shilling freeholder' legislation that made financial independence a prerequisite to vote. Edmund Burke had underscored the 'necessity' of property being passed on through inheritance, relating men's investment in their nation-state to their emotional ties towards their families. In America in the first decades after the Revolutionary War, voting rights in most states still rested on property ownership. But land was much cheaper, and 70 to 80 per cent of the adult white male population of newly settled areas gained the vote.[47] Some British radicals criticized the fact that the American constitution still linked political power to property ownership, but many celebrated the accessible economic opportunities that challenged the old world's uneven distribution of material wealth. America offered an abundance of land for purchase and improvement, new commercial markets, and promised to make any (white, male) emigrant possessed of enough energy and nous financially independent.[48]

Imlay had diligently mined America's potential. Until 1786 he had worked as a surveyor and land speculator in Kentucky, which, he claimed, had seen around 12,000 new settlers in 1784 alone.[49] He also dabbled in various import and export ventures, exploiting the 'capital circumstances in our favour when [European nations] meet us in our own markets': an abundance of raw materials, low taxes, and no middlemen.[50] But speculation could destroy as quickly as it could create wealth. By 1792, Imlay had been forced to liquidate his property holdings, and set up afresh in London. He published *A Topographical Description of the Western Territory of North America*, designed to tout Kentucky's attractions. And by the time he arrived in Paris in early 1793, he was writing a novel, *The Emigrants*, which also advertised America as the ideal destination for reform-minded citizens who were tired of Britain dragging its heels over parliamentary reform but dissuaded from living in France by its political instability.

The Emigrants appealed to – perhaps it even bore the stamp of – Wollstonecraft's sensibilities. Imlay clearly understood the pain of loneliness and exile: he and Wollstonecraft both knew how it felt to be, like his novel's protagonists, 'torn from the bosom of their friends and dear relatives. – banished from their country into the wilds of a desert'.[51] Imlay articulated what Wollstonecraft considered a promisingly progressive attitude to marriage and relationships, criticizing double standards of sexual virtue that 'expect the exercise of a temperance on the part of women, for which [men's] conduct affords such bad examples'.[52] Imlay's novel portrayed how unmarried women who try to form 'tender ties' with men – 'ties which spring from the finest feelings, and which characterize the most humane and exalted souls' – are unfairly treated as social pariahs, 'branded with contempt, and condemned to live in poverty, unnoticed, and unpitied'.[53] These lines would have spoken to Wollstonecraft, who was still nursing her bruises after Fuseli's rejection.

Imlay and Wollstonecraft seem to have swiftly become lovers. Revolutionary Paris took on a new erotic topography, as they arranged night-time sexual assignations at 'the barrier': one of the old toll barriers where taxes on incoming goods had been collected, which became obsolete following the removal of the tolls in 1791.[54] In September 1793 Wollstonecraft agreed to return from the relative tranquillity of Neuilly to the capital to 'live together' with Imlay at his lodgings in Saint-Germain, despite her fear of the Terror's unpredictable violence.[55] Imlay was collaborating with Joel Barlow in a scheme to sequestrate the state of Louisiana and place it under French control, with the tacit agreement of the American government, who feared its seizure by the British. The project offered Imlay the opportunity to return to the United States, and he paraded visions before Wollstonecraft of purchasing a farm, where her two sisters could join them.

Wollstonecraft, now in her thirties, had endured a dismissive family; a violent and drunken father; the effects of marital coercion, rape, and mental breakdown in her sister's marriage; the death of her mother, and of her best friend, Fanny Blood; solitude, isolation and daily drudgery in Ireland; and, most recently, painful rejection by Fuseli. She had learned the hard way about the risks of exposing herself to disappointment by investing hope unwisely, borne on a tide of blind, unregulated emotion. But Imlay offered tenderness, where Fuseli had only leered and postured. Imlay's pioneering independence appealed to her own essentially solitary self-image. He was sexually adept, having had a 'girl' in Kentucky and, more recently, one in Paris too; he kindled the glimmers of erotic desire that seem to have been smouldering in Wollstonecraft. Imlay agreed that marriage was corrupt, and appeared to offer to alleviate her family responsibilities too, which completed Wollstonecraft's enraptured vision of a man who saw how a pair of lovers might reform political society. She fell hard for him, soon writing that 'I love you fondly', and that her 'affection . . . signifies something habitual'; she may have despised marriage, but was no fan of promiscuity, and long-term commitment was the framework in which she thought her robust passions might be best braced by a 'manly' exercise of reason.[56] She and Imlay seem to have kept their passionate liaison secret for the first four months. But soon the unpredictable nature of revolutionary France conspired against them, and they were forced to make their relationship public.

After the Girondins' demise in early summer 1793, uprisings against the Jacobin ascendancy took place in the French cities of Lyon, Avignon, Nîmes and Marseille. In Toulon, the Jacobins were ousted, but royalist forces took advantage of the instability and summoned aid from the British and Spanish navies, who sent 13,000 troops to guard the naval arsenal at Toulon's military harbour. A young captain, Napoleon Bonaparte, was given partial responsibility for countering the siege. The Jacobins outlawed the presence of British citizens in France, ordering the imprisonment of any who remained. Around 250 were thrown into the Luxembourg prison, including Wollstonecraft's friend Helen Maria Williams.[57]

Wollstonecraft was in a bind. Even if she had a passport, she was unwilling to abandon Imlay to slink back to safety in Britain, but nor did she want to marry him and lose her British citizenship. Godwin would later describe how she was nervous about involving Imlay 'in certain family embarrassments to which she conceived herself exposed'; she worried about transferring her family's debts to her lover.[58] And the pair had opposed themselves to the institution of marriage. But this did not prevent Wollstonecraft eventually approaching the American ambassador and requesting a certificate claiming she was the wife of an American. She took the name 'Imlay', and soon realized the name-change was expedient for a very different reason: she was pregnant, and before long was likely to attract raised eyebrows from observers. 'I have felt some gentle twitches,' she wrote to Imlay, 'which make me begin to think, that I am nourishing a creature who will soon be sensible of my care. – This thought has not only produced an overflowing of tenderness to you,' she continued, 'but made me very attentive to calm my mind and take exercise, lest I should destroy an object, in whom we are to have a mutual interest'.[59] She was citing a popular eighteenth-century belief that maternal distress might harm a foetus, and she even endeavoured, with little success, to quieten her revulsion at the sight of fresh blood on the pavement surrounding the Place de Louis Quinze, where an execution had just taken place.

Just as Wollstonecraft's spirits were rising, Imlay left. He went to the port of Havre de Grace (now Le Havre), on the north coast of France, to oversee the shipping of some goods. With a nonchalance that wounded Wollstonecraft to the quick, he mentioned that he would be gone several months. Imlay's departure marked the beginning of an agonizing correspondence between the pair that would last for over two years, in which Wollstonecraft flogged their fading relationship with the fervour of one refusing to relinquish not just her lover, but all the political and personal hopes she had invested in him. Imlay and she had very different expectations of their relationship. A woman with Wollstonecraft's critical attitude to marriage may well have seemed, to Imlay, fair game for a fling in the volatile atmosphere of revolutionary Paris, where its inhabitants existed on a knife-edge between intense life and sudden death, where temporary pleasures were grabbed with both hands. But for women at the end of the eighteenth century, the ever so slight loosening of marriage's patriarchal grip (as aspirations of pleasure joined the acquisition of property as motives for marriage), and the rise of liberal attitudes to the regulation of desire, had opened up alternative forms of intimate relationship and the potential for dramatic political change. For men such as Fuseli, Imlay, and James Lawrence, the weakening of the institution of marriage brought primarily sexual benefits: unmarried partnerships presented pleasurable opportunities for men to freely express and satisfy desire, averting the constraints of monogamous 'chastity'. But for their female contemporaries, the benefits of alternative forms of relationship far exceeded the sensual: they offered the possibility of maintaining independent property and economic agency, transforming partnerships into collaborations of equals, rather than states of slavery. Similar success in Wollstonecraft and Imlay's relationship would make it – she hoped – a microcosm of a transformed, egalitarian society.

In a torrent of frustrated, angry, hurt letters, which generally met with a cruel wall of silence or occasional one-line responses, Wollstonecraft tried to bring Imlay to see her vision. She criticized the business ventures that repeatedly took him away from her. 'I hate commerce' and his 'money-getting face', she spat. She alternately pleaded with him – 'I intreat you. – Do not turn from me' – and implied sarcastically that 'these continual separations were necessary to warm your affection ... Crack! – crack! – and away you go'.[60] She threatened to leave too: 'If you do not return soon – ... I will throw your slippers out at window, and be off – nobody knows where.' She searched desperately for rational reasons to continue believing in his enduring affection: 'I think that you must love me, for, in the sincerity of my heart let me say it, I believe I deserve your tenderness, because I am true'. And she tried to 'grow more reasonable' to his desire to be apart from her, despite expressing vocal anxieties that 'grief' was 'derang[ing] her bowels'.[61] Wollstonecraft resorted to simple statements of expectation: 'I do not want to be loved like a goddess; but I wish to be necessary to you.' And she occasionally dismissed him as just another exponent of male supremacy – 'A man is a tyrant!' – before invoking her pregnancy to try to persuade 'her mate' to stay 'to cheer her', and attempting to rouse his sympathy for 'your poor girl'.[62]

Imlay came and went from Paris over the winter. '[A]m I to see you this week, or this month?'[63] Wollstonecraft wrote exasperatedly around Christmas. In January 1794, a letter arrived from one of his business partners, Colonel Blackden, confirming that Imlay would be remaining in Le Havre for another three months. Finally Imlay placated a furious Wollstonecraft by suggesting she join him. They rented a large house on the rue de la Corderie, with grand shuttered windows overlooking the harbour, where she found herself entombed between a display of naval ships readying for battle, the nearby Notre-Dame cathedral – which had been recently turned into a revolutionary 'temple of reason' – and an old prison, perhaps home to outlawed British citizens like herself.[64] Newspapers in Britain reported that Wollstonecraft, too, had been arrested, and she reassured her sisters – and herself – with a show of bravado: 'I am safe, through the protection of an American. A most worthy man, who joins to uncommon tenderness of heart and quickness of feeling, a soundness of understanding, and reasonableness of temper, rarely to be met with'.[65] But by 12 March 1794, Imlay had gone again; and she was left, she confessed to him, 'turn[ing] to your side of the bed, and tr[ying] to make the most of the comfort of the pillow ... but all would not do'.[66]

In Le Havre, Wollstonecraft, now heavily pregnant, countered her loneliness by completing a long manuscript on which she had been working for some time. Despite her dawning realization that life may be shaped more by suffering and failure than a constant advance towards perfectibility, as eighteenth-century optimists had maintained, Wollstonecraft's *An Historical*

and Moral View of the Origin and Progress of the French Revolution
upheld the notion that the grand sweep of history is in a progressive direction. The French Revolution, she wrote, was 'the
natural consequence of intellectual improvement, gradually
proceeding to perfection in the advancement of communities,
from a state of barbarism to that of polished society'.[67] The most
important manifestation of that intellectual improvement was
the rise of 'virtue', behaviour promoting 'sociability', which her
old friend Richard Price had insisted 'oblig[es] us to restrain
our passions, and to practise self-denial'.[68] That the exercise
of reason to regulate the passions was becoming more widespread and effective was borne out by the demise of the ancient
world's immorality, 'barbarism' and despotism, and by successful
'political experiments' in late-eighteenth-century America and
post–1688 Britain, working towards equality, 'the equilibrium
of the whole'.[69]

Revolutionary France was part of the same historical trajectory. But Wollstonecraft placed it at a much earlier, more
primitive stage in human development. She recalled how, when
she had first arrived in Paris, she had entertained high hopes that
she was about to witness 'the fair form of Liberty slowly rising,
and Virtue expanding her wings to shelter all her children'.[70]
But what she had actually been presented with, Wollstonecraft
now realized, was the death throes of the 'volatile' sensuality of
the old regime, 'fading before the attentive eye of observation'.[71]
The 'vicious passions' of 'the hardened children of oppression'
did not represent a new world of politics governed by 'moral
emotion'. Robespierre's 'cold calculat[ion]' – embodied in the
supposedly dispassionate efficiency of the guillotine's method
of execution – had simply led, as Edmund Burke had predicted, to 'lawless passions' refusing government, to 'disorder',
'vice', and eventually, 'evil'.[72] The Jacobins and *sans-culottes*
were more like 'beasts of prey' than Enlightenment citizens,
Wollstonecraft exclaimed.[73] She was not optimistic that the

'change of sentiments' so necessary to bring about emancipation and democracy would materialize before 'some years to come' had been spent 'in a state of anarchy'.[74] And when 'out of this chaotic mass a fairer government' would eventually emerge, it would not be the result of executions, but of 'education'.[75] It was in the crucible of education, of gradual and rational illumination, that 'the atmosphere of manners' would be forged 'in which a character is formed, chang[ing] the natural laws of humanity'.[76]

These were dangerous views to entertain in France during the Terror, let alone to commit to paper and entrust to the post, as Wollstonecraft did in March 1794, when she sent a large portion of her completed manuscript to Johnson for publication. Wollstonecraft admitted that 'my life, would not have been worth much, if it had been found'.[77] In the summer of 1793, Madame Roland (née Marie-Jeanne Phlipon) had been imprisoned and Stéphanie Félicité du Crest de Saint-Aubin, Comtesse de Genlis ('Madame de Genlis') had fled to Switzerland; they had both entrusted their manuscripts to Helen Maria Williams. During the Terror, arbitrary house searches of Girondin supporters and suspected counter-revolutionaries became common, and Williams felt she had no choice but to burn their papers.[78] '[D]eath and misery, in every shape of terror, haunts this devoted country,' Wollstonecraft wrote, knowing she had had a lucky escape.[79]

By April 1794, Wollstonecraft suspected that 'it cannot be long before this lively animal pops on us'.[80] Her baby, a daughter she named Fanny, after the much-loved dead friend of her youth, was born at 2 p.m. on 14 May 1794, and was registered at the local Maison Commune as 'Françoise Imlay'. 'Nothing could be more natural or easy than my labour,' she wrote a week later to Joel Barlow's wife, Ruth, adding proudly that her 'nurse has been twenty years in this employment, and she tells me, she never knew a woman so well – adding, Frenchwoman like, that I ought to make children for the Republic, since I treat it so slightly'. 'I have got a vigorous little Girl,' Wollstonecraft continued: 'I feel great pleasure at being a mother – and the constant tenderness of my most affectionate companion makes me regard a fresh tie as a blessing'.[81]

Her time in revolutionary France had confirmed Wollstonecraft's conviction that virtue was reliant upon rigid control of the passions. The *sans-culottes'* violence, and Imlay's derogations of duty, demonstrated how liberation merely undermined social cohesion, and even freed men to bolster their supremacy over women. But the birth of Fanny brought Imlay home. He played the part of a besotted father well, commenting on Fanny's *'manfully'* vigorous breastfeeding, and 'reckon[ing] saucily on her writing the second part of the R[igh]ts of Woman', Wollstonecraft related with tender amusement.[82] Fuseli may have proved resistant to her attempts to bring male libido under regulation, but now it seemed that her faith in Imlay might not have been so hopelessly bestowed.

Chapter 7

THE MOST DELIGHTFUL
THEORY OF AN ISLAND

Exactly one month after the birth of Fanny Imlay, a new
project began gestating in Britain, in which a utopian
community was suggested as the best means to achieve
radical emotional reform. Its proponents embodied the late-
eighteenth-century attitude to emotion as a moral phenomenon,
agreeing that 'virtue', or sociable behaviour, was motivated by
the passions. Societies were responsible for managing citizens'
competing desires and envious passions through legislation
governing the distribution of property and economic exchanges.
That late-eighteenth-century British society had so far failed,
they considered, was evident in the prevalence of 'deteriorating
passions' like 'wrath, anger, clamour'.[1] The mid-1790s was characterized by residual hope in the wake of the French Revolution
that such negative passions might be ameliorated through drastic
political reform, coupled with suspicion that such change would

have to be pursued elsewhere, given the emerging reactionary backlash in Britain. So the advocates of this project sought to establish their utopian principles not in Britain, but on the relatively blank slate of America.

On 14 June 1794, Samuel Taylor Coleridge – who was a twenty-one-year-old undergraduate at Cambridge university – wrote to a friend that 'Tomorrow morning early I set out on a pedestrian scheme for Oxford'.[2] Four days or so later an undergraduate in Oxford – Robert Southey – was bemoaning the state of his bowels, his 'poor trullibubs'. But Southey had determined to delay the 'pickling of my tripes' with a salt-based remedy until 'the departure of a Cantab[rigian]', Coleridge, 'one whom I very much esteem & admire'.[3]

Samuel Taylor Coleridge and Robert Southey were introduced at Oxford by a mutual friend, Robert Allen, a strikingly handsome, guileless undergraduate at University College. Coleridge's walking tour had been designed partly to visit Allen, an old school friend. Southey and Allen had become acquainted a couple of months previously, when Southey 'introduced myself to him at the Anatomy school because I much liked his physiognomy'.[4] He was not the first to be stopped in his tracks by Allen's appearance. The critic and essayist Leigh Hunt would later recall how Allen was 'so handsome ... that running one day against a barrow-woman in the street, and turning round to appease her in the midst of her abuse, she said "Where are you driving to, you great hulking, good-for nothing, – beautiful fellow, God bless you!"'[5] Coleridge and Southey had actually been in close proximity before: they had both attended the trial of William Frend in Cambridge's Senate House on 28 May 1793. But their meeting in mid-June 1794 marked the first time they had come face-to-face.

One of the first topics of conversation between the two undergraduates seems to have been how 'the passions are not vicious – tis society makes the indulgence of them so. they resemble an assemblage of waters destructive if they run wildly over the country, but the source of abundance if properly guided.'[6] Soon after meeting, Coleridge and Southey formulated a plan 'to regenerate the whole complexion of society ... by excluding all the little deteriorating passions: injustice, "wrath, anger, clamour, and evil speaking," and thereby setting an example of "Human Perfectability [*sic*]".'[7] They sought neither to set the passions entirely free from regulation, nor to stifle them completely in favour of reason, but to guide them towards more virtuous human interactions than those that existed in their current society. In particular, these two young men hoped to establish an experimental political colony in which revolutionized laws of property ownership and political representation would underpin a rejuvenated approach to emotion that would allow man, and the political state, to flourish to their full capacity. Coleridge and Southey were typical late-eighteenth-century citizens in perceiving that political revolutions went hand in hand with 'revolutions of feeling' (in the words of their friend Joseph Cottle, a Bristol bookseller).[8]

When they first met, both Coleridge and Southey considered themselves 'more persecuted' than most, struggling for 'chearfulness' amid disappointments 'enough to break a dozen hearts'.[9] Coleridge had spent over two years in a state of frustrated affection for a woman called Mary Evans, the sister of one of his schoolfriends. He sent her mother wistful, forlorn poems, such as 'To Disappointment', in which he yearned for 'Hope on Wisdom's wing' to 'whisp[er] pure delight' and rid himself of disappointment's 'cank'rous blight'.[10] He was consumed by 'ardour', and believed Mary reciprocated it, but felt prevented from proposing marriage by his inability to support her financially. Coleridge would afterwards admit to indulging in 'unchastities' instead. His later nightmares would resurrect visions of the prostituted men and women he had paid in this period: a 'fat sturdy Boy', 'a little weak contemptible wretch offering his services', and 'a university harlot', 'the Cambridge Girl (Sal Hall)'.[11] Coleridge entertained a long-standing contempt for 'sensuality', and wrote subsequently of his loss of his own 'inward sense of Dignity', his self-loathing and *'Disgust'*.[12] When William Godwin came to make notes on Coleridge's life, he suggested that after a 'night in a house of ill fame' in 1793, Coleridge was found 'ruminating in a chair: next morning meditates suicide'.[13]

Coleridge had a troubled relationship with his family. His father, John, vicar of St Mary's Church in Ottery St Mary, died suddenly when Coleridge was nine years old. His mother, Ann, then engineered a place for her youngest son at Christ's Hospital school. The school's spartan environment, in the City of London, contrasted brutally with the intimacy of Coleridge's upbringing in the Devon village of Ottery St Mary, and he nursed aggrieved resentment towards his mother, coupled with 'anguish' at the prospect of letting down 'those who love me': 'does it not plant my pillow with thorns, and make my dreams full of terrors?'[14]

By the end of 1793, Coleridge's 'unchastities' had helped to run up debts amounting to over £150 – the equivalent of around £8,000 today. His elder brothers tried to bail him out, but Coleridge started spending their contribution before it reached his creditors. Coleridge's financial straits, combined with his inability to 'even in a whisper avow my passion' to Mary Evans, drove him to desperation.[15] After contemplating suicide, he decided, on 4 December 1793, to swear himself in at Reading as a recruit in the King's Light Dragoons, for a bounty of six-and-a-half guineas (about £300 today). This was a withdrawal from adult responsibility, not a proactive effort to forge a career. The 'Ebb and Flow of my hopes & fears has stagnated into recklessness,' Coleridge wrote despairingly.[16] Painfully ashamed, anticipating his family's censure and wanting to conceal his whereabouts, he gave his name as 'Silas Tomkin Comberbache'.

Coleridge's disappearance from Cambridge did not go unnoticed. A friend at St John's College, George Lowman Tuckett, rightly guessed that Coleridge had disclosed his plans to old schoolfriends, and persuaded them to break the confidence.[17] Tuckett tracked Coleridge down and passed the information on to Coleridge's older brother George and his commanding officer.[18] Whilst his brothers negotiated with the army, Coleridge festered in his military quarters, wallowing in the thought that 'a man once corrupted will ever remain so, unless some sudden revolution, some unexpected change of Place or Station shall have utterly altered his connection'.[19]

By late March 1794, the army was still dragging its heels. The terms of Coleridge's Rustat Scholarship – a grant dedicated to the sons of clergymen – stipulated that he had to be back in residence at Cambridge by Easter. Upon pressing his commanding officer, George Coleridge was told that twenty-five guineas, four times the initial bounty, was the price of his discharge. Whether Coleridge's family paid or the commanding officer relented is unclear, but on 10 April 1794, the regiment's muster roll reads 'discharged S. T. Comberbach/Insane'. Coleridge returned to Cambridge in disgrace. His brother paid for new clothes, and Jesus College confined him to its grounds for a month and tasked him with translating the works of the Athenian orator Demetrius of Phalerum into English. The 'pedestrian scheme' to Oxford in June 1794 was a cry of freedom to mark that penance's conclusion.[20] But Coleridge embarked upon his 'peregrination' not with light-hearted abandon, but burdened by the shame and guilt of his recent past, and watchful for the 'unexpected change of Place or Station' that might precipitate the 'sudden revolution' in his morals and sentiments.

Robert Southey, too, was dogged by dejection. Three weeks prior to meeting Coleridge, he had written to his closest friend, Grosvenor Bedford, that he seemed to have reached a crossroads in which there was little alternative to 'emigration': 'either in six months I fix myself in some honest means of living or I quit my country – my friends – & every fondest hope I indulge, for ever'.[21] Like Coleridge, Southey had also found his family a disappointment. In 1790, his father, a tradesman, had become, in Southey's words, 'the dupe of artifice & was ruined'. He 'was arrested not for his own debts but for a bill endorsed for a deceitful friend' and Southey 'saw him releas[e]d just in time to reach home – meet fresh misfortunes & die of a broken heart' on 26 December 1792. 'Home you may easily imagine could be no longer agreable [*sic*],' Southey confessed to Bedford. He had long lived with an aunt, for whom 'unmerited injuries – & generosity (even prodigal) ill requited have soured her temper'. But her house nevertheless seemed preferable to 'the lodging house which my Mother supports herself by at Bath, [which] is still more unpleasant'.[22]

In the wake of his father's death, Southey was painfully aware of his responsibility for the 'future support' of his mother and brothers. These obligations stifled his own aspirations: the burden 'witholds me either from seeking happiness in France in America or in the grave'. Southey had heard rumours that, 'at the deaths of my father[']s elder brother & of Lord Somerville', a distant relation, 'a very large estate reverts to me'. He remained fixated for the next few years on this mysterious inheritance, which hovered tantalizingly, offering instant release from his financial anxieties. In the event, his hopes would come to nothing: there was no such entail. The heavy cares of Southey's early life gave him a reputation for 'cool & composed' dignity, which he wore wearily, his 'Stoic' exterior barely concealing the 'natural ardor of [his] temper'.[23]

When Southey was fourteen years old, his uncle arranged for him to attend Westminster School, as a precursor to Oxford University and a career in the church. In March 1792, shortly before he was due to leave Westminster and enter Christ Church college, Southey contributed an essay to a student periodical that he and his friends had established, *The Flagellant*. His essay characterized corporal punishment as an invention of the devil. William Vincent, by implication the satanically inclined headteacher of Westminster, promptly expelled Southey, who enthusiastically embraced his new identity as a persecuted defender of 'conscious merit' and 'liberty' in the face of 'Stupidity – Insolence Despotism'.[24] When Tom Paine's publisher pleaded guilty to sedition for printing Part Two of the *Rights of Man* at the end of May, the seventeen-year-old Southey aligned himself with Paine as a protector of free speech, against Vincent, an exponent of the same repressive regime as Pitt:

> *Nor I alone in this eventful year*
> *Of wicked libels & sedition hear*
> *To hope that Truth would shelter me how vain*
> *When Truth & Eloquence both faild for Paine!*[25]

And he bragged to a school friend that 'a good flaming libel is wanted very much & were there a possibility of publishing it safely I would sweat the whole system of government'.[26]

In September 1792, Southey realized to his horror that 'Dr Vincent[']s arts' had 'shut me out' from Christ Church. His old adversary had written to the college, warning them against accepting Southey. He would have to wait until January, to 'enter at' a different college that was oblivious to Vincent's attempts.[27] Once ensconced at Balliol in January 1793, Southey made the 'pious resolution ... of rising every morning at five to study [so] that the rest of the day may be at my own disposal'.[28] He spent his free time with old and new friends, particularly with Edmund Seward, a young man from Sapey in Worcestershire, now also at Balliol. Southey had met Seward two years previously in Bath, gratefully availing himself of Seward's hospitality as an escape from his aunt's uncongenial house.

At Easter 1793, during a return to the West Country, Southey

was dismayed to see the dramatic impact on Bristol and Bath
of Britain's entry in the French Revolutionary Wars two months
earlier. He lamented how 'several of the first merchants are
ruined & a total stop put to the circulation of country paper'.
Southey remarked on the deteriorating atmosphere, noting in
July that 'the militia are here & the crowd of dissolute people
continually about them': within a couple of months, the discontent would erupt into the Bristol Bridge Riots.[29] In the midst
of those unruly crowds, there was one face in particular 'whom
[Southey] earnestly wish[e]d to see'.[30] In mid-July 1793, he wrote
how 'my hopes were raised to the highest pitch when I thought
I recognized the dress but disappointment soon checked them
& the rest of the evening passed heavily & sadly'.[31]

The longed-for face belonged to Edith Fricker: one of five
daughters of Stephen Fricker, a sometime publican who had
died in 1789 after going bankrupt, and Martha, who after her
husband's death had opened a school and dress shop in Bristol.
Southey had begun the summer of 1793 at his mother's boarding-
house in Bath, where she had employed the Fricker girls – Edith,
Eliza, Mary, Martha and Sara – in needlework. Although he was
keen to know Edith better, that summer Southey's principal
romantic hopes were invested elsewhere, in Augusta Roberts,
who lodged with his friend Seward, nearly one hundred miles
away in Sapey.[32] In August he received the disheartening news
that Roberts was engaged to Seward's brother John. In the cold
light of dejection, Edith seemed a poor alternative: despised by
his supercilious aunt and, Southey admitted, only 'partly educated', with a family history 'as melancholy as my own'.[33]

By winter 1793, Southey's disappointment in Westminster
and Oxford, in Augusta Roberts, and in his family, had peaked.
His mother's health was 'declining,' and he felt the increased
financial pressure acutely. Southey failed to return to Balliol
that term. 'At the age of nineteen I have known more calamity
than many who deserve it more, meet with in long lives,' he

wrote, somewhat hyperbolically, to his friend Bedford's brother Horace.[34] Emigration had long been a subject of fantasy in Southey's imagination, and now it intensified. However, he had two younger brothers, whom 'I must & will protect . . . otherwise the first vessel that sails for America should bear with it one more emigrant'.[35]

The only consolation at this time was a promising new friendship with the son of a Quaker minister and her husband, a wealthy Quaker cabinet-maker and pin manufacturer. Robert Lovell was three years Southey's senior, and a refreshing contrast to some of the gauche young men he had encountered at Oxford. Lovell was a perceptive critic of the ill effects of Bristol's commercial exploits on the moral character of its inhabitants. He was working on a lengthy poem, *Bristol: A Satire*, known colloquially as the *Bristoliad* – a play on Pope's satire, the *Dunciad* – in which he attacked the 'varied passions' that were exacerbated by the city's 'avarice', which 'binds their groveling hearts in golden chains': a reference to the moral corruption that Lovell saw as both the consequence and cause of Bristol merchants' involvement in the slave trade.[36] Southey prolonged his stay in Bristol to get to know Lovell better – 'you know the no-ceremony I stand upon when I wish to make a friend' – and the two began to plot future writing projects.[37]

Perhaps influenced by Lovell, who was fascinated by natural science, Southey returned to Oxford in January 1794, newly determined to embark on 'anatomical & chemical studies . . . & then commence – Doctor Southey!!!'[38] Despite Southey's supplications, Lovell refused to leave Bristol with him. On 20 January, he had married Mary Fricker, Edith's sister. After her father's bankruptcy, Mary had supplemented her family's meagre income by acting, a trade, like sewing, which was often viewed as a cover for prostitution. Lovell's family were horrified by Mary's low circumstances and virulently opposed the marriage, with devastating repercussions for Mary. Further down the line her marriage to Lovell was almost certainly the catalyst for Southey's renewal of interest in Edith. His attraction to Augusta Roberts the previous year had been partly motivated by desire to formalize his relationship with his friend Edmund Seward, who was her landlord. Now Edith Fricker presented the possibility of cementing his friendship with her brother-in-law Robert Lovell. Southey was grasping at opportunities to craft a new family, bonding himself to friends by means of marital ties to near relations. He was soon thinking of Edith as 'a woman whom I have long esteem[e]d as a sister & for whom I now indulge a warmer sentiment'.[39]

By the end of May, with the conclusion of another Oxford term, Southey was back in Bristol and had declared his intention to 'unite' himself to Edith. Previously he had wearily accepted his family's expectation that he would go into the church, but now this prospect loomed too close for comfort: 'there is no alternative I will not prefer to taking orders,' Southey wrote desperately, imploring Bedford to find him a situation at his office.[40] The French Revolution's path shaped both Southey and Coleridge's interior lives throughout the early 1790s, and Southey had even once fantasized about leaving Britain to fight for the French Revolutionary Army.[41] Many of his childhood friends, including Grosvenor Bedford and Thomas Phillips Lamb, were conservatives. Southey defined himself in opposition to their apparently staid pragmatism, as an authentic, passionate, occasionally hot-headed sympathizer with the most down-trodden members of society: a figure whom today we might today call a true bleeding-heart liberal. He proudly declared himself a 're-publican and sinner', a 'victim of affection – my heart is too often consulted where the head should have determined'.[42] His passions ricocheted in response to news from France. The execution in October 1793 of Brissot, with whom Southey identified as a charismatic defender of moderate reform, 'completely harrowed up my faculties,' he wrote in desolation; 'oppression is

triumphant every where & the only difference is that it acts . . .
in France [through the organ of] a Revolutionary Tribunal & in
England of a prime minister'.[43] By summer 1794, revolutionary
France's transition into Terror, combined with Southey's personal disillusionments, had convinced him that 'there is no place
for virtue' on earth.

When Southey and Coleridge met, both men were hankering
after an escape from their personal and political dissatisfactions,
a retreat into a 'place for virtue'. In August 1793 the reformer
Thomas Muir had been given an unprecedentedly brutal sentence of fourteen years' transportation for seditious activity, and
Southey seized on Muir's optimistic prediction that his punishment would provide him with an opportunity to 'contemplate an
infant empire, a new Europe in embryo'.[44] Renovation of existing political societies no longer seemed so certain a possibility,
and retreat to an untainted land began to preoccupy Southey's
imagination. Coleridge, too, was seeking a 'change of Place or
Station' that would precipitate a revolution in his own moral
character, to atone for his recent failings. The meeting between
the two young men would catalyse their incipient discontent
into a project to become, like Muir, 'virtuous exiles'. But their
ambitious project was born, not of the 'spirit strong in hope'
that fuelled the very start of the decade, but of the uncertainty
and discomfiture – the 'hope discouraged' – that was becoming
endemic by its mid-point. Emigration to a utopian community
was 'the last resource' of personal and political 'disappointment'
for the two men.[45]

Between autumn 1792 and summer 1793, Southey had become
preoccupied by island retreats, and one colony in particular. On
28 October 1792, three men had been hanged from the yard-
arm of HMS *Brunswick* in Portsmouth dock. Thomas Burkett,
Thomas Ellison and John Millward had been able seamen on
board the *Bounty*, on an expedition to source breadfruit on the

island of Otaheiti (now Tahiti) in the south Pacific. About thirty nautical miles off the island of Tofua, east of Otaheiti, the ship's 'Foremast-man' Fletcher Christian had led a mutiny. He had cast the *Bounty*'s commander, Lieutenant William Bligh, and loyal members of the crew, off the ship into a dangerously overloaded vessel, in which they were left to make their treacherous way to Indonesia. Bligh and the other survivors finally found a safe passage home to England, where they landed on 14 March 1790. He was swiftly acquitted for the loss of the *Bounty*; and a frigate, the HMS *Pandora*, was dispatched to bring back the mutineers.

After a brief failed attempt at settling on the island of Tubuai, 450 nautical miles further south, over half the mutineers had returned to Otaheiti, where, in 1792, they were discovered, arrested and summarily returned to Britain. The remaining men's whereabouts were not discovered until 1808, when an American sealing ship, the *Topaz*, happened upon an island a long way to the east of Tahiti, called Pitcairn. There the American crew discovered a settlement founded by nine mutineers, who had abducted fourteen Tahitian women into sexual and reproductive slavery, and six Tahitian men into manual slavery. After three years of the women being 'passed around from one "husband" to another' on Pitcairn, the Tahitians had revolted and by the time that the *Topaz* came upon the community, only two of the *Bounty* mutineers, and none of the Tahitian men, had survived. They were accompanied by nine Tahitian women and nineteen children.[46]

In January 1793, the testimonies of the *Bounty* mutineers struck a chord with Robert Southey, as they did with many revolutionary sympathizers. British radicals commonly saw Bligh's alleged tyranny towards his crew as a microcosm of institutional oppression, and romanticized the mutiny as a storming of the Bastille on the high seas. In November 1792, Fletcher Christian's brother Edward had formed a committee to publicly investigate the mutiny, hoping to absolve his brother. The majority of his

committee were passionate abolitionists, and they discovered
that the apparently innocuous 'scientific' expedition to collect
breadfruit may have been partially motivated by a commercial
desire to cut the costs of maintaining slave plantations, by providing 'a wholesome and pleasant food to our negroes, which
would have the great advantage of being raised with infinitely
less labour than the plantain'.[47]

One evening, a committee member and radical lawyer called
James Losh started a conversation with friends about 'the real
state of Christian's mutiny' and 'all agreed that were there any
place to go emigration wou'd be a prudent thing for ... the
friends of freedom' – for the increasingly discouraged radicals
of the 1790s.[48] Robert Southey was among those present, who
discussed how the *Bounty* mutineers' colonies on Tubuai and
Otaheiti showed that retreat in the face of oppression might be
a constructive, dignified enterprise. Southey also reflected on
the sexual reputation of the Otaheiti women. Ever since the
return of the *Endeavour* expedition in 1771, Joseph Banks – the
ship's doctor who, as President of the Royal Society, organized
the *Bounty* expedition – had fuelled titillating rumours about
the sexually liberated behaviour of Tahitian women.[49] Inspired
by the idea that colonial projects might provide an opportunity
for regenerating the most intimate aspects of society's passions,
in February 1793 Southey 'form[ed] the most delightful theory
of an island peopled by men,' where 'all [should be] sati[s]fied
without profusion'. 'Otaheitii [*sic*],' he continued, 'independent
of its women had many inducements[,] not only for the sailor but
the philosopher ... [H]e might be truly happy in himself ... he
might introduce the advantages & yet avoid the vices of cultivated society.'[50]

Emigration continued to shape Southey's utopian fantasies
in the ensuing months. Reading about Plotinus' 'experiment'
to regenerate a ruined city in Campania, he 'rhapsodize[d]' to
Bedford: 'Southeyopolis' would have 'no palaces no hovels'.[51]

Two weeks later, Southey reflected that the desire for exile had historically been found among royalists as well as radicals, and that it had been 'the favorite intention' of the seventeenth-century Royalist poet Abraham Cowley – who had exiled himself to Paris for twelve years during the Civil War – 'to retire with his books to a cottage in America & seek that happiness in solitude which he could not find in society'. In the face of insurmountable obstacles, such as a political tide that could not be turned, emigration was a logical response, whatever one's politics, he concluded. Southey even fantasized about his dream colony's aesthetics: a house built in the 'prettiest Doric stile', with a garden matching that of Monsieur and Madame de Wolmar's garden in Rousseau's *La Nouvelle Héloïse*.[52] But until June 1794, Southey admitted that his colonial fantasy 'was built in the air [and] falls to pieces & leaves me like most such visionary projectors staring at disappointment'.[53]

Many of Southey's early daydreams were spurred on by a friend at Balliol, George Burnett, who was also intended to enter the church after finishing university. The son of a respectable Somerset farmer, and an apparently even-tempered teetotal devotee to agrarian radicalism and the redistribution of land, Burnett had become close to Southey shortly after the former's matriculation at Balliol in March 1793.[54] By the time of Coleridge's arrival in Oxford, Southey had surrounded himself with a group of fashionably dissident friends – George Burnett, Edmund Seward and Robert Allen at Oxford; Robert Lovell in Bristol – with whom he indulged his fantasies of emigration from his disappointing family life and the gloomy prospects awaiting him after university. All that was needed was a spark to kindle this youthful enthusiasm and escapist longing into an incendiary utopian project.

On 19 June 1794, or thereabouts, that spark ignited into a 'hallowed Fire'. Immediately after the summer term's end, Coleridge blazed into Oxford with his travelling companion, a

Cambridge graduate named Joseph Hucks. He rekindled his childhood friendship with Robert Allen, and was introduced to Southey. Both men instantly impressed one another. Coleridge was attracted by Southey's 'moral Excellence' and *'perpendicular Virtue'*. In turn, Southey was struck by Coleridge's 'most uncommon merit – of the strongest genius the clearest judgment & the best heart. my friend he already is,' he concluded joyfully, mere days after their first meeting.[55] Southey's friendship group was temporarily realigned around Coleridge at the centre. The undergraduates often idled in the rooms of a man called Bloxham, at Worcester College, and it was here, in Coleridge's presence, that Southey and Burnett reignited their favourite conversation about establishing a political utopia.[56] Coleridge seized delightedly on their idea. Southey and Burnett had discussed how such a colony might revolutionize property ownership, but it was probably Coleridge who showed the wider possibilities of thereby ridding society of 'deterioriating' antisocial passions. Coleridge conjured up the name 'pantisocracy' for the imaginary community, from the Greek *pan* and *isocratia*, meaning 'equal government by all'. Pantisocracy slanted into his field of vision like a chink of early morning light. The 'change of Place' after which Coleridge had hankered for months was finally visible.

Two-and-a-half weeks later, ten of Southey's friends left Oxford on foot, heading west towards Eynsham and Witney. Six peeled off to return to town, but Southey, Burnett, Coleridge and Hucks continued. Burnett later described how, during 'our journey, S. & myself discoursed of no other subject but that of Pantisocracy. We first considered whether it were practicable. Having settled this point with ourselves, we examined whether it were practicable in this country. This question we soon determined in the negative, and perceived that America was the only place in which it is *possible* that such a scheme should be re-alized'.[57] America's more egalitarian system of property ownership and political representation provided the ideal setting for a colony seeking to reform the passions by radically redistributing private property. After 'fifteen or sixteen miles', around Northleach in the Cotswolds, Southey and Burnett headed south towards Cirencester, en route to Bristol, while Coleridge and Hucks carried on towards the Welsh border. Within twenty-four hours, Coleridge was toasting 'Health & Republicanism!' in a letter to Southey, and neologizing afresh, inventing 'aspheterism' – from the Greek *a* and *spheteros*, 'not one's own' – to refer to the eradication of private ownership of 'the Bounties of Nature'.[58]

Over the next month, Coleridge and Southey thrashed out the rudiments of their project in correspondence. Coleridge excitedly recounted how he had 'preached Pantisocracy and Aspheterism' at a public house in 'Llanvillin' (Llanfyllin) 'with so much success that two great huge Fellows, of Butcher like appearance, danced around the room in enthusiastic agitation'. 'I have done nothing but dream of the System of no Property every step of the Way since I left you,' he promised.[59] Characteristically pragmatic, Southey applied himself to the colony's practical details. He recruited among his friends and family, and consulted Edmund Seward, at home in Worcestershire, and Robert Lovell in Bristol, about 'the best mode of settling in America'.[60] By the beginning of August, Southey had 'full convinced Lovell of the propriety' of the scheme and, a few days later, his own mother and two younger brothers, Edward and Henry Herbert. This was a huge relief: pantisocracy's chief attraction for Southey was that it answered the question of how to provide for his family without taking orders. '[N]ever did so delightful a prospect of happiness open upon my view before,' Southey wrote to Bedford; 'to go with all I love ... to live with them in the most agreable & most honourable employment. to eat the fruits I have raised, & see every face happy around me. my Mother sheltered in her declining years from the anxieties which have pursued her. my brothers educated to be useful &

virtuous'.[61] Southey began considering how to fund the expedition, and took his newly composed republican poem *Joan of Arc* to a printer, hoping that the proceeds will 'get me some few acres a spade & a plough'.[62] Coleridge helpfully suggested that Southey might consider applying for 'the office of a Clerk in a Compting House'.[63]

By the first week of August, the walking tour concluded, Coleridge unexpectedly arrived in Bristol, having cleared his future plans to make way for pantisocracy.[64] Southey, Lovell, Burnett and he promptly arranged shared lodgings at 48 College Street, in the centre of Bristol. Now preparations got underway in earnest. Southey had initially thought they would set up in Kentucky, but by the end of August Coleridge reported that 'our plan is, to settle at a distance, but at a convenient distance, from Cooper's Town on the banks of the Susquehannah'.[65] This revision was influenced by two writers in particular. In 1792, *A Topographical Description of the Western Territory of North America*, by Mary Wollstonecraft's lover Gilbert Imlay, had described how a 'fair river', 'fertility so astonishing', and 'nature robed in all her charms' had drawn emigrants to Kentucky since 1774, when the first permanent colony was founded at Harrod's Town by order of the Virginia assembly.[66]

But Coleridge's research, much of which derived from books borrowed from Bristol Library, drew him towards Pennsylvania.[67] He was entranced by Thomas Cooper's very recent *Some Information Respecting America*, and probably responsible for an enthusiastic review of Cooper's book in the *Critical Review* in early 1795.[68] Cooper assured his readers that America offered 'an asylum from civil persecution', but also acknowledged that many exiles were motivated by personal and financial reasons – *'the total absence of anxiety respecting the future success of a family'* – rather than a search for political refuge.[69] The historian James Horn has described how the 1790s' harvest failures and economic crises were responsible for a sharp increase in emigration from across the political spectrum.[70] Coleridge was writing poetry in this period in which the search for 'Domestic Peace' was every bit as important as the political motivations for 'high-souled Pantisocracy'. And Southey, too, sought a pastoral existence in which he 'could till the earth, and provide by honest industry the meat which my wife would dress with pleasing care'.[71]

Pennsylvania was especially attractive to Coleridge because Cooper's father-in-law was Joseph Priestley, the most famous political refugee from reactionary forces in Britain in the 1790s. Priestley resigned himself to leaving Britain in June 1792, when it became apparent that there was no ebb in the 'increasing bigotry of the high-church party' that had materialized in the Birmingham Riots of 1791. By June 1793, he 'consider[ed] my stay in this country as very uncertain. All my sons will soon, I hope, be in America, and I shall probably follow them'.[72] After consulting Jedidiah Morse's *The American Geography*, Priestley sent his son Joseph, his son-in-law Thomas Cooper and two friends to America to scout for a suitable location for 'a large settlement for the friends of liberty in general'.[73] He briefly considered moving to France, but Cooper warned that its instability and increasing authoritarianism made it 'rather to be admired at a distance, than fit for a peaceable man to reside among'.[74] America, though, and specifically Pennsylvania were ideal, Cooper assured him: the state did not permit slavery, servants were easy to come by, there was peace with the Native Americans, the climate was similar to England, a high proportion of English settlers resided there already, and a large amount of land was available for purchase.

Pennsylvania was especially attractive as, five years previously, it had nearly housed a very similar political settlement to that now being proposed by Priestley. In 1788, shortly after establishing an abolitionist 'Society of the Friends of the Blacks' in France, Brissot de Warville had been paid by the financier Étienne Clavière to assess sites in America for a 'Eutopia': a place of well-being, rather than the 'no place' (*u*, not, + *topos*, place) of 'Utopia'. Clavière had stressed that the settlement must generate profit. The scheme was called off when Brissot returned to France for the convening of the Estates-General in May 1789, but he had written up his impressions in 1791 in *Travels in the United States*. In the wake of Brissot's execution in October 1793, Priestley hoped his own settlement might commemorate Brissot's earlier efforts by offering asylum to French Girondins and their British supporters. (Priestley's son-in-law Cooper had been expelled from the Jacobins in late 1792 for his allegiance to Brissot, so he was highly sympathetic to the cause of other exiled Girondins.) Cooper recommended that Priestley should pay heed to Clavière's emphasis that emigration should be undertaken with economic pragmatism. Pennsylvania offered an opportunity for speculation as well as political utopianism, and by mid-1795 the acquisitions of Priestley and his family would extend to 700,000 acres.[75]

On 5 June 1794, the *American Daily Advertiser* reported that 'Dr. Priestley, with about one hundred other passengers, are on board the Sansom, which may be hourly expected.' Priestley and his wife had actually arrived the previous day. After two enjoyable weeks of being welcomed in New York, Priestley and his family travelled ninety miles south-west to Philadelphia, before heading for their final destination over 150 miles to the north-west. Through painstaking consultation of the land patents bestowed in this era, the literary historian Mary Park discovered that Cooper and Priestley were part of a consortium that purchased swathes of land midway between the north and west branches of the Susquehanna river. The headquarters of Priestley's settlement – 'Cooper's Town', now called Forksville – was situated in the luxuriant, frequently flooded valley through which Loyalsock Creek veins into two, while Priestley himself settled in the nearby town of Northumberland.[76]

Priestley's widely publicised departure in 1794 for a region replete with radical history convinced the pantisocrats of their destination. They abandoned Kentucky, and set their sights on the lands that Priestley himself was selling. Pennsylvania presented an unmissable opportunity to forge a new life alongside an Enlightenment icon, celebrated by Coleridge as 'patriot, and saint, and sage'.[77] On 1 September 1794, Coleridge left Bristol and breakfasted in London with George Dyer, author of *The Complaints of the Poor People of England*, published the previous year. Coleridge reported that Dyer 'was enraptured' by the scheme, 'pronounced it impregnable – He is intimate with Dr Priestley – and doubts not, that the Doctor will join us'.[78] In the Salutation and Cat tavern on Newgate Street, Coleridge also met, repeatedly, a land agent who had spent the last five years in America, and also 'recommend[ed] the Susqusannah [*sic*] from it's [*sic*] excessive Beauty, and it's security from hostile Indians'.[79] The only affordable remaining land for sale was in unimproved territory on 'the extreme corner of the river-front land': on the southern and western sides of the Susquehanna, across from a small settlement now called Wyalusing. Just eight miles south of the land intended for French Girondin refugees, less than a day's walk from Cooper's Town, and marketed by Thomas Cooper as facing 'a river about half a mile broad, running at the foot of bold and steep mountains, through a valley ... rich, beautiful, and variegated', the location must have seemed absolutely perfect.[80]

The land agent confirmed that £2,000 (roughly £80–90,000 today) would acquire well over 1,000 acres and cover the costs of passage across the Atlantic.[81] Banking on at least sixteen 'gentlemen' subscribers, alongside their presumably non-paying wives and children, Coleridge and Southey calculated that '£125 [each] will be sufficient to carry the scheme into execution'.[82] Lovell related how the pantisocrats discussed 'freight[ing] a ship, carrying out with us, ploughs, and all other implements of husbandry'.[83] And in typically fastidious fashion, Southey drew up an exhaustive packing list of clothes: 'two or three pairs' of 'common blue trowsers' for his 'working winter dress. & as many jackets either blue or grey', 'two cloth jackets – four linen ones – six brown holland pantaloons & two nankeen', 'two new waistcoats,' and he made the abstemious resolution that 'I shall not wear brogues'.[84]

The pantisocrats primarily turned to writing to raise the funds. Southey and Lovell planned to write a poetry collection under the pseudonyms 'Bion and Moschus'. Through Lovell, Coleridge was introduced to the Bristol bookseller and publisher Joseph Cottle, and begged him for a loan of five pounds to pay the rent on their College Street rooms, 'which is indeed much higher than we expected': an indication of how short of their total the young men were falling.[85] Cottle was privately horrified by the plan to transport heavy agricultural equipment across the Atlantic, convinced it would be more 'economical' to 'purchase such articles in America'. But the loan request reassured him that 'the spectre of the ship! the ship!' was unlikely to ever materialize. Seeing in the pantisocrats' desperation an opportunity to capitalize on literary talent, Cottle offered Coleridge an advance of twenty, then thirty, guineas for a volume of poetry: 'the silence and the grasped hand, showed, that, at that moment, one person was happy'.[86] He then visited Southey, offering him the same, plus a further fifty guineas for his new poem *Joan of Arc*, and was accepted on both counts.[87] Coleridge, Southey and Lovell began working on a tragedy that Coleridge took to Cambridge to be printed in September, optimistic that 'it will repay us amply'.[88] And they mooted a course of lectures each at Bristol: Coleridge 'to disseminate Truth by three political Lectures', Southey to offer 'a course of historical Lectures at Bristol, teaching what is right by showing what is wrong'.[89] Lectures might drum up much-needed revenue, whilst also disseminating pantisocracy's ideology to potential recruits. With that latter aim, the two men also hoped to get 'our plan & principles ready for printing to distribute privately'.[90]

Pantisocracy's signed-up members came and went around the committed core of Southey, Coleridge and Burnett. An initial list comprised seven of the requisite sixteen gentlemen, and included Robert Allen and Southey's naval brother Tom. Edmund Seward and Robert Lovell's commitment wavered between 'doubtful' and '*going partners*'.[91] Southey's and Lovell's relationships with Edith and Mary Fricker turned the colony into a proto-family, but equally, the colony would need to reproduce itself, and marriage had a pragmatic role in the project too. By mid-August, Coleridge was muscling in on the new '*fraternal* Love' between Southey and Lovell, and impulsively proposed to Edith and Mary's sister Sara Fricker.[92] Lovell knew of Coleridge's prior attachment to Mary Evans, disapproved of his hasty transferral of affection, and the two men temporarily fell out. Cottle commented sarcastically on their 'marked coolness ... so inauspicious in those about to establish a "Fraternal Colony;" and, in the result, to renovate the whole face of society!'[93] George Burnett, too, tried his luck with Martha, another of the Fricker sisters, but was rebuffed.[94]

The engagements swelled the total of potential emigrants, and when Coleridge arrived in London in early September 1794, the pantisocrats numbered over twenty, including all five Fricker sisters and their mother, Southey's younger brothers and mother, Lovell's three siblings, Southey's cousin Margaret 'Peggy' Hill, and two nineteen-year-old undergraduates, Samuel Favell and Samuel Le Grice, who promised to join them after graduating. The pantisocrats also sensibly invited Charles Heath, an 'apothecary & man-midwife'.[95] By 12 October, the colony's '27 adventurers' were finalized: Seward had pulled out, but an acquaintance of Southey's friend Charles Collins had registered interest, along with five other friends, and 'Mary Baker who ardently wishes to be of our party'. Although they had initially hoped to set sail for America 'very shortly', by the beginning of the autumn they all agreed that 'next March' – March

1795 – would be the most suitable 'time of emigration'. Coleridge admitted that many of the pantisocrats' 'bodies, from habits of sedentary study or academic indolence, have not acquired their full tone and strength', and he wanted to spend the winter in training, and learning 'the theory and practice of agriculture and carpentry'.[96] In October 1794, Southey wrote buoyantly to his brother that 'our plan is in great forwardness, nor do I see how it can be frustrated'.[97] All that remained was to thrash out their utopian community's political ideology. How exactly would they reform the political, economic and sexual structures of the old, corrupted world, and how would this lead to the renovation of the passions?

Chapter 8

THE ORGASM OF
THE REVOLUTION

By mid-October 1794, the pantisocrats were giddy with anticipation. The remaining element of the colony's 'battle array', as Coleridge put it, was the structure of their day-to-day lives in Pennsylvania, which would be dictated by the settlement's political purpose.[1] Different members were enthused by different, sometimes conflicting, rationales. Coleridge was driven by eclectic interests in theology, psychology and education; Burnett was a devotee of seventeenth-century agrarianism; and Southey hoped the colony would defend the moderate-left politics of Brissot and the Girondins. But all participants agreed that 'the leading Idea of Pantisocracy is to make men *necessarily* virtuous by removing all motives to Evil'.[2]

At the beginning of their project, Southey insisted that the passions were not evil in themselves: 'indulgence of the passions

is only vicious as the organization of society renders it so'.[3]
George Burnett was heavily influenced by the seventeenth-
century radical politician James Harrington, who had formulated
the constitution of a utopian republic, Oceana, during the
Interregnum. Harrington considered citizens' passions a barom-
eter of the state's efficacy and a reflection of its division of
property: 'good orders make evil men good, bad orders make
good men evil', and an 'equal and well-ordered commonwealth'
was one in 'which the whole people be landlords'.[4] The pantisocrats' aim was to remove material inequality as the first step
to remedying antisocial passions that stemmed from a chronic
frustration of desire, which affected all citizens to some extent,
but some classes more than others. They wanted to nurture
virtuous passions by radically redistributing property.

'Pantisocracy' meant 'equal government by all' and the pantisocrats agreed that their community would do without a ruling
body or leader. Formal government was only rendered necessary
by antisocial behaviour resulting from 'Avarice and appetites!'
and would become redundant once inequality had been remedied and 'the unsocial Passions' had melted away. 'Let us exert
over our own hearts a virtuous despotism, and lead our own
Passions in triumph, and then we shall want neither Monarch
nor General,' Coleridge would soon proclaim magnificently.[5] He
also realized that material inequality was especially visible in
the unequal division of labour: 'the necessaries of twenty men
are raised by one man, who works ten hours a day exclusive of
his meals'. Coleridge described to the other pantisocrats how the
labouring classes undertook a disproportionate amount of society's vital manual work, while affluent classes pursued sensual
gratification, resulting in labourers' material deprivation through
low wages and cultural undervaluation, and their exclusion from
the creative arts. The pantisocrats enthusiastically consulted
other political theorists' schemes to draw up a blueprint for the
colonists' daily timetable to combat this inequality. Southey

reported how, 'according to the computation of Adam Smith', if the total quantity of necessary labour for a community of twenty was divided equally, 'the sum of work is half an hour to each individual' per day.[6] Robert Wallace's utopian design in *Various Prospects of Mankind, Nature and Providence* (1761) suggested three to six hours of manual labour a day per person. Eventually the pantisocrats agreed that 'the demand on their labour would not exceed two hours a day; that is, for the production of absolute necessaries. 'The leisure still remaining' would be devoted to improving the land adjoining their residences and felling trees, leaving 'a large portion of time ... for their own individual pursuits, so that they might read, converse, and even write books'.[7]

The matter of private property provoked more conflict among the colonists. Should the colony completely eradicate private property, placing everything in common possession? Or might they enforce a less dramatic *equalization* of ownership? Coleridge traced the descent into inequality of property back to the Book of Judges' account of the moment when the ancient confederation of Israelite tribes first demanded a king, around 1050 BCE. Under the earlier Mosaic constitution, Coleridge wrote, 'Property is Power and equal Property equal Power': 'the Jewish [state] has been the only Republic that can consistently boast of Liberty and Equality'.[8] But Coleridge thought that ultimately 'the Jews were too ignorant a people, too deeply leavened with the Vices of Aegypt to be capable of so exalted a state of Society' and had failed to establish a perfect equality. Christ's mission was to succeed where the Mosaic constitution had failed, and Coleridge would soon lecture that 'Jesus Christ forbids to his disciples all property' and stressed that '[w]hile I possess anything exclusively mine, the selfish Passions will have full play, and our Hearts will never learn'.[9]

For most radicals of the 1790s, arguments for the eradication of private property recalled a much more recent book than the Bible. In September 1791, just two months before his first meeting with Mary Wollstonecraft at Johnson's, William Godwin had started composing *An Enquiry Concerning Political Justice and its Influence on Morals and Happiness*. It took him sixteen months to complete and, when it appeared on 15 February 1793, Godwin predicted that it would meet a reading 'public that is panic struck', wound up into a frenzy of hopeful passion by popular political societies and establishment politicians all exacerbating the British populace's 'strongest impressions of fear and hope, apprehension and desire, dejection and triumph'.[10] In the face of this emotional mania, Godwin had intended to 'look with indifference upon the false fire of the moment, and to foresee the calm period of reason which will succeed'.[11] In the early 1790s, after shrugging off religion and adopting the mantle of a public intellectual, Godwin had constructed himself as the archetypal Enlightenment rationalist, eschewing the vagaries of passion for cool reason. He was a perfect exponent of the tradition of left-wing political thought that looks askance on emotion and attachment – encapsulated in the family – as hindrances to progress. *Political Justice* provided a lengthy account of how the current system of private property, contractual obligations (especially marriage), and government relied on and drummed up passions that undermined 'the individual's independence' and progression towards a 'perfectly voluntary state'.[12]

The book was a hit. Its contents were disseminated via unauthorized versions, extracts in radical journals and summarized in popular lectures by the radical John Thelwall. The essayist William Hazlitt later described how 'no work in our time gave such a blow to the philosophical mind of the country'. Robert Southey 'all but worshipped' it and the young Henry Crabb Robinson claimed that it 'directed the whole course of my life'. Godwin claimed contentedly that the ideas expounded in *Political Justice* must have 'coincided in a great degree with the sentiments then prevailing in English society'. Perhaps, he speculated optimistically, by 1793 the British public were becoming nauseated by the passionate turmoil of the last few years, and seeking a more 'tranquil', reasoned alternative.[13]

In *Political Justice*, Godwin argued that 'we have in reality nothing that is strictly speaking our own': we live in a state of fundamental dispossession. All property already had 'a destination prescribed to it by the immutable voice of reason and justice': a purpose to which it would be best put to increase 'the absolute production of happiness' in society.[14] Individuals into whose hands possessions fell became custodians with 'no right to dispose' of those goods at their own 'caprice': 'every shilling of [property] is appropriated by the laws of morality'.[15] 'Justice' required that property was divided as equally as possible according to the fundamental 'equality of mankind'. If one man found himself owning more property than an estimated average, he was morally compelled to redistribute the excess without an expectation of gratitude.

Godwin's pronouncements on property and the passions reflected his fascination with the ancient philosophy of Stoicism. In the wake of the French Revolution, Godwin had shored himself up against the tide of 'violence and passion' on both sides of the Channel by consulting the works of the Greek Stoic and slave Epictetus.[16] Stoicism taught that earthly events and objects were all 'indifferent', unworthy of emotional investment; and that passions were irrational judgements that wrongly accorded value to meaningless things. But Stoics also believed that each individual was able to 'dissent' from a passion, to refuse to follow through its impulse towards expression and action. In his early religious life, Godwin had preached that it was the 'dictates of religion' that allowed individuals to attain this Stoic indifference: to detach themselves from the 'trials of this life' by focusing on religious virtue and the afterlife, and, in doing so, to manifest heroism, 'valour and fortitude' in the face of fear.[17] By the time he wrote *Political Justice*, Godwin had come to believe that it was (atheist) reason, not religion, that facilitated such disinterest.

Edmund Burke had claimed that private ownership of property uniquely aroused enough emotional attachment in individuals to make them enact a duty of care towards their property. But Godwin affirmed that duty of care towards property must come from 'intellectual resolution' instead: the rational capacity to 'perceiv[e] what is eligible and right'.[18] One of the greatest threats to 'the genuine and wholesome exercise of an intellectual nature' in the rational disposal of property, he argued, was the 'contract' or 'promise'. Contracts made duty to 'property' a matter not of reasoned 'conscience' or 'understanding', but of strict enforcement imposed through the irrational fear of the consequences of reneging. And they compelled attachment and responsibility long after any initial emotional investment had petered out.[19] For Godwin, marriage was one of the worst examples of irrational contracts. Marriage was 'a monopoly, and the worst of monopolies', which transformed women into jealously guarded 'possessions' and men into 'despotic' tyrants: 'It is absurd to expect that the inclinations and wishes of two human beings should coincide through a long period of time. To oblige them to act and to live together, is to subject them to some inevitable portion of thwarting, bickering and unhappiness.'[20] Godwin's 'New Philosophy', as it came to be known, called for the abolition of marriage along with other types of 'accumulated property'. Godwin was optimistic that, freed from this unnatural, irrational, stifling contract, humanity would govern sexual relationships according to 'the dictates of reason and duty'. Sexual partners would come and go as they pleased, and the cultural importance of fatherhood – in his eyes, a chronic state of contractually enforced duty towards property (children) – would dissolve because 'such knowledge [as to who a child's father is] will be of no importance'.[21]

Coleridge was attracted by Godwin's arguments for abolition of property in so far as they coincided with the biblical justifications he had read. But he worried that Godwin's reforms would not eradicate the passions or desires: they would merely free them from duty of care to the goods (including women and children) under men's protection. Godwin's own private life, the rumours of sensuality that came to surround him, seemed to bear out Coleridge's contemptuous summary of *Political Justice*'s principles: 'filial Love is a Folly, Gratitude criminal, Marriage Injustice, and a promiscuous Intercourse of the Sexes our wisdom and our duty'.[22] Without a system of emotional regulation – such as marriage – prescribing men's duties towards their possessions, men's self-interest would run rampant, reinforcing the inequalities of power created by the pre-existent system of private property and accumulation, and manifesting the selfish, sensuous nature of untamed passions. Despite the book's seductive popularity, Coleridge condemned *Political Justice* as 'a System of gloomy and cold blooded Selfishness'.[23] And when it came to thinking about the system of property that would be adopted in their pantisocratic utopia, Coleridge was concerned about the implications that property reform had for sexual relationships, which Godwin's book had made very clear. In September 1794, Coleridge's and Southey's mutual friend, the Somerset autodidact, tanner and tradesman Thomas Poole, described how 'the regulations relating to the females strike [the pantisocrats] as the most difficult; whether the marriage contract shall be dissolved if agreeable to one or both parties, and many other circumstances, are not yet determined'.[24] They were not the only ones in the late eighteenth century to find the question of sexual reform tantalizing, if troubling, and inextricably coupled to the redistribution of property.

What Southey, not entirely metaphorically, called 'the orgasm of the [French] Revolution' intensified the links between political and sexual reform.[25] The historians Lynn Hunt and Margaret Jacob describe how the revolution 'released a kind of seismic affective energy' that impelled young men like the pantisocrats to 'explicitly challeng[e] authoritarianism in politics and personal life' through bodily and sexual experimentation.[26] The intimate connection between sexual 'ownership' and economic property was encapsulated by marriage laws, and the use in the late-eighteenth century of the term 'the commodity' to refer to female genitalia.[27] Sexual utopians frequently worried about the restraint of libido in terms akin to anxieties about economic regulation. To many men, marriage seemed to constrain male libido, confining its energies to the family unit, consigning men to boredom, frustration and lack of 'productivity'. Although eighteenth-century marriage laws demarcated women's bodies, possessions and children as the property of their husbands, most male sexual utopians criticized marriage not from the perspective of women's rights, but in terms of the deleterious effects of private property and proprietorship on male 'virtue'. They proposed sexual liberation as the principal means of stamping out unsocial passions that stemmed from sexual frustration.

In a utopian novel published in 1798, *The Captive of the Castle of Sennaar*, George Cumberland, a friend of the artist William Blake, devised a fictional sexual utopia on 'the island of Sophis, at the head of the lake Zambree' in central Africa, in which all economic, legal and social customs were founded on 'the principle of human love'. 'Suppression of the natural fires' of sexual desire was thought 'danger[ous]', and 'every man and woman' was permitted to 'act freely; subject to no restraint while they *violate not the innocent will of another*'. When the narrator tells the Sophians about the British marital system, they recoil from it as an unnatural 'check' to 'the first genuine irresistible impulse of tender desire'. They consider the British trend towards late marriage as a postponement of 'the great unerring and explicit laws of procreation'. And in Godwinian fashion, the Sophians point out that the difficulty of obtaining a divorce has the effect of 'continuing a brutal commerce between, what you call married people, after the affections are dead and cold ... reconcil[ing] them to such legal prostitution'.[28]

Although sexual liberation on Sophis purportedly applied to 'every man and woman', the energy of the Sophian sexual marketplace was entirely male. Men have 'natural fires', the 'suppression' of which is dangerous, but women are only able to offer 'soft denials' designed to 'fa[n] the mysterious flame' of male libido.[29] Sophian women were therefore 'naturally' condemned to the status of passive property, their exclusion from active economic or sexual agency further justified by their apparently innate aptitude for domesticity and child-rearing. For Sophian women, liberation merely 'freed' them to continue occupying the same status as passive property and domestic slaves as always. The property laws that dictated that '[e]very man, by being born in the island, had a title to a certain portion of land' applied as much to women's sexual 'commodity' as to land. Men's access to both land and women's bodies was allocated on the basis that men 'must consider nothing as your own but what is necessary to your being, and those whom you preserve'. Burke had cast women as men's property in a highly regulated sexual and economic marketplace; radicals like Cumberland envisioned the lifting of restrictions on sexual and economic energy – but, in both men's systems, women were relegated to the status of property. In a Burkean landscape, a woman was the property of one man; in Cumberland's, she was the property of many. The same pattern was identified 170 years later, when the sex educator Shere Hite asked a survey respondent about the 1960s' sexual revolution, to be told that it 'was late sixties bullshit. It was about *male* liberation, women being shared property instead of private property.'[30]

Marriage, free love and the redistribution of property were the subjects of another exotic utopian treatment by the writer James Henry Lawrence, who published 'An Essay on the Nair System of Gallantry and Inheritance' in 1793 and later a novel entitled *The*

Empire of the Nairs; or, the Rights of Women: An Utopian Romance.
The reportedly polyandrous customs of the 'mighty empire' of
the Nair, or Nayar, group of Indian castes on the Malabar coast
fascinated travel writers in the early nineteenth century, notably James Forbes, whose *Oriental Memoirs* described how 'Nair
women allowed a plurality of husbands'.[31] Lawrence was a fan of
William Godwin, as well as 'the principles of Mrs. Wollstonecraft'
and French Enlightenment philosophy. He praised the Nairs,
who recognized man's 'passion for variety' by allowing divorce
and polygamy, for freeing 'the restraints imposed on love'. And
he recommended the founding of 'a country where there were
no wives', in which marriage was abolished altogether.[32] Unlike
Cumberland, Lawrence attacked the 'domestic yoke' of marriage for how it 'debases the female into a slave', as well as for
its 'cramp[ing of] the genius and vigor of the male'.[33] Marriage,
Lawrence wrote, was 'ordained exclusively for the comfort of the
man, that of the woman being disregarded'. Its abolition 'would
be the abolition of the servitude' of women.[34]

Cumberland and Lawrence both thought that sexual reform
needed to go hand in hand with – indeed, was a version of – radical reforms of the distribution of property. Lawrence compared
the Nairs' 'natural system [of] uninterrupted felicity' in sexual
commerce to 'agrarian law'. James Caulfeild, first Earl of
Charlemont, made a similar connection. In 1789, he had written
(critically) about the matriarchal Greek island of Lesbos, populated by 'manly ladies [who] seem to have changed sexes with
the men' and were exhibiting active, autonomous sexual agency.
He described how 'casual and unrestrained' 'connexion between
the sexes' required a radically different attitude to property
than in societies in which marriage and primogeniture was the
norm. The claim that free love would absolve men from the
responsibilities of fatherhood was repeatedly made in the 1790s,
notably by Godwin and Cumberland; Caulfeild too thought that
sexual liberation on Lesbos meant that 'who the real father was

could scarcely be known with any degree of certainty'.[35] This, Caulfeild argued, required not the abolition of property, but its investment in the female line of families, through matrilineal inheritance.

Unsurprisingly there were marked differences between men's and women's utopian projects in the late eighteenth century. Men like Cumberland, Lawrence and the pantisocrats imagined the wholesale restructuring of all society's systems of property, inheritance, economics, political representation and sexuality, in one fell, all-encompassing and rather vague swoop. In contrast, the literary critic Alessa Johns has pointed out that, in the eighteenth century, many women's utopias were small-scale, potentially achievable projects to resist the male-dominated status quo.[36] The travel writer Mary Wortley Montagu mined forms of female sociability that she witnessed in countries like Turkey, in order to devise 'feminotopias': idealized versions of female independence and pleasure.[37] The female educationalist Clara Reeves described how each and every girls' school might help the country as a whole approach to a moral 'Utopia'.[38] It is arguable that the smaller scale of many eighteenth-century female utopias reflected not women's constrained domestic experience, but the need to escape from their domestic 'slavery', a far more pressing imperative than for utopian-minded men.

Many of those female utopias took the form of secluded, female-only communities. In 1779, the *Lady's Magazine* published a short story: 'Matilda; or, the Female Recluse'. After being 'left a wanderer, young and inexperienced' by the death of her father, and encountering the 'treachery and inconstancy' of men in their predatory approaches to her inherited fortune, Matilda decides to retire, 'remote from the busy world'. She purchases a 'solitary retreat' on a gentleman's estate, and devotes herself to 'philosophy' and friendship with 'one unalterable friend, who shares with her every joy and pang of life'.[39] There were plenty of real-life Matildas. In 1751 Sarah Robinson married a family friend, George Scott, whom she left after a year of unconsummated marriage, amid rumours of abuse and extra-marital affairs. Denied financial assistance from her father, Sarah and her close friend Lady Bab Montagu settled abstemiously in Bath, where they established a programme of aid for vulnerable women and children. In 1762, Sarah published *A Description of Millenium Hall*: a utopian novel about a community of widows and spinsters engaged, like themselves, in scholarship and practical forms of social reform.[40]

Pursuing a life without men, in the company of a close female friend, was also the utopian aspiration of the young poet Anna Seward. In 1766, when she was fourteen, Anna's father adopted the five-year-old Honora Sneyd, whose mother had recently died. They lived together in Lichfield for fourteen years: Honora's presence transformed the house into 'an Edenic scene', wrote Seward.[41] The two girls fantasized about living together permanently, but when Honora reached nineteen years of age her father called her home, and two years later she was married – to Richard Lovell Edgeworth. She would become an adored stepmother to Edgeworth's first son, Dick, and a perhaps less revered stepmother to his third daughter, Anna, who would go on to marry Thomas Beddoes. To Anna Seward, Honora's marriage – and her early death in 1780, aged twenty-nine, from consumption – betrayed all their youthful utopianism. Even before their separation, Seward wrote that 'should that cruel time arrive',

> *I cou'd not learn my struggling heart to tear*
> *From thy lov'd form, that thro' my memory strays;*
> *Nor in the pale horizon of Despair*
> *Endure the wintry and the darken'd days.*[42]

In 1778, a more hopeful example of an idealized female-only community presented itself. One night in March, a usually shy and awkward twenty-three-year-old Irishwoman called Sarah Ponsonby dressed herself in men's clothes, armed herself with a pistol, and – with her small dog, Frisk, under one arm – lifted the bottom sash of the parlour window and clambered out. She eloped with her friend, Eleanor Butler, a thirty-nine-year-old upper-class Catholic, and the pair intended to 'go to England, take a house and live together'.[43] They were soon brought back home, but Sarah and Eleanor eventually persuaded their families to allow them to move into a cottage, Plas Newydd, in Llangollen Vale, near Wrexham, in north Wales, in early 1780. Friends of the family initially professed disgust – 'I never saw anything so confident as their behaviour' – but the 'Ladies of Llangollen' soon acquired a reputation as respectable retirees from the corrupt and male-dominated sexual and economic marketplace. The king bestowed a royal pension upon Sarah, and an influx of visitors – Wordsworth, Southey, Josiah Wedgwood, Edmund Burke, Hester Thrale Piozzi, Walter Scott – poured into Llangollen to witness their 'romantic' way of life. Anna Seward saw their domestic project as a success where her own attempt had failed: it was 'the blest reality of Hope's fond dream'. In October 1797, when Anna came across a portrait that reminded her of her lost love, she purchased it and sent it to Llangollen, hoping that the Ladies would hang it and that Honora's 'form should be enshrined in the receptacle of grace and beauty and appear there distinctly as those of Lady E. Butler and Miss Ponsonby'.[44]

Male sexual utopians were usually open about their communities' authorization of blatant polygamy, but most who encountered the Ladies of Llangollen refused to countenance the possibility of lesbian sexual activity. A relative of Sarah Ponsonby was adamant that her 'conduct, though it has an appearance of imprudence, is I am sure void of serious impropriety. There were no gentlemen concerned, nor does it appear to be anything more than a scheme of Romantic Friendship'.[45]

'Romantic friendship' in the eighteenth century denoted an intense, demonstrative relationship between two women. It was usually perceived as a preparation for, rather than a challenge to, their forthcoming married lives. But the writer and critic Emma Donoghue has pointed out that for a significant minority of women, romantic friendships did present a same-sex alternative to heterosexual marriage. An anonymous female poet of 1720 stated that 'We ... / Despise the [male] sex, and in our selves we find/ Pleasures for their gross senses too refined'.[46] The application of the term 'romantic friendship' has a tendency to sanitize such relationships by insisting on their non-sexual nature.

Dominant medical theories of libido in the eighteenth century had little language or theory to account for autonomous female sexuality or to depict active female desire that did not mirror male wants as anything other than pathological. The literary critic Helen P. Bruder explains that '[t]here was simply no way of writing about (or for that matter visually representing) women's sexuality, in the 1790s', which was not implicated in the pornographic tradition that cast women either as virgin or whore; passive, ill or evil.[47] But this clearly did not mean that healthy, active desire did not exist in late-eighteenth-century women.[48] 'Respectable' women were caught in a bind when faced with conversations about women who were sexually attracted to other women. (The term 'lesbian' only began to be used in this context in the late nineteenth century.) Hester Thrale Piozzi, the diarist, patron and great friend of Samuel Johnson, encapsulated this simultaneous guilty recognition and silencing of female sexuality by referring to female same-sex attraction as 'Impossibilities': ''tis now grown common to suspect Impossibilities – (such I think 'em) whenever two Ladies live too much together'.[49] Piozzi was debarred from openly recognizing the possibilities of the Ladies of Llangollen's attraction to one another by a cultural stigma about female sexuality, and especially about lesbianism, that threatened to turn social censure back onto the woman who acknowledged its existence: a form of 'she who smelled it, dealt it'. It was only in private, in an unpublished diary, that Piozzi voiced her recognition of, and vitriol towards, lesbians, designating the Ladies of Llangollen as 'damned Sapphists' and claiming that unaccompanied women were afraid to stay the night.

Late-eighteenth-century cultural suppression of female sexuality, and particularly of lesbian desire, meant that even if women's utopias were partly motivated by sexual imperatives, those imperatives did not dominate their schemes to anything like the degree that they shaped men's utopias. Female utopians like Sarah Scott (née Robinson) did engage with economic reform: the residents of Millenium Hall instigated a 'perfect equality' in which all financial resources were shared communally. But whereas male utopian thinkers often coupled such property reforms with equal access to women's sexual 'commodities', Millenium Hall's *raison d'être* was to take women's bodies out of the patriarchal economy that cast them as property in the first place. Economic reform was pursued in order to ameliorate women's deprivation – to offer education to working-class girls, to top up wages of low-paid female workers, and to encourage women's personal growth through the creative arts – not to exacerbate that deprivation by casting women's bodies (or men's, for that matter) as somebody else's 'property'. Radical men often focused on lifting regulatory constraints on male sexual desire, but continued to designate women as property in this 'revolutionized' sexual economy. Female sexual utopians were arguably more radical – despite the smaller scale of their projects – in challenging the marriage legislation that demarcated women as the sexual and economic property of men.

The pantisocrats' conversations about their colonies' approach to sexual reform reflected the connection between economic and erotic property. One of the newer recruits, Samuel Favell, wrote

optimistically 'extatic' poems about the free love that would be
on offer to him in Pennsylvania, anticipating the 'Kiss' that the
'mild-eyed Forms' of the settlement would bestow, and looking forward to 'drink[ing] of your love-bowl ... And pluck[ing]
from every Bank the Rose of Bliss!'[50] Southey believed that 'a
resolution of celibacy' was undesirable, even impossible, and
he expressed sympathy for Godwin's position that all domestic
ties were versions of hoarding property, based on irrational self-
interest. Coleridge hinted that Southey, at least temporarily,
supported complete abolition of private property in the pantisocratic community, along with the surrender of every domestic
link to 'his father and mother and wife and children and brethren and sisters, yea, and his own Life also'.[51] (Coleridge saw the
stoic denigration of emotional attachment as a form of nihilism.)
Southey was critical of sexual double standards, commenting in
1793 that 'the inequalities between the sexes is dreadful' and
that 'man may plunge in guilt of the most atrocious nature &
not only escape uncensurd but in some degree derive estimation from his crimes', whilst patriarchal society 'despises woman
when fallen & yet employs every artifice to ruin her'. The sight
of 'courtesans in the streets of London' provided further 'proof'
to Southey that 'we are [not] born in sin', but that 'sin is artificial – it is the monstrous offspring of government & property',
and that 'the origin of both was in injustice'.[52] Pantisocracy's
intended purpose was precisely to eradicate such artificial sin
by reforming government and property in line with principles
of political justice. And Southey appears to have been attracted,
even if just momentarily, by utopias that did so by freeing all
community members from regulations governing economic and
sexual consumption.

   Nevertheless, utopian sexual liberation of the type advocated
by James Lawrence was a minority interest, even among the
most extreme of the British radicals. The literary critic Marilyn
Butler has compared mainstream radicals who opined on the

subject to 'conservative moralists' in their 'advocacy of reason and restraint'.[53] At heart, Coleridge and Southey were both conservative about gender roles and sensuality, and shared an essentialist view of female attributes in which women's 'natural' sphere was the domestic, and emancipation of women's desires would only free them to better occupy this role. Coleridge advocated that 'pregnant Women or nurses' and mothers should do 'what is absolutely convenient and customary' in Pennsylvania, such as 'perform[ing] the little offices of ironing Cloaths or making Shirts'.[54] Southey started composing an epic poem, *Madoc*, around this time, in which a Welsh nobleman fled to establish a new life and colony in America; he imagined the settlement's female members purely as homemakers or reproductive devices.[55] For all his posturing about gendered double standards, Southey remained convinced that women's principal social role was to uphold moral 'decency', especially in periods of political turmoil. 'I am for Liberty & Long Petticoats,' he admitted.[56]

Coleridge's views were less wavering. Marriage was the heart of Coleridge's pantisocratic vision, and he was repelled by Godwin's image of an emotionless sexual economy. Marriage was, for Coleridge, not suitable for transformation into communal property: it was the 'sole propriety', in his words, the very nucleus of community attachment.[57] And unlike Godwin, Coleridge did not idealize the annihilation of the passions, but instead advocated a form of regulation. His writings on the subject reflected a theological tradition in which spiritual virtue depended on successful regulation of emotion. The early Christian philosophers Saint Augustine and Thomas Aquinas had both characterized the passions as forms of love – motions towards an object – that must be turned towards God in the form of obedience, by means of the will. Augustine had rejected Stoicism's acclaim of apathy because it denied humans that opportunity to turn towards God: 'we are rather worse men than better if we have none of these emotions at all'.[58] Right through the eighteenth century, the terminology of 'passions', 'affections' and 'appetites' carried overtly religious connotations; for Augustine, 'love' fell into the category of 'affections of the soul', as a turning towards God. There were clear echoes of this Christian tradition of emotion in Coleridge's – and Wollstonecraft's – insistence on the importance of the passions as 'paternal and filial duties [that] discipline the heart and prepare it for that blessed state of perfection in which all our Passions are to be absorbed in the Love of God'.[59] Godwin maintained that the suppression of emotion was a prerequisite of universal benevolence; Coleridge did not see how either universal benevolence or religious virtue could occur *without* emotion. 'If we love not our friends and Parents whom we have seen – how can we love our universal Friend and Almighty Parent whom we have not seen?'[60] For Coleridge, marriage and the family were both founded on 'chastity', a state of sexual regulation that mirrored a Christian man's turning of his passions towards God.

Coleridge coupled these beliefs to a madonna-whore complex: the women in his life were sorted into chaste marital material and seductive temptresses. Mary Evans, whom Coleridge had cast off to pursue Sara Fricker, began to occupy an idealized role in his sexual imagination as 'Sister' to her 'best-beloved Brother'; a 'pure and heavenly' 'image' rather than a flesh-and-blood woman. Poor Sara Fricker, meanwhile, whom Coleridge confessed to desiring with an 'inward melting away of Soul', acquired the taint of 'low Desire', and he worried that he would 'degrade her' by 'making her the Instrument ... [of] the removal of a desultory Appetite'.[61] Coleridge was repulsed by Godwin's detachment of sexual desire from emotional regulation, and he equated Godwin's 'New Philosophy' with 'promisc[uous] interc[ourse] of the sexes': he saw it as a direct challenge to the 'principles of the *heart*' that were necessary to Christian faith.[62] So marriage became a precondition of joining pantisocracy, along with equalization – rather than abolition – of private property. Both entailed emotional regulation, rather than liberation, in the name of men's duty of care towards their (female) property. Southey instructed his friend Horace Walpole Bedford that '[we] will gladly receive you in Pennsylvania', but only if 'you marry soon'.[63] That the male colonists mostly sought wives among a single family of sisters reflected Coleridge's view that patriotism should be an extension of domestic affection: their experimental state would literally be one family.

By the autumn of 1794, the pantisocrats had confirmed their colony's location, budget, timetable, 'list of adventurers' and had forged the bedrock of their utopian community's theoretical rationale. All that remained was to raise enough money to purchase land and passage, and to summon up enough shared convictions, energy and initiative to tip the 'castle in the air' into actuality.

Chapter 9

THE NEW PHILOSOPHY OF AIR

In March 1794, Thomas Beddoes travelled to Ireland, to Edgeworthstown, or Mostrim, in County Longford. His prospective wife, Anna Edgeworth, did not seem to have been distracted by any local 'Lords, Squires, Captains &c.', as she had feared. In April, she and Beddoes were married, by a 'very careless and negligent' vicar who 'omitted to register the Births and marriages of many persons'.[1] Beddoes wrote optimistically to his father than 'I am certain of living happily with her' and 'I think it more than probable that she will have a considerable addition to her fortune some time. But,' he hastened to add, 'I marry her for her prudence, her good sense and the sweetness of her disposition.'[2] Anna's father, Richard Lovell Edgeworth, was confident that 'Anna is happy with Beddoes' and their mutual friend Erasmus Darwin wrote to Beddoes to congratulate him on 'being on the road to happiness'.[3] But Beddoes still harboured some misgivings. He was anxious that 'for a young person to leave an house where she has always lived happily and a country where her father has been a kind of king is a very serious step', and he worried that his own buttoned-up relations might not offer quite the same exuberant welcome to Anna as Richard had to him.[4]

It was a season of fresh starts. In addition to an interesting – and imminently wealthy – new wife, Beddoes was in possession of a novel freedom, released from the social and professional constraints of Oxford. He had started to make a political name for himself, especially through his analysis of popular violence, and his claim that it originated, hydraulically, as a response to oppression. This had been expressed in *Alexander's Expedition down the Hydaspes*, and in his *Letter on Early Instruction* Beddoes had shown how education could gently guide the passions of both the ruling and ruled classes into more sympathetic and sociable behaviour. Shortly before his move to Bristol, Beddoes had published *The History of Isaac Jenkins, and Sarah His Wife, and Their Three Children*. By January 1793, it had become 'a prodigious favourite'. 'Two editions (near 5000 copies) have been distributed or sold,' Beddoes gleefully informed Giddy that month.[5] *Isaac Jenkins* describes the trials of a poor family near Ludlow, who are exploited by a quack doctor, and suffer the death of a child and the father's descent into alcoholism, before being returned to 'cheerfulness and content' by a good doctor's advice and support.[6] It was one of numerous late-eighteenth-century attempts to educate the poor, in the tradition of the evangelical educationalist Hannah More. But whereas Beddoes thought that More's works were 'calculated to fill the minds of the uneducated with superstition & bigotry & hypocrisy', he wanted education to nurture 'natural benevolence' to create healthy, happy citizens, on the basis that '[u]nless the mass of the people be trained to humanity, no place or person can be fully secure from the effects of popular fury'.[7]

Beddoes' move from Oxford to Bristol was a transition from academic chemistry to practical 'physic', but also a shift from a university environment in which his political principles remained necessarily cloistered, to one in which they could fully inform his work. In *Isaac Jenkins*, Beddoes argued that the country doctor's role – to educate and inform the population's behaviour – was an overtly political one. The close connection between medicine and politics was clear in the use of medical terminology in political language. We speak of the *body politic*, 'the body of the people'; the constitution, the state, the system; and describe political 'disorders' or discomfort using medical analogies: the *Observer* has referred to 'disdain' and 'reflexive sneering' as 'the root of our diseased politics'.[8] But the connection between politics and citizens' physical health went much deeper. Physicians had long considered it within their remit to issue prescriptions about their patients' lifestyles, advising changes to diet, hygiene and clothing. Beddoes thought that physicians' engagement with lifestyle should transcend a simplistic critique of individual patients' behaviour and choices, and explore the structural factors behind the material conditions of the sickest classes of society.

In *Isaac Jenkins*, Beddoes cited the physician George Fordyce's claim that, on average, 25 per cent more children die in cities than in the country, and that 50 per cent of working-class children in London die before the age of five. Beddoes explained that such deaths were caused when 'mothers being almost always obliged to labour for their bread, and often even robbed by their husbands, have no time left to take the necessary care for the rearing of infants, so that they are often left to wallow in dirt – nor can their food be at all attended to'.[9] The living conditions resulting from political and economic deprivation – especially 'insufficient food and cloathing' – were breeding-grounds for disease, so the political remit of the physician's role was obvious: many illnesses could be traced back to political causes. Brissot himself had written that 'the great principle of physical health is the equality of all beings'.[10] This was the beginning of the concept of 'public health', which promotes the health of communities through organized social change, and sees doctors as important political advocates for the most deprived.

Soon after his arrival in Bristol, in the summer of 1793, Beddoes' commitment to ameliorating the worst physical effects of material inequality coalesced into a definite project. During his trip to Cornwall in 1791, in the fields around Giddy's house at Tredrea, Beddoes – full of revolutionary enthusiasm – had had an epiphany about the need to widen access to treatment for consumption. Now he started formulating a plan to establish a private institution, combining medical research with new therapies, which, Beddoes hoped, would improve the health of Bristol's poorest citizens by using his varied expertise and applying chemical advancements to medicine: in particular, by administering gases to consumptives.

Beddoes had been fascinated by 'pneumatic medicine' since the late 1780s, when he visited Dijon, in eastern France, to see the laboratory of the chemist Louis-Bernard Guyton, Baron de Morveau, famous for his 'ingenious investigations for facilitating enquiries in the new philosophy of air'.[11] Beddoes met the chemist and nobleman Antoine-Laurent de Lavoisier on the same trip, and the revolutionary political alignment of pneumatic chemistry soon became clear: Guyton was elected a deputy to the Legislative Assembly, then to the National Convention, and a member of the Committee of Public Safety; and Lavoisier shrugged off his aristocratic heritage, changed his name (to simple 'Antoine Lavoisier'), and chaired a commission to establish a uniform system of weights and measures as part of the revolution's forms. In 1793, Guyton used the results of earlier experiments with hydrogen balloons to form a corps of balloonists for the French Revolutionary Army, and flew one himself during the Battle of Fleurus on 26 June 1794.[12] After his visit to Dijon, Beddoes had dabbled with hot-air ballooning too, in what he reported as 'one of the most perfect and beautiful

experiments I have ever seen'. In June 1791, with James Sadler –
the first English aeronaut – Beddoes had constructed a sphere,
filled it with inflammable gases, lit it with a touchpaper, and
stood back to watch the delicate orb float high above and through
the spires of Oxford. The ball of gas shrugged off its case, and,
'freed from the load, rose sensibly and suddenly. It continued
compact and burnt away with a lambent flame, [until] it was
diminished to a very small size' and resembled an 'igneous
meteor.'[13]

Beddoes intended that his 'Pneumatic Institute' would use
various gases as experimental treatments for a range of conditions, but particularly for respiratory disorders such as 'spasmodic
asthma' and *'phthisis pulmonaris'*, or consumption. He estimated
that consumption was responsible for a staggering quarter of all
deaths in Britain, skewed towards poorer sectors of society.[14]
Beddoes postulated that hyperoxygenation – exposure to excessive levels of oxygen – might be a cause of consumption, and that
treatment might focus on the prolonged breathing of 'a reduced
air'. Before opening an operational institute, he wanted to test
this hypothesis through extensive research and found a suitable
property in Bristol Hotwells, on the aptly named Hope Square.
This was a smart development that had been built since the
1770s, on the sides of the cliff rearing up from the River Avon.
His prospective neighbours initially protested against the presence of a research laboratory belching out potentially noxious
and dangerous gases, but Richard Lovell Edgeworth's influence
helped to calm the waters, and Beddoes wrote in July 1793 that
he had the support of local 'medical people' who 'at present at
least wish me success'.[15]

Beddoes started work swiftly. By late August 1793, he had
made four experiments on kittens. To one animal, he administered gas comprising 50 per cent oxygen and 50 per cent
atmospheric air, and to another, gas entirely comprising atmospheric air. Then he attempted to drown both, finding that the

animal that had been exposed to oxygenated air was the last to fall unconscious and the first to recover.[16] This was an exciting start, and he wrote soon after beginning work that he had 'made airs, and made some experiments upon them, [but] I am not yet in a fit condition to receive patients'. Before he could open his Pneumatic Institute, Beddoes still needed to calculate when doses of particular gases became harmful; and to improve 'the appearance' of the laboratory.[17] Most of all, he needed to be able to account for precisely how the administration of gases might cure disease and, in doing so, improve the conditions of the most oppressed and potentially most emotionally volatile classes.

In 1794, Beddoes found a rationale for his pneumatic researches when the schoolmaster, minister and political writer Samuel Parr suggested that Beddoes might consider producing a popular English edition of *Elementa Medicinae*, a controversial medical work by the Scottish physician John Brown, published in Latin in 1780. Brown had died suddenly in late 1788, and his friends were rallying to raise financial support for his widow and children. Parr hinted that the endeavour would also help publicise Beddoes and his proposed Pneumatic Institute, and the tactic worked.[18] Beddoes was a talented linguist who had translated European medical and chemical texts since his time at Oxford, and he began work straight away on his translation, *Elements of Medicine*.

John Brown had been a pugnacious, divisive figure in Scottish medicine: something of a bruiser, talented at boxing and wrestling, vivacious 'of disposition and strong passions', fond of alcohol and opium, who took on the orthodox Edinburgh medical establishment. Largely self-taught in medicine, Brown worked as a private tutor until his late thirties, including teaching the children of William Cullen, Professor of Medicine at Edinburgh University. The story goes that Cullen encouraged Brown to apply for the chair of the Institute of Medicine, and then stymied his application, denigrating him to colleagues as a rustic 'Jock'. And when Brown sought membership of the prestigious Edinburgh Philosophical Society, Cullen again apparently engineered his rejection, leading to a permanent breach between the two men.[19]

Unsurprisingly, Brown became highly critical of the medical establishment, considering it corrupt, insular, and in implacable 'opposition to improvement'.[20] After qualifying from the University of St Andrews, he started teaching his own system of medicine in the late 1770s, directly refuting the Edinburgh orthodoxy, especially the theories of his former employer, William Cullen. To many, Brown acquired the reputation of a 'quack' but his anti-establishment background made him popular among supporters – 'Brunonians' – drawn from medical outsiders and political reformers. He cultivated this dissident identity in braggadocious fashion, and Beddoes described how 'Brown was the first person I ever saw absurd enough to profess himself a Jacobite'.[21] In 1786, Brown moved himself and his family to London, but quickly ran up debts and endured a spell in the King's Bench Prison. He managed to improve his prospects with a frenzied bout of writing, but was struck down by apoplexy and died on 17 October 1788, either from a fit, or, Beddoes thought more likely, from an overdose of laudanum.

As something of a medical and political outsider himself, Beddoes had been intrigued by Brown's theories since becoming aware of the Brown–Cullen spat during his time at the Edinburgh Medical School in the mid-1780s. Beddoes initially proclaimed his independence from this dispute, loftily declaring that 'between the Brunonians and Cullonians[*sic*] Truth and Nature are too much forgotten'.[22] He attended Cullen's lectures, but was disappointed. Cullen's charisma had waned towards the end of his professional life and Beddoes complained that he 'does nothing but read his text book'.[23] But he was also wary of the cultish 'infatuation' of many Brunonians, and thought they lacked 'perfect use of their senses'.[24] Nevertheless, Brown's

ideas were influential, especially on the continent, where
Beddoes' university friend Christoph Girtanner had been diligent in promoting them. After the French Revolution, Brown's
followers began to align his opponents' theories with the tired
ideas of the old regime, while according Brown himself the
status of a medical revolutionary; and in 1790 even the hitherto
sceptical Beddoes began to write sympathetic articles about
him for the *Monthly Review*. A sketch by the French painter
Carle Vernet captured just how high emotions ran in this
medical conflict, depicting a rabble of Brunonians and anti-
Brunonians as British and French soldiers locked in a 'fierce
battle' for supremacy.[25]

Re-reading Brown in 1794 was revelatory to Beddoes, because
the *Elements of Medicine* not only theorized how gases might
cure disease, but it also offered a startling new version of the
medical ideas underlying the hydraulic theory of emotion which
interested him so much. The two were closely related. Beddoes'
notion that gases might cure disease was predicated on the idea
that something – oxygen, perhaps, or a quite different element or
substance – was present in both the human body and the gases
surrounding it, and could be transferred from one to the other
through respiration. He imagined the universe traversed by
invisible conduits through which a component, fundamental to
health and life, might flow within and between all its constituent
bodies, obeying the laws of fluid dynamics. Obstruction of this
universal flow might, in one manifestation, lead to diseases like
consumption; in another, it might lead to the hydraulic accumulation of psychic pressures, resulting in the outburst of violent
and antisocial passions. Many eighteenth-century physicians
considered disordered passions to fall within their remit, alongside illness: in his hugely popular manual, *Domestic Medicine*,
William Buchan described at great length how 'the passions
have great influence both in the cause and cure of diseases'.[26]

*

John Brown's theory of disease could be traced all the way back to an ancient Greek Hippocratic medical idea, popularized by the physician Galen in the second century AD, which attributed health and disease to the balance of four basic bodily substances known as the 'humours': blood, yellow bile, black bile, and phlegm.[27] The humours were held responsible for the production of both the passions and disease. Galen had attributed emotion to chemical reactions caused by excessive or deficient levels of certain humours: for example, surplus black bile caused 'melancholia', and yellow bile created a 'choleric' disposition characterized by restlessness, ambition and irritability. Passions were equated with diseases, as products of humoral imbalances, or resulting from coagulations of poisons in the body.

Humoral theory continued to dominate medicine through the Middle Ages and early modern period. In the eighteenth century it was brought up to date in the work of the Dutch physician Herman Boerhaave, who helped to found the University of Leiden's medical department. Boerhaave changed the humoral theory of a body coursing with fluids into a more sophisticated Enlightenment image of the human as a hydraulic machine: a 'mechanism, the solid parts of which are ... vessels, capable of encompassing, directing, changing, separating, collecting and secreting liquids'. He claimed that life itself was the product of the constant circulation of fluids, particularly blood, around the body; and that disease was caused when fluids met with blockages or obstructions such as tumours or 'stagnated blood'.[28] Then, in 1733, research into fluid pressure by Blaise Pascal and Daniel Bernoulli, working separately, was used by Stephen Hales to identify blood pressure, 'the force of blood', in his book *Haema Staticks*. Hales' mechanical and medical theories of blood pressure were subsequently used by physicians to describe how blockages in the body's fluid conduits led to a dangerous internal accumulation of 'force'. Ancient humoral theory combined with Enlightenment laws of fluid dynamics to articulate, in fashionably contemporary and mechanistic terminology, the basic hydraulic idea that when the fluid-based passions are obstructed from attaining expression, potentially grievous damage to the body, psyche and body politic results. Older forms of hydraulic theory had aligned the passions with chemical imbalances as forms of disease, corresponding to theological and philosophical views that cast the passions as disturbances, external visitations and disorders of the soul. But in the eighteenth century, when the passions were viewed more positively, it was not always *the passions themselves* that were considered medically malignant, but *the causes of their obstruction*. This attitude chimed with contemporary philosophies advocating careful nurture and liberation of people's innately benevolent passions, and warning of the result of hindrances.

When Brown's nemesis William Cullen was appointed Professor of Medicine at Edinburgh in 1766, he was clear that Boerhaave's hydraulic ideas formed the orthodoxy from which he was not permitted to depart significantly. 'I was taught to think the system of Boerhaave to be very perfect, complete and sufficient,' Cullen wrote, and was requested to 'avoid differing from Dr. Boerhaave', as such behaviour 'was likely to hurt himself and the University'.[29] Cullen duly declared that the human body comprised three entwined networks of solids and fluids, of which the nervous system – chiefly responsible for the passions – was the most crucial. But both Cullen and Boerhaave left Beddoes, as a medical student, cold. Even though he broadly agreed with their account of how emotion was produced in the body, he loathed how they attributed the miraculous 'phaenomena of life' to mundane 'properties of substances'. 'Cullen situated the principle of life in an "imaginary fluid" that coursed through the nervous system,' he wrote disparagingly.[30] Beddoes thought that this mechanistic approach converted the wonder of human life into a series of chemical or dynamic calculations: 'as if to discover the qualities of a horse, the naturalist were to direct his attention to the movements of a windmill'.[31] Life, for Cullen and Boerhaave, Beddoes decided, was merely an accidental by-product of material bodies whose motions conformed to the same physical laws that described the operation of more vulgar automata, like threshing machines and flush toilets.

His predecessors 'having in this manner left Man entirely out of their systems, or assigned him an unimportant place, Brown atchieved [*sic*] the important service of restoring him to his proper station in the centre', Beddoes wrote admiringly.[32] Brown claimed that human life was the result not of the machine-like movements of the skeletal, muscular, nervous and fluid systems of the body – as if operated by an external force – but of the presence of some intrinsic 'vitalist' property propelling the body from within. Brown equated life with a principle that he called 'excitability': a type of natural energy or vitality dispersed throughout the body. It was this location of the life-force *within* the body, not external to it, that set Brown apart from his predecessors, and marked his theory as revolutionary. It chimed with political and economic philosophies that accorded greater agency to the individual – like Adam Smith's laissez-faire theories – and helped pave the way for the importance of the subjective workings of the individual mind that would come partially to define the aesthetic movement of Romanticism.

In the introduction to the edition of Brown's *Elements of Medicine* on which he was working throughout 1794 and 1795, Beddoes cited an analogy for precisely how excitability operated – an analogy that originated with Joseph Johnson's collaborator Thomas Christie, who had once been a student of Brown. Christie compared the human frame – the skeleton, viscera, muscles – to a grate in a fireplace, in which lies a certain amount of reluctantly combustible fuel. This fuel is '*the matter of life*, the *excitability* of Dr. Brown', and there is a pipe travelling into the grate regularly supplying fresh stocks, just as sleep might 'refuel' our energy levels.[33] Also in the fireplace are tubes pouring streams of fresh air into the conflagration. These 'denote the various *stimuli* applied to the excitability of the body', its encounters with sensory experiences. The flame that bursts forth from this interaction is excitement, 'the product of the exciting powers acting upon the excitability'.[34] If the air tubes emit particularly stimulating oxygenated gases, the flame burns brightly, but the stock of energy is consumed more quickly, and remains depleted until it is naturally regenerated. An extraordinarily high dose of stimulation might burn out the fuel completely and kill the fire, just as a person might drop dead upon receiving a particularly dreadful shock. If less stimulating gases are released, the flame is more subdued and possesses greater stamina; but an exceptionally meagre or suffocating gas might cause the fire to go out (like an individual starving to death). The optimum state of combustion, in which a moderate flame burns at the same rate as the fuel is replenished, is a model for perfect health: bodies require enough stimulation to provoke their natural energy into action, but not so much as to wear out that energy. According to this wildly universalizing theory, all disease is the product of too forceful or too weak a stimulation of the body's life-force: too great or too insubstantial demands made on one's energy. Medicine, therefore, is the art of returning the relationship between the body and its external influences to this precarious state of balance, by either increasing or decreasing the amount of stimulation to which the body is exposed. Brown categorized medicines and remedies as either stimulants or sedatives.

For Brown, 'the passions' were important not so much as automatic responses to sensory stimulation, as they had been for exponents of the cult of sensibility; they were important as *stimuli themselves*, affecting the body's energy levels. Brown thought that the passions mostly originated within the body, and powerfully altered 'the state of our different organs, while we are under their influence', especially modifying a person's levels of excitability.[35] Using a rudimentary scale, Brown illustrated how the 'exciting power' of the passions operated in inverse relationship to the amount of excitability left over once the passion had ended. The stronger the stimulus, the greater the excitement and the more it depleted the stock of energy. Forceful passions, such as happiness and joy, were succeeded by a state of exhaustion. But the weaker the emotion, the less it consumed of the body's energy, and the greater was the 'accumulation, increase, or abundance' of leftover excitability. There was therefore, claimed Brown, a significant danger in prolonging low sensory stimulation of the body, indulging 'depressing passions' or not fulfilling desires. If desires – 'the longing for snuff' or 'the want of venereal gratification' – were withheld from satisfaction for any length of time, or if the 'depressing passions' such as fear, grief and anxiety were indulged, then a 'morbid accumulation' of unspent energy resulted, creating a 'superabundance of excitability' that threatened to erupt dangerously and violently, even leading to 'death'.[36]

This was a doctrine based on hydraulics, just like the old regime of Cullen and Boerhaave. They had claimed life was a by-product of a bodily hydraulic machine; Brown thought that the life-force itself followed hydraulic principles.[37] Despite Brown's determinedly fiery metaphors, he still envisaged the body's energy levels operating like 'a fluid issuing from the brain as water from a spring'. In actual fact, that Brown considered excitability to be subject to the laws of fluid dynamics was not surprising. 'Excitability' was Brown's word for what we might now call 'energy', and in the late eighteenth century, the creation and transfer of energy was widely imagined as a process involving the motion of fluids, especially a 'subtle fluid' related to the substance that Lavoisier had called 'caloric' and held responsible for heat. Caloric 'flow' was thought to be governed by fluid dynamics, and its accumulation – like that of excitability – was thought to lead to 'the point of rendering a substance' volatile and explosive, 'red-hot', in the words of a primer published as late as 1843.[38] Fire and water were not so opposite as they appeared: in the eighteenth century, both were considered subject to hydraulic laws.

In fact, at the end of the Enlightenment, the motion of fluids was thought to be responsible for many of the physical forces propelling the earth. Centuries earlier, the Stoics had proposed the existence of a unifying cosmic substance called *pneuma* – a mixture of air and fire; sensory perception occurred through impressions made upon the *pneuma*, like the depression of seals on soft wax.[39] Descartes had envisaged a human body coursing with 'animal spirits' – invisible entities similar to the humours, flowing through hollow nerves – which were partly responsible for the production of the passions in the pineal gland. And in February 1778, a German physician, Franz Anton Mesmer, proclaimed the existence of a superfine universal fluid travelling around and within all physical bodies, through which gravity, heat, light, electricity and magnetism were conveyed; the obstruction of this fluid was responsible for sickness. Mesmer 'cured' such obstructions by massaging the body's 'poles', especially in the upper abdomen – which led to accusations of sexual impropriety in his treatment of female patients – to cause a convulsive 'crisis' in the patient and restore the free flow of fluid around and beyond the body.[40] Mesmerism was not mainstream medicine, but the historian Robert Darnton has pointed out that the concept of invisible universal fluid did not seem strange to a public who had recently been introduced to the presence of other invisible forces – Newton's gravity, Franklin's electricity, imperceptible gases such as Priestley's phlogiston, and Lavoisier's caloric – in the atmosphere all around them, many of which were thought to follow similar hydraulic laws.

Brown's doctrine of excitability provided Beddoes with a sweeping, comprehensive theory of disease. It described how health was a precarious mean, on either side of which excessive or deficient stimulation caused disorders: the former by wearing out a person's energy levels, the latter by causing that energy to accumulate and erupt destructively. Earlier theorists of hydraulic medicine had attributed the passions to accumulations of poisons, tumours, coagulations or obstructions in the body's fluids. Brown offered a seemingly sophisticated and up-to-date transposition of this theory by arguing that it was the body's internal energy that followed hydraulic principles, and that management of the passions – which acted to channel that energy into joy, or subdue it into depression – was a fundamental concern of physicians. Doctors, he implied, were necessarily engaged in ensuring that the body's energy and excitement were kept at the median level requisite to health. Thomas Christie had compared stimulation of energy, through the passions or otherwise, to oxygen levels applied to a fire, but Beddoes wanted to turn this from an analogy into a concrete reality. The stimulus whose effects on the body interested Beddoes was not 'like' oxygen: it *was* oxygen. At the beginning of his researches, Beddoes was focused on the use of pneumatic medicine to dilute the hyperoxygenation that he thought underlay the disease of consumption. But soon he would become interested in the capacity of gases to transmit energy: either to stimulate the body's existent energy into excited activity, or to replenish the stock of energy itself.

Beddoes seems to have envisaged the process which allowed the body to obtain energy through gases as something similar to the 'metabolism', a term coined towards the end of the nineteenth century: the chemical transformations in the body's cells that convert food or fuel into energy. Today we know that breathing contributes to the process of aerobic respiration, in which oxygen helps to release energy from food substances such as glucose. But Beddoes wondered whether gases could themselves *supply* energy in the same way as food.[41] If such a thing were possible, ventilation would effect a transfer of energy from gas to body, in exactly the same way that heat might be transferred from one substance (for example, methylated spirits in a spirit burner) to another (a cup of water placed above the flame). Different fuels could clearly stimulate varying levels of flame, and different foods could provide varying levels of energy to the body, so why couldn't different gases? In time, Beddoes would widen his early experiments into whether oxygen could cure consumption to explore whether pneumatic medicine might provide a 'cure of the palsy and diseases proceeding from a defect of nervous energy': a cure for paralysis that illuminated the workings of the life-force itself.[42]

Beddoes' hopes for his projected Pneumatic Institute had overt political aims. He considered many forms of ill health to be the result of political mismanagement and inequality, correlates of the antisocial, violent passions that were the inevitable result of oppressive behaviour. Beddoes was as appalled by popular violence as by the political oppression that, in his view, caused it. In his political writings, he sought to persuade members of the ruling establishment to act more sympathetically; and his educational interests had the same aim, as well as 'training' the citizenry to channel frustration in more sociable ways, to avoid violence. Now, as a doctor, he was hoping to treat the medical effects of inequality and deprivation by broadening access to cures for diseases caused by hunger and want. John Brown's theory of excitability not only offered a tantalizing rationale for how weakness, debility and diseases like consumption might be immediately remedied through gases; it also bolstered Beddoes' conviction that popular violence was the inevitable hydraulic outcome of the 'accumulation' of energy in the face of oppression, deprivation and 'low spirits'. For Beddoes, hydraulic theory compellingly justified his claims about the ill effects of oppressive state behaviour on the populace, and implicitly supported progressive measures to ameliorate inequality and deprivation. But he seemed oblivious to the fact that hydraulic theory – in the eighteenth century, and today too – was most often used to reinforce inequality, not as a weapon to tackle it.

*

Most of those in the eighteenth century who thought and wrote on the passions supposed that thwarting men's desires was fraught with danger in a way that did not apply to women. Male sexual desire was conceived of as an unstoppable force, a tide seeking an outlet, which, in the face of obstruction, would inevitably accumulate and explode in rape, violence and murder. This gendered distinction was based on the idea that the hydraulic structures of male and female bodies differ, and that male physiology (and psychology) is peculiarly subject to hydraulic pressures accumulating in its fluids.

In the sixteenth and seventeenth centuries, female sex organs were considered to be structurally similar, albeit inverted, forms of male ones. But by the eighteenth century, physicians and anatomists began to conceive of male and female anatomy as having distinct characteristics, especially in their hydraulic structures, the conduits through which bodily fluids travelled.[43] By the latter half of the century, some physicians were arguing that – in addition to the fluids of the nervous system – the vascular system responsible for producing, transmitting and ejaculating semen was the most influential bodily component involved in forming a man's emotional character and the urgency of his desires. Such Enlightenment theories of the 'spermatic economy' were recruited to justify the claim that, due to the peculiarly hydraulic nature of male physiology, the forcefulness of men's desires radically outstripped those of women.

In 1795, the physician and occultist Ebenezer Sibly theorized that puberty was a crucial stage in the emergence of these sexed characteristics. He posited that the transformation of the pubescent male form was due to the amassing of sperm in the body: 'The flesh and skin, from being tender, delicate, and irritable, become coarse and firm; the body in general loses its succulency; ... and the mind itself ... acquires distinctly new propensities and passions'.[44] For Sibly, 'spermatic liquor' was the elixir of life, 'an elaborate tincture' on which men's and women's bodily health depended: 'The seat of life – of the brain, the seat of the soul – and of the whole powers of the body, [were] concentrated and impelled, as it were, through the genital system'. But whereas men produced their own life-giving elixir, women's health relied on persuading men to ejaculate that elixir into their vaginas (which possessed a 'strong power of absorption') and Sibly worried that 'the want of coition ... induces many disorders in females'.[45] A decade before Sibly, the physician James Graham had set up a 'Temple of Health and Hymen' on London's Pall Mall, and charged customers for using its 'Celestial or Magnetico-electrico bed', which, Graham claimed, guaranteed 'superior ecstasy' to couples paying to have sex in the bed, and would turn the 'barren' 'fruitful'.[46] Graham had similar ideas to Sibly about the life-giving properties of sperm: the 'luminous, ever-active balsam of life'.[47] The early eighteenth century saw the emergence of huge cultural anxieties about masturbation, related to the act's secrecy, the potential for excessive indulgence, and the possibility that its reliance on fantasy would undermine awareness of reality.[48] But Graham feared masturbation for the effect on the body of the loss of semen: 'Every seminal emission out of nature's road,' he wrote, 'is an earthquake – a blast – a deadly paralytic stroke' that compromises the physical health that is reliant upon semen's vital properties.[49]

Men like Sibly held men and women's distinct fluid economies responsible for their wildly different emotional characteristics. Women – dependent creatures, lacking their own spermatic tincture – were 'Lunar': cool, passive, receptive and 'vegetative'.[50] Sibly reasoned that 'strong' emotions such as 'anger and joy' were 'masculine or solar diseases', involving the dynamic and 'expulsive force' of fluids throughout the body, and resulting in increased excretions in males in the form of uniquely abundant perspiration, urination and ejaculation.[51] Obstructions to men's ejaculations were thought to lead to accumulation of pressure

followed by haemorrhages and violent explosions of bodily fluids
and passions. For many, this presented a compelling biological
justification for society to pander more to male desires than to
those of women; Beddoes would later describe how 'the universal facility of credit' was specifically aimed at facilitating every
male whim.[52] But hydraulic theory also threatened to undermine
the traditional stereotype of cool, rational masculinity and irrational, emotional femininity.

Some writers got around this potential contradiction by claiming that, as well as having a more potent physiology of desire,
men were blessed with a superior rational faculty in the brain,
and more vigorous musculature in the body, to rein in the force
of their wants. Those concerned about masturbation fretted
that it 'relaxed' the 'seminal vessels', weakening the 'tone' of
'the erectories, the nerves, and glans, of the penis' and bringing about 'an universal lassitude of the body' that eroded that
manly strength necessary to regulate desire.[53] Others claimed
that men were capable of greater virtue than women, because of
the vigorous moral, rational and physical force that was required
to tame their uniquely powerful desires. And some did argue
that women's bodies were as riddled with 'spermatic' conduits
as men's, equally susceptible to irrational passion. The writer
M. D. T. De Bienville described female orgasm as a process as
fluid as male ejaculation, portraying women's ovaries as 'seminal
vesicles, designed to pour into the *matrix* [the womb] a mucilag-
inous and spermatic liquor, which the vesicles pump, and draw
from the testicles, or *ovaria* of the woman' causing 'pleasure'.
De Bienville thought that obstruction of female orgasm caused
'too great an abundance of the *semen*' inside her, leading to the
ultimately fatal condition 'furor uterinus' or 'nymphomania' that
was characterized by swellings and explosive haemorrhages:
'violent burning and aridity in sexual organs, making them open
up to receive impressions of the air; swelled and large clitoris;
an ovary . . . puffed up with viscous, purulent and thick humour

and ... virulent flux'.[54] But unlike men, women were thought to lack the rational, moral or physical capacity to rein in their unruly wants.

In the course of the 1790s, many conceptions of the passions fell away, to be replaced by a new emotional landscape in which the foundations of contemporary attitudes can be traced. But it was the decade that forged the modern temperament in terms of the theories that did not fall away, too – the approaches to emotion that remained consistent throughout the eighteenth century, into the nineteenth, and right up to today. Hydraulic theory is one of those attitudes to emotion that was colliding and fusing with others in the 1790s' cultural ferment, and has continued to do so to the present day. It has endured due to its defence of the irresistible force of male desire.

The popular book *Men are from Mars, Women are from Venus*, published in 1992, describes how frustration and disappoint-ment make a man 'about to explode' – whereas, in women, they merely cause sadness and resentment.[55] The Nobel prize-winning Japanese novelist Kenzaburo Oe's novella *Seventeen* attributes 'orgies of violence' in extremist terrorism to male 'sexual deprivation', and the reviewer Ian Buruma asks, 'Can sexual inadequacy or deprivation turn angry young men into killers?'[56] A male commentator claims that 'internet porn reduces sex crimes', implying that male desire needs to find an outlet somewhere, and, if hindered, will result in rape.[57] And there is no female equivalent for the so-called 'blue balls' syndrome – the idea that sexual frustration in men causes 'excruciating pain' and testicular swelling 'to the size of coconuts', apparently after retention of blood in the face of 'withheld' orgasm.[58] Even though twenty-first-century readers no longer tend to think that emotions are literally produced by the motion of fluids in the body, male sexual desire is frequently linked to the fluid motion of semen. The psychoanalyst Theodore Reik claimed that 'the

crude sex drive is a biological need which ... is dependent
on inner secretions ... If it is strongly excited, it needs, in its
urgency, an immediate release. It cannot be deflected from its
one aim to different aims, or at most can be as little diverted as
the need to urinate or as hunger and thirst. It insists on gratification in its original realm.'[59]

   The chief assumptions of hydraulic theory – that fluid-based
desires are uniquely forceful and, if obstructed, erupt in violence – appear today in many different guises. Just as John
Brown did, many think of emotional health in terms of 'energy',
as a substance following hydraulic laws, which can be released
or 'pent-up'. The business analyst Pepe Martínez claims that
emotion depends on a 'flow' of 'energy' that 'always find[s] a way
out ... Remember what the laws of physics teach us: energy is
neither created nor destroyed, it can only be transformed.'[60] In
The Emotional Energy Factor, Mira Kirshenbaum describes 'emotional energy' as a miraculous subcategory of general physical
and psychic energy. 'We all know what energy is,' she writes. 'It's
having fuel in your tank.'[61] The self-help blog *Calm Down Mind*
refers to the 'release of suppressed energy': 'life is energy in play
and the more free flowing the energy is the more vibrant/whole
you feel,' its author claims.[62] 'Pent-up energy' is considered a
danger, both to the individual psyche and to society. 'Pockets
of energy which are suppressed, or "held", within you become
sources of resistance to the free flow of your life expression,'
warns the *Calm Down Mind* blog. Hydraulic claims about the
operation of emotion recruit other physical forces too, and are
highly gendered. Newtonian laws of physics are evoked to refer
to people – usually men – being under 'tension', 'stress', being
'wound up', and eventually 'snapping'. The male narrator of
Todd J. Colberg's novel *Self Booked*, for example, recounts how
he 'felt the tension of my pent up frustration, wound up like a
coil, ready to unleash into a tirade'. His tension unleashes into
an outburst of misogynistic hatred: 'You two fucking bitches ...

You're fucking fired . . . You are the dumbest, chicken-headed bitch I've ever met!'[63]

Hydraulic theory is most often used to justify male violence against women as the inevitable result of men's frustration, 'tension' or withheld satisfaction. The *Liverpool Echo* used metaphors of tension to describe how 'a husband who was "nagged ceaselessly" *suddenly snapped* and stabbed his wife to death with a bread knife'.[64] The *Mirror* reported on 8 April 2016 that 'Stuart Andrews, 54, *snapped following months of tension* over their money woes and throttled his wife of 31 years Caroline Andrews, 52'. The judge, Jeremy Carey, confirmed this interpretation of the causes of Andrews' violence, telling him 'you did indeed *snap*'.[65] On 23 April 2016, the news website *Bossip* carried the headline 'Georgia man *snaps* after learning wife's divorce plan, kills five then shoots self'.[66] In Chicago, the Deputy County Public Defender called for a judge to be lenient to a man who had '*unleashed*' his '*pent-up anger* over his wife and children's departure' in the sexual assault and murder of his wife's niece, who '*lit the fuse*' by refusing to help him find his wife.[67] In Australia, in November 1992, Judge O'Bryan sentenced Paul Stanbrook, who had pleaded guilty to aggravated rape and attempted murder, to a sentence 'significantly less' than the maximum. O'Bryan justified the lenient sentencing on the basis that Stanbrook was suffering from '*pent-up lust*' after having 'unsuccessfully made sexual advances to a former lover'.[68]

Treatment of the issue of prostitution, both in the late eighteenth century and today, is one example in which the strongly gendered assumptions of hydraulic theory come to the fore. Eighteenth-century commentators on the subject were divided as to the root cause of prostitution, debating whether it was the result of some 'ill' women's innate sexual deviance and 'disgusting irregularities', or the consequence of obstacles posed to the hydraulic male sex drive by monogamous marriage. James Lawrence argued that 'in a country where there were no wives, there would be no courtesans' and claimed that men were driven to visit prostituted women by 'the chastity which the married woman and every creditable female is forced to maintain'.[69] Today, men's reviews of women on the prostitution review site Punternet.com express, starkly and exactly, this attitude: that prostituted women are an outlet for male desire in the face of the obstruction posed by wifely sexual virtue. One punter described an 'escort' as 'a milf – girl next door that does things your wife wouldn't'; another sex buyer elsewhere boasted that 'if my fiancée won't give me anal, I know someone who will'.[70] The term 'wife experience' ('WE') is repeatedly used in Punternet reviews to slate insufficiently adventurous prostituted women who manifest the 'vanilla' virtue associated with wives: 'Avoid unless you want a wife experience'.[71] One punter claimed that 'escorting' should be 'available on the NHS if you can prove a need: "My wife doesn't understand me, Dr." "Take two doses of Carolina three times a week etc etc"' – as if obstruction of pene-trative ejaculation is as dangerous to health as bodily tumours.[72] The writer, 'sexpert', and campaigner for legalizing prostitution, Theresa 'Darklady' Reed, agrees that most male punters want 'things they often were unable to experience in their private lives or receive from their primary partners'.[73]

A frequently made inference from hydraulic theory is that prostitution acts as a 'safety valve', preventing the outburst of pent-up male desire in rape. The 'unretired call girl' Maggie McNeill writes on her blog that '[s]ince Western society has apparently decided that it is no longer the responsibility of wives to provide for their husbands' sexual needs ... we need Vestals to tend the fires of male passion in order to keep them from becoming dangerous conflagrations'. Without the outlet of prostituted women, McNeill claims that 'the most common way in which the uncontrolled male sex drive can be dangerous is of course rape'.[74] The sociologist Catherine Hakim makes a similar argument, claiming that men experience an 'undeniabl[y]' superior level of sexual desire to women, which cannot be socially constructed, she says, because it occurs internationally.[75] This leaves men with a 'sexual deficit', Hakim writes, that turns female sexuality into a rare and precious commodity, which some men have no choice but to steal through rape. Complete legalization of prostitution, she argues, would prevent male sexual violence by neutralizing the pressure of sexual frustration.[76]

Not everyone, in the eighteenth century or today, accepts these hydraulic arguments. Martin Madan was the son of the poet Judith Cowper Madan, who had published a poem on illicit desire entitled *Abelard to Eloisa* in 1721. Madan himself was said to have lived 'an uninhibited life', before being converted to evangelical Christianity by John Wesley and becoming chaplain at the Lock Hospital in London, an institution for 'penitent' prostitutes. In 1780 Madan published *Thelyphthora; or, A Treatise on Female Ruin*, which shone a light on the behaviour of a hitherto shadowy, obscured demographic in debates about prostitution: male sex buyers, or, in Madan's words, 'the lust, treachery, cruelty, and mean artifices of licentious and profligate men'. Prostitution was not the result of innate female perversion, he wrote, but of 'a want of good government among us' that let male sexual desire 'loose to ravage' on the basis of hydraulic beliefs about the dangers of its confinement.[77] According to Madan, prostitution was not the result of *over*-regulation of hydraulic male desire, leading to its eruption in illicit forms, but of its *under*-regulation, coupled with a political climate centred on male entitlement.

Madan's proposed solution was to reinforce the principal social mechanism designed to regulate sexual desire: marriage. Using scriptural authority, Madan argued that marriage was constituted not by the rituals of the ceremony, but by 'the *union* of the *man* and *woman* as *one body*', and that British laws should therefore compel male buyers to take responsibility for the women whose bodies they had purchased, by considering them husband and wife. Madan's treatise principally caused controversy because it advocated polygamy. And his cousin, the poet William Cowper, criticized him for the naïve assumption that marriage was devoid of the same patriarchal inequalities that he identified in prostitution. In a poetic retort, *Anti-Thelyphthora*, Cowper anticipated that Madan's 'feverish' 'dreams' would result in 'Large population on a liberal plan,/ And woman trembling at the foot of man'.[78] But Madan demonstrated that it was possible to deviate from the hydraulic justification of male sexual entitlement that dominated mainstream opinion. Madan faced censure and vilification for his views, but he showed that in the eighteenth century, as now, it was possible to imagine a world in which male desire is not granted uniquely free rein.

Contemporary research into the mechanism of sexual desire undermines hydraulic theory's conclusion that male libido is a primal craving whose supplications are ignored at society's peril. Many present-day sex researchers reject claims that libido is even a basic drive. The body's genuine drives – hunger, thirst, fatigue, thermoregulation – exist to motivate behaviour that keeps the body at a healthy baseline: fed but not too full, rested but not continually unconscious. Without these drives, the body would be at risk of starvation, dehydration, dangerous overheating, or hormone imbalances destroying tissues. But, as the animal behaviourist Frank Beach wrote in 1956, 'no one has ever suffered tissue damage for lack of sex'.[79] The sexologist Alfred Kinsey demolished the prevalent assumption that withheld male orgasm was physically dangerous because of the 'painful' fluid 'pressures which have accumulated in the testes', pointing out that 'blue ball syndrome' or 'stone-ache' was a fallacy, and that women too experience very similar physical symptoms from 'unrelieved erotic arousal' that derived only from 'muscular tensions in the perineal area': not from the obstruction of fluid force.[80] Both were harmless, he stressed.

In her refreshing book *Come As You Are: The Surprising New*

Science That Will Transform Your Sex Life, the sex educator and researcher Emily Nagoski argues unequivocally that sexual desire is not a drive. It is in fact, she writes, an 'incentive motivation system': desire is motivated by the incentive of an 'attractive external stimulus'. Arousal and desire are not impelled by some sort of internal bodily force – fluid or otherwise – driving inexorably towards a particular object. Instead, arousal arises from the interplay between the body's Sexual Excitation System (its sensitivity to ideas and sensations stimulating arousal) and its Sexual Inhibition System (the sensitivity to ideas and sensations diminishing arousal). A person's level of sexual desire at any one moment is the result of this negotiation in the light of context: 'the circumstances of the present moment – whom you're with, where you are, whether the situation is novel or familiar, risky or safe, etc – and your brain state in the present moment – whether you're relaxed or stressed, trusting or not, loving or not, right now, in this moment'.[81]

Sexual desire as described by Nagoski has much more in common with David Hartley's theory of how the association of ideas structures sexual desire than with the hydraulic theory that constructs sex as a drive. Associationism is an approach to emotion that, like hydraulics, continues to survive to the present day, most obviously in the guise of CBT. The idea of sex as a drive is so tenacious, Nagoski writes, partly because the mind contains a 'monitor' that assesses people's progress in attaining their expectations, and triggers frustration, anger and despair when that progress is slowed. It makes the experience of unsatisfied sexual desire *feel like* a thwarted drive, a tidal flow of longing crashing against its obstructions, even though it emphatically is not. But Nagoski also shows that the principal reason for the enduring popularity of sex-drive theory is political – 'men's sense of sexual entitlement' constructs, at the deepest level, how many men and women anticipate, experience, explain and self-narrate their encounters with male sexual desire. 'If you think of sex as a drive, like hunger or thirst, that has to be fed for survival,' she writes; 'if you think that men in particular ... need to relieve their pent-up sexual energy, then you can invent justifications for any strategy a man might use to relieve himself. Because if sex is a drive, like hunger, then potential partners are like food. Or like animals to be hunted for food. And that's both factually incorrect and just *wrong*'.[82] Shere Hite also described the extent to which the conception of male sexual desire as a drive – and particularly the assumption that male orgasm must take place in a vagina – is 'psychologically conditioned' by a patriarchal, heteronormative culture.[83] Hite also concluded that '[o]ne of the worst forms of this pressure' on women to consent to sex against their wishes 'comes from the idea that a man's need for "sex" is a strong and urgent "drive," which, if not satisfied, can lead to terrible consequences'. The concept of the sex drive, she emphasizes, 'amounts to justifying men in whatever they have to do to get intercourse – even rape'.[84]

As well as demolishing the principal medical claims and political deployments of hydraulic theory, recent research also discredits the 'safety-valve' argument that visiting prostituted women reduces incidences of male sexual violence. There is, in fact, a direct correlation not between paying for sex and reduced sexual aggression, but between punting and *increased* rates of rape and misogyny. A 2015 study shows that male 'sex buyers' are 'more likely to express a preference for impersonal sex, had greater hostile masculinity, had greater self-reported likelihood of raping, and had a greater history of sexual aggression'. Far from providing a hydraulic relief for antisocial tendencies, the attitudes shown by punters to prostituted women – attitudes encapsulated by the man who compared 'a prostitute' to 'a cup of coffee, when you're done, you throw it out' – exacerbate their misogynistic beliefs and behaviours elsewhere, and those men are more, not less, likely to rape.[85]

Hydraulic theory and the language of physical laws of tension, stress, fluid dynamics and electrical energy to depict how emotion operates are most often deployed to align male violence or libido with inevitable unstoppable forces of nature. To question this is not to reject the application of such laws to the physical world, but to reject their application to the workings of emotion and desire. The psychologist Susan Aylwin emphasizes that 'the mind is not a tangible mechanism with tangible structures, even if the brain is'. Emotion does not function 'as a kind of mental clockwork, with tension in the wound-up spring'. Such theories, explains Aylwin, confuse 'mind' – cognitive faculties, such as consciousness, perception, memory, judgement – with the physical 'brain'.[86] Most contemporary neuroscientists, psychologists, psychiatrists, psychotherapists and philosophers agree today that emotion is emphatically not the product of the motion of fluids, or tension in the nerves, which might be described using physical laws. Instead, emotion is generally thought to be produced by, variously, mental feedback on the body's homeostatic mechanisms (hunger and illness are likely to generate negative emotions); sensory responses such as pain; physical symptoms and changes such as crying or sweating; and the mind's perception of such behavioural changes occurring in the body. Emotion is believed to reflect both trans-historical impulses, such as recoiling in fear from an adder – the evolutionarily embedded response that Darwin experienced – and cultural mores and shibboleths characteristic of particular moments in time and place. Emotion and lust are considered to comprise both physiological changes and cognitive ideas, rather than being produced by a tangible bodily substance or fluid. So they cannot be subject to the same laws of nature governing waterfalls, steam, coiled springs, or any of the other physical phenomena to which they are so frequently compared.

John Brown's *Elements of Medicine* seemed to provide Thomas Beddoes with the cutting-edge medical theory he needed to describe how pneumatic medicine might treat ill health, and why the people's desires, when suppressed, so often erupted into violent protest. The weaknesses of hydraulic theory would become apparent to him in the near future. But, by the end of 1794, Beddoes had found a venue in Hope Square for the preliminary researches that were needed before he could open his proposed 'Pneumatic Institute'; he had alighted on a comprehensive theory on which his hypothesis for health might rest; and he had a specific question to investigate: could gases successfully treat consumption and/or paralysis? If fruitful, Beddoes' work would go down in the annals of medicine as the first systematic experiments to confirm Brown's revolutionary identification of the life-force as a fluid substance within the body, and the most resounding proof of the medical use of 'airs'. It would secure a place in political history, too, providing incontrovertible scientific evidence to reject authoritarian government as a dangerous provocation of hydraulic outbursts. All that remained was to locate enough money to obtain premises for the Pneumatic Institute itself, and to fund its staff and expensive pneumatic experiments. Beddoes' hopes for his scheme were to be lifted by an upturn in the political mood: after the prospect of crushing defeat, out of the clouds came a renewal of hope, thanks to events in Britain and France that would take reformers' optimism about their projects' chances of success to levels unseen since the heady days between the French Revolution's outbreak in 1789 and the summer of 1792.

Chapter 10

COME NOW, YE GOLDEN TIMES

t the end of September 1794, the *Times* blazoned across its front page: 'Detection of a plot to assassinate the King'.[1] The *True Briton* reported tremulously that 'it is with a degree of emotion which it is impossible for us to describe, and which True Britons alone can feel, that we communicate to the public the existence of a *plot* for the assassination of our most gracious and excellent King'. It fleshed out the story in tones of similar indignation:

> This horrid attempt was to be carried into execution at the theatre, and in a manner of entirely their own device. The British nation will hear with equal horror and amazement, that a poisoned arrow was to be aimed at the breast of our beloved and amiable Monarch. This was to be directed from the pit through an air machine, or a particular construction, while a riot should have been raised, which would of course have attracted the general attention of the audience.[2]

The *Oracle* traced the blame back to the London Corresponding Society, which, they said, had 'broach[ed] such doctrines as induced the young enthusiasts to believe such a crime would be beneficial to the country ... they hate, and they despise, and they destroy'.[3] A few days later, the Privy Council – the formal body of advisors to the monarch, comprised of the nation's most senior politicians – called a meeting. As a result, between 4 and 7 October 1794, four men were arrested for their part in the 'Pop-Gun Plot': Paul Thomas Lemaitre, a watch-case maker from Soho; John Smith, a Westminster bookseller; George Higgins, a warehouseman at a Fleet Street druggist; and a mechanic and watchmaker, Thomas Upton. All four were members of the LCS. The first three were committed to prison, but Upton was released – suspiciously, the others may have thought – with financial assistance from the Treasury towards his family's maintenance.

Brass-founders around the Fleet Street area would later testify that on 8 September 1794, Upton and two other men had visited their shops, asking 'for a tube three foot long, and of five-eighths of an inch diameter in the bore'. It was also alleged that, on the same day, they had visited John Hill, a woodturner, and commissioned him to make 'a bit of wood like a ruler to cast from, with marks to shew it was to be cast hollow'. The Pop-Gun Plot was laid at the feet of Lemaitre, Smith and Higgins, who were said to have concocted the idea of making a 'certain instrument for the purpose of discharging an arrow and also a certain arrow to be charged and loaded with poison ... to kill and put to death our said Lord the King', and that they had employed Upton to oversee the project.[4] The arrests occurred at the end of a summer that had seen the authorities come head-to-head with the reform movement.

In 1793, the Prime Minister William Pitt had established the Alien Office as a subsidiary of the Home Office. The Alien

Office had set up a secret network of government spies, who included MPs, postal officials, local police forces and 'ordinary patriotic members of the public who wrote in'.[5] The remit was to identify French émigré spies concealed as refugees, and also to unearth British supporters of the revolution. The informers were adept at infiltrating radical political organizations. The Home Office politician William Wickham, who employed informers to monitor the LCS, praised the Alien Office as 'the most powerful means of Observation & Information ... that was ever placed in the hands of a Free Government': it was a 'System of *Preventitive* [*sic*] Police'.[6] Its establishment ushered in a climate of paranoia among Britain's political societies, in which members looked upon their former friends with suspicion, and took measures to conceal their activities.

They were not worrying for nothing. In June 1793, the Unitarian Thomas Fyshe Palmer, a pastor in Dundee, one of the Scottish centres of reform, attended a meeting of a recently founded society, the Friends of Liberty, mostly comprised of working men. Another member, a weaver called George Mealmaker, addressed the meeting, voicing the key aims of reformers – wider suffrage, annual parliaments – and criticizing increased taxation after the declaration of war with France. Palmer helped Mealmaker to revise his address for publication as a handbill, and it was sent to printers in Edinburgh in July. News of Mealmaker's pamphlet quickly reached the authorities, who arrested Palmer on 2 August, on suspicion of leading revolutionary activity in Britain. He was confined to jail in Edinburgh, released on bail, and then summoned to appear at court in Perth on a charge of treason on 12 September 1793. To almost everybody's surprise – considering that Mealmaker and other society members testified that Palmer was not the pamphlet's author – he was found guilty and sentenced harshly, to seven years' transportation, which was upheld even after many in the House of Lords and Commons tried to procure a reversal.[7]

Palmer's trial followed hot on the heels of another harsh sentencing of a Scottish reformer. Thomas Muir – the tall, stocky lawyer son of a Glasgow hop merchant and grocer – had helped to found the Association of the Friends of the People in Edinburgh in late 1792. He became vice president of various Edinburgh reform societies, assisted in establishing others around Scotland, and entered into correspondence with the Society of United Irishmen, a coalition of Irish Anglicans, Catholics, dissenters, Whigs and reformers founded by the barrister Theobald Wolfe Tone in October 1791. The United Irishmen had similar objectives to the British reform associations, coupled with an emphasis on Irish national sovereignty. When Muir attended a convention of delegates from Scottish reform societies in mid-December 1792, he read out a printed address from the United Irishmen calling for the organization of conventions in all three kingdoms, to bring together the British Isles' reform movement as a whole. Alarmed at the prospect of this potentially revolutionary activity, the authorities arrested Muir for sedition in early January 1793. After being released on bail, he travelled to London and then to Paris, where the declaration of war between France and Britain prevented him from returning to Britain for his trial on 25 February. In his absence, Muir was outlawed and struck off as a lawyer. He seems to have decided to emigrate to America, boarded a ship bound for Baltimore, but disembarked at Belfast, and travelled to Dublin to meet the city's prominent United Irishmen. By 30 July 1793, Muir was back in Scotland; he was immediately arrested and thrown into Edinburgh prison. His trial took place on 30 August, for exciting disaffection through seditious speeches and reading out seditious writings, encouraging the reading of seditious publications, and circulating seditious papers. Muir decided to defend himself, and he used the sixteen-hour trial to make rousing political speeches. But the jury was packed with militant loyalists, and on 31 August Muir was found guilty by unanimous

verdict, and was sentenced to the unusually stringent punishment of fourteen years' transportation. He remained imprisoned
in Edinburgh until November, when he was shipped to a prison
hulk on the Thames to await his transportation to Botany Bay.[8]

While Muir and Palmer were awaiting transportation, the
type of unifying convention for which the United Irishmen had
called took place in Edinburgh. The third of a series of Scottish
Conventions, this 'British Convention' was also open to English
delegates. It began on Tuesday 19 November 1793 with admin-
istrative house-keeping: a roll-call, a committee appointed to
devise rules, and the shuffling of managerial roles. Over the following fifteen days, the delegates debated, in orderly, minuted
fashion, historical, theoretical and practical issues ranging from
the precedent set in Saxon England for universal suffrage, to the
disappointing nature of Pitt's leadership, strategies for 'diffusing
political knowledge through the Highlands of Scotland', maintaining connections between all Britain's reform societies, and
assisting Irish 'friends of liberty' who 'have a sham Parliament,
which lords it over them'. The voice of Maurice Margarot –
chairman of the LCS and representative of the United Political
Societies of Norwich – was one of the loudest. On 2 December,
Margarot rallied the delegates by emphasizing that the sheer
numbers of reform society members – over 25,000 from the
London, Sheffield and Norwich societies alone – 'would shew
their enemies, that the Convention was not to be despised'.
But two days later his tone had sobered. 'Spies' were present
at the Convention in the guise of 'strangers', he warned, and
'are using every endeavour to put a stop to our meetings'. In
revolutionary France, conventions of like-minded activists had
formed an alternative to conventional political power, so the
authorities were suspicious of this British Convention. When
the delegates arrived the following day, the panic-stricken secretary informed them that his papers had been seized by the
sheriff; that Margarot – along with another LCS representative,

Joseph Gerrald; William Skirving, the co-founder of the Scottish
Society of the Friends of the People; and various other leading
delegates – had been arrested and charged with sedition; and
that the apparently 'illegal and unconstitutional meeting' was
now 'dissolved'.[9]

Before the trials of Margarot, Gerrald and Skirving, William
Godwin wrote to Gerrald. Despite the unpromising outcome
of Muir's trial a few months earlier, he encouraged Gerrald to
make 'use of this opportunity of telling a tale upon which the
Happiness of Nations depends'. The publicity surrounding
Gerrald's trial, Godwin anticipated, might allow him to 'conver[t]
thousands & progressively of Millions to the cause of Reason
& public Justice. You have a great stake,' he continued: 'You
represent us all.'[10] The gamble did not pay off. Gerrald gave an
eloquent speech in his own defence, but on 30 December 1794,
he was sentenced, like Muir, to fourteen years' transportation.
Godwin could only write to the papers in protest, comparing
the behaviour of Pitt and Dundas to Robespierre: 'We declaim
against the French, & we imitate them in their most horrible
atrocities.'[11]

In the wake of the convictions of the 'Scottish Martyrs', as
Margarot, Gerrald and Skirving came to be known, the spring
and summer of 1794 were edgy and warped by ubiquitous
mistrust. The Society for Constitutional Information and the
LCS reported sudden upsurges in membership, but suspicion
of the presence of informers played on old members' minds.
Citizens across the political spectrum were fearful for their
lives. Reactionaries, whipped into frenzied paranoia by biased
newspapers, were terrified of apparently continual eruptions of
violence and threats of radical plots. The discovery in Edinburgh
and London in spring 1794 of a hoard of pikes intended, it was
said, for a revolutionary coup plotted by Robert Watt, a member
of the Scottish Friends of the People, seemed to confirm their
worst fears: that supporters of the British reform movement were

'Jacobins' intent on 'insurrection, rebellion and revolution', as the *Dumfries Weekly Journal* reported.[12] For reformers, the Pitt administration's increasingly repressive measures – the prosecution of Paine, for example, after the 1792 Royal Proclamation against Seditious Writings and Publications – was an affront to a hard-won, fragile and still extremely limited democracy; and they became tensely vigilant, on the lookout for informers who would consign them to trial for thought-crime, for merely 'imagining the death of the king'.[13]

On 22 May 1794, Pitt suspended Habeas Corpus, legitimized by 'An act to empower his Majesty to secure and detain such persons as his Majesty shall suspect are conspiring against his person and government'. Suspension of Habeas Corpus meant that radicals could be imprisoned for long periods without trial. And following the successful arrest and prosecution of Muir, Palmer, Margarot, Gerrald and Skirving in Scotland, and suspecting that the LCS was about to call a General Convention, the authorities now made a move on the leaders of the principal English political societies. On 12 May 1794, the LCS's chair, Thomas Hardy, was arrested by a team of Bow Street Runners and king's messengers; he was interrogated before the Privy Council, along with six others, and committed to the Tower of London. The following day, the political lecturer John Thelwall was arrested at his lecture rooms in Beaufort Buildings off the Strand, his books and papers were confiscated, and he was also placed in the Tower. John Horne Tooke, aged fifty-seven, had a long history of involvement with the reform movement: he had recently joined the Friends of the Liberty of the Press, as well as helping found reform clubs in London, in Aldgate and Southwark, organizing a dining club for the Society for Constitutional Information, and assisting Hardy in drafting the LCS's constitution. A few days after Hardy's arrest, Horne Tooke sent a letter to Jeremiah Joyce, a Unitarian minister and member of the Society for Constitutional Information, wondering if it was 'possible to get ready by Thursday'. The note referred to the preparation of a pamphlet for print, but it was intercepted by an informer and interpreted as the clarion call for an insurrection, and Horne Tooke and Joyce were both arrested and confined to the Tower too.

Under the suspension of Habeas Corpus, there was no rush to move to trial, and the leading lights of England's reform movement lingered in prison until October. The intervening months saw further arrests and imprisonment for treason, conspiracy and armed rebellion across the country, particularly among the artisans of Norwich's and Sheffield's political societies. Towards the end of the summer, the people reacted. Rioting began in London in August 1794 against the practice of 'crimping' – kidnapping, essentially – to raise recruits for the army in the new war against revolutionary France, and influential members of the police force believed that the LCS was responsible, forcing the LCS to issue a reiteration of its non-violent position, *Reformers not Rioters*.[14] On 9 October Godwin read in a newspaper that his great friend Thomas Holcroft – a warrant for whose arrest had been issued when Hardy, Horne Tooke and Thelwall were rounded up – had turned himself in. Horrified, Godwin applied to the Privy Council for permission to visit him, and applied himself to securing the imprisoned radicals' release in the way he knew best: through careful, rational argument. On 21 October, Godwin's *Cursory Strictures on the Charge Delivered by Lord Chief Justice Eyre to the Grand Jury, October 2, 1794* was published in the *Morning Chronicle*, to much greater interest and effect than the muted title suggests. Godwin pointed out that there was no evidence that the LCS or the Society for Constitutional Information were republican or regicidal organizations, and that the Lord Chief Justice, Sir James Eyre, was therefore attempting to unlawfully expand the definition of treason to encompass mere criticism of the government, or he was requiring the Grand Jury 'to discover, if they can, a secret purpose, totally unlike that which the associators profess'. 'This is the most important crisis, in the history of English liberty, that the world ever saw,' Godwin concluded resoundingly.[15]

Godwin's attack on Eyre was still ringing in the ears of everyone in the courtroom when the first of the imprisoned radicals, Thomas Hardy, was called to trial, on 25 October 1794, four days later. Hardy had been imprisoned, first in the Tower and then in Newgate, for five months after his arrest. His defence barrister was Thomas Erskine, who had lost his position as Attorney General to the Prince of Wales when he had offered to represent Tom Paine in 1792. In his defence of Hardy, Erskine followed Godwin's lead, denying the LCS had any aim beyond parliamentary reform, and he deftly reminded the jury that those bastions of the establishment, Pitt and Lennox, had themselves, until recently, been enthusiasts for reform – the very political position they now sought to criminalize. He also soberly informed the jury of the tragic news that Hardy's wife had died in childbirth and her baby was stillborn, possibly due to the shock of Hardy's arrest and the invasion of their house by a loyalist crowd. The trial lasted twelve days, and on 5 November the jury retired for three hours (a very long time for an eighteenth-century jury). They returned a verdict of not guilty.[16]

Twelve days later, the trial of John Horne Tooke began. Also defended by Erskine, his trial lasted six days. This time the jury only retired for two minutes, before finding him not guilty. John Thelwall was tried next, from 1 to 5 December. And he, too, was acquitted. Jubilant, applauding crowds met each of the friends of liberty outside the courtroom, and carried Hardy through the streets of London, past his old shop. The LCS issued commemorative medals, and established a tradition of anniversary dinners to mark Horne Tooke's acquittal. Erskine became famous as 'the incomparable defender of national liberty', commemorated by hundreds of medals, images and busts distributed as insignia of liberty and reform. In Sheffield, the

Constitutional Society organized a procession through the city
to greet the return of William Camage and Henry Hill, two
likewise 'long-confined and much-injured friends ... who were
arrested in May last for *Treasonable Practices*'. The Sheffield procession was led by 'the bright blaze of upwards of 200 flambeaus
and torches', and its participants carried a silk flag embroidered
with the slogan 'The Liberty of the Press' and lanterns inscribed
with the names of sympathetic jurors. Camage and Hill's coach
carried an 'emblematical transparent painting, supported by two
patriotic swine' – a reclaiming of Burke's 'swinish multitude' –
and depicting the Goddess of Liberty holding 'a medallion of
Thomas Erskine resting on an altar, on the base of which was
inscribed this motto – REFORMATION TO THE WORLD'.[17] Horne
Tooke dared to suggest that the arrest, prolonged imprisonment
and trial of radicals had been 'the best thing our prosecution
could have done, for the cause of freedom': drumming up publicity for their cause, and showing Pitt's administration in a terrible
light. The 'still better thing which they' could do, he concluded
provocatively, was 'namely [to] hang us'.[18]

Those accused of the Pop-Gun Plot were not so lucky as this
first wave of acquitted radicals. The suspension of Habeas
Corpus meant that John Smith could be moved to Newgate
Prison without evidence of guilt, and for an indefinite period
of time, until the case came to trial. In October 1794, Smith
was initially placed in the 'felons' side' of the prison, where 'the
walls were naked, damp, and mouldy, with one chair only and a
broken table' and 'without any hope of being brought to trial'.[19]
It soon took its toll, and Smith became intensely ill, especially
during the harsh winter that he spent in a cell with no window
panes.

Smith and his family had been friends with the physician
James Parkinson, who practised in Hoxton, in east London, for
nearly twelve years before they both became active members

of the LCS. Parkinson was shocked by Smith's plight, and visited him so frequently in jail that some newspapers began reporting that Parkinson himself was 'implicated with [Smith] in the horrible plot'. Parkinson was astounded to find that 'a near relation actually received a condolatory visit from a friend, who had heard, from various persons, that I was in DOUBLE IRONS in Newgate'.[20] He had been friends with the leaders of the LCS since before it was founded, and counted John Thelwall and the radical publisher Daniel Isaac Eaton (who had lived nearby in Hoxton until 1792) among his closest associates. Parkinson shared Beddoes' obsession with the inextricable relationship between political and medical reform, and he had also been motivated to publish political pamphlets in the years immediately after the French Revolution. In 1794, Parkinson was made a member of a 'Committee of Correspondence', a secret subsidiary of the LCS, after eleven previous members were confined to the Tower for suspected sedition following the suspension of Habeas Corpus in May. The Committee of Correspondence was responsible for coordinating certain LCS publications, managing internal relations and disputes between members, and arranging financial support for the families of victims of Pitt's repressive legislation. One of Parkinson's first responsibilities was to mediate a dispute between the men accused in the Pop-Gun Plot: Thomas Upton, John Smith, Paul Thomas Lemaitre and George Higgins. Upton, who had only recently joined the society in early summer 1794, was accused by Smith and Higgins of having set 'fire to his house in order to defraud the insurance office' and his responsibility for collecting subscriptions for the families of imprisoned radicals was summarily suspended.[21] '[I]n a great rage', Upton accused Smith, Higgins and the rest of the Committee of Correspondence of making dangerously unsubstantiated claims. Paul Thomas Lemaitre described how Upton's 'countenance behaviour and language gave him more the appearance of a madman' and admonished that 'he does not deserve the name of *"Citizen"*.[22] Lemaitre seconded a proposal to expel Upton from the LCS, and two days later Upton challenged him to a duel. A mutual acquaintance apparently persuaded the two men to apologize and shake hands.

When those same four men – Upton, Smith, Higgins and Lemaitre – were arrested for allegedly plotting to murder the king with a poisoned arrow blown through a gun, Parkinson interceded with the Privy Council, and, after five months' confinement, Smith was finally moved to the more comfortable 'state side' of Newgate prison. Parkinson accused Pitt of manifesting the absolutist tyranny of the French old regime, combined with 'a daring imitation of that *system of terror*, which Frenchmen, during a revolutionary government, had, by the diabolical machinations of internal and external conspirators, been driven to adopt'.[23] Eventually, in early May 1795, after seven months' imprisonment and no date set for his trial, the Privy Council agreed to release Smith on bail, but refused to return many of his possessions.

Around the time of Smith's release, the Privy Council received a letter from a man they had been attempting to locate for some time: one of Upton's companions as he walked around Fleet Street to commission manufacturers of different elements of the 'pop-gun'. This man had been identified as another physician with a radical political bent. Robert Thomas Crosfeild wrote to the Privy Council to confirm that Upton had told him he was making an airgun, but not its purpose.[24] After the arrests of Lemaitre, Smith and Higgins, Crosfeild had travelled to Bristol, where he considered setting up as a physician, as Beddoes had done.[25] But debts had impelled him to 'go abroad as the surgeon of a ship' and he had signed up for eighteenth months aboard the *Pomona*, employed in South Sea whale fishing.[26] Within a short time, the *Pomona* was boarded and captured by French ships, and Crosfeild taken prisoner and incarcerated on a temporary prison ship at Brest, along with around 240 others. Crosfeild's fellow prisoners would later testify that Crosfeild introduced himself as 'Tom Paine', 'sang some very bad seditious songs', and that the Pop-Gun Plot 'was his constant subject every day after dinner ... for five months together'.[27] In August 1795, Crosfeild was repatriated to Britain under a prisoner-exchange agreement with revolutionary France, and was immediately arrested at Fowey, in Cornwall, after a fellow detainee reported him to the magistrate at Mevagissey. He was put in the Tower of London, where he wrote a medical treatise on scurvy, based on his experiences in France, and five months later, on 14 January 1796, he, Lemaitre, Smith and Higgins – but not Upton – were all formally indicted for 'being moved and seduced by the instigation of the devil as false traitors against our said Lord the King', and placed in Newgate. They were arraigned on 6 April, pleaded not guilty, and the first case – Crosfeild's – was tried on 11 May 1796.

Crew members of the *Pomona* and fellow prisoners from Brest all testified to Crosfeild's boasts of his vital role in a treasonous conspiracy, and parish constables at Fowey described his attempts to bribe them to allow him to escape. James Parkinson testified to the tensions in the LCS that had given Upton a motive for falsely implicating Lemaitre, Higgins and Smith.[28] The prosecution had an insurmountable problem: a charge of high treason required at least two witnesses and formal proof. Upton was a vital witness to the others' purportedly treasonous conspiracy, but he was nowhere to be seen. His wife reported that nearly three months previously, Upton had left their house early in the morning, very drunk, having handed her his wax seal. The next day, the watchman brought her his hat, which had been found by the side of the Thames. 'I believe he is dead,' she said. The jury deliberated for an hour and forty minutes and brought back a verdict of not guilty against Crosfeild. A week later the cases against Lemaitre, Smith and Higgins were dismissed, and the men released, twenty months after their initial arrest.

The likelihood is that the story of the trip around Fleet Street to commission components of an air gun was the foundation of an elaborate attempt by Upton to frame Lemaitre, Higgins and Smith, in revenge for their attempts to expel him from the LCS. There was no evidence to implicate Lemaitre, Higgins or Smith in the incident. But much later, Lemaitre would raise the possibility that the 'Pop-Gun Plot was concocted by' at least three informers who had infiltrated the LCS 'to get [Lemaitre] out of the way before he could expose them fully to the Society'.[29] His suspicions were partly correct. Documents in the National Archives show that 'spy Metcalfe' and 'spy Groves' were reporting back from the LCS's most secret niches. It is unlikely that the whole Pop-Gun Plot was fabricated by Pitt's administration, as Lemaitre hinted. But it was certainly in the Privy Council's interests to fail to unpick Upton's accusations, and to use his fabricated plot to their advantage: as evidence to support the picture the reactionary press was painting of the reform movement as fomenting a violent, regicidal revolution. In the first part of the *Rights of Man*, Paine had described how, in Britain, it is from 'plots *against* the Revolution ... that all the mischiefs have arisen'.[30] This had basis in truth: Pitt, Dundas and Grenville, and various loyalist newspapers, seem to have been intent on fleshing out a stereotype of the violent, seditious radical, to justify repressive moves against the reform movement's aims. If the so-called Pop-Gun Plot did really exist, the mastermind was not Lemaitre, Smith or Higgins, but William Pitt, the prime minister, himself.

The collapse of the Treason Trials was met with a public response that temporarily bore out John Horne Tooke's prediction that the trials were 'the best thing our prosecution could have done, for the cause of freedom'. Thousands of new members flocked to the London Corresponding Society and the Society for Constitutional Information. The outcome of the Pop-Gun Plot was unknown as yet, but Pitt's failure to suppress the radical movement by successful prosecutions contributed to a climate of unexpected optimism at the beginning of 1795. Many reformers dared to hope that change was in the air: that the reactionary backlash to the progress of reform was now on the wane. A long parliamentary debate at the end of December 1794 raised the possibility of ending the war with France: 'Was Denmark, Sweden, or even Genoa ... in a state of anarchy, in consequence of being at peace with France?' demanded Charles James Fox. 'To him it was astonishing how any set of men ... could have so worked themselves up, as to risk such a War on the wild theories they had nourished' that 'we were fighting for our Constitution, our liberties, religion and lives'.[31] Some were optimistic after the Treason Trials that Habeas Corpus would be reinstated.[32] And the Whig politician Charles Grey, and the MP for Norfolk, Thomas Coke, were both hopeful that a 'change' had 'taken place in the sentiments of ... constituents', and that there was now a 'universal' hostility to the 'profligate views of Ministers, and the ruinous tendency of their measures', which extended across 'nine-tenths of the country'.[33]

This feeling that the wind was changing was coupled with new-found hope about France. On 26 July 1794, Maximilien Robespierre had given a speech to the National Convention in France, indicating that he suspected Convention members of plotting a conspiracy against the Republic. Alarmed that they would be next for trial and execution, on 27 July the Convention ordered the arrest of Robespierre and five supporters, declaring them outlaws, which meant they could be executed within twenty-four hours, without trial. Robespierre tried to shoot himself, but only shattered his jaw; and he lay bleeding on a table in the Committee of Public Safety until the next day, when he was guillotined without trial in the Place de la Révolution. Wordsworth recalled first hearing the news that 'Robespierre was dead' and 'That he and his supporters all were fallen' as one of the happiest moments of his life:

Great was my glee of spirit, great my joy
In vengeance, and eternal justice, thus
Made manifest. 'Come now, ye golden times',
Said I, forth-breathing on those open sands
A hymn of triumph, 'as the morning comes
Out of the bosom of the night, come ye.'

Of the Jacobins, he declared:

Their madness is declared and visible;
Elsewhere will safety now be sought, and earth
March firmly towards righteousness and peace.

Robespierre's fall compounded the optimism of many British supporters of the revolution, that, now, at last, 'The mighty renovation would proceed'.[34] Since the September Massacres, the hopeful mood among radicals and reformers had been qualified by concerns about the suitability of France as a political model. But now that hope – that the French Revolution was part of an inexorable extension across the world of wider suffrage and more representative government, since the Glorious Revolution – reasserted itself with vigour.

The political upturn coincided with an exciting time for Beddoes. At the end of July 1794, he had begun openly soliciting subscriptions for his Pneumatic Institute, hoping that some £4,000 (roughly equivalent to £150,000 today) would be sufficient to get it underway.[35] Back in 1792, three of Beddoes' childhood friends – the Shropshire ironmaster William Reynolds, his half-brother Joseph Reynolds, and the Shifnal physician William Yonge – had pledged £200 each 'to bear a part of the expence attending the construction of a pneumatic apparatus, and the salary of a person to construct and superintend it'.[36] On 12 August 1794, Beddoes turned his incipient friendship with the wealthy pottery heir Tom Wedgwood into a professional arrangement. He wrote to Wedgwood fully explaining his pneumatic project and successes to date, and asked him to help circulate his calls for subscriptions. Beddoes drafted a 'Proposal for the Improvement of Medicine', to ascertain the medical power of synthetic 'airs' by establishing an institution dedicated to that research. Wedgwood helped distribute that proposal and publicised its claim 'that the permanently elastic fluids [i.e. gases] seemed possessed of considerable powers upon the human system; and that it is highly desirable to ascertain, how far these powers can be applied or modified so as to afford relief to suffering humanity'.[37] And he contemplated a greater investment too. 'I think I shall contribute,' Wedgwood wrote to his brother Jos, 'as the attempt must be successful if it only goes to show that "airs" are *not* efficacious in medicine.'[38]

At the turn of the new year, Wedgwood's powers of patronage were suddenly enormously augmented. In November 1794, his father, Josiah, consulted Erasmus Darwin: his face had swollen, with excruciating pain in his jaw, which was initially attributed to a decayed tooth. On 2 January 1795, Josiah asked his wife, Sally, and his daughter Susan not to disturb him. When they could not open the door the following morning, a local carpenter scaled a ladder to enter through the window – and found Josiah dead in bed, probably from cancer of the jaw.[39] His fortune (around £25 million in today's money) was divided among his children, and, at the age of twenty-three, Tom Wedgwood found himself very rich indeed. But he had little idea of how to spend such a vast sum. He had no inclination to get married, and his own mental and physical health had deteriorated since his breakdown almost three years previously. He was experiencing rapid and bewildering mood-swings, from 'almost manic elation to incapacitating depression', dread of being left alone, and his physical symptoms included utter exhaustion and weakness, dizziness, sensitivity to the cold, and excruciating stomach pains.[40] Wedgwood's brother-in-law Robert Darwin, Erasmus's son, was convinced that Wedgwood's illness was caused by the mind, not the body, and encouraged him to consult Beddoes, whose interest in the connection between the two was well known. But Wedgwood, who was anticipating little relief in his symptoms, decided that a job or career was likely impossible, even if a miraculous cure were found, and resolved 'to exert myself for the good of my fellow creatures' by helping to fund worthwhile projects.[41] At first, he corresponded with the Quaker bookseller Samuel Phillips about distributing books – with a ban on fiction – among the labouring poor. But Beddoes' Pneumatic Institute offered a much more exciting, innovative prospect: one that, perhaps, might even shed light on the cause, and cure, of his own mysterious illness. So Wedgwood donated a staggering £1,000 to Beddoes' project (the equivalent of around £40,000 today), over a quarter of the required total. His investment took the Pneumatic Institute much closer to the point of opening.

In the autumn of 1794, Beddoes had published his first sustained piece of research on the subject: *Considerations on the Medicinal Use and Production of Factitious Airs*. Part One of what became a six-part work described his early experiments in which kittens were exposed to oxygen and then drowned. Part Two was written by an influential new collaborator. In 1775, the Scottish inventor, engineer and chemist James Watt had entered into partnership with Matthew Boulton, and the new firm of Boulton and Watt became the major producer of steam engines throughout the Industrial Revolution. Watt came up with the concept of horsepower, and the 'watt' unit of power was named after him. Watt had become aware of Beddoes' research through the Lunar Society, of which he was a member, as were Erasmus Darwin and Richard Lovell Edgeworth. In June 1794, Watt's beloved daughter Janet had died, aged fifteen, from tuberculosis. In the wake of her death, he threw himself into supporting Beddoes' research into the use of synthetic gases as a cure for consumption. Within a few months, he had drummed up subscriptions from Boulton, from the botanist and physician William Withering (who discovered the cardiac uses of digitalis), the gun manufacturer Samuel Galton, all the major physicians in Birmingham, and Beddoes' long-standing friend, the chemist James Keir. In 1795 subscriptions also came from illustrious people such as Beddoes' father-in-law Richard Lovell Edgeworth; seven further members of the Wedgwood family, who subscribed '50 pounds each'; influential members of the Edinburgh medical establishment, including the chemist Joseph Black, the physician Andrew Duncan, and the anatomist Alexander Munro; the geologists James Hutton and James Hall; and the entire Royal Medical Society of Edinburgh.[42]

James Watt did more than simply mobilizing subscriptions. One of the first major obstacles to the Pneumatic Institute's success was its lack of equipment. Soon after his daughter's death in 1794, Watt began planning and making apparatus that could be used to collect and wash poisonous and medicinal gases. He quickly became preoccupied by Beddoes' technical problems, trying out substances that might be used to generate particular gases, and devising methods to cool gases and regulate the quantity administered to patients. Beddoes had been dispensing 'factitious airs' via an oiled silk bag, but Watt described his idea of a 'beehive' helmet that could be placed over the head of patients too weak to hold the bag. Before long, Watt suggested that his firm might become formal partners with the Pneumatic Institute, responsible for the manufacture of all its instruments. He reassured Beddoes that his appetite was for medical advancement, not financial profit.[43]

Beddoes stressed to Watt that he was not certain of the curative effects of the airs, but that the Pneumatic Institute was merely intended to test a hypothesis. Watt's enthusiasm remained unabated. Part Two of *Considerations on the Medicinal Use and Production of Factitious Airs* was published in October 1794, including a letter from Watt minutely describing his proposed apparatus. Copies of the *Considerations* sold rapidly, and Beddoes seized on this as a sign 'of a rising disposition in mankind' to improvement.[44] He also knew that 'the speedy sale of my pamphlet' was 'owing to the great name of Watt'.[45] By the end of 1794, the collapse of the Treason Trials contributed to Beddoes' optimism. It was reported swiftly in provincial newspapers, and his sister Rosamund wrote jubilantly from Shifnal to their aunt about Horne Tooke's acquittal, and planned to order shoes from Hardy in support. Beddoes himself wrote to Hardy to assure him that 'every man ... is rejoicing at your hon[oura]ble acquittal ... You had fallen upon times when the violence of a sanguinary faction in a foreign country had rendered the very name of reformation odious here ... You have escaped!'[46] He even started making plans to generate a new petition in favour of parliamentary reform. Suddenly there seemed everything to play for.

Across the Channel, Mary Wollstonecraft, too, sensed herself to be in a state of suspense at the end of 1794. She was soon to write that 'the slow march of time is felt very painfully. – I seem to be counting the ticking of a Clock, and there is no clock here'.[47] In December Little Fanny was seven months old, and had grown to look 'very like' her father, Gilbert Imlay. Wollstonecraft was taken aback at the love she felt for her small daughter, which had begun in a 'very reasonable' vein, 'more the effect of reason, a sense of duty, than feeling'. She set great store by exercising reason over emotion in the name of virtue. But 'now', Wollstonecraft wrote with some concern, Fanny 'has got into my heart and imagination, and when I walk out without her, her little figure is ever dancing before me'.[48] Her maternal sentiments seemed to be exceeding their remit, threatening her rational control. To onlookers, too, Wollstonecraft's new maternal role undermined their previous conception of her as an austere, independent, essentially solitary agent. The lawyer

Archibald Hamilton Rowan, a United Irishman who escaped to France from a Dublin prison, was surprised to encounter Wollstonecraft and Fanny at a fête for Jean-Paul Marat in September. Rowan recalled: "'What!" said I within myself, "this is Miss Mary Wollstonecraft, parading about with a child at her heels ... So much for the rights of women," thought I.'[49]

In August 1794, Imlay's business dealings in Le Havre had come to an end, and he longed to return to Paris, to witness the fallout of Robespierre's execution. From their shared family house, he came and went, and eventually persuaded Wollstonecraft to return to Paris with Fanny. She arrived after a gruelling journey, in which her carriage had overturned four times, to find a ghost city: Paine in prison, Helen Maria Williams in Switzerland, the Barlows in Hamburg. She implored her sister Everina to visit and fill the void that winter: 'I want you to see my little girl, who is more like a boy.'[50] And then Imlay, too, departed: for London. Wollstonecraft pleaded for him to 'Bring me then back your barrier-face,' alluding to their sexual assignations at Paris' old toll barriers. 'Or,' she threatened, 'you shall have nothing to say to my barrier-girl; and I shall fly from you, to cherish the remembrances that will ever be dear to me.'[51] Fanny unwittingly stoked Wollstonecraft's imagination to keep alive her passionate hopes for her relationship with Imlay. Fanny 'often has a kiss, when we are alone together, which I give her for you, with all my heart,' Wollstonecraft assured Imlay; 'I am kissing her for resembling you'.[52]

Fanny's eerie resemblance to Imlay seems to have helped Wollstonecraft to forget, temporarily, her isolation in Paris; the erosion of her hopes. And the sheer joy she found in raising Fanny placed her, despite her serious anxieties, often in a 'sprightly vein'.[53] But she could not remain oblivious to the gathering storm clouds for long. Imlay was engrossed by new business schemes and Wollstonecraft was coming to suspect that he was not the rational defender of women's rights that she had once thought. As 1794 hovered on the verge of 1795, Wollstonecraft was left contemplating the dilemma that taxed all radicals and reformers in the 1790s. When the wind begins to change, and the likelihood of hope materializing is dusted away to reveal disappointment's darkening outline, at what point should one adapt or jettison those once bright hopes?

Towards the end of 1794, pantisocracy, too, was hanging in the balance. The pantisocrats had settled on their colony's chief tenets and its basic practical arrangements, but money was still woefully short. Coleridge returned to Cambridge in October 1794, and without his charismatic intensity, the balance of power within the group shifted towards Robert Southey; with that shift, many of the agreed terms of the project began to come into question. It was no longer clear what form pantisocracy would take; or, indeed, whether it would happen at all.

In late October, shortly after Coleridge's departure, Southey made an eccentric new acquaintance who contributed to the widespread feeling that, as the year drew to a close, the world was on the cusp of a new and uncertain era. 'Tomorrow,' Southey wrote to Grosvenor Bedford on 24 October, 'I am to be introduced to a prophet!!'[54] This was almost certainly a Bristolian called William Bryan: a mellifluously spoken man with 'clear and gentle' eyes, of whom Southey would later write that his 'resemblance to the pictures of our Lord' was 'so striking as truly to astonish'.[55] Bryan had felt himself to be 'favoured with a knowledge of the Divine Goodness' since the age of four, and he had spent much of his first thirty years experimenting with different religious sects, including the Quakers. In October 1788, Bryan had been introduced to another seeker, John Wright, a carpenter who had moved his family from Leeds to London to find his spiritual home. Both men came together for the first time at the New Church, or the church of the New Jerusalem, on Eastcheap, in the City of London.

The New Church was a religious movement informed by the writings of the Swedish theologian and mystic Emanuel Swedenborg, whose works inspired a number of utopian speculations in the late eighteenth century. Many of the proponents of these utopias predicted that radical political and sexual change would occur at the time of an impending, apocalyptic 'millenium': a Second Coming of Christ that would entail the destruction, and miraculous transformation, of the old corrupt world. At around the same time that Southey met Bryan, Southey's friend William Gilbert, a poet living in Bristol, was working on a millenarian poem, *The Hurricane*, based on Swedenborg's claim that Africa was the source of a potent spiritual and sexual energy that facilitated 'conjunction of man with the God of the universe'.[56] Gilbert argued that the American and French Revolutions were the results of the dissemination of this virile African 'potency' via the slave trade, and were preliminary stages in the millennium's arrival.[57]

Swedenborg's claim about Africa had stimulated real-life colonial projects too. On Christmas Day 1788, the Swedish abolitionist Carl Bernhard Wadström was baptised in the New Church in Great Eastcheap. Soon after, he helped to draw up the constitution for a colony in Sierra Leone based on Swedenborg's views on sexuality and marriage.[58] Although Swedenborg was enthusiastic about the spiritual potential of sex, he was virulently opposed to promiscuity. For Swedenborg, God had provided marriage as the conduit through which passionate desire might be channelled towards 'the Lord alone'. Energetic monogamy in marriage – 'love truly conjugial; that ... cannot exist otherwise than between two' – was the counterpart to spiritual love of one god.[59] Polygamy was a form of adultery with God Himself. Wadström followed Swedenborg in envisaging the married unit as the nucleus of his colony, the 'representative, in miniature, of the Civil Society'.[60] Southey was fascinated by Swedenborgianism, even choosing Philip James de

Loutherbourg – faith healer, co-founder of the Swedenborgian Theosophical Society, and millenarian – to draw the frontispiece for his poem *Joan of Arc* in mid-1795.[61] It is possible that Swedenborg's views on marriage influenced the pantisocrats by providing a model of liberated sexuality that did not undermine the institution of monogamous marriage.

Shortly after William Bryan met John Wright in 1788, at the same New Church of which Wadström was a member, he was informed by 'the Spirit that I should be required to go to Avignon'.[62] In the four volumes of his *Memoirs Illustrating the History of Jacobinism*, published in Britain in 1797, the French Jesuit Abbé Augustin Barruel would claim that at Avignon there was a secret masonic society in which 'pupils of Swedenborg' came 'to mingle their mysteries with those of the Rosicrucians and other Masons both ancient and sophisticated'.[63] According to Barruel, 'the Illuminées of Avignon' were the 'parent stock of all those that have since spread over France with their abominable mysteries', and their 'secret dens of conspiracy' were the birthplace of 'Jacobin clubs'.[64] When Bryan received his mystical instruction to visit Avignon, he was working in London as a bookseller and copperplate engraver. His wife had recently given birth to a stillborn infant and she was 'extremely weak' and distressed by his imminent departure.[65] John Wright, who was lodging on Tottenham Court Road, experienced the same revelation as Bryan, but his wife was more encouraging: she gave him half a guinea towards his journey to Avignon, and promised to nurse and reconcile Bryan's wife.

On 23 January 1789, Bryan left London for Dover. He had initially planned to wait for Wright, but the voice of God boomed to '*Stop for no man*'.[66] The two men reconvened the following evening in Dover, set sail at 9 a.m. the next morning, and proceeded to walk over 150 miles from Calais to Paris, then travelled 400 miles further south. Bryan later told Southey that, once in Avignon, the two men 'proceeded to the house of the prophets' and met with a friendly reception.[67] For seven months, Bryan and Wright lived with the Avignon society. Every evening at 7 p.m. they congregated to commemorate Jesus' death, and Wright recounted that, 'very often' 'the furniture in the room . . . shook' and 'we were told that it announced the presence of angels'. One day, they met the 'ARCHANGEL RAPHAEL' sitting under a tree, eating bread.[68] The weather was unseasonably cold; four inches of snow fell in Lyon in May, which Wright interpreted as a sign of the impending apocalypse, especially given the increasing tensions that preceded the fall of the Bastille. Towards the end of the summer, the two men were granted permission to return home, and they arrived in Britain in September 1789. Wright easily fell back into his former employment as a carpenter, but Bryan had acquired a reputation for insanity. After two years of dabbling in small engraving and printing projects, he trained as an apothecary, dedicated to dispensing 'the Spirit of Truth' alongside more traditional 'physic'.

In 1791, Bryan made his first major prophecy. During his time with the Avignon brethren, he declared, the Holy Word had informed him that great revolutions would take place across the globe before 1800. The Turkish Empire would be destroyed by a boy living in Rome, the Pope would die and be replaced by a candidate who would 'close the scene of Papal Tyranny and Authority', and the Jews would be restored to the Holy Land. In France, the revolution would lead France to an even 'greater Degree of Purity and Perfection' and Britain would emerge from the early-1790s 'as or more glorious than France'.[69] Similar predictions of global upheaval occur throughout history: the journalist and author Oliver Burkeman has pointed out that the phrase 'these uncertain times' has punctuated newspapers, journals and books in every decade since the seventeenth century.[70] But, as the *Times* noted in early 1795, millenarian prophecies are particularly seized upon in times of 'great political convulsions'.[71] Millenarianism provides an account of historical progress that allows many people to comprehend dramatic geopolitical changes whose trajectory otherwise seems baffling and terrifying.

Three years later, in late December 1794, William Bryan repeated his prophecies in a published pamphlet; and Robert Southey heard 'the whole system from his own mouth'.[72] Bryan's restatement of his apocalyptic predictions had been motivated by the advent of a rival prophet called Richard Brothers: a tall, good-looking ex-naval officer who had become convinced in 1791 that he was hearing God's judgements against London's corruption. Brothers had written letters to the British government, warning that the French Revolution was one of these judgements against corruption, and that to support the French monarchy was to oppose God. In 1794, Brothers published the two-volume *A Revealed Knowledge of the Prophecies and Times*, in which he thundered that the following year would see the ten 'lost tribes' of Israel reconvene in the midst of a global crisis in which Brothers himself would seize the throne from George III, leading to an exodus to Palestine and the rebuilding of Jerusalem. He predicted that the 'English Government ... will, by the fierce anger and determined judgement of the Lord God, be removed, annihilated, utterly destroyed'; and that the 'King and Parliament of Great Britain' would be decimated if they did not give up the war with France.[73]

Brothers and Bryan both interpreted the French Revolution as an optimistic, if tempestuous and apocalyptic, materialization of God's will and the Second Coming. Not all prophets espoused such radical politics. Another self-styled prophet, Mrs S. Eyre of Cecil Street, London, published long letters testifying to Brothers' role as a harbinger of decay and destruction, and advocating, not greater liberty and equality, but the stricter regulation of women's behaviour in particular, to fend off such cultural decline, 'as [women] are the authors of all wickedness'.[74] But on the whole, millenarians found themselves aligned with radicals. Joseph Priestley was not opposed to millenarianism, considering that prophecies like Bryan's were testimonies to the divinely ordained direction of history.[75] In 1795, the satirical cartoonist James Gillray portrayed Brothers as a *sans-culotte* in his print *The Prophet of the Hebrews*. Bryan's friend William Sharp was called as a witness during the Treason Trials, and nonplussed the court by asking those present to subscribe to his engraving of the Polish patriot Kościuszko, who had led a failed uprising against Imperial Russia.[76] (Southey too was mesmerized by the 'gallant Kosciusko [*sic*]' at the end of 1794, and described how 'every feeling of Nature militate[s] against – Russia'.[77])

As with working-class radical societies – of which many were members – millenarians were open to censure for demonstrating emotional 'enthusiasm'. The literary critic Jon Mee explains that 'enthusiasm' originally connoted actions carried out under 'the *inspiration* of God', such as, in its most extreme form, the shaking and quaking of certain religious sects. By the eighteenth century, 'enthusiasm' referred, in Mee's words, to 'perversions of feeling and experience' resulting from unregulated exercise of the emotions (and sometimes the imagination), often under the misapprehension of being divinely inspired.[78] By the 1790s, men such as Edmund Burke and Horace Walpole were charging the popular political societies with secular enthusiasm: 'enthusiasm without religion'.[79] Many reformers and radicals consciously distanced themselves from precisely that type of unruly, violent behaviour. Godwin and Thelwall emphasized the rational, enquiring nature of political involvement; Beddoes and others repeatedly pointed out that the most anarchic and violent demonstrations had been conducted by Church and King groups, not the popular reform societies; and Coleridge and Wollstonecraft stressed the need to firmly regulate and direct emotion in the name of virtue, rather than 'letting it all hang out'. But the revolutionary bent of millenarians like Bryan and Brothers, with their air of insanity and credulous accounts of furniture shaking under the influence of angels, helped to cement the association, propagated by reactionaries, between radical politics and dangerous enthusiasm that threatened to degenerate from liberty to anarchy.

William Bryan was initially not convinced by Brothers' *Revealed Knowledge*. His old friend John Wright had been converted when a co-worker brought him a copy, and even published his own pamphlet supporting Brothers' prophecies.[80] Wright introduced Bryan to Brothers in December 1794, but Bryan had a dream vision shortly before the meeting, which he interpreted to mean that Brothers was a dark power sent to test his faith in his own prophetic powers. Brothers' fame had grown significantly beyond Bryan's; the former was piqued by the latter's insubordination, and he wrote a peeved letter to him.

Over the following days, all the tension that had been building towards the end of 1794 came to a head. Bryan resolved to prove conclusively that Brothers was not Christ but was mundanely mortal 'by plunging my *knife* into his *heart*'. And on 12 December, on a coach travelling between Marlborough and Devizes on the way to Bristol, at 7 p.m., Bryan 'heard a voice pronounce in a very awful tone, the following words: '*Woe to the city of Bristol! the cry of innocent blood is against it: it shall be shaken, and fall.*' The Corporation of Bristol's incursions against liberty, in the Bridge Riots of September 1793 and in its merchants' encouragement of slavery, warranted its imminent destruction, Bryan explained. He predicted that on 31 December 1794, 'the Lord shall reign with his saints upon the earth' and 'many whom you have despised in their low estate, shall ... trample under their feet, as a vile thing, as the small pebbles, those treasures which you have most prized'.[81]

The prophecy came in the midst of unexpected relief and sudden optimism among radicals in the wake of the collapse of the Treason Trials; uncertainty as to how Pitt would now proceed; consciousness that revolutionary France was balanced on a knife-edge between anarchy and order after Robespierre's execution; hope for the conclusion of the war; and discombobulation in strange weather – 'autumnal flowers continued till December' to be abruptly obliterated by 'a severe ... frost, falling and melting snows, and floods'.[82] For Southey, on the cusp of translating pantisocracy from an insubstantial idea to a living reality – as for radicals across Britain, including Beddoes, and Wollstonecraft in France – Bryan's prophecy occurred at a moment of tense hiatus. The nation was precariously poised between progress and reaction. And the radical movement knew itself to be suspended, for a moment in time, between hope and whatever comes after hope: would it be realization and joy for their projects' successes, or disappointment and despair?

III

Disappointment Sore

Chapter 11

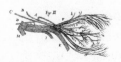

FALLING INTO THE
COMMON LOT OF HUMANITY

New Year's resolutions have a 4,000-year old history,
and citizens of eighteenth-century Britain seem to
have been as diligent as we are today in making resolutions – and failing to stick to them. In 1792, G. M. Woodward's
series of illustrations, *A Long String of Resolutions for a New Year*,
poked fun at citizens doomed to failure in their efforts at self-
improvement, many of which involved taking better control
of their own and others' passions. An ancient man 'resolv'd to
lead a new life'; a sot 'resolv'd not to drink so much in future';
and a coiffed, painted lady 'resolv'd to bid farewell to Scandal'.
A downtrodden housewife, gripping a club in resentful fury,
and 'resolv'd to be meek no longer', was perhaps more likely
to realize her hopes.[1] Across historical and global cultures,
the start of a new year consistently raises high expectations –
coupled with silent acknowledgement of the poor odds of the

materialization of those hopes. The advent of 1795 was no exception. Wollstonecraft, Beddoes, Coleridge and Southey all dared to hope that the upbeat months at the end of 1794, after the fall of Robespierre and the collapse of the Treason Trials, offered a more promising climate for their individual aspirations. But, for most of them, the new year was to usher in nothing but disappointment.

In Bristol, 31 December 1794 – the date that William Bryan had prophesied that the city would 'be shaken, and fall' – came and went with little event. William Bryan gave up his plan to murder his rival prophet Richard Brothers when he missed the coach that was going to transport him across town. That coach went on to overturn in thick fog, and Bryan took it as a portent that, had he attempted to knife Brothers, it would have been in opposition to God's will. After another visit to the more famous prophet, Bryan began to warm to him. Brothers, for his part, seems to have put on a performance of humility, and Bryan finally published a testimony to his authenticity, having been delivered, in his own words, 'from the power and operation of the spirits of darkness'.[2]

After the failed prophecy of 31 December, Bryan was joined in his proselytizing on behalf of Brothers by a Member of Parliament, Nathaniel Brassey Halhed, who circulated 1,000 copies of *The Whole of the Testimonies to the Authenticity of the Prophecies and Mission of Richard Brothers* around the House of Commons and beyond. Sales of Brothers' *Revealed Knowledge* rocketed in the strange atmosphere of early 1795, going through four editions; in the midst of this decade of revolutions, citizens could believe equally in a future of apocalyptic punishment or blissful reward. Bryan adapted his original prophecy: now, he proclaimed, it was London, not Bristol, that would be destroyed by earthquake, and not on 31 December 1794, but on 4 June 1795, the king's official birthday. This concurred with a prediction made by Brothers, that on a day between 25 October 1794 and 'the Beginning of the Month called June 1795', London will 'burn like an oven, and . . . consume the wicked from the face of the earth – like the stubble of the field'.[3]

On 23 May 1795, twelve days before the assigned date, the *St James' Chronicle* reported that 'Several families have actually left their residences in various parts of Rutland, and set out for London, on their intended journey to Jerusalem with Richard Brothers!!!' Some flocked to London in the days before 4 June, but many others fled. The religious writer William Huntington recorded that numerous Londoners tried to 'escape Mr. Brothers' predicted destruction of this city'. Businesses across the capital were shut up. The retired soldier John Stedman characterized the climate as 'disloyal, superstitious . . . Many leave town.'

At around 7.30 p.m. on the allotted day, the heavens opened. The city streets resounded with heavy rain and hail, while thunder and lightning tore apart the skies above London. John Binns, a member of the LCS who was on his way to a meeting, took shelter in a hotel and found over fifty other citizens, along with their children, huddling amid 'a general feeling and expression of alarm'. 'It seemed to me,' Binns continued, 'that every one in the room knew something of Brothers' prophecy'. The prophet himself was watching the storm from a private insane asylum in Islington, where he had been transferred at the end of March, having been arrested at the beginning of that month for treasonable practices.

The storm passed, and London remained standing. A few days later, Binns visited Brothers, who assured him that 'the earthquake had, at his earnest and oft-repeated intercession, been, by the Almighty postponed, and the destruction of London averted'. By August, Brothers' followers had started to melt away, and the *Analytical Review* recorded that '[p]ublic curiosity, with respect to the *prophecies* of Mr. Brothers, is, we apprehend, by this time nearly exhausted'.[4] Brothers would remain in the asylum for another eleven years.

In 1954, the young social psychologist Leon Festinger, together with two colleagues, Henry Riecken and Stanley Schachter, conducted an experiment into the conditions under which individuals might jettison, cling onto, or shore up their collapsed hopes in the face of failed prophecies. (Schachter's interest in hope and prophecy was directly related to his fascination with emotion more generally: he would go on to formulate the influential 'Schachter-Singer' hypothesis of emotion, which states that when physiological arousal occurs, the brain searches its environment for clues about how to label the emotion – occasionally leading to its misinterpretation of an emotional situation.) In late September 1954, the *Chicago Herald* reported on its back page that a 'SUBURBANITE' had received a 'PROPHECY FROM PLANET' that a flood will 'SWAMP US ON DEC. 21'. The researchers infiltrated a small apocalyptic cult that gathered around a housewife, Dorothy Martin (given the pseudonym 'Marion Keech' in Festinger's resulting book, *When Prophecy Fails*), who claimed to be receiving messages from 'superior beings from a planet called "Clarion"', who predicted a flood 'from the Arctic Circle to the Gulf of Mexico', from which believers would be rescued by alien craft. Festinger and his colleagues observed the behaviour of individual cult members as 21 December 1954 came and went, once the 'promised pickup at midnight had not materialized'.[5]

Festinger formulated the theory of 'cognitive dissonance' to describe the cult members' psychological process in the wake of this instantaneous 'disconfirmation' of their hopes. He showed that, if a belief has been invested in significantly – by the believer making large sacrifices, such as financial investment, exposure to social ridicule, or loss of career – then the pain of realizing the erroneousness of that belief in the wake of a disconfirmation will be too great to bear. Such believers will instead adopt a position of 'cognitive dissonance': they will attempt to reinforce the belief, despite the disconfirmation's evidence that it is false. That shoring up of faith often takes place through increased proselytizing, and sometimes by adapting particular details (such as delaying the date on which the flood would happen, as Brothers had done). For many believers, especially those who have invested heavily in a particular outcome, it is preferable to subsist in a wilfully adopted state of delusion than to face the 'sunken costs' of their unsuccessful gamble and accept that 'I am not always right in the choices I make'.

After the flood of 21 December and the alien pickup failed to materialize, the Clarion cult members who had made the largest sacrifices redoubled their commitment to the group. They engaged for the first time in seeking new recruits, telephoning newspapers and making further preparations for a later alien collection. But those whose investments in the cult had been far less significant found it easier to enter a state of disillusionment. They gave 'up on Marian and her beliefs', accepted they had been wrong, and simply never attended another meeting.[6]

Festinger stressed how important it was to forge a community of like-minded believers through proselytizing, in order to sustain faith.[7] For the Clarion cult, enlarging their community became a priority after the 21 December disconfirmation. They began to engage in 'increased proselyting' through 'publicity seeking'; 'personal proselyting'; 'secrecy', which made the group more secluded; and 'the persistence of prediction'. Festinger noted that this followed a historical pattern: increased enthusiasm for proselytizing had also taken place in 1666 after the arrest of Sabbatai Zevi, who had proclaimed himself the promised Jewish Messiah; and in the mid-1840s, after the 'Great Disappointment' of the prophecy by William Miller of Christ's Second Coming in 1843–4. '*If more and more people can be persuaded that the system of belief is correct,*' reflected Festinger, '*then clearly it must, after all, be correct.*'[8] The more people who believe, the more likely it seems that the prophecy is accurate.

Festinger's theory of cognitive dissonance is useful to

understand responses to the disconfirmation of William Bryan's prophecy that Bristol would be destroyed on 31 December 1794, and Richard Brothers' prediction that London would be devastated by an earthquake six months later. Bryan had invested significantly in the millenarian movement. He had sacrificed his career and reputation to pursue his role as prophet, and had given up his own relative fame to devote himself to boosting Brothers' profile. After the disconfirmation of his initial prophecy, Bryan engaged in significantly increased proselytizing, publishing a testimony in favour of Brothers' prophecy and circulating his writings, adapting his original forecast and revising the date of the predicted apocalypse. It was less painful to shore up his faith than to accept his error and face the 'sunken costs' of his investment – the loss of his career, finances and reputation – for nothing.

Beliefs, such as those of the Clarion cult, only finally collapse when the believers themselves drift away: when the weight of evidence provided by repeated disconfirmations proves too dissonant to sustain the faith necessary to make a group cohere. Richard Brothers' popularity would melt away when the prophet was no longer at liberty to form the centre of a community of followers. And the erosion of community would temporarily prove fatal to the reform movement too. Festinger's theory offers a way of thinking about the disappointment that eroded radicalism in the second half of the 1790s. The years from 1789 to 1794 showed how the radicals' faith in the moral rightness and practical viability of their aims could withstand numerous 'disconfirmations' of their feasibility. Popular political societies and the press offered opportunities for sociability and the exchange of ideas that allowed discouraged radicals to shore up their faith in their principles and in their 'attainableness'. But from 1795 onwards, Pitt and his administration turned their attention to dismantling community structures, with fatal consequences for the radical movement and its hopes.

*

It did not take long for the pantisocrats' high hopes of mid-to-late 1794 to begin to crumble. In late October, Coleridge received a letter from Southey, warning him that there had been 'a Revolution in the College Green', at his aunt's house. Southey had finally plucked up the courage to divulge his plans to marry Edith Fricker and emigrate to America, and his aunt, Elizabeth Tyler, had responded by 'declar[ing] she will never see my face again or open a letter of my writing' and turned him 'out of doors in a wet night'. As Southey was leaving, Tyler's servant Shadrach Weeks had apparently taken him to one side, conspiratorially whispering, 'send for me when you are going'. Weeks' enthusiasm prompted Southey to reflect on the possible advantages that a cohort of servants might present to the pantisocratic community. If servants could take over the necessary manual labour, he mused, the original pantisocrats would be freed to concentrate on philosophizing. Instead of the equal division of labour, property, time and political representation that the pantisocrats had initially advocated, Southey now suggested an alternative: that servants might be allowed to 'dine with us and be treated with as much equality as they would wish – but perform that part of Labor for which their Education has fitted them'.[9]

Coleridge – who had returned to Cambridge, making frequent visits to London – was horrified. He had assumed that the pantisocrats were all equally committed to stripping away the inequalities of eighteenth-century society manifested in material wealth, familial assets, suffrage, and access to education, in order to reform the passions. And here was Southey, apparently eager to reinforce those socially constructed disparities. '*Southey* should not have written this sentence,' Coleridge exclaimed angrily, charging him with using the word 'Equals' when he really meant 'Slaves': '*this* is *not our* Plan – nor can I defend it'.[10]

Southey's suggestion was soon accompanied by more proposed modifications to the scheme. Until 1794, America had declared neutrality in the French Revolutionary Wars between Britain and France, but the relationship between the French republic and the US began to disintegrate when the latter refused to pay its debts to the new French administration. By the autumn, Southey thought that war between Britain and America also seemed 'inevitable' and that the Atlantic crossing was now potentially too dangerous. Coleridge had also become anxious about discrepancies between the attractive land prices quoted by Thomas Cooper and the much higher costs now being asked by London agents. At the beginning of December, Southey wrote to Grosvenor Bedford that 'my feelings strongly plead' for 'settl[ing] in Wales', adding that 'it will be exactly upon the same plan as to America. – that of establishing among ourselves the generalization of property & the equalization of labour'.[11] Wales offered cheaper and safer passage; more easily obtainable and familiar land; proximity to necessary supplies, and to friends and family reluctant to join the colony itself; and a quick and easy escape in the event of failure. But it was a much more conservative suggestion. America was a blank slate, ideal for utopian imaginings, with constitutional foundations conducive to the pantisocrats' political principles. Wales was tainted with the same political inequalities they were attempting to escape. '[I]t is nonsense,' wailed Coleridge in desperation: 'We must go to America, if we can get Money enough.'[12]

Southey's change of heart was partly prompted by his mother's growing reluctance to emigrate across the Atlantic. It seemed a huge, irrevocable step and pantisocracy was attracting increasing criticism and ridicule around Bristol and Bath. With Coleridge still in Cambridge and London, the scheme's political imperatives receded behind its domestic aims. Southey's mother and younger brothers could only be persuaded to accept a much less radical version of the plan. But Coleridge censured the idea of shifting to Wales as 'the sickly offspring of disgusted Pride', and the inclusion of a servant class as the means through which

'a System so impregnable in itself should be thus blasted'.[13] He
worried that 'taking a Welch Farm' would convert the high ideals
of the male pantisocrats' fraternity into a bland business proposition to develop land, 'some 5 men *going partners* together'.[14]
Towards the end of the year, these fears were joined to further
concerns, when George Burnett told Coleridge that Southey had
also suggested dramatic modifications to the policy to equalize
private property. Southey's 'private resources were to remain
[his own] individual property, and every thing to be separate
except on five or six acres. In short,' Coleridge wrote with scorn,
'we were to commence Partners in a petty Farming Trade. This
was the Mouse of which the Mountain Pantisocracy was at last
safely delivered!'[15]

At the end of December 1794, handsome Robert Allen –
who had wavered since the start – definitively pulled out of the
scheme. Coleridge sensed that pantisocracy was on the verge
of collapsing, and decided, reluctantly, that compromise was
preferable to complete renunciation. He wrote to Southey that
he had seen 'the wretchedness, that would fall on the majority
of our party from any delay, in so forcible a Light – that . . . I am
most willing to give up all my other views and embark immediately with you'; even to Wales. Southey dispatched his brother
Thomas to 'the coast of Caernarvonshire or Merioneth in North
Wales' to scout for a suitable spot. Lovell estimated that a total
of only £300 would be sufficient to set up a rudimentary form of
their original plan. And they agreed to depart in three months'
time, in March 1795 – the date originally set for emigration to
America.[16] Coleridge applied himself to finding a job to fund his
contribution, and decided to accept 'the Reporter's place to the
Telegraph – live upon a guinea a week – and transmit' the rest
to the pantisocrats.[17]

Pantisocracy had always been a far greater gamble for
Coleridge than for Southey. The stakes he had risked and lost
were clear when, towards the end of October 1784, he received a

letter from his old love-interest, Mary Evans, who had heard the rumours about the 'absurd and extravagant' emigration scheme. Following news of Coleridge's engagement to Sara Fricker, Evans had herself become engaged to someone else. Coleridge was distraught by this 'disappointed *Affection*'.[18] He wrote a sonnet, 'Thou bleedest, my poor Heart!', rebuking himself for having 'listen[ed] to Hope's whisper', and for having failed to nurse his love for Evans 'with an agony of Care'. To Southey, he wrote anguished letters, admitting to having 'mistaken the ebullience of *schematism* for affection' for Sara Fricker. Coleridge wrote off his 'whole Life' as 'a series of Blunders!' and described how 'my Heart is withered within me – and Life seems now to give me disgust rather than pain'.[19]

Southey's own commitment to Edith Fricker remained firm: their relationship had preceded, rather than been instrumental to, pantisocracy. He now accused Coleridge of 'neglect respecting' Sara. Coleridge was aghast at the horror of his situation, entirely of his own making. 'To lose her!' he cried, referring to Evans; 'I can rise above the selfish Pang. But to marry another – O Southey!'[20] Coleridge's reckless gamble had also put Sara in a grim situation. Two other men, 'one of them of large Fortune', were paying 'Addresses' to her, and she was left with the unenviable dilemma of breaking her engagement and marrying a rich man, which would incur social disapproval and the loss of Coleridge; or seeing out her engagement, though she was painfully aware of Coleridge's diminished affections and the public ridicule surrounding his project. '[S]he vainly endeavors to conceal from me how heavy her heart is with anxiety, how disquieted by Suspense,' Coleridge wrote guiltily, and resolved to '*do my Duty*'.[21] At the end of 1794, another sonnet summed up his state of mind: 'O pleasant days of Hope – forever flown!/ Could I recall you! – But that thought is vain.'[22]

By January 1795, Coleridge was still in London, hiding from the evidence of his declining hopes. Southey had been pleading, cajoling, reprimanding and ordering him to return to Bath since November, to do his 'duty' to Sara Fricker, as he had promised, and to help plan the new Welsh iteration of pantisocracy; but with no success. '[I] am resolved, whatever be the consequence, to be at Bath by Saturday [3 January]', Coleridge assured Southey.[23] But on 2 January, he recited a litany of excuses: 'The roads are dangerous – the horses soon knock'd up . . . I have a sore throat – and am not well'.[24] Wednesday 7 January was mooted instead. Southey and Lovell walked over thirty miles to meet his coach at Marlborough, but Coleridge was not on it. After passing the rest of the week in an unpleasant 'state of expectation [that] totally unfits me for anything', by 'Friday night' the coach had still yielded 'no Coleridge!' Southey wrote. 'I am kept in exercise by walking to meet the coaches,' he continued in wry frustration; 'why will he ever fix a day if he cannot abide by it'.[25]

Finally Southey warned Coleridge that, if he would not get on a coach, Southey would come to London himself to 'reclaim his stray'. 'Come to me at the Angel Inn,' Coleridge replied sheepishly: 'It was total Want of Cash that prevented my Expedition'.[26] On or around 12 January, after Southey had travelled for thirty hours to London and unsuccessfully scoured Coleridge's city haunts, he finally found him with an old school friend, the essayist Charles Lamb. Southey and Coleridge had a frank conversation about pantisocracy's future, in which 'Coleridge objected to Wales & thought it best to find some situation in London till we could prosecute our original plan'. Southey still personally 'lean[ed] strongly to Wales in spite of his very strong arguments' but calmly acknowledged that it might not 'be . . . practicable', in which case he planned to 'get a place in some public office of 80 or 100 per year on which with some 50 more by writing for reviews &c'. he and Edith 'can live with frugality & happi[ness]'. By 19 January, Coleridge was ensconced back in Bristol; and '*nor would he, I believe, have come back at all*, if I had not gone to London to look for him,' Southey later wrote.[27]

Both men returned to the West Country having emotionally detached themselves from the fate of their utopian scheme. Seven months earlier, in summer 1794, pantisocracy had appeared to be the sole solution to Southey's and Coleridge's anxieties stemming from past domestic, financial and political failures and disappointments. But by early 1795, they were both making personal accommodations that reflected the decade's political trajectory. Coleridge and Southey were now seeking solutions within Britain, rather than in the utopian setting of Pennsylvania. 'America is still the place to which our ultimate views tend,' Southey wrote unconvincingly in February, 'but it will be years before we can go. [A]s for Wales it is not practicable.'[28]

Coleridge's return to Bristol, however, temporarily rejuvenated the flagging plan. Southey came back from Bath, and he, Coleridge and George Burnett took up their lodgings on College Street again. In the second week of February, Southey was oscillating between abandoning pantisocracy, and full commitment. In the same breath, he described how he was seeking a place for 'I' alone to 'best subsist' – not a community of twelve married couples – yet declared that Coleridge and his own 'names are written in the book of destiny on the same page' through their 'American Plan'.[29] With or without pantisocracy, money was a pressing concern for both men, and they devised numerous plans to drum up the £150 they estimated sufficient for a rudimentary form of Welsh pantisocracy. They had initially hoped subscriptions to Coleridge's *Imitations from the Modern Latin Poets* and Southey's *Joan of Arc* would serve, but when the works failed to raise enough money, they proposed circulating their poetry through a joint literary review, the *Provincial Magazine*, and hoped for posts on a political magazine called *The Citizen*.

The *Provincial Magazine* and *The Citizen* are chalked down in Coleridge's and Southey's biographies as 'unrealized venture[s]'.[30] When it became clear that neither would materialize, Southey and Coleridge pursued an idea that dated from September 1794. Inspired by lucrative public lectures that had recently been given in London by F. A. Nitsch on Kant, and the political lectures of religious ministers such as Richard Price and Joseph Fawcett, Coleridge and Southey had considered giving their own 'lay-sermons'. The most important precedent for successful public lectures had been set by the writer and journalist John Thelwall – according to Pitt, the most dangerous man in Britain – who had begun lecturing on 'the French doctrines of the day' in the early 1790s.[31] Coleridge enthusiastically approved of political lecturing, for reasons beyond money. Lectures articulated faith in achieving political change through the gradual and rational education of the public, a principle in which Coleridge was heavily invested as an alternative to sudden revolutionary violence.

Towards the end of January, Coleridge started to advertise his course of political lectures, and they began shortly after, probably in early February 1795. The first two took place in a room over Bristol's Cornmarket, but the third was relegated to an empty house near Castle Park, most likely because they were gaining a reputation for being inflammatory. Coleridge delivered each lecture from a rough manuscript, frequently departing into fiery ad libs that prompted his astonished audience to describe his arrival onto the Bristol scene as 'like a comet or meteor in our horizon'.[32] Coleridge's audience, and even he himself, worried that, in the midst of his 'turbid Stream of wild Eloquence,' he had a tendency to get 'entirely led away by the feelings of the moment', making outrageous claims out of hunger for effect rather than conviction.[33] Coleridge's lectures each lasted around an hour, for which he charged his audience one shilling each – the same as the cost of the last two lectures that Thelwall delivered at the Beaufort Buildings in London in December 1795. On being challenged about the undemocratic nature of 'tak[ing] money at the door', Coleridge retorted that it was necessary 'to keep out blackguards' who heckled.[34]

Into all three lectures Coleridge poured his thoughts about the political relevance of emotion and its regulation that had provided the rationale for pantisocracy. Coleridge's lectures interrogated the very nature of political conviction. They described how commitment to ideological movements was entirely dependent on participants' idiosyncratic temperaments. In Coleridge's first talk, entitled simply 'A Moral and Political Lecture', he divided the British 'Friends of Liberty' into four groups, according to the nature of their emotional investment in politics. The first category of radicals, he claimed, supported reform on the basis of kneejerk, changeable and superficial emotional reactions to news of 'French Victories' or 'French Excesses': their commitment fluctuated each time they consulted a newspaper. The third class conversely possessed 'fixed Principles', but, Coleridge sneered, they were all 'narrow and self-centering views': their activism was solely aimed at issues by which they were directly affected.[35]

It was the second group of radicals who met the full force of Coleridge's excoriation. He described how their political engagement was motivated by the passions. But whereas the temperament of the first group was 'indolent', theirs was violent and bloody: 'Unilluminated by Philosophy and stimulated to a lust of Revenge by aggravated wrongs, they would make the Altar of Freedom stream with blood, while the grass grew in the desolated Halls of Justice'. Their anger, violence, 'viciousness' and 'want [of] humanity' were the product of poverty, hunger, inequality of material resources, and deprivation of education, Coleridge surmised. In the second part of his second lecture, *Conciones ad Populum* [*Addresses to the People*], entitled 'On the Present War', Coleridge elaborated that this political faction was comprised of the uneducated labouring classes, the 'multitude, who ignorant and needy must necessarily act from the impulse of inflamed Passions'.[36] He was replicating the age-old alignment of the passions with everything politically and physically 'low', base and inferior, associating the labouring classes with displays of emotion unregulated by the 'higher' faculty of reason. Coleridge argued that Pitt's administration had dangerously exacerbated their wild passions, and he used the same hydraulic language as Thomas Beddoes, who believed that authoritarian counter-revolutionary measures were responsible for an accumulation of psychic pressure among the poorer sectors of society. The material deprivation of the poor was increased by rising taxes due to the war, Coleridge explained, and this caused 'the dark Tide of Passions [to] swell', and to 'rush from despair into guilt'.[37] This group of unruly working-class radicals was only small, he admitted, but he maintained that they were dangerous, and that their behaviour provided Pitt's administration with examples that they could use to discredit the entire radical movement.

Against these undesirables, Coleridge opposed his fourth group of radicals: 'thinking and disinterested Patriots'. These men exhibited the rational capacity to regulate their passions that was traditionally considered symptomatic of superior, refined, virtuous classes. In *Conciones ad Populum*, Coleridge celebrated how 'private attachments' in the form of 'paternal and filial duties' motivated this class of political activists to 'discipline the Heart and prepare it for the love of all Mankind'.[38] Such men (they were all men in Coleridge's imagination) had used their rational assessment of the benefits provided by 'home-born feeling' to subdue rampant self-interest, and 'encourag[e] the sympathetic passions till they have become irresistible habits'. To Coleridge, the Patriots' harmonious reconciliation of sociable sentiments and rational judgement was vastly preferable to Godwin's subjugation of emotion in favour of 'promiscuous' reason, and, at the other extreme, the 'enthusiasm ... of an unkindly order' demonstrated by the political societies, populated by Burke's 'swinish multitude'.[39]

Emotional regulation was self-evidently a political issue,

Coleridge emphasized, because the 'intensity of private attachments encourages, not prevents, universal Benevolence'. He thought Pitt's increasingly repressive legislation was so dangerous because it broke up marriages – for Coleridge, the core of community spirit – by throwing radical writers in prison, 'torn from the bleeding breast of domestic affection'.[40] Coleridge described how sympathetic care for one's fellow-citizens was an extension of familial love, rippling outwards through parishes, villages, counties, regions, nations and ultimately across the globe. Burke had arguably implied that domestic affections might be a substitute for political engagement, but Coleridge showed how they led directly to it. Coleridge found an example of such celebrated benevolence in men like the 'Scottish Martyrs': Thomas Muir, Thomas Fyshe Palmer, William Skirving, Maurice Margarot and Joseph Gerrald. This implies that Coleridge was beginning a process of reconciliation with his surroundings, finding pantisocratic virtue within British patriots rather than in American fantasies.

As Coleridge's 'moral and political' lectures ended, Robert Southey's historical lectures began. On 14 March 1795, an advertisement appeared in *Felix Farley's Bristol Journal* stating that a course of lectures 'unconnected with – at least not *immediately* relative to – the politics of the Day' would take place on Tuesdays and Fridays through the latter half of March and April. Coleridge later published his own lectures, but Southey dismissed his as 'only splendid declamation'; and no copies of his scripts survive.[41] Southey gave twelve or thirteen lectures in total, ending in late April. The intended fourth lecture, on the Roman Empire, appealed to Coleridge, who pleaded with Southey to let him deliver it instead. Southey agreed, and Joseph Cottle described how at 'the usual hour, the room was thronged. The moment of commencement arrived. No lecturer appeared!' Coleridge had simply forgotten, and Southey, furious, expressed 'his deep feelings of regret, that his audience should have been disappointed'. Cottle, with some glee, identified this moment as the disintegration of pantisocracy: when 'these two friends, about to exhibit to the world a glorious example of the effects of concord and sound principles, with an exemption from all the selfish and unsocial passions, fell, alas! into the common lot of humanity, and, in so doing, must have demonstrated, even to themselves, the rope of sand, to which they had confined their destinies!'[42]

Pantisocracy nevertheless limped on for a few more months. In mid-June 1795, the scheme lost another participant, in tragic circumstances. On 14 June Southey received a letter informing him of the death of Edmund Seward, who had been unwell for just '6 weeks'. From the beginning of their friendship, Southey had admired Seward's morally uncompromising nature.[43] In October 1794, when Seward, anxious about leaving his mother alone in Britain, had become reluctant to commit himself to pantisocracy, Southey had experienced his hesitancy as a disappointment of his expectations of Seward's moral clarity. Seward sensed this, writing to their mutual friend Nicholas Lightfoot that 'Southey seems to look upon my retraction from the scheme as a dereliction of Christianity itself'.[44] Upon hearing of Seward's death, Southey began idolizing his old friend. '[H]e taught me all that I have of good,' he wrote sadly: 'I have lost a friend – & such a one!'[45] His death was the start of a heartbreaking period for the Seward family. Edmund's brother John died two-and-a-half years later, in December 1797, and shortly after that the eldest brother, William, a lawyer in Hertfordshire, shot himself, leaving only one surviving brother, a Methodist farmer.

Within six weeks of Seward's death, Southey received a letter from his uncle, Herbert Hill, chaplain to a British factory in Lisbon. After paying for Southey's university education, Hill intended Southey to take orders, and now he forced the issue. Southey defined himself as a 'decided Humanist', an 'advocate of that Christianity ... in its native & simple beauty', and opposed to the hierarchical structure and dogma of the church.[46] Coleridge was adamant that he could not take orders. 'Southey!' he exclaimed; 'the point is, whether or no you can *perjure* yourself ... you disapprove of [the church] altogether ... It is impossible that *you* could uphold it by assuming the badge of Affiliation!'[47] By this point, in early August 1795, Coleridge had relegated the realization of his pantisocratic hopes to 'a miraculous Millenium', but he held out the prospect of 'Domestic Happiness' as 'the greatest of things sublunary' as a consolation to Southey.[48] This was one of the last mentions of pantisocracy in their letters of the time. Southey duly informed his uncle that he had 'relinquished all intentions of taking Orders' and 'meant ... to study the Law'.[49] Appalled by his nephew's recalcitrance, and by rumours of his engagement to one of the disreputable Fricker family, Hill curtly informed Southey that he was on his way from Lisbon to Bristol.

On Sunday 4 October 1795, Coleridge and Sara Fricker were '*married* – at St Mary's Red Cliff – poor Chatterton's Church,' Coleridge added as a melancholy afterthought.[50] The young poet Thomas Chatterton had committed suicide at the age of seventeen, disappointed by his failure to make a living from writing. Cottle would later describe Coleridge as the inverse of Chatterton, who was loved by his family but ignored by the literary marketplace. Coleridge was a rising star in British poetry and political journalism, but seemed completely estranged from his relations. In the years in which he lived in and around Bristol, Cottle noticed that Coleridge 'never once visited (that I could learn) any one of his relations nor exchanged a letter with them'.[51] But Coleridge hoped to forge a new family by marrying Sara. The couple took a cottage – 'our comfortable Cot' – in the village of Clevedon in Somerset, thirteen miles from Bristol, facing the Bristol Channel. Coleridge gave 'up all thoughts of the Magazine', *The Citizen*, that he and Southey had planned.

Coleridge had done a good job of convincing himself that

Sara Fricker – not Mary Evans – was 'the woman, whom I love best of all created things'. But he was acutely aware of the huge internal struggle that had been necessary to convert an engagement that had originated in 'Principle not Feeling' into a state in which he felt himself to be in 'love and ... beloved, and ... happy!'[52] In the weeks following his wedding, Coleridge began a mental enumeration of the sacrifices he had made for pantisocracy and for Southey. With the hurt feelings of a discarded lover, Coleridge wrote an angry, accusatory letter to him on 13 November 1795, tracing the respects in which Southey had disappointed him by *fall[ing] back into the Ranks* of the conservative and conventional.[53]

Southey, he claimed, had receded from 'those broad Principles, in which Pantisocracy originated' into 'self-centering Resolve': he had become obsessed with 'I and I'. Coleridge had come to suspect that Southey's proposed modifications to pantisocracy were part of a cynical, devious plan to lay *'a Plot* of Separation' by 'proposing such a vile mutilation of our Scheme, as you must have been conscious, I should reject decisively & with scorn'. Within a few months, Coleridge alleged, Southey had 'altered' from enthusiastic literary and political collaborator, 'brother' and friend, into a sham, who 'unsaluting' blanked Coleridge on the street and, to new acquaintances, denied any connection to him. And when he had pointed out these awful changes, Coleridge wrote, Southey had turned the blame back on his former friend: 'you said – I was intoxicated with the novelty of a System!' Worse, when Coleridge had reconciled himself to the weedy Welsh version of pantisocracy, Southey had opted out on the basis that the 'Plan you are going upon is not of sufficient Importance to justify me to myself in abandoning a family, who have none to support them but me'. But 'was not this *your own Plan*?' Coleridge cried in frustration; 'the plan, for which I abandoned my friends, and every prospect & certainty, and the Woman whom I loved to an excess which you in your warmest dream of fancy could never shadow out?' For pantisocracy, Coleridge had given up not only Mary Evans, but a job offer to tutor 'the Earl of Buchan's Family', and he had 'dedicated [his] whole mind & heart' to Southey's historical lectures, writing 'one half in *Quantity*', he claimed, when Southey's share in his own lectures had been 'little more than Transcription'. Coleridge's icy parting shot made it clear that Southey had disappointed all the expectations bound up with pantisocracy, communal living, and friendship: 'You have left a large Void in my Heart', he concluded. '[N]ever do I expect to meet another man, who will make me unite attachment for his person with reverence for his heart and admiration of his Genius ... But these Things are past by, like as when an hungry man dreams, and lo! he feasteth – but he awakes, and his Soul is empty!'[54]

The psychoanalyst and writer Adam Phillips has pointed out the close affiliation of disappointment with deception, citing the first English dictionary, Robert Cawdrey's *A Table Alphabeticall* of 1604, and its definition of 'frustrate' as to 'make voyde, deceive', which, in turn, meant 'to trick' and 'to disappoint'. To be disappointed was to be tricked out of a contract, to suffer the frustration of an expectation, the voiding of a desire, that once appeared on solid footing. 'He contrary his promesse dyd disapoynte them, and nothynge ayded them,' wrote Robert Fabyan regretfully in 1516, in his *Newe Cronycles of England and Fraunce*.[55] Coleridge certainly experienced his disappointment in Southey as the latter's deceitful breaking of an implicit contract, whose terms had laid out their future plans and political convictions, but also their expectations of who they really were as moral characters.

Southey received Coleridge's letter on 16 November 1795. The finality of its content was echoed in the events of the surrounding days. Southey's uncle had arrived in Bristol and made clear his intention to return to Lisbon with Southey in tow. Coleridge's letter arrived the night before his departure. Southey protested about the forced trip – 'I am not happy' – but his emotional and political attachments were painfully uncertain, and he may have secretly appreciated the opportunity to escape the contested scene. Concerned about forsaking Edith Fricker to 'calumny' and poverty if he should die abroad, on Saturday 14 November Southey and she were married in a ceremony 'performed with the utmost privacy'.[56] Now his family were, unknown to them, committed to assisting Edith if it became necessary.

Nine months earlier, Southey had written to Grosvenor Bedford describing enviously how he had 'look[ed] over your letters & find but little alteration of sentiment from the beginning of 92 to the end of 94. [W]hat a strange mass of matter is in mine during [that] period,' he reflected.[57] It had been an extraordinary couple of years. Southey had been transformed from a gloomy young man, burdened by responsibility for his family, into an eager participant in one of the most notorious radical and utopian schemes in Britain, full of optimism about his capacity to rescue not only his family, but potentially the whole of Western civilization through pantisocracy's revolutionary eradication of unsocial passions. But that 'revolutio[n] of feeling', as Cottle put it in February 1795, had not been permanent. Just nine months later the scheme was buried, and Southey's temperament, expectations and priorities had reverted to the mean. However, he did not feel as pessimistic or helpless as in 1793, and he was now resigned to the juggernaut of forces larger than himself, intent on fulfilling his responsibilities to Edith and his family, rather than transcending them. In retrospect, what had appeared to be a revolution of feeling now seemed to Southey little more than a blip, a momentary 'upheaval of thought'.[58] Shortly before leaving for Lisbon, he described to Bedford how 'my mind is considerably expanded – my opinions are better grounded' since 1792. Southey sensed that he had grown up. In particular, he added meaningfully, experience of 'error' – in the shape of

Coleridge – had done him 'much good'. Southey couldn't resist a parting shot. Of course, he concluded, despite the good that Coleridge had done him, Southey knew that 'I [had done] him more'.[59]

Chapter 12

AWAKING IN FETTERS

As the days began to grow longer in the spring of 1795, as radicals in Britain waited expectantly to discover whether the climate of renewed hope after the Treason Trials' failure would bear fruit, Mary Wollstonecraft travelled north, to seek the outcome of her own hopes for herself and her lover. By mid-April, she had returned to London, to lodgings on Charlotte Street, in Bloomsbury, that Imlay had arranged. A bad cough that had lingered throughout the winter was beginning to fade, and with a mixture of pragmatic relief and deep sorrow she deprived herself 'of my only pleasure' by weaning Fanny to bolster her health.[1] Wollstonecraft had come back to London 'with a heavy heart, not daring', after all the uncertainties and disappointments she had endured, 'to trust to the suggestions of hope'.[2] It was in response to Imlay's suggestion, but he was engrossed in a new business venture, and she swiftly suspected that his invitation was designed to stem her angry, frustrated letters rather than re-establish intimacy. But to her sisters, she

put on a show of bravado. Imlay is 'the most generous creature in
the world', she wrote, and the new opportunity that had brought
him back to London will 'enable me to be useful to you and
Everina'.[3]

In reality, Wollstonecraft was anguished – although not necessarily surprised – to discover that Imlay had 'formed another
connection; as it is said, with a young actress from a strolling
company of players'.[4] She found herself alone with Fanny, in the
apartments she had hoped would be a new family home. Unable
to relinquish her past hopes entirely, she fended off her sisters'
enquiries after the promises of a new life together, in Paris or
America, that she had made them, and she dissuaded them
from visiting. 'I know you will think me unkind,' Wollstonecraft
began, 'But Eliza it is my opinion' that 'the presence of a third
person interrupts or destroys domestic happiness.'[5] She could
not bear to reveal her vulnerability and grief made her blind to
the wounding tactlessness of her letter. Eliza had given up her
position as a governess, and had been learning French from an
émigré priest in preparation for joining Wollstonecraft and Imlay
in Paris. She was floored: 'Good God what a letter! how have I
merited such pointed cruelty?'[6]

At the beginning of May, Wollstonecraft issued Imlay an
ultimatum: live with her and Fanny, or separate. 'How can you
love to fly about continually – dropping down, as it were, in a
new world – cold and strange! – every other day?' she demanded
incredulously. 'Why do you not attach those tender emotions
round the idea of home'?[7] She blamed commerce for having
'embrute[d]' his passions: 'satiety had ... close[d] up every
tender avenue of sentiment'.[8] Wollstonecraft was railing against a
nascent change that was taking place in sex roles, against which
she would prove powerless. Earlier in the eighteenth century,
much business had been conducted from within the home, as a
'family enterprise': in cottage industries, like textile production,
women might spin and wind the yarn, while men weaved it into

cloth. The home was the site of both domesticity and business, and men and women participated in both. By the century's end, industrialization and the rise of opportunities linked to commercial speculation were causing a 'provincial middle class' to take shape, in which work – and men – were increasingly brought out of the home.[9] The labour market was becoming a masculine realm. And while 'respectable' means of earning an income were therefore increasingly closed off to women, the war with France also entrenched more rigid norms of masculinity: British men were encouraged to oppose themselves to the French and their 'effeminacy'.[10] Gillray's satirical print of 1806, *Tiddy-doll, the Great French-Gingerbread-Baker, Drawing out a New Batch of Kings*, showed Napoleon in women's clothes and apron, bodging the baking of 'gingerbread' monarchs as part of his imperialistic plan.[11]

Amid anxieties that the increasingly masculine commercial economy was lacking in morality, the home was taking on a new significance in late-eighteenth-century middle-class culture as a feminized haven of virtue. Evangelical writers stressed the importance of women's management of their husbands' spiritual progress, and of maintaining high standards of cleanliness in hygiene, bodily functions and sexual practices.[12] By the early nineteenth century, the middle-class home was governed by strict patriarchal 'manners'. The preacher John Angell James declared that 'every family ... has a sacred character, inasmuch as the [male] head of it acts the part of both the prophet and the priest of his household ... by supporting a system of order, subordination and discipline' and that 'to be a good wife is ... *woman's brightest glory since the fall*'.[13]

Even committed male radicals upheld the emerging new order's entrenchment of patriarchal sex roles. The historians Leonore Davidoff and Catherine Hall describe how James Luckock, a Birmingham jeweller who professed himself a fan of Paine and Priestley and won the title 'Father of Birmingham

Reform', declared that he and his wife were 'Equal in property –
equal in importance – equal in good intentions – equal in fidelity
and affection – equal in the estimation and favour of Heaven'.[14]
But Davidoff and Hall show how, despite these protestations of
equality, 'the Luckocks were a family organized around the idea
of sexual difference, expressed through the proper forms of masculinity and feminity'. As a married woman, Mrs Luckock (we
don't know her first name) had no property rights, and her husband devoted himself to pursuing politics whose chief purpose
was to ensure political representation for male heads of house-
holds, while 'hunt[ing] the world for business' to establish and
maintain a home in which his wife lived in obscure retirement.[15]
Earlier in the century, Rousseau's celebration of breastfeeding
and maternal sentiments had presented a revolutionary vision
of liberated natural emotion and women's important (albeit
limited) role in society, but by the end of the century, such
celebrations of women's domestic and familial roles were being
put to more conservative ends.

Wollstonecraft also found herself exposed to the great lie
of the sexual free market: the myth that it set everyone free,
as equals, in an evenly accessible landscape of opportunity.
Her female body had born the consequences of the liberation
of male desire, and she found herself confined to home while
Imlay was swaggering around the globe freely pursuing financial
and sexual openings. Wollstonecraft was opposed to marriage
because it entrenched women's disenfranchisement. She had
conceived of emotional reform as a type of work: a cottage
industry to which men and women would apply themselves in
the home, with regulated fervour. That 'unison of affection and
desire' was entirely distinct from the 'common' pursuit of sexual
'satiety' that she now saw in Imlay's behaviour.

By May 1795, Wollstonecraft had 'not only lost the hope, but
the power of being happy'. She had started to fantasize about
suicide, impressing upon Imlay 'how much active fortitude it

requires to labour perpetually to blunt the shafts of disappointment' stemming from his derogations of duty, and, at the end
of the month, she resolved to take an overdose of poison.[16] She
may have followed through.[17] Godwin later attributed her survival and determination 'to continue to exist' to Imlay's efforts.[18]
But Wollstonecraft's suicide attempt or intention came at a
time in which Imlay was absorbed in business preoccupations.
Back in France, he had purchased a cargo ship, *La Liberté*, and
with the help of a man called Peder Ellefsen he had certified it
as Norwegian and renamed it *Maria and Margaretha*, possibly
after Wollstonecraft and her Parisian maid, Marguerite. Imlay
planned for Ellefsen to sail the ship and its £3,500-cargo of
Bourbon silver from Le Havre to Norway, bearing a Danish flag
to evade the English blockade, and to exchange the silver for
grain. Ellefsen had gone worryingly silent. It became apparent
that, on arrival in Norway, he had filched both the ship and its
lucrative cargo, transferred ownership to his own family, and
moved it between harbours. Panicked, Imlay and his business
partner Elias Backman arranged for a merchant in the Swedish
city of Strömstad, Christoffer Nordberg, and the district judge,
A. J. Ungar, to investigate through a Board of Inquiry. Ellefsen
denied all knowledge of either the ship or the silver, so Backman
escalated the matter and it was brought by a Swedish minister
before the Danish government. A royal commission was established to scrutinize the matter, and now Imlay needed a trusted
agent to press legal proceedings against Ellefsen, or to settle.
It was decided that Wollstonecraft herself would go. She was
glad to be useful to Imlay, and he was relieved to be rid of her
depressing, critical presence. So in June 1795, she, Fanny and
Marguerite set off from Hull across the North Sea, clutching a
testimony from Imlay stating that she was 'Mary Imlay my best
friend and wife' and authorizing her 'to take the sole management and direction of all my affairs and business'.[19]

The captain initially intended to land in Arendal, in southern

Norway, or in Gothenburg, near to Backman's house, but a strong wind blew their boat further south along the Swedish coast, towards the Onsala peninsula. As they sped past the small inlets and harbours, Wollstonecraft saw her personal anxieties mirrored in the landscape, in which 'every cloud that flitted on the horizon was hailed as a liberator, till approaching nearer, like most of the prospects sketched by hope, it dissolved under the eye into disappointment'.[20] When no pilot boat emerged from the harbour, she persuaded the captain and a few sailors to row her, Fanny and Marguerite to shore. There they were met by a local English-speaking lieutenant, who hosted them for a few nights, before hiring an open carriage to take the trio twenty miles to Backman in Gothenburg. Wollstonecraft did some sightseeing while Fanny played with Backman's children, and she reflected that the Swedish 'peasantry' embodied an emotional 'golden age', demonstrating 'so much overflowing of heart, and fellow-feeling, that only benevolence, and the honest sympathy of nature, diffused smiles over my countenance'.[21] It was good to be away, she realized: to forget 'the horrors I had witnessed in France, which had cast a gloom over all nature' and to rescue the 'character' that had been 'too often, gracious God! damped by the tears of disappointed affection, to be lighted up afresh'.[22]

But the trip was primarily for business, and soon Backman was pointing Wollstonecraft in the direction of her next stop: Strömstad, where she needed to consult two judges on the Board of Inquiry. Next, she had to continue up the coast and over the Norwegian border to Tønsberg, to interview Backman's former agent Jacob Wulfsburg, who had accompanied Nordberg and Ungar during their original investigation into the ship's disappearance. The seventy-mile road from Gothenburg to Strömstad was notoriously poor, and a better alternative was to go by sea, across the deceptively titled 'Skagerrak': a name probably deriving from *rak*, 'straight waterway' and Skagen, the town on the northern cape of Denmark. In reality, the Skagerrak is far from 'straight' or indeed straightforward: its tricky currents and concealed reefs and rocks make it arduous to navigate. So Wollstonecraft sent Fanny and Marguerite back to Backman's house, while she pressed on alone. Upon arriving at Tønsberg, Wollstonecraft realized with a heavy heart that her investigations and negotiations would take at least a few weeks, and require a trip to Christiania (the city of Oslo) at the tip of the Oslofjord.

It was the longest she had been separated from her fourteen-month-old daughter, and Wollstonecraft noticed the quiet and solitude acutely: a 'sort of weak melancholy ... hung about my heart'. But as she sailed alone past the steep, densely forested coastline, which occasionally flattened into beaches and inlets, where rabbits frolicked among ruined monasteries, she witnessed the arrival of an inner calm. The isolation Wollstonecraft had felt in Paris, Le Havre and London, amid the noisy bustle of Imlay and his business associates – or, in his absence, among those to whom she was largely indifferent – had been intolerable. 'I ... then considered myself as a particle broken off from the grand mass of mankind,' she wrote in a notebook. But now, in true solitude, she realized that 'I was still a part of a mighty whole, from which I could not sever myself'.[23]

Wollstonecraft turned her attention away from the frustrations of her pursuit of Imlay, to her own 'soul'. And she realized that the emotions were more than an eloquent testimony to want and inequality, or the currency through which societies were formed, as eighteenth-century philosophers had maintained. Using the emerging vocabulary of the 'emotions' rather than the older language of the 'passions', Wollstonecraft described how they could be spontaneous 'transient sensations', formed in 'responsive sympathy' to 'a quick perception of the beautiful and sublime'; they arose in the 'harmonized soul' as a natural, pleasurable response to her surroundings, 'just as the chords are touched, like the aeolian harp agitated by the changing wind'.[24]

Wollstonecraft's reflections mark the birth of the Romantic sensibility: an attitude to emotion that differed from its Enlightenment precursor by emphasizing the interior and imaginative aspects of affective experience, rather than its social 'propriety' and responsiveness to material conditions. That same cultural shift could be seen in poems such as 'The Aeolian Harp' – originally published as a poetic 'Effusion' – which Coleridge was writing in his 'cot' in Somerset as Wollstonecraft was traversing the Skagerrak. In Coleridge's poem, 'love' and 'joyance' are produced when the poet's 'tranquil' mind is stimulated into imaginative activity by the sound of the wind playing the strings of an outdoor harp. The resulting emotion is the spontaneous product of transient sensation, not a testimony to a political state's efficacy in meeting its citizens' needs. And the emotion's effects are predominantly confined to the individual mind. The result of emotional turbulence is poetry, rather than – for example – the charitable behaviour that Laurence Sterne envisaged in *A Sentimental Journey* thirty years previously. For Coleridge, emotion's principal interest lies in what it reveals about the operation of the individual's imagination and mind.

As Wollstonecraft enjoyed the rare sensation of emotions that were pleasurable rather than tormenting, she began to wonder if she had been mistaken in her attempts to firmly regulate her emotional behaviour. Had she been striving to 'calm an impetuous tide – labouring to make my feelings take an orderly course ... striving against the stream'?[25] She concluded that she had been led to 'forget the respect due to my own emotions – sacred emotions, that are the sure harbingers of the delights I was formed to enjoy'.[26] And so Wollstonecraft tried to put her ear to the shell of her soul, straining to listen to the very process through which her emotions bubbled up within her, finding 'moments of bliss' as 'the imagination bodies forth its conceptions unrestrained, and stops enraptured to adore the beings

Oil sketch attributed to Jacques-Louis David, 1790–1794. *The Tennis Court Oath* shows deputies representing the French Third Estate (commoners), meeting in defiance of Louis XVI, and taking an oath not to disband before formulating a new French constitution.

John Opie, *Mary Wollstonecraft*, painted when she was in her early thirties.

Thomas Lawrence, *Thomas Holcroft and William Godwin*, 1794. Lawrence's drawing shows Holcroft (left) and Godwin (right) as spectators during the 'treason trial' of their friend and radical John Thelwall, in early December 1794.

John Opie, *Henry Fuseli*, exhibited in 1794.

A portrait of Joseph Priestley by Ellen Sharples, made in *c.*1797, after his arrival in America.

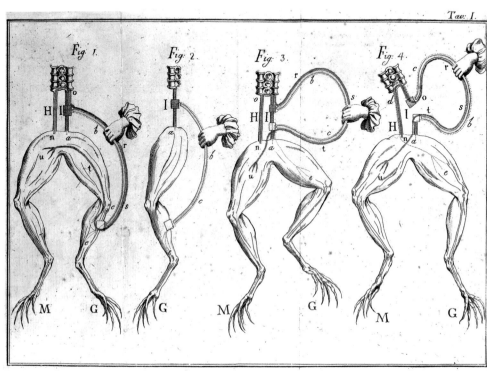

In the 1780s and 1790s, the Italian physician Luigi Galvani discovered that dead frogs' legs twitched when stimulated by electricity. Images of the frogs' legs chimed with earlier eighteenth-century representations of the body as a machine, driven by physical laws; but Galvani was also important to vitalists, who claimed that bodies were driven by innate vital energy.

Angelica Kauffman's *Monk from Calais* depicts a scene from Laurence Sterne's
A Sentimental Journey through France and Italy (1768), in which a monk begs for
donations: the narrator, Yorick, initially refuses but later changes his mind, and he
and the monk exchange snuff-boxes. Kauffman's painting emphasises the emotional
nature of charity and communication: the exchange between Yorick and the monk is
conducted through heightened, emotive gestures, typical of the 'cult of sensibility'.

Sampson Towgood Roche's portrait of Thomas Beddoes was made in 1794, when Beddoes was in his mid-thirties; and shortly after his move to Bristol.

From a chalk portrait of Thomas Wedgwood – artist unknown – which forms the frontispiece to a 1903 biography of Wedgwood.

Burning of Dr. Priestley's House at Fairhill.*

Engraving showing the looting and destruction of Joseph Priestley's house
at Fairhill, Birmingham, from 14–17 July 1791.

Miniature portrait of the educationalist and inventor Richard Lovell Edgeworth, made in 1785, when Edgeworth was in his late thirties.

Portrait of Anna Beddoes (née Edgeworth), daughter of Richard Lovell Edgeworth and wife of Thomas Beddoes.

Adolphe and Émile Rouargue's engraving of the Temple Prison in Paris shows part of the revolutionary panorama that Mary Wollstonecraft viewed from the top floor of her apartments on the Rue Meslée.

The engraver and artist Robert Hancock's 1796 chalk and pencil portraits of Samuel Taylor Coleridge (above) and Robert Southey (below) show them in their early and mid-twenties, shortly after the collapse of pantisocracy.

Drawn & Etched by   Lieut. Col. Batty.

George Young, & his Wife (Hannah Adams),
of Pitcairns Island.

From Sketches by Lieut. Smith, of H.M.S. Blossom.

Published by John Murray, Albemarle Street, 1831.

The frontispiece to John Barrow's *Eventful History of the Mutiny and
Piratical Seizure of HMS Bounty* (1831), entitled 'George Young and his
Wife', shows how the sexual relationships of the mutineers and the
indigenous population occupied an important place in the mythologising of
the *Bounty* mutiny, and the idealisation of the island settlement as a realm
of sexual freedom.

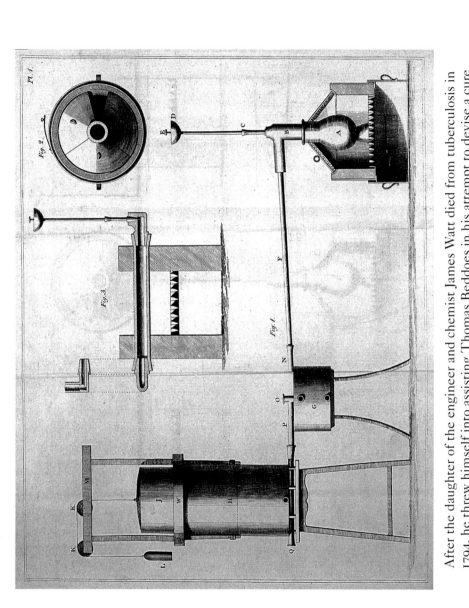

After the daughter of the engineer and chemist James Watt died from tuberculosis in 1794, he threw himself into assisting Thomas Beddoes in his attempt to devise a cure for the disease through the 'medicinal use of airs'. Watt constructed apparatus to collect, cool and administer gases to patients.

The *PROPHET of the HEBREWS,— the PRINCE of PEACE,— conducting the JEWS to the PROMISD-LAND*.

James Gillray's satirical print of 1795 – subtitled 'the prince of peace, conducting the Jews to the Promis'd-Land' – depicts the millenarian prophet Richard Brothers, known to his followers as 'Prince of the Hebrews'. Trampling on royalty, to a backdrop of London burning, Brothers is shown as a *sans-culottes* carrying politicians including Charles James Fox on his back, and is clearly being identified with revolutionary politics.

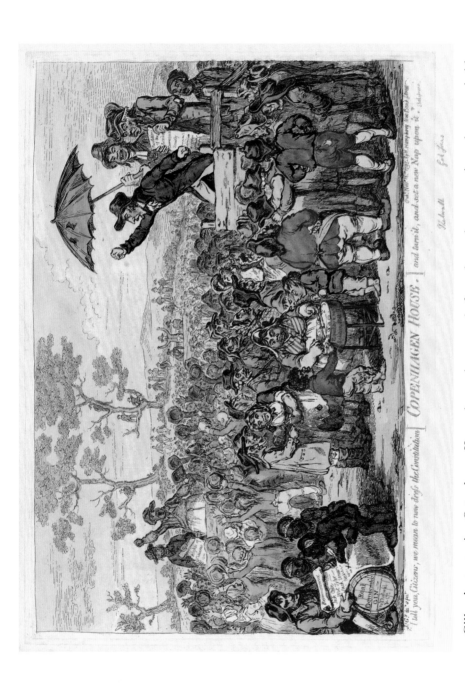

Gillray's 1795 print *Copenhagen House* shows the second of two large demonstrations that were held in October–November 1795, in Copenhagen Fields, in Islington in London, around the time of the Gagging Bills' introduction.

Cruikshank's satirical print *Talk of an Ostrich!* was published in December 1795, as the Gagging Acts were becoming law. It shows the prime minister William Pitt ramming the repressive legislation down the throat of a choking 'Johnny Bull', a personification of a 'true Briton'.

Gillray's 1802 print *Scientific Researches!* mocks the afterlife of Thomas Beddoes' work on pneumatics. It shows a demonstration at the Royal Institution, in which Humphry Davy figures as a parochial idiot savant, sniggering as the physician Thomas Garnett administers nitrous oxide to the institution's founder member Sir John Coxe Hippisley, whose trousers explode in an enormous fart.

of its own creation', and storing them up for the 'memory [to] recal[l] with delight'.[27]

But, on the return voyage, as Wollstonecraft sailed down the Oslofjord into the Skagerrak on her way back to Gothenburg at the end of August 1795, her optimism about the possibility of maintaining such a passive, joyful experience of emotion receded. 'These sentiments' could not be fostered 'in such an imperfect state of existence' as the flawed reality of her life. Such subjective introspection and passive acceptance was only possible in retreat. 'My imagination . . . seek[s] an asylum in such a retreat from all the disappointments I am threatened with,' she wrote; 'but reason drags me back, whispering that the world is still the world, and man the same compound of weakness and folly.'[28] 'How am I altered by disappointment!' Wollstonecraft despaired, recognizing the profound difference not only in her feelings, but in her feelings about feeling. Ten years previously, just before Fanny Blood died, she had valued the experience of disappointment for what it revealed about the true nature of providence. The loss of Blood made her less sanguine, more intent on tempering her hopes with reason to avert disappointment in the first place. But despite her best efforts, the repeated failure to make Imlay love her had left Wollstonecraft unable to imagine a future in which beauty and satisfaction were real, not 'illusive', and in which emotion might be pleasurable and liberated, rather than a painful but potentially purifying disturbance to be contained. For Wollstonecraft, the Romantic sensibility – with its introspection, its conscious detachment from the material world, its fixation on emotion as a product of imagination, preserved in the storehouse of memory, and its emphasis on freedom and spontaneity – was an illusory reaction to disappointment and despair, and only viable in retreat.

In Gothenburg, at the end of August, Wollstonecraft was reunited with her '*Fannikin*'.[29] She was also greeted by a pile of letters from Imlay, to whom she had been dashing off angry missives complaining at his lack of attention. Imlay's replies grew increasingly cold, until he made it clear that he would no longer be meeting the trio at Hamburg, as arranged. It seemed that Wollstonecraft's homecoming would be marked by the deprivation that she had foreseen on her voyage down the Oslofjord. She made her way to Copenhagen, where she presented Count Andreas Peter Bernstorff – the 'real sovereign' of Norway, to whom the regent, Crown Prince Frederik, the son of Christian VII, had delegated power in the 1780s – with her investigation into Imlay's affairs, and was advised to settle with Ellefsen out of court. Her duties now discharged, Wollstonecraft arranged for herself, Fanny and Marguerite to take the ferry to Lübeck, in Germany. But the crossing was longer than Wollstonecraft had anticipated, she hadn't packed any food, and Fanny 'began to cry so bitterly for bread, that . . . I, literally speaking, enveloped myself in sympathetic horrours, augmented by every tear my babe shed'.[30] It was a woeful return.

In Hamburg, Imlay, true to his word, was nowhere to be seen. Finally a letter arrived: the harshest rejection to date. 'To the fiat of fate I submit,' Wollstonecraft replied. 'I am content to be wretched; but I will not be contemptible. – Of me you have no cause to complain, but for having had too much regard for you – for having expected a degree of permanent happiness, when you only sought a momentary gratification.' But she was still unable to bring herself to end their communication for good: 'I shall take no step, till I see or hear from you.'[31] Ultimately, though, she had no choice but to depart: the French armies were advancing. Instead of returning home via Switzerland, as she had hoped, she sailed down the Elbe and out into the North Sea. Wollstonecraft had received no payment for her fourteen-week expedition; and her recompense from Imlay was the discovery, back in London, that he had 'formed some new attachment' and had prepared a 'ready-furnished house . . . for his new mistress'.[32]

After momentarily dabbling with the idea of purchasing a

small estate in France for herself and Fanny, Wollstonecraft
decided that 'she would sooner suffer a thousand deaths,
than pass another [night] of equal misery' to her first back
in London.[33] She wrote to Imlay, this time quite calmly. She
instructed him to 'let the maid have all my clothes' and to 'pay
the cook her wages'. 'May you never know by experience what
you have made me endure,' she concluded.[34] Wollstonecraft
walked to Battersea Bridge but, discomfited by the crowds, she
continued another few miles, to Putney Bridge. It was raining
hard, and she traced and retraced her steps back and forth across
the bridge, while her clothes grew sodden and heavy. And then
she jumped. When she did not sink, Wollstonecraft gathered her
clothes tighter, bunching herself into a small dense weight, and
as she sank beneath the fast-flowing black water of the Thames,
she fell unconscious.

A few weeks later, on 26 October 1795, a protest took place
in Islington, in Copenhagen Fields – the grounds around
Copenhagen House, a seventeenth-century residence of the
Danish ambassador. The London Corresponding Society
erected three platforms, which attracted 150,000 protestors –
over a sixth of London's entire population; the equivalent today
would be a protest involving 1.3 million demonstrators.[35] The
rally had been organized to demonstrate against parliamentary
corruption, and the 'misery and want' that was now all too visible across Britain. To those who could hear him, John Thelwall
made a speech from one of these makeshift stages, professing
'the most inviolable attachment to the *principles* for which you
associate'.[36] Nearby, the publisher Richard 'Citizen' Lee was
selling copies of his recent regicidal pamphlet *King Killing*,
which led to his arrest within a few weeks.[37] A satirical print by
James Gillray of an even larger demonstration in Copenhagen
Fields two weeks later captured the atmosphere of the protests. They were part political rallies, with wildly gesticulating

orators hammering home the 'Resolutions of the LCS' and petitioners seeking signatures for 'Remonstrance' against a host of grievances. And they were part fairgrounds, fuelled by 'Real Democratic Gin', with stalls selling 'Thelwall' hair ribbons and a roulette table at which speculators gambled on the most pertinent issues of the day.

The year leading up to the demonstration of 26 October had seen rapidly rising prices of wheat and grain following poor harvests, a particularly harsh winter, and a blockade on imports through France, which resulted in a dramatic rise in poverty and civil unrest. In Bristol, riots had again broken out, nearly two years after the Bridge Riots. Beddoes had suspended advertising for subscriptions for the Pneumatic Institute 'from the necessity of contributions to keep the poor alive this hard winter'.[38] Increased taxation to fund the war made the situation even harder; many working families were unable to afford bread, and children descended into malnutrition and then starvation. The Privy Council advised reducing the consumption of grain and the *Bristol Gazette* included an insert, 'In the Time of Dearth', advising how to eke out leftovers.

At the beginning of June, crowds started protesting in the evenings, congregating around the offices of traders and the city corporation. Even during such terrible shortages, the corporation had refused to restrict middlemen who bought grain from suppliers and sold it on at grossly inflated prices to bakers. On 6 June, a crowd assembled outside a butcher's shop and, as darkness fell, some began to smash windows to seize the meat inside. The historian Trevor Levere has pointed out that this was the first food riot in Bristol for forty years. It demonstrated the extent to which trust between the citizens – the butchers and their starving customers – and the city authorities had entirely dissolved.[39]

For Bristol citizens like Thomas Beddoes, anxiety about 'a general fermentation among the working class' combined in the summer of 1795 with heightened fears of a French invasion.[40] The militia was put on alert, and the Home Office drew up a plan, 'In Case of Invasion', which stressed that 'every attempt at Sedition or Disturbance shall be repressed with a High Hand'. By October, Beddoes' hydraulic theory that obstruction of the people led to eruptions of violence was apparently confirmed. The mayor received an anonymous letter warning that corn warehouses and bakers' shops would be raided if prices didn't fall, and local colliers prepared for armed conflict, along with 'three regiments of soldiers on our side'.[41] In London, three days after the protest at Copenhagen Fields, a crowd gathered outside parliament for the state opening, crying 'Down with Pitt!', 'No King!', 'No Pitt!', 'No war!', 'Peace!' and 'Bread!'. As the king drew up in his carriage and prepared to alight, a stone was thrown and shattered the window. *The Times* reported the next day that his groom had been hurt; upon entering the House of Commons, George himself reportedly gasped to an aristocratic bystander, 'My Lord, I, I, I've been shot at!'[42]

The attack on the king's coach made Pitt bold. On 4 November 1795, a Royal Proclamation was issued, preventing large meetings for 'seditious' purposes, and forbidding the circulation of 'treasonable' papers. Two days later, the proclamation's reach was extended. Pitt introduced a motion in the House of Commons: a proposal for the 'Seditious Meetings Bill', to outlaw any meetings of fifty or more taking place without a magistrate's consent. Gatherings like the protest at Copenhagen Fields were outlawed. Such meetings now required prior notice, the consent of seven local householders, and had to take place in premises licensed for political activity by two magistrates. Pitt's bill also empowered local Justices of the Peace and magistrates to disperse any meetings, even licensed ones, if they appeared remotely 'seditious'. Resistance to a meeting's dispersal might incur the death sentence. The explicit aim of Pitt's bill was to protect the state from political activity among the labouring class – from those 'who, of all men, are, by education and habits of life, and means of information, the least capable of exercising a sound judgement on such subjects, and who are most likely to be imposed upon by others'.[43]

The Secretary of State for Foreign Affairs – William Wyndham Grenville, Lord Grenville – introduced a second bill, this time into the Lords: the Treasonable Practices Bill. Grenville's bill altered the legal definition of treason to encompass 'inciting the people to hatred or contempt of his Majesty' through speech or publication, even if no action had followed. It potentially criminalized republican political theory. The 'Two Bills', as they were popularly known, would maim the radical movement. They would criminalize large political meetings, shut down radicals' access to the political elite, and prompt many moderates to retreat from the political societies, leaving radical factions who appeared to confirm the most extreme stereotypes that the reactionary press had been propagating throughout the decade. As many angry protestors pointed out, the legislation eroded the freedom of speech enshrined in the 1689 Bill of Rights. At the end of 1794, the unsuccessful prosecution of famous radicals like Thelwall, Hardy and Horne Tooke in the Treason Trials had given the radical movement temporary heart that the worst of the political disappointments were over, and that the tide might turn in their favour after all. But just over a year later, the Two Acts – once the bills had passed through parliament – were a devastating follow-up and, many feared, a conclusive disappointment, curtailing civil liberties more dramatically than had ever been thought possible.

Thomas Beddoes was not the only one to be shocked into political activity as vital as in the heady early years of the 1790s. But whereas Beddoes' earlier writings were fuelled by genuine hope and possibility, now he was reduced to defending the century-old rights secured by the Bill of Rights of 1689. Beddoes' new tone was reckless. The pamphlets he hastily scribbled in late 1795 and early 1796 were last-ditch attempts to assert the value of freedom of speech, the right to petition the monarch without fear of retribution, frequent elections, protection from cruel and unusual punishment, and the free election of members of parliament. Rights they had once considered impregnable, radicals were now having to defend with all their energy.

Beddoes' first pamphlet of this panicked period appeared on 17 November 1795. *A Word in Defence of the Bill of Rights, against Gagging Bills* was one of the most influential responses to Pitt's legislation, and Beddoes' reference to 'the Gagging Bills' – or 'Gagging Acts', as they would become – coined a phrase that immediately entered popular currency and is still used by historians today. Beddoes emphasized how the effects of ministers' decisions were felt by every citizen, at the level of housing, the cost and availability of bread, diseases stemming from poverty, and what today we would call emotional well-being. The passions were barometers for the state's levels of compassion. Progressive policies ensured 'the poor man' feels 'more comfortable by his fire-side', but the Gagging Acts would cause widespread distress. Citizens would 'know by feeling rather than reason' that 'the possessors of power are ever on the watch to encroach; that a nation which slumbers over its rights, will be fortunate if it awake not in fetters'. The curtailment of free speech would have especially egregious effects on emotional health, Beddoes predicted, drawing on Enlightenment ideas, like Adam Smith's, about the importance of the free exchange of sentiments to social cohesion.[44] The Gagging Acts' restriction of speech would cause 'all the kindly feelings of the heart [to] retire inward and die', leading to 'death of freedom', 'mournful silence of despair' across the land, in the face of which 'the noble attributes of the British character' would wither.[45] Smith's vision of a society built upon self-regulated emotional exchanges was threatened by Pitt's ministers, who seemed intent on 'damping the reason, and firing the passions, of the uninstructed'. Authoritarian measures like the Gagging Acts, combined with the inevitable consequence of hindering the education of the poor and eroding the basis of sociability, would incite 'black revengeful thoughts' among the populace, and 'set neighbour to worry neighbour, as if they were so many tygers'.[46]

On the same day that his *Defence of the Bill of Rights* appeared, Beddoes attended a large public meeting in the medieval Guildhall in Bristol's Old City. The mayor had called the meeting to pass a 'very loyal and dutiful, and affectionate Address' to the king, congratulating him on his escape from assassination. But radicals wanted to interrogate and challenge the Two Bills. Soon after the meeting began, a young man with wild hair and fervid voice stood up to speak. Beddoes, a long-standing abolitionist, is likely to have known this man by sight and name from a lecture that he had delivered attacking the slave trade, five months earlier, in mid-June 1795: it was Samuel Taylor Coleridge.

We don't know exactly when Beddoes and Coleridge first encountered one another. Beddoes had probably attended Coleridge's lectures on politics, as well as his talk on slavery. His warning in the *Defence of the Bill of Rights*, that a 'nation which slumbers over its rights, will be fortunate if it awake not in fetters', clearly echoed Coleridge's claim in his third political lecture that 'the Sleep of Nations is followed by their Slavery'.[47] Whenever it occurred that autumn, their meeting brought together two of the most intellectually original radicals in Bristol, and the agitation around the Gagging Bills enabled them to form a friendship. But Coleridge and Beddoes were at very different stages of their projects. In late 1795, Coleridge was reeling from pantisocracy's failure, and starting to draw away from the radical movement to find an accommodation with the emerging political climate. Beddoes, almost ten years older, was experiencing a second wind of radical outrage, and was still developing his own method of emotional reform. The months in which Coleridge and Beddoes came together in Bristol marked a brief, exciting moment of overlap and collaboration, before the two men would go their separate ways.

Coleridge had decided that his Clevedon cottage was too removed from the political heat. He had lasted only six weeks there, before abandoning Sara to return to Bristol.[48] At the Guildhall meeting on 17 November 1795, with Beddoes in the audience, Coleridge delivered 'the most elegant, the most pathetic, the most sublime Address', and no doubt reminded his audience of the warning that Beddoes had echoed. He was shouted down by loyalists and the Mayor 'refused to hear' him.[49] Others tried to speak too, and were similarly stifled. The ex-pantisocrat Robert Lovell was 'purposely' silenced. And Edward Long Fox – a physician at the Bristol Infirmary, who had very recently taken over a psychiatric asylum at Cleve Hill – was also barred from speaking. Edward Long Fox had significant standing in Bristol. During the Bridge Riots in September 1793, he had led the campaign to hold the authorities to account, acquiring a reputation among radicals and reformers as 'one of the most upright and benevolent characters'. But to Tories and other reactionaries, Fox appeared a 'Jacobin' who wished 'to throw over all order, and established Government', and his carriage was even pelted with stones when he travelled around Bristol.[50]

Immediately after the public meeting, Beddoes 'recommend[ed] the Citizens to meet and frame a Petition, to shew their disapprobation of the measures likely to be adopted by Government' and Fox 'requested of the Mayor the use of the Guildhall, as a proper place to assemble, which was granted'. On 20 November, a second meeting took place, with Fox now in the chair, and Beddoes in the audience, probably accompanied by Coleridge. The participants congregated to 'consider the Propriety of Petitioning Parliament against certain Bills now pending in the House of Commons, by which Bills it is conceived that the Bill of Rights will be invaded'. This meeting's audience and atmosphere was very different from the first. Full of righteous fury, a Bristol banker, Mr Savery, presented a petition against the Two Bills. Beddoes seconded it. He 'is no Orator', reported William Wordsworth's friend Azariah Pinney, who was in the audience, but he 'spoke to the purpose'.[51]

Outside, a military parade created a raucous disturbance. Protestors distributed leaflets warning of the dangers of 'Jacobin' sentiment, and charged Fox with provoking the populace 'in a way calculated to mislead their judgment, inflame their passions, and excite their resentment'. At the beginning of December 1795, a Bristol citizen, 'A.W.', published *A Letter to Edward Long Fox M.D.*, attacking him and Beddoes for cynically 'work[ing] upon' the people's 'passions' in their speeches and political publications, twisting the poor into 'enthusiastic delusion'.[52] Coleridge leapt to the defence of Fox and his new friend Beddoes – semi-anonymously, under the pseudonym 'C.T.S.' – in *An Answer to a Letter to Edward Long Fox*. He alleged that Edmund Burke and other counter-revolutionaries were drumming up violent sentiment among those liable to join Church and King mobs, to a far more dangerous extent than radicals, through reactionary rhetoric that functioned like 'boiling lead'.[53] And he claimed that this was a deliberate political strategy, to provoke the labouring classes as a whole to a permanent state of 'appetite and passion', making them 'toil like brutes and be dumb like brutes', debarring them from 'all power and exercise of reason' and excluding them from the benefits of education and political representation.[54]

The scene in Bristol was replayed across the country, in meetings dominated by 'hissings' that articulated 'the hall's abhorrence of the bills'.[55] The Gagging Bills were a crisis, an erosion of civil liberties. They prompted different political factions to unite in opposition to Pitt's legislation, from establishment

Whig politicians to the artisanal and labouring-class members of many of the Corresponding Societies. The *Morning Post* printed the bills' long text on its front page, demanding debate among its readers. John Thelwall and William Frend, the Unitarian lecturer who had been banished from Cambridge University, presented the king and House of Commons with a petition in opposition to the Two Bills; there were ninety-four petitions in total, comprising 131,284 signatures. Sixty-five petitions were offered in support, with only 29,922 signatures: less than a quarter of their rivals.[56] The satirical cartoonist Isaac Cruikshank published *Talk of an Ostrich!*, a print in which Pitt is gagging John Bull, shoving the legislation down his throat with the butt of a musket. On 26 November 1795, Coleridge delivered a blistering lecture against the Two Bills, 'in the Great Room at the Pelican Inn, Thomas Street', in Bristol; it would later be published under the title *The Plot Discovered*. Coleridge saw the legislation as a direct attack on Thelwall, whom he represented as the 'voice of tens of thousands', and he and Thelwall were among the first to compare the Two Bills to the French Terror.[57]

Nevertheless, the bills passed into law in mid-December 1795. Now Pitt's opponents predicted that the acts would have the opposite effect to his intention. Instead of repressing working-class activism, they predicted, the Gagging Acts would incite members of political societies to violent revolution. This was the moment that Beddoes' hydraulic theory of violent retorts to oppression would be put to the test. Would poorly educated sectors of the population respond to the incursions of the Gagging Acts with outbursts of violence? On 26 November 1795, James Gillray published *Retribution*, a cartoon showing Fox and Sheridan exacting a 'Patriots['] Revenge' on Pitt: they are tarring the prime minister with the 'Remonstrance of the People' and feathering him with the plumes of 'Libertas', prior to hanging him from a lamp post resembling a French guillotine, while the Sedition Bill burns beneath the 'Rights of the People'.

'Nay & you'll stop Our Mouths, beware Your Own', reads the menacing motto.

An immediate retort to the Gagging Acts was peaceful, however. On 8 December 1795, the *Morning Chronicle* printed an advertisement for a society formed to help 'sav[e] the Country' through 'an immediate Junction of the Whig Interest and the Corresponding Society'.[58] The new affiliation would meet in London at 8 p.m. at Westminster Forum in Panton Street, Haymarket. The idea of setting up a 'Grand National Association' specifically to defend the Bill of Rights had first been mooted by the politician James Burgh in his *Political Disquisitions* (published in 1774, before the bill was as threatened as it was in 1795), which Coleridge had been re-reading whilst composing *The Plot Discovered*. Now Whig politicians advocated a long-term approach. They hoped that popular opposition would lead to Pitt's downfall at the next election, followed by the acts' repeal; and they sought unprecedented collaboration with the popular political societies to maintain pressure. The societies, for their part, saw an opportunity for access to the political elite. So, on 18 December, the day that the Gagging Bills passed into law and became the Gagging Acts, the 'Whig Club' was formally founded with the aim of procuring their repeal. A reactionary satire published at the beginning of January 1796 denounced this new 'Catenation of Clubs' as 'the great Jacobin Den of England', 'the common receptacle of all the political abominations of which the French had drunk largely and fatally', set up with the exclusive purpose 'to overawe and intimidate the government'.[59] Its author scorned the claim made by Beddoes, among others, that the Two Bills eroded the fellow-feeling essential to social cohesion, dismissing the emphasis on '*Love*' as a 'trifling' 'absurdity'.[60] The wind was changing, and the eighteenth-century consensus that the passions were intrinsic to political commitment and change was apparently dissolving.

Coleridge fully supported the Whig Club's aims. He and

Beddoes had both considered that a new provincial radical magazine might be extremely useful in propagating political theory and events among readers who might struggle to attend the societies, and might improve the state of political education. The Revolutionary War, and Pitt's earlier repressive measures against freedom of speech, had stimulated the founding of journals such as James Montgomery's *Sheffield Iris* in 1794, and Benjamin Flower's *Cambridge Intelligencer* in 1793, and in Norwich, *The Cabinet* had propagated French Revolutionary ideals from 1795.[61] In late 1795, almost certainly after conversations with Beddoes, Coleridge decided to set up a magazine with the express purpose 'to co-operate (1) with the WHIG CLUB in procuring a repeal of Lord Grenville's and Mr Pitt's bills, now passed into laws, and (2) with the PATRIOTIC SOCIETIES, for obtaining a Right of Suffrage general and frequent'. Whereas many equivalent newspapers were mostly comprised of advertisements, Coleridge's would be 'dedicate[d] *entirely* to this work' of 'proclaim[ing] the State of the Political Atmosphere, and preserv[ing] Freedom and her Friends from the attacks of Robbers and Assassins'. He would call it *The Watchman*, likening himself to the watchman of Isaiah and Ezekiel – 'For thus hath the LORD said unto me, Go, set a watchman, let him declare what he seeth', and 'Son of Man, I have made thee a watchman unto the house of Israel' – who preserved freedom from attack. Its motto would ring loud: 'That all may know the Truth, and that the Truth may make us free'.[62]

On Saturday 9 January 1796, Coleridge boarded a coach to Worcester, as the first stage of a tour of the Midlands and North to procure subscribers to *The Watchman*, to add to the 270 he had already garnered in Bristol. He did not have an auspicious start: he was crammed next to a man so fat that he would need 'elbow room if he was walking on Salisbury Plain'.[63] Over the next month, Coleridge travelled from Worcester to Birmingham (where a potential subscriber refused the '*four-pence*' subscription because '*Thirty-two pages*' was 'more than I ever reads, Sir! all the year round'); to Derby (where he met Joseph Wright, the painter, and Erasmus Darwin); to Nottingham, Sheffield, Manchester and Lichfield, leaving out Liverpool and London to come home to Sara, who was pregnant, nauseous, lonely and had moved back in with her mother in Bristol. By 13 February 1796 Coleridge had returned, buoyed up, with enough energy and subscriptions to dedicate himself '*entirely*' to *The Watchman*. He found Sara's 'groans, and complaints & sickness!' an irritating distraction, but the 'gloomy prospect of so many mouths to open & shut' concentrated his mind.[64] He found a new residence for Sara and himself in Kingsdown, a suburb of Bristol, and set to. The first issue was promised for 5 February; it finally emerged on 1 March 1796.

Coleridge conceived of his newspaper as a 'miscellany', a popular magazine form in the eighteenth century. The first ten issues of *The Watchman* comprised an assortment of overtly political essays, historical accounts, reports of further Treason Trials, reviews of Burke, extracts from Coleridge's lectures, poems, summaries of national news items and parliamentary proceedings, and digests of 'Foreign Intelligence'. Beddoes contributed: possibly an attack on Pitt on 19 April, probably general news items and medical curiosities, such as an account of a case of hydrophobia, and he objected to one piece in which Coleridge romanticized consumptive patients.[65] In turn, *The Watchman* favourably reviewed Beddoes' new pamphlet *Essay on the Public Merits of Mr. Pitt*, approving of how its 'Author wages war with the Minister and nowhere degrades his cause'.[66] But overall Coleridge's publication was something of a 'muddle', reflecting his distracted state of mind. Sara had become 'dangerously ill', 'expected hourly to miscarry', and he had started 'taking Laudanum almost every night' to ease the pain of an 'alarmingly inflamed' eye.[67] He was bogged down in queries about distribution costs and the price of paper, whilst also trying to finish the volume of poems that Cottle had commissioned in 1794, which would become *Poems on Various Subjects*.

Successful late-eighteenth-century miscellanies had a clear, unifying theme, such as the *Lady's Magazine*, with its overall objective of female education and improvement.[68] But Coleridge undermined any unique selling point or unifying message that his readership might have expected. He had expressly sought subscribers among dissenters, but aside from a satire on religious fasting (citing Isaiah, 'Wherefore my Bowels shall sound like an Harp'), none of *The Watchman*'s essays tackled dissenting issues. Soon Coleridge was haemorrhaging subscribers, losing 'near five hundred ... at one blow' after the essay on fasts. *The Watchman* had never made more than 'a *bread-and-cheesish* profit', but by May it was making a loss of 'exactly five pounds more than the whole amount of my receipts'. In the tenth issue, Coleridge had no choice but to sadly proclaim: 'This is the last Number of the WATCHMAN.—Henceforward I shall cease to cry the State of the political Atmosphere ... if the words of the Prophet be altogether applicable to me, *"O Watchman! thou hast watched in vain!"*'[69]

There was another sector of *The Watchman*'s audience who found themselves alienated by Coleridge's tone: the political radicals who formed its core readership. From the beginning of his political engagement, Coleridge had declared his ideological independence from any grouping: 'though I may be classed with a party, I scorn to be of a faction'. True to this spirit, *The Watchman*'s third number included his essay 'Modern Patriotism', in which he denounced Godwin's views on marriage as 'vicious', those of a 'pimp' and a 'Pandar to Sensuality'. John Thelwall, too, came under fire for popularizing Godwin's *Political Justice* through his lectures and his own journal, *The Tribune*.[70] Thelwall retorted by accusing Coleridge's essay of 'illiberal dogmatism', 'abuse', 'outrageous violence' and 'intolerant prejudice'.[71]

Coleridge's political lectures of 1795, and his editorship of *The Watchman*, marked the peak of his career as a radical. But even as early as November 1794, he had begun to baulk at being publicly identified as a 'Friend of Liberty'. 'People have resolved, that I am a Democrat,' he wrote to his brother, 'and accordingly look at every thing I do through the Spectacles of Prejudication ... Solemnly, my Brother! I tell you – I am *not* a Democrat.' He defined himself instead as a 'perfectibilist', who can 'see evidently, that the present is *not* the *highest* state of Society, of which we are *capable*'.[72] *The Watchman* was important in cementing Coleridge's reputation as a radical. But it also expressed his increasingly strenuous attempts to separate himself from the movement and assert his ideological and practical independence. Arguably, Coleridge's political autonomy would save him from the heat of Pitt's retribution and from being tainted by association with some of the most infamous radicals in 1790s' Britain. But it would also subject him to charges of betrayal, denial and desertion from his former political collaborators. The seeds of Coleridge's 'apostasy' had been sown, and his attempts to separate himself from the radical movement were replicated by others, too, across Britain, as the Gagging Acts raised the stakes involved in overt radical political participation. Eventually, such ideological reversals would help lead to that movement's erosion, the death of hope, and a revolution in the very understanding of hope and disappointment.

Chapter 13

REVOLUTIONS BY MOURNING
AND ACCOMMODATION

A few days after Mary Wollstonecraft's suicide attempt in October 1795, *The Times* reported that 'a Lady elegantly dressed' had gone 'upon Putney Bridge, [and] threw herself from the frame of the central arch into the Thames'. 'Fortunately,' the article continued, 'she was picked up by a fishing-boat, and being carried to an inn at Fulham, was soon restored by the skill of one of the medical persons belonging to the Humane Society.'[1] *The Times* may not have been referring to Wollstonecraft herself – female suicides were common – but she, too, was 'brought back to life and misery' from the bottom of the Thames. She wrote haughtily to Imlay that 'I [will not] allow that to be a frantic attempt, which was one of the calmest acts of reason.'[2]

His compassion roused, Imlay did not visit Wollstonecraft initially, but he sent a physician to attend her, and arranged with

her old friend Thomas Christie and his wife for Wollstonecraft
to stay at their house in Finsbury Square while she recovered.
Imlay downplayed his current liaison as 'merely a casual, sensual connection', and faint hope revived in Wollstonecraft,
resulting in more letters to him. She drew on the language of
financial failure to capture her level of devastation, her emotional
bankruptcy, her misplaced investment: 'I have loved with my
whole soul, only to discover that I had no chance of a return.'[3]
Towards the end of the year, trudging the streets of London as
if 'buried alive' in a gleamless 'tomb', she called on Fuseli. 'I
vainly imagined you would have called upon me,' she berated
him later, but 'I have long ceased to expect kindness or affection
from any human creature.'[4] She weakly requested that he return
her old letters, but met with a flat refusal.

By the new year of 1796, Wollstonecraft had moved into her
own lodgings in London, but she was half-heartedly considering
'settling in France, because I wish to leave my little Girl there'. In
the immediate aftermath of the Gagging Acts' implementation,
'the state of public affairs here are not in a posture to assuage
private sorrow'.[5] Towards the end of the winter, Wollstonecraft
called upon Mrs Christie and found her in a fluster. Imlay was
in the parlour, in a business meeting with Thomas, and Mrs
Christie vainly tried to conceal his presence. But Wollstonecraft
swung open the door, and coolly led little Fanny to her father's
knee. Imlay ushered Wollstonecraft into a side room, promising
to call on her the following day. Recognizing the dangerous reap-
pearance of futile hope, she wisely decided to absent herself,
and went off with Fanny to rural Berkshire, to visit a friend, Mrs
Cotton. There, after receiving another dampening letter from
Imlay, she decided, once and for all, to renounce her hopes. She
had made similar resolutions before, of course. But this time she
allowed for no caveat.

Wollstonecraft's biography draws attention to the close
connection between disappointment, death and mourning.

Twentieth-century psychoanalysts have written extensively on the pain of disappointment and disillusionment as forms of loss and mourning, and have related those states to the first significant loss that each and every individual faces: separation from the mother in infancy. The twentieth-century child psychologist Donald Winnicott, for example, has described early infancy (between nought and five months) as a period of illusory, inchoate oneness. In that period, the anarchically emotive baby's only dependable structure is the mother and her breast, who appear to the baby to be the same entity as itself, conjured into presence by cries of need. The infant's realization of its separateness from the mother, Winnicott writes, is a process that takes place when she or he tests boundaries, utilizes 'transitional objects' such as toys or blankets, and is weaned from the breast.[6] The separation that wrenches the baby apart from the mother is both a disappointment – in the word's earliest meaning of 'to deprive of an appointment, office, or possession' – and a disillusionment, revealing the infant state of oneness to be an enchanted dream. Heinz Kohut, the Austrian-American psychoanalyst, also saw the engineering of 'tolerable disappointments' as a principal responsibility of parents, to gently disillusion the infant of its false sense of omnipotence in its early months.[7] It was only through experiencing the frustration of its needs that the child would begin to sense its separation from the world. And, by implication, that first separation propels each individual into a life subsequently lived in a state of permanent disillusionment, punctuated frequently by painful nostalgic reminders of the loss of the satiety of infancy and the inexorable frustrations of adulthood.

Not every writer on child development considered that growing up necessarily involved growing out of the illusions of infancy. The mid-twentieth-century psychologist John Bowlby echoed Jean-Jacques Rousseau in envisaging infancy not as illusion, but as truth, a hearkening to a pure and primitive version of humanity. Forcing a child to separate too fast, too brutally, from this archaic reality was 'dangerous', Bowlby warned, and the infant's maturing must be eased by the mother's sensitive attention to the child's 'instinctive' 'attachment' to her.[8] For Bowlby, all subsequent disappointments recall this first, traumatic divorce of the child not only from its mother, but from its connection to humanity's primitive state.

It was the Austrian-British psychoanalyst Melanie Klein who captured the full trauma of infantile disillusionment, and its proximity to bereavement and to mourning. Klein described the process of the infant's separation from the mother as a state of deathly hunger after the loss of the breast and the collapse of the baby's fantasy that its desires would always be met. Disillusionment flung the infant into a depression characterized by guilt, anxiety about the death of loved ones, and fear of deprivation and loss of control. Recovery was a process of grief and mourning, requiring the individual to undertake a reordering of her or his 'internal objects', a reconfiguration of the ideas, memories, emotions, connections and attachments between the lost, loved object and its survivors. Mourning in the wake of disappointment was only successful, Klein wrote, amid 'greater trust in actual people and things, and help received from the external world'.[9] Connection and community, she emphasized, were essential to allow the reconstruction of one's internal attachments after loss and grief have ripped a hole in the fabric of one's identity.

Wollstonecraft's disappointment in Imlay had been felt with the full force of bereavement. This was not just metaphor: disappointments literally entail the death of part of oneself, the death of cherished hopes. And recovery from disappointment is a process of mourning not only for the lost, loved object, but for the part of oneself that has died. Psychoanalysts might interpret Wollstonecraft's account of her time in Scandinavia – and, indeed, Romantic poetry that emphasized the sensation of being 'part of a mighty whole, from which I could not sever myself' – as a wishful resurrection of the infantile state of oneness, which was lost when Wollstonecraft was precipitated into brutal separation from Imlay. And, indeed, her temporary inability to recover from that separation was manifested in the suicidal, 'transitory manic-depressive state' that Klein identifies as the stage between brutal loss and commencement of the productive work of mourning. Mourning was written into the fabric of the second half of the 1790s: most radicals suffered devastating losses, ranging from loss of possessions to the deaths of loved ones. Klein points to the significance of community in recovering from disappointment and grief – but in the wake of the Gagging Acts, it was community that was perhaps under most threat.

In January 1796, a couple of months before her final meeting with Imlay, Mary Wollstonecraft was reintroduced to William Godwin. They were both friends of the novelist Mary Hays, who was in mourning, like Wollstonecraft, for unrequited affection – for the sacked Cambridge lecturer William Frend. Hays declared herself torn 'by conflicting passions, & wasted in anguish'.[10] Godwin recoiled, urging Hays to strongly resist her distracting passions. 'It is a mistake to suppose that the heart is not to be compelled,' he lectured; 'had you worshipped at the altar of reason but half as assiduously as you have sacrificed at the shrine of illusion, your present happiness would have been as enviable, as your present distress is worthy of compassion.'[11] Wollstonecraft, too, had written to Hays, pronouncing herself to 'have been most hurt at your not *labouring* to acquire more contentment'.[12] Hays might understandably have raised an eyebrow at this somewhat hypocritical advice, which Wollstonecraft was far from taking herself.

Godwin was not initially delighted at the prospect of seeing 'Mrs Wolstencraft, of whom I know not that I ever said a word

of harm, & who has frequently amused herself with depreci-
ating me'.[13] But both had changed since their first meeting in
November 1791. Wollstonecraft had been about to embark on
writing *A Vindication of the Rights of Woman*, she was infatuated
with Fuseli, and fervent about the possibility of political change
through 'a revolution in female manners'. Just over four years
later, her reiterated disappointments had left Wollstonecraft
with little optimism for reforming the emotional behaviour of
other people, especially men. The suffering she had endured in
the attempt – combined with the revelation in Scandinavia of an
alternative attitude to emotion that was becoming entrenched in
the Romantic sensibility – had changed her view of the passions.
Once she had considered them active forces for change, but now
she saw how emotions could be the passive medium onto which
pain and inequality were stamped. Wollstonecraft was working
on a new novel, *Maria: or The Wrongs of Woman*, in which the
'agonizing emotions' of its protagonist bear the imprint of suffering resulting from the 'despotic' rule of her brother; her father's
cavorting with the housekeeper; her marriage to a libertine who
abducts her child and consigns her to an insane asylum; and
seduction by another inmate, Darnford, whose 'every desire
became a torrent that bore down all opposition'.[14] To Godwin,
this revolution in Wollstonecraft's attitude to feeling – a revolution wrought by defeat, disappointment and mourning – seemed
to be manifested in a softer, more acquiescent demeanour. He
was soon to read her *Letters Written During a Short Residence in
Sweden, Norway and Denmark*, published in January 1796, and
later would approvingly record how the 'occasional harshness
and ruggedness of character, that diversify her Vindications of
the Rights of Woman, here totally disappear. If ever there was
a book calculated to make a man in love with its author, this
appears to me to be the book.'[15]

Godwin, too, was much changed. The dour, ascetic divine
of the 1770s and 1780s was gone, and in his place had emerged

something of a flirt and a dandy. Godwin had capitalised on the aesthetic transformation he had wrought earlier – shrugging off his dissenters' black clothes in favour of blue coat and stockings, yellow breeches and waistcoat – to acquire distinctive spectacles and the smooth, solicitous manner that had made an impression on women across London, including the novelist and actor Elizabeth Inchbald, the novelist Amelia Alderson (to whose father he offered a 'proposal'), his friend Maria Reveley, wife of the architect Willey Reveley, and the actor and poet Mary Robinson, known as 'the English Sappho'. Godwin had found a pleasurable undercurrent of sexuality in his new persona, which had softened him to the presence of the emotions in human life. In the first edition of *Political Justice*, published in 1793, Godwin had proclaimed that the passions 'cloud, instead of illuminate my understanding'.[16] But since then he had been busily revising *Political Justice*, striking out words like 'reasonings' and replacing them with 'pleasure and pain'. He now declared that universal benevolence might be attained not through reason, but through 'feeling ripened into virtue'.[17]

Godwin was not apologetic for changing his mind: after all, he had done so before, in the wake of meeting Fawcett in the late 1770s, after which he had gradually abandoned Toryism for radicalism. Changes of opinion were simply the result of the mind approaching closer to perfectibility, Godwin argued, through paradigm shifts involving the recognition of error and subsequent correction. And he was coming to think, amid the darkening political climate, that uncompromising political purity – clinging rigidly to every ounce of a belief – was supremely counterproductive. In revisions made to *Political Justice* that would be published in 1798, he wrote that 'a corrupt state of society ... forces the most enlightened and the most virtuous unwillingly to participate in its justice'. And he stressed that '[i]t would be weakness, and not magnanimity ... to refuse to be useful because no usefulness is pure'.[18] 'Accommodation' could be a radical activity in itself, Paine had argued in the first part of the *Rights of Man*: 'it would be an act of wisdom to ... produce Revolutions by reason and accommodation, rather than commit them to the issue of convulsions'.[19] In the second half of the 1790s, when organizations – like the popular political societies – that would promote such 'convulsions' were being dismantled, political change through 'reason and accommodation' was all that many could hope for.

Godwin had made recent significant accommodations himself. Tom Wedgwood had given him a copying machine after being enraptured by the first edition of *Political Justice*, enthusiastically distributing copies among his friends, and engineering a meeting with its author. Godwin had returned Wedgwood's gift, on the basis that the 'giving & receiving' of presents was 'erroneous', and presented no challenge to the unequal distribution of property.[20] Over the following years, Wedgwood had taken issue with Godwin's 'impracticable' attempts 'to build all our actions on motives of vestal purity'.[21] It led to prickly conversations. The increasingly impecunious Godwin was chary of offending the enormously wealthy Wedgwood, who wanted to be recognized as simultaneously useful and philosophically adroit. An unspoken arrangement resulted by the middle of the decade, in which Wedgwood forwarded generous loans to Godwin, even prepaying the postage for his return letters; and Godwin himself was left muttering about Wedgwood's 'infallible way of conferring benefits on me to which I can have no exception', without ever explicitly saying 'thank you'.[22]

The meeting between Godwin and Wollstonecraft in January 1796 was a success. Godwin reported that, as well as reminding him of 'the respect I had always entertained for her talents', he had felt pity at Wollstonecraft's defeated demeanour.[23] While Wollstonecraft was in Berkshire in March, he called at the Christies' house, hoping to find her. On her return, she repaid the favour, calling at his lodgings on 25 Chalton Street, in Camden.

This was 'a deviation from etiquette', Godwin wrote; 'but she had through life trampled on those rules which are built on the assumption of the imbecility of her sex'.[24]

Before long, Wollstonecraft and Godwin had started to feel affection and desire for one another, feelings that progressed in each other at exactly the same rate, Godwin claimed, so that neither was 'the agent or patient, the toil-spreader or the prey'. Despite his recent flirtations, the forty-year-old Godwin was sexually inexperienced, and Wollstonecraft was cautious of her own emotional vulnerability. They negotiated their fledgling relationship in intermittent phases of daring openness and retreat. Often one misjudged the other's intentions and withdrew into wounded umbrage. Wollstonecraft was offended by Godwin's slight criticism of her writings, and indignantly retorted that 'there is something in my writings more valuable, than in the productions of some people on whom you bestow warm elogiums'.[25] And one evening, when Wollstonecraft's mood, 'full of gaiety & life', clashed with Godwin's earnest solemnity, he felt mocked, reporting curtly the next morning that 'I have been very unwell all night. You ... unintentionally impressed upon me a mortifying sensation.'[26]

In July, Godwin and Wollstonecraft decided to forge 'a space for the maturing of inclination'.[27] Godwin left for Norfolk, to visit the physician James Alderson (Amelia's father), and his mother. He promised to write poetry for Wollstonecraft, and she exhorted him playfully 'not to choose the easiest task, my perfections, but to dwell on your own feelings – that is to say, give me a bird's-eye view of your heart'.[28] Not as adept at subjective introspection as Wollstonecraft, Godwin listed 'every thing that constitutes the bewitching *tout ensemble* of the celebrated Mary'. And he penned a parody of his own passions: 'when I make love, it shall be with the eloquent tone of my voice, with dying accents, with speaking glances (through the glass of my spectacles), with all the witching of that irresistible, universal passion'.[29] On his return, those promises were put to the test. On 15 August 1796, 'chez moi' appears in his diary; and, the next day, 'chez elle': coded indications of their first sexual encounters. On 21 August: 'chez moi toute' and finally, in October, 'chez moi, bonne'.[30] After their first sexual encounters, Godwin found himself able to lay out before Wollstonecraft the bird's-eye view of his heart she had requested. 'You set my imagination on fire on Saturday,' he wrote. 'For six & thirty hours I could think of nothing else. I longed inexpressibly to have you in my arms ... I see nothing in you but what I respect & adore.'[31]

Towards the end of January 1797 Tom Wedgwood wrote to Godwin again. Chronic pain had overshadowed the last five years of Wedgwood's life, but he was starting to formulate a plan: not only to ameliorate his own suffering, but to alter the experience of pleasure and pain for all humanity. Their correspondence, even in the dark days of 1797, raised the possibility of finally realizing Enlightenment philosophers' fading hopes for the transformative power of the passions through a new scheme. It was a project that promised to bring together the figures in this book – Godwin, Wollstonecraft, Wedgwood, Beddoes and Coleridge – who, between them, most thoughtfully and poignantly reflected the dying of an old regime of 'the passions' and the advent of a new attitude to 'emotion'.

By 1797, Wedgwood's brother Jos had produced three daughters and a son, aged four and under, and Wedgwood had taken to sitting in a dark corner of their nursery, watching them play, and surreptitiously scribbling observations in a red notebook. He didn't find it wholly enjoyable, on one occasion jotting down that to 'a bachelor, and especially one of sensibility, the cry of a child is extremely disagreeable'.[32] Like innovators such as Beddoes and Edgeworth, Wedgwood was critical of what he perceived as the strict and controlling nature of mainstream 'modern education', and thought that tutors and nurses 'tie[d] down the freedom of judgment by a thousand prejudices'.[33] He was particularly sensitive to their apparently cavalier exposure of infants and young children to unnecessary pain. Wedgwood hated seeing Jos's children being chastised for bad behaviour, considering it counterproductive, and that it 'just adds to the sum of pain in the world'. He flinched as the family's nurse proceeded with 'daily washings and dressing' while the children 'supplicate for liberty and a cessation to their pain', the nurse paying 'the least attention to their entreaties'. 'What a picture of brute insensibility,' he wrote.[34]

Wedgwood had begun to think that a new system of education might diminish and even eradicate distress. Education might eliminate children's exposure to unnecessary episodes of pain, and enable them to cope with unavoidable instances. Observing Jos's children convinced Wedgwood that fussing over a tearful child exacerbated its suffering, and he concluded that 'the futility of all repining should be urged' by simply leaving the child alone. Parents and tutors might habituate children to painful sights by taking them to visit prisons, hospitals and insane asylums, and by deliberately engineering terrifying experiences, such as provoking a bull to charge before scaring it off at the last minute by opening an umbrella in its face.[35] Wedgwood's frame of reference was his own pain-saturated life: the griping in his intestines; the perpetual migraine clamped to his skull like a dull iron visor, hampering his efforts to move or see; the grief for his lost potential that lanced him unexpectedly, rendering him breathless. In hours spent prone in darkened rooms, Wedgwood had realized that his pain originated in his earliest childhood experiences, in an upbringing that had somehow rendered him particularly sensitive to life's dissatisfactions; and he wanted to learn from his own past, to protect his nieces and nephews from enduring the same suffering.

Wedgwood had become fascinated by the association of ideas, which caused otherwise pleasurable states to cloud over into pain. He remembered an occasion the previous November, when he had been travelling from Burton-upon-Trent to Leek, near the family pottery at Etruria. Getting out of his light carriage, Wedgwood heard church bells chiming. He knew that, for most people, this was a pleasurable sound; but he experienced it as an 'oppressive influence'. After much self-reflection, Wedgwood realized that his 'melancholy feeling' was the result of an association dating back to his childhood, to 'a natural timidity which was alarmed more or less every Sunday by my being forced into crowded streets and highways, the bells chiming at the same time'.[36] The philosopher David Hartley had argued that all sensations were, 'in their original state, either pleasures or pains'.[37] Pleasure he attributed to the vibration of the nervous system's particles at an optimum level, but vibrations at a frequency or intensity above or below this pitch – usually when multiple sensations, ideas, memories and emotions become associated with one another – 'pass into pain'. Wedgwood surmised that the association of the simple sound of the bells' chimes with his painful childhood memory had caused his nervous system's vibrations to exceed the level of pleasure and become painful. But he hoped that an innovative educational system might avert such trauma for less unfortunate children, by ranking sensations according to the intensity of pleasure or pain they generated, and exposing the child to them in an orderly, rational fashion, with the aim of entrenching only neutral or pleasurable associations.[38]

Wedgwood wanted to discuss his idea with Godwin, because *Political Justice* was one of the most important developments of Hartley's ideas in the 1790s. Godwin had described how the association of ideas was a process as regular, predictable and deterministic as the collision of 'a ball upon a billiard-board ... upon a second ball'.[39] To correctly predict the outcome of a shot in billiards it was necessary to know the angle that the cue, or 'mace', made with the ball; the Newtonian laws of motion; the force with which the ball was struck; the other balls' positions;

and the friction and incline of the billiard-board. Godwin proposed that the 'Mind', and its collision and association of ideas, could be described by similar laws, which he called 'the doctrine of necessity'. 'The character of any man,' Godwin wrote, 'is the result of a long series of impressions, communicated to his mind and modifying it in a certain manner, so as to enable us, a number of these modifications and impressions being given, to predict his conduct.'[40]

Godwin's theory made *Political Justice* famous, to the extent that Wordsworth exhorted a student to discard his books on chemistry, and 'read Godwin on Necessity' instead.[41] Godwin hoped that the doctrine of necessity would enable readers to consider themselves bystanders to chains of sensations, ideas and intentions running through their minds, over which they had very little control. He hoped this would free them from 'the tumult of passion' that accompanies the delusion of completely free will. But Wedgwood wanted to discuss with Godwin whether such tranquillity might be achieved not by detaching oneself from one's own ideas and sensations, but by manipulating them to maximize pleasure and minimize pain. Wedgwood wanted to order the infant's mind like a set of well-placed billiard balls in a rack, to predispose it to the most pleasurable 'hit' in life. Godwin pointed Wedgwood in the direction of the philosophy of David Hume too.[42] Hume had identified pleasure and pain as 'the chief spring and moving principle of all ... actions': it was pleasure and pain that motivated people to pursue behaviour prolonging the former and averting the latter.[43] How might we be driven into action, without the stimulus of pain, Godwin asked in response to Wedgwood's plan to eradicate suffering.

In February 1797, Godwin frankly informed Wedgwood that he wanted to 'borrow money of you': £50, to discharge the debts that Wollstonecraft had accrued during her relationship with Imlay.[44] Wollstonecraft had a long-standing interest in educational theories – she had written *Thoughts on the Education of*

Daughters in the late 1780s and was working on a book on 'the management of infants'. In her earlier work, she had expressed a similar aversion to the painful and 'injudicious correction' of children that came to preoccupy Wedgwood, although her conclusion was less dramatic: 'Restrain them ... but never ... without a very sufficient cause,' she advised. But she was hostile to the micro-management of children's sensory experiences, and 'recommended the mind's being put into a proper train, and then left to itself'.[45] It is likely that Wollstonecraft and Godwin, perhaps with Wedgwood present too, discussed his project in some depth and that, although she would not directly participate, Godwin's views of the scheme were partially shaped by her objections. Wollstonecraft, personally, did not warm to Wedgwood, tracing his precise, somewhat aloof character to the 'half spoilt' product of privilege: 'I am afraid that all men are materially injured by inheriting wealth, and, without knowing it, become important in their own eyes.'[46]

But Wollstonecraft's aversion did not stop Godwin approaching Wedgwood for 'a further supply of fifty pounds' two months later, in April.[47] This extra injection of cash was needed because, on 29 March 1797, Godwin and Wollstonecraft had married, at the church of St Pancras in London. Godwin hoped that Wedgwood's donation would 'enable us to start fair'.[48] By early April the couple's marriage had become public knowledge. Fuseli gossiped conspiratorially to the historian, abolitionist, collector and patron of the arts William Roscoe – who had commissioned a portrait of Wollstonecraft in 1791 – 'You have not, perhaps, heard that the assertrix of female rights has given her hand to the *balancier* of political justice.'[49] Both Godwin and Wollstonecraft were acutely aware that their marriage disappointed expectations raised by their previous public pronouncements against the institution. Godwin marshalled his justifications: Wollstonecraft was pregnant and 'unwilling, perhaps with reason, to incur that exclusion from the society of many valuable and excellent individuals'. There was 'no way so obvious for her to drop the name of Imlay, as to assume the name of Godwin'.[50]

To Wedgwood, Godwin denied that there was 'an inconsistency between my practice in this instance & my doctrines'. 'The doctrine of my Political Justice,' he explained, 'is, that an attachment, in some degree permanent, between two persons of opposite sexes is right, but that marriage, as practised in European countries is wrong. I still adhere to that opinion,' he asserted. Godwin still wanted to see marriage 'abolished' and would never 'recommend [it] to my fellow men ... but with the greatest caution'. But on this occasion, the rational arguments in favour of protecting Wollstonecraft from further social ostracism outweighed his 'abhorrence' of 'the European institution of marriage'.[51] To another correspondent, he rationalized that '[e]very day of my life, I comply with institutions & customs which I ardently wish to see abolished'.[52] Godwin homed in on the question of *accommodation*, with which so many radicals and reformers were preoccupied in the latter years of the 1790s. No man or woman, he felt now, was required to martyr their daily well-being on the altar of unpopular political principles: everybody makes their own negotiations between hope, and the 'judgment of attainableness' of those hopes, in a 'corrupt world'.

Godwin's profoundly altered views about marriage and emotion were evident in further revisions he made to *Political Justice* in preparation for a third edition in 1798. In the first edition, he had described how rational intent hastens people into action: they 'foresee' 'certain consequences to result'. But the trajectory of the 1790s had taught him that predictions did not always materialize, and that intent did not necessarily translate into action. Furthermore, it is likely that conversations with Tom Wedgwood had focused Godwin's attention on the importance of pleasure and pain, hope and emotion, in translating intention into action. Godwin revised the earlier paragraph, now writing

that it is 'hope or fear of the event' that predominantly moti-
vates action, instead of simply 'foreseeing . . . consequences'. In
the third edition of *Political Justice*, action is based on 'passion',
rather than on confident rational prediction.[53]

Godwin also made changes to the views expressed in *Political
Justice* on the unequal distribution of property. In the first edition, he had advocated abolition of private property and had
praised emotional detachment from worldly objects, to which,
Stoicism advised, we should all be indifferent. But in April
and May 1797 major naval mutinies took place at Spithead,
near Portsmouth, and the Nore, in the Thames Estuary, where
the mutineers blockaded London, in protest at the poor living
conditions aboard Royal Navy vessels. The provincial press
stressed that the 'mutiness [*sic*] infection' was a major threat to
the nation's first line of defence against French invasion, leaving
British property vulnerable to attack; and conspiracy theorists
speculated that they were the result of plotting by United
Irishmen.[54] Around this time, Godwin started making the case
for the necessary *protection* of private property. He had come to
think that the bloody revolutionary force necessary to ameliorate
inequality of wealth was 'more injurious to the common welfare' than inequality itself. Debates about property in the 1790s
were closely connected to the status of women as property. So
Godwin's more conservative emphasis in the third edition of
Political Justice on resignation to injustice and inequality, and
his fear of 'acrimon[ious]' popular protest and violent disruptions
of property, may well have been linked to his recent softening
towards the institution of marriage.[55] Ambitious sexual reform
threatened a social upheaval of as great a magnitude as the abolition, or redistribution, of private property, and Godwin was now
wary of both revolutionary changes.

Despite the significant ideological accommodations they had
both made, Wollstonecraft and Godwin still found themselves
ostracized when news of their marriage became public knowledge.

Wollstonecraft's marriage to Godwin did not salvage her respectability after her past with Imlay. It simply revealed that her pretence that she had been 'Mrs Imlay' was a lie. Her friends, the Twisses, stopped inviting her to dinner. And when she, Godwin, Amelia Alderson, Maria Reveley, Eliza Fenwick and Elizabeth Inchbald congregated for a trip to the theatre, Inchbald announced that she wanted nothing to do with Wollstonecraft, passing an arch note to Godwin that 'I have entreated another person to supply your place ... If I have done wrong, when you next marry, I will act differently'.[56] Even radicals commonly entertained conventional views about the respectability of marriage and its patriarchal gender relations. In the mid-eighteenth century, a greater emphasis had been placed on affection between husband and wife, and greater egalitarianism had emerged in men and women's business dealings and domestic involvement. But very few questioned the continuing supremacy of marriage, and even fewer actively pursued alternatives. By the end of the century, significant changes in the economy and labour market, combined with the rising tide of Evangelicalism, which asserted the moral importance of the feminine domestic sphere, strengthened the institution of marriage even further. Wollstonecraft and Godwin's capitulation to respectability, for fear of criticism by their radical cohort, testified to the failure of sexual utopianism and to the pervasiveness of the emerging emphasis on stricter regulation of desire.

By May 1797, Godwin's lukewarm responses to Wedgwood's educational 'master-stroke' – his commitment to using education to diminish pain – combined with his persistent entreaties for money, provoked an irritated letter from Wedgwood. Godwin, surprised and concerned, admitted that 'it is very probable that the habits of both of us have ... made a proceeding of unmixed confidence & frankness more difficult than it ought to be'.[57] Godwin suggested that he and his pupil, the young lawyer and philosophy enthusiast Basil Montagu, should visit Wedgwood at Etruria to discuss his proposed scheme in more detail, and rebuild their friendship. Wedgwood agreed, and on 5 June, Godwin and Montagu were en route; at Hampton Lucy in Warwickshire, they 'concluded the Sunday evening' with a bout of 'drinking', after which, Godwin informed Wollstonecraft in a letter home, 'Montagu has just had a vomit, to carry off a certain quantity of punch'.[58] He soon began missing her, and asked that she 'tell [Fanny] I have not forgotten her little mug & that I shall chuse a very pretty one' from the Wedgwoods' pottery factory. Once arrived at 'the land of mugs', Godwin was relieved to find a 'cordial' reception from Tom Wedgwood. Wollstonecraft's sister, Everina, was employed as governess to Jos's children, and they toured Etruria together, where Godwin chose a mug for Fanny, with the letter 'F' 'shaped in a garland of flowers, of green & orange-tawny alternately'. At the precise moment that Wedgwood was devising a scheme to rigorously control every experience to which a child might be exposed, Godwin was realizing the significant consolations of relinquishing control to another person. 'We love,' he wrote to Wollstonecraft that night, 'to multiply our consciousness & our existence, even at the hazard of ... opening new avenues for pain & misery to attack us.'[59] Godwin began to worry that, in his zeal to eradicate pain, Wedgwood's grand plan might inadvertently eliminate the most profound source of pleasure available to humanity.

Nevertheless, Godwin's visit helped Wedgwood to crystallize his intentions. By July, Wedgwood's project was now two-fold: first, to counter the 'host of half formed impressions & abortive conceptions' that mainstream education had 'blended into a mass of confusion', resulting in 'disorder ... in the Passions' and, crucially, in unnecessary pain. Secondly, the scheme would unite all the recipients of his financial support into a 'master stroke which should anticipate a century or two upon the large-paced progress of human improvement'. It would bring together radical and intellectual thinkers in one last-ditch attempt to change the world by effecting a revolution of feeling, by setting up a school designed to put Wedgwood's ideas into practice. Wedgwood hoped that Godwin and Beddoes, perhaps along with Holcroft and Horne Tooke, would form a philosophical advisory body charged with assessing 'how to connect high degrees of pleasure' with 'vivid objects for sight & touch'. And 'Wordsworth & Coleridge', whom he knew by reputation only, would be employed as 'superintendents' over the school itself: a space of 'plain grey walls' in which children would be taught 'the extreme importance of connecting their chief pleasures with rational objects'. Wordsworth and Coleridge would be directly responsible for prohibiting the trivial pleasures of '[r]omping, tickling & fooling', warding off 'the slightest indication of Desp[air]' in children, and creating 'an individual with these endowments, [capable of] producing a general revolution of sentiment' in the world at large.[60] Even towards the dusk of the 1790s, radical projects were still being proposed, couched in the eighteenth-century language of optimism, and in which the passions were conceived to possess a transformative political potential.

Chapter 14

THE NURSERY OF GENIUS

On 31 July 1797, whilst writing his proposal for what he would call the 'Nursery of Genius', Tom Wedgwood admitted that he 'never saw or had any communication with either' Wordsworth or Coleridge, to whom he was intending to entrust the day-to-day running of the project.[1] Wedgwood had first heard Wordsworth's virtues extolled by his brother Jos, who had dined with Wordsworth and Montagu in Bath back in March. Montagu had been Wordsworth's pupil, as well as Godwin's, since 1795, and probably sang Wordsworth's praises during his visit to Etruria with Godwin in June 1797. In September of that year, Wedgwood decided to visit Wordsworth and Coleridge in person, to inform them of his hopes. That summer, Coleridge and Sara had moved to a small thatched cottage in the village of Nether Stowey, forty miles south-west of Bristol, at the gateway to the Quantock Hills. Coleridge's friend Thomas Poole had introduced him to the region. Coleridge had hoped to move to a cottage with six acres of land, at Adscombe, three miles away, but his plans had fallen through at the last minute, possibly because Poole developed cold feet about the erratic Coleridge living in close proximity to his own family. But Coleridge was desperate and the 'little hovel' at Nether Stowey was found as a replacement. There, Coleridge described how 'from seven to half past eight I work in my garden; from breakfast till 12 I read & compose; then work again – feed the pigs, poultry &c., till two o'clock – after dinner work again till Tea – from Tea till supper *review*. So jogs the day; & I am happy.'[2] The life he had once thought only possible in a pantisocratic utopia, he had finally forged for himself, Sara and their young son Hartley (named after David Hartley), not in a distant island retreat, but in the heart of the English countryside.

In Clevedon, back in 1795, Coleridge had started to write poetry in which he had come to see his secluded idyll, his 'cot o'ergrown/ With white-flowered jasmin', as the nucleus from which his benevolence could extend outwards 'to love all things in a world so filled'.[3] He had once envisaged pantisocracy as a settlement clearly removed from the corrupt old world. Coleridge now realized – as Wollstonecraft had done in Scandinavia in 1795 – that even secluded communes in Pennsylvania were 'caressed' by the same 'intellectual breeze' as every other place on earth. He was coming to terms with residing, in Wordsworth's words,

> *Not in Utopia – subterraneous fields,*
> *Or some secreted island, heaven knows where –*
> *But in the very world which is the world*
> *Of all of us, the place in which, in the end,*
> *We find our happiness, or not at all.*[4]

Such accommodation necessitated a dilution of his earlier radicalism, a shift from pantisocracy's emphasis on sudden wholesale change to a concentration on forging individual happiness in secluded retreat. Large, lively political assemblies were a thing of the recent past; it seemed Coleridge no longer hankered after the buzz of the front line of Bristol politics.

In summer 1797, Coleridge's school friend Charles Lamb visited the tiny, damp, draughty cottage at Nether Stowey, which was invaded by mice and, occasionally, by the stream running through the garden. Lamb had a tragic and recent personal history of pain. He had spent six weeks in a Hoxton asylum in 1795, and in September the following year his sister, Mary, in a state of mania, had stabbed her mother to death with a kitchen knife, after which Charles had become responsible for her life-long care.[5] In an epigraph to his poem 'This Lime-Tree Bower my Prison', Coleridge wrote about 'an accident, which disabled him from walking' with Lamb during his visit. Coleridge used his accident and its consequence as the catalyst for reflecting on disappointment, gesturing implicitly towards the recent failure of his pantisocratic gamble and the spirit of frustration that was dogging the reform movement:

> *. . . sometimes*
> *'Tis well to be bereft of promised good,*
> *That we may lift the Soul, and contemplate*
> *With lively joy the joys we cannot share.*

'This Lime-Tree Bower my Prison' was a milestone in the collapse of Enlightenment hopes for 'perfectibility' – the continual material improvement of humanity's circumstances – and the emergence of the Romantic sensibility. The poem raised the possibility that desire for material objects might be consoled by the imagination; that 'fancy' might replace the 'joy' of satisfaction with a joy existing primarily in the imagination. When the material world proved disappointing, the imagination possessed a remarkable capacity to generate consolatory worlds and emotions.

In June 1797, a month before Lamb's visit, Coleridge had reignited his friendship with William Wordsworth. Coleridge and Wordsworth had first met in Bristol in late September 1795, as pantisocracy was limping to a close.[6] Southey was thinking of pursuing a law career, but then left for Portugal. Wordsworth, shortly after meeting Coleridge, wrote that 'I saw but little of him. I wished indeed to have seen more – his talent appears to me very great.'[7] But Coleridge and Wordsworth did not meet again for another eighteen months, until Wordsworth and his sister Dorothy were living at Racedown Lodge at the foot of Pilsdon Pen in West Dorset. One morning in early June 1797, Dorothy looked across the kitchen garden to see Coleridge careering through the corn field towards the house.

Wordsworth had been in revolutionary France itself in 1790, when that country was 'standing on the top of golden hours,/ And human nature seeming born again'.[8] Back in Britain in 1791, he had attended Fawcett's lectures, mixed with dissenters, immersed himself in the pamphlets discussing the French Revolution controversy, and made sense of the scenes he had witnessed in France as the birth of a bright new society. 'Bliss was it in that dawn to be alive,' he would write retrospectively, 'But to be young was very heaven!'[9] Wordsworth returned to France at the end of the year, where he remained until December 1792, furthering his political and personal education primarily through a friendship with an older soldier, Michel de Beaupuy.[10] Upon his return to Britain in December 1792, Wordsworth wrote unmistakeably anti-monarchist poetry in *Descriptive Sketches*, and, in early 1793, *A Letter to the Bishop of Llandaff* 'by a republican', in indignation at the declaration of war between Britain and France that had torn 'By violence at one decisive rent/ From the best Youth in England, their dear pride,/ Their joy, in England'.[11] But within two-and-a-half years, Wordsworth had come to doubt many of the anchors of his self-proclaimed 'democratic' identity. From late September 1795, when he and his sister Dorothy moved into the house at Racedown, Wordsworth increasingly found Godwinian rationalism a sterile account of human motivation, and considered the grand, universalizing gestures of the French Revolution controversy to be blind to details of the mundane suffering of Britain's poorest. Around the time that his friendship with Coleridge was reignited in summer 1797, Wordsworth had begun to write poems on precisely that subject, such as 'Salisbury Plain', with its interwoven accounts of personal woe. Eventually, Wordsworth's long poem *The Prelude* would provide one of the most famous narratives of the subjective effects of the 1790s' disappointments, and of the ideological changes and accommodations that, for many, became necessary during that decade.

On 16 July 1797, two days after Lamb's departure, after being bombarded by Coleridge's persuasive rhetoric, William and Dorothy Wordsworth moved into the beautiful, airy, expansive house of Alfoxden, three miles into the Quantocks. The next day the political lecturer John Thelwall arrived at Nether Stowey. Perhaps strangely, despite Coleridge's excoriation of Thelwall in his *Watchman* essay on 'Modern Patriotism', the two men had become friends. In April 1796, Coleridge had written to him, pointing out that, as political lecturers, '[p]ursuing the same end by the same means, we ought not be strangers to each other', and acknowledging that his *Watchman* piece had been 'unfortunate' and 'offensive'.[12] By May, he had sent him a sonnet, 'To John Thelwall', pleading with him not to 'refuse' his 'song of grateful praise' for his 'patriot zeal'. Thelwall replied approvingly to Coleridge's 'very handsome favour'.[13]

The friendly letters had continued over the next year, and in June 1797, Thelwall set off from London on a tour of the West Country. Although he had resisted longer than most, the Gagging Acts had ultimately ended his political career. He had continued to lecture on politics under the guise of Roman history, but in East Anglia in 1796, Church and King mobs had besieged his lectures; local magistrates had refused protection;

and, terrifyingly, the crew of a man-of-war were given shore leave and bludgeons to confront Thelwall face-to-face. Twenty years later, Thelwall recalled how he had been 'proscribed and hunted – driven like a wild beast, and banished like a contagion, from society'. He 'never did desert the public', Thelwall swore; 'the public deserted him'.[14] Finally he cancelled his lectures, ceased publication of *The Tribune* (the organ he had founded to print his political speeches), and recognized that his activism was 'concluded'.[15]

In Stowey, the group of five – Sara and Samuel Taylor Coleridge, William and Dorothy Wordsworth, and John Thelwall – made a 'most philosophical party'. They hiked, dissected 'religion ... morals ... politics and philosophy', and Wordsworth read aloud his new verse tragedy *The Borderers* under the trees at Alfoxden Park. Thelwall appreciated Nether Stowey as 'a place to make a man forget that there is any necessity for treason!'[16] By the time he left Somerset at the end of June, to continue his walking tour through Bristol and into South Wales, all five felt that 'we like each other uncommonly well' and that Thelwall would make an excellent addition to their group. Coleridge volunteered to find him a nearby residence, with Thomas Poole's help.

On 15 August, a government spy called John Walsh arrived in Nether Stowey, alerted to the possible presence of French informers by reports of two men making maps of local rivers and talking about 'spy nosey'. Wordsworth and Coleridge had actually been talking about *Spinoza*, and making '*studies*' for a topographical poem called 'The Brook', but Walsh's surveillance rattled them and their neighbours. Wordsworth's landlord threatened to evict them, especially once he heard that the notorious Thelwall had recently visited. 'You cannot conceive the tumult, calumnies, & apparatus of threatened persecutions which this event has occasioned round about us,' Coleridge reported, perhaps with a little hyperbole, to Thelwall. Faced with losing

Wordsworth as a neighbour, Coleridge was prepared to sacrifice his friendship with Thelwall to placate the Wordsworths' landlord, the local community, and Poole. On 21 August, Coleridge wrote to Thelwall, postponing their agreed plan that he should take a cottage in Stowey too: 'Come! but not yet!'[17]

Thelwall ended up settling at Llyswen Farm, near Brecon, and Coleridge, William and Dorothy Wordsworth visited him in August 1798. But he felt Coleridge's rejection acutely long after. In the 'Prefatory Memoir' that Thelwall included in his *Poems, Chiefly Written in Retirement*, published in 1801, he identified erosion of friendship as one of the most painful consequences of Pitt's crackdowns on radicalism. The Gagging Acts engendered a paranoia that pitted former friends against one another, stifled opportunities for collaboration, and eroded privacy through surveillance: 'the intercourses of the closest relationship [have been] violated and impeded, and the recesses of the utmost obscurity have been disturbed'.[18]

Thelwall's departure from Stowey left Wordsworth and Coleridge free to cement their friendship, and on 15 September 1797, Tom Wedgwood descended on the village too, to propose his Nursery of Genius scheme to the two men upon whom he had settled as its most likely superintendents.[19] But Wedgwood swiftly became disappointed in Wordsworth, with whose views on education he clashed. In *The Prelude*, Wordsworth would ridicule pedagogical methods that, like Wedgwood's, sought to

> ... *range the faculties*
> *In scale and order, class the cabinet*
> *Of their sensations, and in voluble phrase*
> *Run through the history and birth of each*
> *As of a single independent thing.*

It was a 'Hard task to analyse a soul', Wordsworth stressed, and 'Who knows the individual hour in which/ His habits were first sown, even as a seed?' Wordsworth instead recommended cultivating 'the filial bond/ Of Nature that connect[s] [the child] with the world': a bond that manifested itself 'in all sentiments of grief,/ Of exultation, fear and joy'. Pain as well as pleasure – negative as well as positive emotions – were spontaneous results of opening the 'mind' to the 'Poetic spirit' of Nature.[20] Pain and distress were not to be plucked out of human life like unwanted hairs.

Coleridge defended Wordsworth against Wedgwood's aggrieved reaction, declaring that 'he strides on so far before you that he dwindles into the distance'.[21] But Coleridge, personally, got on well with Wedgwood. He relished his sensitivity, his deep and prolonged reflection into the life of the passions, his analysis of the 'sore place[s] in his mind'.[22] And Wedgwood's money was an undeniable attraction for the permanently impecunious poet: Coleridge had none of Godwin's ethical qualms about accepting gifts. So Coleridge began to entertain the possibility of putting Wedgwood's Nursery of Genius plan into action. Wordsworth was clearly out of the picture, but Coleridge proposed 'joining with Mr Montague [sic] in a project of Tuition'. By November, Coleridge had put together 'the Sketch of a Plan of General Study', outlining how, 'in three years', his students would 'go systematically, yet with constant reference to the nature of *man*, thro' the mathematical Branches, chemistry, Anatomy, the laws of Life, the laws of Intellect, & lastly, thro' universal History'.[23] Notably, Coleridge's plan seems to have contained little mention of Wedgwood's obsession with the elimination of pain. Coleridge proposed to begin with eight students, for a fee of £100 per pupil, the revenue from which would pay his salary along with Wedgwood's subsidy. The Nursery of Genius was taking shape.

Thomas Beddoes, too, was likely sympathetic to Wedgwood's scheme at first: indeed, it may have originated from one of his own works. In the early 1790s, Beddoes had written *Observations on the Nature of Demonstrative Evidence*. It was dedicated to his great friend Davies Giddy and explored 'whether objects appear to the senses of others as they appear to his senses'.[24] Beddoes explained that his interest in whether different people perceive the same object in the same way was intended to provide a foundation for 'a plan of education which shall pay some attention to the senses and understanding': the exact remit of Wedgwood's Nursery of Genius.[25] Whereas Wedgwood was interested in the manipulation of early sensory experiences to manage pleasure and pain, Beddoes' treatise focused on how geometric and mathematical principles might be taught through sensory objects. He suggested that 'models would make the study infinitely more engaging'; that solid shapes might prompt children to have ideas about volume, extension and quantity.[26]

In 1796, Beddoes had returned to these thoughts about mathematical toys, and had discussed with Wedgwood a project to make models to 'smooth the difficulties which render the study of geometry so repulsive to young people'.[27] Beddoes' sister-in-law, Maria Edgeworth, had helped him to find a manufacturer to build prototype models, and Wedgwood may have assisted financially. But it had proved impossible to persuade anyone to go into mass production. Beddoes' efforts were not a complete failure, however. Two years later, in 1798, the manual on *Practical Education* on which Maria, Richard Lovell Edgeworth and his now deceased second wife, Honora Sneyd, had been working for twenty years, was finally published. It was a success; a second edition was printed in 1801, and it was translated across the Continent, making the Edgeworths internationally famous. Its preface acknowledged that the 'first hint of the chapter on Toys was received from Dr. Beddoes'.[28]

But Beddoes did not turn out to be a willing participant in the Nursery of Genius, for, in June 1796, he had witnessed the demise of Enlightenment optimism about the revolutionary potential of education close at hand, when Beddoes' father-in-law, Richard Lovell Edgeworth, received a distraught message from his son Dick, in whom his Rousseauvian educational hopes had once been invested. The previous autumn, Dick had once again made the long voyage from North Carolina to the British Isles, to visit the family with whom he had been reconciled only three years earlier. Dick had consulted Beddoes about a lingering illness. And he had thrown himself into his father's 'perpetual' attempts to construct a telegraph network. His sister Maria had written approvingly of how 'in all his actions he has been so happy as to please my father Mother & every Individual in the family beyond even my sanguine expectations'. In the spring of 1796, Dick had set sail again. Edgeworth's educational experiment had undoubtedly failed in the short-term, but Dick's resilience and apparent success in America appeared partially to vindicate his father's efforts.

A badly water-damaged, mouldy letter from Dick to Edgeworth in the family archive describes how he returned to America to find that, in his absence, his crops had been destroyed by a flood, his workers drowned, and his horses killed by an epidemic. After begging a basic annuity of £50 from his father, Dick promised to now turn his attention to law. But within two months, he was dead. In August 1796, Dick's friend John Hardwick wrote from North Carolina to Edgeworth in Ireland, informing him that Dick had 'never got over the complaint he had at Bristol ... he appeared to grow weaker every day'. In 1792, Dick had agreed with his father that his eldest son, Lovell, would be sent to Edgeworth to be educated in Ireland. But in the wake of Dick's death, Edgeworth reneged. He wrote to Dick's widow that the children would be better off being educated in America, and concluded that Dick's 'way of life was become such as promised no happiness to himself or his family – it is therefore better for both, that he has retired from the scene – [he was] a very promising boy!' Edgeworth's project was now shown to have irretrievably failed: after the disappointment of Dick's unruliness in his youth, Edgeworth may have latterly found vindication for his Rousseauvian educational scheme, with its emphasis on cultivating *Robinson Crusoe*-style adventurousness, in Dick's apparently successful management of an American farm. But now that, too, had collapsed, with fatal consequences. While Edgeworth had proved adept at detaching himself from the aftermath of his project, his son had not been so lucky. And the now definitive failure of one of the most famous Enlightenment experiments in education may have played a part in turning Beddoes' attention to less ambitious educational projects, which sought to effect small, gradual improvements rather than the large-scale transformations envisaged by Wedgwood.

In October 1797, an opportunity to materialize some of Beddoes' ambitions for medical education presented itself in a way that seemed more feasible than the Nursery of Genius. He was approached by 'a practitioner in Surgery', 'desirous of giving a Course of Anatomical Lectures in Bristol'. Beddoes described how to 'furnish individuals with so much knowledge of themselves as should enable them to guard against habitual sickliness ... had been long an object of contemplation with me'. Lectures, open to the general public, might widen access to medical knowledge and treatment. So he agreed to organize the series. 'The purpose of the course', Beddoes explained, 'will be to exhibit the structure of the human body', 'to explain the functions of the parts' and 'to illustrate by specimens the principal deviations of these parts from their healthy conformation'.[29] But Beddoes did not plan to deliver the lecture series himself, beyond an introductory lecture, which he would dedicate to Wedgwood, in recognition of his educational efforts. Beddoes knew that his own Jacobin taint might deter audience members and prompt negative reviews, so he hired the Bristol anatomist F. C. Bowles and the Bristol Infirmary surgeon Richard Smith:

reassuring establishment figures.[30] The course would comprise twenty-four lectures, three evenings per week, over an eight-week period, on basic anatomy and physiology, along with 'some hints on the subject of Diseases'. They would be open to medical pupils & 'scientific persons in general', cost 2 guineas per person for the whole course, and begin around November.

But the anatomical lectures were not open to *all* 'persons in general'. Reflecting the increasing confinement of women to the home, and their exclusion from the formal clubs and institutions that would characterize nineteenth-century urban and provincial topography, females were banned by Bowles and Smith. They overruled Beddoes, who had 'no objection' to women attending the lectures. Ever the subversive, Beddoes used his introductory lecture to describe the importance of anatomical knowledge to women's health. He described how the eighteenth century's relatively liberal approach to emotional regulation was paralleled by relaxation in dress. Around the 1780s, the hoops, panniers and wigs of earlier fashions were replaced by the informal 'deshabille' or 'undress' pioneered by Marie Antoinette. Beddoes correlated the 'abolition of that severe system of constriction' with better physical health for women.[31] He worried that the constraints of 'the best secured fortress of effeminacy' left women with an accumulation of energy that made them prone to violent reactions when the restrictions were temporarily lifted. On rare immersions in nature, he claimed, women were left 'shiver[ing] more at the inclemencies of the seasons, than the mountaineer who is exposed to all the blasts of winter'.[32] But where men's hydraulic outbursts endangered all society, the eruption of women's accumulated energy tended to threaten their own bodies alone.

At the beginning of January 1798, after the conclusion of the men's anatomical lectures, Beddoes announced a series designed purely for women (and male chaperones), carefully excluding 'every topic which might, by possibility, afford room for a perverted imagination to lay hold of'.[33] Beddoes soon wrote happily that 'the ladies' anatomical lectures succeed perfectly. The number exceeds 30 and I hope will reach 40.'[34] The course consisted of ten lectures on subjects ranging from general physiology, the sensory organs, teeth and bones, the heart and circulation of the blood, the nervous system, and lungs and other organs. Beddoes was proud that his lectures demonstrated that nothing could alarm 'female delicacy, or excite disgust'.[35]

After the success of his two lecture series, Beddoes threw himself into organizing further courses, first on chemistry, and then on geology. He hoped that such events would diffuse the hostility accumulating after the Gagging Acts by bringing together opposing political factions, and thereby 'spar[ing] some acts of barbarity in the times that are approaching'.[36] He tried to expand the lectures' remit by setting up a permanent 'Bristol Philosophic Theatre'.[37] But Beddoes' 'Jacobin' reputation again kiboshed his intentions: the dean and chapter of Bristol cathedral refused to grant permission for the theatre, since the proposed venue was within sight of the cathedral. Nevertheless, the lectures themselves had been a success, though they represented a more modest aspiration for education than projects in which Beddoes had previously been involved, and diverted his energies away from Wedgwood's Nursery of Genius.

The demise of Godwin's already lukewarm interest in Wedgwood's project was prompted by personal reasons. By the summer of 1797, he, Wollstonecraft and little Fanny had moved in together in Somers Town, in London. The Polygon was a relatively new housing block, roughly circular but with fifteen sides and three storeys. Wollstonecraft and Godwin agreed 'that it was possible for two persons to be too uniformly in each other's society', so Godwin rented another apartment twenty doors down, ostensibly to use as his study, but where he ensconced himself every day from morning until dinner.[38] By

June, Wollstonecraft was six months pregnant. She and Godwin referred to the foetus as 'Master William', and she had begun 'to love this little creature, and to anticipate his birth as a fresh twist to a knot, which I do not wish to untie'. To Godwin, she confessed that 'I love you better than I supposed I did, when I promised to love you for ever' and 'on the whole I may be termed happy'.[39] Combined with philosophical doubts about the propriety of eradicating pain from human existence, Godwin's impending family responsibilities may have compelled him to extricate himself from the Nursery of Genius; the upbringing of Fanny and Master William must have appeared more pressing than the hypothetical children at Wedgwood's imaginary grey-walled school.

Having experienced a relatively easy birth with Fanny, Wollstonecraft was relaxed about her second labour. On 25 August, she felt some dull, low pains in her uterus. It turned out to be a false alarm, but five days later, she had 'no doubt of seeing the animal to day'.[40] Wollstonecraft's contractions started at 5 a.m. in the morning of 30 August, and by 9 a.m. her midwife, Mrs Blenkensop, at the Westminster Lying-In Hospital, had been sent for. 'Every thing is in a fair way,' Wollstonecraft wrote to Godwin, who had absented himself to his study down the road; 'there is no fear of the event being put off another day.' A few hours later: 'Mrs Blenkensop tells me that I am in the most natural state, and can promise me a safe delivery – But that I must have a little patience,' echoing her mother's dying words – 'A little patience – and then all will be over!'[41]

At 2 p.m. Wollstonecraft made her way upstairs to prepare for the delivery. But, for a second labour, it was proceeding very slowly, and the baby was not born until 11.20 at night. By now, Godwin was waiting in the parlour, where Wollstonecraft had instructed him to remain until she was ready to present 'Master William'. By 2 a.m., he had still not been called in. Then Mrs Blenkensop emerged with the disquieting news that,

although the baby – not 'William', but 'Mary' – had been born
safely, the placenta had not yet been expelled. Godwin sent for
the physician and man mid-wife Dr Poignand, from the same
hospital, who arrived within the hour. He set about extracting
Wollstonecraft's placenta in pieces, rummaging inside her until
'he was satisfied that the whole was removed'.[42] Wollstonecraft
haemorrhaged badly, losing consciousness in 'an almost uninterrupted series of fainting fits'. By 4 a.m., though, the operation
seemed a success, and Wollstonecraft, although weak, was lying
quietly against her pillow; Godwin wrote that she bestowed
upon him 'one of those smiles which so eminently illuminated
her countenance' and declared herself 'determined not to leave
me'. The removal of the placenta had been terrible – 'she had
never known what bodily pain was before' – but the danger
appeared to be consigned to the past.[43]

Later that morning, Poignand visited again; and Wollstonecraft
requested that Godwin also send for her friend George Fordyce,
the distinguished Scottish physician. Both proclaimed the
patient weak, but out of danger. And although Godwin remained
by her side that day, the following morning – 1 September – he
was confident enough to travel across London on business,
returning home just before dinner to be told that the patient
was in a 'promising state'. Two days later, Godwin ventured out
again, accompanying a friend on some calls as far as Kensington.
But on his return, Godwin was met by 'a degree of anxiety in
every face, and was told that she had had a sort of shivering fit'.[44]
Wollstonecraft succumbed to chills again that evening: 'every
muscle of the body trembled, the teeth chattered, and the bed
shook under her ... for five minutes'. The terrifying realization
dawned on her and Godwin that the placenta had not been
entirely removed, as Poignand had assured them, but was decay-
ing inside her – the poor, damaged surface of her uterus was
killing her from within. Godwin sent for Fordyce, who prohibited breastfeeding and located puppies to suckle her milk and

relieve her engorged discomfort, 'occasion[ing] some pleasantry of Mary with me and the other attendants'. The following day, Fordyce recruited Dr John Clarke, a specialist in 'the Epidemic Disease of Lying-in Women', and the two men discussed the propriety of a further operation, to locate the remaining placental fragment.[45] But Wollstonecraft was too weak to endure such intervention, and they instead charged Godwin with overseeing the regular application of sips of wine, hoping to stimulate her ailing frame.

'I now fought to suppress every idea of hope,' Godwin would remember. 'The greatest anguish I have any conception of, consists in that crushing of a new-born hope.'[46] By 8 September, nine days after giving birth, Wollstonecraft had become delirious. Godwin gently pressed her about her wishes for her two children. After he had 'repeated this idea to her in a great variety of forms, she at length said, with a significant tone of voice, "I know what you are thinking of," but added, that she had nothing to communicate to me upon the subject'.[47] She held on for another two days, and then, at 6 a.m. on 10 September 1797, her friend Carlisle woke Godwin to summon him to her chamber. Wollstonecraft died at 7.40 a.m. She was buried five days later, at the churchyard of St Pancras Old Church. Godwin was too distressed to attend her funeral.

After Wollstonecraft's death, Godwin devoted himself to the care of Fanny, then three years old, and to the newborn Mary. He also began to organize Wollstonecraft's papers, to take charge of her legacy. At her death, she had left unpublished the beginnings of a book 'on the Management of Infants', as well as the manuscript of *Maria*, and reams of letters, including those tortured missives to Imlay. Godwin organized her papers into four volumes of *Posthumous Works of the Author of a Vindication of the Rights of Woman*, which Johnson published in 1798. And he wrote a biography too: *Memoirs of the Author of a Vindication of the Rights of Woman*.

Godwin had so recently urged the wisdom of accommodating ideas to the changing climate. But he showed himself to be tone deaf to the emerging emotional culture that would come to define the new century, in which marriage, domesticity, 'modesty' and strict emotional regulation were being urged on women, especially, with a new vigour. In this increasingly conservative atmosphere, Godwin's *Memoirs* and *Posthumous Works* laid bare Wollstonecraft's extra-marital sexuality, and reduced her complex and nuanced approach to emotional regulation to an image of someone who simply 'gave a loose to all the sensibilities of her nature'.[48] In writing and in life, Wollstonecraft had robustly challenged the 'feminine' associations of 'the passions'. And Godwin himself had shrugged off the masculine mantle of 'the coldest blooded metaphysician of the age', as the essayist Isaac d'Israeli dubbed him, to make greater space for emotion, desire and intimate attachments.[49] But now Godwin took it upon himself to reinscribe the gendered conventions surrounding emotion that, in life, Wollstonecraft had so vigorously countered. His *Memoirs* asserted that 'the two sexes are particularly distinguished from each other' in their experiences of the passions: 'one is accustomed more to the exercise of its reasoning powers, and the other of its feelings. Women have a frame of body more delicate and susceptible of impression than men, and . . . are more unreservedly under the empire of feeling.' In the example of 'Mary and myself', Godwin continued, 'each carried farther than to its common extent the characteristics of the sexes to which we belonged'.[50] He himself, he thought, had lived up to the criticism he had once received for being too 'masculine' in his reason: 'thou ungrateful, unfeeling, cruel, insulting, barbarous man, or to sum up thy iniquities in one word, thou Philosopher'.[51] But Wollstonecraft's 'feelings had a character of peculiar strength [which . . .] she found herself unable to control'. He did compare her to a Romantic emotional male – a 'female Werther' – but the qualities Godwin assigned to Wollstonecraft were more enduringly associated with the stereotype of the quintessential emotional female.[52]

Godwin's eulogy did a disservice to Wollstonecraft's lifelong attempts to attain 'virtue' by harmonizing reason and emotion. And he betrayed her efforts to undermine the rigid gendering of emotion, by portraying her as an embodiment of the incontinent 'sensibility' she had derided for inflaming women's senses, neglecting their understanding, and rendering them prey to 'every momentary gust of feeling'.[53] Godwin's sexually explicit revelations were also responsible for ensuring that Wollstonecraft became a cultural figure of fear and loathing in the early nineteenth century, the nadir against which feminine virtue was defined. The historian Barbara Taylor describes how 'the decade after [Wollstonecraft's] death saw the publication of dozens of works – some authored by women, including erstwhile admirers and associates – satirizing her as an addlebrained fanatic addicted to utopian system-mongering while abusing or neglecting everyone around her'.[54] The Rev. Dr Thomas Binney maligned Wollstonecraft's perceived 'masculinisation' of women, and 'feminisation' of men in her attempts to erode the force of gender, and proclaimed that women's mission was to inspire, animate, soothe and resuscitate men, so that 'the mighty engine of masculine life might be aided in its action and its results'.[55] The *Anti-Jacobin Review* listed Wollstonecraft's name under 'prostitution' in its index, proclaiming that 'it is our province, and our duty, to meet the legion of Wollstonecrafts . . . [who] diffuse the poison of corruption through the mass of society . . . and to endeavour to cast them out!'[56] And the *European Magazine* labelled her a 'philosophical wanton', driven by Jacobin immoderation.[57] The 1790s had brought about a revolution of feeling in both Wollstonecraft's and Godwin's philosophies of emotion. But he sacrificed the reputation of Wollstonecraft and her writings to the changing climate. Not permanently, but for a very long time – until the early twentieth century – he was responsible for relegating her memory to the wrong side of history.

Even Coleridge, who was most invested of all the potential participants in the Nursery of Genius, fell away from Tom Wedgwood's scheme. In the autumn of 1797, following his visit to Stowey, Wedgwood spent a great deal of time at his brother John's residence, Cote House, at Westbury on Trym, forty miles or so from Coleridge's cottage. John had married Louisa Jane Allen, whose sister, Catherine, was engaged to be married to Sir James Mackintosh, a Whig politician and journalist. In April 1791, Mackintosh had published one of the most lauded radical responses to Burke: *Vindiciae Gallicae: Defence of the French Revolution and its English Admirers.*[58] But since then, Mackintosh had done an ideological about-turn. He had been an eye-witness to the September Massacres, and by 1796 openly admitted that he had come to hold his old opponent Burke in the 'most affectionate veneration'. Mackintosh spent nearly every weekend at Cote House, attacking the 'perfectibilist speculations' of Godwin – and of his prospective brother-in-law Tom Wedgwood – as 'part of the dangerous disease associated with the spread of the "new philosophy" since the French revolution'.[59] Coleridge was also a frequent visitor to Cote House while he and Wedgwood were thrashing out the logistics of the Nursery of Genius. He and Mackintosh had a fierce argument, and Coleridge left Cote House in a huff, although some reported that he had been driven out after losing the argument.

Coleridge's enthusiasm for Wedgwood's project was also waning for less personal reasons. By the end of 1797, it had been announced that Pitt planned to triple assessed taxes – a combined tax, covering a duty on inhabited houses, on carriages and servants, and on horses and game, which was intended to weigh more heavily on the wealthy – even quadrupling them for the most affluent, to fund the continued war with France.

Such a tax increase would reduce many families' ability to pay the Nursery's proposed fees. Coleridge decided to jump ship and 'made up my mind to be a Dissenting Minister' instead. He contacted a local minister in Shrewsbury, and arranged to 'supply [his] place for a few Sundays'.[60] On his return to Stowey, Coleridge – still dithering – presented Basil Montagu with an ultimatum: find eight pupils at speed and 'I would join him gladly'; otherwise 'I should accept some situation, as Dissenting Minister'. Wedgwood was informed and conferred with his brother Jos. Around Christmas Day, two letters arrived at Coleridge's cottage. One, from Shrewsbury, invited him to apply for a vacancy as Unitarian minister. The other, from Tom and Jos Wedgwood, offered him an annual payment of £100, for the rest of Coleridge's life. But Coleridge became anxious that, 'if I accept it, I certainly bind myself to ... the co-execution of the Plan of general Study with Montague'.[61] Coleridge feared it was not an unconditional offer, but was dependent on carrying out Wedgwood's plan. The Nursery of Genius had offered a temporary opportunity for a secure wage, but Coleridge had never been genuinely enthused by the idea of teaching, sneering that '*They* who had to teach, can *never afford* to learn'.[62] Now there was a preferable, and more viable, career option on the table.

In early January 1798, Coleridge replied to Wedgwood, turning down the annuity. He set off for Shrewsbury, preaching a sermon there on 14 January, in anticipation of being offered a permanent position. Back in Stowey, a letter arrived for him. Jos had written to Coleridge, describing how 'My brother and myself are possessed of a considerable superfluity of fortune' and were 'earnestly desirous to convert this superfluity into a fund of beneficence ... we have no hesitation in declaring that your claim upon the fund appears ... to be every way more unobjectionable, than we could possibly have expected ... I have only to state the proposal we wish to make to you,' he continued: 'It is that you shall accept an annuity for life of £150, *to be regularly paid by us, no condition whatsoever being annexed to it.* Thus your liberty will remain entire,' Jos assured Coleridge, recognizing his concerns about being bound to the Nursery of Genius. '[Y] ou will be under the influence of no professional bias, and will be in possession of a *"permanent income not inconsistent with your religious and political creeds."* [63]

Whilst Coleridge was being interviewed for a permanent position as Unitarian minister, the Wedgwoods' letter – and its promise of permanent financial security for the rest of his life – was sitting unopened on his table. Luckily Poole took it upon himself to open Jos's proposal, and immediately forwarded it to Coleridge in Shrewsbury. On opening it, Coleridge was, as he described to Thelwall, 'astonished, agitated, and feeling as I could not help feeling, I accepted the offer in the same worthy spirit, I hope, in which it was made'. Impressed, Wordsworth declared it an act of 'unexampled liberality'. [64] Tom and Jos's formal patronage of Coleridge would free him from the financial anxiety that had dogged him throughout the decade and had restricted his ability to pursue poetic or philosophical projects at length. But it also put an end to Tom Wedgwood's hopes for his Nursery of Genius. A few weeks previously, Coleridge had recorded that the plan now 'appeared absolutely romantic' and was to be given up. [65] Wedgwood had hoped that uniting all the beneficiaries of 'the Wedgwood fund' – Godwin, Beddoes, Wollstonecraft and Coleridge – would result in an ambitious educational scheme that could not fail to transform children's experiences of emotion, pleasure and pain. 'How animating is the thought that if by the labour of my life I should add one idea to the stock of those concerning Education, my life has been well spent!' Wedgwood had exulted. [66] But the project never got off the ground, and now everyone seemed destined to go their separate ways. The climate was no longer conducive to such radical, optimistic schemes.

IV

The Age of Despair

Chapter 15

RULING OVER THE CAUSES
OF PAIN AND PLEASURE

On Saturday 19 May 1798, a proclamation was issued by the Lord Lieutenant of Ireland and the Privy Council, declaring 'the County of the City of Dublin to be in immediate danger of becoming in a state of disturbance'.[1] Within days, English newspapers were breathlessly reporting that 'the advices received' about 'a plan of a general rising of the people for subverting the Government' had been correct. On 24 May, a rebellion began but was narrowly aborted in Dublin, when government informers related details about rebel assembly points; the leaders were swept up, whilst everyone else dispersed, dumping their weapons. But in the surrounding districts and counties of Dublin, the uprisings went ahead as planned. Fierce fighting soon spread through Leinster and County Kildare. The *Dublin Mail* reported that 'the village of Lacklan, in the County of Wicklow, consisting of 27 houses, was consumed in the course of last week', the local blacksmith having been 'apprehended . . . for making pikes'.[2] The rebels had most success in Wexford, where they seized control of the county until 21 June, when the uprising there was put down by 20,000 loyalist troops.

The 1798 Irish Rebellion was the result of preparations made by the Society of United Irishmen: the broad coalition of Protestant liberals, Catholics, Presbyterians and other dissenters that had been founded in 1791. During the latter half of the eighteenth century, the same principles that had invigorated parliamentary reform associations in England had led to an Irish reform movement that sought greater autonomy from Britain. During the American War of Independence, thousands of Irish volunteers had responded to a call from London to form militias in order to defend Ireland from a potential French invasion. This gave the volunteers a valuable bargaining position, and, along with Henry Grattan of the Irish Patriot Party, they negotiated for limited self-rule with an independent parliament. In 1793, suffrage was extended in Ireland to Catholics who possessed enough property, although they continued to be barred from standing for election or appointment as state officials. The Society of United Irishmen aimed to further this progress, and proposed policies for greater democratic reforms and Catholic emancipation. By 1797, the United Irishmen numbered 200,000 members. 'To subvert the tyranny of our execrable Government, to break the connection of England, the never-failing source of all our political evils, and to assert the independence of my country – these were my objects,' declared their founding member, Wolfe Tone: 'To unite the whole people of Ireland, to abolish the memory of all past dissensions, and to substitute the common name of Irishman in the place of the denominations of Protestant, Catholic and Dissenter – these were my means.'[3]

But after the early 1790s, the climate was hostile to calls for greater reform, and after the outbreak of war with France, the United Irishmen began to set their sights on an armed

insurrection, assisted by the French military. In 1796, Tone –
who had been exiled to Philadelphia, in America – travelled
to France to invite their troops to land in Ireland and assist an
uprising. In December that year, 14,450 troops paused off the
coast of Bantry Bay, with another 17,000 following in reserve.
They had eluded the Royal Navy, but a storm had hit, and,
under a combination of irresolute leadership and inadequate
seamanship, a decision was made to turn back. Tone commented, ruefully, that 'England has had its luckiest escape since
the Armada'.[4] The abortive invasion took England entirely by
surprise and provoked a major political crisis.

By 1797, France had altered its policy: it would no longer assist
foreign revolutionaries unless they had launched an uprising
first, alone. Seemingly unaware of this shift, Tone exhorted the
United Irishmen to maintain their strength until the French
arrived. But that strength was eroded throughout 1797 and
1798 by the arrest of rebel leaders on the basis of information
gathered by government infiltrators. In March 1798, martial
law was imposed throughout Ireland, and the depleted United
Irishmen were under pressure to act before the moment had
passed. Militants, under the leadership of Samuel Neilson and
Lord Edward Fitzgerald, set the date for the rebellion, for 23
May 1798. A reward of £1,000 was offered for Fitzgerald's capture
on 11 May, and he managed to avoid arrest for another week,
lodging with a feather merchant. But on 19 May, he was discovered, prone on an upstairs bed, and in the following struggle he
shot and killed one man, before he himself sustained a shot to
the shoulder. Imprisoned in Newgate Gaol, in Dublin, as the
rebellion took off in the counties surrounding him, his wounds
grew infected and turned into septicaemia. Fitzgerald died in
his cell, on 4 June.[5]

Nearly two weeks later, Tone, in France, learned of the
outbreak of the rebellion. Rushed preparations were made to
mount a French invasion, and a few small units of troops were

dispatched to spots on the Irish coast. On 16 September, a much larger force, including Tone, left France, but in the time it had taken to assemble it, the British press had printed details of its course. Even as he was embarking, Tone knew that 'his life was gone'. On 12 October, the ships were simultaneously buffeted by a storm and attacked by the Navy, and surrendered after a battle lasting three hours. Tone was captured, tried by military court for treason, and, after being sentenced to hang, cut his own throat on 19 November 1798. 'I have attempted to establish the independence of my country; I have failed in the attempt; my life is in consequence forfeited,' he had acknowledged before the court.[6]

For many English radicals, the fate of the United Irish Rebellion marked the definitive failure of the reform movement. English, Scottish and Welsh Corresponding Societies had forged close alliances with the United Irishmen, and considered their aims and destinies closely entwined. Lord Edward Fitzgerald was the first cousin of Caroline Fitzgerald, Lady Kingsborough, Mary Wollstonecraft's employer in Ireland; and he had arrived in Paris in 1792, just weeks before she herself had become involved with the British Club of Jacobins at White's Hotel, making friends there, too, with Archibald Hamilton Rowan, another United Irishman. In the aftermath of the Irish rebellion's defeat, small pockets of rebels subsisted in various counties across Ireland for a number of years. But the British government pushed through the Act of Union, which came into force on 1 January 1801, partly as a response to the rebellion. The Act of Union eroded the limited autonomy that had been won for the Protestant Ascendancy, and marked the definitive end of any aspirations, either in England or in Ireland, that the 1790s might witness radical political change.

In the wake of the United Irish Rebellion, in the autumn of 1798, Thomas Beddoes finally had enough money to announce the imminent opening of the Pneumatic Institute. The project dated back to the summer of 1791, when Beddoes had first realized the need to widen access to treatment for consumption, and proposed an innovative new treatment based on 'the airs'. It was Beddoes' reading of John Brown's theory of 'excitability' that had convinced him of the greater possibilities of pneumatic cures: not only might they alter levels of oxygen in the body to treat tuberculosis, but they might be the conduit through which the body's very life-force was renewed. Beddoes had procured premises for his preliminary research in 1793, and the following year he had begun disseminating accounts of his methods and hinting at exciting early results. He had secured the collaboration of the firm of Watt and Boulton in manufacturing instruments for his proposed institute, and had acquired famous and wealthy patrons and supporters, including Tom Wedgwood and even Georgiana, the Duchess of Devonshire. On 21 March 1797, Beddoes circulated a formal plan for the Pneumatic Institute, *Suggestions Towards Setting on Foot the Projected Establishment for Ascertaining the Powers of Factitious Airs in Medicine.*[7] All that remained was to locate premises for receiving patients, and an assistant. Beddoes negotiated to acquire a house in the corner of Dowry Square in Bristol Hotwells, and in April 1798 he identified a candidate for the post of assistant: a twenty-year-old chemistry enthusiast and apprentice apothecary from Penzance, whom his old friend Davies Giddy had taken under his wing.[8]

Humphry Davy was a fearsomely acute young man, with a rapt, unwavering gaze. Giddy had found him swinging on his gate at Tredrea and invited him in to use his library. Davy had become entranced by Lavoisier's work on caloric theory, which attributed heat to the presence of a fluid, 'caloric', that flowed from hot objects to cooler ones. In the late 1790s, the caloric theory was being attacked in experiments by the physicist Benjamin Thompson, Count Rumford. When watching the manufacture of a cannon, Rumford noticed that heat was generated when the hole was bored by a tool creating friction. Rumford conducted an experiment in which a cannon was immersed in water, and bored by a specially blunted tool to generate exceptionally large amounts of friction. After around two-and-a-half hours, the water began to boil, and Rumford showed that the supply of frictional heat from the boring of the cannon did not reduce but seemed inexhaustible. Heat was not caused by the release of a finite substance like caloric, he concluded, but by motion and mechanical work. This became the 'mechanical theory of heat', which gradually developed in the nineteenth century into the science of thermodynamics, and, in the twentieth century, contributed to the kinetic theory of gases. These theories attributed heat to motion and position, not to the presence of a chemical element like Lavoisier's 'caloric'. Davy had been sceptical about Lavoisier's claims when he first read his *Traité élémentaire de chimie*, and he devised his own experiment – rubbing lumps of ice together to melt them – to prove the alternative theory of kinetic heat. When Davy became interested in a copy of Beddoes' *Considerations*, which linked 'muscular motion' to the presence of both bodily 'heat' and 'oxygen', Giddy introduced the two men – one nearly forty and bearing an air of resigned disappointment; one not quite twenty, with everything to play for.[9]

Davy arrived in Bristol in October 1798. It was the first time he had left home, and he wrote to his mother from Rodney Place that 'Our house is capacious and handsome; my rooms are very large, nice and convenient; and, above all, I have an excellent laboratory.' But, he continued, 'Dr Beddoes ... is one of the most original men I ever saw – uncommonly short and fat, with little elegance of manners, and nothing characteristic *externally* of genius or science; extremely silent, and in a few words, a very bad companion. His behaviour to me, however, has been particularly handsome.' On the other hand, Davy reflected, 'Mrs Beddoes is the reverse of Dr Beddoes – extremely cheerful, gay and witty; she is one of the most pleasing women I have ever met with ... We are already great friends.'[10]

With Davy's arrival, the opening of the Pneumatic Institute became imminent. On 21 March 1799, the first day of spring, its doors were finally unlocked and patients began queuing. Beddoes announced in a prospectus published that day in the *Bristol Gazette* that ailments such as 'Consumption, Asthma, Palsy, Dropsy, obstinate Venereal Complaints, Scrophula or King's Evil' would be treated with a combination of common and pneumatic remedies, and the outcomes carefully documented. Beddoes and Davy were in attendance to meet patients 'from Eleven till One o'clock' each day. Many patients were wary of the gases: the untested remedies for which they would be guinea pigs, and the unfamiliar apparatus that made the laboratory resemble a factory. But when 'ordinary means ha[d] failed to remove' their suffering, patients usually became more amenable to the strange new pneumatic treatment.[11]

Beddoes' and Davy's first experiments in Dowry Square presented patients with oxygen to inhale. Beddoes had noticed that the blood and complexions of consumptives appeared bright red, hyper-oxygenated, and surmised that a cure might be found in the application of gases with a different proportion of oxygen to that in atmospheric air. He trialled a number of gases, including hydrogen. But soon Beddoes' energies were diverted from focusing on the link between gases and the cure of consumption when the results were not as promising as he had hoped. He began to investigate a different gas – nitrous oxide – with the intention of exploring not its power to cure consumption, but whether it might be the gas that Brown had envisaged in his theory of excitability: could nitrous oxide transmit energy to those who inhaled it? Davy and Beddoes had both read a paper written by the New York physician Samuel Latham Mitchill, who warned that inhalation of nitrous oxide could lead to a speedy demise. But Davy had disproved Mitchill's claim by inhaling the gas himself in Cornwall. In October 1798, Beddoes and Davy began their systematic experiments on the gas that Lavoisier had called 'the gaseous oxyd of azote', which Priestley had referred to as 'dephlogisticated nitrous air', and which today we colloquially call 'laughing gas'.[12]

On 8 April 1799, in their first formal trial of nitrous oxide, Davy used a method to produce the gas pioneered by Lavoisier's colleague Claude Louis Berthollet. He used an alembic, or distilling apparatus. Davy placed the crystals of ammonium nitrate in the 'cucurbit', one of the sealed glass vessels of the still, and slowly heated them to around 350 degrees, until gas rose into the head of the alembic and flowed down through a tube into a trough filled with water, which cooled the gas to a stable temperature. Davy sat in front of the alembic, attached a breathing tube to an outlet, pinched his nostrils, bowed his head, and inhaled deeply.

As the unexpectedly sweet taste of the gas hit his tongue, Davy, who was haphazardly jotting notes throughout the trial, described the 'first definite sensation' as a momentary 'dizziness, a fulness in the head, such as to induce a fear of falling'.[13] After the initial head rush, nitrous oxide commonly causes a feeling of elevation and disembodiment, a detachment from one's surroundings, followed by inebriated giddy clumsiness. Davy described how, after detaching himself from the breathing tube, 'I immediately laughed. The laugh was involuntary but highly pleasurable, accompanied by a thrill all through me; and a tingling in my toes and fingers, a sensation perfectly new and delightful. I felt a fulness in my chest afterwards; and during the remainder of the day, imagined that my taste and hearing were more than commonly quick. Certain I am that I felt myself more than usually strong and chearful.'[14] The experiment had been a delicious success, and in the second trial Davy inhaled the gas for longer. Protracted exposure, he found, seemed to stimulate muscular motion: 'I felt a thrill in my teeth; and breathing still

longer the third time, became so full of strength as to be compelled to exercise my arms and feet.'[15]

Beddoes, who was just observing, was astounded and thrilled.
One thing was certain: Mitchill's scaremongering about the fatal
effects of the gas were palpably untrue: the experiment had
proven 'the respirability ... of nitrous oxide'.[16] The gas appeared
to kindle life, not stifle it. Was it the result of transferred energy
from the gas to the body, as John Brown had predicted? After
more trials, Beddoes wrote to Jos Wedgwood that the 'species of
air' certainly 'seems to act by giving excitability or life'. He even
raised the longed-for possibility that 'we could now stimulate
Tom's torpid machine'.[17] He had once hoped that the Pneumatic
Institute's research would show a connection between oxygen
and health, but his and Davy's experiments seemed to reveal
that nitrous oxide was *a more powerful form of oxygen gas*, the
basis of *an infinite series of power,*' and that 'the possibility of
exalting the bodily and mental powers, and of renovating excitability ... seems now more feasible than ever'.[18]

Over the next two years, Beddoes and Davy devoted themselves to the life-stimulating properties of nitrous oxide.[19] Since
the arrival of Coleridge and Southey had animated the radical
political community in Bristol, Thomas Beddoes had become
the middle-aged centre of a social group of sparky, talented,
impulsive young men. Once news of the nitrous oxide experiments began to circulate, many turned up on the doorstep of
the Dowry Square house, wanting a trial. Now that the object
of Beddoes' and Davy's researches was not to research consumption but to examine the connection between nitrous oxide
and life itself, anybody, healthy or infirm, might be a useful
subject for experimentation. On 12 July 1799, Robert Southey
wrote ecstatically to his brother Thomas after trialling the gas:
'O Tom such a gas has Davy discovered, the gaseous oxyde!
O Tom! I have had some of it, it made me laugh and tingle
in every finger tip ... I am sure the air in heaven must be this

wonder working gas of delight.'[20] Beddoes recounted that 'Mrs Beddoes had frequently seemed to be ascending like a balloon up the hill to Clifton'.[21] Thomas Poole described how, during his inhalation, 'all the faculties' seemed to be 'absorbed by the fine pleasing feelings of existence without consciousness'. And Coleridge, who tried the gas at least four times, reported feeling 'an highly pleasurable sensation of warmth over my whole frame', 'distended' eyes, a heart beating 'as if it were leaping up and down', dim eyesight 'as if I had seen ... through tears', and 'unmingled pleasure'.[22]

Almost every trial of the gas at the Pneumatic Institute seemed to confirm John Brown's hypothesis that there was a ghost in the Enlightenment machine – not a soul inhabiting the body, but a vital force, an independent source of energy, on which nitrous oxide had a uniquely stimulating effect. But when Beddoes and Davy took the gas outside Bristol, their elation faded. The ecstatic reactions it had elicited in Bristol proved elusive elsewhere.[23] Even in Bristol, Tom Wedgwood and Davy himself discovered that their responses changed after long-term exposure to the gas. Robert Southey found that an interruption in his regular inhalations, caused by a period of illness, meant that, on returning to it, 'half the quantity affects me, and its operation is more violent' and not 'in the slightest degree pleasurable'.[24] Women also seemed less enraptured by the 'atmosphere of heaven'. Beddoes' later assistant John Stock reported how some female volunteers fell into trances and mild hysterics; and one woman became so ill with paroxysms that Beddoes had to take her home for prolonged treatment.

Today we don't fully understand nitrous oxide's effects on the brain, but some neuroscientists think they are due to its inhibition of the NMDA receptors, a type of glutamate receptor in the brain involved in learning and memory; its promotion of the release of certain neurotransmitters that inhibit the transmission of pain; and its stimulation of the GABA receptors involved in cognition. This creates an anaesthetic and dissociative effect combined with apparently heightened cognition and euphoria.[25] But it is certain today that inhaling nitrous oxide is not responsible for a transfer of energy from the gas to the body, resulting in unusual stimulation, as Beddoes had hoped. When his volunteers inhaled the gas over the long term, and when it was administered to subjects outside the hothouse environment of the Pneumatic Institute, this became clear to Beddoes. It pointed to the importance of the Pneumatic Institute itself in fostering enthusiastic responses to nitrous oxide. In Bristol, Beddoes had formed the nucleus of a group of fiery enthusiasts for radical change, and then, by the end of the decade, he had provided a pharmaceutical retreat from the reactionary political tide they had failed to turn back. For Coleridge, Southey, Poole, Wedgwood and many others, their heightened emotional response to nitrous oxide was like a badge of solidarity among their community of politically like-minded men. It was also a marker of the Romantic sensitivity, ardour and introspection that they believed set them apart from the increasingly repressed, authoritarian mainstream. That Southey's and Davy's responses to nitrous oxide waned was probably as closely related to the difficulty of maintaining that heightened emotional response as to the physiological process of habituation. And women's more subdued reactions to nitrous oxide were probably less related to biological difference than to the emerging emotional culture's insistence on female 'modesty' and domestic virtue, and its opposition to uninhibited emotion. As Beddoes' sister-in-law Maria Edgeworth put it in her characteristically acerbic tone, 'faith, great faith, is I believe necessary to produce any effect upon the drinkers'.[26]

After witnessing the diminishing effect of nitrous oxide, Beddoes realized – doubtless with quite a crash – that the theory of excitability on which the Pneumatic Institute was built had been disproved. John Brown's theory had suggested that gaseous stimuli might provoke the body's energy into full flame. But Coleridge was one among many who reported that nitrous oxide's effects on energy were haphazard: once or twice he felt 'violently' stimulated and 'could not avoid . . . beating the ground with my feet', but other times 'my heart did not beat so violently', and 'the only motion which I felt inclined to make, was that of laughing'.[27] This had devastating implications for the cure of consumption and paralysis ('palsy'). But it also had revolutionary consequences for medical and mainstream understanding of how the passions operate in the body.

On 26 December 1799, Davy reported that the elusive sensation of disembodiment that accompanied inhalation of nitrous oxide became pronounced with prolonged exposure. After a particularly large dose, the young man described how 'I lost all connection with external things . . . I existed in a world of new connected and newly modified ideas . . . When I was awakened from this semi-delirious trance . . . I exclaimed "Nothing exists but thoughts". The universe is composed of impressions, ideas, pleasure and pain.'[28] Most influential eighteenth-century writers on the passions had agreed that they were deeply embedded in the material world. David Hume saw the passions as part of a detailed linear progression from sensation to action. David Hartley, William Cullen, physicians treating nervous disorders, and the followers of the cult of sensibility all linked the passions to the sensitive body's contact with matter; they traced every trembling, quivering communication of sensation through the cords and fluids of the nervous system, to the central 'sensorium' at the body's heart and back to its outer edges, where emotion was manifested in blushing, fainting, weeping and flinching. Adam Smith described emotional transactions in strikingly similar terms to the truck, barter and exchange of commodities in the marketplace, and compared their management to the self-regulating financial economy. James Harrington, Jean-Jacques Rousseau and Beddoes saw passions as barometers of the state's ability to meet the needs of its citizenry. But the Pneumatic Institute's nitrous oxide experiments divorced emotion from this intimate connection with the world of matter. Davy's pharmaceutically engineered state was not a response to deprivation or the unequal distribution of property; it was not the result of sympathetic communication, nor was it displayed purposely to stimulate compassion and establish sociability. On the cusp of the nineteenth century, Davy showed that emotion *might have no moral purpose at all.*

The implications of the nitrous oxide trials extended to the cultural importance of pleasure and pain. For most of the eighteenth century, pain was a largely unavoidable consequence of material deprivation, war, sickness and childbirth. Optimists like Joseph Priestley and the clergyman William Paley had assured readers that pain of disappointment was a salutary experience revealing hitherto unknown information about Providence's true course. Religious devotees had rationalized pain as 'an opportunity to submit to God's will, or even to be purged of sin'.[29] But the Pneumatic Institute's experiments demonstrated that gases might annihilate, as well as stimulate, feeling. Davy was struck by the observation that 'nitrous oxide in its extensive operation appears capable of destroying physical pain' and suggested that, in the future, it might find a use 'with advantage during surgical operations'.[30] Coupled with Beddoes's discovery that medicines could be inhaled as well as ingested, Davy's remark paved the way for the first use, in 1844, of nitrous oxide as an anaesthetic drug during a dental extraction. Now it is used around the globe as an anaesthetic during childbirth, as a component of the medicinal gas Entonox.

Beddoes' and Davy's recognition that feeling could be artificially dulled contributed to a wider shift in cultural attitudes to pleasure and pain. Beddoes hoped fervently that, 'by ascertaining the action of the elements entering into his composition, man may sometime come to rule over the causes of pain or pleasure, with a dominion as absolute as that which he at present exercises over domestic animals and the other instruments of his convenience'.[31] In the eighteenth century, pleasure had been understood as an avowedly political phenomenon. Shaftesbury had claimed that 'pleasure' originated from 'perceiving the order to which we belong'. But the literary critic Rowan Boyson has shown how pleasure became divorced from political philosophy in the early nineteenth century.[32] In the mid-eighteenth century, 'the man of pleasure' was an exemplar of sociability; but a hundred years later, pleasure was being criticized by Karl Marx, among others, as a solipsistic *challenge* to society.

Tom Wedgwood had sought to eradicate pain through education; but the Pneumatic Institute's discovery that it could be eliminated pharmaceutically traced a radical shift in cultural attitudes to pain. As pain became avoidable, and therefore a matter of choice, suffering became, for some, a niche, fetishized experience, as is arguably visible in today's exaltation of 'natural' childbirth or BDSM practices. But, in the mainstream, pain – like pleasure – would lose its moral value. On 2 November 1804, Beddoes' great friend Davies Giddy wrote of his desire to find 'euthanasia' for pain, and Beddoes' wife, Anna, responded with incredulity: 'Tell me, you Mimosa, how you could possibly wish to be without feeling!' The conversation – with which this book begins – reveals two people at the end of the Enlightenment on either side of a cultural divide. Feeling, Anna assured Giddy, looking back to eighteenth-century philosophical justifications for the passions, was the basis of being 'morally invulnerable'.[33] But for Giddy, who was looking forward to the new century, psychological and physical distress were morally neutral, pointless accidents, which might be obliterated pharmaceutically.

The advent of the pharmaceutical treatment of pain and emotional disorder was also reflected in changing approaches to mental ill health. In the 1790s, both Thomas Beddoes and the great French psychiatrist Philippe Pinel recognized the close connection of madness with politics. Pinel described how the 'mental alienation' of 27 per cent of his 113 patients at the Bicêtre asylum, to the south of Paris, was directly caused by, or manifested itself in, muddled beliefs concerning 'events connected with the revolution'. French revolutionary events directly led to madness by entailing loss of possessions, shock, trauma, destitution, 'frustrated ambition', or unexpected fame. The historian Laure Murat also describes how the Terror produced 'a very specific climate of threat and fear, easily detectable in the causes of admission to the asylum'; many inmates suffered delusions and fears based around images specific to the revolution, especially terror of the guillotine and decapitation.[34] In Britain, Beddoes noted a case of a 'quiet character and calm politician' who suffered a 'couple of days' of 'insanity' after the implementation of the Gagging Acts, hallucinating that Pitt appointed his arch-rivals the Whig statesmen Charles James Fox and Lord John Russell to prominent places in the cabinet.[35] Beddoes knew that the 1790s had driven many of its victims mad: it provided the elements, figures and events upon which imaginations displaying tendencies to fearful paranoia seized.

But, ironically, Beddoes' own research at the Pneumatic Institute reflected the advent of a new attitude to madness that would divorce it from politics and rely more heavily on the 'chemical cosh' instead of Pinel's pioneering 'moral therapies' in the treatment of insanity.[36] Throughout the eighteenth century, apothecaries had offered herbal medicines to treat 'weak nerves', but the medicalization of madness was formalized in the following century as the disorders of 'neurasthenia', 'nervous breakdown' and 'nervous exhaustion' became embedded in psychiatric discourse. Nineteenth-century entrepreneurs patented an enormous variety of 'nerve tonics' – often including strychnine, morphine, opium, quinine, lithium salts and cocaine – with names such as 'Antineurasthin', 'Sanotogen', 'Glycolactophos' and 'Bromocarpine'. Bromide, paraldehyde and chloral hydrate were developed in the mid-nineteenth century as sedatives.[37] The adoption of Beddoes and Davy's 'excellent air-bag' of nitrous oxide by upper-class parties in the summer of 1799 marked a beginning of recreational drug culture, but it also denoted a paradigm shift taking place in the pharmaceutical instigation of pleasure or tranquillity for psychiatric purposes.[38]

The most important revelation of Beddoes' nitrous oxide trials, however, was that Brown's hydraulic account of the passions' operation in the body was shown to be incorrect. Brown had defined fear and grief as 'sedative passions', characterized by a meagre burning of the body's fuel, with physical effects such as 'benumbing' of the sensations, 'debility' or 'a state of permanent torpor', and leading to an accumulation of energy. They were felt with far less force than 'high spirits', Brown claimed, which animate and elevate up 'to the warmth of summer'.[39] By the end of the 1790s, Beddoes knew this to be untrue. Throughout that decade, his temperament had violently oscillated between hope and despair, settling into resignation, disappointment and, finally, what Beddoes described in a letter to Giddy as 'the Hamlet tone of mind ... what Solomon calls the "vanity" & Darwin the "nihility" of all things': a chronic state of depression characterized by 'odious selfishness' and 'the self-humiliation of the melancholy'.[40] But Beddoes knew that this was not a 'torpid' state, as Brown had claimed. When 'hope is finally destroyed', Beddoes wrote, it leads to an 'intensity of thought' in which 'some train of ideas is pursued' as animatedly as 'animals in full chance of their prey'.[41] '*Torpid* melancholy! *torpid* grief!' he mocked sarcastically; 'they may as well apply the epithet to the boisterous state of passion or insanity, and speak of *torpid* anger or *torpid* phrenzy.' In grief and melancholy, Beddoes knew, there was 'an internal agitation far beyond the average warmth of sane and complacent mortals'.[42] His experience of the 1790s had made this painfully clear.

Not only were grief and melancholy 'depressing passions',

claimed Brown, their low consumption of the body's energy resulted in a hydraulic 'accumulation, increase, or abundance' – a 'superabundance of excitability' – that threatened to erupt dangerously. 'High spirits', in contrast, Brown surmised, depleted excitability and created a state of 'debility', or lack of energy. Early on in his trials, Beddoes had noticed that inhalation of nitrous oxide had pronounced effects on his patients' emotional states. He himself had been initially 'rendered [too] timid' by his 'apoplectic make' to try the gas.[43] But when twenty-two volunteers inhaled it simultaneously at the Pneumatic Institute, Beddoes threw caution to the wind. In notes written straight away, he described how, 'after the first moments of surprise it was impossible not to recognize the expressions of the most extatic pleasure'. He compared its effects to 'feelings, excited by a piece of joyful and unlooked for news': he found himself 'bathed all over with a bucketfull [sic] of good humour'.[44] But Beddoes was most struck by the observation that even 'after innumerable trials' of nitrous oxide, even after its provocation of violent happiness, 'he had never once felt lassitude or depression'.[45] He knew this was 'an exception so striking to the general laws' of hydraulics governing 'the expenditure of a quality, or a substance, or a spirit, and its renewal or accumulation'. Beddoes could only conclude that the hydraulic theory of emotion was 'a grievous baneful error'. The trials' results, combined with his own experience of 'melancholy' in the late 1790s, made him think that 'it often happens that excitement and excitability increase, and still oftener that they decrease together': that vigorous, impassioned emotion generates more of the same, as does dull, flaccid melancholy. Beddoes remembered that, once, while observing young children, he had remarked on how 'nurses when they play with infants of a lively temperament, late in the evening, so as to raise strong emotions, frequently find that they soon awake disturbed': overstimulation begat further animation, not exhaustion.[46] This was the opposite of hydraulic theory's description of emotion. Brown's 'doctrine' of accumulating energy in the face of withheld 'gratification' was wrong.

In 1794, John Brown's doctrine of excitability had been attractive to Beddoes, because its hydraulic account of the passions had made sense of recent outbreaks of popular violence in response to state oppression: in the Priestley Riots, the Saint-Domingue revolution, the Bristol Bridge Riots, and in revolutionary France after the fall of the old regime and in response to Jacobin authoritarianism. Hydraulic theory argued that 'sympathetic' government was necessary to ease popular tensions; it implied a key political role for education in 'channelling' emotions into a 'sociable' and 'virtuous' manner of expression; and it threatened the inevitability of violent eruptions if these failed. But the Pneumatic Institute's trials disconfirmed hydraulic theory's explanation of how emotional energy operates in the body, and this paralleled the discomfiting suspicions growing among radicals that its account of how emotion functions in the *body politic* was also fallacious. The Gagging Acts, and the increasingly conservative, authoritarian political tide, especially after the United Irish Rebellion, were arguably resulting in a more, not less, docile population in Britain, as membership of political associations fell, or fell out of overt visibility into a 'radical underground'.[47] Justifications for protecting rights and liberties would need to be sought elsewhere than in hydraulic theory. Today such justifications are chiefly found in, for example, 'interests theory' – which argues that the central function of human rights is to protect and promote certain essential human interests – or in 'will theory' – which argues that a right gives its holder control over another's duty – but not in the hydraulic threat of violence if certain inalienable human needs or rights are not met.

Today the mainstream political application of hydraulic theory is to provide a biological justification for gendered stereotypes of men and women's emotional traits, and to bolster claims that male desire warrants far greater attention and entitlement than female desire. As the plethora of contemporary examples demonstrates, the popularity of hydraulic theory in this context survived the revolution of feeling at the end of the 1790s and continued to hold sway in the nineteenth century and beyond. Beddoes' trials had disproved its medical basis, and he was himself anxious about gendered emotional tropes that compared female patients to 'blossom nipped by untimely frost' – he disliked the implication of such stereotypes that 'drooping' women feel and suffer 'no more than the drooping vegetable expresses'.[48] But hydraulic theory has remained impervious to sound scientific, psychological, linguistic, theoretical and political objections throughout history. And its cultural power has not been undermined by medical evidence, such as Beddoes' nitrous oxide trials, that disproved its account of how emotion operates in the body. Hydraulic theory remains such a dominant 'quack' theory of gendered emotion because it is founded on, and justifies, male political, economic and sexual supremacy. Hydraulic theory's strange cultural allure will not fade until the material inequalities and oppressions that it serves begin to fade too.

GOD WITHDRAWS
HIS PROTECTION

In a different era, the Pneumatic Institute's two-year life-span might have been the brightest period of Thomas Beddoes' professional life. It offered the chance to investigate ambitious claims about the nature of human life itself, buoyed up by the funding of illustrious supporters, the technological help of one of Britain's most prestigious inventors, and the research assistance of a brilliant young man. At the end of the 1790s, Humphry Davy was at the beginning of his career, uncontaminated by the taint of radicalism, and would go on to occupy the highest echelons of European science. But Beddoes, who was almost forty, felt he was approaching the end of his life. He was emotionally dispirited, at odds with the medical and political establishment. In more optimistic times, he might have seen that the Pneumatic Institute's discoveries about human energy and emotion were contributing to a paradigm shift in medical and cultural attitudes to those subjects. But instead his discoveries simply confirmed Beddoes' disjunction from the world in which he had once felt at home. For him, they signalled the end to a familiar way of life; not a new beginning.

The autumn of 1799 saw persistent, prolonged rain followed by an unseasonably early arrival of frost and snow, devastating the late harvest. Some tried to find reason in the random cruelty, weakly claiming that 'such changes and uncertainties are wisely intended by Providence to impress us with a sense of our constant dependence on God; to teach us that, at no season, and at no period, should we deem ourselves secure'.[1] Optimists like Priestley and Paley had considered history's trajectory to be inexorably aimed at perfectibility, but now the Reverend Thomas Watson impressed a more uncertain view upon his readers: 'Our brightest prospects in life may soon be clouded, if God withdraws his protection.'[2] The image of God as a rational watchmaker was fading, and in its place was emerging a conception of the Creator as capricious and harsh, occasionally and unpredictably swayed by human pleas and sacrifices. By spring 1800, that pessimistic image of God was reinforced when the wholesale price of wheat doubled and malnutrition contributed to the spread of putrid fevers and typhus around Bristol. Beddoes put the Pneumatic Institute's trials on hold, focusing instead on providing emergency relief for the sick. He published a handbill giving advice on hygiene, stressing the importance of vigorous washing after coming into contact with invalids, and keeping houses clean and well ventilated.[3]

This small project may have been a welcome diversion from the Pneumatic Institute, which was attracting the unwelcome attention of the reactionary press. In May 1800, George Canning's *Anti-Jacobin Review* printed a satirical poem, 'The Pneumatic Revellers: An Eclogue'. Beddoes, Davy and their circle were depicted, in the words of the historian Jan Golinski, as 'a coterie of utopians and freethinkers indulging in orgies of intoxication and sexual license, and peddling quack therapies whose benefits were entirely delusional'.[4] The poem was published with the motto, 'Trifles, light as air,/ Are to the *Theorist* confirmation strong', linking the 'air' of the Pneumatic Institute's gaseous experiments with the insubstantial 'air' of Othello's false 'proofs'. At around the same time, a barrel of frogs intended as experimental subjects for the Pneumatic Institute was dropped on Bristol Quay. It burst and hundreds of frogs escaped, prompting onlookers to conclude that the amphibians were 'meant as food for the French revolutionaries concealed' in Beddoes' laboratory.[5] Two years later, the satires, parodies and criticisms of the Pneumatic Institute's work continued. In his 1802 print *Scientific Researches! – New Discoveries in Pneumaticks!* the satirical printmaker James Gillray portrayed Davy as a parochial idiot savant, sniggering as the physician Thomas Garnett – who lectured at the Royal Institution and continued to defend Brunonian theory even after Beddoes' disillusionment – administered nitrous oxide to the politician and founder member of the institution, Sir John Coxe Hippisley, the seat of whose trousers duly exploded in an enormous fart. Where once Beddoes and his endeavours had been attacked for posing a serious threat to social order, now they had become trivial laughing stocks.

A few months after the appearance of 'The Pneumatic Revellers' in May 1800, Humphry Davy published the first conclusions from the nitrous oxide trials, in *Researches Chemical and Philosophical, Chiefly Concerning Nitrous Oxide, or Dephlogisticated Nitrous Air, and its Respiration*, which was printed by Joseph Johnson. The *Researches* contained a section, 'Observations on the Effects of Nitrous Oxide', written by Beddoes. Here he made public, in print, for the first time, his suspicion that Brown's hydraulic doctrine of the accumulation of excitability was incorrect. But he shrugged off the responsibility of formulating a new theory of the physiology of emotion, wearily delegating this to 'the observers of some distant generation'.[6]

Davy's *Researches* were a rather ill-thought-out enterprise. He had rushed into print when the Pneumatic Institute's experiments had been underway for little more than a year. Without any tangible discoveries to report, the Pneumatic Institute and Beddoes himself inevitably appeared as failures. Beddoes had worried about premature publication of their investigations, when he circulated 'Notice of Some Observations Made at the Medical Pneumatic Institution' in 1799. He had fretted then about admitting 'those partial failures which had disappointed some of his previous expectations', and rightly suspected that inability to present a compensating theory would be taken 'as conclusive evidences of the total inefficacy of his plans'. In 1799, risk of public censure had been outweighed by 'the necessity ... of forcibly awakening the attention of the community' to the Pneumatic Institute's inconclusive but enthralling activities.[7] But in 1800, satires like the 'Pneumatic Revellers' poem showed the nitrous oxide trials had garnered public interest, yet there were still no proofs to present. Davy admitted that the trials' theoretical basis was 'false', and that 'pneumatic chemistry in its application to medicine is an art yet in its infancy, weak, almost useless'. He hinted at potential developments of pneumatics, indicating that 'an account of [nitrous oxide's] agency in paralytic affections, will be speedily published by Dr. Beddoes', who would also publish 'observations' on the use of nitrous acid in 'venereal complaints'.[8] But Davy knew that Beddoes was soon to admit that these experiments had failed: he had tried nitrous oxide on three paralysed patients, none of whom had shown any improvement.[9]

In fact, the most important research on paralysis at that time was conducted by another radically minded physician: James Parkinson, who had played such an important role in the Pop-Gun Plot of 1794. Within the first two decades of the nineteenth century, Parkinson had demolished Beddoes' attempt to attribute all disease to the single, universal cause of deviation from a moderate state of stimulation. Parkinson correctly identified that different medical conditions usually originate in separate, often localized, causes. He rejected Beddoes' conjecture that paralysis might be 'a mere consequence of constitutional debility' – the result of weak energy – and curable with 'tonic medicines, and highly nutritious diet', or with stimulating gases. Parkinson spent years observing patients with the 'shaking palsy' – a neurological condition progressing to paralysis – and surmised that it was produced by 'interruption of the flow of the nervous influence to the affected parts'.[10] The existence of neurotransmitters wasn't identified until over a century later, when the 'shaking palsy' was recognized as a deficiency of dopamine and the abnormal aggregation of protein called Lewy bodies developing inside nerve cells. But James Parkinson's sustained analytic focus on the distinctive characteristics and symptoms of the condition, and his fight to identify it as a discrete medical disorder, led to it being christened 'Parkinson's disease'.

Davy's *Researches* relegated Beddoes and the Pneumatic Institute to the speculative optimism and wild 'generalisation' of the past. Davy himself professed 'rational scepticism' towards its work and emerged in the *Researches* as a sophisticated, techno-logically advanced chemist, engaging in original and systematic work within the constraints of the Pneumatic Institute's obso-lete structures: a 'misemployed genius', as he later referred to his role under Beddoes.[11] The *Annals of Medicine* lauded Davy's readiness to sacrifice his own health to his projects and heartily praised 'the industry and genius' of the *Researches*' author.[12] Before long Davy would be working on projects at the vanguard of the chemical revolution: building batteries and identifying the presence of silica in grasses. His notebooks from this period reveal 'a deep ideal feeling of good, a look towards future great-ness' and in September 1800, he wrote to his mother, somewhat enigmatically, about 'prospects of a very brilliant nature'.[13] The lambent flame of Beddoes and the Pneumatic Institute might be diminishing, but Davy knew himself to be rising in the firmament, freed from the load.

A few months later, in January 1801, shortly after his twenty-second birthday, Davy wrote again to his mother. He had accepted an offer to join 'the Royal Philosophical Institution established by Count Rumford and others of the aristocracy'. 'You will all I dare say,' he remarked knowingly, 'be glad to see me getting among the royalists.'[14] At a meeting at Joseph Banks' house on 7 March 1799, Count Rumford had concocted a proposal to establish a 'national institution' to diffuse scientific knowledge and introduce useful innovations.[15] Rumford appointed the physician Thomas Garnett as the institution's chemistry professor, but he had reservations: Garnett was a proponent of the now outdated Brunonian theory, and moreover he had been an established lecturer since 1790 and was exerting an independence irksome to his employer.[16] Rumford engaged Davy as chemical lecturer to keep Garnett in check, and stressed that the new position must 'be kept distinct from party politics'. He did not want the Royal Institution tarnished by the political controversies that had dogged the Pneumatic Institute. Davy emphatically agreed: 'I sincerely wish that this may be the case.'[17] Beddoes did not put any obstacles in Davy's way, and by March 1801 Davy had left Bristol and started a new phase of his life in London. It marked the beginning of the end of the Pneumatic Institute.

A month later, on 19 April 1801, Anna Beddoes sat down, in quite a state of nervousness, to write to her husband's closest friend, Davies Giddy. The two had begun corresponding a few months earlier, after Davy's departure had relegated Anna to the loneliness and boredom she had experienced before his arrival in 1798. Giddy had stayed with Anna and Thomas Beddoes in the late summer of 1800, believing himself to be suffering from consumption. He and Anna swiftly became close. After his return to Tredrea, she penned long, frank letters, calling him her 'dear new found Brother', teasing the taciturn Giddy about attractive mutual acquaintances, and dissecting her own ambivalence to the life in which she found herself. She described – often indirectly, sometimes openly – how she was married to a fascinating but frequently absent man; she was mostly excluded from his professional and political sphere; and although she lived in a large, fashionable, modern townhouse, she was socially a *persona non grata* because of her husband's political opinions. Anna confessed to Giddy that 'I feel [Beddoes'] views are larger, his soul nobler than mine; yet there are moments when I am selfish enough to wish, not that I should be equal to him, but that he were humbled to my level'.[18]

Anna directly requested Giddy's advice. 'When you came last summer,' she reminded him, 'you saw for a few moments only I believe, a man whom you pronounced a very silly fellow.' Anna now begged Giddy to 'burn the letter' immediately after reading. She described how this man – a 'Mr. W.', 'more than 20 years older than' she – had 'married very young, contrary to the wishes of his friends', to a woman with 'a violent temper' and 'no money'.[19] Their 'beautiful & accomplished' daughter had been 'partly educated by' Anna Laetitia Barbauld, the poet and children's author. Afterwards the daughter was married 'it seems to escape from her mother' to 'an uncommonly clever man with the most insinuating manner', but he 'turned out to be extremely wicked . . . he beats, locks up, drags his poor wife about the house by the hair of her head'. 'When Mr. W. first heard of his wickedness,' Anna wrote sadly, 'he was instantly driven out of his senses, & was under Dr. Williams['] care for some time'.[20] A few years later, in the summer of 1800, Mr W. himself temporarily escaped his family anxieties by fleeing to Bristol, where he 'took shelter in our society'. 'We became so intimate,' Anna confessed, 'that not a day passed in which more than half our time was not spent in sauntering somehow or some where with him.' Despite Giddy's contempt for this man, Anna herself had concluded that he had 'great generosity of character and much sensibility'.[21] He stayed until well into the winter.

'Mr. W.' is possibly William Wynch, a civil servant for the East India Company, who was twenty-three years Anna's senior and had married Rhoda Crocket around 1774. Wynch's daughter Flora was Anna Laetitia Barbauld's first paying pupil; in 1794, Barbauld addressed her essay, 'Fashion: A Vision', to her 'dear Flora', before the young woman married James Legge Willis in January 1795.[22] Barbauld's essay lamented that the young, free and 'light' Flora Wynch was soon to become victim to such 'dreadful instruments of torture' as the 'the shackles of oppression' exercised by women's fashions and male 'tyrant[s]'.[23]

After a season of Mr W.'s companionship, Anna gradually became convinced that 'my company' had 'become necessary to his happiness; this he assured me with such strong expressions of affection, that I could not mistake his meaning'. He had even 'told me when at Clifton that he had made a will in which he had left me a large legacy'.[24] She found herself attracted by 'the softened voice, gentle manner, and the tears of a man not effeminate', and indulged her romantic fantasies by reading the popular collection of romantic poetry *Colin's Kisses*.[25] She told Beddoes of Mr W.'s attachment to her, but, she admitted to Giddy, 'the Dr. has some singular peculiarities in constitution & character'. She and Beddoes had been married for seven years, and no children had resulted. Neither party seemed particularly attracted to the other. Anna was embarrassed that Beddoes, keen to avoid scandal, 'made me promise ... that nothing of this kind' – her relationship with Mr W. – 'should pass'; she was surprised to find, in the wake of her confession, that Beddoes 'seemed to become fonder of me, tho he said he could not exactly tell why', and gave her permission to 'contin[ue] the visits' of Mr W.[26]

The upright Giddy initially sympathized with Anna's loneliness, confessing that he too suspected she and Beddoes were
not 'perfectly suited in disposition or character', and acknowledging that sexual incompatibility can obstruct 'that complete
happiness which young women fancy they can attain'.[27] But he
instructed Anna to immediately cut contact with Mr W. She
did so, sending Giddy a copy of her final letter, in which she
reminisced to Mr W. that 'when you first expressed yourself in
a manner that I ought to have heard with indignation, I told you
that most women would have thought themselves insulted, but
that in these things I did not think with the generality of my
sex'. Nevertheless, fearing that 'I am the wife of the best of men,
[and] I have been unworthy of his extreme tenderness', Anna
commanded Mr W., *'think of me no more'* and *'do not* leave me the
legacy you proposed'.[28] After a few minor relapses, a permanent
separation was established.

The split between Anna and Mr W. was made easier, and
indeed necessary, by the fact that by June 1801, two months
after their final meeting, and two months after Beddoes'
increased fondness, she realized she was pregnant with their
first child. Anna was embarrassed about telling Giddy, aware
that 'a cruel doubt I know will come across your mind', but she
asked him to 'do me the justice to believe I have no reason to
be ashamed'.[29] The question of disputed paternity faded into
temporary insignificance as Beddoes became severely ill, with
an infection that turned into a lymphatic swelling in his chest.
He had been dogged by rasping breath for years – unalleviated
by his own medicinal airs – but now he was suffocating, and
begged Anna 'in the most serious manner to let him put himself out of pain – he repeated this too other times, saying he
could bear it no longer'.[30] Now all Anna's attention was on her
husband. 'I believe I love him better,' she wrote to Giddy, a few
weeks after Beddoes' merciful recovery, 'for I was so unhappy
and anxious when he was ill I did not know what to do.' Little

Anna Frances Emily Beddoes was born on Christmas Eve 1801. Her mother was enraptured, looking on her as her 'guardian angel'. But Anna could not shrug off her painful awareness of Giddy's suspicions about the baby's parentage. Although she protested that 'my little Anna's untutored countenance speaks most eloquently' to Beddoes' paternity, and urged Giddy, 'if you have any doubts "Look on her face, and you'll forget them all"', her letters to him dwindled until they reconnected in person, eighteen months later.[31]

In the wake of Davy's departure, and the damning effects of his *Researches*, Beddoes' Pneumatic Institute wound down. The nitrous oxide trials came to an end, and Beddoes concentrated on treating the illnesses of the poor with more conventional methods. In summer 1802, Robert Southey recorded that 'The Pneumatic Institute continues. The name should be changed as they do little with gases, on account chiefly of the expense of experiments. Beddoes now chiefly supports it' financially.[32] The Pneumatic Institute became a dispensary and an out-patients' clinic; and Beddoes' assistant who had come to the institute around 1798 – a Swiss refugee called Johann Koenig, who anglicized his name to John King – gradually took over as its principal doctor, alongside a newcomer, Dr Stock. In 1803, these altered priorities were cemented when Beddoes moved the institute from Dowry Square to Bristol's quay and renamed it 'the Medical Institution for the Sick and Drooping Poor'. He introduced astute innovations, such as a deposit scheme, whereby patients paid two shillings and sixpence upon com-mencing treatment, ensuring they saw the course of treatment right to the end, when the deposit was returned. And Beddoes published a handbook, the 'Rules', advising how to establish a healthy lifestyle through hygiene, good diet and fresh air.

In Beddoes' medical writings at the beginning of the 1790s, he had attributed disease to material conditions that politicians' decisions had caused or failed to address, and had been optimistic that agitating for change would soon lead to improved health among the poor. Now, in the first years of the nineteenth century, the political solution had failed and Beddoes instead tried to avert illness by encouraging alterations to lifestyle. His focus had shifted from petitioning politicians for structural reform to help the poorest in society, to combining his work at the Medical Institution with berating individual middle-class patients to make changes in their personal habits. In 1802, he published a three-volume text called *Hygëia: Or Essays Moral and Medical*, which analysed 'causes affecting the personal state of our Middling and Affluent Classes'.

In his later years, Beddoes also made contributions to the emerging field of statistics and probability. In early autumn 1797, he was trialling the use of nitrous acid in treating syphilis and developed the survey method of research by requesting that doctors across Britain write to him with their own experiences. During his work on consumption, Beddoes turned to Bristol's parish records. He scoured numerical data, comparing prevalence of the disease in those who had lived in hot climates to long-term British residents, concluding that climate made no difference. He analysed the records by occupation, noticing that workers in trades involving exposure to dust or poor ventilation – especially needle-grinders – were particularly prone to consumption. Butchers, however, seemed miraculously resistant. Beddoes read about Edward Jenner's breakthrough, which was published in 1798: that exposure to cowpox appeared to naturally inoculate dairymaids against the far more serious smallpox. And Beddoes wondered if cows' breath might also bestow resistance to consumption. Over the winter of 1799, while the nitrous oxide experiments were energetically underway, he decided to trial the theory, encouraging six patients with 'desperate cases of consumption' to 'liv[e] with cows'. Soon he was gleefully reporting 'much promise of success' to Giddy, and hypothesizing that bovine 'fumes' contained a component that stimulated his patients' excitability.[33] But Giddy refused him a loan of '£400 to £500' to bring his vision to life.[34]

The outcome of Beddoes' immersion in the parish records was a failure, but his research practices were in tune with the times. Statistical research and survey methodology had been gaining in popularity since the Scottish politician and financier Sir John Sinclair had published his *Statistical Account of Scotland* between 1791 and 1799, importing the German word 'statistics' into the English language, and attempting to measure Scotland's 'quantum of happiness'. In 1799, Jenner used the results of a nationwide survey establishing his hypothesis about smallpox inoculation to set up a national vaccination programme. Statistics implied a different perspective on historical progress to the view that had been entertained through the second half of the eighteenth century. As faith in Providence and perfectibility waned, many turned to probability and statistics to help predict the future. The philosopher Ian Hacking locates the erosion of determinism and the rise of statistics in the last decade of the eighteenth century and first decade of the nineteenth. He directly relates it to the effects of the French Revolution: to the 'avalanche of printed numbers' that resulted from the French Revolutionary and Napoleonic state's bureaucratic endeavours, and to the surveys conducted during the early industrial revolution in Britain.[35] Statistics and probability provided a firmer footing for hope – 'the data for calculating individual happiness', as Beddoes himself put it – than providential gambles relying on the now outdated concept of a benevolent God.[36] Beddoes' later work reflected the advent of a new, cautious and even pessimistic approach to historical progress. It was an attitude that had been partly brought about by the backlash to radical politics after the French Revolution, and Beddoes himself had directly borne the brunt of that reversal of hope.

*

On 30 June 1803, Anna gave birth to their second child, Thomas Lovell Beddoes, after a difficult labour. Anna renewed her correspondence with Giddy, writing that little Thomas seemed 'inclined to be nothing but skin and bone like his mama'.[37] Giddy's sister invited the weakened Anna down to Tredrea to recuperate, and Beddoes was delighted to find that she returned a different person, riding 'a tide of pleasurable feeling'.[38] Anna fleshed out the nature of that pleasure in a 'female billet' that she sent to Giddy straight after her homecoming. She conjured up the memory of a 'dangerous situation' she and Giddy had found themselves in one night: his 'beating heart' had been pressed 'to mine ... when your languid head rested upon my shoulder, when I fearfully sought in your eyes, what I trembled lest you should find in mine ... As we sat together,' she recalled lovingly, 'your arm pressed round me, I knew not what we were saying, when I turned towards you, our eyes asked each other life's leave to meet – they did meet, and from that moment I slept no more.'[39]

When Giddy visited Bristol a few months later, Anna openly suggested they enter into a long-term adulterous relationship. The ascetic Giddy recoiled, retorting that he and Anna were 'two parallel straight lines [that] can never meet'.[40] Despite their intimacy in Tredrea, he had come to idealize their friendship as 'the relation of a Brother and Sister', 'pure from any mixture of sexual desire, the sole species of Platonic love that can be indulged with truth and without danger'. Anna suffered terribly from this disappointment. She wrote sorrowfully to Giddy that 'I used to be told I was a very modest woman[.] I have forfeited this title entirely.'[41] She proved less adept at ending the entanglement with Giddy than she had been with Mr W. back in 1800, and they continued to sidestep one another in a frustrating dance of surrender and guilt for the next six years. She came to think of herself as 'unworthy ... of any good person[']s affection ... a good for nothing woman', convinced that Giddy 'may love me, but at the same time ... secretly despise me'.[42] She wrote sad, fervid memories of their time together, fancying him 'sitting beside me with your head on my pillow & your lips close to mine', and was horrified to find one morning 'when I wakened that I had clung round the Dr as close as possible & exclaimed, My God ... thinking I was speaking to someone else'. Anna now saw in her daughter's 'cherished image', a reminder not of her dalliance with Mr W. or her return to fidelity with Beddoes, but of the intimacy that had first been established between her and Giddy in 1800.[43]

In late spring 1806, Beddoes became gravely ill, afflicted by chronic rheumatism and an infection affecting the nerves in his chest and nostrils – possibly what would be identified today as Guillain-Barré syndrome. He and Anna now had four children: Charles Henry and Mary Eliza had joined Anna Frances and Thomas Lovell. Seeing Beddoes approach the 'very point of death', Anna became convinced that she would soon be free to marry Giddy. When Beddoes disappointed her by recovering again, she contemplated dramatic action. 'If it could be done without injury to little Anna or her father,' she wrote in desperation to Giddy, 'I would deliberately destroy myself' – her reputation or her life – 'to be yours for once'.[44] Giddy eventually extricated himself by proposing marriage to a wealthy heiress, Mary Ann Gilbert, in August 1807. Anna was deeply hurt. She wrote a bitter poem, 'Disappointment', accusing him of having initiated their intimacy – 'He clasped me in the ivied Tower' – before leaving her 'to repine/ And seek a wealthier fair!'[45] And she remonstrated with him about how there was 'too great a dissimilarity of character & habits' between himself and Gilbert, with which 'you hazard all the future happiness of your life'.[46] Within six months of Giddy's proposal, he appears to have come to agree with Anna. After the exchange of a few coded letters in which he presumably admitted his feelings for her, Anna finally wrote that 'I can never for a moment doubt the kindness and strength of your affection' but admonished him to 'act as you ought'. She had been prepared to endanger her own reputation, but would not do the same to another woman. Anna reassured Giddy that 'I think of you often very often' and bade him a final 'farewell'.[47] He and Gilbert were married at Easter, 1808.

Eight months later, at 9 p.m. on 23 December, the day before little Anna's seventh birthday, Thomas Beddoes died of a 'dropsy in his chest'. An autopsy, conducted by his assistants Stock and King at the Medical Institution, revealed he had suffered throughout his life from a congenital heart defect. Since his illness in the summer of 1801 this had been coupled with a collapsed left lung, causing his right lung to become dangerously swollen.[48] Shortly before his death, Anna noted, in a double-edged compliment, that 'in illness Dr. B. appears to advantage in many respects . . . he expresses much more feeling and has less appearance of selfishness than when his mind is occupied upon larger objects'.[49] While Beddoes was unwell, she was finally able to enjoy being the focus of her husband's interest and affection.

Beddoes was buried on New Year's Eve, 'in the North Western Corner of a Burial Ground between Clifton and Bristol'.[50] He had nominated Davies Giddy as guardian to the children. Anna and Giddy found themselves co-parenting, locked into a chaste, familial relationship. They were both painfully aware that, had Giddy only waited eight months before marrying, it might have been Anna at the altar rather than Gilbert. She lashed out at him in frustration, and he recorded sadly in his diary that 'I this day much offended'. Two months later, on 14 February 1809, Giddy and Gilbert's first child, of five in total, was born. The little girl, Mary, suffered from a rare and extremely serious congenital condition, now called acalvaria, in which the dura mater, the thick membrane surrounding the base of the brain and spinal cord, is absent. When she died seventeen years later, Giddy described how Mary had been 'released from a merely vegetable existence, having never held up her head, put her feet to the ground, nor her hand to her mouth, nor uttered an articulate syllable. She

was moreover quite blind, and becoming more and more distressed every day,' having suffered convulsions since birth.[51] But
Mary Ann Gilbert proved to be a more compatible wife than
Giddy and Anna had initially predicted, and after his election to
the Board of Agriculture in 1809, she instigated some successful
social experiments, teaching the poor to feed themselves using
unwanted land around Beachy Head.

After Beddoes' death, Anna Edgeworth returned often to her
family home in Ireland, at Edgeworthstown. She saw Giddy for
the last time in Bath in 1818, when he returned 'a large bundle
of letters' to her; and they corresponded for the final time five
years later, in January 1823. 'I thank you most heartily for all
you have done for me,' she wrote, 'and with equal gratitude for
what you have foreborne to do, for nothing can be more kind
and gentle than your manner of writing to me, although you have
more reason than any other for expressing yourself differently.'[52]

In 1824, aged fifty-one, Anna and her daughters, Anna Frances
and Mary, set off on a European tour. Her son Thomas Lovell
had become a poet, and was studying physiology at Göttingen
University, convinced that knowledge of anatomy was essential
for the 'correct and masterly delineations of the passions'.[53]
He exemplified the Victorian understanding of emotion as a
medical pathology rather than a moral or political phenomenon:
an approach that his own father's researches had unwittingly
reflected. That summer, Thomas Lovell wrote doleful, morbid
poems, finding in the 'starry' nights over 'Geneva's sea' only a
mirror of his own black depression. He became fixated on death
as a means of happiness for 'they,/ Who have no body but the
beauteous air,/ No body but their minds'.[54] In 1849, aged forty-
five, he would commit suicide, after losing a leg to gangrene.
In his deathbed letter, he reflected that 'I ought to have been
among other things a good poet; Life was too great a bore on
one peg & that a bad one'.

At the end of the summer of 1824, in Florence, Anna herself

became ill. Thomas Lovell rushed to her side, but arrived too late. She was buried at the Old English Cemetery in Livorno. Her daughter – little Anna – returned to Edgeworthstown, and nearly lived to see the dawn of the twentieth century, dying in 1896 at the age of ninety-five, having lived, and died, in a very different emotional culture to her mother.

Chapter 17

TREACHERY AND DESERTION

At the beginning of the 1790s, Wollstonecraft's friend and publisher Joseph Johnson reissued a pamphlet written in 1783 by Charles Lennox, the 'radical Duke'.[1] Lennox had called for 'parliamentary reform' giving the right to 'ALL the Commons of Great Britain (Infants, Persons of insane Mind, and Criminals incapacitated by Law, only excepted) to vote in the Election of their Representatives in Parliament'. (The continued exclusion of women from suffrage was so self-evident to Lennox as to go unsaid.) Alongside 'universal' male suffrage, he had also called for 'restoring annual Parliaments', electing Scottish peers, and the establishment of free and fair elections. 'A long exclusion from any share in the legislature of their country, has rendered the great mass of the people indifferent,' Lennox explained.[2] Reformed representation would reinvigorate citizens' emotional investment in their nation, he hoped. That Lennox's aspirations were widely considered viable was borne out by the presentation before parliament of reform bills in 1780, 1783 and 1785. But these had failed, and by the time Johnson reissued Lennox's rallying cry in 1792, the formerly 'radical Duke' had 'signified his intention to oppose any scheme of reform that might be proposed, upon the stale pretence that this is not the proper time'.[3]

Over the remainder of the 1790s, radicals' expectations that the objectives of the parliamentary reform movement would soon be achieved were repeatedly disappointed. The government's response to the Church and King riots demonstrated that, whilst loyalists could seemingly rampage with impunity, the same did not apply to anti-establishment protests, as was evinced by the harsh suppression of the Bristol Bridge Riots in 1793. That freedom of speech and the right to assemble were under threat was hinted at as early as 1792, when Paine was prosecuted for the *Rights of Man*. The Gagging Acts of 1795 decisively stifled the publication of radical political theory; Coleridge held the Treasonable Practices Act responsible for stunting the development of the 'human intellect'.[4] Its partner, the Seditious Meetings Act, nearly killed the popular political societies that had flourished in the first half of the decade. In mid-1797, the radical Francis Place described how the majority of moderate reformers who had led the London Corresponding Society had either been arrested or had resigned.[5] A more violent and revolutionary movement emerged, leading directly to the United Irish Rebellion of 1798. But in its wake, the government redoubled its efforts, and between 1798 and 1799, most of the leaders of the United Irish movement and the LCS were arrested.

Habeas Corpus had been suspended in 1794, and then again, during the Irish crisis, in 1798 and 1799, to facilitate the arrest, prolonged detention and trial of suspected revolutionary leaders, often on flimsy pretences and without evidence. Harsh sentences of transportation had been doled out to the 'Scottish Martyrs', and suspects in the Treason Trials endured years of incarceration, even if many were eventually acquitted. The Seditious Meetings Act's legacy extends right until the present day: legislation prohibiting unlicensed assemblies existed in similar form until the Public Order Act of 1986, and was reinstated in the 1994 Criminal Justice and Public Order Act, which was criticized for containing badly defined restrictions on parties, raves, squatting, football culture and hunt-saboteur meetings. Section 63 of the act was used in 2009 to close down a birthday barbecue for fifteen people that the authorities feared might expand into an 'illegal rave'.[6]

After 1799, political meetings continued to take place 'underground', but Britain did not see open agitation for reform until after the Napoleonic Wars, in the 1820s, after a twenty-year hiatus. The aims of the eighteenth-century reform movement did not come to fruition until the Great Reform Act of 1832, which finally redrew the boundaries of new parliamentary constituencies to eliminate so-called 'rotten boroughs' (constituencies containing a tiny electorate, many of whom were voting under the influence of patrons) and extended suffrage to male householders living in properties worth at least £10 a year. The Reform Act was partly drafted by the Whig MP John George Lambton – 'Radical Jack'. As a young boy, he and his brother lived for a few years as pupils of Anna and Thomas Beddoes; Beddoes' hope that education could effect significant political change was finally realized by someone whom he had himself taught. But even the Great Reform Act achieved a much less ambitious vision than Lennox had entertained in the 1780s. Universal manhood suffrage was not instigated in Britain until 1918, while women were not granted the vote on equal terms to men until 1928. Slavery abolitionists, too, were disappointed in the slow progress of their movement in the 1790s. Upper Canada passed an anti-slavery law in 1793, but Britain would not follow suit until 1807. Even the 1807 Act only fined captains continuing with the trade, designating them pirates; slavery wasn't decisively abolished on the basis of principle until 1833.

In 1789, France had offered a beacon of hope for radical political change, but by the end of the 1790s it appeared a desperate disappointment to many British citizens. Most reformers, who upheld the purportedly 'bloodless' values of the 1688 Glorious Revolution, decried the violence of the Tuileries attack, the September Massacres, the execution of Louis XVI and the Terror. By 1798, Napoleon's ascendancy, France's transformation into a military empire, and its own practice of censorship meant that few looked across the Channel any longer for a model of Enlightenment democracy. Prolonged war between Britain and Revolutionary and Napoleonic France not only seemed to radicals to confirm the British administration's opposition to republican values, but was interpreted by many as the cause of economic crisis and increasing poverty in Britain throughout the decade. The war was initially predicted to be over swiftly, but in fact lasted twenty-two years, from 1793 until 1815 (with a brief hiatus in 1802–3) – enough time, as the historian Jenny Uglow points out, for babies born at the beginning of the war to be fighting at Waterloo.[7]

Very few of the figures who appear in this book came through the decade relatively unscathed. But some did. Richard Lovell Edgeworth, true to form, recovered from his early failed experiment in Rousseauvian education and the death of his eldest son Dick and of his first two wives, to marry Elizabeth Sneyd, the sister of his second wife, Honora. When Elizabeth died in 1797, he married again, to Frances Anne Beaufort, with whom he had six further children. Edgeworth continued to engage in a plethora of outlandish and inventive projects, including manufacturing a prefabricated church spire, composing a practical manual on road construction, and experimenting with the design of wheels and carriages. He died at home, at the age of seventy-three, on 13 June 1817, outliving by nearly ten years his son-in-law Beddoes, who had hoped to reap a substantial inheritance. The first object of Mary Wollstonecraft's emotional hopes, Henry Fuseli, died on 16 April 1825, aged eighty-four, after enjoying robust health, a solid, if scandalous, reputation, and a lifelong marriage to Sophia; he was buried in St Paul's Cathedral. And Wollstonecraft's second lover, Gilbert Imlay, Fanny's absent father, disappeared from the historical record around 1801, when he moved to the Isle of Jersey, where he died, apparently after twenty-seven uneventful years, on 20 November 1828.

A small minority of radicals managed to maintain their political principles without incurring significant social penalties. George Dyer was an active member of the LCS. In 1789 he praised French republicanism and declared it to be 'the most complete form of government' for Britain, later excoriating the inequality of the late-eighteenth-century British state, in which 'one man possessed three or four magnificent houses ... while many of the industrious poor can scarcely get the necessaries of life'. After 1795, Dyer turned to less overtly political journalism and writing, composing histories of the University of Cambridge, numerous volumes of poetry, contributions to works on classical literature, and essays on 'the English Constitution', showing he hadn't completely abandoned his convictions. Despite being 'very dirty' in appearance – his friend Charles Lamb noted that his 'Pantaloons ... were absolutely ingrained with the accumulated dirt of ages' – and despite his history of 'Jacobinism', Dyer managed to forge a reasonable living from writing, and died aged eighty-six in 1841, after seventeen happy years of being 'affectionately tended' by his wife, Honour Mather.[8]

The active radical John Horne Tooke, a member of the Society for Constitutional Information, also continued in politics beyond the mid-1790s. In 1796, he stood as Member of Parliament for Westminster against Charles James Fox, but ended up accepting the position of MP for Old Sarum. (The

irony of an ardent reformer representing a rotten borough was
not lost on him.) Tooke sat in parliament for the first time on
16 February 1801 and kept his seat for a year. But his health
was declining, and in his final decade he suffered from gout,
kidney stones and gangrenous legs, dying on 18 March 1812,
aged seventy-six. In death, as in life, Tooke was celebrated and
denounced in equal measure.[9]

Most radicals, though, were forced by the events of the 1790s
to confront – and often alter or relinquish – their investment
in their political principles. The literary scholar Kenneth R.
Johnston has provided a magisterial survey of the accommodations made by disillusioned radicals from the second half
of the 1790s onwards – and the consequences of refusal to
adapt, of sticking fast to principle – in his recent study, *Unusual
Suspects: Pitt's Reign of Alarm and the Lost Generation of the 1790s.*
'Disappointment' and 'disillusionment' describe two very different paths that radicals found open to them. Both entailed
significant loss: either the jettisoning or significant adaptation of
past beliefs, by dismissing them as false, illusory, childish (disillusionment); or the maintenance of those principles, but coupled
with a pessimistic 'judgment of attainableness', the abandonment of hope that they might come to fruition (disappointment).

In the late 1790s, there were many who were disappointed –
who were left subsisting in the shadows of reactionary Britain,
clinging to their old beliefs, out of place, on the wrong side of
history; or they had been flung off altogether, to foreign countries; or were left dying or dead. By 1801, William Godwin was
admitting that 'I have fallen (if I have fallen) in one common
grave with the cause and the love of liberty'.[10] He described
how the passionate 'zeal' with which many pursued utopian
hopes inspired by the French Revolution could not withstand
the frustrations of the 1790s, and 'without a continual supply
of fuel [did] speedily cool'.[11] Godwin found himself demoted
from intellectual celebrity to obscurity. When the young poet

Percy Bysshe Shelley admiringly brought up *Political Justice* in conversation with Southey in 1812, he was astounded to discover Godwin was still alive. 'I had enrolled your name on the list of the honourable dead,' he wrote to his hero, rather tactlessly.[12] But Shelley professed himself grievously disappointed that *Political Justice*'s objectives had failed to materialize: 'What has followed? have men ceased to fight, have vice and misery vanished from the earth?'[13]

By 1810, Godwin was remarried, to Mary Jane Clairmont, with whom, in 1805, he had established a bookshop and publishing house four years after their marriage, specializing in works for children, with financial assistance from Tom Wedgwood. He remained impecunious for almost the rest of his life, until 1833, when he was rescued by a government sinecure that tided him over until his death three years later. Godwin had adopted Wollstonecraft's '*Fannikin*', who was just three years old when her mother died. On the night of 9–10 October 1816, at the age of twenty-two, Fanny committed suicide, alone in a coaching inn, the Mackworth Arms, on Wind Street, in Swansea. 'I have long determined that the best thing I could do was to put an end to the existence of a being whose birth was unfortunate, and whose life has only been a series of pain to those persons who have hurt their health in endeavouring to promote her welfare,' her suicide note read. The circumstances of Fanny's suicide are not clear, but it seems that she had craved a home alongside the brave new world that her sister Mary – the baby to whom Wollstonecraft had given birth shortly before her death in 1797 – appeared to be forging with her lover, Shelley, but had been rejected. As her biographer Janet Todd points out, Fanny's last journey, from Bath to Swansea, was a wretched mirror image of the intrepid Scandinavian adventure on which she and her mother had embarked twenty-one years earlier, the account of which, in *Letters Written During a Short Residence in Sweden, Norway, and Denmark*, Fanny had clung to as soon as she could read.[14]

Imminent death was woven into the fates of the many radicals who were active in the 1790s, and mourning became part and parcel of political engagement, as a response to death and disappointment. The 'Scottish Martyrs' – Thomas Fyshe Palmer, Thomas Muir, Joseph Gerrald, William Skirving and Maurice Margarot, who were arrested in 1793 for sedition, the latter three for their role in organizing the National Convention in Edinburgh in November of that year – were all sentenced to transportation. Thomas Fyshe Palmer died in 1802, two years after his sentence expired. He tried to return home from Australia via the Ladrones (or Mariana) Islands in the Pacific Ocean, but they were under the rule of Spain, with whom Britain was at war. Palmer was taken prisoner of war, and died from dysentery on Guguan island. Thomas Muir made it back to France after an eventful escape from the Australian penal colony, via a Pacific crossing to Nootka Sound on an American trading ship, a Spanish ship to California, then across the Mexican border and onto another voyage to Cuba. He finally boarded a Spanish frigate to Cadiz, where the ship was attacked by the British Navy, and a flying splinter left Muir with a missing left eye and permanently disfigured. Veiled in blood, he evaded the British authorities and, unrecognized, went on shore, where he was initially detained as a prisoner of war, before the French helped to secure his release and offered him a home. Hailed at first as a revolutionary hero in Paris, Muir soon fell into debt and temporary obscurity; he died in Chantilly in 1799. Joseph Gerrald and William Skirving both died in Australia in 1796: the former from consumption, probably contracted during his long voyage, and the latter from dysentery. Maurice Margarot alone made it back to Britain, and continued to urge restoration of the Saxon constitution, the curtailing of commerce, and the redistribution of land. He spent the summers of 1813 and 1814 in France, attempting to revive his business, which had been destroyed during his sentence in the penal colony, but his health was failing and his sight deteriorated, and he was forced to call on Godwin, begging for charity.[15] He died on 11 November 1815, aged seventy, in London.

Many of those implicated in the Treason Trials faced similar fates. Pitt's politicking in the Pop-Gun Plot had devastating effects on its scapegoats. Paul Lemaitre's mother died 'a victim to grief at the imprisonment and ill treatment of her beloved son'. George Higgins was 'restored to the world with a load of suspicion on his back to look out for a new employment'. James Parkinson's friend, John Smith, described how his 'employment was taken from him – great part of his stock in trade was seized; he returned to his family just time enough indeed to keep them from ruin; but what from his illness, the unavoidable confusion in his affairs, and the loss of his employment, is not without daily solicitude for his support'.[16] In February 1797, Smith was sentenced to two years' hard labour for publishing a text critical of the government, A Summary of the Duties of Citizenship. In April 1798, after the second suspension of Habeas Corpus, Robert Crosfeild was imprisoned for three years. His consumption grew worse in prison, and he died shortly after his release, in 1802, aged forty-four, and was buried in Hendon, north London.

By the time of his acquittal, the most famous victim of the Treason Trials, Thomas Hardy, had lost his wife, their infant child, and his business. He failed to revive his shoe shop and, after his home again faced loyalist attacks, he retreated from the front line of radical politics. However, when Habeas Corpus was suspended in 1798, and again in 1810, Hardy acted as treasurer of a fund to help radicals under arrest. He died on 11 October 1832, having lived just long enough to see the Great Reform Act passed. The biblical scholar Gilbert Wakefield, who had attacked Pitt for being in league with the anti-Christ, was indicted after he published a pamphlet in 1798 arguing that the British government had provoked war with France and rendered Britain open to invasion by destroying the health of the poor.

After representing himself at trial, Wakefield was convicted and sentenced to two years in Dorchester jail. During his prison term, his mother and his youngest child died, and a chronic shoulder ailment recurred. He was released in May 1801, but had contracted typhus fever and died only a few months later, on 9 September 1801. And John Binns, the member of the LCS who witnessed the London thunderstorm on the date predicted by Richard Brothers as the Second Coming, was arrested for sedition in 1796, acquitted two years later, arrested again for High Treason in 1798 for his support of the United Irish Rebellion, was again acquitted, but was finally arrested and imprisoned at the end of 1798 while Habeas Corpus was suspended. He was confined without charge in Gloucester jail until February 1801, after which he left for America and headed to Joseph Priestley's settlement in Northumberland, Pennsylvania, where Priestley presided over his wedding to another British emigrant, Mary Ann Bagster. Binns died in obscurity on 16 June 1860, aged eighty-seven.

Priestley, himself, had been 'dis-appointed' from Britain – in the literal sense of being deprived of an 'office, appointment or profession' – when Church and King protestors burned his house to the ground in July 1791 and shortly after he emigrated to Pennsylvania, to help establish Cooper's Town. His American residence proved to be disappointing too. Overwhelmed by the work of building a house and intellectual community from scratch in Northumberland, Priestley's intention to establish a nearby haven for Girondins fleeing from France 'was given up', he wrote shortly after his arrival. (However, 'several philanthropic persons in Pennsylvania' do seem to have sponsored 'a place of retreat for the unfortunate French emigrants who fled to America', twenty-four miles to the north-east of Cooper's Town, on the west bank of the Susquehanna. It was christened French Town and now bears the evocative name 'Asylum'.[17]) Priestley's wife died before his house had been built, and he found himself isolated, in failing health, five or six days' rough travel from Philadelphia, the nearest large settlement and intellectual community. He hoped that 'a readier communication will be opened with Philadelphia, and that the place will improve, and become more eligible'.[18] But Priestley died in 1804, over ten years after leaving Britain. Two years later, Northumberland was overlooked as capital of Pennsylvania in favour of Harrisburg, over 100 miles south. The lands that his son-in-law Thomas Cooper had advised Priestley to purchase did not turn into the burgeoning intellectual centre or worthwhile financial investment that he had hoped. In 1811, Priestley's son Joseph admitted defeat and returned to Britain, where he sold off most of Priestley's surviving library and scientific instruments, and destroyed his father's correspondence. As early as 1795, the *Gentleman's Magazine* was warning that stories anticipating Priestley's experience showed that America, 'this land of universal promise is a land of general disappointment'.[19]

Land of disappointment or not, many had no choice but to forge a new life abroad after the mid-1790s. Tom Paine returned to America during the Peace of Amiens, the brief truce in 1802–3 between Britain and France; he published positive comments on Napoleon in *Remarks on English Affairs* and essays, such as *Constitutional Reform*, and died on 8 June 1809, after suffering repeated apoplectic fits, losing the use of his legs, and requiring constant care. The classical scholar John Tweddell, a member of the Friends of the People, who was a friend of Godwin, Dyer, Frend, Holcroft and Losh, was driven by the French Revolution's 'eternal injury to the cause of freedom' to leave Britain for incessant travel around Europe. In letters home, he wrote of preferring 'to remain in a corner unnoticed, than to take any active part in the busy scenes of this silly world'.[20] He died of fever in Athens on 25 July 1799.[21] After the Scottish authorities attempted to arrest the writer James Thomson Callender for sedition for the pamphlet *The Political Progress of*

Britain, he exiled himself to America in 1793, where he continued publishing radical tracts. The American pamphleteer Joel Barlow was also back in the United States by 1805. In 1811, he was appointed envoy to France to negotiate trade relations, and headed to Vilna, Poland, to finalize a treaty. He got caught up in Napoleon's retreat from Russia in October 1812, and died of pneumonia in a village near Cracow in December. Helen Maria Williams also maintained her exile from Britain, remaining in France throughout the Napoleonic Wars, with a brief sojourn in Amsterdam between 1823 and 1827. She died in Paris on 15 December 1827. And in 1798, Robert Southey's friend William Gilbert, the Bristol poet, completely disappeared after having been driven into religious mania by the French Revolution's apparent materialization of the 'preliminary stages of humanity's progress towards millenarian fulfilment'. Familiar with his idealization of Africa, Southey suspected he had gone to find 'Gibberti' (modern Djibouti), whose inhabitants Gilbert believed were his relatives. Southey made enquiries among captains involved in trade there, but failed to uncover any information, and wrote him off as dead. But Gilbert didn't die until around 1825, not in Africa, but in Charleston, South Carolina, where he had been resident for around twenty-six years. The successful proprietor of land there, he was resentful of his characterization by Southey as 'the most insane person I have ever known at large'.[22]

Many disappointed radicals who remained in Britain did so at the expense of their careers and reputations. The physician and poet William Drennan, whose literary career effectively ended after his trial for seditious libel on 29 June 1794, retired to Belfast in 1807. Elizabeth Inchbald, the actor and writer, close friends with Holcroft and Godwin, withdrew her historical play *The Massacre* from publication because of its obvious commentary on the French Revolution. She later destroyed her four-volume autobiography, foregoing the publisher's £1,000 fee, because of anxieties about its frank portrayal of her political radicalism.[23] William Frend lost his university career after the publication of his *Peace and Union* pamphlet, but continued to actively support reform, especially in the run-up to the Great Reform Bill of 1832. He died in February 1841, after suffering two strokes. The once best-selling works of the Enlightenment physician, poet and Lunar Society member Erasmus Darwin were also victims of the increasingly reactionary climate of the late 1790s: in the first two decades of the nineteenth century, Darwin's works were not published at all.[24] And at the end of 1799, his eldest son, Erasmus II, 'became the victim of secret and utter despair', and died after throwing himself into the 'partially frozen' River Derwent.[25] Darwin was criticized for displaying an inhumanly 'stoic' response to his eldest son's death; he spent the following two years putting Erasmus II's affairs in order, before dying himself, on 18 April 1802, after finishing 'a very sprightly letter' to his great friend Richard Lovell Edgeworth.[26]

Many of the victims of disappointment listed above were in their middle age during the 1790s, having pursued reform since the original reigniting of that movement in the 1760s. For them, the failures of the 1790s entailed retreat into a more solitary, melancholy later life. But a vocal few were much younger during that decade, and experienced its disappointments as the premature amputation of youthful hopes and energy. After Edmund Seward's tragic death in June 1795, the pantisocrat Robert Lovell died less than a year later, on 3 May 1796, aged only twenty-five, after contracting a fever and undertaking a long journey against medical advice. After his death, Lovell's father refused to provide any financial assistance either to Lovell's widow, Mary (née Fricker), or to their son; Mary turned to Southey for help, living with him and then with his daughter until her death at the age of ninety. For George Burnett, the collapse of pantisocracy marked the end of his sustained commitment to any scheme, and he drifted for decades, dabbling as a medical student, assistant to the census-taker John Rickman, hack writer, domestic tutor, opium-addict and naval surgeon. He died aged thirty-six, in 1811, in poverty, having begged Southey for support.

The historian E. P. Thompson describes the later trajectory of 1790s radicals as 'disenchantment' or 'apostacy'; he praises the former as a state in which principles are maintained or even lost, but which does not entail any subsequent search for an alternative certainty. Thompson writes that disenchantment, as a state of suspension, can create conditions for 'the creative impulse [to] be felt', by maintaining, but not attempting to resolve, the 'tension between a boundless aspiration – for liberty, reason, *égalité*, perfectibility – and a peculiarly harsh and unregenerate reality'.[27] Thompson's idea of disenchantment has much in common with that psychological and creative state defined by the poet John Keats in 1817 as 'negative capability': 'when a man is capable of being in uncertainties, Mysteries, doubts, without any irritable reaching after fact & reason ... remaining content with half knowledge'.[28] And certainly the ability to recall, sympathetically, the attractions of the revolutionary mindset, while narrating the conditions under which it collapsed and was succeeded by an alternative reality, was the basis for extraordinary bursts of creativity in a plethora of literary texts that came out of the 1790s, including Wordsworth's *Prelude*, his *Excursion*, his poem 'Ruth', and Coleridge's 'Fears in Solitude'.

In *The Excursion*, published in 1814, Wordsworth embodied radicals' trajectory from hope to disappointment in the figure of the 'Solitary'. At the beginning of the 1790s, the Solitary was buoyed up by 'the unlooked-for dawn,/ That promised everlasting joy to France!'[29] But a few years later, having 'forfeited/ All joy in human nature,' he lives as a hermit, 'Tormented thus, after a wandering course/ Of discontent, and inwardly opprest/ With malady – in part ... provoked/ By weariness of life'.[30] The Solitary was said to be mostly modelled on the Unitarian preacher Joseph Fawcett, Godwin's old friend, whom William

Hazlitt described as 'one of the most enthusiastic admirers of the French Revolution'.[31] In 1795, Fawcett had retired from London to Hertfordshire in a depression caused by the progress of the French Revolution and the British reform movement. He threw himself into farming and poetry, dying nine years later, in his mid-forties; his death was 'hastened', said Hazlitt, by 'the disappointment of the hopes he had cherished of the freedom and happiness of mankind [which] preyed upon his mind'.[32] It is notable, though, that Fawcett himself did not benefit from the creative flourishing that Thompson links to disappointment: he was merely inspiration for the poetic endeavours of Wordsworth, who had followed a different psychological trajectory towards accommodation and apostasy.

The figure perhaps most associated with disappointment throughout the whole course of the 1790s was the prime minister, William Pitt, who had once been the focus of radicals' hopes for translating their political ambitions into reality. In the 1780s, Pitt had championed reformist campaigns: the abolition of slavery, the cause of the American colonists during the American War of Independence, and he had seen three reform bills through parliament. But within a few years of the French Revolution, Pitt had disappointed these hopes to become the most infamous political apostate, who had betrayed his earlier enthusiasm for parliamentary reform to impose restrictions on 'the rights of man' and pursue a costly war with France. Thomas Beddoes was one of his chief accusers. In late 1795, Beddoes published *Where Would be the Harm of a Speedy Peace?*, describing Pitt and the Home Secretary, William Grenville – Pitt's cousin and ally – as 'Inquisitors general'. Beddoes painted a bleak dystopian picture of late 1790s Britain 'strewed over with ruins' after 'the effects of popular indignation [had] burs[t] forth in all its undistinguishing fury'.[33] In his *Essay on the Public Merits of Mr Pitt* (1796), Beddoes reproached Pitt with 'the failure of every scheme that he had formed, and the disappointment of every result that he had anticipated'.[34]

Beddoes' reaction to Pitt's ideological volte-face was typical of a wider change that was taking place in the conception of disappointment. Novels published before the 1790s used the word 'disappointment' to describe a temporary emotional state ('stark mad with disappointment'), an impermanent mood ('if she personated pride, she maintained it even in disappointment'), or a personified emotion ('Disappointment's cruel pain'). It designated the outcome of a specific project ('research ... terminating in uncertainty and disappointment'), the thwarting of a precise desire ('the disappointment of her wishes'), or a single event that had deflated hopes ('this intelligence operated as a disappointment').[35] Accusations of disappointment or failure were generally levelled at a single facet of a person, who was generally acknowledged to otherwise transcend such individual flaws. In Samuel Richardson's gargantuan epistolary novel *Clarissa*, the protagonist berates herself for being 'guilty of a failure', but stops short of disdaining herself *as* a total failure.

Towards the end of the century, 'failure' and 'disappointment' were being deployed with more terminal implications. In perhaps the first use of 'disappointment' to write off an entire life, in 1765 the poet William Cowper – who suffered depression, insanity, and attempted suicide three times – described himself as having 'been a disappointment and a vexation to [his family] ever since he has been of consequence enough to be either'.[36] By 1800, Charles Dibdin characterized the playwright Dryden's entire early life as a 'success or disappointment'. By the mid-nineteenth century, this terminal association of 'disappointment' and 'failure' had become a standard figure of speech. 'Whose life is not a disappointment?' wondered Thackeray in 1849. 'I am a failure,' mourned Gissing in *New Grub Street*. Dickens, in *Little Dorrit*, in 1857, stated, 'I am a disappointment as I very well know', and Somerville, in *The Real Charlotte*, in 1894, objected that 'Mrs Lambert was a failure.' The despondent, accusatory phrase 'I am disappointed in you' was infrequently used in the eighteenth century, but Gaskell's *North and South*, in 1855, deploys it twice: 'he was disappointed in her'; 'I am disappointed in him'.

This changing linguistic convention mirrors how, by the mid-nineteenth century, the value of individual lives had become synonymous with the outcome of single projects. Dramatic failure of the latter was enough to erode the former. A hundred years earlier, in the mid-eighteenth century, the figure of the 'projector' had been embodied by Beddoes' father-in-law, Richard Lovell Edgeworth. Edgeworth was an energetic schemer, an enthusiast hopping from venture to venture, sometimes in pursuit of profit, or intellectual aggrandisement, or scientific discovery. Edgeworth, with his generous private income from his landed estate, was hardly affected by individual failures, such as his Rousseauvian project; they were like water off a duck's back. But in the late-eighteenth and early nineteenth centuries, the rise of the middle classes, with their financial independence, arguably placed a new urgency on the success of individual enterprises. The definition of 'speculator' was changing too, in the same period, from an emphasis on intellectual reflection and philosophical wondering, to commercial gambles. The *Oxford English Dictionary* cites the physician Alexander Hamilton's reference to 'speculators in the city' in 1778 as the first use of 'speculator' to designate 'one who engages in commercial or financial speculation' instead of metaphysical wondering.

The historian Scott Sandage ascribes the dramatic linguistic change that reflected how projectors' and speculators' enterprises were shrinking to the pursuit of profit, and in which 'failure' and 'disappointment' were taking on a more terminal significance to the rapidly increasing authority of credit-rating agencies in America in the early nineteenth century.[37] Credit agencies identified individuals as successes or failures according to the outcome of specific projects. In Europe, the linguistic shift appears to have occurred earlier than in America. There 'a bankrupt' had been used, as a noun, to refer to a person since the mid-sixteenth century. And in the 1790s, in a description of Dutch financial laws, the clergyman John Trusler referred to 'when a person fails in Holland'.[38] His use of overtly financial language to dismiss a whole person reflected how the words 'failure' and 'disappointment' were taking on a new nuance in general usage, implying the potential termination of the possibilities of an entire life, as exhibited in Beddoes' criticisms of Pitt.

The rise of credit was also arguably responsible for propagating an idea – utterly opposed to Joseph Priestley's welcoming of instructive disappointment – that failure and disappointment were psychologically intolerable states. The social psychologist Erich Fromm describes how credit itself is predicated on the premise *'that every desire must be satisfied immediately, no wish must be frustrated'*. It touts the image of an individual as *'a system of desires and satisfactions'* who should never have to deal with states of non-satisfaction. The capitalist 'economic machine' can only exist by stimulating 'synthetic' appetites and prescribing 'commodities, sights, food, drinks, cigarettes, people, lectures, books, movies' as satisfactions for the pain of longing. Credit systems ensure that satisfaction can be obtained without delay. But the economic machine also relies upon that satisfaction being continually withheld, through the prescription of fundamentally unsatisfying objects. 'The world is one great object for our appetite,' writes Fromm: 'a big apple, a big bottle, a big breast; we are the sucklers, the eternally expectant ones, the hopeful ones – and the eternally disappointed ones. How can we help being disappointed if our birth stops at the breast of the mother, if we are never weaned, if we remain overgrown babes, if we never go beyond the receptive orientation?' Fromm describes how the rise of credit fails to wean us from the infant state of permanent hunger and expectation, and fails to accustom us to the experience of disappointment – a crucial stage in infant development. Not only this, but credit agencies' very survival is predicated on characterizing the state of disappointment as the most intolerable imaginable, which may only be relieved by the Next Big Thing.[39] In the popular imagination disappointment shifted from salutary correction or temporary blip to unbearable tragedy, which corresponded with the linguistic change that ascribed it greater import and permanency. Both reflected, and assisted, global changes in commerce, but it is arguable that widespread experience of disappointment in 1790s Britain – in which political and personal disappointments were increasingly felt to terminate rather than inform future possibilities – reinforced that cultural and economic shift.

Pitt may have proved a disappointment to many, but he himself showed that there was an alternative route to permanent disappointment, to maintaining principles with no hope of materialization. Despite the shame of mirroring his behaviour, many radicals came – like Pitt – to abandon their former ideology: they converted from a pro-revolutionary to a staunchly anti-revolutionary stance. Often, they came to see this as a process of 'disillusionment', a developmental process of awakening and maturation, shrugging off the illusions of childhood to adopt a worldly wise, adult point of view. Disillusionment was a very different trajectory to the dislocation and dejection involved in disappointment. In 1805, Wordsworth's *Prelude* reflected the process of disillusionment by pronouncing the optimism, 'hope and joy' of the early 1790s as symptoms of 'a country in romance', overseen by a 'prime enchanter', to which '[t]hey who had fed their childhood upon dreams – / The playfellows of fancy' were especially susceptible.[40] Disapppointed radicals experienced the failure of hope as a process of dislocation, which cut them off from their 'appointed' places in society and history. But disillusioned radicals used the failure of hope as the basis of personal transformation, adaptation and accommodation to the changing climate.

The disillusioned ranged from outright apostates, who experienced a sincere and dramatic conversion of political ideology, to those who made pragmatic ideological accommodations to maintain earnings and reputation. Among the latter was John Thelwall, who resumed lecturing in November 1801, but renounced political subjects, chiefly addressing his audience on elocution and speech. By 1809, he had established the Institute of Elocution in London, which flourished until 1818. After the end of the Napoleonic Wars, he resumed his career as an itinerant lecturer, but confined his topics to elocution, poetry and the poet John Milton. In January 1834, Thelwall started complaining of 'an unpleasant symptom of the chest' and 'astmha [*sic*], or whatever it is'; he died three weeks later, on 17 February 1834.[41] After his acquittal in the Treason Trials, Godwin's friend Thomas Holcroft devoted time to pursuits including riding, music, collecting foreign-language books and pornography. He wrote plays, many of which flopped, such as the *Man of Ten Thousand*, which finished its run at Drury Lane after just seven performances. After spending three years in Hamburg, Holcroft returned to Britain in 1802, relaunching a literary career based on philosophical travel writing, comedies, novels and more plays. He penned an autobiography, portraying himself as the living embodiment of 'how difficulties may be endured, how they may be overcome, and how they may at last contribute, as a school of instruction, to bring forth hidden talent'. He died on 23 March 1809, at the age of sixty-four.[42]

Many radicals' 'apostasies' were more dramatic. Tom Wedgwood's brother-in-law, James Mackintosh, underwent a volte-face from the vanguard of radicalism to become a standard-bearer of the establishment. Robert Southey emerged from his sojourn in Portugal with fainter, although not completely demolished, radical sympathies. When France invaded Spain and Portugal in 1808, Southey's fondness for those countries set him against most radicals' opposition to Britain's war with France.

Over the next few years, collaborations with Tory journals such as the *Quarterly Review*, anxiety over George III's declining mental health, and horror at a new government's potentially weaker resolve regarding the war led Southey to call for strong leadership coupled with continued military action against France. He was so intent on 'keep[ing] the peace-party out [that] Pitt himself,' Southey admitted, 'should have my support . . . against any ministry that would abandon Spain and treat with Bonaparte'.[43] The extent of Southey's accommodation with the Tory establishment was confirmed in 1813, when he was offered, and accepted, the post of Poet Laureate and, eight years later, composed *A Vision of Judgement*, commemorating George III's death. He imagined the king welcomed in heaven by a host of Tory worthies, and linked political opposition to Satan. Byron memorably denounced Southey as a 'pitiful renegado' with a 'shifting and turncoat existence', who had:

> *. . . written praises of a regicide;*
> *He had written praises of all kings whatever;*
> *He had written for republics far and wide,*
> *And then against them bitterer than ever;*
> *For pantisocracy he once had cried*
> *Aloud; a scheme less moral than t'was clever;*
> *Then grew a hearty anti-jacobin –*
> *Had turn'd his coat – and would have turn'd his skin.*[44]

Alongside Pitt, one of the most famous disillusioned apostates of 1790s Britain was Southey's fellow pantisocrat, Coleridge. In 1795, before pantisocracy had completely collapsed, Coleridge had reproached Pitt (that 'calumniated Judas Iscariot'), Lennox and Burke for their political betrayals by evoking the 'Fable of the Maddening Rain'. In that fable, a man, who had escaped exposure to a rainstorm that turned his compatriots mad with lust, greed and envy, decided in the face of the discomfort of living on the wrong side of history, to conform and turn himself mad too.[45] Coleridge used the fable to parallel 'the Fate of more than one Reformer' who 'began his career with high efforts of zealous Patriotism, till finding his exertions fruitless and himself calumniated, from despair he has sunk into acquiescence, and from hopeless Conformity into active Guilt'.[46]

But Coleridge would find himself the target of accusations of such Judas-like behaviour by the decade's end. 'I have ... snapped my squeaking baby-trumpet of sedition, and have hung up its fragments in the chamber of Penitences,' he wrote, as early as October 1796.[47] And in 'Religious Musings', a poem he began on Christmas Eve 1794 but revised until its publication in 1796, he referred to his pantisocratic hope to see Priestley with his 'fleshly eye' as a *'childish* pang'.[48] Nicholas Roe, the biographer of Wordsworth's, Coleridge's and Thelwall's 'radical years', has described Coleridge's jettisoning of Thelwall for Wordsworth in summer 1797 as 'a formative stage in the process towards apostasy, which would eventually lead Coleridge to deny the reality of his political opinions'.[49] In a letter to his then patrons, Sir George and Lady Margaret Beaumont, on 1 October 1803, Coleridge made the bombastic claim that during the 1790s he had been 'utterly unconnected with any party or club or society – (& this praise I must take to myself, that I disclaimed all these Societies, these Imperia in Imperio [states within the state], these Ascarides [parasitic worms] in the Bowels of the State, subsisting on the weakness & diseasedness, & having for their final Object the Death of that State, whose Life had been their Birth & growth, & continued to be their sole nourishment. – All such Societies, under whatever name, I abhorred as wicked Conspiracies – and to this principle I adhered immoveably, simply because it was a principle'.[50] In 1809, in his second attempt to found a newspaper – this time called *The Friend* – Coleridge's essay 'Enthusiasm for an Ideal World' fondly denigrated the pantisocratic project as a 'gradually exhausted

balloon of youthful enthusiasm'.[51] And when Coleridge's autobiographical 'sketches', *Biographia Literaria*, were published in
1817, he reiterated the declaration that even at the high point of
radical fervour, from 1794 to 1796, 'my principles were [opposite]
to those of jacobinism, or even democracy'.[52]

Coleridge's grandiose denials of his apostasy met with scorn.
The *Monthly Magazine* quoted an associate from Coleridge's
Bristol days, who spluttered, 'I very well remember what his
sentiments were, at the time that he, Southey, Lovell, Burnett,
and some others, talked of going to America . . . positively and
decidedly democratic.'[53] Thelwall scribbled a furious comment
beside the *Biographia Literaria* passage, alleging that 'Mr C. was
indeed far from Democracy, because he was far beyond it . . .
a down right zealous leveller & indeed . . . a Jacobin, a man of
blood'.[54] Certainly Coleridge's lectures and publications of 1795
to 1796 had explicitly rallied behind reformers and opponents of
the Two Acts, and from the perspective of most contemporary
observers he was active in what has been called the 'Golden Age'
of Bristol politics.[55] Pantisocracy may have been partially driven
by Coleridge's domestic objectives, but he did not correct those
who interpreted it as an apotheosis of Enlightenment optimism
about human perfectibility and the liberation of desire, and of
seventeenth-century radical theories about the redistribution of
private property.

In a crucial respect, Coleridge's was a literal apostasy: a sincere
shift of opinion, based on religious differences between himself
and the radical movement, propelled by a changing spiritual climate. In summer 1795, Coleridge followed his political lectures
with six talks on 'revealed religion', setting out the cornerstones
of his religious thought at that time. In those lectures he demonstrated his allegiance to Priestley's and Paley's optimistic belief
that 'every event however calamitous is the necessary means of
the best possible end'. Coleridge emphasized that 'We offer petitions, not as supposing that we influence the immutable – but

because to petition the Supreme Being is the way ... to stir up the benevolent affection in our own heart.'[56] God was unpersuadable, because the world was on a path towards perfectibility. Prayers and sacrifices were all rituals whose effects were only felt in the human temperament. By mid-1797, however, Coleridge had changed his mind. He proclaimed 'the propriety of offering *petitions* as well as thanksgivings to Deity'.[57] He had come to associate Priestley's view of an immutable God with Godwin's atheist indifference. As he separated himself from the latter, he relinquished his sympathy for the former.

The shift in Coleridge's religious attitudes reflected the emerging influence of the Christian movement of evangelicalism. Whereas the optimistic eighteenth-century view was that good works were necessary to attain religious virtue, early evangelicals like John and Charles Wesley were influenced by the Moravians' conviction that individuals' emotional experiences of faith could alone testify to salvation. From the 1730s onwards, the reach of this 'religion of the heart' expanded, based on central notions such as the innate depravity of humanity, for whom life is an 'arena of moral trial', in which redemption from sinfulness may be attained through the conscience. Christ's Atonement on the Cross provided sinners with the means to attain redemption from their fundamental guilt, through profound internal faith and reflection.[58] One of evangelicalism's chief proponents, the abolitionist William Wilberforce, wrote in a letter in 1803 that evangelical 'Christianity appears to me to consider the world as in a state of alienation from God, as lost in depravity and guilt', and that writers were responsible for persuading readers 'to obtain deliverance from ... the power of sin'.[59] Coleridge had once derided the Doctrine of the Atonement as 'the most irrational and gloomy Superstition that ever degraded the human mind'. It ran counter to Joseph Butler's optimistic 'sentiment', emphasized fervently by Coleridge in his 1795 lectures, that 'repentance and a good life are, *of themselves*, sufficient to recommend us to the divine favour'.[60] But by the early nineteenth century, Coleridge was defining 'my Faith' as 'simply this – that there is an original corruption of our nature, from which & from the consequences of which we may be redeemed by Christ ... in a mysterious manner as an effect of his Crucifixion – and this I believe,' he continued, 'not because I *understand* it; but because I *feel*, that it is not only suitable to, but needful for, my nature.'[61]

By the end of the 1790s, optimistic religious narratives proclaiming the rational, perfectible direction of the universe no longer provided an adequate means of interpreting that decade's events. They did not seem 'suitable' or 'needful' any more. Nobody had emerged unscathed from the 1790s. Radicals, reformers, reactionaries and political indifferents all lived in fear of violent demonstrations, invasion, war, poverty, famine and civil unrest. Evangelicalism's emphasis on humanity's fundamental depravity and guilt, its denial that history moves on a positive, progressive trajectory, coupled with its image of a God doling out rewards mysteriously, provided an account that fitted many Britons' experiences of the recent past. Daniel Wilson, vicar of Islington, who released an edition of *The Analogy of Religion* by the early eighteenth-century moral philosopher and theologian Joseph Butler in 1825, thought the fact that Butler had not lived through the French Revolution had given him an 'inadequate view of the fallen state of man'.[62] The 1790s in Europe were thought to have revealed something especially dark about the nature of humanity. Evangelicalism charted a shift into internal and subjective realms of feeling, to emphasize faith and 'heart' rather than moral actions. This was part and parcel of a revolution of feeling in which many of the eighteenth century's dominant assumptions about the passions were overturned, to usher in a very different emotional landscape: one whose contours undergird our contemporary approach to emotion.

Chapter 18

THE REVOLUTION OF FEELING

In 1817, the poet Percy Bysshe Shelley – who had married William Godwin and Mary Wollstonecraft's daughter Mary – reflected on the climate of post-1790s Britain: 'methinks, those who now live have survived an age of despair'. He thought that the French Revolution had triggered changes in the 'general state of feeling'. The decade's early years had been characterized by 'sympathy' and 'unmingled good'; then by frustration and 'revulsion'; and finally by 'reverses of hope', moral 'ruin' and 'melancholy desolation' from 1795 onwards. By 1817, barely any of the older generation of 1790s radicals were still alive; and those who were had, for the most part, retreated from the British political scene. '[G]loom and misanthropy have become the characteristics of the age in which we live,' intoned Shelley: 'the solace of a disappointment that unconsciously finds relief only in the wilful exaggeration of its own despair'.[1]

The collapse of Enlightenment hopes for the passions, and the ushering in of a new emotional landscape, was precipitated both by acute events – the French Revolution – and by trends that had been gestating since the middle of the century but accelerated in the 1790s – including the rise of evangelicalism, burgeoning industrialization, enthusiasm for laissez-faire economics, the erosion of determinism, and the rise of statistics. The decade also brought to a head the eighteenth-century philosophical attitude to the passions as drivers of political change, in the projects described in this book. The failure of those projects, and the acute events and long-term trends that coalesced in the 1790s, brought about a paradigm shift in the cultural understanding of emotion itself: what it is, how it functioned, and its relationship to politics. Even after the initial period of mourning had passed, even after citizens had emerged from what Shelley described as their 'trance of grief' for the decade's losses, the effects of this revolution of feeling still remained. And its legacy can be felt in the present day.

'Hydraulic' explanations of the passions were recruited for multiple political purposes towards the end of the eighteenth century: some sexual and 'utopian', others warning against the dangers of authoritarian government. But after the defeat of the 1798 United Irish Rebellion, the legacy of Pitt's repressive legislation was not further rebellion but the erosion of radical political activism for two decades. History gave the lie to hydraulic predictions of the inevitability of violent reaction. Pitt achieved his ends, not through education, but through the suppression of free speech and the right to assemble, the suspension of Habeas Corpus, and by rounding up remaining radicals. Repression, it became clear, did not always result in accumulation of pressure leading to rebellion. Defenders of the rights of man, like Beddoes, would have to recruit alternative arguments. This is not to say that deprivation or oppression does not cause profound damage to the individual or society, but the hydraulic assumption that the damage always manifests itself in violent reaction no longer seemed so certain. At the same time that he reached this conclusion, Beddoes' own scientific research revealed the fallacy of the hydraulic paradigm as an explanation for how emotional energy operates in the body.

In May 1798, hydraulic theory, as an argument for the liberation of desire, received another decisive blow. Reverend Robert Malthus, a cleric and scholar, published, anonymously, a deceptively slight volume entitled *An Essay on the Principle of Population*. Malthus explained in the preface that it derived from one of Godwin's essays, 'On Avarice and Profusion', published the previous year, in which Godwin had proclaimed that, when 'each man [was] trusted with a discretionary power', the world's direction 'will conduce to the improvement and happiness of each'.[2] Malthus thought that 'the great question . . . now at issue' at the close of the eighteenth century was 'whether man shall henceforth start forwards with accelerated velocity towards illimitable, and hitherto unconceived improvement' – as Godwin had predicted – or whether humanity was really 'condemned' to a much more gloomy future: 'a perpetual oscillation between happiness and misery, and after every effort remain still at an immeasurable distance from the wished-for goal'.[3]

Malthus launched a devastating blow to eighteenth-century optimism. Godwin's vision of a continually progressive course of history was impossible, he wrote, because of the simple fact that 'the power of population is indefinitely greater than the power in the earth to produce subsistence for man'. Malthus explained that 'population, when unchecked, increases in a geometrical ratio'. Data on American settlement had shown that, in a land with profuse opportunities for agriculture, the population doubled roughly every twenty-five years. But subsistence, Malthus claimed, 'increases only in an arithmetical ratio': agricultural productivity increased every twenty-five years by the addition of the original output. This meant that after a century of observing a country in which the population begins at 7 million, the population would number 112 million, but agricultural productivity would suffice to feed only 35 million. The gloomy result of such overpopulation relative to resources, Malthus predicted, would be 'great emigration', famine, disease and war, the spectre of which put the kibosh on Godwin's relentlessly optimistic vision. In the first edition of his essay, Malthus was cautious about recommending 'restraints upon matrimony', suspecting that the inhibition of male libido led to 'vicious customs'. But by 1803, he had incorporated revisions urging that 'moral restraint' was necessary to check population growth and fend off the misery, illness and death that he saw as the inevitable consequences of overpopulation.[4]

Malthus' *An Essay on the Principle of Population* accelerated the sense that was emerging at the end of the 1790s that, far from facilitating sociability, as Adam Smith had once argued, the unregulated passions and desires were its chief threat: the source of bloody revolutions, antisocial riots and apocalyptic overpopulation. This was a dramatic turnaround from the predominant concern in the eighteenth century about *under*population, and it relegated emotion to the status that the passions had occupied in the seventeenth century and before, as social disturbances. In 1889, the surgeon Robert Lawson Tait would write that 'the sexual instinct has become ... the great weapon of evolution. That it should be curbed, properly restrained and judiciously directed is now one of the great objects of civilization.'[5] Malthus' teleological warning reinforced the incentives for delayed marriage and sexual abstinence that had been growing since the late eighteenth century, including financial reasons to delay intercourse, such as the expense of bringing up children making it harder to obtain luxury goods. Evangelicals like Hannah More and William Wilberforce promoted the spiritual virtue of sexual continence through organizations such as the Society for the Suppression of Vice, founded in 1802.

The revolution in attitudes to the regulation of sexual desire was so noticeable that the radical Francis Place recorded how, by the 1820s, many of the landmarks of late-eighteenth-century erotic topography – 'cock-and-hen clubs' (drinking and sex clubs), bawdy songs, drinking, gambling, visiting prostitutes – had completely disappeared. They hadn't, but a change had clearly taken place. Enlightenment philosophies defending the passions' intrinsic benevolence were replaced by an overweening sense that, in the words of the philosopher John Stuart Mill, 'nearly every respectable attribute of humanity is the result, not of instinct, but of victory over instinct'.[6] Some Victorian writers disinterred the early Christian vision of the hierarchical soul to advocate subordinating the lower, animal elements – including the passions – to the higher intellect. In 1872, William Pratt wrote that 'to get the body under, and to keep it in perfect subjugation to a resolute and chaste will, is certainly the first duty of every one who aspires to anything here or hereafter'.[7] In train with the gendered implications of the hierarchical soul, the stricter emphasis on emotional regulation was counterpointed by increased stress on women's role in managing male moral virtue, entrenchment of the patriarchal family unit, a prevalence of the madonna-whore complex, and the shrinking of women's opportunities in the public sphere.

The stereotypical image of the Victorian period as one of emotional repression was played out in the changing conception of childhood and education between the eighteenth and nineteenth centuries. If children had sometimes been understood in the seventeenth century as deficient adults of little interest, during the Enlightenment theories of the development of the mind, like Locke's and Hartley's, allowed the adult's ideas, personality traits and emotional behaviour to be traced back to early formative experiences during childhood; the child might be valued as the bedrock of the adult persona. But the stricter emphasis on sexual regulation and the perceived consequences of its failure in the Victorian period led, on the one hand, to the idealized, sometimes cloyingly sentimental construction of childhood as an innocent, asexual arena quite distinct from adulthood; and, on the other, to the paranoid policing of children's emotional behaviour. As the satirical writer Saki put it, 'people talk vaguely about the innocence of a little child, but they take mighty good care not to let it out of their sight for twenty minutes'.[8] The commitment to childhood piety and regulated physical health was evident in the works of writers such as Charles Kingsley and Thomas Hughes (author of *Tom Brown's School Days*), in the movement subsequently labelled 'muscular Christianity', and in the educational ethos centred around 'Christian and moral and political philosophy' at Rugby School, where Thomas Arnold was headmaster from 1828 to 1841; it was founded on the principle that 'a man's body is given him to be trained and brought into subjection'.[9]

Nineteenth-century writers did not necessarily recommend the complete eradication of the passions. Male virtue was thought to be forged in the furnace of sexual self-control, and the Victorian writer Thomas Carlyle equated 'heroism' with the act of a man 'perfect[ing] himself into victory over mere Desire'.[10] Carlyle dismissed the mechanistic, atheist, pleasure-obsessed, liberal eighteenth century as 'effete', and attributed heroic virtue to rigorous containment of 'general force of soul' through 'struggle'.[11] As the historian John Tosh has pointed out, the containment of sexual desire in Carlyle's philosophy had far more to do with the imperative to 'perfect manhood – rather than a moral obligation towards women' or with population control.[12] It chimed with the evangelical emphasis on self-improvement. The literary critic Trev Broughton has described how Carlyle's friend James Anthony Froude and his heirs published volumes of *Reminiscences* and biographies of Carlyle after his death, accusing him of negating his role as husband through temperamental incompetence, but also, crucially, through sexual impotence. Whilst 'celibacy models a kind of virtuoso manliness, the highest and finest instance of that discipline of desire, that turn from pleasure to productivity that defines industrial manhood', Carlyle's alleged impotence – his lack of passion – undermined his claims to hard-won victory, and hinted at his indulgence in incontinent masturbation. Regulation of weak, impotent desire was a poor moral struggle in contrast to the heroism of the task of taming the passions of a man like Robert Burns, with his 'generous valour and manfulness'.[13]

The blow that Malthus' *Essay* dealt to the hydraulic paradigm did not demolish it – and nor did it seek to. Hydraulic explanations of the passions could be used to justify the complete liberation of male sexual desire, or to argue for the channelling of desire into more civilized forms of expression. The transition from the eighteenth to the nineteenth century did not see the annihilation of the hydraulic paradigm, but, rather, a swing in emphasis from advocating greater liberation to greater repression and stricter management of desire. By the late Enlightenment, 'vitalism' was gaining ground against mechanism, linking emotion to an internal principle of life or energy, instead of the machine-like movements of nerves or fluids. But, as Beddoes' experiments showed, even vitalist ideas could lead to the same conclusions as hydraulic theory. What remained constant from the eighteenth to the nineteenth centuries, from mechanism to vitalism, from an attitude of greater liberation to one of greater repression, was hydraulic theory's insistence on the unique force of male desire. Hydraulic theory was – and still is – recruited to justify and absolve occasions when men engage in sexual and physical violence and greedy consumption.

Testimony to the resilience of the hydraulic paradigm can be found in the fact that it continued to define both mainstream cultural attitudes promoting the vigorous management of emotion in the nineteenth century, and counter-cultural ones fostering a more liberal approach. During the 1830s, followers of the utopian socialist Robert Owen set up communities in which the reform or abolition of marriage was a key element of the intention to detach kinship ties from the nuclear family and extend them across the entire membership of the community. Some male Owenites argued for the liberation of libido from repressive conventions and legislation using hydraulic language, depicting sexual desire as 'an instinct of reproduction' that laws couldn't and shouldn't confine: 'like steam', it would always 'force its way'.[14] But, as with eighteenth-century women's responses to male sexual utopias, female Owenites were often more circumspect, fearing the social and physical consequences of multiple pregnancies outside marriage.[15]

The revolution of feeling at the end of the eighteenth century cannot be reduced to a simple switch from liberation to repression: that shift of emphasis is only one aspect of the change in cultural attitudes to emotion. Malthus' *Essay* was not just important for its implications for the management of libido. It also contributed to the collapse of optimistic Enlightenment hopes for the passions. One of the most important resonances of Malthus' *Essay* was its implications for the theory of perfectibility. After the 1790s, many found it hard to sustain belief in Priestley's nonchalant dismissal of disappointments as minor blips in an otherwise progressive teleology. The mood shifted, from optimism to pessimism, from hope to an 'age of despair'.

In 1804, the Liverpool physician James Currie wrote about treating a patient whose mind had become deranged by optimistic Enlightenment belief in 'the improvement of the human race, and the perfectibility of man'. This patient had devised a scheme to enlarge the earth's surface to assist human perfectibility, and had sent it to William Pitt. Currie prescribed Malthus' *Essay* as a remedy for this psychotic – and, by 1804, outdated – state of optimism, hoping that the patient would be disillusioned into sanity by 'the objection, that when men became so happy as he proposed to make them, they would increase too fast for the limits of the earth'. But Currie underestimated the devastating psychological effects of such a brutal, rapid demolition of old, loved beliefs. He described how, 'After finishing the perusal, [his patient] got pen, ink, and paper, and sat down, seemingly with an intention to answer it, or to write notes upon it. But he did not finish a single sentence ... his mind had taken a melancholy turn. One afternoon he retired into his room, on the pretence of drowsiness. The keeper ... entered, and found the sleep he had fallen into was the sleep of death. He had "shuffled off this mortal coil".'[16]

Most readers did not die upon understanding the import of Malthus' *Essay*. But it did help usher in a new emotional climate for which the gathering force of evangelicalism provided a 'needful' emotional vocabulary: an atmosphere of guilt, sin, punishment and atonement.[17] The new pessimistic mood was visible in attitudes towards laissez-faire economics in the nineteenth century. Malthus suggested that the liberation of desire in the economic as well as the sexual realm could not be assumed to tend towards the maximization of productivity that Adam Smith had predicted, but would likely bring about financial crises. Evangelicals rationalized that such crises would instigate periods of spiritual reflection leading to self-denial, in a vision of a self-regulating market that was much darker than Smith's optimistic idea of the 'invisible hand' channelling self-interest towards sociably desirable ends.[18]

Along with an altered, more ominous approach to free-market economics went a new perception of emotions' relationship to historical change. Emotions like hope are forms of investment in the world and in the future. Priestley and Paley had entertained an optimistic vision of hope as a light-hearted gamble that, if disappointed, would reveal new knowledge about God's immutable laws. At the end of the eighteenth century, this was eroded by a turn to statistics and probability as attempts to ward off disappointment, which was now considered almost intolerable. In the place of determinism emerged the idea of an obscure, capricious God with no evidently beneficial plan for the universe, who was not susceptible to human supplication. As hope was approached on a more conservative basis than in the previous century, so too were the emotions in general subject to a tighter reining in. This was closely connected to the most important and long-lasting legacy of the 1790s' revolution of feeling: the divorce of emotion from the material world, and from politics.

During the eighteenth century, philosophers and writers had conceptualized the passions as responses to inequality and deprivation, instigators of moral behaviour, forms of attachment to property and family, the result of sensory responses to matter, and the equivalent of commodities that might be exchanged or withheld in the emotional marketplace. The passions' significance was predominantly social, and political reform was thought to proceed hand in hand with emotional reform. This was not just to say that most people recognized that seismic disruptions to the political landscape had profound emotional effects, but that emotional attachments were considered subject to redistribution, along with property. Political reform's purpose, for many, was to renew the passions – to create a state in which needs were met, passions calmed, and sociable sentiments nurtured. Burke was not the only one in the 1790s to designate the French Revolution as a 'revolution of sentiments', illuminating the indissoluble relationship between historical and emotional change. The French politician Joseph Lakanal wrote that Rousseau had effected 'an immense revolution in our institutions and in our manners'.[19] The Bristol publisher Joseph Cottle encapsulated the purpose and effect of pantisocracy as instigating 'revolutions of feeling'. Tom Wedgwood had hoped that the Nursery of Genius would bring about 'a general revolution of sentiment'. The evangelical reformer and educationalist Hannah More wanted her *Strictures on Female Education* to effect 'a thorough reformation' in the 'hearts and lives' of young women: a 'revolution of manners'.[20] This echoed Mary Wollstonecraft's hopes that *A Vindication of the Rights of Woman* would produce 'a revolution in female manners'.

At the end of the eighteenth century, a number of historical trends coincided to divorce emotion from such political relevance. The events of the 1790s and the evangelical 'awakening' fostered the widespread sense that human emotions were not, as Shaftesbury and Hutcheson had argued at the century's beginning, an innately benevolent foundation for a kinder society, but sources of negative and painful experiences. Evangelicalism's emphasis on self-perfection helped to transform emotional management into a solipsistic task of self-improvement, rather than a utopian, communitarian project of reform. This mirrored the rising importance of the individual in left-wing, as well as right-wing, political movements, arguably assisted by the erosion of radical community after 1795. The historian Lawrence Stone finds the seeds of 'affective individualism' were sown in the late seventeenth century, in the form of growing introspection and interest in the individual personality, demands for personal autonomy and the individual right to privacy and self-expression, and in the Bill of Rights' recognition of the immorality of coercing the individual for political ends.[21] The optimism of early laissez-faire economics was obscured by Malthus' predictions of catastrophe, and what remained was the focus on the individual's economic agency and self-interest. Physicians like Beddoes had long been interested in emotional disorders as symptoms of material inequality, but by the end of the eighteenth century many were offering solutions that placed an onus on individuals to adapt their behaviour, rather than wider political reforms.

That the shift to an individualist approach to emotion shaped left-wing writings too was evidenced by a famous description of emotion by William Wordsworth in the 1800 edition of the *Lyrical Ballads*. In the preface, Wordsworth described how, 'in tranquillity', memories of a past emotion might be 'recollected' and 'contemplated till, by a species of reaction, the tranquillity gradually disappears, and an emotion, kindred to that which was before the subject of contemplation, is gradually produced, and does itself actually exist in the mind. In this mood,' Wordsworth continued, 'successful composition' of poetry 'generally begins'.[22] Using the new vocabulary of 'emotion' instead of the eighteenth-century discourse of 'passions', 'appetites', 'sentiments' and 'affections', Wordsworth displaced emotion from a direct reaction to material circumstances. He described how it is conjured up through memory, not through immediate sensation, and that its purpose is not to instigate moral behaviour but to result in an act of imaginative creation, in the form of poetry. Emotion's causes and consequences all begin and end in the individual consciousness.

The literary critic Thomas Pfau has argued that the turn to the subjective, interior, individual experience of emotion was the mirror image of the eighteenth-century approach to the passions as bound up with and constructed by history. If the mind can be made by history, as eighteenth-century writers thought, then the reverse can also be true: history can be approached as a production of the mind.[23] The Romantics did engage in fierce historical and political commentary and analysis, but with an emphasis on its subjective effects and interpretations. Wordsworth's narrative of the French Revolution in *The Prelude* is contextualized by the part it played in the 'growth of the poet's mind'. And the Romantics did propose that acts of imaginative creation could have political import, with Shelley defending poets' role as 'unacknowledged legislators of the world'.[24] But they reflected the nineteenth-century turn to emotion as an individual, subjective experience, relocating political change to the utopian imagination or to secluded retreats such as the Lake District, in the face of the disappointment of hopes for widespread material change.

The turn to individualism, pessimism, caution and conservatism in attitudes to emotion, and its divorce from politics, was clearly visible in the emerging field of psychology. In

1820, *Lectures on the Philosophy of the Human Mind* by Thomas
Brown, Doctor of Medicine and Professor of Moral Philosophy
at Edinburgh University, were posthumously published. Brown
popularized the term 'emotions' in place of the eighteenth-
century (and older) vocabulary of 'passions', 'sentiments', and
'affections'. The literary historian Thomas Dixon has described
how that older nomenclature offered a 'differentiated typology'
that allowed commentators to speak with 'subtlety about the
nature and value of the enormous range of passionate, affectionate, sentimental, felt and committed mental states and
stances of which we are capable'.[25] The term 'emotion' had
historical connotations of civil unrest and disorder. In the early
nineteenth century, some of these connotations were imported
into psychology when Thomas Brown suggested that emotion
was produced, passively, by an involuntary association of ideas.
This was a much less optimistic view than that entertained by
David Hartley about the individual's power to control, shape
and educate emotional responses. In 1833, the Scottish minister
and economist Thomas Chalmers extrapolated that emotion
was largely irrelevant to cognition, useless in the process of
acquiring knowledge; he reiterated that it was an involuntary
state 'altogether unmodified by the will'. Emotion was closely
connected to 'mental pathology,' Chalmers continued, and was
produced when 'the mind is either wholly powerless or wholly
inactive'.[26] Emotion was becoming, as the contemporary philosopher Martha Nussbaum puts it, an 'upheaval of thought', a cause
of mental unrest – very different from Hume's identification of
the passions as the slave-driver of reason.

In 1884, one of the most famous essays on emotion ever to be
published, simply entitled 'What is an Emotion?', by the philosopher, psychologist and physician William James (brother of the
novelist Henry James), was printed in the journal *Mind*. Emotion
was not a reaction to sensory perception or new knowledge,
James declared: it was merely a form of physiological feedback,

a response to changes that had occurred in the disposition of the body's limbs, muscles and viscera.[27] James's essay was hotly debated and not representative of mainstream opinion, but the fact that it had been written at all encapsulated the dramatic shift in attitudes to emotion that had occurred in the preceding century. Since 1799, emotion had been progressively stripped of its cognitive role – its role in learning and education – its sensitivity to inequalities and deprivations in the material world, and its part in making judgements about the propriety of investment and attachment. By the early nineteenth century, 'emotion' was increasingly understood by psychologists to be random, involuntary, evolutionarily and cognitively redundant. With the erosion of the passions' spiritual role, and the disappearance of the vocabulary of 'passions', 'affections' and 'appetites', emotion emerged as a primarily secular phenomenon. This transition was captured in 1850 when Wordsworth revised the 1805 version of *The Prelude*. In the earlier version, he had reflected on the 'hard task' of educating a '*soul*', but in the later revisions, this was changed to the 'hard task, vain hope' of educating the '*mind*'.[28] The secular and subjective face of the concept of 'emotion' was also revealed in *The Varieties of Religious Experience* (1902), a partly autobiographical dissection by William James of minute temperamental variegations during experiences of religious conversion, mysticism and using drugs like alcohol and nitrous oxide.[29] In an essay on 'The Subjective Effects of Nitrous Oxide' (1882), James described the 'immense emotional sense of *reconciliation* which characterizes the "maudlin" stage of alcoholic drunkenness' when breathing nitrous oxide.[30] James' account was the direct heir of autobiographical accounts of nitrous oxide's effect on the emotions by Thomas Beddoes, some ninety years previously. Both showed emotion to be spontaneous and involuntary, amoral and apolitical, superficial to the self rather than its chief constituent.

Yet James' *Varieties* and Wordsworth and Coleridge's *Lyrical*

Ballads show that one of the new emotional climate's great successes was its insight into subjective experience. By concentrating on the material circumstances that gave rise to the passions, and their operation *between* people, eighteenth-century writers had frequently neglected their effects *within* the individual. In Coleridge's 'Dejection: An Ode', John Keats' 'Fancy' and 'Ode on Melancholy', De Quincey's minute-by-minute analysis of the changes wrought by opium, or James Clarence Mangan's 'Sixty-Drop Dose of Laudanum', that neglect was remedied. Through their profound and detailed analysis of emotional and imaginative experience as a naturalistic, spontaneous, unstructured phenomenon, the Romantics especially – and later Victorian poets too – offered a counter-cultural retort to the dominant nineteenth-century narrative of rigorous emotional control and repression. Keats compared 'melancholy' to 'a weeping cloud', but the relationship went much further than simile. In 'Frost at Midnight', for example, Coleridge describes the fluttering 'thin blue flame' of the 'low-burnt fire' in the grate as a 'companionable form' – an 'Echo or mirror' – of the imagination: the human mind and the natural world are suffused by the same 'idling Spirit'. The monolithic category 'emotion' can be criticized for obscuring the nuances of meaning contained in the older terminology of 'passions', 'sentiments' and 'affections'. But a significant consolation for the quietening of the passions' moral and political role was the rousing of the voices of, among others, poets, novelists and biographers, bearing witness to the interior turmoil of emotional experience with unprecedented insight and originality.

The development of that emotional insight was luminously visible in the later life of the man who forms the quiet centre of this book: Tom Wedgwood. After establishing a £150 annuity on Coleridge for the rest of his life, Wedgwood's health worsened. Perhaps inspired by conversations with Beddoes about the idealist philosophical writings of Immanuel Kant, Coleridge started planning a trip to Germany. Before he departed, with the Wordsworths, in September 1798, he and Wedgwood engaged in months of experimentation with various pharmaceutical remedies for the latter's chronic pain. Wordsworth's brother John, a sea captain, was recruited to supply hashish and opium; and Coleridge approached the President of the Royal Society, Joseph Banks, to obtain a 4 oz parcel of bhang, edible cannabis paste.[31] Wedgwood sampled some of Beddoes' nitrous oxide, too.[32] He was turning to the new century's antidotes for pain, in which tranquillity and even pleasure might be procured through pharmaceutical intervention.

Over the following years, as Wedgwood's mental and physical health deteriorated further, he began to suspect that the Enlightenment account of the passions was missing something crucial. Godwin's portrayal of the association of ideas, for example, presented the collision of ideas, sensations, memories and emotions as a phenomenon as regular, visible and logical as billiard balls obeying Newtonian laws of motion. But Wedgwood became fascinated by the degree to which the passions undermined – not obeyed – the best efforts of reason and intention. 'Shyness,' he scribbled in his notebook, 'is always a fear of our real character being known.'[33] Perhaps, he thought, 'real character' was not the simple result of reason's relationship with the passions, but was produced by an internal civil war between superficial self-image and a mass of disobedient emotions bubbling beneath the surface. People weren't as full of 'honesty and candour' as they made out, either to others, or to themselves – especially women, Wedgwood thought, who seemed to him expressly to 'avoid candour' (a word whose meaning was itself undergoing transition at the end of the eighteenth century, from 'tolerant whitewashing or covering up' to 'brutal frankness').[34] He reflected on his friends' apparent readiness to ignore their associates' obvious failings and 'vice'. And he realized that, on an occasion when he had gained pleasure from writing to a friend, he had misattributed the cause: it was not the pleasure of altruism, he saw now, but something far less admirable – 'that self-congratulation and intoxicating influence of a flattered self-love'.[35]

People *lied*, Wedgwood began to realize – not intentionally, but because their conscious aims and self-images were so frequently at odds with their emotions, which he came to see as an untrustworthy undercurrent eroding the foundations of conscious identity. Wedgwood's reflections paralleled a more systematic development, on the Continent, of understanding the 'unconscious'. The word *Unbewusste* was coined by the German Romantic philosopher Friedrich Schelling, and was brought into English usage by Coleridge, in his description of 'unconscious' elements of the 'self' and subjective 'intelligence' in his autobiographical work of 1817, *Biographia Literaria*.[36] Wedgwood was grappling his way towards describing how the association of ideas frequently took place out of sight of the conscious mind. 'With what an inadequate ignorance we judge of the nature of our happiness!' he exclaimed in exasperation.[37]

This significant revelation, which undermined the received knowledge of the Enlightenment, and occurred almost a century before the birth of psychoanalysis, does not seem to have helped Wedgwood: he knew that his conscious mind was barely aware of the causes or extent of his emotional disorder, but he had no tools with which to excavate better health. He grew worse, physically and emotionally, and the physician Matthew Baillie offered a diagnosis to Jos: 'Your brother's complaint seems to me to be hypochondriasis.'[38] This came as no surprise to Tom himself, who knew that his ailments were produced at the intersection between mind and body. Coleridge wrote to Wedgwood, admitting that he had come to think that the widespread 'hope' of the past decade had been 'a disease'. But 'Life was so flat a thing without enthusiasm,' Coleridge reflected sadly in the newly subdued climate.[39] Beddoes suggested a 'warm-room plan' to ease Wedgwood's symptoms: sealing a room, by tightly fastening doors and windows, with a stove that maintained a temperature of seventy degrees, for seventy-two hours.[40] In early 1800, Wedgwood decided to seek a permanently warm climate, and sailed for the West Indies. At first, the trip seemed a success. Martinique was, Wedgwood wrote to Jos, 'a paradise' in which 'the little by-streams of those rapid and full currents of thought' could come to consciousness, and be soothed.[41] But within a month or so, the headaches and indigestion returned, and by late June, Wedgwood was home again. Jos, distraught at the failure of this last-ditch attempt, staunchly declared, 'I will not despair of a brother so dear to my heart.'[42]

Robert Darwin wrote to Wedgwood: 'As your disorder affects your mind, let your mind affect your disorder, try travelling,' he exhorted, 'change of climate, & collect circumstances that amuse your mind.'[43] So Wedgwood continued his restless, irritable travel. During the Peace of Amiens, he set off on a Continental tour with an Italian violinist, Giovanni Bianchi; he soon fell out with his companion, proceeded to Brussels alone, then to Paris, where he joined up with James Mackintosh and Thomas Poole, followed the latter to Italy, and returned home after a renewed bout of sickness. Beddoes prescribed a litany of drugs – valerian, chloroform, strychnine – with no success. Wedgwood attempted domesticity, taking an apartment in London with a young flautist called Frederic, and throwing himself into cooking and chores, but he soon became bored. By 1804, when Mackintosh was knighted and dispatched to India as 'recorder of Bombay', Wedgwood was too unwell to attend his farewell parties, suffering blindness in one eye, 'constant fever & headache ... & have lost 4 lbs of flesh'. Coleridge recommended another visit to a 'hot climate' where he would have uninhibited access to 'large doses of opium', and Wedgwood began planning a return to the Caribbean.[44] He became fixated on transporting the sounds of the British countryside with him, procuring larks, blackbirds, robins, nightingales and thrushes as musical companions for the voyage. But a few days before the allotted date of departure, in July 1805, Wedgwood took a balmy summer evening's ride in an open carriage with his ten-year-old nephew Joe. A sudden, unexpected shower induced a chill, and Wedgwood died at 7 p.m. on 10 July, barely two months after his thirty-fourth birthday.

Around five years before his death, while living in an apartment near the Wedgwood pottery showrooms on St James's Square in London, Wedgwood had begun dabbling in photography. Using paper and white leather coated with light-sensitive chemicals, he successfully created 'photographs' by exposing the surface to direct sunlight falling on objects such as leaves. The areas drenched in unobstructed sunlight darkened rapidly, leaving a sharp white silhouette of the intervening object. Silver nitrate was found to be a particularly sensitive chemical in the creation of these 'Silver Pictures'. In 1802, Wedgwood and Humphry Davy together wrote up his researches for the *Journal of the Royal Institution* in 'An Account of a Method of Copying Paintings Upon Glass, and of Making Profiles, by the Agency of Light upon Nitrate of Silver. Invented by T. Wedgwood, Esq.' But Wedgwood was unable to 'fix' his pictures, noting in dismay that, unless 'kept in some obscure place', the white image would begin to darken under the effect of the light, fading to a page of undifferentiated black.[45]

After Wedgwood's death, Jos asked Coleridge to write a biographical sketch of Tom's life, and Mackintosh to prepare his notebooks and writings for publication. Coleridge had dismissed Mackintosh as 'one of those men with whom the meaning to do a thing means nothing', and Mackintosh was true to his reputation: no posthumous works appeared.[46] Coleridge, too, ignored Jos' request, but four years later he expressed particular regret for 'two things which I exceedingly wished, and in both have been disappointed: to have written the Life and prepared the Psychological Remains of my revered friend and benefactor, T.W.: and to have been intrusted [*sic*] with the biography, etc., of Dr B'.[47] It fell to Beddoes' assistant, Stock, to write his biography, but he composed an apologetic whitewash of his former employer's political activities, to the dismay of Beddoes' friends.

Today, Wedgwood is most frequently memorialized either as Romanticism's patron, the nucleus around whom Godwin, Beddoes and Coleridge branched like the dendrites of nerves; or as 'the first photographer', whose experiments anticipated the pioneering work of Henry Fox Talbot in the 1840s.[48] But Wedgwood's photographs may also be read as visualizations of the part he played in the revolution of feeling at the end of the eighteenth century. Wedgwood's confessional writings depict emotion not as an easily discernible system obeying rational laws, but as a nebulous and murky terrain, warranting a refined, descriptive language, which operates below the level of consciousness, rising to the surface only to impair individuals' attempts at self-control – and at wider political reform. Wedgwood lost faith in the optimistic approach to pain as a motivation for moral action, and turned instead to promises of pharmaceutical and narcotic oblivion, seeking – not eighteenth-century sociability – but tranquillized solitude, which, he commented, is 'not in itself above half the evil which we ingeniously make it'.[49] On Wedgwood's watch, the Enlightenment's bright image of the passions faded like the silhouettes of his silver pictures, receding into the obscurity and darkness of the age of despair's fixation on guilt, sin and unconscious disturbance.

At the beginning of *Civilization and its Discontents* (1930), Sigmund Freud imagines the human mind as a city in which 'nothing that has once come into existence will have passed away and all the earlier phases of development continue to exist alongside the latest one'. In Rome, in Freud's formulation, the 'palaces of the Caesars and the Septizonium of Septimius Severus' would coexist alongside 'the castle of S. Angelo', and 'the Palazzo Caffarelli' alongside 'the Temple of Jupiter Capitolinus' on the same site. Freud uses the image of a city in which each and every historical stratum is present simultaneously as a spatial visualization of the claim that 'everything past is preserved' in the mind.[50] It also serves as a metaphor for the emotional landscape of our present day. It is not true that *nothing* crumbles into dust and disappears. For example, widespread belief in the existence of the 'superfine universal fluid' proposed by Franz Anton Mesmer had faded by the twentieth century, and, along with it, the conviction that emotional disturbances may be cured by massaging the 'poles' of the body. But so many of the landmark philosophies of emotion that were colliding with one another at the end of the 1790s can still be traced beneath the contour lines of our twenty-first-century, Anglophone emotional landscape.

Some eighteenth-century frameworks proved particularly resilient, and survived the seismic shifts of the revolution of feeling almost intact. As we have seen, hydraulic theory offers a shape-shifting explanation of emotion that can adapt to periods of greater repression or liberation, and can take on a range of physiological and physical guises ('tension', 'energy', 'stress') in the name of buttressing male desire. The collapse of liberal Enlightenment attitudes to the passions met with a shift towards repression in the Victorian era. But hydraulic theory never went away, and at the end of the nineteenth century, it came into the ascendancy again when psychoanalysts warned that repression's attempts to confine certain desires to the unconscious were ineffectual. 'The libido behaves like a stream whose main bed has become blocked. It proceeds to fill up collateral channels which may hitherto have been empty,' wrote Freud; sexual repression fills up those channels in the form of 'perversions in persons who might perhaps otherwise have remained normal'.[51]

Today psychoanalysis is one of the main therapies for emotional distress. The British Psychoanalytic Council – a professional association and voluntary regulator – numbers around 1,400 practitioners of psychoanalytic and psychodynamic psychotherapies. The predominance of psychoanalytic concepts (such as 'repression', 'ego', 'narcissism', 'libido', 'projection', 'Oedipus complex') in mainstream discourse about emotion, combined with liberal attitudes towards sexuality dating from the 1960s, means that Victorian repression of emotion is certainly not celebrated in contemporary Anglo-American mainstream culture. Repression is one legacy of the late-1790s revolution of feeling which has not endured. The *New York Times* published a report on the 'Health Dangers of Repressing Emotional Turmoil'; online psychology magazines warn men, especially, of the 'dangers of repression'; and health forums caution that 'holding things in leads to psychosomatic illnesses' and 'speaking up [is the] key to emotional release'.[52] Among the elements of the 1790s revolution of feeling that are preserved in present-day mainstream attitudes, repression and strict emotional control are overshadowed by the predominant, lasting structure of hydraulic theory, which has persisted intact as an argument for emotional freedom from the work of Galen in the second century AD, through the nineteenth and twentieth centuries, and into the twenty-first.

Despite the survival of certain theories of emotion, like hydraulics, the 1790s did represent a cataclysmic earthquake in which many other philosophical structures were damaged, displaced or jostled by the emergence of new (and the return of much older) viewpoints, coming up through the seismic cracks. The religious view of the 'affections' as kinetic movements of the soul towards God receded from mainstream thought, displaced by a secular language of 'emotion' as a psychological pathology.[53] Unlike repression, many of the new frameworks and attitudes that came to light in the wake of the 1790s have survived to dominate our present-day Anglo-American emotional panorama, forging the modern temperament as we know it today. Of the ideas that emerged in the 'age of despair', the conviction that emotion is fundamentally rooted in the individual body and in individual interests holds most sway in the contemporary landscape.

Psychologies magazine contains subsections on 'self', 'wellness' and immediate 'relationships'. *Marie Claire* advises readers 'how to be happier' by smiling more; connecting more with, and hugging, friends; exercising; and practising gratitude and self-care. Popular online blogs encourage readers to approach emotion as a 'pure and natural' phenomenon, whose cultivation, as part of a process of self-perfection, allows us to appreciate 'each emotion [as] a beautiful sculpture that is formed when we let ourselves feel'.[54] Gone is the eighteenth-century view of the emotions as symptoms of social deprivation, forms of attachment to property, motivations for revolution, whose significance lies primarily in their ability to be transmitted across the public sphere through 'sympathy' and 'fellow-feeling'. With the rise of the discourse of 'identity' and the 'self', contemporary academics think about 'Me, My Self and Emotion' and bloggers reflect on how an individual's 'emotional identity' is predominantly formed by 'innate personality, desires, and motivations'.[55] Most contemporary emotional therapies focus primarily on the idiosyncratic facets of emotion: on the childhood experiences that forged them, or their expression in the individual behaviours. The clinical psychologist Eliot Brenner and the social psychologist Peter Salovey go so far as to define the expression, purpose and effect of emotion as solely situated within the individual. 'Emotions', they write, are 'responses that guide the individual's behaviour and serve as information that helps the individual achieve goals'.[56]

The turn to the individual in today's culture generally goes hand in hand with a depoliticization of emotion. Mindfulness and CBT can be invaluable for individuals: their techniques offer respite from engagement with a frustrating, traumatizing world. But, as political philosophies, they articulate conservative or apolitical approaches to change, seeking to reconcile individuals to wanting only what they are likely to get. Lecturers, encouraged by their workplace mindfulness programme to 'change' or rid themselves of their expectations that 'I should be treated with respect' and 'my work should be appreciated', might be better off consulting a trade union to seek workplace reform. Some mindfulness therapists advocate detaching oneself from one's emotions, on the basis that although emotions and thoughts may be 'valuable', 'they are not "you" or "reality"' – thereby silencing, or distancing oneself from, negative emotions' testimony to the discomforting or unsatisfying nature of one's surroundings. Even when emotion and desire are considered in contemporary political contexts, there is frequently a glaring disjunction between emotional attitudes and economic or political philosophies. Certain socialists advocate strict economic regulation in order to reduce material inequality, to rein in the exploitative desires of those with most material power, and to curtail 'the free market ... in favour of intervention'. But, in the emotional marketplace, they defend individualism and the liberation of male sexual desire, via the decriminalization of prostitution and pimping, on the basis of making sex workers individual 'free agents'.

As this book has repeatedly indicated, feminists have an especial interest in the politics of emotion. Emotional stereotypes are recruited to exclude women from positions of power, and to compel women to take on disproportionate responsibility for caring for children, the sick and the elderly. Misogynistic and incorrect beliefs about innate disparities in men and women's levels of sexual desire are used to absolve men of sexual violence and the purchase of sex, and leave women surviving in a culture in which male pleasure is almost uniquely centred on intercourse and in which glaring gaps still characterize research on the female reproductive system. Forms of 'emotional labour' – remembering birthdays, office pleasantries, relationship management, offering sympathy, smiling when male passers-by demand, 'Give us a smile, love' – have recently been designated 'repeated, taxing and under-acknowledged acts of gendered performance'.[57] Yet the trend towards the depoliticization of emotion, and the heightened perception of emotion as an individual rather than a social phenomenon, discourages women from challenging the way in which emotions and emotional negotiations are infected with highly gendered inequalities of power. There is much to learn from the lost legacy of the 1790s' philosophy of emotion: from the decade when the passions were collective political experiences and forces, when emotional regulation was a social negotiation between individuals'claims and desires, and when revolutions were driven by feeling.

NOTES

INTRODUCTION: THE HISTORY OF EMOTION

1 Anna Beddoes to Davies Giddy, Archive of the Davies Gilbert Family of Trelissick, Feock, Cornwall Record Office (CRO), DG89, 6 May 1802 and 2 Nov 1803.

2 Marcel Proust, *Swann's Way; The First Part of Remembrance of Things Past*, trans. C. K. Scott Moncrieff (Harmondsworth: Penguin, 1957; first published 1913), p. 56.

3 Cf. Joseph LeDoux, *The Emotional Brain: The Mysterious Underpinnings of Emotional Life* (London: Phoenix, 1999; first published New York: Simon & Schuster, 1998), pp. 73–103. LeDoux outlines MacLean's influential theory, before offering a counter-view.

4 Charles Darwin, *The Expression of the Emotions in Man and Animals* (1872), pp. 1249–477, in *From So Simple a Beginning: The Four Great Books of Charles Darwin*, ed. Edward O. Wilson (New York and London: Norton, 2006), p. 1272.

5 John Bowlby, *Attachment and Loss* trilogy: Vol. I, *Attachment* (London: Pimlico, 1997; first published London: Hogarth Press and Institute of Psychoanalysis, 1969); Vol. II, *Separation: Anxiety and Anger* (London: Pimlico, 1998; first published London: Hogarth Press and Institute of Psychoanalysis, 1973), I, p. 58.

6 Khaled Hosseini, *The Kite Runner* (London: Bloomsbury, 2003), p. 105.

7 Simo Knuuttila, *Emotions in Ancient and Medieval Philosophy* (Oxford: Clarendon Press, 2004), pp. 214–15.

8 Galen, *On the Doctrines of Hippocrates and Plato*, 4.2.9–18, in *The Stoics Reader*, trans. Brad Indood and Lloyd P. Gerson (Indianapolis: Hackett, 2008).

9 'What is the purpose of anxiety?' www.sharecare.com/health/anxiety/what-purpose-anxiety (accessed 6 March 2017).

10 Cited under the definition of 'emotion, n.', *OED Online*, Dec 2016, Oxford University Press, www.oed.com/view/Entry/61249?rskey=TPA1J3&result=1&isAdvanced=false (accessed 23 Dec 2016).

11 Thomas Dixon, *From Passions to Emotions: The Creation of a Secular Psychological Category* (Cambridge: Cambridge University Press, 2003).

12 Cited in Susan James, *Passion and Action: The Emotions in Seventeenth-Century Philosophy* (Oxford: Clarendon, 1997), p. 11.

13 Thomas Wedgwood to William Godwin, cited in William Godwin, *The Letters of William Godwin*, Vol. I: *1778–1797*, ed. Pamela Clemit (Oxford: Oxford University Press, 2011), p. 198.

14 Pei-Ying Lin, 'Untranslatable Emotions in Languages other than English, vs Parrott's Emotion Classification' (2013) http://unspeakableness.net (accessed 30 Dec 2016).

15 http://metro.co.uk/2015/06/13/13-signs-that-youre-homesick–5237381/ (accessed 30 Dec 2016).

16 I am very grateful to Marina Strinkovsky for a fascinating discussion about '*tocka*'.

17 Lin, 'Untranslatable Emotions'.

18 Erich Fromm, *Beyond the Chains of Illusion: My Encounter with Marx and Freud* (New York: Continuum, 1990; first published 1962), p. 88.

19 René Descartes, *The Passions of the Soul*, trans. Stephen Voss (Indianapolis: Hackett, 1989), §57–8; Charles Le Brun, *Méthode pour apprendre à dessiner les passions* (Amsterdam: François van der Plaats, 1698).

20 'Recognising and Managing Emotions' www.skillsyouneed.com/ps/ managing-emotions.html (accessed 19 March 2017).

21 Definition of 'manner, n. (and int.)', *OED Online*, Dec 2016, Oxford University Press, www.oed.com/view/Entry/113569?redirectedFrom= manners (accessed 24 Dec 2016).

22 Edmund Burke, *Reflections on the Revolution in France*, ed. Conor Cruise O'Brien (Harmondsworth: Penguin, 1968; first published London: J. Dodsley, 1790), pp. 151–2, 175.

23 William Wordsworth and Samuel Taylor Coleridge, *Lyrical Ballads*, ed. R. L. Brett and A. R. Jones (London and New York: Routledge, 2005), pp. 286–314.

24 Percy Bysshe Shelley, *The Revolt of Islam*, in *The Major Works*, ed. Zachary Leader and Michael O'Neill (Oxford: Oxford University Press, 2009), p. 132.

25 Definition of 'disappoint, v.', *OED Online*, March 2017, Oxford University Press, www.oed.com/view/Entry/53508 (accessed March 19, 2017).

26 Burke, *Reflections*, p. 175.

1: The Unlooked-For Dawn

1 William Godwin, *The Diary of William Godwin*, ed. Victoria Myers, David O'Shaughnessy and Mark Philp (Oxford: Oxford Digital Library, 2010) http://godwindiary.bodleian.ox.ac.uk Dep. e.199, fol. 6r., 13 November 1791 (accessed 8 Nov 2016).

2 Conal Condren, *The Politics of Language in Seventeenth-Century England* (Basingstoke: Palgrave Macmillan, 1994), pp. 155–8.

3 Walter Thornbury, *Old and New London* (London, 1878), I, pp. 262–74, *British History Online* www.british-history.ac.uk/old-new-london/vol1/ pp262-274 (accessed 6 Oct 2016).

4 Alexander Gilchrist, *Life of William Blake* (London: John Lane The Bodley Head, 1907; first published 1863), p. 94.
5 William Godwin, *Collected Novels and Memoirs of William Godwin*, ed. Mark Philp, 8 vols (London: Pickering, 1992), I, p. 30.
6 Alan Ruston, 'Fawcett, Joseph (*c.*1758–1804)', *Oxford Dictionary of National Biography*, Oxford University Press, 2004; online edition, Jan 2008, www.oxforddnb.com/view/article/9225 (accessed 10 Nov 2016).
7 Cited in William Godwin to Joseph Fawcett, May 1782–?1785, in Godwin, *Letters*, p. 17.
8 William Wordsworth, *The Excursion*, ed. Sally Bushell, James A. Butler and Michael C. Jaye (Ithaca and London: Cornell University Press, 2007), ll. 692–4 (p. 97).
9 William Godwin, *Thoughts Occasioned by the Perusal of Dr. Parr's Spital Sermon, Preached at Christ Church, April 15, 1800* (London: Taylor and Wilks, 1801), p. 2.
10 *The New Annual Register, or, General Repository of History, Politics and Literature for the Year 1780* (London: G. Robinson, 1781).
11 William St Clair, *The Godwins and the Shelleys* (London: Faber, 1989), p. 56.
12 Anon., 'Wm Godwin B. 1756. D. 1836', New York Public Library, Pforzheimer Collection, C 198b.
13 *London Chronicle*, 18 July 1789, issue 5116.
14 Mary Wollstonecraft, *An Historical and Moral View of the Origin and Progress of the French Revolution; and the Effect it has Produced in Europe*, 2nd edition (London: Johnson, 1795), pp. 12, 50.
15 Lynn Hunt, 'Pornography and the French Revolution', pp. 301–40, in Lynn Hunt, ed., *The Invention of Pornography* (New York: Zone Books, 1993), pp. 305–29.
16 Wollstonecraft, *Historical and Moral View*, p. 50.
17 Wollstonecraft, *Historical and Moral View*, pp. 63, 38.
18 Wollstonecraft, *Historical and Moral View*, p. 110.
19 Wollstonecraft, *Historical and Moral View*, pp. 113–14.
20 Simon Schama, *Citizens: A Chronicle of the French Revolution* (London: Viking, 1989), pp. 125–81, 153.
21 Wollstonecraft, *Historical and Moral View*, pp. 192–3.
22 Günther Lottes, 'Radicalism, Revolution and Political Culture: An Anglo-French Comparison', pp. 78–98, in Mark Philp, ed., *The French Revolution and British Popular Politics* (Cambridge: Cambridge University Press, 1991), p. 81.
23 *London Chronicle*, 14 July 1789, issue 5114, 55.
24 Alison Gilbert Olson, *The Radical Duke: Career and Correspondence of Charles Lennox, third Duke of Richmond* (Oxford: Oxford University Press, 1961), p. 48
25 Cited in Albert Goodwin, *The Friends of Liberty: the English Democratic Movement in the Age of the French Revolution* (London: Hutchinson, 1979), p. 63.
26 J. P. W. Ehrman, Anthony Smith, 'Pitt, William (1759–1806)', *Oxford Dictionary of National Biography*, Oxford University Press, 2004; online

edition, May 2009, www.oxforddnb.com/view/article/22338 (accessed 19 March 2017).

27 Richard Price, *A Discourse on the Love of our Country* (1790), pp. 39–56, in Iain Hampsher-Monk, ed., *The Impact of the French Revolution: Texts from Britain in the 1790s* (Cambridge: Cambridge University Press, 2005), pp. 54, 49.

28 Cited in Goodwin, *Friends of Liberty*, pp. 136–70, 208–87, 167.

29 Goodwin, *Friends of Liberty*, p. 193.

30 Thomas Hardy, 'Sketch of the History of the London Corresponding Society', British Library Add. MSS 27814, 2 July 1795–30 November 1797, fo. 39.

31 William Hazlitt, *The Life of Napoleon Bonaparte* (1828), in *The Complete Works of William Hazlitt*, ed. P. P. Howe, 21 vols (London: J. M. Dent and Sons, 1930), XIII, p. 38.

32 David Duff, 'Burke and Paine: Contrasts', pp. 47–70, in *The Cambridge Companion to British Literature of the French Revolution in the 1790s*, ed. Pamela Clemit (Cambridge: Cambridge University Press, 2011), p. 56.

33 Thomas Paine, *Rights of Man: Being an Answer to Mr Burke's Attack on the French Revolution* (London: J. S. Jordan, 1791), pp. 83–197, in Thomas Paine, *Rights of Man, Common Sense and Other Political Writings*, ed. Mark Philp (Oxford: Oxford University Press, 1995; 2008), p. 135.

34 Paine, *Rights of Man* (1791), pp. 140, 142–3.

35 Étienne Dumont, cited in John Keane, *Tom Paine: A Political Life* (London: Bloomsbury, 1995), p. 311, cited in Mark Philp, 'Paine, Thomas (1737–1809)', *Oxford Dictionary of National Biography*, Oxford University Press, 2004; online edition, May 2008, www.oxforddnb.com/view/article/21133 (accessed 10 Nov 2016).

36 Godwin to Thomas Paine, 7 Nov 1791, in Godwin, *Letters*, p. 65.

37 William Godwin, *Memoirs of the Author of a Vindication of the Rights of Woman*, 2nd edition (London: J. Johnson, 1798), p. 83.

38 Thomas Wedgwood, *The Value of a Maimed Life: Extracts from the Manuscript Notes of Thomas Wedgwood*, ed. Margaret Olivia Tremayne (London: C. W. Daniel, 1912), p. 46.

39 Godwin, *Memoirs*, pp. 98, 97.

40 Godwin, *Memoirs*, pp. 75–7.

41 Jean-François Senault, cited in James, *Passion and Action*, p. 3.

42 Thomas Paine, *The Age of Reason: Being an Investigation of True and Fabulous Theology* (London: Daniel Eaton, 1794).

43 William M. Reddy, *The Navigation of Feeling: A Framework for the History of Emotions* (Cambridge: Cambridge University Press, 2001), pp. 124–6.

44 Price, *Discourse*, pp. 40–42.

45 Paul Langford, 'Burke, Edmund (1729/30–1797)', *Oxford Dictionary of National Biography*, Oxford University Press, 2004; online edition, Sept 2012, www.oxforddnb.com/view/article/4019 (accessed 19 March 2017).

46 Burke, *Reflections*, pp. 140, 105, 150, 135.

47 Burke, *Reflections*, pp. 169–70, 244.

48 Burke, *Reflections*, pp. 173, 194, 165.

49   Cited in Gregory Claeys, 'The *Reflections* Refracted: The Critical Reception of Burke's *Reflections on the Revolution in France* During the Early 1790s', pp. 40–50, in John Whale, ed., Edmund Burke's *Reflections on the Revolution in France* (Manchester: Manchester University Press, 2000), p. 41.

50   Hampsher-Monk, *Impact*, p. 58.

51   Edmund Burke, *The Correspondence of Edmund Burke*, 10 vols (Cambridge: Cambridge University Press, 1958–78), VI, pp. 85–7.

52   Mary Wollstonecraft, *A Vindication of the Rights of Men, in a Letter to the Right Honourable Edmund Burke* (London: Joseph Johnson, 1790), pp. 1–68, in Mary Wollstonecraft, *A Vindication of the Rights of Woman & A Vindication of the Rights of Men*, ed. Janet Todd (Oxford: Oxford World's Classics, 1993), pp. 29, 45, 6, 27, 44.

53   Wollstonecraft, *Vindication of the Rights of Men*, p. 22.

54   Ole Riis and Linda Woodhead, *A Sociology of Religious Emotion* (Oxford: Oxford University Press, 2010), p. 50.

55   Chris Doyle, 'Logic of "Remain" Must Triumph Over the Emotion of "Leave" in British Referendum', *Al Arabiya English* http://english. alarabiya.net/en/views/news/middle-east/2016/06/23/Logic-of-remain-must-triumph-over-the-emotion-of-leave-in-British-referendum.html (accessed 19 March 2017); 'Brexit: Emotion the Driving Factor as Britain Decides to "Remain or Leave"', *Hindustan Times* www.msn.com/en-in/news/other/brexit-emotion-the-driving-factor-as-britain-decides-to-'remain-or-leave'/ar-AahuveK (accessed 19 March 2017).

56   Jasmin Lavoie, 'EU Referendum: The Words Used Most by Brexit and Remain Camps – and What They Say About the Campaigns', *Independent*, 31 May 2016 www.independent.co.uk/news/uk/politics/eu-referendum-brexit-remain-camps-britain-stronger-in-europe-vote-leave-a7057826.html (accessed 19 March 2017).

57   Paine, *Rights of Man* (1791), pp. 161, 89.

2: THE DISTRIBUTION OF HUMAN HAPPINESS

1   Mary Wollstonecraft to Jane Arden, early 1780, in Mary Wollstonecraft, *The Collected Letters of Mary Wollstonecraft*, ed. Janet Todd (New York: Columbia University Press, 1993), p. 22.

2   Wollstonecraft to Jane Arden, early 1780, in Wollstonecraft, *Collected Letters*, p. 22.

3   Godwin, *Memoirs*, p. 34.

4   William Paley, *Natural Theology or Evidences of the Existence and Attributes of the Deity* (Philadelphia: John Morgan, 1802), chapters 1–3.

5   Robert E. Schofield, *The Enlightened Joseph Priestley: A Study of his Life and Work from 1773 to 1804* (University Park, Penn.: Pennsylvania University Press, 2004), pp. 80–81.

6   Joseph Priestley, 'On Faith and Patience', in *Four Discourses* (1806), in *Memoirs of Dr. Joseph Priestley, to the Year 1795* (London: J. Johnson, 1807), II, pp. 27–9.

7   William Godwin, *Enquiry Concerning Political Justice*, 3rd edition, ed. Isaac
    Kramnick (Penguin: Harmondsworth, 1976; first published 1798), pp.
    341–3.
8   Wollstonecraft to Jane Arden, early 1780, in Wollstonecraft, *Collected
    Letters*, p. 23.
9   Wollstonecraft to Jane Arden, early 1780, in Wollstonecraft, *Collected
    Letters*, pp. 24–5.
10 Godwin, *Memoirs*, pp. 26–7.
11 Janet Todd, *Mary Wollstonecraft: A Revolutionary Life* (London: Phoenix,
    2000), p. 40.
12 Wollstonecraft to Eliza Bishop, late Nov 1785, in Wollstonecraft, *Collected
    Letters*, p. 63.
13 Mary Wollstonecraft, *Letters Written During a Short Residence in Sweden,
    Norway, and Denmark*, ed. Jon Mee (Oxford: Oxford University Press,
    2009), p. 39.
14 Wollstonecraft to Jane Arden, ?April 1781, in Wollstonecraft, *Collected
    Letters*, p. 29.
15 Wollstonecraft to George Blood, 4 Feb 1786, in Wollstonecraft, *Collected
    Letters*, p. 65.
16 Todd, *Wollstonecraft*, pp. 75–6.
17 Mary Wollstonecraft, *Thoughts on the Education of Daughters* (Oxford and
    New York: Woodstock Books, 1994; facsimile of London: J. Johnson,
    1787).
18 Wollstonecraft to Everina Wollstonecraft, 17 Nov 1786, in Wollstonecraft,
    Collected Letters, p. 90.
19 Wollstonecraft to Everina Wollstonecraft, 17 Nov 1786, in Wollstonecraft,
    Collected Letters, p. 91.
20 Cited in Todd, *Wollstonecraft*, p. 104.
21 Wollstonecraft to Everina Wollstonecraft, 9 Oct 1786, in Wollstonecraft,
    Collected Letters, p. 80.
22 Wollstonecraft to George Blood, 7 Nov 1786, and Wollstonecraft to
    George Blood, 4 Dec 1786, in Wollstonecraft, *Collected Letters*, pp. 89–90,
    93.
23 Mary Wollstonecraft, 'Letters to Mr. Johnson, Bookseller, in St Paul's
    Church-Yard', pp. 59–95, in *Posthumous Works of Mary Wollstonecraft
    Godwin*, ed. William Godwin, 4 vols (London: J. Johnson, 1798), IV, pp.
    75, 65.
24 Wollstonecraft, *Historical and Moral View*, pp. 61–2.
25 Mary Wollstonecraft, *Of the Importance of Religious Opinions Translated
    from the French of Mr. Necker* (Dublin: M. Mills, 1789), p. 20.
26 C. S. Salzmann, *Elements of Morality; for the Use of Young Persons. To Which
    is Prefixed, an Address to Parents*, trans. Mary Wollstonecraft (Edinburgh:
    Oliver and Boyd, 1821), p. 1.
27 Mary Wollstonecraft, review of *The Happy Recovery*, in *Analytical Review*,
    in Mary Wollstonecraft, *The Works of Mary Wollstonecraft*, ed. Janet Todd
    and Marilyn Butler (London: Pickering & Chatto, 1989), VII, p. 19; cited
    in Todd, *Wollstonecraft*, p. 139.

28 Wollstonecraft to George Blood, 16 May 1788, in Wollstonecraft, *Collected Letters*, p. 155.

29 Joseph Priestley, 'On Faith and Patience', pp. 26–45, in Priestley, *Memoirs*, II, p. 29.

30 Joseph Priestley, 'The Institutions of Moses and those of the Hindoos, &c. Compared', in *The Theological and Miscellaneous Works of Joseph Priestley*, ed. John Towill Rutt, 25 vols (London: 1817–31), XVII, pp. 317–18.

31 Joseph Priestley, *The Evidences of Revealed Religion*, pp. 3–409, in Priestley, *Theological and Miscellaneous Works*, XVI, p. 21.

32 William Godwin, *Notes on Philosophical Topics*, Abinger Collection, Bodleian Library, Abinger c. 30, ff. 8–39 (f. 13).

33 Erich Fromm, *The Sane Society* (London: Routledge, 2002; first published 1956), pp. 30–50; Simone Weil, *The Need for Roots: Prelude to a Declaration of Duties Towards Mankind* (London: Routledge, 2002; first published Paris: 1949; first published in English, 1952), pp. 9–19.

34 Sarah Edelman, *Change Your Thinking with CBT: Overcome Stress, Combat Anxiety and Improve Your Life* (London: Vermilion, 2006), p. 22.

35 Fromm, *Sane Society*, p. 164.

36 Andrew Cayton, *Love in the Time of Revolution: Transatlantic Literary Radicalism and Historical Change, 1793–1818* (Chapel Hill: University of North Carolina Press, 2013), p. 33.

37 Godwin, *Memoirs*, p. 93.

38 John Knowles, *The Life and Writings of Henry Fuseli*, 3 vols (London: Colburn & Bentley, 1831), I, pp. 161–2.

39 Eudo C. Mason, *The Mind of Henry Fuseli: Selections from his Writings* (London: Routledge and Kegan Paul, 1951), p. 155.

40 Cited in Todd, *Wollstonecraft*, p. 153.

41 Henry Fuseli, 'Lecture IV: Invention – Part II', II, pp. 189–235, in Knowles, *Life and Writings*, p. 196.

42 Knowles, *Life and Writings*, I, p. 164.

43 Wollstonecraft to Henry Fuseli [speculative reconstruction of letter], late 1792, in Wollstonecraft, *Collected Letters*, p. 205.

44 Wollstonecraft to Jane Arden (late 1782), in Wollstonecraft, *Collected Letters*, p. 38.

45 Cited in Lawrence Stone, *The Family, Sex and Marriage in England 1500–1800* (London: Penguin, 1979), p. 165.

46 Randolph Trumbach, *The Rise of the Egalitarian Family: Aristocratic Kinship and Domestic Relations in Eighteenth-Century England* (New York: Academic Press, 1978).

47 Anon., *The Laws Respecting Women, as They Regard Their Natural Rights, or Their Connections and Conduct* (London: 1777), p. 65.

48 Cited in Joanne Bailey, 'Favoured or Oppressed? Married Women, Property and "Coverture" in England, 1660–1800', *Continuity or Change*, 17 (3), (2002), 351–72, 351, 360.

49 Wollstonecraft to Everina Wollstonecraft, 11, 18, or 25 Jan 1784, in Wollstonecraft, *Collected Letters*, pp. 44–5.

50 Wollstonecraft to Everina Wollstonecraft, 11, 18, or 25 Jan 1784, in Wollstonecraft, *Collected Letters*, pp. 44–5.

51 Wollstonecraft to Jane Arden, mid-late 1773 to 16 Nov 1774, in Wollstonecraft, *Collected Letters*, p. 13.

52 Wollstonecraft to Joseph Johnson, summer 1790; and Wollstonecraft to anon., summer 1790; in Wollstonecraft, *Collected Letters*, pp. 172–5.

53 Knowles, *Life and Writings*, I, p. 163.

54 Cited in Lyndall Gordon, *Vindication: A Life of Mary Wollstonecraft* (London: Virago, 2005), p. 178.

55 Samuel Taylor Coleridge, 'A Moral and Political Lecture', in *Lectures 1795: On Politics and Religion*, ed. Lewis Patton and Peter Mann, *The Collected Works of Samuel Taylor Coleridge* (London: Routledge and Kegan Paul, 1971), I, p. 12.

56 Knowles, *Life and Writings*, I, p. 166.

57 Wollstonecraft to Everina Wollstonecraft, 21 Aug 1790, in Wollstonecraft, *Collected Letters*, p. 176.

58 Wollstonecraft to Everina Wollstonecraft, 10 Sept 1790, in Wollstonecraft, *Collected Letters*, p. 181.

59 Wollstonecraft to Everina Wollstonecraft, 4 Sept 1790, in Wollstonecraft, *Collected Letters*, p. 178.

3: A Revolution in Female Manners

1 Wollstonecraft to William Roscoe, 3 Jan 1792, in Wollstonecraft, *Collected Letters*, p. 193.

2 Helen P. Bruder, *William Blake and the Daughters of Albion* (Basingstoke: Macmillan, 1997), p. 140. I am grateful to Pete Newbon for pointing me in the direction of this excellent book.

3 *Feuille du Salut Public* (1793), cited in Bruder, *William Blake*, pp. 141–2.

4 Olympe de Gouges, *The Rights of Woman*, trans. Val Stevenson (London: Pythia, 1989), p. 13.

5 Thomas Cooper, 'Propositions Respecting the Foundation of Civil Government' (1790), pp. 93–109, in *A Reply to Mr. Burke's Invective against Mr. Cooper and Mr. Watt*, 2nd edition (London: Johnson, 1792), p. 98 (fn.), cited in Bruder, *William Blake*, pp. 93–4.

6 Mary Wollstonecraft, *A Vindication of the Rights of Woman*, 2nd edition (London: Johnson, 1792), pp. 63–282, in Mary Wollstonecraft, *A Vindication of the Rights of Woman & A Vindication of the Rights of Men*, ed. Janet Todd (Oxford: Oxford World's Classics, 1993), p. 133.

7 Augustine of Hippo, *The City of God*, trans. Marcus Dods (Mass.: Hendrickson, 1999), p. 251.

8 Plato, *Republic*, cited in John Cottingham, *Philosophy and the Good Life: Reason and the Passions in Greek, Cartesian and Psychoanalytic Ethics* (Cambridge: Cambridge University Press, 1998), p. 37.

9 Cited in Cottingham, *Philosophy*, p. 41.

10 Augustine, *City of God*, p. 255.

11 Cayton, *Love in the Time of Revolution*, p. 33.

12 Wollstonecraft, *Vindication of Woman*, p. 130.

13 Wollstonecraft, *Vindication of Woman*, p. 100.

14 Wollstonecraft, *Vindication of Woman*, p. 113.

15 Wollstonecraft, *Vindication of Woman*, pp. 104, 133.

16 Descartes, *Passions*, §§ 12, 34.

17 Julien Offray de La Mettrie, *Man a Machine*, trans. Jean Baptiste de Boyer (Dublin: Brien, 1794; first published in French as *L'Homme Machine*, 1747).

18 George Cheyne, *The English Malady: Or, a Treatise of Nervous Diseases of All Kinds, as Spleen, Vapours, Lowness of Spirits, Hypochondriacal, and Hysterical Distempers &c.* (London: G. Strahan, 1733), pp. 4–5.

19 David Hartley, *Observations on Man: His Frame, His Duty, And His Expectations*, 4th edition (London: Joseph Johnson, 1801; first edition 1748), pp. 58, 11–12, 64.

20 Robert Whyte, *Observations on the Nature, Causes, and Cure of those Disorders Which Have Been Commonly Called Nervous, Hypochondriac, or Hysteric: To Which are Prefixed Some Remarks on the Sympathy of the Nerves* (London and Edinburgh: 1765), p. 1.

21 William Battie, *A Treatise on Madness* (London: Whiston and White, 1758), p. 55.

22 Laurence Sterne, *A Sentimental Journey through France and Italy* (London: Penguin, 2001; first published 1768), p. 111.

23 Whyte, *Observations*, pp. 10–12.

24 Cheyne, *English Malady*, p. 96.

25 Wollstonecraft, *Vindication of Woman*, pp. 133, 146, 115.

26 Wollstonecraft, *Vindication of Woman*, pp. 88, 135.

27 Edmund Burke, *A Philosophical Enquiry into the Origin of Our Ideas of the Sublime and Beautiful*, ed. Adam Phillips (Oxford: Oxford University Press, 1990; first published London: R & J Dodsley, 1757), p. 100.

28 Wollstonecraft, *Vindication of Men*, p. 46.

29 John Gray, *Men are from Mars, Women are from Venus* (London: Thorsons, 1993), pp. 12, 16–18.

30 Carol Tavris, *The Mismeasure of Woman: Why Women Are Not the Better Sex, the Inferior Sex, or the Opposite Sex* (New York: Touchstone, 1993), p. 44.

31 Cited in Cordelia Fine, *Delusions of Gender: The Real Science Behind Sex Differences* (London: Icon, 2010), pp. 147–50.

32 Simon Baron-Cohen, *The Essential Difference: Male and Female Brains and the Truth about Autism* (New York: Basic Books, 2004).

33 Louanne Brizendine, *The Female Brain* (New York: Broadway Books, 2007), p. 121.

34 Fine, *Delusions*, Part Two.

35 Robyn Bluhm, 'New Research, Old Problems: Methodological and Ethical Issues in fMRI Research Examining Sex/Gender Differences in Emotion Processing', *Neuroethics* 6 (2), (Aug 2013), 319–330 (327) (my emphases). I am very grateful to Caroline Criado-Perez for sending me this article.

36 Deborah Cameron, *The Myth of Mars and Venus* (Oxford: Oxford University Press, 2007, 2008), pp. 5–7, 11. I am very grateful to Deborah Cameron for links to the research in this paragraph.

37 Janet S. Hyde, 'The Gender Similarities Hypothesis', *American Psychologist* (Sept 2005), 581–92; cited in Cameron, *Myth*, pp. 41–4.

38 Clive Seale and Jonathan Charteris-Black, 'The Interaction of Class and Gender in Illness Narratives', *Sociology* 42 (3), (June 2008), 453–69.

39 Oscar Rickett, 'If Only More Men Could Express Emotion Like Professor Green', *Guardian*, 29 Oct 2015 www.theguardian.com/commentisfree/2015/oct/29/men-express-themselves-professor-green-suicide-express-feelings (accessed 20 March 2017).

40 World Health Organization, *Preventing Suicide: A Global Imperative* (2014) www.who.int/mental_health/suicide-prevention/world_report_2014/en/ (accessed 25 Nov 2016); Nisha Lilia Diu, 'Suicide is Now the Biggest Killer of Teenage Girls Worldwide', *Telegraph*, 25 May 2015 www.telegraph.co.uk/women/womens-health/11549954/Teen-girls-Suicide-kills-more-young-women-than-anything.-Heres-why.html (accessed 25 Nov 2016).

41 Daniel Freeman and Jason Freeman, 'Why Are Men More Likely Than Women to Take Their Own Lives?', *Guardian*, 21 Jan 2015 www.theguardian.com/science/2015/jan/21/suicide-gender-men-women-mental-health-nick-clegg (accessed 25 Nov 2016); referencing Office for National Statistics, *Suicides in the United Kingdom: 2012 Registrations* (2014), p. 1 http://webarchive.nationalarchives.gov.uk/20160105160709/www.ons.gov.uk/ons/dcp171778_351100.pdf (accessed 25 Nov 2016).

42 Paul Bebbington, et al., *Adult Psychiatric Morbidity in England, 2007: Results of a Household Survey*, 4.3.1 http://content.digital.nhs.uk/catalogue/PUB02931/adul-psyc-morb-res-hou-sur-eng–2007-rep.pdf (accessed 25 Nov 2016).

43 Daniel Freeman and Jason Freeman, 'Let's Talk About the Gender Differences That Really Matter – in Mental Health', *Guardian*, 13 Dec 2013 www.theguardian.com/science/blog/2013/dec/13/gender-differences-mental-health (accessed 25 Nov 2016); Denis Campbell and Haroon Siddique, 'Mental Illness Soars Among Young Women in England – Survey', *Guardian* 29 Sept 2016 www.theguardian.com/lifeandstyle/2016/sep/29/self-harm-ptsd-and-mental-illness-soaring-among-young-women-in-england-survey (accessed 25 Nov 2016).

44 Sigmund Freud, 'Three Essays on the Theory of Sexuality' (1905), pp. 123–245, in *The Standard Edition of the Complete Psychological Works of Sigmund Freud*, Vol. VII (1901–05), trans. James Strachey in collaboration with Anna Freud, Alix Strachey and Alan Tyson (first published in Britain, London: Hogarth Press, 1953; this edition London: Vintage, 2001), pp. 163–4, 170.

45 Jordi Quoidbach, Moïra Mikolajczak, Ilios Kotsou, June Gruber, Alexsandr Kogan, and Michael I. Norton, 'Emodiversity and the Emotional Ecosystem', *Journal of Experimental Psychology: General*, 143 (6), (2014), 2057–66 (2057). I am very grateful to Tiffany Watt-Smith

for this link; and to Joe Wilson for conversations about the pitfalls of measuring happiness.

46 Andrew Halpern-Manners, Landon Schnabel, and Elaine M. Hernandez, 'The Relationship Between Education and Mental Health: New Evidence from a Discordant Twin Study', *Social Forces*, 95 (2), (2016), doi: 10.1093/sf/sow035, 1. This article notes that the correlation between education and mental health is complicated by the fact that participation in education is itself subject to social selection, and those suffering early onset mental-health problems and health conditions may be excluded from education and liable to suffer poor mental health. The authors cite the following papers in support of the correlation between education and mental health: Yu and Williams (1999); Kessler et. al (1995); Lantz et al. (2005); Mirowsky and Ross (2003); Ritsher et al. (2001); Schieman and Plickert (2008); Turner, Wheaton and Lloyd (1995).

47 Deborah Cameron, *Good to Talk?* (London: Sage Publications, 2000), p. 149.

48 Carol Tavris, *Anger: The Misunderstood Emotion* (New York and London: Touchstone, 1989), pp. 152–3. I am very grateful to Ophelia Benson for suggesting I look at this book.

49 Rory C. O'Connor and Matthew K. Nock, 'The Psychology of Suicidal Behaviour', *Lancet Psychiatry*, 1 (1), (June 2014), 73–85 (77). I am very grateful to Sarah Ditum for pointing me in the direction of this article.

50 For an account of Rachel Prescott, see Harriet Guest, *Unbounded Attachment: Sentiment and Politics in the Age of the French Revolution* (Oxford: Oxford University Press, 2013), pp. 109–12.

51 Cited in Todd, *Wollstonecraft*, p. 184.

52 Godwin, *Memoirs*, p. 76.

53 Cited in Todd, *Wollstonecraft*, p. 185.

54 Maria Edgeworth, *Belinda*, ed. Kathryn J. Kirkpatrick (Oxford: Oxford University Press, 1994; first published London: Johnson, 1801), p. 49.

55 Knowles, *Life and Writings*, p. 167.

56 Wollstonecraft to Everina Wollstonecraft, 20 June 1792, in Wollstonecraft, *Collected Letters*, p. 200.

4: The Inhumanity of Kings

1 Richard Lovell Edgeworth to Mrs Ruxton, 21 July 1793, in Maria Edgeworth, *The Life and Letters of Maria Edgeworth*, ed. Augustus J. C. Hare, 2 vols (London: Edward Arnold, 1894), I, pp. 30–31. Cited in Mike Jay, *The Atmosphere of Heaven: The Unnatural Experiments of Dr Beddoes and his Sons of Genius* (New Haven and London: Yale University Press, 2009), p. 91.

2 Davies Giddy, Almanac 1791, CRO, DG15, note written 1826. Cited in Jay, *Atmosphere*, p. 8.

3 Cited in Trevor H. Levere, 'Dr. Thomas Beddoes (1750–1808): Science and Medicine in Politics and Society', *The British Journal for the History of Science*, 17:2, (July 1984), 187–204 (193).

4   R[ichard] Beddoes to Thomas Beddoes, CRO, DG41/31, 21 Aug 1791.

5   Richard Polwhele, *Biographical Sketches in Cornwall*, 3 vols (Truro: J. B. Nichols & Son, 1831), III, p. 104.

6   Thomas Beddoes, 'Verses on a Cornish Lady Who was Prevailed Upon to Dance with a National Cockade, in 1790', cited in John Edmonds Stock, *Memoirs of the Life of Thomas Beddoes, M.D. with an Analytical Account of his Writings* (London, Bristol, Edinburgh, Dublin: John Murray, J. M. Gutch, William Blackwood, M. N. Mahon, 1811), Appendix No. 10, p. lvi. Although Stock dates the poem to 1790, Richard Polwhele, in *Biographical Sketches in Cornwall*, III, p. 104, dates the episode to 1791. Beddoes' biographer Mike Jay agrees.

7   Thomas Beddoes to Davies Giddy, CRO, DG41/52, n.d. [1790/1791].

8   Beddoes to Davies Giddy, CRO, DG41/51, n.d. [1790/1791].

9   Roy Porter, *Doctor of Society: Thomas Beddoes and the Sick Trade in Late-Enlightenment England* (London and New York: Routledge, 1992), pp. 37–57.

10   Cited in Jay, *Atmosphere*, p. 27.

11   Beddoes to Davies Giddy, CRO, DG41/40/1, 9 Jan [1792/1793].

12   Beddoes to Davies Giddy, CRO, DG41/41, 4 Nov 1791.

13   Beddoes to Davies Giddy, CRO, DG41/41, 4 Nov 1791.

14   Beddoes to Davies Giddy, CRO, DG41/34, 6 June [1792?].

15   Jay, *Atmosphere*, p. 125.

16   Thomas Paine, *Rights of Man; Part the Second* (London: Symonds, 1792), pp. 20, 18, 59, 13.

17   Gouverneur Morris, *Diary of the French Revolution by Gouverneur Morris 1752–1816*, ed. Beatrice Cary Davenport, 2 vols (London: George Harrap & Co., 1939), II, p. 368, 16 Feb 1792.

18   Beddoes to Davies Giddy, cited in Dorothy A. Stansfield, *Thomas Beddoes M.D. 1760–1808: Chemist, Physician, Democrat* (Dordrecht, Boston and Lancaster: D. Reidel Publishing Company, 1984), p. 131.

19   Adam Smith, *Theory of Moral Sentiments*, Glasgow edition of the *Works and Correspondence of Adam Smith*, ed. D. D. Raphael and A. L. Macfie (Indianapolis: Liberty Fund, 1982; exact photographic reprint of Oxford: Oxford University Press, 1976; first published Edinburgh: Andrew Millar, 1759), chapter 3.

20   Thomas Beddoes, *Alexander's Expedition down the Hydaspes & the Indus to the Indian Ocean* (London: John Murray, 1792), p. 28.

21   Beddoes to Davies Giddy, CRO, DG41/52 [Sept? 1791].

22   *An Authentic Account of the Riots in Birmingham, Also ... the Trials of the Rioters.* (Birmingham: n.p., 1791), p. 2.

23   Goodwin, *Friends of Liberty*, pp. 65–98.

24   John E. Archer, *Social Unrest and Popular Protest in England 1780–1840* (Cambridge: Cambridge University Press, 2000), p. 60.

25   Joseph Priestley, *An Appeal to the Public on the Subject of the Riots in Birmingham* (Birmingham: Thompson, 1791), p. 30; cited in Ian Haywood, *Bloody Romanticism: Spectacular Violence and the Politics of Representation* (Basingstoke: Palgrave Macmillan, 2006), p. 195.

26 William Hutton, *The History of Birmingham*, 6th edition (London: George Berger, 1836), p. 432.

27 William Hutton, *The Life of William Hutton* (London: Baldwin, 1816), p. 200.

28 *Cobbett's Parliamentary History of England from the Earliest Period to the Year 1803* (London: Hansard, 1817), XXIX, p. 1441.

29 Cited in Schofield, *Enlightened Joseph Priestley*, p. 288.

30 C. L. R. James, *The Black Jacobins* (London: Penguin, 2001; first published 1938), p. 67.

31 Anne Stott, *Hannah More: The First Victorian* (Oxford: Oxford University Press, 2003; reprinted 2007), pp. 87–8.

32 Stott, *Hannah More*, pp. 92–3.

33 Cited in Stansfield, *Thomas Beddoes*, p. 75; Jay, *Atmosphere*, p. 50.

34 Beddoes to Davies Giddy, CRO, DG41/52, [Sept? 1791].

35 Thomas Beddoes, *Extract of a Letter on Early Instruction, Particularly That of the Poor* (n.p., 25 Jan 1792), p. 7.

36 Paine, *Rights of Man; Part the Second*, p. 55.

37 Barbara Rosenwein, 'Worrying About Emotions in History', *American Historical Review*, 107:3, (June 2002), 821–45 (834).

38 Freud, 'Three Essays on the Theory of Sexuality', in *Standard Edition*, VII, p. 170.

39 William Frend, *Peace and Union Recommended to the Associated Bodies of Republicans and Anti-Republicans*, 2nd edition (Cambridge: B. Flower, 1793), p. 60.

40 Paine, *Rights of Man; Part the Second*, p. 476.

41 Beddoes to Davies Giddy, CRO, DG41/13, 2 Feb 1792.

42 *World*, 5 Jan 1791, issue 1252.

43 *St James's Chronicle, or the Evening Post*, 7–9 July 1791, issue 4725.

44 *Evening Mail*, 5 Aug 1791, issue 382.

45 Ruth Scurr, *Fatal Purity: Robespierre and the French Revolution* (London: Vintage, 2007), p. 126.

46 Cited in David Bell, *The First Total War: Napoleon's Europe and the Birth of Warfare as We Know It* (Boston: Houghton Mifflin Harcourt, 2007), p. 118.

47 Beddoes to Davies Giddy, CRO, DG41/16, 4 July 1792.

48 Schama, *Citizens*, p. 602; Eric Hobsbawm, *The Age of Revolution: Europe 1787–1848* (London: Abacus, 2003; first published London: Weidenfeld & Nicolson, 1962), p. 84.

49 Beddoes to Davies Giddy, CRO, DG41/16, 4 July 1792. For a history of 20 June 1792, cf. François Mignet, *History of the French Revolution from 1789–1814* (London: 1826); Schama, *Citizens*, pp. 608–10; Albert Soboul, *The French Revolution: 1787–1799*, trans. Alan Forrest and Colin Jones (London: Unwin Hyman, 1989); Albert Soboul, *The Parisian Sans-Culottes and the French Revolution, 1793–4*, trans. Gwynne Lewis (Oxford: Clarendon Press, 1964); Marisa Linton, *Choosing Terror: Virtue, Friendship, and Authenticity in the French Revolution* (Oxford: Oxford University Press, 2013); Gwynne Lewis, *The French Revolution: Rethinking the Debate* (London: Routledge, 1993).

50　Beddoes to Davies Giddy, CRO, DG41/14, 18 July 1792; Beddoes to
　　Davies Giddy, CRO, DG41/16, 4 July 1792.

51　Cited in R. R. Palmer, *The Age of the Democratic Revolution: A Political
　　History of Europe and America, 1760–1800* (Princeton and Oxford:
　　Princeton University Press, 2014), p. 402.

52　Beddoes to Davies Giddy, CRO, DG41/18, Aug 1792.

53　Beddoes to Davies Giddy, CRO, DG41/18, [15] Aug 1792.

54　Beddoes to Davies Giddy, CRO, DG41/19, 12 Sept 1792.

55　Thomas Beddoes, 'Reasons', CRO, DG41/25, 9 Oct 1792.

56　Cited in Levere, 'Dr. Thomas Beddoes (1750–1808)', 193.

57　Stansfield, *Thomas Beddoes*, pp. 58, 76.

58　Frend to Lady Byron, 7 Jan 1838, Lovelace–Byron deposit, Bodleian
　　Library, 71, fol. 114; cited in Nicholas Roe, 'Frend, William (1757–1841)',
　　Oxford Dictionary of National Biography, Oxford University Press, 2004
　　www.oxforddnb.com/view/article/10169 (accessed 29 Nov 2016).

59　*An Account of Mr. Whiston's Prosecution at, and Banishment from, the
　　University of Cambridge* (London: J. Roberts, 1718), p. 15.

60　Guilford to [Dundas], [7] July 1792; C. Willoughby to Guilford, 11 July
　　1792; J. Cooke to Guilford, 1 July 1792; in National Archives, HO 42/21,
　　42/208. Beddoes to Davies Giddy, CRO, MS DG41/22, 1793. Willoughby
　　to Dundas, 21 July 1792, National Archives, HO 42.208. All cited in
　　Levere, 'Dr. Thomas Beddoes (1750–1808)', 190. Latter quote cited in
　　Stansfield, *Thomas Beddoes*, pp. 77–8.

61　Beddoes to Davies Giddy, CRO, DG41/2, 7 April 1793.

62　Beddoes to Davies Giddy, CRO, DG41/22, Spring 1793.

63　Wedgwood MS 17760, 30 April 1768; cited in Robin Reilly, 'Wedgwood,
　　Josiah (1730–1795)', *Oxford Dictionary of National Biography*, Oxford
　　University Press, 2004; online edition, Sept 2013, www.oxforddnb.com/
　　view/article/28966 (accessed 20 March 2017).

64　Tom Wedgwood to Josiah Wedgwood, 8 May 1790, cited in R. B.
　　Litchfield, *Tom Wedgwood: The First Photographer* (London: Duckworth &
　　Co., 1903), p. 13.

65　Cited in Litchfield, *Tom Wedgwood*, p. 18.

66　Cited in Litchfield, *Tom Wedgwood*, p. 15.

67　Wedgwood, *Value of a Maimed Life*, p. 37.

68　Wedgwood, *Value of a Maimed Life*, p. 64.

69　Cited in Litchfield, *Tom Wedgwood*, pp. 25–6.

70　Cited in Litchfield, *Tom Wedgwood*, p. 28.

71　Cited in Barbara and Hensleigh Wedgwood, *The Wedgwood Circle 1730–
　　1897: Four Generations of a Family and their Friends* (London: Cassell,
　　1980), p. 102.

72　Beddoes to Davies Giddy, CRO, DG41/19, 12 Sept 1792.

73　James K. Chandler, *Wordsworth's Second Nature: A Study of the Poetry and
　　Politics* (Chicago and London: University of Chicago Press, 1985), p. 98.

74　Beddoes, *Extract of a Letter*, p. 3.

75　Beddoes, *Extract of a Letter*, pp. 6, 9.

76　Beddoes, *Extract of a Letter*, pp. 5–6.

77   Beddoes to Davies Giddy, CRO, DG41/16, 4 July 1792; DG41/14, 18 July
     1792.
78   Beddoes to Davies Giddy, CRO, DG41/13, 2 Feb 1792.
79   William Wordsworth, *The Prelude* (1850), in Wordsworth, *The Prelude, 1799,
     1805, 1850*, ed. M. H. Abrams (New York: Norton, 1979), X, ll. 165–6; I, l.
     124.

5: THE PURIFYING ALCHEMY OF EDUCATION

1   Jean-Jacques Rousseau, *Émile: Or, on Education*, trans. Allan Bloom
     (London: Penguin, 1979; first published 1762), p. 203.
2   Richard Lovell Edgeworth and Maria Edgeworth, *Memoirs of Richard
     Lovell Edgeworth: Begun by Himself and Concluded by His Daughter Maria
     Edgeworth*, 2 vols (Shannon: Irish University Press, 1969), I, pp. 72–3.
3   Edgeworth and Edgeworth, *Memoirs*, I, p. 178.
4   Edgeworth and Edgeworth, *Memoirs*, I, pp. 177–8.
5   *Essai sur l'opinion consideire comme une des principales causes de la
     Revolution de 1789* (Paris, 1789), 35; *Moniteur*, 30 Aug 1791; for a
     consideration of Rousseau's influence on the French Revolution, see
     David Williams, 'The Influence of Rousseau on Political Opinion, 1760–
     95', *English Historical Review*, 48:191, (1933), 414–30.
6   Edmund Burke, *A Letter to a Member of the National Assembly* (London: J.
     Dodsley, 1791), pp. 46–7.
7   Samuel von Pufendorf, cited by Nicholas Phillipson, *Adam Smith: An
     Enlightened Life* (London: Allen Lane, 2010), pp. 43–4.
8   Thomas Hobbes, *Leviathan*, ed. Richard Tuck (Cambridge: Cambridge
     University Press, 1991; first published 1651), chapters 13–14.
9   Bernard Mandeville, *The Fable of the Bees: Or, Private Vices, Publick
     Benefits*, 6th edition, 2 vols (Oxford: Clarendon Press, 1924; facsimile of
     London: J. Tonson, 1732), pp. 47, 68, 73.
10   Francis Hutcheson, *A Short Introduction to Moral Philosophy*, 2nd edition
     (Glasgow, 1753), cited by Phillipson, *Adam Smith*, p. 46.
11   Anthony Ashley Cooper, Third Earl of Shaftesbury, *Characteristicks
     of Men, Manners, Opinions, Times*, 4 vols (London, 1758), I, p. 73. See
     also Rowan Boyson, *Wordsworth and the Enlightenment Idea of Pleasure*
     (Cambridge: Cambridge University Press, 2012), p. 32.
12   Hutcheson, *Short Introduction*, p. 119; Cooper, *Characteristicks*, I, pp. 75–6.
13   William Godwin, *Notes on Philosophical Topics*, Abinger Collection,
     Bodleian Library, Abinger c. 30, ff. 8–39 (f. 29).
14   Jean-Jacques Rousseau, *Discourse on the Origin and Foundations of
     Inequality Among Men*, pp. 23–109, in Jean-Jacques Rousseau, *The Basic
     Political Writings*, trans. Donald A. Cress (Indianapolis & Cambridge:
     Hackett, 1987; first published 1755), p. 46; Rousseau, *Émile*, p. 85.
15   Rousseau, *Discourse*, p. 46.
16   Rousseau, *Discourse*, p. 55.
17   Mandeville, *Fable of the Bees*, cited in Boyson, *Wordsworth*, p. 25.
18   Jean-Jacques Rousseau, *The Social Contract*, pp. 1–158, in Jean-Jacques

Rousseau, *Political Writings*, trans. Frederick Watkins (Madison: University of Wisconsin Press, 1986; first published 1762), p. 20.

19 Rousseau, *Émile*, p. 37; Rousseau, *Social Contract*, p. 3.

20 Rousseau, *Émile*, pp. 60, 48.

21 Rousseau, *Émile*, pp. 203–5.

22 Rousseau, *Émile*, pp. 359, 443.

23 William Godwin, 'Of Deception and Frankness', Pforzheimer Collection, New York Public Library, G 0374 (c. 1797).

24 'Vous dites très bien qu'il est impossible de faire un Emile. Mais je ne puis croire que vous preniez le Livre qui porte ce nom pour un vrai traitté d'Education. C'est un ouvrage assez philosophique Sur ce principe avancé par l'Auteur dans d'autres écrits *que l'homme est naturellement bon.*' Rousseau, cited in Jeffrey Sworowski, 'Condorcet's Education: Haunted by the Ghost of Rousseau', *International Journal of Lifelong Education*, 14:4, (1995), 320–30.

25 Rousseau, letter to Mme. la Maréchale de Luxembourg, cited in Jean Guehénno, *Jean-Jacques*, 3 vols (Paris: 1948–52), II, p. 57f. For a discussion of Rousseau's treatment of his own children, see William Kessen, 'Rousseau's Children', *Daedalus*, 107:3, (1978), 155–66.

26 Edgeworth and Edgeworth, *Memoirs*, I, pp. 178–9.

27 Rousseau, *Émile*, p. 206; Edgeworth and Edgeworth, *Memoirs*, I, p. 35.

28 Edgeworth and Edgeworth, *Memoirs*, I, pp. 178–9.

29 Edgeworth and Edgeworth, *Memoirs*, I, p. 180.

30 Thomas Day to Richard Lovell Edgeworth, 'Correspondence Relating to a Biography of Thomas Day', National Library of Ireland, MSS 22470, 1, December 1774.

31 Edgeworth and Edgeworth, *Memoirs*, I, p. 226.

32 Wendy Moore, *How to Create the Perfect Wife: The True Story of One Gentleman, Two Orphans, and an Experiment to Create the Ideal Woman* (London: Weidenfeld & Nicolson, 2014).

33 Rousseau, *Émile*, pp. 358, 396.

34 Rousseau, *Émile*, pp. 359, 361.

35 Rousseau, *Émile*, p. 397.

36 Mary McAlpin, *Female Sexuality and Cultural Degradation in Enlightenment France: Medicine and Literature* (Farnham: Ashgate, 2012), pp. 1, 24.

37 Edgeworth and Edgeworth, *Memoirs*, I, p. 214.

38 Edgeworth and Edgeworth, *Memoirs*, I, pp. 226, 224; Rousseau, *Émile*, p. 358.

39 John Blackman, *A Memoir of the Life and Writings of Thomas Day, Author of 'Sandford and Merton'* (London: J. B. Lewis, 1862), cited in Peter Rowland, *The Life and Times of Thomas Day, 1748–1789* (Lewiston, New York, and Lampeter: Edwin Mellen Press, 1996), p. 20; Edgeworth and Edgeworth, *Memoirs*, I, pp. 217–18.

40 Rowland, *Life and Times*, p. 21.

41 Edgeworth and Edgeworth, *Memoirs*, I, p. 339.

42 Edgeworth and Edgeworth, *Memoirs*, II, pp. 109–11, 113.

43 Edgeworth and Edgeworth, *Memoirs*, I, pp. 257, 258–9.

44 Maria Edgeworth, note on letter from Richard Lovell Edgeworth to Margaret Ruxton, 14 Oct 1790, Edgeworth Papers, NLI, P. 9026, f. 69.

45 Cited in Edgeworth and Edgeworth, *Memoirs*, I, p. 226; Thomas Day to Richard Lovell Edgeworth, 'Correspondence Relating to a Biography of Thomas Day', NLI, MSS 22470, 1 December 1774.

46 Cited in Edgeworth and Edgeworth, *Memoirs*, I, pp. 273, 353–4.

47 Mary Louise Medley, *History of Anson County, North Carolina, 1750–1976* (Baltimore, MD: Anson County Historical Society, 1976), p. 80.

48 Edgeworth and Edgeworth, *Memoirs*, I, pp. 353–4; Richard Lovell Edgeworth to Thomas Day, 5 Feb 1787, Edgeworth Papers, NLI, P. 9026, f. 57; Richard Lovell Edgeworth to Margaret Ruxton, 4 Jan 1780, Edgeworth Papers, NLI, P. 9026, f. 17; Richard Lovell Edgeworth to Margaret Ruxton, 9 March 1781, Edgeworth Papers, NLI, P. 9026, f. 43.

49 Beddoes to Davies Giddy, 21 Nov 1792, CRO, DG41/48/1.

50 Richard Lovell Edgeworth to Thomas Day, 8 July 1784, in Edgeworth Papers, NLI, MSS P. 9026, f. 52.

51 Edgeworth and Edgeworth, *Memoirs*, I, p. 341.

52 Thomas Day, *The History of Sandford and Merton*, 3 vols (Dublin: 1787).

53 Richard Lovell Edgeworth to Esther Day, 29 Nov 1789, Edgeworth Papers, NLI, MSS 22470 (1), f. 11; Esther Day to Richard Lovell Edgeworth, 21 Jan 1790, Edgeworth Papers, NLI, MSS 22470 (2), f. 5.

54 Sabrina Bicknell to Maria Edgeworth, 29 Oct 1818, Edgeworth Papers, NLI, MSS 22470 (4), f. 8.

55 Richard Lovell Edgeworth to Margaret Ruxton, 3 Nov 1791, Edgeworth Papers, NLI, MSS P. 9026, f. 85; Edgar E. MacDonald, *The American Edgeworths: A Biographical Sketch of Richard Edgeworth (1764–1796) with Letters and Documents Pertaining to the Legacy of His Three Sons* (Richmond, Virginia: 1970); Dick Edgeworth to Richard Lovell Edgeworth, 28 Feb 1792, copy included in letter from Maria Edgeworth to Margaret Ruxton, 20 April 1792, Edgeworth Papers, NLI, MSS P. 9026, f. 91.

56 Maria Edgeworth to Margaret Ruxton, 13 Dec 1792, Edgeworth Papers, NLI, MSS P. 9026, f. 99; Maria Edgeworth to Sophy Ruxton, 14 Aug 1792, Edgeworth Papers, NLI, MSS P. 9026, f. 94.

57 Maria Edgeworth to Margaret Ruxton, 21 July 1793, Edgeworth Papers, NLI, MSS P. 9026, f. 105.

58 Georges-Louis Leclerc, Comte de Buffon, cited in Julia V. Douthwaite, *The Wild Girl, Natural Man and the Monster: Dangerous Experiments in the Age of Enlightenment* (Chicago and London: University of Chicago Press, 2002), p. 27.

59 Douthwaite, *Wild Girl*, pp. 31–2.

60 Nancy Yousef, 'Savage or Solitary?: The Wild Child and Rousseau's Man of Nature', *Journal of the History of Ideas* 62 (2), (April 2001), 245–63 (248).

61 William Lawrence, cited in Douthwaite, *Wild Girl*, p. 28.

62 For the tight regulation of the British economy at the beginning of the nineteenth century, see Alvin Rabushka, *From Adam Smith to the Wealth of America* (New Brunswick and Oxford: Transaction Books, 1985), pp. 72–3.

63 Beddoes to Davies Giddy, CRO, DG41/27, 25–26 May 1793.

64 Beddoes to Davies Giddy, CRO, DG41/27, 25–26 May 1793.

65 Jay, *Atmosphere*, p. 90.

66 Beddoes to Davies Giddy, CRO, DG41/27, 25–26 May 1793.

67 Jay, *Atmosphere*, pp. 81–2. Stock, *Memoirs*, Appendix, p. 8.

68 Richard Lovell Edgeworth and Maria Edgeworth, *Practical Education*, 3 vols (London: Joseph Johnson, 1798), I, pp. 8–9.

69 John Locke, *An Essay Concerning Human Understanding*, ed. Peter H. Nidditch (Oxford: Oxford University Press, 1975; first published 1689), p. 104.

70 Hartley, *Observations*, pp. 80, 368.

71 Hartley, *Observations*, pp. 368–9.

72 Hartley, *Observations*, pp. 240–41.

73 Hartley, *Observations*, p. 81; Coleridge, *Lectures, 1795*, p. 10.

74 Edelman, *Change Your Thinking*, p. ix.

75 R. T. Fancher, *Cultures of Healing: Correcting the Image of American Mental Health Care* (New York: W. H. Freeman, 1995), p. 231.

76 Coleridge, 'A Moral and Political Lecture', *Lectures, 1795*, p. 12.

77 Hannah More, *Strictures on the Modern System of Female Education*, 3rd edition, 2 vols (London: T. Cadell, 1799), I, p. 64.

78 Joseph Priestley, cited in Dixon, *From Passions to Emotions*, p. 119.

79 Thomas Beddoes, *The History of Isaac Jenkins, and Sarah His Wife, and Their Three Children*, 6th edition (London: H. Murray and J. Johnson, 1794), pp. iii–v.

80 Beddoes to Davies Giddy, CRO, DG41/21, 26 May 1793.

81 Thomas Beddoes, cited in Stock, *Memoirs*, p. 94.

82 Beddoes to Davies Giddy, CRO, DG41/7, 3 July 1793.

83 Richard Lovell Edgeworth to Mrs Ruxton, 21 July 1793, in Maria Edgeworth, *Life and Letters*, I, pp. 30–31; cited in Jay, *Atmosphere*, p. 91.

84 Beddoes to Davies Giddy, CRO, DG41/28, 15 June 1793.

85 Samuel Seyer MSS, 'Chronicle of Events 1760–1813', Bristol Reference Library, B4533, pp. 39–41; cited in Mark Harrison, '"To Raise and Dare Resentment": The Bristol Bridge Riot of 1793 Re-Examined', *Historical Journal*, 26 (3), (1983), 557–85 (562).

86 Harrison, '"To Raise and Dare Resentment"', 557–85.

87 Beddoes to Davies Giddy, CRO, DG41/4, 29 Oct 1793.

6: Neck or Nothing

1 Wollstonecraft to William Roscoe, 12 Nov 1792, in Wollstonecraft, *Collected Letters*, p. 208.

2 Theresa McBride, 'Public Authority and Private Lives: Divorce after the French Revolution', *French Historical Studies*, 17:3, (1992), 747–68 (749–50); James F. Traer, *Marriage and the Family in Eighteenth-Century France* (Ithaca, NY: Cornell University Press, 1980), pp. 120–21; Laura Emerson Talamante, 'Creating the Republican Family: Political and Social Transformation and the Revolutionary Family Tribunal', *Proceedings*

of the Western Society for French History, 38, (2010), 143–62; Lynn Hunt, *The Family Romance of the French Revolution* (Berkeley: University of California Press, 1992), pp. 41–2.

3   Wollstonecraft to William Roscoe, 12 Nov 1792, in Wollstonecraft, *Collected Letters*, p. 208.

4   R. C. Christie, 'Christie, Thomas (1761–1796)', rev. Alexander Du Toit, *Oxford Dictionary of National Biography*, Oxford University Press, 2004, www.oxforddnb.com/view/article/5365 (accessed 20 March 2017).

5   Stephen Gill, *William Wordsworth: A Life* (Oxford: Oxford University Press, 1989), pp. 57, 58, 68.

6   James Lawrence, *The Empire of the Nairs; or, the Rights of Women: An Utopian Romance, in Twelve Books* (London: T. Hookham, 1811), p. xl.

7   Lawrence, *Empire*, pp. xxxvi–vii.

8   Gill, *William Wordsworth*, pp. 66–7.

9   'How to Control Your Anger' www.nhs.uk/conditions/stress-anxiety-depression/pages/controlling-anger.aspx (accessed 2 Dec 2016).

10   Amy Fleming, 'The Science of Craving', *The Economist: 1843*, May–June 2015, www.1843magazine.com/content/features/wanting-versus-liking (accessed 20 March 2017).

11   Adam Smith, *An Inquiry into the Nature and Causes of the Wealth of Nations* (London: Strahan and Cadell, 1776), Book 1, chapter 2.

12   Smith, *Moral Sentiments*, Part 1, Section 1, chapter 1, §5.

13   Smith, *Moral Sentiments*, Part 1, Section 1, chapter 4, §5.

14   Smith, *Wealth of Nations*, Book 4, chapter 2.

15   Rafael Torres Sanchez, 'The Triumph of the Fiscal-Military State in the Eighteenth Century', pp. 25–34, in Rafael Torres Sanchez, ed., *War, State and Development* (Pamplona: Universidad de Navarra, 2007); John Brewer, *The Sinews of Power: War, Money and the English State, 1688–1783* (Cambridge, Mass.: Harvard University Press, 1990).

16   Smith, *Wealth of Nations*, Book 1, chapter 10; Book 1, chapter 8.

17   Philip Connell, *Romanticism, Economics and the Question of 'Culture'* (Oxford: Oxford University Press, 2001), p. 144. I am very grateful to Pete Newbon for pointing me in the direction of this book.

18   Emma Rothschild, 'Adam Smith and Conservative Economics', *Economic History Review*, 2nd set, 45 (1992), 74–96; Iain McLean, *Adam Smith: Radical and Egalitarian – An Interpretation for the 21st Century* (Edinburgh: Edinburgh University Press, 2006).

19   Wollstonecraft to Henry Fuseli, late 1792, *Collected Letters*, p. 205.

20   Knowles, *Life and Writings*, I, pp. 167–8.

21   Knowles, *Life and Writings*, I, p. 167.

22   Knowles, *Life and Writings*, I, p. 168.

23   Wollstonecraft to William Roscoe, 12 Nov 1792, *Collected Letters*, pp. 206–7.

24   Wollstonecraft to Joseph Johnson, 26 Dec 1792, *Collected Letters*, p. 217.

25   Wollstonecraft to Everina Wollstonecraft, early Dec 1792, *Collected Letters*, p. 212.

26   Mary Wollstonecraft, 'Letter on the Present Character of the French Nation', IV, pp. 37–51, in *Posthumous Works*, IV, p. 39.

27 Wollstonecraft to Everina Wollstonecraft, 24 Dec 1792, *Collected Letters*, pp. 214–15.

28 J. G. Alger, 'The British Colony in Paris, 1792–93', *English Historical Review*, 13:52, (1898), 672–94 (672–3).

29 Rachel Rogers, 'White's Hotel: A Junction of British Radical Culture in Early 1790s Paris', *Caliban: French Journal of English Studies*, 33, (2013), 153–72.

30 Gary Kates, *Cercle Social, the Girondins and the French Revolution* (Princeton: Princeton University Press, 1985), p. 191.

31 Richard Buel, *Joel Barlow: American Citizen in a Revolutionary World* (Baltimore: Johns Hopkins University Press, 2011).

32 Keane, *Tom Paine*, pp. 345–6.

33 Helen Maria Williams, *Letters Written in France*, ed. Neil Fraistat and Susan S. Lanser (Ormskirk: Broadview, 2001), pp. 176–7, 216; Wollstonecraft to Everina Wollstonecraft, 24 Dec 1792, *Collected Letters*, p. 215; Godwin, *Memoirs*, p. 105.

34 Wollstonecraft to Joseph Johnson, 26 Dec 1792, *Collected Letters*, p. 216.

35 'Indictment of Louis XVI, 11 December 1792', in John Hall Stewart, ed., *A Documentary Survey of the French Revolution* (New York: Macmillan, 1951), pp. 386–9, 391.

36 Wollstonecraft to Joseph Johnson, 26 Dec 1792, *Collected Letters*, pp. 216–17.

37 Wollstonecraft, *Letter on the Present Character*, p. 46.

38 Buel, *Joel Barlow*, p. 163.

39 Wollstonecraft to Joseph Johnson, 26 Dec 1792, *Collected Letters*, pp. 216–17.

40 Eliza Wollstonecraft to Everina Wollstonecraft, *Collected Letters*, p. 221, fn. 514.

41 Cited in Todd, *Wollstonecraft*, p. 241; Godwin, *Memoirs*, p. 121.

42 Wollstonecraft to Eliza Wollstonecraft, 13 June 1793, *Collected Letters*, p. 226.

43 Wollstonecraft to Eliza Wollstonecraft, 13 June 1793, *Collected Letters*, p. 226.

44 Eliza Wollstonecraft to Everina Wollstonecraft, 14 July 1793, *Collected Letters*, p. 227, fn. 531.

45 Godwin, *Memoirs*, p. 111.

46 Wollstonecraft to Eliza Wollstonecraft, 13 June 1793, *Collected Letters*, p. 225.

47 Donald Ratcliffe, 'The Right to Vote and the Rise of Democracy, 1787–1828', *Journal of the Early Republic*, 33, (Summer 2013), 219–54.

48 Nancy E. Johnson, '"Seated on her Bags of Dollars": Representations of America in the English Jacobin Novel', *Dalhousie Review*, 82 (3), (2002), 423–39.

49 Gilbert Imlay, *A Topographical Description of the Western Territory of North America* (London: J. Debrett, 1797), pp. 16–17.

50 Imlay, *Topographical Description*, p. viii.

51 Gilbert Imlay, *The Emigrants, &c., or the History of an Expatriated Family,*

Being a Delineation of English Manners, Drawn from Real Characters, Written in America (London: A. Hamilton, 1793), p. 6.

52 Imlay, *Emigrants*, p. 17.

53 Imlay, *Emigrants*, p. 66.

54 Mary Wollstonecraft, 'Letters', III, pp. 1–190, and IV, pp. 1–37, in *Posthumous Works*, III, p. 61.

55 Wollstonecraft, *Posthumous Works*, III, p. 3.

56 Wollstonecraft, *Posthumous Works*, III, pp. 28, 3–4, 23; Claire Tomalin, *The Life and Death of Mary Wollstonecraft* (London: Penguin, 1974; 1992), pp. 184–90.

57 Todd, *Wollstonecraft*, p. 239.

58 Godwin, *Memoirs*, p. 110.

59 Wollstonecraft, *Posthumous Works*, III, p. 11.

60 Wollstonecraft, *Posthumous Works*, III, pp. 24, 15, 28, 9.

61 Wollstonecraft, *Posthumous Works*, III, pp. 25, 16, 18, 35.

62 Wollstonecraft, *Posthumous Works*, III, pp. 27, 26, 40.

63 Wollstonecraft, *Posthumous Works*, III, p. 19.

64 Aline Lemonnier-Mercier, *Les Embellissements du Havre au XVIIIe siècle: projets, réalisations, 1719–1830* (Rouen and Le Havre: Presses Universitaires de Rouen et du Havre, 2013).

65 See Gordon, *Vindication*, chapter 10, for Gordon's interesting comments on how extraordinary it was that Wollstonecraft was not arrested.

66 Wollstonecraft to Everina Wollstonecraft, 10 March 1794, *Collected Letters*, p. 249; Wollstonecraft, *Posthumous Works*, III, p. 45.

67 Wollstonecraft, *Historical and Moral View*, p. 220.

68 Richard Price, 'Of the Happiness of a Virtuous Course', pp. 19–40, in *Sermons by Richard Price and Joseph Priestley* (London: British and Foreign Unitarian Association, 1830), p. 24.

69 Wollstonecraft, *Historical and Moral View*, p. 8.

70 Wollstonecraft, *Historical and Moral View*, p. 19.

71 Wollstonecraft, *Letter on the Present Character*, pp. 41, 42, 45.

72 Wollstonecraft, *Historical and Moral View*, pp. 21, 256; Wollstonecraft, *Letter on the Present Character of the French Nation*, pp. 42, 49–4.

73 Wollstonecraft, *Historical and Moral View*, pp. 256–8.

74 Wollstonecraft, *Historical and Moral View*, p. 72.

75 Wollstonecraft, *Historical and Moral View*, pp. 73, 132.

76 Wollstonecraft, *Historical and Moral View*, p. 132.

77 Wollstonecraft to Everina Wollstonecraft, 10 March 1794, *Collected Letters*, p. 248.

78 Deborah Kennedy, *Helen Maria Williams and the Age of Revolution* (Lewisburg: Associated University Presses, 2002), pp. 211–12.

79 Wollstonecraft to Everina Wollstonecraft, 10 March 1794, *Collected Letters*, p. 249.

80 Wollstonecraft to Ruth Barlow, 27 April 1794, *Collected Letters*, p. 252.

81 Wollstonecraft to Ruth Barlow, 27 April 1794, *Collected Letters*, pp. 252–3.

82 Wollstonecraft to Ruth Barlow, 20 May 1794, *Collected Letters*, p. 254.

7: THE MOST DELIGHTFUL THEORY OF AN ISLAND

1 Joseph Cottle, *Early Recollections; Chiefly Relating to the Late Samuel Taylor Coleridge, During His Long Residence in Bristol*, 2 vols (London: Longman, Rees & Co., 1837), I, pp. 2–3.

2 Samuel Taylor Coleridge to Samuel Butler, 14 June 1794, *Collected Letters of Samuel Taylor Coleridge*, Vol. I: *1785–1800*, ed. Earl Leslie Griggs (Oxford: Clarendon Press, 1956; 2002), I, p. 82.

3 Robert Southey to Grosvenor Bedford, 12–19? June 1794, *The Collected Letters of Robert Southey: Part One, 1791–1797*, ed. Lynda Pratt, Romantic Circles Electronic Edition, www.rc.umd.edu/editions/southey_letters.

4 Southey to Grosvenor Bedford, 11–18 May 1794, *Collected Letters of Robert Southey*.

5 Leigh Hunt, *Autobiography*, cited in Mark Storey, *Robert Southey: A Life* (Oxford: Oxford University Press, 1997), p. 45.

6 Southey to Grosvenor Bedford, 12–19? June 1794, *Collected Letters of Robert Southey*.

7 Cottle, *Recollections*, I, pp. 2–3.

8 Cottle, *Recollections*, I, p. 136.

9 Southey to Grosvenor Bedford, c. 5 May 1792, *Collected Letters of Robert Southey*; Coleridge to Anne Evans, 10 Feb 1793, *Collected Letters of Coleridge*, I, p. 55; Southey to Thomas Phillips Lamb, c. 6 Oct 1792, *Collected Letters of Robert Southey*.

10 Coleridge to Mrs Evans, 13 Feb 1792, *Collected Letters of Coleridge*, I, p. 12.

11 Samuel Taylor Coleridge, *The Notebooks of Samuel Taylor Coleridge*, ed. Kathleen Coburn (London: Routledge and Kegan Paul, 1957), Vol. I: *1794–1804*, Text, #1726.

12 Coleridge to George Coleridge, 23 Feb 1794, *Collected Letters of Coleridge*, I, p. 67.

13 Godwin's MS notes on Coleridge's life up to 1799, cited in Nicholas Roe, *Wordsworth and Coleridge: The Radical Years* (Oxford: Clarendon, 1988), pp. 109–10.

14 Coleridge to G. L. Tuckett, 6 Feb 1794, *Collected Letters of Coleridge*, I, pp. 62–3.

15 Coleridge to G. L. Tuckett, 6 Feb 1794, *Collected Letters of Coleridge*, I, p. 61.

16 Coleridge to George Coleridge, 5 Feb 1794, *Collected Letters of Coleridge*, I, p. 63.

17 Naomi Clifford, 'George Lowman Tuckett', *All Things Georgian* georgianera.wordpress.com/tag/samuel-taylor-coleridge/ (accessed 15 Sept 2016).

18 Coleridge to G. L. Tuckett, 6 Feb 1794, *Collected Letters of Coleridge*, I, pp. 62–3.

19 Coleridge to George Coleridge, 23 March 1794, *Collected Letters of Coleridge*, I, p. 74.

20 Richard Holmes, *Coleridge: Early Visions* (London: Penguin, 1989), p. 60.

21 Southey to Grosvenor Bedford, 1 June 1794, *Collected Letters of Robert Southey*.

22 Southey to Grosvenor Bedford, 11 Dec 1793, *Collected Letters of Robert Southey*.

23 Southey to John Horseman, before 3 Feb 1794, *Collected Letters of Robert Southey*; Southey to Grosvenor Bedford, 11–18 May 1794, *Collected Letters of Robert Southey*.

24 Southey to Grosvenor Bedford, c. 3 April 1792, *Collected Letters of Robert Southey*.

25 Southey to Grosvenor Bedford, 30 Dec 1792, *Collected Letters of Robert Southey*.

26 Southey to Charles Collins, c. 4 June 1792, *Collected Letters of Robert Southey*.

27 Southey to Grosvenor Bedford, c. 29 Sept 1792, *Collected Letters of Robert Southey*.

28 Southey to Grosvenor Bedford, 25 Jan–8 Feb 1793, *Collected Letters of Robert Southey*.

29 Southey to Grosvenor Bedford, *Collected Letters of Robert Southey*.

30 Southey to Grosvenor Bedford, 14–21 July 1793, *Collected Letters of Robert Southey*, 14–21 July 1793.

31 Southey to Grosvenor Bedford, 14–21 July 1793, *Collected Letters of Robert Southey*.

32 Southey to Grosvenor Bedford, 28 May 1794, *Collected Letters of Robert Southey*.

33 W. A. Speck, *Robert Southey: Entire Man of Letters* (New Haven and London: Yale University Press, 2006), p. 36, fn. 58.

34 Southey to Horace Walpole Bedford, 11 Dec 1793, *Collected Letters of Robert Southey*.

35 Southey to Horace Walpole Bedford, 12–15 Dec 1793, *Collected Letters of Robert Southey*.

36 Robert Lovell, *Bristol: A Satire* (London: printed for the author, 1794), pp. 6, 1.

37 Southey to Horace Walpole Bedford, 22–24 Dec 1793, *Collected Letters of Robert Southey*.

38 Southey to Horace Walpole Bedford, 24 Jan–18 Feb 1794, *Collected Letters of Robert Southey*.

39 Southey to Grosvenor Bedford, before 28 May 1794, *Collected Letters of Robert Southey*.

40 Southey to Grosvenor Bedford, before 28 May 1794, *Collected Letters of Robert Southey*.

41 Southey to Horace Walpole Bedford, 12–15 Dec 1793, *Collected Letters of Robert Southey*.

42 Southey to Grosvenor Bedford, 31 July–6 Aug 1793, *Collected Letters of Robert Southey*; Southey to Grosvenor Bedford, 12 June 1794, *Collected Letters of Robert Southey*.

43 Southey to Grosvenor Bedford, 12–15 Nov 1793, *Collected Letters of Robert Southey*.

44 Southey to Robert Lovell, 5–6 April 1794, *Collected Letters of Robert Southey*.

45 Southey to Horace Walpole Bedford, 22 Aug–3 Sept 1794, *Collected Letters of Robert Southey*.

46 For details about the mutiny on the *Bounty*, see Caroline Alexander, *The Bounty: The True Story of the Mutiny on the Bounty* (London: HarperCollins, 2003); Richard Hough, *Captain Bligh and Mr Christian: The Men and the Mutiny* (London: Hutchinson, 1972).

47 Cited in Alexander, *Bounty*, pp. 321–9.

48 Cited in Alexander, *Bounty*, pp. 321–9; cf. James C. McKusick, '"Wisely Forgetful": Coleridge and the Politics of Pantisocracy', pp. 107–28, in *Romanticism and Colonialism: Writing and Empire, 1780–1830*, ed. Tim Fulford and Peter Kitson (Cambridge: Cambridge University Press, 1998), p. 110.

49 Alexander, *Bounty*, pp. 38–9.

50 Southey to Grosvenor Bedford, 25 Jan–8 Feb 1793, *Collected Letters of Robert Southey*.

51 Southey to Grosvenor Bedford, 26–27 Oct 1793, *Collected Letters of Robert Southey*.

52 Southey to Horace Walpole Bedford, 13–16 Nov 1793, *Collected Letters of Robert Southey*.

53 Southey to Horace Walpole Bedford, 13–16 Nov 1793, *Collected Letters of Robert Southey*.

54 Cottle, *Recollections*, I, pp. 6–7.

55 Coleridge to George Dyer, later Feb 1795, in Coleridge, *Collected Letters*, I, pp. 152–3; Southey to Grosvenor Bedford, 12–19 June 1794, in Southey, *Collected Letters* .

56 George Burnett to Nicholas Lightfoot, 22 Oct 1796, Bodleian Library, MS Eng. Letters c. 453.

57 George Burnett to Nicholas Lightfoot, 22 Oct 1796, Bodleian Library, MS Eng. Letters c. 453.

58 Coleridge to Robert Southey, 6 July 1794, in Coleridge, *Collected Letters*, I, p. 84.

59 Coleridge to Robert Southey, 13 July 1794, in Coleridge, *Collected Letters*, I, p. 88–90.

60 Southey to Grosvenor Bedford, 20–21 July 1794, in Southey, *Collected Letters*.

61 Southey to Grosvenor Bedford, 1–21 Aug 1794, in Southey, *Collected Letters*.

62 Southey to Grosvenor Bedford, 20–21 July 1794, in Southey, *Collected Letters*.

63 Coleridge to Robert Southey, 13 July 1794, in Coleridge, *Collected Letters*, I, p. 85.

64 The *Oxford Dictionary of National Biography* gives the date of Coleridge's arrival in Bristol as 21 August, but seeing that he's engaged to Sara Fricker two weeks before 1 September (i.e. 19 August), he probably arrived in Bristol around the end of July or the beginning of August. When Coleridge leaves Bristol on 2 September, Robert Southey says he's been there for 'nearly five weeks' (7 September 1794). John Beer, 'Coleridge,

Samuel Taylor (1772–1834)', *Oxford Dictionary of National Biography*, Oxford University Press, 2004; online edition, Oct 2008, www.oxforddnb. com/view/article/5888 (accessed 21 March 2017).

65 Southey to Horace Walpole Bedford, 1 Aug 1794, in Southey, *Collected Letters*; Coleridge to Charles Heath, 29 Aug 1794, in Coleridge, *Collected Letters*, I, p. 97.

66 Imlay, *Topographical Description*, pp. 21, 29.

67 George Whalley, 'The Bristol Library Borrowings of Southey and Coleridge, 1793–8', *Library*, IV (1949), 114–31.

68 Nigel Leask, 'Pantisocracy and the politics of the "Preface" to *Lyrical Ballads*', pp. 39–58, in *Reflections of Revolution: Images of Romanticism*, ed. Alison Yarrington and Kelvin Everest (London and New York: Routledge, 1993), p. 42.

69 Thomas Cooper, *Some Information Respecting America* (London: Johnson, 1794), cited in Mary C. Park, *Joseph Priestley and the Problem of Pantisocracy*, in *Proceedings of the Delaware County Institute of Science*, XI, (1947), 1–60 (25).

70 James Horn, 'British Diaspora: Emigration from Britain, 1680–1815', pp. 28–52, in P. J. Marshall and Alaine Low, eds, *The Oxford History of the British Empire*, Vol. II: *The Eighteenth Century* (Oxford: Oxford University Press, 1998), cited in Carol Bolton, *Writing the Empire: Robert Southey and Romantic Colonialism* (London: Pickering and Chatto, 2007), p. 73.

71 Coleridge, 'Domestic Peace', from Coleridge, *The Fall of Robespierre* (Cambridge: Benjamin Flower, 1794), Act I, l. 210; Coleridge, 'To a Young Ass', *Morning Chronicle*, 9 December 1794; Southey to Horace Walpole Bedford, 13–16 Nov 1793, Southey, *Collected Letters*.

72 Joseph Priestley to Rev. W. Turner, 13 June 1793, cited in Park, *Joseph Priestley*, 12.

73 Joseph Priestley, *Memoirs*, p. 133, cited in Colin Jager, 'A Poetics of Dissent; or, Pantisocracy in America' *Theory & Event* (10:1), (2007), doi: 10.1353/tae.2007.0042, 23.

74 Cooper, *Some Information*, pp. 76–7.

75 See *Plan du vente*, a pamphlet found by Maurice W. Kelley in the Bibliothèque Nationale de France in the early twentieth century, which implies that Cooper and Priestley were more set on selling land than on reforming society. The pamphlet is cited in Eugenia Logan, 'Coleridge's Scheme of Pantisocracy and American Travel Accounts', *PMLA* 45 (1930), 1069–84. Park, in *Joseph Priestley and the Problem of Pantisocracy*, claims that the Priestley family acquired 70,000 acres of land, 17–18.

76 Cooper, *Some Information*, p. 75; cited in Logan, 'Coleridge's Scheme of Pantisocracy', 1074; Park, *Joseph Priestley*, 31.

77 Coleridge, 'Religious Musings', in Coleridge, *Poems on Various Subjects* (London: Robinsons and Cottle, 1796), p. 165, l. 395.

78 Coleridge to Robert Southey, 1 Sept 1794, in Coleridge, *Collected Letters*, I, p. 98.

79 Coleridge to Robert Southey, 1 Sept 1794, in Coleridge, *Collected Letters*, I, p. 98.

80 Cooper, *Some Information*, p. 75; cited in Logan, 'Coleridge's Scheme of Pantisocracy', 1074.
81 Coleridge to Robert Southey, 1 Sept 1794, in Coleridge, *Collected Letters*, I, pp. 98–9.
82 Mrs Henry Sandford, *Thomas Poole and his Friends*, 2 vols (London: Macmillan, 1888), I, p. 98.
83 Cottle, *Recollections*, I, p. 3.
84 Southey to Tom Southey, 7 Sept 1794, in Southey, *Collected Letters*.
85 Cited in Cottle, *Recollections*, I, p. 16.
86 Cottle, *Recollections*, I, p. 17.
87 Cottle, *Recollections*, I, p. 18.
88 Coleridge to Robert Southey, 1 Sept 1794, in Coleridge, *Collected Letters*, I, p. 98; Coleridge to Robert Southey, 11 Sept 1794, in Coleridge, *Collected Letters*, I, p. 101.
89 Coleridge to George Dyer, late Feb 1795, in Coleridge, *Collected Letters*, I, p. 152; Southey to Tom Southey, 21 March 1795, in Southey, *Collected Letters*.
90 Southey to Tom Southey, 7 Sept 1794, in Southey, *Collected Letters*.
91 Coleridge to Robert Southey, 19 Jan 1795, in Coleridge, *Collected Letters*, I, p. 150.
92 Coleridge to Robert Southey, 1 Sept 1794, in Coleridge, *Collected Letters*, I, p. 99.
93 Cottle, *Recollections*, I, p. 30.
94 Thompson Cooper, 'Burnett, George (1774/5–1811)', rev. David Kaloustian, *Oxford Dictionary of National Biography*, Oxford University Press, 2004; online edition, May 2009, www.oxforddnb.com/view/article/4071 (accessed 21 March 2017).
95 Coleridge to Charles Heath, 29 Aug 1794, in Coleridge, *Collected Letters*, I, pp. 96–7; Southey to Tom Southey, 7 Sept 1794, in Southey, *Collected Letters*.
96 Coleridge to Charles Heath, 29 Aug 1794, in Coleridge, *Collected Letters*, I, pp. 96–7.
97 Southey to Tom Southey, 12 Oct 1794, in Southey, *Collected Letters*.

8: THE ORGASM OF THE REVOLUTION

1 Coleridge to Robert Southey, 18 Sept 1794, in Coleridge, *Collected Letters*, I, p. 103.
2 Coleridge to Robert Southey, 21 Oct 1794, in Coleridge, *Collected Letters*, I, p. 114.
3 Southey to Grosvenor Bedford, 20–21 July 1794, in Southey, *Collected Letters*.
4 James Harrington, *The Political Works of James Harrington*, ed. J. G. A. Pocock (Cambridge: Cambridge University Press, 1977), p. 164, cited in Leask, 'Pantisocracy', p. 48.
5 Coleridge, 'Lecture Six', *Six Lectures on Revealed Religion, Its Corruptions and Political Views*, in Coleridge, *Lectures 1795*, I, p. 228.
6 Southey to Horace Walpole Bedford, 22 Aug–3 Sept 1794, in Southey, *Collected Letters*.

7   Robert Lovell, cited in Cottle, *Recollections*, I, p. 9.

8   Coleridge, 'Lecture Two', *Six Lectures on Revealed Religion*, in *Lectures 1795*, I, p. 128. For eighteenth-century political interpretations of the Mosaic constitution, see also Graham Hammill, *The Mosaic Constitution: Political Theology and Imagination from Machiavelli to Milton* (Chicago: University of Chicago Press, 2012).

9   Coleridge, 'Lecture Six', *Six Lectures on Revealed Religion*, in *Lectures 1795*, I, pp. 218, 226, 288; 'Lecture Two', *Six Lectures on Revealed Religion*, in *Lectures 1795*, I, p. 128.

10 Godwin, *Political Justice* (1798), p. 271.

11 Godwin, *Political Justice* (1798), p. 71.

12 Godwin, *Political Justice* (1798), pp. 79, 127.

13 Cited in *The Carl H. Pforzheimer Library: Shelley and his Circle, 1773–1882*, ed. Kenneth Neill Cameron (Cambridge, Mass.: Harvard University Press, 1961), I, pp. 9–12.

14 Godwin, *Political Justice* (1798), pp. 193–4; Godwin, *Notes on Philosophical Topics*, Abinger Collection, Bodleian Library, Abinger c. 30, ff. 8–39 (f. 15).

15 Godwin, *Political Justice* (1798), p. 199.

16 Godwin, *Diary*, April 1790.

17 William Godwin, 'Sermon on Heroism', Abinger Collection, Bodleian Library, Abinger c. 30, Dep. c. 532/9, ff. 83–6.

18 Godwin, *Political Justice* (1798), p. 135.

19 Godwin, *Political Justice* (1798), pp. 218, 229.

20 William Godwin, *An Enquiry Concerning Political Justice* (London: Robinson, 1793), I, p. 849.

21 Godwin, *Political Justice* (1793), I, 852.

22 Coleridge, 'Lecture Three', *Six Lectures on Revealed Religion*, in *Lectures 1795*, I, pp. 164–5.

23 Coleridge, 'Lecture Three', *Six Lectures on Revealed Religion*, in *Lectures 1795*, I. p. 157.

24 Sandford, *Thomas Poole*, I, p. 98.

25 Southey to Samuel Taylor Coleridge, 16 Jan 1800, in Kenneth Curry, ed., *New Letters of Robert Southey* (New York: Columbia University Press, 1965), p. 215.

26 Lynn Hunt and Margaret Jacob, 'The Affective Revolution in 1790s Britain', *Eighteenth-Century Studies*, 34 (4), (2001), 491–521 (496–7).

27 Bruder, *William Blake*, p. 77.

28 George Cumberland, *The Captive of the Castle of Sennaar, an African Tale: Containing Various Anecdotes of the Sophians Hitherto Unknown to Mankind in General* (London: Printed for the Author, 1798), pp. 77–8, 88, 149–50.

29 Cumberland, *Captive*, p. 151.

30 Shere Hite, *The Hite Report: A Nationwide Study on Female Sexuality* (New York and London: Macmillan, 1976), p. 311.

31 James Forbes, *Oriental Memoirs*, 4 vols (London: White, Cochrane & Co., 1813), I, 385.

32 Lawrence, *Empire*, pp. xviii, vii, xvi.

33 Lawrence, *Empire*, pp. iv, vii, xl.

34   Lawrence, *Empire*, pp. x.
35   James Caulfeild, Earl of Charlemont, 'Account of a Singular Custom at Metelin, with some Conjectures on the Antiquity of its Origin', *Transactions of the Royal Irish Academy*, 3, (1789), 3–20.
36   Alessa Johns, *Women's Utopias of the Eighteenth Century* (Urbana and Chicago: University of Illinois Press, 2003), p. 3.
37   Mary Louise Pratt, *Imperial Eyes: Travel Writing and Transculturation* (London: Routledge, 1992), pp. 16–17.
38   Clara Reeves, *Plans of Education; with Remarks on the Systems of Other Writers* (London: Hookham and Carpenter, 1792), cited in Johns, *Women's Utopias*, p. 9.
39   'Ophelia', 'Matilda; or, the Female Recluse: An Anecdote', *Lady's Magazine*, April 1779, 201–24.
40   Sarah Scott, *A Description of Millenium Hall* (London: 1762).
41   Anna Seward to Mrs. T., 19 June 1796, in Anna Seward, *Letters of Anna Seward: Written between the Years 1784 and 1807*, 6 vols (Edinburgh: George Ramsay, 1811), IV, p. 217.
42   Anna Seward, 'Sonnet X' (April 1773), cited in Emma Donoghue, *Passions Between Women: British Lesbian Culture 1668–1801* (London: Scarlet Press, 1993), p. 118.
43   Cited in Elizabeth Mavor, *The Ladies of Llangollen: A Study in Romantic Friendship* (Ludlow: Moonrise Press, 1971; this edition 2011), p. 27.
44   Cited in Lilian Faderman, *Surpassing the Love of Men: Romantic Friendship and Love Between Women from the Renaissance to the Present* (London: Women's Press, 1981), pp. 137–8.
45   Cited in Faderman, *Surpassing the Love of Men*, p. 75.
46   Cited in Donoghue, *Passions*, pp. 2, 123–4.
47   Bruder, *William Blake*, p. 84.
48   For example, see Roy F. Baumeister and Jean M. Twenge, 'Cultural Suppression of Female Sexuality', *Review of General Psychology*, 6:2, (2002), 166–203.
49   Cited in Mavor, *Ladies of Llangollen*, p. 79.
50   Samuel Favell, cited in letter from Coleridge to Robert Southey, 1 Sept 1794, in Coleridge, *Collected Letters*, I, p. 100.
51   Coleridge to Robert Southey, 13 Nov 1795, in Coleridge, *Collected Letters*, I, p. 164.
52   Southey to Horace Walpole Bedford, 12–15 Dec 1793, in Southey, *Collected Letters*.
53   Marilyn Butler, cited in Bruder, *William Blake*, p. 86.
54   Coleridge to Robert Southey, 21 Oct 1794, in Coleridge, *Collected Letters*, I, p. 114.
55   Bolton, p. 89.
56   Southey to Grosvenor Bedford, 31 July–6 Aug 1793, in Southey, *Collected Letters*.
57   Cited by Lewis Patton and Peter Mann, 'Editors' Introduction', to Coleridge, *Lectures 1795*, p. 10.
58   Augustine, *City of God*, p. 410.

59 Coleridge, *Conciones ad Populum*, in *Lectures 1795*, I, p. 46.

60 Coleridge, 'Lecture Three', *Six Lectures on Revealed Religion*, in *Lectures 1795*, I, pp. 162–3.

61 Coleridge to Robert Southey, 21 Oct 1794, in Coleridge, *Collected Letters*, I, p. 112; Coleridge to Robert Southey, 29 Dec 1794, in Coleridge, *Collected Letters*, I, p. 145.

62 Coleridge, 'Lecture Three', *Six Lectures on Revealed Religion*, in *Lectures 1795*, I, p. 164.

63 Southey to Horace Walpole Bedford, 3 Sept 1794, in Southey, *Collected Letters*.

9: The New Philosophy of Air

1 Cited in Stansfield, *Thomas Beddoes*, p. 122.

2 Cited in Stansfield, *Thomas Beddoes*, p. 122.

3 Cited in Stansfield, *Thomas Beddoes*, p. 123.

4 Cited in Stansfield, *Thomas Beddoes*, p. 122.

5 Beddoes to Davies Giddy, CRO, DG41/53, 7–12 Jan 1793.

6 Beddoes, *Isaac Jenkins*, p. 33.

7 Beddoes to Davies Giddy, CRO, DG42/30, 14 March 1795; Beddoes, *Isaac Jenkins*, pp. iii–v.

8 Roy Porter, *Doctor of Society*, p. 158; Andrew Eil, 'Disdain: The Root of Our Diseased Politics', *Observer*, 5 March 2016 http://observer.com/2016/05/disdain-the-root-of-our-diseased-politics/.

9 Beddoes, *Isaac Jenkins*, p. vi.

10 Cited in Robert Darnton, *Mesmerism and the End of the Enlightenment in France* (Cambridge, Mass.: Harvard University Press, 1968), p. 112.

11 Cited in Stansfield, *Thomas Beddoes*, p. 33.

12 Stansfield, *Thomas Beddoes*, p. 34.

13 Stock, *Memoirs*, pp. 10–11.

14 Beddoes to Davies Giddy, CRO, DG41/4, 29 Oct 1793; Thomas Beddoes, cited in Jay, *Atmosphere*, p. 28.

15 Stansfield, *Thomas Beddoes*, pp. 99; Jay, *Atmosphere*, p. 80; Beddoes to Davies Giddy, CRO, DG41/7, 3 July 1793.

16 Cited in Stock, *Memoirs*, p. 94.

17 Cited in Stock, *Memoirs*, pp. 93–4.

18 Jay, *Atmosphere*, p. 101; Stock, *Memoirs*, pp. 109–10.

19 William Cullen, cited by Christopher Lawrence, 'Brown, John (*bap.* 1735, d. 1788)', *Oxford Dictionary of National Biography*, Oxford University Press, 2004, www.oxforddnb.com/view/article/3623 (accessed 1 July 2016).

20 Thomas Beddoes, 'Observations on the Character and Writings of John Brown, MD', pp. xlii–clxii, in John Brown, *The Elements of Medicine of John Brown*, trans. Thomas Beddoes, 2 vols (London: J. Johnson, 1795), I, p. lxv.

21 Christopher Lawrence, 'Brown, John (bap. 1735, d. 1788)', *Oxford Dictionary of National Biography*, Oxford University Press, 2004, www.oxforddnb.com/view/article/3623 (accessed 1 July 2016).

22 Cited in Stansfield, *Thomas Beddoes*, p. 23.

23 Cited in Stansfield, *Thomas Beddoes*, p. 24.

24 Cited in Stansfield, *Thomas Beddoes*, p. 25.

25 Carle Vernet, 'A Fierce Battle Between the Supporters of John Brown (Bruno), Opposed to Blood-letting, and Those of F. J. V. Broussais, in Favour of Blood-letting', Wellcome Library, London, no. 24101i.

26 William Buchan, *Domestic Medicine: Or, a Treatise on the Prevention and Cure of Diseases by Regimen and Simple Medicines. With an Appendix Containing a Dispensatory for the Use of Private Practitioners. The Eleventh Edition* (London: A. Strahan, T. Cadell, J. Balfour, W. Creech, 1790), p. III.

27 Rosenwein, 'Worrying About Emotions', 833–4.

28 Herman Boerhaave, cited in Rina Knoeff, *Herman Boerhaave (1668–1738): Calvinist Chemist and Physician* (Amsterdam: Royal Netherlands Academy of Arts and Sciences, 2002), p. 169; pp. 170–72.

29 William Cullen, cited in G. A. Lindeboom, *Boerhaave and Great Britain: Three Lectures on Boerhaave with Particular Reference to his Relations with Great Britain* (Leiden: E. J. Brill, 1974), p. 19.

30 Beddoes, 'Character and Writings of John Brown, MD', I, pp. clxi–xii.

31 Beddoes, 'Character and Writings of John Brown, MD', I, p. clxi; cited in Christopher Lawrence, 'Cullen, Brown and the Poverty of Essentialism', pp. 1–21, in W. F. Bynum and Roy Porter, eds, *Brunonianism in Britain and Europe*, Supplement No. 8 to *Medical History* (London: Wellcome Institute, 1988), p. 10.

32 Beddoes, 'Character and Writings of John Brown, MD', I, pp. clxi–xii.

33 Beddoes, 'Character and Writings of John Brown, MD', I, p. cxxix.

34 Beddoes, 'Character and Writings of John Brown, MD', I, p. cxxix–cxxx.

35 Beddoes, 'Character and Writings of John Brown, MD', I, pp. clv.

36 John Brown, *Elements of Medicine*, I, p. 28–9; Beddoes, 'Character and Writings of John Brown, MD', I, p. clv.

37 Beddoes, 'Character and Writings of John Brown, MD', I, p. cxxxix; John Brown, *Elements of Medicine*, I, p. 29.

38 J. L. Williams, *The Boy's Own Book: A Compendium of All the Sports and Recreations of Youth* (Paris: Baudry's European Library, 1843), p. 281.

39 Sextus Empiricus, *PH*, 2.70–2.159, in *The Stoics Reader*, trans. Brad Indood and Lloyd P. Gerson (Indianapolis: Hackett, 2008), 2.70–2.73; 2.83.

40 Darnton, *Mesmerism*, pp. 1–10.

41 Humphry Davy, *Researches Chemical and Philosophical, Chiefly Concerning Nitrous Oxide, or Dephlogisticated Nitrous Air, and its Respiration* (London: Joseph Johnson, 1800), p. 549.

42 Stansfield, *Thomas Beddoes*, p. 163.

43 McAlpin, *Female Sexuality*, p. 24; Thomas W. Laqueur, *Making Sex: Body and Gender from the Greeks to Freud* (Cambridge, Mass.: Harvard University Press, 1990), p. 149.

44 Ebenezer Sibly, *The Medical Mirror; or, Treatise on the Impregnation of the Human Female* (London: Sibly, [1795]), p. 42.

45 Sibly, *Medical Mirror*, pp. 15, 34, 55, 44.

46 Roy Porter, 'Sex and the Singular Man: The Seminal Ideas of James Graham', *Studies on Voltaire and the Eighteenth Century*, 228, (1984), 3–24 (9).

47 Roy Porter, 'The Sexual Politics of James Graham', *British Journal for Eighteenth-Century Studies* 5 (2), (1982), 199–206 (202).

48 Laqueur, *Making Sex*, p. 21.

49 James Graham, cited in Porter, 'Sexual Politics', 202; Sibly, *Medical Mirror*, p. 145.

50 Sibly, *Medical Mirror*, pp. 64–5.

51 Sibly, *Medical Mirror*, p. 125.

52 Thomas Beddoes, *Hygëia: or Essays Moral and Medical, on the Causes Affecting the Personal State of our Middling and Affluent Classes*, 3 vols (Bristol: J. Mills, 1802), II, p. 29.

53 James Graham, cited in Porter, 'Sexual Politics', 202; Sibly, *Medical Mirror*, p. 145.

54 M. D. T. De Bienville, *Nymphomania, or, a Dissertation Concerning the Furor Uterinus*, trans. Edward Sloane Wilmot (London: J. Bew, 1775), pp. 21, 72–4.

55 Gray, *Men Are from Mars*, p. 217.

56 Kenzaburo Oe, cited in Ian Buruma, 'Extremism: The Loser's Revenge, or Can Sexual Inadequacy or Deprivation Turn Angry Young Men into Killers?', *Guardian*, 25 Feb 2006, www.theguardian.com/world/2006/feb/25/terrorism.comment (accessed 3 July 2016).

57 Steven E. Landsburg, 'How the Web Prevents Rape', www.slate.com/articles/arts/everyday_economics/2006/10/how_the_web_prevents_rape.html (accessed 4 July 2016).

58 'Blue Balls', *Urban Dictionary*, www.urbandictionary.com/define.php?term=Blue%20Balls (accessed 3 July 2016).

59 Theodore Reik, cited in Hite, *Hite Report*, pp. 316–17.

60 Pepe Martinez, *The Consumer Mind: Brand Perception and the Implication for Marketers* (London and Philadelphia: Kogan Page, 2012), p. 56.

61 Mira Kirshenbaum, 'What is Emotional Energy?', *The Emotional Energy Factor: The Secrets High Energy People Use to Fight Fatigue* www.chestnuthillinstitute.com/books/eef/faqs.php (accessed 17 Aug 2016).

62 'Sen', 'Allowing the Release of Suppressed Energy', *Calm Down Mind*, 5 March 2012, www.calmdownmind.com/allowing-the-release-of-suppressed-energy/ (accessed 16 Aug 2016).

63 Todd Colberg, *Self Booked: Empty Bottles, Germs Burns and Bootneck Dreams* (Todd Colberg, 2012), p. 92.

64 'Man murdered "nagging wife"', *Liverpool Echo*, 31 May 2001, www.liverpoolecho.co.uk/news/liverpool-news/man-murdered-nagging-wife-3564270 (accessed 19 Aug 2016; *my emphasis*).

65 'Caroline Andrews Murder: Banker Husband Admits Killing Supply Teacher Wife and £267,000 Theft from Father-in-law with Dementia', 8 April 2016, *Mirror*, www.mirror.co.uk/news/uk-news/caroline-andrews-murder-banker-husband–7717587 (accessed 19 Aug 2016).

66 http://bossip.com/1306591/

snapped-georgia-man-fatally-shoots-five-before-setting-house-on-fire-after-learning-wife-wanted-a-divorce/ (accessed 19 Aug 2016).

67 'Man Gets Life Sentence in Murder', *Lincoln Journal Star*, 31 July 2005, http://journalstar.com/news/local/man-gets-life-sentence-in-murder/article_f8a75c8c–463d–58c2-a1e4-a67bef110bca.html (accessed 19 Aug 2016).

68 'Judges Accused of Anti-female Bias: Anger in Australia as Victims Blamed for Rapes', *Independent*, 19 May 1993, www.independent.co.uk/news/world/judges-accused-of-anti-female-bias-anger-in-australia-as-victims-blamed-for-rapes–2323987.html (accessed 19 Aug 2016).

69 Lawrence, *Empire*, p. xix.

70 www.punternet.com/index.php/reviews/104517-Review-of-Sally-of-Dudley?fs=2 (accessed 29 Sept 2016); latter two cited in Melissa Farley, Jacqueline M. Golding, Emily Shuckman Matthews, Neil M. Malaluth, and Laura Jarrett, 'Comparing Sex Buyers with Men Who Do Not Buy Sex: New Data on Prostitution and Trafficking', *Journal of Interpersonal Violence* (2015), 1–25 (13).

71 www.punternet.com/index.php/reviews/120610-Review-of-Divya-of-Ilford?fs=2 (accessed 29 Sept 2016).

72 www.punternet.com/index.php/reviews/107149-Review-of-Carolina-of-Central-London?fs=2 (accessed 29 Sept 2016).

73 Theresa A. Reed (aka Darklady), 'Private Acts vs Public Art: Where Prostitution Ends and Pornography Begins', pp. 249–57, in Jessica Spector, ed., *Prostitution and Pornography: Philosophical Debate about the Sex Industry* (Stanford: Stanford University Press, 2006), p. 256.

74 Maggie McNeill, 'Out of Control', *The Honest Courtesan*, 24 Sept 2010 maggiemcneill.wordpress.com/2010/09/24/out-of-control/ (accessed 2 Sept 2016).

75 There is a wealth of research into the socially constructed nature of female desire, and also its inhibition in response to unequal division of domestic labour. See, for example, Sinikka Elliott and Debra Umberson, 'The Performance of Desire: Gender and Sexual Negotiation in Long-Term Marriages', *Journal of Marriage and the Family*, 70:2, (May 2008), 391–406; Darlene L. Pina & Vern Bengtson, 'The Division of Household Labor and Wives' Happiness: Ideology, Employment and Perceptions of Support', *Journal of Marriage and the Family*, 55:4, (Nov 1993), 901–12; P. Voydanoff and B. W. Donnelly, 'The Intersection of Time in Activities and Perceived Unfairness in Relation to Psychological Distress and Marital Quality', *Journal of Marriage and the Family*, 61, (1999), 739–51. I am grateful to Jackie Scott for the links in this paragraph.

76 Catherine Hakim, 'The Male Sexual Deficit: A Social Fact of the 21st Century', *International Sociology* (2015), 1–22.

77 Martin Madan, *Thelyphthora; or, A Treatise on Female Ruin*, 2 vols (London: J. Dodsley, 1780), I, pp. viii, xvii, 52, 7.

78 William Cowper, *Anti-Thelyphthora: A Tale in Verse* (London: Joseph Johnson, 1781).

79 Frank Beach, 'Characteristics of Masculine "Sex Drive"', IV, pp. 1–32,

in *Nebraska Symposium on Motivation* (Lincoln: University of Nebraska Press, 1956).

80 Alfred Kinsey, cited in Hite, *Hite Report*, p. 318.

81 Emily Nagoski, *Come as You Are: The Surprising New Science That Will Transform Your Sex Life* (London: Scribe, 2015), pp. 230, 75.

82 Nagoski, p. 232.

83 Hite, *Hite Report*, p. 318.

84 Hite, *Hite Report*, pp. 316, 317.

85 Farley, et al., 'Comparing Sex Buyers', 13, 16.

86 Susan Aylwin, *Structure in Thought and Feeling* (London: Methuen, 1985), pp. 73–4.

10: Come Now, Ye Golden Times

1 Cited in [John Smith], *Assassination of the King! The Conspirators Exposed, or an Account of The Apprehension, Treatment in Prison, and Repeated Examinations Before the Privy Council, of John Smith and George Higgins, on a Charge of High Treason* (London: John Smith, 1795), p. 71.

2 Cited in [Smith], *Assassination*, pp. 70–71.

3 Cited in [Smith], *Assassination*, pp. 71–3.

4 Joseph Gurney, *The Trial of Robert Thomas Crosfeild, for High Treason, at the Sessions House in the Old Bailey, on Wednesday the Eleventh, and Thursday the Twelfth of May, 1796* (London: Martha Gurney, 1796), p. 26; [Smith], *Assassination*, p. 52; Gurney, *Trial*, p. 7.

5 Bernard Porter, *Plots and Paranoia: A History of Political Espionage in Britain 1790–1988* (London and New York: Routledge, 1989; 1992), p. 30.

6 William Wickham, Letter to Portland, in Pelham Papers, BL, Add. MS 33107, fol. 3, 3 Jan 1801.

7 A. H. Millar, 'Palmer, Thomas Fyshe (1747–1802)', rev. G. M. Ditchfield, *Oxford Dictionary of National Biography*, Oxford University Press, 2004; online edition, Jan 2008, www.oxforddnb.com/view/article/21220 (accessed 11 Dec 2016).

8 H. T. Dickinson, 'Muir, Thomas (1765–1799)', *Oxford Dictionary of National Biography*, Oxford University Press, 2004; online edition, Sept 2010, www.oxforddnb.com/view/article/19498 (accessed 12 Dec 2016).

9 *An Account of the Proceedings of the British Convention, Held in Edinburgh, the 19th of November, 1793* (London: D. Eaton, [1793]).

10 Godwin to Joseph Gerrald, 23 Jan 1794, in Godwin, *Letters*, pp. 90–91.

11 Godwin to Editor of the *Morning Chronicle*, 3 March 1794, in Godwin, *Letters*, p. 98.

12 Cited in Bob Harris, *The Scottish People and the French Revolution* (London: Routledge, 2015), p. 58.

13 See John Barrell, *Imagining the King's Death: Figurative Treason, Fantasies of Regicide 1793–1796* (Oxford: Oxford University Press, 2000).

14 Clive Emsley, 'The Pop-Gun Plot, 1794', pp. 56–68, in Michael T. David, ed., *Radicalism and Revolution in Britain, 1775–1848: Essays in Honour of Malcolm I. Thomis* (Basingstoke: Macmillan, 2000), p. 67.

15 William Godwin, *Cursory Strictures on the Charge Delivered by Lord Chief Justice Eyre to the Grand Jury, October 2, 1794. First Published in the Morning Chronicle October 21* (London: C. and G. Kearsley, 1794).

16 For the history of the 1794 Treason Trials, see John Barrell and Jon Mee, eds., *Trials for Treason and Sedition, 1792–1794*, 8 vols (London: Pickering and Chatto, 2006–7); Barrell, *Imagining*; Marilyn Butler, *Romantics, Rebels and Reactionaries* (Oxford: Oxford University Press, 1981); Clive Emsley, '"An Aspect of Pitt's Terror": Prosecutions for Sedition during the 1790s', *Social History*, 6:2 (1981), 155–84; Goodwin, *Friends of Liberty*, pp. 307–58; E. P. Thompson, *The Making of the English Working Class* (London: Penguin, 1991; first published London: Victor Gollancz, 1963), pp. 135–50; Alan Wharam, *The Treason Trials, 1794* (Leicester: Leicester University Press, 1992).

17 'Extract of a Letter from Sheffield', *Morning Chronicle*, 27 Dec 1794, issue 7865.

18 Thomas Holcroft, *A Narrative of the Facts Relating to a Prosecution for High Treason* (1795), p. 87.

19 [Smith], *Assassination*, pp. 7, 26.

20 Cited in A. D. Morris, *James Parkinson: His Life and Times* (Boston: Birkhauser, 1989), p. 44.

21 Gurney, *Trial*, p. 193; Mary Thale, *Selections from the Papers of the London Corresponding Society 1792–1799* (Cambridge: Cambridge University Press, 1983), p. 221.

22 Thale, *Selections*, p. 221.

23 [Smith], *Assassination*, p. 68.

24 [Smith], *Assassination*, p. 27.

25 Gurney, *Trial*, p. 64.

26 R. T. Crosfeild, MD., *Remarks on the Scurvy as it Appeared Among the English Prisoners in France in the Year 1795; with an Account of the Effects of Opium in that Disease, and of the Methods Proper to Render Its Use More Extensive and Easy; (Written During His Confinement in the Tower)* (London: J. Ridgway, 1797), pp. iii–iv.

27 Gurney, *Trial*, pp. 110–14.

28 Morris, *James Parkinson*, p. 44.

29 Emsley, 'Pop-Gun Plot, 1794', p. 61; cf. also Francis Place, *The Autobiography of Francis Place*, ed. Mary Thale (London: Cambridge University Press, 1972).

30 Paine, *Rights of Man* (1791), p. 110.

31 Fox, cited in *Morning Chronicle*, 1 Jan 1795, issue 7868.

32 *Morning Chronicle*, 24 Jan 1795, issue 7888.

33 Cited in *Morning Chronicle*, 26 Jan 1795, issue 7889.

34 Wordsworth, *Prelude* (1805), X, ll. 539–44, 550–2, 556.

35 Trevor H. Levere, 'Dr Beddoes and the Establishment of his Pneumatic Institute: A Tale of Three Presidents', *Notes and Records of the Royal Society of London*, 32:1, (July 1977), 43.

36 Thomas Beddoes, *Considerations on the Medicinal Use and Production of Factitious Airs* (Bristol: Joseph Johnson, 1794), p. 3.

37 Beddoes, cited in Stock, *Memoirs*, p. 104.

38 Wedgwood, cited in Litchfield, *Tom Wedgwood*, p. 35.

39 See Robin Reilly, 'Josiah Wedgwood'.

40 Cited in Barbara Wedgwood, *Wedgwood Circle*, p. 107.

41 Cited in Litchfield, *Tom Wedgwood*, p. 45.

42 Beddoes to Davies Giddy, CRO, DG42/4, Jan or Feb 1795; Levere, 'Dr Thomas Beddoes (1750–1808)', 196.

43 James Watt, in Beddoes, *Considerations*, Part 2, p. 2.

44 Beddoes, cited in Stock, *Memoirs*, p. 105.

45 Beddoes to Davies Giddy, CRO, DG42/36, 12 Feb 1795.

46 Beddoes to Thomas Hardy, enclosed in letter to Davies Giddy, CRO, DG42/4, Jan or Feb 1795.

47 Wollstonecraft to Archibald Hamilton Rowan, April 1795, in Wollstonecraft, *Collected Letters*, p. 287.

48 Wollstonecraft, *Posthumous Works*, III, p. 53.

49 Wollstonecraft to Archibald Hamilton Rowan, April 1795, in Wollstonecraft, *Collected Letters*, p. 287 (fn.).

50 Wollstonecraft, *Posthumous Works*, III, p. 30.

51 Wollstonecraft, *Posthumous Works*, III, p. 61.

52 Wollstonecraft, *Posthumous Works*, III, pp. 78–9.

53 Wollstonecraft, *Posthumous Works*, III, p. 75.

54 Cited in Clarke Garrett, *Respectable Folly: Millenarians and the French Revolution in France and England* (Baltimore and London: John Hopkins University Press, 1975), p. 175.

55 Robert Southey, *Letters from England* (London: Cresset Press, 1951; first published 1807), p. 417.

56 Emanuel Swedenborg, *The Delights of Wisdom Pertaining to Conjugial Love*, trans. Samuel M. Warren (West Chester, Pennsylvania: Swedenborg Foundation, 2009), p. 142 (§113).

57 Marsha Keith Schuchard, 'Rediscovering William "Hurricane" Gilbert: A Lost Voice of Revolution and Madness in the Worlds of Blake and the Romantics', *BARS Conference: Romantic Revelations*, July 1999.

58 Robert Rix, 'Carl Bernhard Wadström (1749–1799)', www.brycchancarey.com/abolition/wadstrom.htm (accessed 16 Dec 2016); Robert Rix, *William Blake and the Cultures of Radical Christianity* (London: Routledge, 2007), chapter 5.

59 Swedenborg, *Delights of Wisdom*, p. 379 (§332).

60 [August Nordenskjöld & Carl Wadström], *Plan for a Free Community Upon the Coast of Africa, Under the Protection of Great Britain; but Intirely Independent of All European Laws and Governments. With an Invitation, Under Certain Conditions, to All Persons Desirous of Partaking the Benefits Thereof* (London: Hindmarsh, 24 June 1789), pp. v–vi.

61 Southey to Joseph Cottle, 26 Feb 1836, in Southey, *New Letters*, II, p. 442; Southey to Richard Duppa, [12 July 1795], in Southey, *Collected Letters*.

62 William Bryan, *A Testimony of the Spirit of Truth, Concerning Richard Brothers* (London: J. Wright, 1795), p. 20.

63   Abbé Barruel, *Memoirs Illustrating the History of Jacobinism*, 4 vols
     (London: T. Burton, 1797), IV, p. 347.
64   Barruel, *Memoirs*, IV, pp. 143–4 (fn.), 347; I, p. xiv.
65   Bryan, *Testimony*, p. 20.
66   Bryan, *Testimony*, p. 23.
67   Southey, *Letters from England*, pp. 420–21.
68   John Wright, *A Revealed Knowledge of Some Things That Will Speedily be
     Fulfilled in the World* (London: 1794), p. 19.
69   Cited in Garrett, *Respectable Folly*, p. 177.
70   Oliver Burkeman, *The Antidote: Happiness for People Who Can't Stand
     Positive Thinking* (Edinburgh: Canongate, 2012), p. 131.
71   Cited in Garrett, *Respectable Folly*, p. 196.
72   Cited in Garrett, *Respectable Folly*, p. 175.
73   Richard Brothers, *Revealed Knowledge of the Prophecies and Times*, 2 vols
     (London: 1794), II, pp. 66–7.
74   Cited in Garrett, *Respectable Folly*, p. 196.
75   Garrett, *Respectable Folly*, p. 126.
76   Garrett, *Respectable Folly*, p. 161.
77   Southey to Grosvenor Bedford, 22 Nov 1794, in Southey, *Collected Letters*;
     Southey to Grosvenor Bedford, 7 June 1794, in Southey, *Collected Letters*.
78   Jon Mee, *Romanticism, Enthusiasm and Regulation: Poetics and the Policing
     of Culture in the Romantic Period* (Oxford: Oxford University Press, 2003),
     pp. 3, 5, 10.
79   Cited in Mee, *Romanticism*, p. 84.
80   Wright, *Revealed Knowledge*, pp. 27–31.
81   Bryan, *Testimony*, pp. 8–9, 14.
82   Thomas Barker, cited in John Kington, 'The Severe Winter of 1794/1795
     in England', *Weather*, 49:12, (1994), 419–20.

11: Falling into the Common Lot of Humanity

1   G. M. Woodward and Isaac Cruikshank, *A Long String of Resolutions for
     a New Year* (London: S. W. Fores, 1792); images are reproduced in Emily
     Brand, 'Some Familiar C18th New Year's Resolutions', historyofloveblog.
     wordpress.com/2013/12/31/some-familiar-c18th-new-years-resolutions/
     (accessed 21 March 2017).
2   Cited in Garrett, *Respectable Folly*, p. 178.
3   Brothers, *Revealed Knowledge*, I, p. 180.
4   Cited in Garrett, *Respectable Folly*, pp. 203–7.
5   Leon Festinger, Henry W. Riecken, Stanley Schachter, *When Prophecy
     Fails* (London: Pinter & Martin, 2013; first published 1956), pp. 32–3, 167.
6   Festinger, et al., *When Prophecy Fails*, pp. 209–10.
7   Festinger, et al., *When Prophecy Fails*, pp. 32–3.
8   Festinger, et al., *When Prophecy Fails* , pp. 210–17, 30.
9   Southey to Tom Southey, 19 Oct 1794, in Southey, *Collected Letters*.
10   Coleridge to Robert Southey, 21 Oct 1794, in Coleridge, *Collected Letters*,
     I, p. 114.

11 Southey to Grosvenor Bedford, 3 Dec 1794, in Southey, *Collected Letters*;
   Southey to Tom Southey, 5 Jan 1795, in Southey, *Collected Letters*.

12 Coleridge to Robert Southey, 9 Dec 1794, in Coleridge, *Collected Letters*, I,
   p. 132.

13 Coleridge to Robert Southey, 19 January 1795, in Coleridge, *Collected
   Letters*, I, p. 150; Coleridge to Robert Southey, 23 Oct 1794, in Coleridge,
   Collected Letters, I, p. 120.

14 Coleridge to Robert Southey, 19 Jan 1795, in Coleridge, *Collected Letters*, I,
   p. 150.

15 Coleridge to Robert Southey, 13 Nov 1795, in Coleridge, *Collected Letters*,
   p. 165.

16 Southey to Tom Southey, 31 Dec 1794, in Southey, *Collected Letters*.

17 Coleridge to Robert Southey, 19 Jan 1795, in Coleridge, *Collected Letters*, I,
   p. 150.

18 Coleridge to Robert Southey, [3 Nov 1794], in Coleridge, *Collected Letters*,
   I, p. 123.

19 Coleridge to Robert Southey, 9 Dec 1794, in Coleridge, *Collected Letters*, I,
   p. 132.

20 Coleridge to Robert Southey, 29 Dec 1794, in Coleridge, *Collected Letters*,
   I, p. 145.

21 Coleridge to George Dyer, late Feb 1795, in Coleridge, *Collected Letters*, I,
   p. 151.

22 Coleridge, 'Sonnet (Thou gentle Look)', in *Samuel Taylor Coleridge: The
   Complete Poems*, ed. William Keach (London: Penguin, 1997).

23 Coleridge to Robert Southey, 29 Dec 1794, in Coleridge, *Collected Letters*,
   I, p. 146.

24 Coleridge to Robert Southey, 2 Jan 1795, in Coleridge, *Collected Letters*, I,
   p. 148.

25 Southey to Sara Fricker, 9 Jan 1795, in Southey, *Collected Letters*.

26 Coleridge to Robert Southey, [mid-Jan 1795], in Coleridge, *Collected
   Letters*, I, p. 149.

27 Robert Southey, cited in Coleridge, *Collected Letters*, I, p. 149.

28 Southey to Grosvenor Bedford, 8–9 Feb 1795, in Southey, *Collected Letters*.

29 Southey to Grosvenor Bedford, 8–9 Feb 1795, in Southey, *Collected Letters*.

30 Coleridge, *Collected Letters*, I, p. 161 (fn. 2), cited in Nicola Trott,
   'Coleridge's City', *Coleridge Bulletin*, New Series 19 (2002), 41–57.

31 'Obituary: Mr. Thelwall', *Gentleman's Magazine*, 156 (1831), 549–50.

32 'Q', *Monthly Magazine*, 48, (1819), 203; cited in Lewis Patton and Peter
   Mann, 'Editors' Introduction', in Coleridge, *Lectures 1795*, p. 27.

33 Coleridge to Sir George and Lady Beaumont, 1 Oct 1803, in Coleridge,
   Collected Letters, II, p. 1001; Charlotte Poole, cited in Sandford, *Thomas
   Poole*, I, p. 124.

34 Cited in Henry Crabb Robinson, *Henry Crabb Robinson on Books and their
   Writers*, ed. Edith J. Morley, 3 vols (London: J. M. Dent & Sons, 1938), I,
   p. 59.

35 Coleridge, 'A Moral and Political Lecture', in Coleridge, *Lectures 1795*, I,
   pp. 5–19.

36 Coleridge, *Conciones ad Populum*, in Coleridge, *Lectures 1795*, I, p. 51.

37 Coleridge, *Conciones ad Populum*, in Coleridge, *Lectures 1795*, I, p. 70.

38 Coleridge, *Conciones ad Populum*, in Coleridge, *Lectures 1795*, I, pp. 12, 46.

39 Coleridge, *Conciones ad Populum*, in Coleridge, *Lectures 1795*, I, pp. 46, 12, 35.

40 Coleridge, *Conciones ad Populum*, in Coleridge, *Lectures 1795*, I, pp. 46, 62.

41 Southey, cited in Coleridge, *Lectures 1795*, I, p. 34.

42 Cottle, *Recollections*, I, pp. 41–2.

43 Robert Southey, Bodleian MSS. Eng. Letters, c. 22, f. 80, November 1793.

44 Edmund Seward, cited in Christopher J. P. Smith, *A Quest for Home: Reading Robert Southey* (Liverpool: Liverpool University Press, 1997), p. 73.

45 Southey to Grosvenor Bedford, 14 June 1795, in Southey, *Collected Letters*.

46 Southey to Grosvenor Bedford, c. 22 Aug 1795, in Southey, *Collected Letters*.

47 Coleridge to Robert Southey, [early Aug 1795], in Coleridge, *Collected Letters*, I, p. 158.

48 Coleridge to Robert Southey, early Aug 1795, in Coleridge, *Collected Letters*, I, p. 158.

49 Coleridge to Joseph Cottle, 22 Aug 1795, in Coleridge, *Collected Letters*, I, p. 159.

50 Coleridge to Thomas Poole, 7 Oct 1795, in Coleridge, *Collected Letters*, I, p. 160.

51 Cottle, *Recollections*, I, pp. 147–8.

52 Coleridge to Robert Southey, 13 Nov 1795, in Coleridge, *Collected Letters*, I, p. 164.

53 Coleridge to Robert Southey, 13 Nov 1795, in Coleridge, *Collected Letters*, I, p. 166.

54 Coleridge to Robert Southey, 13 Nov 1795, in Coleridge, *Collected Letters*, I, pp. 163–73.

55 Adam Phillips, *Missing Out: In Praise of the Unlived Life* (London: Hamish Hamilton, 2012), p. 4.

56 Southey to Grosvenor Bedford, 17 Nov 1795, in Southey, *Collected Letters*.

57 Southey to Grosvenor Bedford, 8–9 Feb 1795, in Southey, *Collected Letters*.

58 Martha C. Nussbaum, *Upheavals of Thought: The Intelligence of Emotions* (New York: Cambridge University Press, 2001), p. 45.

59 Southey to Grosvenor Bedford, 1–10 Oct 1795, in Southey, *Collected Letters*.

12: Awaking in Fetters

1 Wollstonecraft, *Posthumous Works*, III, pp. 115–16.

2 Godwin, *Memoirs*, p. 127.

3 Wollstonecraft to Eliza Wollstonecraft, 23 April 1795, in Wollstonecraft, *Collected Letters*, p. 290.

4 Godwin, *Memoirs*, p. 128.

5 Wollstonecraft to Eliza Wollstonecraft, 23 April 1795, in Wollstonecraft, *Collected Letters*, p. 290.

6 Cited in Wollstonecraft, *Collected Letters*, p. 291 (fn.).

7 Wollstonecraft, *Posthumous Works*, III, p. 124.

8 Wollstonecraft, *Posthumous Works*, III, p. 127.

9 Leonore Davidoff and Catherine Hall, *Family Fortunes: Men and Women of the English Middle Class, 1780–1850* (London: Hutchinson 1987), p. 18.

10 Davidoff and Hall, *Family Fortunes*, p. 19.

11 James Gillray, *Tiddy-doll, the Great French-Gingerbread-Baker, Drawing out a New Batch of Kings*, etching with hand colouring, 1806 (Fitzwilliam Museum, Cambridge).

12 Davidoff and Hall, *Family Fortunes*, p. 399.

13 Cited in Davidoff and Hall, *Family Fortunes*, p. 114.

14 Cited in Davidoff and Hall, *Family Fortunes*, p. 18.

15 Davidoff and Hall, *Family Fortunes*, pp. 17–18.

16 Wollstonecraft, *Posthumous Works*, III, pp. 130–131.

17 Todd, *Wollstonecraft*, pp. 286–7.

18 Godwin, *Memoirs*, p. 74.

19 Todd, *Wollstonecraft*, pp. 303–50.

20 Wollstonecraft, *Letters Written During a Short Residence*, p. 5.

21 Wollstonecraft, *Letters Written During a Short Residence*, pp. 8–9.

22 Wollstonecraft, *Letters Written During a Short Residence*, p. 10.

23 Wollstonecraft, *Letters Written During a Short Residence*, pp. 11–12.

24 Wollstonecraft, *Letters Written During a Short Residence*, p. 39.

25 Wollstonecraft, *Letters Written During a Short Residence*, p. 50.

26 Wollstonecraft, *Letters Written During a Short Residence*, p. 163.

27 Wollstonecraft, *Letters Written During a Short Residence*, pp. 57–8.

28 Wollstonecraft, *Letters Written During a Short Residence*, p. 36.

29 Wollstonecraft, *Letters Written During a Short Residence*, p. 73.

30 Wollstonecraft, *Letters Written During a Short Residence*, p. 118.

31 Mary Wollstonecraft, cited Todd, *Wollstonecraft*, p. 349.

32 Godwin *Memoirs*, 135.

33 Wollstonecraft, *Posthumous Works*, IV, p. 7; Godwin, *Memoirs*, p. 136.

34 Wollstonecraft, *Posthumous Works*, IV, pp. 10–11.

35 The estimated numbers at the meeting of 26 October 1795 vary. Susan Manly estimates between 100,000 and 150,000, in *Language, Custom and Nation in the 1790s: Locke, Tooke, Wordsworth, Edgeworth* (Aldershot: Ashgate, 2007), p. 66. For the topography of the meeting, see Samuel Lewis, *The History and Topography of the Parish of Saint Mary, Islington* (London: J. H. Jackson, 1842), p. 41.

36 Cited in Roe, *Wordsworth and Coleridge*, p. 146.

37 Mee, *Romanticism*, p. 103.

38 Cited in Levere, 'Dr. Thomas Beddoes (1750–1808)', 194.

39 Cited in Levere, 'Dr. Thomas Beddoes (1750–1808)', 199; see also Jay, *Atmosphere*, pp. 122–4.

40 Beddoes to Davies Giddy, CRO, DG42/30, 14 March 1795.

41 Cited in Levere, 'Dr. Thomas Beddoes (1750–1808)', 200.

42 Cited in Roe, *Wordsworth and Coleridge*, p. 148; Thompson, *Making of the English Working Class*, p. 158; *The Times*, 30 Oct 1795.

43 *Parliamentary Register: or History of the Proceedings and Debates of the House of Commons* (London: J. Debrett, 1796), 43, pp. 243–4.

44 Thomas Beddoes, *A Word in Defence of the Bill of Rights, Against Gagging Bills* (Bristol: N. Biggs, 1795), p. 4.

45 Beddoes, *Word in Defence*, p. 4.

46 Beddoes, *Word in Defence*, p. 3.

47 Coleridge, *Conciones ad Populum*, in Coleridge, *Lectures 1795*, p. 57.

48 Adam Sisman, *Wordsworth and Coleridge: The Friendship* (London: Harper Perennial, 2007), p. 129.

49 Cited in Stansfield, *Thomas Beddoes*, p. 129; Azariah Pinney to Wordsworth, 26 Nov 1795, cited in Patton and Mann, 'Editors' Introduction', in Coleridge, *Lectures 1795*, p. xlvi (citing Pinney Papers, in Bristol University Library).

50 *Felix Farley's Bristol Journal*, 1793; cited in Leonard Smith, 'A Gentleman's Mad Doctor in Georgian England: Edward Long Fox and Brislington House', *History of Psychiatry*, 19, (June 2008), 163–84 (168).

51 Patton and Mann, 'Editors' Introduction', in Coleridge, *Lectures 1795*, p. xlvi.

52 Patton and Mann, 'Editors' Introduction', in Coleridge, *Lectures 1795*, p. xlvi. Patton and Mann argue that the true target of A. W.'s *Letter* was Beddoes, not Fox.

53 Coleridge, *Lectures 1795*, p. 331.

54 Coleridge, *Lectures 1795*, pp. 331–2.

55 Cited in John Bugg, *Five Long Winters: The Trials of British Romanticism* (Stanford: Stanford University Press, 2014), p. 33.

56 Bugg, *Five Long Winters*, p. 33.

57 Cited in Nicholas Roe, 'Coleridge and John Thelwall: The Road to Nether Stowey', pp. 62–80, in *The Coleridge Connection: Essays for Thomas McFarland*, ed. Richard Gravil and Molly Lefebure (London: Macmillan, 1990) p. 68.

58 Cited in Patton and Mann, 'Editor's Introduction', in Coleridge, *Lectures 1795*, p. l.

59 *Remarks on the Declaration of the Whig Club, on the 23d of January, 1796, in a Postscript to the Second Edition of a Satire, Entitled, The Political Dramatist of the House of Commons, in 1795* (London: J. Parsons, 1796), pp. 7–8.

60 *Remarks on the Declaration of the Whig Club*, p. 13.

61 Betty T. Bennett, *British War Poetry in the Age of Romanticism, 1793–1815*, ed. Orianne Smith, www.rc.umd.edu/editions/warpoetry/intro.html (accessed 22 March 2017).

62 Nicholas Roe, 'Coleridge's Watchman Tour', *Coleridge Bulletin*, 21, (2003) 35–46.

63 Cited in Roe, 'Coleridge's Watchman Tour', 37.

64 Cited in Roe, 'Coleridge's Watchman Tour', 38–40.

65 Stansfield, *Thomas Beddoes*, p. 132; Stuart Andrews, *The British Periodical Press and the French Revolution, 1789–99* (London: Palgrave Macmillan, 2000), pp. 56–68.

66 Cited in Stansfield, *Thomas Beddoes*, p. 141.

67 Cited in Roe, 'Coleridge's Watchman Tour', 43.
68 Jennie Batchelor, '"To Cherish *Female* Ingenuity and to Conduce to *Female* Improvement": The *Lady's Magazine* and the Birth of the Women's Magazine', Centre for Eighteenth Century Studies Research Seminars, University of York, 18 Oct 2016.
69 Cited in Roe, 'Coleridge's Watchman Tour', 43–4.
70 Cf Deirdre Coleman, 'The Journalist', in *Cambridge Companion to Samuel Taylor Coleridge*, ed. Lucy Newlyn (Cambridge: Cambridge University Press, 2002), pp. 126–41.
71 Cited in Roe, 'Coleridge and John Thelwall', pp. 69–70.
72 Coleridge to George Coleridge, 6 Nov 1794, in Coleridge, *Collected Letters*, I, pp. 125–6.

13: Revolutions by Mourning and Accommodation

1   Cited in Todd, *Wollstonecraft*, p. 356.
2   Wollstonecraft, *Posthumous Works*, IV, p. 14.
3   Wollstonecraft, *Posthumous Works*, IV, p. 25.
4   Wollstonecraft to Mary Hays, April–May 1796, in Wollstonecraft, *Collected Letters*, p. 340. This letter is a speculative reconstruction. Wollstonecraft to Henry Fuseli, Monday Morning, late 1795, in Wollstonecraft, *Collected Letters*, p. 336.
5   Wollstonecraft to Archibald Hamilton Rowan, 26 Jan 1796, in Wollstonecraft, *Collected Letters*, p. 338.
6   D. W. Winnicott, *Playing and Reality* (London: Routledge, 2008; first published London: Tavistock Publications, 1971).
7   Heinz Kohut, *The Analysis of the Self: A Systematic Approach to the Psychoanalytic Treatment of Narcissistic Personality Disorders* (Chicago and London: University of Chicago Press, 2009; first published 1971), p. 64; cited in Donald Carveth, 'Is There a Future in Disillusion? Constructionist and Deconstructionist Approaches in Psychoanalysis', *Journal of American Academy of Psychoanalysis*, 27: 2, (1999), 325–58.
8   Bowlby, *Attachment and Loss* trilogy, I, pp. 152, 40.
9   Melanie Klein, 'Mourning and its Relation to Manic-Depressive States' (1940), pp. 344–69, in *Love, Guilt and Reparation; and Other Works 1921–1945* (New York: Free Press, 1975), p. 359.
10 Cited in Todd, *Wollstonecraft*, p. 375.
11 Godwin to Mary Hays, 2 Feb 1796, in Godwin, *Letters*, I, p. 155.
12 Wollstonecraft to Mary Hays, 1796, in Wollstonecraft, *Collected Letters*, p. 344.
13 Godwin to Mary Hays, 5 Jan 1796, in Godwin, *Letters*, I, p. 145.
14 Mary Wollstonecraft, *Mary, A Fiction and The Wrongs of Woman, or Maria*, ed. Michelle Faubert (London: Broadview, 2012), p. 180.
15 Godwin, *Memoirs*, p. 133.
16 Godwin, *Political Justice* (1793), p. 319; cited in Mark Philp, *Godwin's Political Justice* (London: Duckworth, 1986), p. 31.
17 Philp, *Godwin's* Political Justice, pp. 202–25.

18 Cited in Philp, *Godwin's* Political Justice, p. 198.
19 Paine, *Rights of Man* (1791), p. 197.
20 Godwin to Thomas Wedgwood, 5 Nov 1795, in Godwin, *Letters*, I, p. 130.
21 Cited in Litchfield, *Tom Wedgwood*, pp. 29–30.
22 Cited in Litchfield, *Tom Wedgwood*, pp. 30–31.
23 Godwin, *Memoirs*, p. 154.
24 Godwin, *Memoirs*, p. 155.
25 Wollstonecraft to William Godwin, 4 Sept 1796, in Wollstonecraft, *Collected Letters*, p. 358.
26 Godwin, *Memoirs*, p. 156.
27 Godwin, *Memoirs*, p. 158.
28 Wollstonecraft to William Godwin, 1 July 1796, in Wollstonecraft, *Collected Letters*, pp. 342–3.
29 Godwin to Mary Wollstonecraft, 13 July 1796, in Godwin, *Letters*, I, p. 171.
30 Cited in Philp, *Godwin's* Political Justice, p. 176.
31 Godwin to Mary Wollstonecraft, 17 Aug 1796, in Godwin, *Letters*, I, p. 173.
32 Wedgwood, *Value of a Maimed Life*, p. 56.
33 Wedgwood, *Value of a Maimed Life*, p. 44.
34 Wedgwood, *Value of a Maimed Life*, pp. 78–80.
35 Wedgwood, *Value of a Maimed Life*, p. 86.
36 Wedgwood, *Value of a Maimed Life*, pp. 51–2.
37 Hartley, *Observations*, pp. 35, 38, 41.
38 David V. Erdman, 'Coleridge, Wordsworth and the Wedgwood Fund', *Bulletin of the New York Public Library*, 60:9, (1956), 425–43; 487–507 (488).
39 Godwin, *Political Justice*, p. 351.
40 Godwin, *Political Justice*, pp. 352, 340.
41 Cited in Peter H. Marshall, *William Godwin* (New Haven and London: Yale University Press, 1984), p. 130.
42 Godwin to Thomas Wedgwood, 30 Jan 1797, in Godwin, *Letters*, I, p. 192.
43 David Hume, *A Treatise of Human Nature*, ed. Ernest C. Mossner (London: Penguin, 1985; first published 1739–40), p. 168.
44 Godwin to Thomas Wedgwood, 28 Feb 1797, in Godwin, *Letters*, I, p. 194.
45 Wollstonecraft, *Thoughts*, pp. 15, 55.
46 Cited in Erdman, 'Coleridge, Wordsworth and the Wedgwood Fund', 429.
47 Godwin to Thomas Wedgwood, 19 April 1797, in Godwin, *Letters*, I. p. 200.
48 Godwin to Thomas Wedgwood, 19 April 1797, in Godwin, *Letters*, I. p. 200.
49 Cited in Todd, *Wollstonecraft*, p. 405.
50 Godwin, *Memoirs*, p. 162.
51 Godwin to Thomas Wedgwood, 19 April 1797, in Godwin, *Letters*, I. pp. 199–200.
52 Godwin [addressee unknown], 3 May 1797, in Godwin, *Letters*, I, p. 205.
53 William Godwin, 'Holograph Proof Revisions of Political Justice', Vol. I, New York Public Library, Pforzheimer, SC17: ?March–?December 1797.
54 Philip MacDougall, 'Reporting the Mutinies in the Provincial Press',

pp. 161–78 (p. 161), and Christopher Doorne, 'A Floating Republic? Conspiracy Theory and the Nore Mutiny of 1797', pp. 179–93, in Ann Veronica Coats and Philip MacDougall, eds, *The Naval Mutinies of 1797: Unity and Perseverance* (Woodbridge: Boydell Press, 2011).

55 Philp, *Godwin's* Political Justice, pp. 194–5.

56 Cited in Todd, *Wollstonecraft*, p. 420.

57 Godwin to Thomas Wedgwood, 30 May 1797, in Godwin, *Letters*, I, p. 207.

58 Godwin to Mary Wollstonecraft, 5 June 1797, in Godwin, *Letters*, I, pp. 209–10.

59 Godwin to Mary Wollstonecraft, 9–10 June 1797, in Godwin, *Letters*, I, p. 215.

60 Wedgwood to William Godwin, 31 July 1797, cited in Erdman, 'Coleridge, Wordsworth and the Wedgwood Fund', 430–3.

14: THE NURSERY OF GENIUS

1 Cited in Erdman, 'Coleridge, Wordsworth and the Wedgwood Fund', 431.

2 Cited in Roe, 'Coleridge and Thelwall', p. 74.

3 Coleridge, 'The Eolian Harp'.

4 Wordsworth, *Prelude* (1805), X, ll. 723–27.

5 Peter Swaab, 'Lamb, Charles (1775–1834)', *Oxford Dictionary of National Biography*, Oxford University Press, 2004, www.oxforddnb.com/view/article/15912 (accessed 22 March 2017).

6 There are three contradictory accounts of Coleridge and Wordsworth's first meeting. By one account, the two men were introduced at the house of John Pretor Pinney, one of Bristol's wealthiest merchants, whose fortune was built on numerous Caribbean slave plantations. But Coleridge's staunch abolitionist stance, recently reinforced at his 'Lecture on the Slave Trade' on 16 June 1795, makes this unlikely. The painter Joseph Farington recalled that the two men first made each other's acquaintance at a political debating society, 'where on one occasion Wordsworth spoke with so much force & eloquence that Coleridge was captivated by it & sought to know Him'. But Coleridge professed never to have been a member of any political societies. And fifty years later, when Wordsworth himself was asked to relate the circumstances of their meeting, he confessed that he did not have 'as distinct a remembrance as he could wish', but thought he'd probably met Coleridge at 'a lodging in Bristol' (the Fricker family house, perhaps), together with Southey, Edith and Sara. But Southey and Coleridge's friendship was distinctly strained by the end of September 1795, with Southey feeling that Coleridge 'has behaved wickedly towards me', and Coleridge angry at Southey's desertion of pantisocracy 'to study the Law' (*Letters*, 1 Oct 1795; Coleridge to Joseph Cottle, 22 Aug 1795, p. 159). However Wordsworth and Coleridge met, the biographer Adam Sisman has narrowed it down to 21 or 22 September 1795, in a politically charged Bristolian context (see *The Friendship: Wordsworth and Coleridge*).

7 Wordsworth to Mathews, cited in Sisman, *The Friendship*, p. 112.

8   Wordsworth, *Prelude* (1805), VI, ll. 353–4.
9   Wordsworth, *Prelude* (1805), X, ll. 692–3.
10 David V. Erdman, 'The Man Who Was Not Napoleon', *Wordsworth Circle*, 12 (1), (1981), 92–6.
11 Wordsworth, *Prelude* (1805), X, l. 275–7.
12 Roe, 'Coleridge and John Thelwall', pp. 68–9; 70.
13 Coleridge, 'To John Thelwall', cited in Roe, 'Coleridge and John Thelwall', p. 70.
14 E. P. Thompson, 'Disenchantment or Default? A Lay Sermon', pp. 33–74, in E. P. Thompson, *The Romantics: Wordsworth, Coleridge, Thelwall* (Woodbridge: Merlin Press, 1997); originally given as one of the Albert Schweitzer lectures at New York University, 1968; originally published in O'Brien and Vaneck, eds, *Power and Consciousness* (New York: New York University Press, 1969), pp. 44–5.
15 Cited in Roe, 'Coleridge and John Thelwall', p. 74; cf. Kenneth R. Johnston, *Unusual Suspects: Pitt's Reign of Alarm and the Lost Generation of the 1790s* (Oxford: Oxford University Press, 2013).
16 Cited in Roe, 'Coleridge and John Thelwall', p. 75.
17 Cited in Roe, 'Coleridge and John Thelwall', pp. 76–7.
18 Cited in Roe, 'Coleridge and John Thelwall', p. 78.
19 Erdman, 'Coleridge, Wordsworth and the Wedgwood Fund', p. 434.
20 Wordsworth, *Prelude* (1805), II, ll. 229–33, 212–13, 265–78.
21 Cited in Litchfield, *Tom Wedgwood*, p. 53 (fn.).
22 Wedgwood, *Value of a Maimed Life*, p. 62.
23 Coleridge, cited in Erdman, 'Coleridge, Wordsworth and the Wedgwood Fund', p. 438.
24 Thomas Beddoes, *On the Nature of Demonstrative Evidence* (London: Joseph Johnson, 1793), p. iii.
25 Beddoes, *Demonstrative Evidence*, p. 129.
26 Beddoes, *Demonstrative Evidence*, p. vii.
27 Thomas Beddoes, cited in Stansfield, *Thomas Beddoes*, p. 94.
28 Maria Edgeworth and Richard Lovell Edgeworth, *Practical Education* (London: Joseph Johnson, 1798), I, p. ix.
29 Thomas Beddoes, 'Lectures on Anatomy and the Preservation of Health', CRO, DG42/29, 8 Oct 1797.
30 Mary E. Fissell, *Patients, Power and the Poor in Eighteenth-Century Bristol* (Cambridge: Cambridge University Press, 1991), pp. 130, 199.
31 Thomas Beddoes, cited in Stock, *Memoirs*, pp. 137–8.
32 Thomas Beddoes, cited in Stock, *Memoirs*, p. 139.
33 Cited in Stock, *Memoirs*, p. 144.
34 Cited in Stansfield, *Thomas Beddoes*, p. 190.
35 Cited in Stock, *Memoirs*, p. 145.
36 Cited in Stansfield, *Thomas Beddoes*, p. 191.
37 Levere, 'Dr Thomas Beddoes (1750–1808)', 196.
38 Godwin, *Memoirs*, p. 173.
39 Wollstonecraft to William Godwin, 6 June 1797, in Wollstonecraft, *Collected Letters*, pp. 416–17.

40 Wollstonecraft to William Godwin, 30 Aug 1797, in Wollstonecraft, *Collected Letters*, p. 436.

41 Wollstonecraft to William Godwin, 30 Aug 1797, in Wollstonecraft, *Collected Letters*, p. 437 (and fn.).

42 Godwin, *Memoirs*, p. 181.

43 Godwin, *Memoirs*, p. 182.

44 Godwin, *Memoirs*, p. 185.

45 John Clarke, *An Essay on the Epidemic Disease of Lying-In Women* (London: Johnson, 1788); see also Candace Ward, *Desire and Disorder: Fevers, Fictions, and Feeling in English Georgian Culture* (Lewisburg: Bucknell University Press, 2007), p. 57.

46 Godwin, *Memoirs*, p. 193.

47 Godwin, *Memoirs*, pp. 196–7.

48 Godwin, *Memoirs*, p. 116.

49 Marshall, *William Godwin*, p. 214.

50 Godwin, *Memoirs*, pp. 200–202.

51 Cited in Barbara Taylor, *Mary Wollstonecraft and the Feminist Imagination* (Cambridge: Cambridge University Press, 2003), p. 192.

52 Godwin, *Memoirs*, p. 203.

53 Wollstonecraft, *Vindication of Woman*, p. 131.

54 Taylor, *Wollstonecraft*, p. 28.

55 Taylor, *Wollstonecraft*, p. 118.

56 Cited in Anna Clark, *Scandal! The Sexual Politics of the British Constitution* (Princeton: Princeton University Press, 2006), p. 137.

57 Cited in Taylor, *Wollstonecraft*, p. 28.

58 James Mackintosh, *Vindiciae Gallicae: Defence of the French Revolution and its English Admirers* (London: Robinson, 1791).

59 Christopher J. Finlay, 'Mackintosh, Sir James, of Kyllachy (1765–1832)', *Oxford Dictionary of National Biography*, Oxford University Press, 2004; online edition, Jan 2010, www.oxforddnb.com/view/article/17620 (accessed 22 March 2017).

60 Cited in Erdman, 'Coleridge, Wordsworth and the Wedgwood Fund', p. 439.

61 Cited in Erdman, 'Coleridge, Wordsworth and the Wedgwood Fund', p. 441.

62 Cited in Erdman, 'Coleridge, Wordsworth and the Wedgwood Fund', p. 441 (fn. 21).

63 Cited in Litchfield, *Tom Wedgwood*, pp. 55–6.

64 Cited in Litchfield, *Tom Wedgwood*, pp. 57, 59.

65 Cited in Erdman, 'Coleridge, Wordsworth and the Wedgwood Fund', p. 439.

66 Cited in Barbara Wedgwood, *Wedgwood Circle*, p. 129.

15: RULING OVER THE CAUSES OF PAIN AND PLEASURE

1 *Evening Mail*, 25–8 May 1798.

2 Reported in *Morning Chronicle*, 25 May 1798, issue 9049.

3 Wolfe Tone, Trinity College Dublin, MS 2046/41*v*.

4 Wolfe Tone, cited in Frank McLynn, *The Road Not Taken: How Britain Narrowly Missed a Revolution, 1381–1926* (London: Bodley Head, 2012), p. 486.

5 For the life of Edward Fitzgerald, see Stella Tillyard, *Citizen Lord: Edward Fitzgerald, 1763–1798* (London: Chatto & Windus, 1997).

6 Marianne Elliott, *Wolfe Tone*, 2nd edition (Liverpool: Liverpool University Press, 2012; first published 1989), p. 380.

7 Levere, 'Dr Thomas Beddoes (1750–1808)', 196.

8 J. A. Paris, *The Life of Sir Humphry Davy, Bart. Ll. D.*, 2 vols (London: 1831), I, pp. 52–66; cited in Levere, 'Dr Thomas Beddoes and the Establishment', 46.

9 Beddoes, *Considerations*, I, 79.

10 Cited in Stansfield, *Thomas Beddoes*, pp. 160–61.

11 'New Medical Institution', *Bristol Gazette*, 21 March 1799; cited in Levere, 'Dr Thomas Beddoes and the Establishment', 46.

12 Stock, *Memoirs*, p. 176.

13 Cited in Stansfield, *Thomas Beddoes*, p. 166.

14 Cited in Stansfield, *Thomas Beddoes*, p. 166.

15 Cited in Stansfield, *Thomas Beddoes*, p. 166.

16 Davy, *Researches*, p. xi; see also Thomas Beddoes, *Notice of Some Observations Made at the Medical Pneumatic Institute* (Bristol: 1799).

17 Beddoes to Jos Wedgwood, in Keele University Wedgwood Archives, Etruria and Liverpool, 564–1; cited in Mike Jay, 'The Atmosphere of Heaven: The 1799 Nitrous Oxide Researches Reconsidered', *Notes and Records of the Royal Society of London*, 63:3, (2009), 297–309 (298).

18 Stock, *Memoirs*, p. 178.

19 Cited in Stansfield, *Thomas Beddoes*, p. 167.

20 Cited in Stansfield, *Thomas Beddoes*, p. 166.

21 Cited in Stansfield, *Thomas Beddoes*, p. 164.

22 Cited in Stansfield, *Thomas Beddoes*, pp. 166–7.

23 Davy, *Researches*, p. 552.

24 Davy, *Researches*, pp. 508–9.

25 I am very grateful to the neuroscientist Molly Crockett for clarifying the effects of nitrous oxide on the brain.

26 Cited in Jay, *Atmosphere*, p. 186. The importance of the placebo effect in the Pneumatic Institute's trials was also revealed when Davy placed a thermometer beneath a patient's tongue, to be met with the patient's ecstatic declaration that the instrument had cured him. For a fortnight, he attended the Pneumatic Institute, and Davy took his temperature, after which he announced himself 'satisfied and cured' (Barbara Wedgwood, *Wedgwood Circle*, p. 112).

27 Davy, *Researches*, pp. 517–18.

28 Cited in Stansfield, *Thomas Beddoes*, p. 165.

29 Louise Hide, Joanna Bourke, and Carmen Mangion, 'Perspectives on Pain: Introduction', *19: Interdisciplinary Studies in the Long Nineteenth Century*, (15), (2012), http://doi.org/10.16995/ntn.663.

30 Davy, *Researches*, p. 556.

31 Beddoes, *Notice*, p. 27.
32 Boyson, *Wordsworth*, p. 13.
33 Anna Beddoes to Davies Giddy, CRO, DG89/1, 2 Nov 1803.
34 Laure Murat, *The Man Who Thought He Was Napoleon: Toward a Political History of Madness*, trans. Deke Dusinberre (Chicago and London: University of Chicago Press, 2014), pp. 56, 3.
35 Beddoes, *Hygëia*, III, pp. 54–5.
36 Henry R. Rollin, 'Psychiatry in Britain One Hundred Years Ago', *The British Journal of Psychiatry*, (183:4), (2003), 292–8 (298).
37 Rollin, 'Psychiatry in Britain', 292–8.
38 Robert Southey, 12 July 1799, in Eliza Meteyard, *A Group of Englishmen (1795–1815): Being Records of the Younger Wedgwoods and their Friends* (London: 1871), p. 85.
39 Brown, *Elements of Medicine*, I, p. clvi.
40 Beddoes to Davies Giddy, CRO, DG42/24, 3 March 1803.
41 Brown, *Elements of Medicine*, I, pp. 13–14; Beddoes, 'Of the Brunonian Doctrine', in Brown, *Elements of Medicine*, I, pp. clviii–clix.
42 Beddoes, *Hygëia*, III, p. 33.
43 Cited in Jay, *Atmosphere*, p. 173.
44 Cited in Stansfield, *Thomas Beddoes*, pp. 163–4.
45 Cited in Stock, *Memoirs*, p. 182.
46 Beddoes, *Hygëia*, III, p. 104.
47 Iain McCalman, *Radical Underworld: Prophets, Revolutionaries and Pornographers in London, 1795–1840* (Oxford: Clarendon Press, 1993).
48 Cited in Stock, *Memoirs*, p. 164.

16: God Withdraws His Protection

1 Thomas Watson, *Popular Evidences of Natural Religion and Christianity* (London: Longman, Hurst, Rees and Orme, 1805), p. 142.
2 Watson, *Popular Evidences*, p. 142.
3 Jay, *Atmosphere*, p. 201.
4 Jan Golinski, 'Humphry Davy: The Experimental Self', *Eighteenth-Century Studies*, 45 (1), (2011), 15–28 (19); 'The Pneumatic Revellers: An Eclogue', *Anti-Jacobin Review and Magazine*, 4, (1800), 109–18.
5 C. C. Abbott, 'The Parents of T. L. Beddoes', *Durham University Journal*, 3 (1941–2), 159–75 (168); cited in Levere, 'Dr. Thomas Beddoes (1750–1808)', 197.
6 Thomas Beddoes, 'Observations on the Effects of Nitrous Oxide', pp. 541–8 (542), in Davy, *Researches*.
7 Stock, *Memoirs*, p. 177.
8 Davy, *Researches*, pp. 555, 580.
9 Stansfield, *Thomas Beddoes*, p. 164.
10 James Parkinson, *An Essay on the Shaking Palsy* (London: Sherwood, Neely and Jones, 1817), pp. 63, 34, 63.
11 Davy, *Researches*, p. 579; Robert Hunt, 'Humphry Davy', *Dictionary of National Biography* (London: Smith, Elder & Co., 1888).

12 Cited in W. D. A. Smith, *Under the Influence: A History of Nitrous Oxide and Oxygen Anaesthesia* (London: Macmillan, 1982), p. 30.

13 Humphry Davy, cited in David Knight, *Humphry Davy: Science and Power* (Cambridge: Cambridge University Press, 1992), p. 41.

14 Humphry Davy, cited in June Z. Fullmer, *Young Humphry Davy: The Making of an Experimental Chemist* (Philadelphia: American Philosophical Society, 2000), pp. 328–9.

15 David Knight, 'Thompson, Sir Benjamin, Count Rumford in the nobility of the Holy Roman empire (1753–1814)', *Oxford Dictionary of National Biography*, Oxford University Press, 2004; online edition, Jan 2008 www.oxforddnb.com/view/article/27255 (accessed 28 Aug 2016).

16 Robert Fox, 'Garnett, Thomas (1766–1802)', *Oxford Dictionary of National Biography*, Oxford University Press, 2004; online edition, Jan 2015 www.oxforddnb.com/view/article/10395 (accessed 28 Aug 2016).

17 Humphry Davy, 8 March 1801, in Paris, *Life of Sir Humphry Davy*, I, p. 87.

18 Anna Beddoes to Davies Giddy, CRO, DG89, 29 April 1801.

19 Anna Beddoes to Davies Giddy, CRO, DG89 [n.d.].

20 Anna Beddoes to Davies Giddy, CRO, DG89 [n.d.; Spring 1801?].

21 Anna Beddoes to Davies Giddy, CRO, DG89/11, 19 April 1801.

22 William McCarthy, *Anna Letitia Barbauld: Voice of the Enlightenment* (Baltimore and London: John Hopkins University Press, 2008), p. 266. I am very grateful to Professor McCarthy for suggesting William Wynch as a likely candidate for the unknown 'Mr. W.'.

23 Anna Laetitia Barbauld, 'Fashion: A Vision', in *A Legacy for Young Ladies, Consisting of Miscellaneous Pieces, in Prose and Verse, by the Late Mrs. Barbauld*, ed. Lucy Aikin (Boston: 1826). Thomas Beddoes had made similar links between the political emancipation of women and the safeguarding of female health through reforms to fashion in his introductory lecture to the series of Anatomical Lectures in 1797. Barbauld's essay wasn't published until the 1820s, and it is likely that Beddoes' comments were inspired instead by writers like Wollstonecraft. But it's possible that he was guided by William Wynch's description of Barbauld's essay. And Beddoes and Wynch did have other shared interests, which may have stemmed from their acquaintance. In 1804, Wynch subscribed to the posthumous publication of Thomas Garnett's *Popular Lectures on Zoonomia*, which expressed unqualified support for Brunonian medical theory and referenced Beddoes' work on the importance of moderation in diet and temperature. An acquaintance between Wynch, Beddoes and his wife Anna would account for the former's otherwise incongruous interest in Brunonian excitability.

24 Anna Beddoes to Davies Giddy, CRO, DG89 [n.d.; Spring 1801].

25 Anna Beddoes to Davies Giddy, CRO, DG89, 1 June 1801; and scrap of paper in same, DG89 [n.d.].

26 Anna Beddoes to Davies Giddy, CRO, DG89 [n.d.]; Anna Beddoes to Davies Giddy, CRO, DG89/11, 19 April 1801.

27 Davies Giddy to Anna Beddoes, 23 April 1801; in A. C. Todd, *Beyond the Blaze: A Biography of Davies Gilbert* (Truro: D. Bradford Barton, 1967), p. 48.

28 Anna Beddoes to Davies Giddy, CRO, DG89, 14 May 1801.

29 Anna Beddoes to Davies Giddy, CRO, DG89, 1 July [1801].

30 Beddoes to Davies Giddy, CRO, DG89, 1 July 1801.

31 Anna Beddoes to Davies Giddy, CRO, DG89/1, 20 May 1802.

32 Southey to John Rickman, 1802, in W. J. Warter, ed., *Selections from the Letters of Robert Southey* (1856); cited in Stansfield, *Thomas Beddoes*, pp. 169–70.

33 Beddoes to Davies Giddy, CRO, DG42/34, Dec 1799; Beddoes to Josiah Wedgwood, Keele University Special Collections, Wedgwood Etruria and Liverpool Manuscripts, W E/L 566–1, 12 November 1799.

34 Beddoes to Davies Giddy, CRO, DG42/34, Dec 1799.

35 Ian Hacking, *The Taming of Chance* (Cambridge: Cambridge University Press, 1990; 1991), p. 5.

36 Beddoes, *Hygëia*, I, p. 78; cf. David S. Shields, 'Happiness in Society: The Development of an Eighteenth-Century American Poetic Ideal', *American Literature*, 55 (4), (Dec 1983), 541–59; Caroline Winterer, *American Enlightenments: Pursuing Happiness in the Age of Reason* (Cambridge, Mass.: Yale University Press, 2016).

37 Anna Beddoes, 1 Aug 1803, cited in Todd, *Beyond the Blaze*, p. 49.

38 Beddoes to Davies Giddy, CRO, DG42/21, 2 Oct 1803.

39 Anna Beddoes to Davies Giddy, CRO, DG90 [1803].

40 Anna Beddoes to Davies Giddy, Nov 1803, cited in Todd, *Beyond the Blaze*, p. 49.

41 Anna Beddoes to Davies Giddy, CRO, DG89/1, [23 Oct 1803?].

42 Anna Beddoes to Davies Giddy, CRO, DG90, 23 Oct 1803.

43 Anna Beddoes, 'Little Anna', CRO, DG90 [n.d.].

44 Anna Beddoes to Davies Giddy, CRO, DG90, 31 Jan [1806?].

45 Anna Beddoes, 'Disappointment', CRO, DG90.

46 Anna Beddoes to Davies Giddy, CRO, DG89/2, 21 Feb 1806.

47 Anna Beddoes to Davies Giddy, CRO, DG89/2, 17 Feb 1808.

48 Jay, *Atmosphere*, p. 249.

49 Anna Beddoes, cited in Stansfield, *Thomas Beddoes*, p. 238.

50 Davies Giddy, Diary, 31 Dec 1808, cited in Todd, *Beyond the Blaze*, p. 51.

51 Davies Giddy, Diary, 14 Feb 1826, cited in Todd, *Beyond the Blaze*, p. 52.

52 Anna Beddoes to Davies Giddy, Diary, 20 Jan 1823, cited in Todd, *Beyond the Blaze*, p. 55.

53 Thomas Lovell Beddoes, cited in Ute Berns, *Science, Politics and Friendship in the Works of Thomas Lovell Beddoes* (Newark: University of Delaware Press, 2012), p. 18.

54 Thomas Lovell Beddoes, 'Lines Written at Geneva, July 16 [1824]', in Thomas Lovell Beddoes, *Poems by the Late Thomas Lovell Beddoes* (London: Pickering, 1851), p. 211.

17: Treachery and Desertion

1 Olson, *Radical Duke*, p. 48.
2 Charles Lennox, *An Authentic Copy of the Duke of Richmond's Bill, for a Parliamentary Reform* (London: J. Stockdale, 1783).
3 Charles Lennox, *A Letter from His Grace the Duke of Richmond to Lieutenant Colonel Sharman, Chairman to the Committee of Correspondence Appointed by the Delegates of Forty-five Corps of Volunteers, Assembled at Lisburn in Ireland; with NOTES, by a Member of the Society for Constitutional Information* (London: J. Johnson, 1792), p. 8 (fn.).
4 Samuel Taylor Coleridge, *The Plot Discovered; or an Address to the People Against Ministerial Treason* (Bristol: 1795), p. 45; cited in Bugg, *Five Long Winters*, p. 41.
5 Place, *Autobiography*, cited in McCalman, *Radical Underworld*, p. 8.
6 'Police Helicopter Sent to Rave', 17 July 2009 http://news.bbc.co.uk/1/hi/england/devon/8155441.stm (accessed 20 Dec 2016).
7 Jenny Uglow, *In These Times: Living in Britain Through Napoleon's Wars 1793–1815* (London: Faber, 2014), p. 1.
8 Nicholas Roe, 'Dyer, George (1755–1841)', *Oxford Dictionary of National Biography*, Oxford University Press, 2004, www.oxforddnb.com/view/article/8347 (accessed 20 Dec 2016); M. R. Adams, *Studies in the Literary Backgrounds of English Radicalism* (Lancaster, Pennsylvania: 1947); Johnston, *Unusual Suspects*, p. 14.
9 Michael T. Davis, 'Tooke, John Horne (1736–1812)', *Oxford Dictionary of National Biography*, Oxford University Press, 2004; online edition, Oct 2009, www.oxforddnb.com/view/article/27545 (accessed 20 Dec 2016); Christina Bewley and David Bewley, *Gentleman Radical: A Life of John Horne Tooke, 1736–1812* (London: Tauris, 1998).
10 Godwin, *Thoughts*, p. 2.
11 Godwin, *Thoughts*, p. 9.
12 Percy Bysshe Shelley, cited in Desmond King-Hele, *Shelley: His Thought and Work* (London: Macmillan, 1962, 1971), pp. 18–19; from *The Letters of Percy Bysshe Shelley*, ed. Frederick L. Jones, 2 vols (Oxford: Clarendon Press, 1964), I, p. 220.
13 Cited in St Clair, *Godwins and Shelleys*, p. 106.
14 Janet Todd, *Death and the Maidens: Fanny Wollstonecraft and the Shelley Circle* (London: Profile, 2007), pp. 3, 11.
15 St Clair, *Godwins and Shelleys*, p. 303.
16 [Smith], *Assassination*, pp. 76–7.
17 Isaac Weld the Younger, *Travels Through the States of North America*, 2 vols (London: 1807), II, 350–5; cited in Park, *Joseph Priestley*, 32 (fn. 78).
18 Priestley, *Memoirs*, cited in Park, *Joseph Priestley*, 15.
19 'Letters on Emigration from a Gentleman Lately Returned from America', *Gentleman's Magazine*, 65:2, (Sept 1795), 760, cited in Logan, 'Coleridge's Scheme of Pantisocracy', 1081.
20 Robert Tweddell, ed., *The Remains of John Tweddell* (London: J. Mawman, 1815), pp. 47, 162–3.

21   Nicholas Roe, 'Tweddell, John (1769–1799)', Oxford Dictionary of National Biography, Oxford University Press, 2004, www.oxforddnb.com/view/article/27902 (accessed 22 March 2017).

22   Southey to William Sidney Walker, unpublished letter; cited in Richard Garnett, 'Gilbert, William (1763?–c.1825)', rev. S. C. Bushell, *Oxford Dictionary of National Biography*, Oxford University Press, 2004; online edition, Jan 2009, www.oxforddnb.com/view/article/10706 (accessed 21 Dec 2016).

23   Johnston, *Unusual Suspects*, pp. xx, 14.

24   Erasmus Darwin, cited in J. Browne, 'Botany for Gentlemen: Erasmus Darwin and "The Loves of the Plants"', *Isis*, 80 (4), (1989), 592–621 (601).

25   Anna Seward, *Memoirs of the Life of Dr. Darwin* (London: Johnson, 1804), pp. 404–5.

26   Seward, *Memoirs*, pp. 408–9; 426.

27   Thompson, 'Disenchantment or Default?', p. 38.

28   John Keats, *The Letters of John Keats*, ed. H. E. Rollins, 2 vols (Cambridge: Cambridge University Press, 1958), I, pp. 193–4.

29   Wordsworth, *Excursion*, II, ll. 212–13.

30   Wordsworth, *Excursion*, II, ll. 296–7, 304–6.

31   William Hazlitt, *Memoirs of the Late Thomas Holcroft*, 3 vols (London: Longman, 1816), II, p. 247 (fn.).

32   Hazlitt, *Memoirs*, with manuscript annotations in the hand of William Godwin, New York Public Library, Pforz (BT) Godwin 01 (G 0338); ff. 246–7n, post-1816.

33   Beddoes, cited in Stock, *Memoirs*, p. 118.

34   Stock, *Memoirs*, p. 124.

35   Charles Dibdin, *A Complete History of the English Stage*, 5 vols (London: Dibdin, 1797–1800), VIII, chapter 14; Robert Bloomfield, *The Farmer's Boy* (London: Bensley, 1800); Charles Brockden Brown, *Ormond* (London: Minerva, 1800).

36   William Cowper to Lady Hesketh, 1 Aug 1765, in William Cowper, *The Life and Letters of William Cowper*, ed. William Hayley (Chichester: Johnson, 1809), p. 25.

37   Scott A. Sandage, *Born Losers: A History of Failure in America* (Cambridge, Mass.: Harvard University Press, 2005), pp. 9–10.

38   John Trusler, *The Habitable World Described* (London: Trusler, 1788–1797).

39   Fromm, *Sane Society*, pp. 160–61.

40   Wordsworth, *Prelude* (1805), X, ll. 105–35.

41   Nicholas Roe, 'Thelwall, John (1764–1834)', *Oxford Dictionary of National Biography*, Oxford University Press, 2004; online edition, Sept 2012, www.oxforddnb.com/view/article/27167 (accessed 22 March 2017).

42   Gary Kelly, 'Holcroft, Thomas (1745–1809)', *Oxford Dictionary of National Biography*, Oxford University Press, 2004, www.oxforddnb.com/view/article/13487 (accessed 22 March 2017).

43   Southey, cited in Speck, *Robert Southey*, p. 138.

44   George Byron, *The Vision of Judgement*, ll. 769–76; cited in Speck, *Robert Southey*, p. 188.

45 Coleridge, *Lectures 1795*, p. 215.
46 Coleridge, *Lectures 1795*, p. 217 (fn. 1).
47 Coleridge, cited in Thompson, *Romantics*, p. 45.
48 Coleridge, 'Religious Musings', ll. 396–7.
49 Roe, 'Coleridge and John Thelwall', p. 78.
50 Coleridge to Sir George and Lady Margaret Beaumont, in Coleridge, *Collected Letters*, II, p. 1001; cited in Roe, *Wordsworth and Coleridge*, pp. 2–3.
51 Coleridge, 'Enthusiasm for an Ideal World', *The Friend*, ed. Barbara Rooke, 2 vols (Princeton University Press: Princeton, 1969), I, p. 223.
52 Cited in Roe, 'Coleridge and John Thelwall', p. 62.
53 Cited in Roe, 'Coleridge and John Thelwall', p. 62.
54 Cited in Roe, 'Coleridge and John Thelwall', p. 64.
55 Joseph Cottle, cited in Lynda Pratt, '"Let not Bristol be ashamed"?: Coleridge's Afterlife in the Early Recollections of Joseph Cottle', pp. 20–35 in James Vigus and Jane Wright, eds, *Coleridge's Afterlives* (Basingstoke and New York: Palgrave, 2008), p. 35.
56 Coleridge to Joseph Cottle, 15 March 1797, cited in *Lectures 1795*, p. 203 (fn.).
57 Cited in *Lectures 1795*, p. 203 (fn.).
58 Boyd Hilton, *The Age of Atonement: The Influence of Evangelicalism on Social and Economic Thought, 1785–1865* (Oxford: Clarendon Press, 1988), p. 8.
59 Wilberforce to Ralph Creyke, 8 Jan 1803, *Correspondence of William Wilberforce* (1840), I, 247–53, cited in Hilton, *Age of Atonement*, p. 5.
60 Cited in Coleridge, *Lectures 1795*, p. 204 (fn.).
61 Cited in Coleridge, *Lectures 1795*, p. 206.
62 Cited in Hilton, *Age of Atonement*, p. 180.

18: The Revolution of Feeling

1 Percy Bysshe Shelley, Preface, *The Revolt of Islam; A Poem, in Twelve Cantos* (London: C. and J. Ollier, 1818), pp. viii–xi. The literary critic Thomas Pfau has, similarly, characterized the 1790s as a period of 'paranoia', leading to 'trauma' between 1800 and 1815, resolving into a state of 'melancholy' that lasted until 1840. Thomas Pfau, *Romantic Moods: Paranoia, Trauma, and Melancholy, 1790–1840* (Baltimore: Johns Hopkins University Press, 2005), p. 17.
2 William Godwin, 'On Avarice and Profusion', *The Enquirer: Reflections on Education, Manners, and Literature. In a Series of Essays* (London: G. G. and J. Robinson, 1797), p. 169.
3 Thomas R. Malthus, *An Essay on the Principle of Population*, ed. Geoffrey Gilbert (Oxford: Oxford University Press, 2008; first published London, 1798), p. 9.
4 Malthus, *Essay*, pp. 17, 32.
5 Robert Lawson Tait, *Diseases of Women and Abdominal Surgery* (Leicester: Richardson & Co., 1889); cited in Robert Darby, *A Surgical Temptation: The Demonization of the Foreskin and the Rise of Circumcision in Britain* (Chicago and London: University of Chicago Press, 2005), p. 73.

6   Cited in Darby, *Surgical Temptation*, p. 78.

7   Cited in Darby, *Surgical Temptation*, p. 79.

8   Cited in Darby, *Surgical Temptation*, p. 86.

9   Thomas Hughes, *Tom Brown at Oxford* (New York: John W. Lovell Company, n.d.), pp. 129–30.

10   Thomas Carlyle, *On Heroes, Hero-Worship and the Heroic in History*, ed. Michael K. Goldberg (Berkeley and Los Angeles: University of California Press, 1993), p. 159.

11   Carlyle, *On Heroes*, p. 164.

12   John Tosh, *A Man's Place: Masculinity and the Middle-Class Home in Victorian England* (Newhaven and London: Yale University Press, 1999), p. 189.

13   Trev Lynn Broughton, *Men of Letters, Writing Lives: Masculinity and Literary Auto/Biography in the Late Victorian Period* (London and New York: Routledge, 1999), pp. 144–5.

14   Charles Southwell, cited in Barbara Taylor, *Eve and the New Jerusalem: Socialism and Feminism in the Nineteenth Century* (London: Virago, 1983), p. 214.

15   Taylor, *Eve and the New Jerusalem*, pp. 47–8.

16   James Currie and W. W. Currie, *Memoir of the Life, Writings, and Correspondence of James Currie*, 2 vols (London: Longman, 1831), II, pp. 249–51; cited in Hilton, *Age of Atonement*, pp. 73–4.

17   In *Age of Atonement*, Boyd Hilton points out that evangelicalism dominated both cultural and counter-cultural approaches to history's trajectory (p. 3, fn. 2).

18   Peter Mathias, 'Malthus and the Transition from Optimism to Pessimism in Classical Economic Thought', unpublished paper, 1981; cited in Hilton, *Age of Atonement*, pp. 31–2.

19   Cited in Chandler, *Wordsworth's Second Nature*, p. 100.

20   More, *Strictures*, I, pp. 17, 25.

21   Stone, *Family, Sex and Marriage*, pp. 150–80.

22   Wordsworth and Coleridge, *Lyrical Ballads*, pp. 286–314.

23   Pfau, *Romantic Moods*, p. 6.

24   Percy Bysshe Shelley, 'A Defence of Poetry', pp. 1–57, in *Essays, Letters from Abroad, Translations and Fragments* (London: Edward Moxon, 1840), p. 57.

25   Dixon, *From Passions to Emotions*, pp. 1–2.

26   Thomas Chalmers, cited in Dixon, *From Passions to Emotions*, p. 131.

27   William James, 'What is an Emotion?', *Mind*, 9, (1884), 188–205.

28   Wordsworth, *Prelude* (1805), II, l. 232; Wordsworth, *Prelude* (1850), II, l. 228.

29   William James, *The Varieties of Religious Experience: A Study in Human Nature* (London: Penguin, 1982; first published USA: Longmans, Green & Co, 1902), pp. 194–257; 379–427.

30   William James, 'Subjective Effects of Nitrous Oxide', *Mind*, 7, (1882), 186–208.

31   Cited in Barbara Wedgwood, *Wedgwood Circle*, p. 127.

32 Cited in Litchfield, *Tom Wedgwood*, pp. 37–8.

33 Wedgwood, *Value of a Maimed Life*, p. 45.

34 Wedgwood, *Value of a Maimed Life*, pp. 49, 57. Valentine Cunningham, *In the Reading Gaol: Postmodernity, Texts and History* (Oxford: Wiley Blackwell, 1994), p. 330.

35 Wedgwood, *Value of a Maimed Life*, p. 56.

36 Matt ffytche, *The Foundation of the Unconscious: Schelling, Freud and the Birth of the Modern Psyche* (Cambridge: Cambridge University Press, 2013).

37 Wedgwood, *Value of a Maimed Life*, p. 58.

38 Cited in Barbara Wedgwood, *Wedgwood Circle*, p. 124.

39 Cited in Litchfield, *Tom Wedgwood*, p. 75.

40 Litchfield, *Tom Wedgwood*, p. 35.

41 Cited in Litchfield, *Tom Wedgwood*, p. 89.

42 Cited in Litchfield, *Tom Wedgwood*, p. 96.

43 Cited in Barbara Wedgwood, *Wedgwood Circle*, p. 124, 9 April 1802.

44 Cited in Barbara Wedgwood, *Wedgwood Circle*, p. 128.

45 Humphry Davy and Thomas Wedgwood, 'An Account of a Method of Copying Paintings Upon Glass, and of Making Profiles, by the Agency of Light upon Nitrate of Silver. Invented by T. Wedgwood, Esq.', *Journal of the Royal Institution*, 1:9, (1802), reprinted in Beaumont Newhall, ed., *Photography: Essays and Images* (New York: Museum of Modern Art, 1980), pp. 15–16.

46 Coleridge to Thomas Wedgwood, in Coleridge, *Collected Letters*, II, p. 931.

47 Cited in Litchfield, *Tom Wedgwood*, pp. 183–4.

48 Litchfield, *Tom Wedgwood*.

49 Cited in Barbara Wedgwood, *Wedgwood Circle*, p. 129.

50 Sigmund Freud, *Civilization and its Discontents*, trans. Joan Riviere (London: Hogarth Press, 1973; first published 1930), pp. 7–8.

51 Freud, 'Three Essays on Infantile Sexuality', in *Standard Edition*, VII, p. 170.

52 Daniel Goleman, 'Health: New Studies Report Health Dangers of Repressing Emotional Turmoil', *New York Times*, 3 March 1988, www.nytimes.com/1988/03/03/us/health-new-studies-report-health-dangers-of-repressing-emotional-turmoil.html (accessed 23 March 2017); Khole, 'Men: Dangers of Repression', *Psych2go*, 18 Jan 2017, www.psych2go.net/dangers-of-repression (accessed 23 March 2017); 'The Dangers of Repressed Emotions', *Step to Health*, steptohealth.com/dangers-repressed-emotions (accessed 23 March 2017).

53 Dixon, *Passions to Emotions*, p. 21.

54 Anna Gragert, 'Emotions Aren't Good or Bad, They Just Are', *Thought Catalog*, 8 April 2014, http://thoughtcatalog.com/anna-gragert/2014/04/emotions-arent-good-or-bad-they-just-are/ (accessed 24 Dec 2016).

55 Nicole M. Verrochi, 'Me, My Self, and Emotion: Identity-Consistent Emotions and Consumption', dissertation research presented at the University of Pennsylvania, 2014; 'Your Emotional Identity – What is Really Important to You, and How Does That Relate to Your Environment?', *Identity and Type*, 18 March 2012, identityandtype.

wordpress.com/2012/03/18/your-emotional-identity-what-is-really-
important-to-you-and-how-does-that-relate-to-your-environment
(accessed 23 March 2017).

56 Eliot M. Brenner and Peter Salovey, 'Emotion Regulation During
Childhood: Developmental, Interpersonal and Individual Considerations',
pp. 168–92, in Peter Salovey and David J. Sluyter, eds, *Emotional
Development and Emotional Intelligence: Educational Implications* (New
York: Basic Books, 1997), p. 183.

57 Rose Hackman, '"Women Are Just Better At This Stuff": Is Emotional
Labor Feminism's Next Frontier?', *Guardian*, 8 Nov 2015, www.
theguardian.com/world/2015/nov/08/women-gender-roles-sexism-
emotional-labor-feminism (accessed 23 March 2017).

BIBLIOGRAPHY

Archives

Abinger Collection, Bodleian Library
Archive of the Davies Gilbert family of Trelissick, Feock, Cornwall
    Record Office
British Library Manuscripts
Correspondence, 16th–20th Century, Bodleian Library
Edgeworth Papers, National Library of Ireland
Fitzwilliam Museum, Cambridge
Pelham Papers, British Library
Pinney Papers, Bristol University Library
Pforzheimer Collection, New York Public Library
Home Office: Letters and Papers, National Archives
Papers of the Noel, Byron and Lovelace Families, Bodleian Library
Trinity College, Dublin
Wedgwood and Etruria Papers, Keele University Special Collections
Wellcome Library

Newspapers

Bristol Gazette
Evening Mail
Felix Farley's Bristol Journal
Gentleman's Magazine
Guardian
Independent
Lincoln Journal Star
Liverpool Echo

London Chronicle
Mirror
Moniteur
Monthly Magazine
Morning Chronicle
The New Annual Register, Or, General Repository of History, Politics and Literature for the Year 1780 (London: G. Robinson, 1781)
New York Times
Observer
St. James's Chronicle
The Times
World

Texts

Abbott, C. C., 'The Parents of T. L. Beddoes', *Durham University Journal*, 3, (1941–2), 159–75

Adams, M. R., *Studies in the Literary Backgrounds of English Radicalism* (Lancaster, Pennsylvania: 1947)

Alexander, Caroline, *The Bounty: The True Story of the Mutiny on the Bounty* (London: HarperCollins, 2003)

Alger, J. G., 'The British Colony in Paris, 1792–93', *English Historical Review*, 13:52, (1898), 672–94

An Account of Mr. Whiston's Prosecution at, and Banishment from, the University of Cambridge (London: J. Roberts, 1718)

An Account of the Proceedings of the British Convention, Held in Edinburgh, the 19th of November, 1793 (London: D. Eaton, [1793])

An Authentic Account of the Riots in Birmingham, Also ... the Trials of the Rioters (Birmingham: n.p., 1791)

Andrews, Stuart, *The British Periodical Press and the French Revolution, 1789–99* (London: Palgrave Macmillan, 2000)

Archer, John E., *Social Unrest and Popular Protest in England 1780–1840* (Cambridge: Cambridge University Press, 2000)

Augustine of Hippo, *The City of God*, trans. Marcus Dods (Mass.: Hendrickson, 1999)

Aylwin, Susan, *Structure in Thought and Feeling* (London: Methuen, 1985)

Bailey, Joanne, 'Favoured or Oppressed? Married Women, Property and "Coverture" in England, 1660–1800', *Continuity or Change*, 17 (3), (2002), 351–72

Barbauld, Anna Laetitia, *A Legacy for Young Ladies, Consisting of Miscellaneous Pieces, in Prose and Verse, by the Late Mrs. Barbauld*, ed. Lucy Aikin (Boston: 1826)

Baron-Cohen, Simon, *The Essential Difference: Male and Female Brains and the Truth about Autism* (New York: Basic Books, 2004)

Barrell, John, *Imagining the King's Death: Figurative Treason, Fantasies of Regicide 1793–1796* (Oxford: Oxford University Press, 2000)

Barrell, John, and Jon Mee, eds, *Trials for Treason and Sedition, 1792– 1794*, 8 vols (London: Pickering and Chatto, 2006–7)

Barruel, Augustin, *Memoirs Illustrating the History of Jacobinism*, 4 vols (London: T. Burton, 1797)

Batchelor, Jennie, '"To Cherish *Female* Ingenuity and to Conduce to *Female* Improvement": The *Lady's Magazine* and the Birth of the Women's Magazine', Centre for Eighteenth Century Studies Research Seminars, University of York, 18 October 2016

Battie, William, *A Treatise on Madness* (London: Whiston and White, 1758)

Baumeister, Roy F., and Jean M. Twenge, 'Cultural Suppression of Female Sexuality', *Review of General Psychology*, 6:2, (2002), 166–203

Beach, Frank, 'Characteristics of Masculine "Sex Drive"', pp. 1–32, in *Nebraska Symposium on Motivation*, Vol. 4, M. R. Jones, ed. (Lincoln: University of Nebraska Press, 1956)

Bebbington, Paul, et al., *Adult Psychiatric Morbidity in England, 2007: Results of a Household Survey* http://content.digital.nhs.uk/catalogue/PUB02931/adul-psyc-morb-res-hou-sur-eng-2007-rep.pdf (accessed 25 November 2016)

Beddoes, Thomas, *Alexander's Expedition down the Hydaspes & the Indus to the Indian Ocean* (London: John Murray, 1792)

Beddoes, Thomas, *Considerations on the Medicinal Use and Production of Factitious Airs* (Bristol: Joseph Johnson, 1794)

Beddoes, Thomas, *Extract of a Letter on Early Instruction, Particularly That of the Poor* (n.p., 25 January 1792)

Beddoes, Thomas, *The History of Isaac Jenkins, and Sarah His Wife, and Their Three Children*, 6th edition (London: H. Murray and J. Johnson, 1794)

Beddoes, Thomas, *Hygëia: Or Essays Moral and Medical, on the Causes Affecting the Personal State of our Middling and Affluent Classes*, 3 vols (Bristol: J. Mills, 1802)

Beddoes, Thomas, *Notice of Some Observations Made at the Medical*

Pneumatic Institute (Bristol: Biggs & Cottle, 1799)

Beddoes, Thomas, 'Observations on the Character and Writings of John Brown, MD', I, pp. xlii–clxii, in John Brown, *The Elements of Medicine of John Brown*, trans. Thomas Beddoes, 2 vols (London: J. Johnson, 1795)

Beddoes, Thomas, 'Observations on the Effects of Nitrous Oxide', pp. 541–8, in Humphry Davy, *Researches Chemical and Philosophical, Chiefly Concerning Nitrous Oxide, or Dephlogisticated Nitrous Air, and its Respiration* (London: Joseph Johnson, 1800)

Beddoes, Thomas, *On the Nature of Demonstrative Evidence* (London: Joseph Johnson, 1793)

Beddoes, Thomas, *A Word in Defence of the Bill of Rights, Against Gagging Bills* (Bristol: N. Biggs, 1795)

Beddoes, Thomas Lovell, *Poems by the Late Thomas Lovell Beddoes* (London: Pickering, 1851)

Beer, John, 'Coleridge, Samuel Taylor (1772–1834)', *Oxford Dictionary of National Biography*, Oxford University Press, 2004; online edition, Oct 2008, www.oxforddnb.com/view/article/5888 (accessed 21 March 2017)

Bell, David, *The First Total War: Napoleon's Europe and the Birth of Warfare as We Know It* (Boston: Houghton Mifflin Harcourt, 2007)

Bennett, Betty T., *British War Poetry in the Age of Romanticism, 1793–1815*, ed. Orianne Smith, www.rc.umd.edu/editions/warpoetry/intro.html (accessed 22 March 2017)

Berns, Ute, *Science, Politics and Friendship in the Works of Thomas Lovell Beddoes* (Newark: University of Delaware Press, 2012)

Bewley, Christina and David Bewley, *Gentleman Radical: A Life of John Horne Tooke, 1736–1812* (London: Tauris, 1998)

De Bienville, M. D. T., *Nymphomania, or, a Dissertation Concerning the Furor Uterinus*, trans. Edward Sloane Wilmot (London: J. Bew, 1775)

Blackman, John, *A Memoir of the Life and Writings of Thomas Day, Author of 'Sandford and Merton'* (London: J. B. Lewis, 1862)

Bloomfield, Robert, *The Farmer's Boy* (London: Bensley, 1800)

Bluhm, Robyn, 'New Research, Old Problems: Methodological and Ethical Issues in fMRI Research Examining Sex/Gender Differences in Emotion Processing', *Neuroethics*, 6 (2), (August 2013), 319–30

Bolton, Carol, *Writing the Empire: Robert Southey and Romantic Colonialism* (London: Pickering and Chatto, 2007)

Bowlby, John, *Attachment and Loss* trilogy: Vol. I, *Attachment* (London: Pimlico, 1997; first published London: Hogarth Press and Institute of Psychoanalysis, 1969); Vol. II, *Separation: Anxiety and Anger* (London: Pimlico, 1998; first published London: Hogarth Press and Institute of Psychoanalysis, 1973)

Boyson, Rowan, *Wordsworth and the Enlightenment Idea of Pleasure* (Cambridge: Cambridge University Press, 2012)

Brenner, Eliot M., and Peter Salovey, 'Emotion Regulation During Childhood: Developmental, Interpersonal and Individual Considerations', pp. 168–92, in Peter Salovey and David J. Sluyter, eds, *Emotional Development and Emotional Intelligence: Educational Implications* (New York: Basic Books, 1997)

Brewer, John, *The Sinews of Power: War, Money and the English State, 1688–1783* (Cambridge, Mass.: Harvard University Press, 1990)

Brizendine, Louanne, *The Female Brain* (New York: Broadway Books, 2007)

Brothers, Richard, *Revealed Knowledge of the Prophecies and Times*, 2 vols (London: 1794)

Broughton, Trev Lynn, *Men of Letters, Writing Lives: Masculinity and Literary Auto/Biography in the Late Victorian Period* (London and New York: Routledge, 1999)

Brown, Charles Brockden, *Ormond* (London: Minerva, 1800)

Brown, John, *The Elements of Medicine of John Brown*, trans. Thomas Beddoes, 2 vols (London: J. Johnson, 1795)

Browne, J., 'Botany for Gentlemen: Erasmus Darwin and "The Loves of the Plants"', *Isis*, 80:4, (1989), 592–621

Bruder, Helen P., *William Blake and the Daughters of Albion* (Basingstoke: Macmillan, 1997)

Le Brun, Charles, *Méthode pour apprendre à dessiner les passions* (Amsterdam: François van der Plaats, 1698)

Bryan, William, *A Testimony of the Spirit of Truth, Concerning Richard Brothers* (London: J. Wright, 1795)

Buchan, William, *Domestic Medicine: Or, a Treatise on the Prevention and Cure of Diseases by Regimen and Simple Medicines. With an Appendix Containing a Dispensatory for the Use of Private Practitioners. The Eleventh Edition* (London: A. Strahan, T. Cadell, J. Balfour, W. Creech, 1790)

Buel, Richard, *Joel Barlow: American Citizen in a Revolutionary World* (Baltimore: Johns Hopkins University Press, 2011)

Bugg, John, *Five Long Winters: The Trials of British Romanticism* (Stanford: Stanford University Press, 2014)

Burke, Edmund, *The Correspondence of Edmund Burke*, 10 vols

(Cambridge: Cambridge University Press, 1958–78)

Burke, Edmund, *A Letter to a Member of the National Assembly* (London: J. Dodsley, 1791)

Burke, Edmund, *A Philosophical Enquiry into the Origin of Our Ideas of the Sublime and Beautiful*, ed. Adam Phillips (Oxford: Oxford University Press, 1990; first published London: R & J Dodsley, 1757)

Burke, Edmund, *Reflections on the Revolution in France*, ed. Conor Cruise O'Brien (Harmondsworth: Penguin, 1968; first published London: J. Dodsley, 1790)

Burkeman, Oliver, *The Antidote: Happiness for People who Can't Stand Positive Thinking* (Edinburgh: Canongate, 2012)

Buruma, Ian, 'Extremism: The Loser's Revenge, or Can Sexual Inadequacy or Deprivation Turn Angry Young Men into Killers?', *Guardian*, Sat 25 February 2006, www.theguardian.com/world/2006/feb/25/terrorism.comment (accessed 3 July 2016)

Butler, Marilyn, *Romantics, Rebels and Reactionaries* (Oxford: Oxford University Press, 1981)

Bynum, W. F., and Roy Porter, eds, *Brunonianism in Britain and Europe*, Supplement No. 8 to *Medical History* (London: Wellcome Institute, 1988)

Cameron, Deborah, *Good to Talk?* (London: Sage Publications, 2000)

Cameron, Deborah, *The Myth of Mars and Venus* (Oxford: Oxford University Press, 2007, 2008)

Cameron, Kenneth Neill, ed., *The Carl H. Pforzheimer Library: Shelley and His Circle, 1773–1882*, 4 vols (Cambridge, Mass.: Harvard University Press, 1961–70)

Campbell, Denis and Haroon Siddique, 'Mental Illness Soars Among Young Women in England – Survey', *Guardian*, 29 September 2016, www.theguardian.com/lifeandstyle/2016/sep/29/self-harm-ptsd-and-mental-illness-soaring-among-young-women-in-england-survey (accessed 25 November 2016)

Carlyle, Thomas, *On Heroes, Hero-Worship and the Heroic in History*, ed. Michael K. Goldberg (Berkeley and Los Angeles: University of California Press, 1993)

Carveth, Donald, 'Is There a Future in Disillusion? Constructionist and Deconstructionist Approaches in Psychoanalysis', *Journal of the American Academy of Psychoanalysis*, 27: 2, (1999), 325–58

Caulfeild, James, Earl of Charlemont, 'Account of a Singular Custom at Metelin, with Some Conjectures on the Antiquity of its Origin',

Transactions of the Royal Irish Academy, 3, (1789), 3–20

Cayton, Andrew, *Love in the Time of Revolution: Transatlantic Literary Radicalism and Historical Change, 1793–1818* (Chapel Hill: University of North Carolina Press, 2013)

Chandler, Abigail, '14 Signs That You're Homesick', http://metro. co.uk/2015/06/13/13-signs-that-youre-homesick–5237381/ (accessed 30 December 2016)

Chandler, James K., *Wordsworth's Second Nature: A Study of the Poetry and Politics* (Chicago and London: University of Chicago Press, 1985)

Cheyne, George, *The English Malady: Or, a Treatise of Nervous Diseases of All Kinds, as Spleen, Vapours, Lowness of Spirits, Hypochondriacal, and Hysterical Distempers &c.* (London: G. Strahan, 1733)

Christie, R. C., 'Christie, Thomas (1761–1796)', rev. Alexander Du Toit, *Oxford Dictionary of National Biography*, Oxford University Press, 2004, www.oxforddnb.com/view/article/5365 (accessed 20 March 2017)

Claeys, Gregory, 'The *Reflections* Refracted: The Critical Reception of Burke's *Reflections on the Revolution in France* during the early 1790s', pp. 40–50, in John Whale, ed., *Edmund Burke's* Reflections on the Revolution in France (Manchester: Manchester University Press, 2000)

Clark, Anna, *Scandal! The Sexual Politics of the British Constitution* (Princeton: Princeton University Press, 2006)

Clarke, John, *An Essay on the Epidemic Disease of Lying-In Women* (London: Johnson, 1788)

Clemit, Pamela, ed., *The Cambridge Companion to British Literature of the French Revolution in the 1790s* (Cambridge: Cambridge University Press, 2011)

Clifford, Naomi, 'George Lowman Tuckett', *All Things Georgian*, georgianera.wordpress.com/tag/samuel-taylor-coleridge/ (accessed 15 September 2016)

Coats, Ann Veronica, and Philip MacDougall, eds., *The Naval Mutinies of 1797: Unity and Perseverance* (Woodbridge: Boydell Press, 2011)

Cobbett, William, *The Parliamentary History of England from the Earliest Period to the Year 1803*, 36 vols (London: Hansard, 1817)

Colberg, Todd, *Self Booked: Empty Bottles, Germs Burns and Bootneck Dreams* (Todd Colberg, 2012)

Coleman, Deirdre, 'The Journalist', pp. 126–41, in *Cambridge Companion to Samuel Taylor Coleridge*, ed. Lucy Newlyn

(Cambridge: Cambridge University Press, 2002)

Coleridge, Samuel Taylor, *Collected Letters of Samuel Taylor Coleridge*, ed. Earl Leslie Griggs, 6 vols (Oxford: Clarendon Press, 1956–71; 2002)

Coleridge, Samuel Taylor, *The Fall of Robespierre* (Cambridge: Benjamin Flower, 1794)

Coleridge, Samuel Taylor, *The Friend*, ed. Barbara Rooke, 2 vols (Princeton University Press: Princeton, 1969)

Coleridge, Samuel Taylor, *Lectures 1795: On Politics and Religion*, ed. Lewis Patton and Peter Mann, *The Collected Works of Samuel Taylor Coleridge* (London: Routledge and Kegan Paul, 1971), Vol. I

Coleridge, Samuel Taylor, *The Notebooks of Samuel Taylor Coleridge*, ed. Kathleen Coburn, 5 vols (London: Routledge and Kegan Paul, 1957)

Coleridge, Samuel Taylor, *The Plot Discovered; or an Address to the People Against Ministerial Treason* (Bristol: 1795)

Coleridge, Samuel Taylor, *Poems on Various Subjects* (London: Robinsons and Cottle, 1796)

Coleridge, Samuel Taylor, *Samuel Taylor Coleridge: The Complete Poems*, ed. William Keach (London: Penguin, 1997)

Condren, Conal, *The Politics of Language in Seventeenth-Century England* (Basingstoke: Palgrave Macmillan, 1994)

Connell, Philip, *Romanticism, Economics and the Question of 'Culture'* (Oxford: Oxford University Press, 2001)

Cooper, Anthony Ashley, Third Earl of Shaftesbury, *Characteristicks of Men, Manners, Opinions, Times*, 4 vols (London: 1758)

Cooper, Thomas 'Propositions Respecting the Foundation of Civil Government' (1790), pp. 93–109, in Thomas Cooper, *A Reply to Mr. Burke's Invective against Mr. Cooper and Mr. Watt*, 2nd edition (London: Johnson, 1792)

Cooper, Thomas, *A Reply to Mr. Burke's Invective against Mr. Cooper and Mr. Watt*, 2nd edition (London: Johnson, 1792)

Cooper, Thomas, *Some Information Respecting America* (London: Johnson, 1794)

Cooper, Thompson, 'Burnett, George (1774/5–1811)', rev. David Kaloustian, *Oxford Dictionary of National Biography*, Oxford University Press, 2004; online edition, May 2009, www.oxforddnb.com/view/article/4071 (accessed 21 March 2017)

Cottingham, John, *Philosophy and the Good Life: Reason and the Passions in Greek, Cartesian and Psychoanalytic Ethics* (Cambridge:

Cambridge University Press, 1998)

Cottle, Joseph, *Early Recollections; Chiefly Relating to the Late Samuel Taylor Coleridge, During his Long Residence in Bristol*, 2 vols (London: Longman, Rees & Co., 1837)

Cowper, William, *Anti-Thelyphthora: A Tale in Verse* (London: Joseph Johnson, 1781)

Cowper, William, *The Life and Letters of William Cowper*, ed. William Hayley (Chichester: Johnson, 1809)

Crosfeild, R. T., *Remarks on the Scurvy as it Appeared Among the English Prisoners in France in the Year 1795; with an Account of the Effects of Opium in that Disease, and of the Methods Proper to Render its Use More Extensive and Easy; (Written During His Confinement in the Tower)* (London: J. Ridgway, 1797)

Cumberland, George, *The Captive of the Castle of Sennaar, an African Tale: Containing Various Anecdotes of the Sophians Hitherto Unknown to Mankind in General* (London: Printed for the Author, 1798)

Cunningham, Valentine, *In the Reading Gaol: Postmodernity, Texts and History* (Oxford: Wiley Blackwell, 1994)

Currie, James, and W. W. Currie, *Memoir of the Life, Writings, and Correspondence of James Currie*, 2 vols (London: Longman, 1831)

'The Dangers of Repressed Emotions', *Step to Health*, www.steptohealth.com/dangers-repressed-emotions (accessed 23 March 2017)

Darby, Robert, *A Surgical Temptation: The Demonization of the Foreskin and the Rise of Circumcision in Britain* (Chicago and London: University of Chicago Press, 2005)

Darnton, Robert, *Mesmerism and the End of the Enlightenment in France* (Cambridge, Mass.: Harvard University Press, 1968)

Darwin, Charles, *The Expression of the Emotions in Man and Animals* (1872), pp. 1249–477, in *From So Simple a Beginning: The Four Great Books of Charles Darwin*, ed. Edward O. Wilson (New York and London: Norton, 2006)

David, Michael T., ed., *Radicalism and Revolution in Britain, 1775–1848: Essays in Honour of Malcolm I. Thomis* (Basingstoke: Macmillan, 2000)

Davidoff, Leonore, and Catherine Hall, *Family Fortunes: Men and Women of the English Middle Class, 1780–1850* (London: Hutchinson 1987)

Davis, Michael T., 'Tooke, John Horne (1736–1812)', *Oxford Dictionary of National Biography*, Oxford University Press, 2004; online

edition, Oct 2009, www.oxforddnb.com/view/article/27545
(accessed 20 Dec 2016)

Davy, Humphry, *Researches Chemical and Philosophical, Chiefly
Concerning Nitrous Oxide, or Dephlogisticated Nitrous Air, and its
Respiration* (London: Joseph Johnson, 1800)

Davy, Humphry, and Thomas Wedgwood, 'An Account of a Method
of Copying Paintings Upon Glass, and of Making Profiles, by the
Agency of Light upon Nitrate of Silver. Invented by T. Wedgwood,
Esq.', *Journal of the Royal Institution*, 1:9, (1802), reprinted in
Beaumont Newhall, ed., *Photography: Essays and Images* (New
York: Museum of Modern Art, 1980), pp. 15–16

Day, Thomas, *The History of Sandford and Merton*, 3 vols (Dublin: 1787)

Descartes, René, *The Passions of the Soul*, trans. Stephen Voss
(Indianapolis: Hackett, 1989)

Dibdin, Charles, *A Complete History of the English Stage*, 5 vols (London:
Dibdin, 1797–1800)

Dickinson, H. T., 'Muir, Thomas (1765–1799)', *Oxford Dictionary of
National Biography*, Oxford University Press, 2004; online edition,
Sept 2010, www.oxforddnb.com/view/article/19498 (accessed 12
Dec 2016)

'disappoint, v.'. OED Online. March 2017. Oxford University Press.
www.oed.com/view/Entry/53508 (accessed March 19, 2017)

Diu, Nisha Lilia, 'Suicide is Now the Biggest Killer of Teenage Girls
Worldwide', *Telegraph*, 25 May 2015 www.telegraph.co.uk/women/
womens-health/11549954/Teen-girls-Suicide-kills-more-young-
women-than-anything.-Heres-why.html (accessed 25 November
2016)

Dixon, Thomas, *From Passions to Emotions: The Creation of a Secular
Psychological Category* (Cambridge: Cambridge University Press,
2003)

Donoghue, Emma, *Passions Between Women: British Lesbian Culture
1668–1801* (London: Scarlet Press, 1993)

Douthwaite, Julia V., *The Wild Girl, Natural Man and the Monster:
Dangerous Experiments in the Age of Enlightenment* (Chicago and
London: University of Chicago Press, 2002)

Duff, David, 'Burke and Paine: Contrasts', pp. 47–70, in *The Cambridge
Companion to British Literature of the French Revolution in the 1790s*,
ed. Pamela Clemit (Cambridge: Cambridge University Press, 2011)

Edelman, Sarah, *Change Your Thinking with CBT: Overcome Stress,
Combat Anxiety and Improve Your Life* (London: Vermilion, 2006)

Edgeworth, Maria, *The Life and Letters of Maria Edgeworth*, ed.
Augustus J. C. Hare, 2 vols (London: Edward Arnold, 1894)

Edgeworth, Richard Lovell, and Maria Edgeworth, *Memoirs of Richard Lovell Edgeworth: Begun by Himself and Concluded by His Daughter Maria Edgeworth*, 2 vols (Shannon: Irish University Press, 1969; first published 1820)

Edgeworth, Richard Lovell, and Maria Edgeworth, *Practical Education*, 3 vols (London: Joseph Johnson, 1798)

Eil, Andrew, 'Disdain: The Root of Our Diseased Politics', *Observer*, 5 March 2016 http://observer.com/2016/05/disdain-the-root-of-our-diseased-politics/

Elliott, Marianne, *Wolfe Tone*, 2nd edition (Liverpool: Liverpool University Press, 2012; first published 1989)

Elliott, Sinikka, and Debra Umberson, 'The Performance of Desire: Gender and Sexual Negotiation in Long-Term Marriages', *Journal of Marriage and the Family*, 70:2, (May 2008), 391–406

'emotion, n.'. OED Online. March 2017. Oxford University Press. www.oed.com/view/Entry/61249?rskey=-OtObro&result=1&isAdvanced=false (accessed March 19, 2017)

Emsley, Clive, '"An Aspect of Pitt's Terror": Prosecutions for Sedition during the 1790s', *Social History*, 6:2, (1981), 155–84

Emsley, Clive, 'The Pop-Gun Plot, 1794', pp. 56–68, in Michael T. David, ed., *Radicalism and Revolution in Britain, 1775–1848: Essays in Honour of Malcolm I. Thomis* (Basingstoke: Macmillan, 2000)

Erdman, David V., 'Coleridge, Wordsworth and the Wedgwood Fund', *Bulletin of the New York Public Library*, 60:9, (1956), 425–43; 487–507

Erdman, David V., 'The Man Who Was Not Napoleon', *Wordsworth Circle*, I2 (1), (1981), 92–6

Essai sur l'opinion consideire comme une des principales causes de la Revolution de 1789 (Paris, 1789)

Faderman, Lilian, *Surpassing the Love of Men: Romantic Friendship and Love Between Women from the Renaissance to the Present* (London: Women's Press, 1981)

Fancher, R. T., *Cultures of Healing: Correcting the Image of American Mental Health Care* (New York: W. H. Freeman, 1995)

Farley, Melissa, Jacqueline M. Golding, Emily Shuckman Matthews, Neil M. Malaluth, and Laura Jarrett, 'Comparing Sex Buyers with Men Who Do Not Buy Sex: New Data on Prostitution and Trafficking', *Journal of Interpersonal Violence*, (2015), 1–25

Festinger, Leon, Henry W. Riecken, and Stanley Schachter, *When*

Prophecy Fails (London: Pinter & Martin, 2013; first published 1956)

ffytche, Matt, *The Foundation of the Unconscious: Schelling, Freud and the Birth of the Modern Psyche* (Cambridge: Cambridge University Press, 2013)

Fine, Cordelia, *Delusions of Gender: The Real Science Behind Sex Differences* (London: Icon, 2010)

Finlay, Christopher J., 'Mackintosh, Sir James, of Kyllachy (1765–1832)', *Oxford Dictionary of National Biography*, Oxford University Press, 2004; online edition, Jan 2010, www.oxforddnb.com/view/article/17620 (accessed 22 March 2017)

Fleming, Amy, 'The Science of Craving', *The Economist: 1843*, May–June 2015, www.1843magazine.com/content/features/wanting-versus-liking (accessed 20 March 2017)

Forbes, James, *Oriental Memoirs*, 4 vols (London: White, Cochrane & Co., 1813)

Fox, Robert, 'Garnett, Thomas (1766–1802)', *Oxford Dictionary of National Biography*, Oxford University Press, 2004; online edition, Jan 2015, www.oxforddnb.com/view/article/10395 (accessed 28 Aug 2016)

Freeman, Daniel, and Jason Freeman, 'Let's Talk About the Gender Differences That Really Matter – in Mental Health', *Guardian*, 13 December 2013, www.theguardian.com/science/blog/2013/dec/13/gender-differences-mental-health (accessed 25 November 2016)

Freeman, Daniel, and Jason Freeman, 'Why Are Men More Likely Than Women to Take Their Own Lives?', *Guardian*, 21 January 2015 www.theguardian.com/science/2015/jan/21/suicide-gender-men-women-mental-health-nick-clegg (accessed 25 November 2016)

Frend, William, *Peace and Union Recommended to the Associated Bodies of Republicans and Anti-Republicans*, 2nd edition (Cambridge: B. Flower, 1793)

Freud, Sigmund, *Civilization and its Discontents*, trans. Joan Riviere (London: Hogarth Press, 1973; first published 1930)

Freud, Sigmund, *The Standard Edition of the Complete Psychological Works of Sigmund Freud*, trans. James Strachey in collaboration with Anna Freud, Alix Strachey and Alan Tyson, 24 vols (first published in Britain, London: Hogarth Press, 1956–74; this edition, London: Vintage, 1999–2001)

Fromm, Erich, *Beyond the Chains of Illusion: My Encounter with Marx and Freud* (New York: Continuum, 1990; first published 1962)

Fromm, Erich, *The Sane Society* (London: Routledge, 2002; first
   published 1956)

Fulford, Tim, and Peter Kitson, eds, *Romanticism and Colonialism:
   Writing and Empire, 1780–1830* (Cambridge: Cambridge University
   Press, 1998)

Fullmer, June Z., *Young Humphry Davy: The Making of an Experimental
   Chemist* (Philadelphia: American Philosophical Society, 2000)

Garnett, Richard, 'Gilbert, William (1763?–c.1825)', rev. S. C. Bushell,
   Oxford Dictionary of National Biography, Oxford University
   Press, 2004; online edition, Jan 2009, www.oxforddnb.com/view/
   article/10706 (accessed 21 Dec 2016)

Garrett, Clarke, *Respectable Folly: Millenarians and the French Revolution
   in France and England* (Baltimore and London: John Hopkins
   University Press, 1975)

Gilchrist, Alexander, *Life of William Blake* (London: John Lane/The
   Bodley Head, 1907; first published 1863)

Gill, Stephen, *William Wordsworth: A Life* (Oxford: Oxford University
   Press, 1989)

Godwin, William, *Collected Novels and Memoirs of William Godwin*, ed.
   Mark Philp, 8 vols (London: Pickering, 1992)

Godwin, William, *Cursory Strictures on the Charge Delivered by Lord
   Chief Justice Eyre to the Grand Jury, October 2, 1794. First Published in
   the Morning Chronicle October 21* (London: C. and G. Kearsley, 1794)

Godwin, William, *The Diary of William Godwin*, ed. Victoria Myers,
   David O'Shaughnessy, and Mark Philp (Oxford: Oxford Digital
   Library, 2010) http://godwindiary.bodleian.ox.ac.uk

Godwin, William, *The Enquirer: Reflections on Education, Manners, and
   Literature. In a Series of Essays* (London: G. G. and J. Robinson, 1797)

Godwin, William, *An Enquiry Concerning Political Justice*, 2 vols
   (London: Robinson, 1793)

Godwin, William, *Enquiry Concerning Political Justice*, 3rd edition, ed.
   Isaac Kramnick (Penguin: Harmondsworth, 1976; first published
   1798)

Godwin, William, *The Letters of William Godwin*, Vol. I: *1778–1797*, ed.
   Pamela Clemit (Oxford: Oxford University Press, 2011)

Godwin, William, *Memoirs of the Author of a Vindication of the Rights of
   Woman*, 2nd edition (London: J. Johnson, 1798)

Godwin, William, *Thoughts Occasioned by the Perusal of Dr. Parr's Spital
   Sermon, Preached at Christ Church, April 15, 1800* (London: Taylor
   and Wilks, 1801)

Goleman, Daniel, 'Health: New Studies Report Health Dangers of Repressing Emotional Turmoil', *New York Times*, 3 March 1988, www.nytimes.com/1988/03/03/us/health-new-studies-report-health-dangers-of-repressing-emotional-turmoil.html (accessed 23 March 2017)

Golinski, Jan, 'Humphry Davy: The Experimental Self', *Eighteenth-Century Studies* 45 (1), (2011), 15–28

Goodwin, Albert, *The Friends of Liberty: The English Democratic Movement in the Age of the French Revolution* (London: Hutchinson, 1979)

Gordon, Lyndall, *Vindication: A Life of Mary Wollstonecraft* (London: Virago, 2005)

de Gouges, Olympe, *The Rights of Woman*, trans. Val Stevenson (London: Pythia, 1989)

Gragert, Anna, 'Emotions Aren't Good or Bad, They Just Are', *Thought Catalog*, 8 April 2014, http://thoughtcatalog.com/anna-gragert/2014/04/emotions-arent-good-or-bad-they-just-are/ (accessed 24 December 2016)

Gravil, Richard, and Molly Lefebure, eds, *The Coleridge Connection: Essays for Thomas McFarland* (London: Macmillan, 1990)

Gray, John, *Men Are from Mars, Women Are from Venus* (London: Thorsons, 1993)

Guehénno, Jean, *Jean-Jacques*, 3 vols (Paris: 1948–52)

Guest, Harriet, *Unbounded Attachment: Sentiment and Politics in the Age of the French Revolution* (Oxford: Oxford University Press, 2013)

Gurney, Joseph, *The Trial of Robert Thomas Crosfeild, for High Treason, at the Sessions House in the Old Bailey, on Wednesday the Eleventh, and Thursday the Twelfth of May, 1796* (London: Martha Gurney, 1796)

Hacking, Ian, *The Taming of Chance* (Cambridge: Cambridge University Press, 1990; 1991)

Hakim, Catherine, 'The Male Sexual Deficit: A Social Fact of the 21st Century', *International Sociology*, (2015), 1–22

Halpern-Manners, Andrew, Landon Schnabel, and Elaine M. Hernandez, 'The Relationship between Education and Mental Health: New Evidence from a Discordant Twin Study', *Social Forces*, 95 (2), (2016), doi: 10.1093/sf/sow035

Hammill, Graham, *The Mosaic Constitution: Political Theology and Imagination from Machiavelli to Milton* (Chicago: University of Chicago Press, 2012)

Hampsher-Monk, Iain, ed., *The Impact of the French Revolution: Texts from Britain in the 1790s* (Cambridge: Cambridge University Press, 2005)

Harrington, James, *The Political Works of James Harrington*, ed. J. G. A. Pocock (Cambridge: Cambridge University Press, 1977)

Harris, Bob, *The Scottish People and the French Revolution* (London: Routledge, 2015)

Harrison, Mark, '"To Raise and Dare Resentment": The Bristol Bridge Riot of 1793 Re-Examined', *Historical Journal*, 26 (3), (1983), 557–85

Hartley, David, *Observations on Man: His Frame, His Duty, and His Expectations*, 4th edition (London: Joseph Johnson, 1801; 1st edition 1748)

Haywood, Ian, *Bloody Romanticism: Spectacular Violence and the Politics of Representation* (Basingstoke: Palgrave Macmillan, 2006)

Hazlitt, William, *The Complete Works of William Hazlitt*, ed. P. P. Howe, 21 vols (London: J. M. Dent and Sons, 1930)

Hazlitt, William, *Memoirs of the Late Thomas Holcroft*, 3 vols (London: Longman, 1816)

Hide, Louise, Joanna Bourke, and Carmen Mangion, 'Perspectives on Pain: Introduction', 19, *Interdisciplinary Studies in the Long Nineteenth Century*, (15), (2012), http://doi.org/10.16995/ntn.663

Hilton, Boyd, *The Age of Atonement: The Influence of Evangelicalism on Social and Economic Thought, 1785–1865* (Oxford: Clarendon Press, 1988)

Hite, Shere, *The Hite Report: A Nationwide Study on Female Sexuality* (New York and London: Macmillan, 1976)

Hobbes, Thomas, *Leviathan*, ed. Richard Tuck (Cambridge: Cambridge University Press, 1991; first published 1651)

Hobsbawm, Eric, *The Age of Revolution: Europe 1787–1848* (London: Abacus, 2003; first published London: Weidenfeld & Nicolson, 1962)

Holcroft, Thomas, *A Narrative of the Facts Relating to a Prosecution for High Treason* (1795)

Holmes, Richard, *Coleridge: Early Visions* (London: Penguin, 1989)

Horn, James, 'British Diaspora: Emigration from Britain, 1680–1815', pp. 28–52, in P. J. Marshall and Alaine Low, eds, *The Oxford History of the British Empire*, Vol. II: *The Eighteenth Century* (Oxford: Oxford University Press, 1998)

Hosseini, Khaled, *The Kite Runner* (London: Bloomsbury, 2003)

Hough, Richard, *Captain Bligh and Mr Christian: The Men and the Mutiny* (London: Hutchinson, 1972)

'How to Control Your Anger', www.nhs.uk/conditions/stress-anxiety-depression/pages/controlling-anger.aspx (accessed 2 December 2016)

Hughes, Thomas, *Tom Brown at Oxford* (New York: John W. Lovell Company, n.d.)

Hume, David, *A Treatise of Human Nature*, ed. Ernest C. Mossner (London: Penguin, 1985; first published 1739–40)

Hunt, Lynn, *The Family Romance of the French Revolution* (Berkeley: University of California Press, 1992)

Hunt, Lynn, ed., *The Invention of Pornography* (New York: Zone Books, 1993)

Hunt, Lynn, 'Pornography and the French Revolution', pp. 301–40, in Lynn Hunt, ed., *The Invention of Pornography* (New York: Zone Books, 1993)

Hunt, Lynn, and Margaret Jacob, 'The Affective Revolution in 1790s Britain', *Eighteenth-Century Studies*, 34 (4), (2001), 491–521

Hunt, Robert, 'Humphry Davy', *Dictionary of National Biography* (London: Smith, Elder & Co., 1888)

Hutcheson, Francis, *A Short Introduction to Moral Philosophy*, 2nd edition (Glasgow: 1753)

Hutton, William, *The History of Birmingham*, 6th edition (London: George Berger, 1836)

Hutton, William, *The Life of William Hutton* (London: Baldwin, 1816)

Hyde, Janet S., 'The Gender Similarities Hypothesis', *American Psychologist*, (September 2005), 581–92

Imlay, Gilbert, *The Emigrants, &c., or the History of an Expatriated Family, Being a Delineation of English Manners, Drawn from Real Characters, Written in America* (London: A. Hamilton, 1793)

Imlay, Gilbert, *A Topographical Description of the Western Territory of North America* (London: J. Debrett, 1797)

Indood, Brad, and Lloyd P. Gerson, eds, *The Stoics Reader* (Indianapolis: Hackett, 2008)

Jager, Colin, 'A Poetics of Dissent; or, Pantisocracy in America', *Theory & Event* (10:1), (2007), doi: 10.1353/tae.2007.0042

James, C. L. R., *The Black Jacobins* (London: Penguin, 2001; first published 1938)

James, Susan, *Passion and Action: The Emotions in Seventeenth-Century Philosophy* (Oxford: Clarendon, 1997)

James, William, 'Subjective Effects of Nitrous Oxide', *Mind*, 7, (1882), 186–208

James, William, *The Varieties of Religious Experience: A Study in Human Nature* (London: Penguin, 1982; first published USA: Longmans, Green & Co, 1902)

James, William, 'What is an Emotion?', *Mind*, 9, (1884), 188–205

Jay, Mike, *The Atmosphere of Heaven: The Unnatural Experiments of Dr Beddoes and his Sons of Genius* (New Haven and London: Yale University Press, 2009)

Jay, Mike, 'The Atmosphere of Heaven: The 1799 Nitrous Oxide Researches Reconsidered', *Notes and Records of the Royal Society of London*, 63:3, (2009), 297–309

Johns, Alessa, *Women's Utopias of the Eighteenth Century* (Urbana and Chicago: University of Illinois Press, 2003)

Johnson, Nancy E., '"Seated on her Bags of Dollars": Representations of America in the English Jacobin Novel', *Dalhousie Review*, 82 (3), (2002), 423–39

Johnston, Kenneth R., *Unusual Suspects: Pitt's Reign of Alarm and the Lost Generation of the 1790s* (Oxford: Oxford University Press, 2013)

Kates, Gary, *Cercle Social, the Girondins and the French Revolution* (Princeton: Princeton University Press, 1985)

Keane, John, *Tom Paine: A Political Life* (1995)

Keats, John, *The Letters of John Keats*, ed. H. E. Rollins, 2 vols (Cambridge: Cambridge University Press, 1958)

Kelly, Gary, 'Holcroft, Thomas (1745–1809)', *Oxford Dictionary of National Biography*, Oxford University Press, 2004, www.oxforddnb.com/view/article/13487 (accessed 22 March 2017)

Kennedy, Deborah, *Helen Maria Williams and the Age of Revolution* (Lewisburg: Associated University Presses, 2002)

Kessen, William, 'Rousseau's Children', *Daedalus*, 107:3, (1978), 155–66

Khole, 'Men: Dangers of Repression', *Psych2go*, 18 January 2017, www.psych2go.net/dangers-of-repression (accessed 23 March 2017)

King-Hele, Desmond, *Shelley: His Thought and Work* (London: Macmillan, 1962; 1971)

Kington, John, 'The Severe Winter of 1794/1795 in England', *Weather*, 49:12, (1994), 419–20

Kirshenbaum, Mira, 'What is Emotional Energy?', *The Emotional Energy Factor: The Secrets High Energy People Use to Fight Fatigue* www.chestnuthillinstitute.com/books/eef/faqs.php (accessed 17 August 2016)

Klein, Melanie, *Love, Guilt and Reparation; and Other Works 1921–1945* (New York: Free Press, 1975)

Knight, David, *Humphry Davy: Science and Power* (Cambridge: Cambridge University Press, 1992)

Knight, David, 'Thompson, Sir Benjamin, Count Rumford in the Nobility of the Holy Roman empire (1753–1814)', *Oxford Dictionary of National Biography*, Oxford University Press, 2004; online edition, Jan 2008, www.oxforddnb.com/view/article/27255 (accessed 28 Aug 2016)

Knoeff, Rina, *Herman Boerhaave (1668–1738): Calvinist Chemist and Physician* (Amsterdam: Royal Netherlands Academy of Arts and Sciences, 2002)

Knowles, John, *The Life and Writings of Henry Fuseli*, 3 vols (London: Colburn & Bentley, 1831)

Knuuttila, Simo, *Emotions in Ancient and Medieval Philosophy* (Oxford: Clarendon Press, 2004)

Kohut, Heinz, *The Analysis of the Self: A Systematic Approach to the Psychoanalytic Treatment of Narcissistic Personality Disorders* (Chicago and London: University of Chicago Press, 2009; first published 1971)

Landsburg, Steven E., 'How the Web Prevents Rape', www.slate.com/articles/arts/everyday_economics/2006/10/how_the_web_prevents_rape.html (accessed 4 July 2016)

Laqueur, Thomas W., *Making Sex: Body and Gender from the Greeks to Freud* (Cambridge, Mass.: Harvard University Press, 1990)

Lawrence, Christopher, 'Brown, John (*bap.* 1735, *d.* 1788)', *Oxford Dictionary of National Biography*, Oxford University Press, 2004, www.oxforddnb.com/view/article/3623 (accessed 1 July 2016)

Lawrence, Christopher, 'Cullen, Brown and the Poverty of Essentialism', pp. 1–21, in W. F. Bynum and Roy Porter, eds, *Brunonianism in Britain and Europe*, Supplement No. 8 to *Medical History* (London: Wellcome Institute, 1988)

Lawrence, James, *The Empire of the Nairs; or, the Rights of Women. An Utopian Romance, in Twelve Books* (London: T. Hookham, 1811)

The Laws Respecting Women, as They Regard Their Natural Rights, or Their Connections And Conduct (London: 1777)

Leask, Nigel, 'Pantisocracy and the politics of the "Preface" to *Lyrical Ballads*', pp. 39–58, in *Reflections of Revolution: Images of Romanticism*, ed. Alison Yarrington and Kelvin Everest (London and New York: Routledge, 1993)

LeDoux, Joseph, *The Emotional Brain: The Mysterious Underpinnings of*

Emotional Life (London: Phoenix, 1999; first published New York: Simon & Schuster, 1998)

Lemonnier-Mercier, Aline, *Les Embellissements du Havre au XVIIIe siècle: projets, réalisations, 1719–1830* (Rouen and Le Havre: Presses Universitaires de Rouen et du Havre, 2013)

Lennox, Charles, *An Authentic Copy of the Duke of Richmond's Bill, for a Parliamentary Reform* (London: J. Stockdale, 1783)

Lennox, Charles, *A Letter from His Grace the Duke of Richmond to Lieutenant Colonel Sharman, Chairman to the Committee of Correspondence Appointed by the Delegates of Forty-five Corps of Volunteers, Assembled at Lisburn in Ireland; with NOTES, by a Member of the Society for Constitutional Information* (London: J. Johnson, 1792)

'Letters on Emigration from a Gentleman Lately Returned from America', *Gentleman's Magazine*, 65:2, (Sept 1795), 760

Levere, Trevor H., 'Dr Thomas Beddoes and the Establishment of his Pneumatic Institute: A Tale of Three Presidents', *Notes and Records of the Royal Society of London*, 32:1, (July 1977), 41–9

Levere, Trevor H., 'Dr. Thomas Beddoes (1750–1808): Science and Medicine in Politics and Society', *The British Journal for the History of Science*, 17:2, (July 1984), 187–204

Lewis, Gwynne, *The French Revolution: Rethinking the Debate* (London: Routledge, 1993)

Lewis, Samuel, *The History and Topography of the Parish of Saint Mary, Islington* (London: J. H. Jackson, 1842)

Lin, Pei-Ying, 'Untranslatable Emotions in Languages other than English, vs Parrott's Emotion Classification' (2013), http://unspeakableness.net (accessed 30 December 2016)

Lindeboom, G. A., *Boerhaave and Great Britain: Three Lectures on Boerhaave with Particular Reference to his Relations with Great Britain* (Leiden: E. J. Brill, 1974)

Linton, Marisa, *Choosing Terror: Virtue, Friendship, and Authenticity in the French Revolution* (Oxford: Oxford University Press, 2013)

Litchfield, R. B., *Tom Wedgwood: The First Photographer* (London: Duckworth & Co., 1903)

Locke, John, *An Essay Concerning Human Understanding*, ed. Peter H. Nidditch (Oxford: Oxford University Press, 1975; first published 1689)

Logan, Eugenia, 'Coleridge's Scheme of Pantisocracy and American Travel Accounts', *PMLA*, 45, (1930), 1069–1084

Lottes, Günther, 'Radicalism, Revolution and Political Culture:

An Anglo-French Comparison', pp. 78–98, in Mark Philp, ed., *The French Revolution and British Popular Politics* (Cambridge: Cambridge University Press, 1991)

Lovell, Robert, *Bristol: A Satire* (London: printed for the author, 1794)

MacDonald, Edgar E., *The American Edgeworths: A Biographical Sketch of Richard Edgeworth (1764–1796) with Letters and Documents Pertaining to the Legacy of His Three Sons* (Richmond, Virginia: 1970)

Mackintosh, James, *Vindiciae Gallicae: Defence of the French Revolution and its English Admirers* (London: Robinson, 1791)

Madan, Martin, *Thelyphthora; or, A Treatise on Female Ruin*, 2 vols (London: J. Dodsley, 1780)

Malthus, Thomas R., *An Essay on the Principle of Population*, ed. Geoffrey Gilbert (Oxford: Oxford University Press, 2008; first published London, 1798)

Mandeville, Bernard, *The Fable of the Bees: Or, Private Vices, Publick Benefits*, 2 vols (Oxford: Clarendon Press, 1924; a reproduction of 6th edition, London: J. Tonson, 1732)

Manly, Susan, *Language, Custom and Nation in the 1790s: Locke, Tooke, Wordsworth, Edgeworth* (Aldershot: Ashgate, 2007)

'manner, n. (and int.)'. OED Online. December 2016. Oxford University Press, www.oed.com/view/Entry/113569 ?redirectedFrom=manners (accessed December 24, 2016)

Marshall, P. J. and Alaine Low, eds, *The Oxford History of the British Empire*, Vol. II: *The Eighteenth Century* (Oxford: Oxford University Press, 1998)

Marshall, Peter H., *William Godwin* (New Haven and London: Yale University Press, 1984)

Martinez, Pepe, *The Consumer Mind: Brand Perception and the Implication for Marketers* (London and Philadelphia: Kogan Page, 2012)

Mason, Eudo C., *The Mind of Henry Fuseli: Selections from his Writings* (London: Routledge and Kegan Paul, 1951)

Mathias, Peter, 'Malthus and the Transition from Optimism to Pessimism in Classical Economic Thought', unpublished paper, 1981

Mavor, Elizabeth, *The Ladies of Llangollen: A Study in Romantic Friendship* (Ludlow: Moonrise Press, 1971; 2011)

McAlpin, Mary, *Female Sexuality and Cultural Degradation in Enlightenment France: Medicine and Literature* (Farnham: Ashgate, 2012)

McBride, Theresa, 'Public Authority and Private Lives: Divorce after the French Revolution', *French Historical Studies*, 17:3, (1992) 747–68

McCalman, Iain, *Radical Underworld: Prophets, Revolutionaries and Pornographers in London, 1795–1840* (Oxford: Clarendon Press, 1993)

McCarthy, William, *Anna Letitia Barbauld: Voice of the Enlightenment* (Baltimore and London: John Hopkins University Press, 2008)

McKusick, James C., '"Wisely Forgetful": Coleridge and the Politics of Pantisocracy', pp. 107–28, in *Romanticism and Colonialism: Writing and Empire, 1780–1830*, Tim Fulford and Peter Kitson, eds (Cambridge: Cambridge University Press, 1998)

McLean, Iain, *Adam Smith: Radical and Egalitarian – An Interpretation for the 21st Century* (Edinburgh: Edinburgh University Press, 2006)

McLynn, Frank, *The Road Not Taken: How Britain Narrowly Missed a Revolution, 1381–1926* (London: Bodley Head, 2012)

McNeill, Maggie, 'Out of Control', *The Honest Courtesan*, 24 September 2010, maggiemcneill.wordpress.com/2010/09/24/out-of-control/ (accessed 2 September 2016)

Medley, Mary Louise, *History of Anson County, North Carolina, 1750–1976* (Baltimore, MD: Anson County Historical Society, 1976)

Mee, Jon, *Romanticism, Enthusiasm and Regulation: Poetics and the Policing of Culture in the Romantic Period* (Oxford: Oxford University Press, 2003)

Meteyard, Eliza, *A Group of Englishmen (1795–1815): Being Records of the Younger Wedgwoods and their Friends* (London: 1871)

de La Mettrie, Julien Offray, *Man a Machine*, trans. Jean Baptiste de Boyer (Dublin: Brien, 1794; first published in French as *L'Homme Machine*, 1747)

Mignet, François, *History of the French Revolution from 1789–1814* (London: 1826)

Millar, A. H., 'Palmer, Thomas Fyshe (1747–1802)', rev. G. M. Ditchfield, *Oxford Dictionary of National Biography*, Oxford University Press, 2004; online edition, Jan 2008, www.oxforddnb.com/view/article/21220 (accessed 11 Dec 2016)

Moore, Wendy, *How to Create the Perfect Wife: The True Story of One Gentleman, Two Orphans, and an Experiment to Create the Ideal Woman* (London: Weidenfeld & Nicolson, 2014)

More, Hannah, *Strictures on the Modern System of Female Education*, 3rd edition, 2 vols (London: T. Cadell, 1799)

Morris, A. D., *James Parkinson: His Life and Times* (Boston: Birkhauser, 1989)

Morris, Gouverneur, *Diary of the French Revolution by Gouverneur Morris 1752–1816*, ed. Beatrice Cary Davenport, 2 vols (London: George Harrap & Co., 1939)

Murat, Laure, *The Man Who Thought He Was Napoleon: Toward a Political History of Madness*, trans. Deke Dusinberre (Chicago and London: University of Chicago Press, 2014)

Nagoski, Emily, *Come As You Are: The Surprising New Science That Will Transform Your Sex Life* (London: Scribe, 2015)

Newhall, Beaumont, ed., *Photography: Essays and Images* (New York: Museum of Modern Art, 1980)

Newlyn, Lucy, ed., *Cambridge Companion to Samuel Taylor Coleridge* (Cambridge: Cambridge University Press, 2002)

[Nordenskjöld, August & Carl Wadström], *Plan for a Free Community Upon the Coast of Africa, Under the Protection of Great Britain; but Intirely Independent of All European Laws and Governments. With an Invitation, Under Certain Conditions, to All Persons Desirous of Partaking the Benefits Thereof* (London: Hindmarsh, 24 June 1789)

Nussbaum, Martha C., *Upheavals of Thought: The Intelligence of Emotions* (New York: Cambridge University Press, 2001)

O'Connor, Rory C., and Matthew K. Nock, 'The Psychology of Suicidal Behaviour', *Lancet Psychiatry*, 1 (1), (June 2014), 73–85

Office for National Statistics, *Suicides in the United Kingdom: 2012 Registrations* (2014), p. 1, http://webarchive.nationalarchives.gov.uk/20160105160709/www.ons.gov.uk/ons/dcp171778_351100.pdf (accessed 25 November 2016)

Olson, Alison Gilbert, *The Radical Duke: Career and Correspondence of Charles Lennox, third Duke of Richmond* (Oxford: Oxford University Press, 1961)

'Ophelia', 'Matilda; or, the Female Recluse. An Anecdote', *Lady's Magazine*, April 1779, 201–4

Paine, Thomas, *The Age of Reason: Being an Investigation of True and Fabulous Theology* (London: Daniel Eaton, 1794)

Paine, Thomas, *Rights of Man: Being an Answer to Mr Burke's Attack on the French Revolution* (London: J. S. Jordan, 1791), pp. 83–197, in Thomas Paine, *Rights of Man, Common Sense and Other Political Writings*, ed. Mark Philp (Oxford: Oxford University Press, 1995; 2008)

Paine, Thomas, *Rights of Man, Common Sense and Other Political Writings*, ed. Mark Philp (Oxford: Oxford University Press, 1995; reissued 2008)

Paine, Thomas, *Rights of Man; Part the Second* (London: Symonds, 1792)

Paley, William, *Natural Theology or Evidences of the Existence and Attributes of the Deity* (Philadelphia: John Morgan, 1802)

Palmer, R. R., *The Age of the Democratic Revolution: A Political History of Europe and America, 1760–1800* (Princeton and Oxford: Princeton University Press, 2014)

Paris, John Ayrton, *The Life of Sir Humphry Davy, Bart. Ll. D*, 2 vols (London: 1831)

Park, Mary C., *Joseph Priestley and the Problem of Pantisocracy*, in *Proceedings of the Delaware County Institute of Science*, XI, (1947), 1–60

Parkinson, James, *An Essay on the Shaking Palsy* (London: Sherwood, Neely and Jones, 1817)

Parliamentary Register: Or History of the Proceedings and Debates of the House of Commons (London: J. Debrett, 1796)

Pfau, Thomas, *Romantic Moods: Paranoia, Trauma, and Melancholy, 1790–1840* (Baltimore: Johns Hopkins University Press, 2005)

Phillips, Adam, *Missing Out: In Praise of the Unlived Life* (London: Hamish Hamilton, 2012)

Phillipson, Nicholas, *Adam Smith: An Enlightened Life* (London: Allen Lane, 2010)

Philp, Mark, ed., *The French Revolution and British Popular Politics* (Cambridge: Cambridge University Press, 1991)

Philp, Mark, *Godwin's* Political Justice (London: Duckworth, 1986)

Pina, Darlene L., and Vern Bengtson, 'The Division of Household Labor and Wives' Happiness: Ideology, Employment and Perceptions of Support', *Journal of Marriage and the Family*, 55:4, (November 1993), 901–12

Place, Francis, *The Autobiography of Francis Place*, ed. Mary Thale (London: Cambridge University Press, 1972)

'The Pneumatic Revellers: An Eclogue', *Anti-Jacobin Review and Magazine*, 4, (1800), 109–18

Polwhele, Richard, *Biographical Sketches in Cornwall*, 3 vols (Truro: J. B. Nichols & Son, 1831)

Porter, Bernard, *Plots and Paranoia: A History of Political Espionage in Britain 1790–1988* (London and New York: Routledge, 1989; 1992)

Porter, Roy, *Doctor of Society: Thomas Beddoes and the Sick Trade in Late-Enlightenment England* (London and New York: Routledge, 1992)

Porter, Roy, 'Sex and the Singular Man: The Seminal Ideas of James Graham', *Studies on Voltaire and the Eighteenth Century*, 228, (1984), 3–24

Porter, Roy, 'The Sexual Politics of James Graham', *British Journal for Eighteenth-Century Studies*, 5 (2), (1982), 199–206

Pratt, Lynda, '"Let not Bristol be Ashamed"?: Coleridge's Afterlife in the Early Recollections of Joseph Cottle', pp. 20–35 in James Vigus and Jane Wright, eds, *Coleridge's Afterlives*, (Basingstoke and New York: Palgrave, 2008)

Pratt, Mary Louise, *Imperial Eyes: Travel Writing and Transculturation* (London: Routledge, 1992)

Price, Richard, *A Discourse on the Love of our Country* (1790), pp. 39–56, in Iain Hampsher-Monk, ed., *The Impact of the French Revolution: Texts from Britain in the 1790s* (Cambridge: Cambridge University Press, 2005)

Price, Richard and Joseph Priestley, *Sermons by Richard Price and Joseph Priestley* (London: British and Foreign Unitarian Association, 1830)

Priestley, Joseph, *An Appeal to the Public on the Subject of the Riots in Birmingham* (Birmingham: Thompson, 1791)

Priestley, Joseph, *A Letter to the Right Honourable William Pitt . . . on the Subjects of Toleration and Church Establishments*, 2nd edition (London: Johnson, 1787)

Priestley, Joseph, *Memoirs of Dr. Joseph Priestley, to the Year 1795* (London: J. Johnson, 1807)

Priestley, Joseph, *The Theological and Miscellaneous Works of Joseph Priestley*, ed. John Towill Rutt, 25 vols (London: 1817–31)

Quoidbach, Jordi, Moïra Mikolajczak, Ilios Kotsou, June Gruber, Alexsandr Kogan, and Michael I. Norton, 'Emodiversity and the Emotional Ecosystem', *Journal of Experimental Psychology: General*, 143 (6), (2014), 2057–66

Rabushka, Alvin, *From Adam Smith to the Wealth of America* (New Brunswick and Oxford: Transaction Books, 1985)

Ratcliffe, Donald, 'The Right to Vote and the Rise of Democracy, 1787–1828', *Journal of the Early Republic*, 33, (Summer 2013), 219–54

Reddy, William M., *The Navigation of Feeling: A Framework for the History of Emotions* (Cambridge: Cambridge University Press, 2001)

Reed, Theresa A. (aka Darklady), 'Private Acts vs Public Art: Where Prostitution Ends and Pornography Begins', pp. 249–57, in Jessica Spector, ed., *Prostitution and Pornography: Philosophical Debate about the Sex Industry* (Stanford: Stanford University Press, 2006)

Reeves, Clara, *Plans of Education; with Remarks on the Systems of Other Writers* (London: Hookham and Carpenter, 1792)

Reilly, Robin, 'Wedgwood, Josiah (1730–1795)', *Oxford Dictionary of National Biography*, Oxford University Press, 2004; online edition, Sept 2013, www.oxforddnb.com/view/article/28966 (accessed 20 March 2017)

Remarks on the Declaration of the Whig Club, on the 23d of January, 1796, in a Postcript to the 2nd Edition of a Satire, Entitled, The Political Dramatist of the House of Commons in 1795 (London: J. Parsons, 1796)

Rickett, Oscar, 'If Only More Men Could Express Emotion Like Professor Green', *Guardian*, 29 October 2015, www.theguardian.com/commentisfree/2015/oct/29/men-express-themselves-professor-green-suicide-express-feelings (accessed 20 March 2017)

Riis, Ole, and Linda Woodhead, *A Sociology of Religious Emotion* (Oxford: Oxford University Press, 2010)

Rix, Robert, 'Carl Bernhard Wadström (1749–1799)', www.brycchancarey.com/abolition/wadstrom.htm (accessed 16 December 2016)

Rix, Robert, *William Blake and the Cultures of Radical Christianity* (London: Routledge, 2007)

Robinson, Henry Crabb, *Henry Crabb Robinson on Books and their Writers*, ed. Edith J. Morley, 3 vols (London: J. M. Dent & Sons, 1938)

Roe, Nicholas, 'Coleridge and John Thelwall: The Road to Nether Stowey', pp. 62–80, in *The Coleridge Connection: Essays for Thomas McFarland*, ed. Richard Gravil and Molly Lefebure (London: Macmillan, 1990)

Roe, Nicholas, 'Coleridge's Watchman Tour', *Coleridge Bulletin*, 21 (2003) 35–46

Roe, Nicholas, 'Dyer, George (1755–1841)', *Oxford Dictionary of National Biography*, Oxford University Press, 2004, www.oxforddnb.com/view/article/8347 (accessed 20 Dec 2016)

Roe, Nicholas, 'Thelwall, John (1764–1834)', *Oxford Dictionary of National Biography*, Oxford University Press, 2004; online edition, Sept 2012, www.oxforddnb.com/view/article/27167 (accessed 22 March 2017)

Roe, Nicholas, 'Tweddell, John (1769–1799)', *Oxford Dictionary of National Biography*, Oxford University Press, 2004, www.oxforddnb.com/view/article/27902 (accessed 22 March 2017)

Roe, Nicholas, *Wordsworth and Coleridge: The Radical Years* (Oxford: Clarendon, 1988)

Rogers, Rachel, 'White's Hotel: A Junction of British Radical Culture in Early 1790s Paris', *Caliban: French Journal of English Studies*, 33, (2013), 153–72

Rollin, Henry R., 'Psychiatry in Britain One Hundred Years Ago', *The British Journal of Psychiatry*, 183:4, (2003), 292–8

Rosenwein, Barbara, 'Worrying About Emotions in History', *American Historical Review*, 107:3, (June 2002), 821–45

Rothschild, Emma, 'Adam Smith and Conservative Economics', *Economic History Review*, 2nd set, 45, (1992), 74–96

Rousseau, Jean-Jacques, *The Basic Political Writings*, trans. Donald A. Cress (Indianapolis & Cambridge: Hackett, 1987; first published 1755)

Rousseau, Jean-Jacques, *Discourse on the Origin and Foundations of Inequality Among Men*, pp. 23–109, in Jean-Jacques Rousseau, *The Basic Political Writings*, trans. Donald A. Cress (Indianapolis & Cambridge: Hackett, 1987; first published 1755)

Rousseau, Jean-Jacques, *Émile: Or, on Education*, trans. Allan Bloom (London: Penguin, 1979; first published 1762)

Rousseau, Jean-Jacques, *Political Writings*, trans. Frederick Watkins (Madison: University of Wisconsin Press, 1986; first published 1762)

Rousseau, Jean-Jacques, *The Social Contract*, pp. 1–158, in Jean-Jacques Rousseau, *Political Writings*, trans. Frederick Watkins (Madison: University of Wisconsin Press, 1986; first published 1762)

Rowland, Peter, *The Life and Times of Thomas Day, 1748–1789* (Lewiston, New York, and Lampeter: Edwin Mellen Press, 1996)

St Clair, William, *The Godwins and the Shelleys* (London: Faber, 1989)

Salzmann, C. S., *Elements of Morality; for the Use of Young Persons. To Which is Prefixed, an Address to Parents*, trans. Mary Wollstonecraft (Edinburgh: Oliver and Boyd, 1821)

Salovey, Peter, and David J. Sluyter, eds, *Emotional Development and Emotional Intelligence: Educational Implications* (New York: Basic Books, 1997)

Sanchez, Rafael Torres, 'The Triumph of the Fiscal-Military State in the Eighteenth Century', pp. 25–34, in Rafael Torres Sanchez, ed., *War, State and Development* (Pamplona: Universidad de Navarra, 2007)

Sanchez, Rafael Torres, ed., *War, State and Development* (Pamplona: Universidad de Navarra, 2007)

Sandage, Scott A., *Born Losers: A History of Failure in America* (Cambridge, Mass.: Harvard University Press, 2005)

Sandford, Mrs Henry, *Thomas Poole and his Friends*, 2 vols (London: Macmillan, 1888)

Schama, Simon, *Citizens: A Chronicle of the French Revolution* (London: Viking, 1989)

Schofield, Robert E., *The Enlightened Joseph Priestley: A Study of His Life and Work from 1773 to 1804* (University Park, Penn.: Pennsylvania University Press, 2004)

Schuchard, Marsha Keith, 'Rediscovering William "Hurricane" Gilbert: A Lost Voice of Revolution and Madness in the Worlds of Blake and the Romantics', *British Association for Romanticism Studies Conference: Romantic Revelations*, July 1999

Scott, Sarah, *A Description of Millenium Hall* (London: 1762)

Scurr, Ruth, *Fatal Purity: Robespierre and the French Revolution* (London: Vintage, 2007)

Seale, Clive, and Jonathan Charteris-Black, 'The Interaction of Class and Gender in Illness Narratives', *Sociology*, 42 (3), (June 2008), 453–69

Seward, Anna, *Letters of Anna Seward: Written Between the Years 1784 and 1807*, 6 vols (Edinburgh: George Ramsay, 1811)

Seward, Anna, *Memoirs of the Life of Dr. Darwin* (London: Johnson, 1804)

Shelley, Percy Bysshe, *Essays, Letters from Abroad, Translations and Fragments* (London: Edward Moxon, 1840)

Shelley, Percy Bysshe, *The Letters of Percy Bysshe Shelley*, ed. Frederick L. Jones, 2 vols (Oxford: Clarendon Press, 1964)

Shelley, Percy Bysshe, *The Major Works*, ed. Zachary Leader and Michael O'Neill (Oxford: Oxford University Press, 2009)

Shelley, Percy Bysshe, *The Revolt of Islam; A Poem, in Twelve Cantos* (London: C. and J. Ollier, 1818)

Shields, David S., 'Happiness in Society: The Development of an Eighteenth-Century American Poetic Ideal', *American Literature*, 55:4, (December 1983), 541–59

Sibly, Ebenezer, *The Medical Mirror; or, Treatise on the Impregnation of the Human Female* (London: Sibly, [1795])

Sisman, Adam, *Wordsworth and Coleridge: The Friendship* (London: Harper Perennial, 2007)

Smith, Adam, *Theory of Moral Sentiments*, Glasgow edition of the *Works and Correspondence of Adam Smith*, ed. D. D. Raphael and A. L.

Macfie (Indianapolis: Liberty Fund, 1982; facsimile of Oxford: Oxford University Press, 1976; first published Edinburgh: Andrew Millar, 1759)

Smith, Adam, *An Inquiry into the Nature and Causes of the Wealth of Nations* (London: Strahan and Cadell, 1776)

Smith, Christopher J. P., *A Quest for Home: Reading Robert Southey* (Liverpool: Liverpool University Press, 1997)

[Smith, John], *Assassination of the King! The Conspirators Exposed, or an Account of the Apprehension, Treatment in Prison, and Repeated Examinations Before the Privy Council, of John Smith and George Higgins, on a Charge of High Treason* (London: John Smith, 1795)

Smith, Leonard, 'A Gentleman's Mad Doctor in Georgian England: Edward Long Fox and Brislington House', *History of Psychiatry*, 19, (June 2008), 163–84

Smith, W. D. A., *Under the Influence: A History of Nitrous Oxide and Oxygen Anaesthesia* (London: Macmillan, 1982)

Soboul, Albert, *The French Revolution: 1787–1799*, trans. Alan Forrest and Colin Jones (London: Unwin Hyman, 1989)

Soboul, Albert, *The Parisian Sans-Culottes and the French Revolution, 1793–4*, trans. Gwynne Lewis (Oxford: Clarendon Press, 1964)

Southey, Robert, *The Collected Letters of Robert Southey: Part One, 1791–1797*, ed. Lynda Pratt, Romantic Circles Electronic Edition www.rc.umd.edu/editions/southey_letters

Southey, Robert, *Letters from England* (London: Cresset Press, 1951; first published 1807)

Southey, Robert, *New Letters of Robert Southey*, ed. Kenneth Curry (New York: Columbia University Press, 1965)

Southey, Robert, *Selections from the Letters of Robert Southey*, ed. John Wood Warter (London: 1856)

Speck, William Arthur, *Robert Southey: Entire Man of Letters* (New Haven and London: Yale University Press, 2006)

Spector, Jessica, ed., *Prostitution and Pornography: Philosophical Debate about the Sex Industry* (Stanford: Stanford University Press, 2006)

Stansfield, Dorothy A., *Thomas Beddoes M.D. 1760–1808: Chemist, Physician, Democrat* (Dordrecht, Boston and Lancaster: D. Reidel Publishing Company, 1984)

Sterne, Laurence, *A Sentimental Journey through France and Italy* (London: Penguin, 2001; first published 1768)

Stewart, John Hall, ed., *A Documentary Survey of the French Revolution* (New York: Macmillan, 1951)

Stock, John Edmonds, *Memoirs of the Life of Thomas Beddoes, M.D. with an Analytical Account of his Writings* (London, Bristol, Edinburgh, Dublin: John Murray, J. M. Gutch, William Blackwood, M. N. Mahon, 1811)

The Stoics Reader, trans. Brad Indood and Lloyd P. Gerson (Indianapolis: Hackett, 2008)

Stone, Lawrence, *The Family, Sex and Marriage in England 1500–1800* (London: Penguin, 1979)

Storey, Mark, *Robert Southey: A Life* (Oxford: Oxford University Press, 1997)

Stott, Anne, *Hannah More: The First Victorian* (Oxford: Oxford University Press, 2003; reprinted 2007)

Swaab, Peter, 'Lamb, Charles (1775–1834)', *Oxford Dictionary of National Biography*, Oxford University Press, 2004, www. oxforddnb.com/view/article/15912 (accessed 22 March 2017)

Swedenborg, Emanuel, *The Delights of Wisdom Pertaining to Conjugial Love*, trans. Samuel M. Warren (West Chester, Pennsylvania: Swedenborg Foundation, 2009)

Sworowski, Jeffrey, 'Condorcet's Education: Haunted by the Ghost of Rousseau', *International Journal of Lifelong Education*, 14:4, (1995), 320–30

Tait, Robert Lawson, *Diseases of Women and Abdominal Surgery* (Leicester: Richardson & Co., 1889)

Talamante, Laura Emerson, 'Creating the Republican Family: Political and Social Transformation and the Revolutionary Family Tribunal', *Proceedings of the Western Society for French History*, 38, (2010), 143–62

Tavris, Carol, *Anger: The Misunderstood Emotion* (New York and London: Touchstone, 1989)

Tavris, Carol, *The Mismeasure of Woman: Why Women are Not the Better Sex, the Inferior Sex, or the Opposite Sex* (New York: Touchstone, 1993)

Taylor, Barbara, *Eve and the New Jerusalem: Socialism and Feminism in the Nineteenth Century* (London: Virago, 1983)

Taylor, Barbara, *Mary Wollstonecraft and the Feminist Imagination* (Cambridge: Cambridge University Press, 2003)

Thale, Mary, *Selections from the Papers of the London Corresponding Society 1792–1799* (Cambridge: Cambridge University Press, 1983)

Thompson, E. P., 'Disenchantment or Default? A Lay Sermon,' pp. 33–74, in E. P. Thompson, *The Romantics: Wordsworth, Coleridge,*

Thelwall (Woodbridge: Merlin Press, 1997); originally given as one of the Albert Schweitzer lectures at New York University, 1968; originally published in O'Brien and Vaneck, eds, *Power and Consciousness* (New York: New York University Press, 1969)

Thompson, E. P., *The Making of the English Working Class* (London: Penguin, 1991; first published London: Victor Gollancz, 1963)

Thompson, E. P., *The Romantics: Wordsworth, Coleridge, Thelwall* (Woodbridge: Merlin Press, 1997)

Thornbury, Walter, *Old and New London* (London, 1878)

Tillyard, Stella, *Citizen Lord: Edward Fitzgerald, 1763–1798* (London: Chatto & Windus, 1997)

Todd, A. C., *Beyond the Blaze: A Biograpy of Davies Gilbert* (Truro: D. Bradford Barton, 1967)

Todd, Janet, *Death and the Maidens: Fanny Wollstonecraft and the Shelley Circle* (London: Profile, 2007)

Todd, Janet, *Mary Wollstonecraft: A Revolutionary Life* (London: Phoenix, 2000)

Tomalin, Claire, *The Life and Death of Mary Wollstonecraft* (London: Penguin, 1974; 1992)

Tosh, John, *A Man's Place: Masculinity and the Middle-Class Home in Victorian England* (Newhaven and London: Yale University Press, 1999)

Traer, James F., *Marriage and the Family in Eighteenth-Century France* (Ithaca, NY: Cornell University Press, 1980)

Trott, Nicola, 'Coleridge's City', *Coleridge Bulletin*, New Series, 19, (2002), 41–57

Trumbach, Randolph, *The Rise of the Egalitarian Family: Aristocratic Kinship and Domestic Relations in Eighteenth-Century England* (New York: Academic Press, 1978)

Trusler, John, *The Habitable World Described* (London: Trusler, 1788–97)

Tweddell, Robert, ed., *The Remains of John Tweddell* (London: J. Mawman, 1815)

Uglow, Jenny, *In These Times: Living in Britain Through Napoleon's Wars 1793–1815* (London: Faber, 2014)

Verrochi, Nicole M., 'Me, My Self, and Emotion: Identity-Consistent Emotions and Consumption', dissertation research presented to University of Pennsylvania, 2014

Vigus, James, and Jane Wright, eds., *Coleridge's Afterlives* (Basingstoke and New York: Palgrave, 2008)

Voydanoff, P., and B. W. Donnelly, 'The Intersection of Time in
    Activities and Perceived Unfairness in Relation to Psychological
    Distress and Marital Quality', *Journal of Marriage and the Family*,
    61, (1999), 739–51

Ward, Candace, *Desire and Disorder: Fevers, Fictions, and Feeling in
    English Georgian Culture* (Lewisburg: Bucknell University Press,
    2007)

Watson, Thomas, *Popular Evidences of Natural Religion and Christianity*
    (London: Longman, Hurst, Rees and Orme, 1805)

Wedgwood, Barbara and Hensleigh Wedgwood, *The Wedgwood Circle
    1730–1897: Four Generations of a Family and their Friends* (London:
    Cassell, 1980)

Wedgwood, Thomas, *The Value of a Maimed Life: Extracts from the
    Manuscript Notes of Thomas Wedgwood*, ed. Margaret Olivia
    Tremayne (London: C. W. Daniel, 1912)

Weld the Younger, Isaac, *Travels Through the States of North America*, 2
    vols (London: 1807)

Whale John, ed., *Edmund Burke's Reflections on the Revolution in France*
    (Manchester: Manchester University Press, 2000)

Whalley, George, 'The Bristol Library Borrowings of Southey and
    Coleridge, 1793–8', *Library*, IV, (1949), 114–31

Wharam, Alan, *The Treason Trials, 1794* (Leicester: Leicester
    University Press, 1992)

Whyte, Robert, *Observations on the Nature, Causes, and Cure of
    those Disorders Which Have Been Commonly Called Nervous,
    Hypochondriac, or Hysteric: To Which are Prefixed Some Remarks on
    the Sympathy of the Nerves* (London and Edinburgh: 1765)

Williams, David, 'The Influence of Rousseau on Political Opinion,
    1760–95', *English Historical Review*, 48:191, (1933), 414–30

Williams, Helen Maria, *Letters Written in France*, ed. Neil Fraistat and
    Susan S. Lanser (Ormskirk: Broadview, 2001)

Williams, J. L., *The Boy's Own Book: A Compendium of All the Sports and
    Recreations of Youth* (Paris: Baudry's European Library, 1843)

Winnicott, D. W., *Playing and Reality* (London: Routledge, 2008; first
    published London: Tavistock Publications, 1971)

Winterer, Caroline, *American Enlightenments: Pursuing Happiness
    in the Age of Reason* (Cambridge, Mass.: Yale University Press,
    2016)

Wollstonecraft, Mary, *The Collected Letters of Mary Wollstonecraft*, ed.
    Janet Todd (New York: Columbia University Press, 1993)

Wollstonecraft, Mary, *An Historical and Moral View of the Origin and Progress of the French Revolution; and the Effect it has Produced in Europe*, 2nd edition (London: Johnson, 1795)

Wollstonecraft, Mary, 'Letter on the Present Character of the French Nation', IV, pp. 37–51, in *Posthumous Works of Mary Wollstonecraft Godwin*, 4 vols, ed. William Godwin (London: J. Johnson, 1798)

Wollstonecraft, Mary, *Letters Written During a Short Residence in Sweden, Norway, and Denmark*, ed. Jon Mee (Oxford: Oxford University Press, 2009)

Wollstonecraft, Mary, *Mary, A Fiction and The Wrongs of Woman, or Maria*, ed. Michelle Faubert (London: Broadview, 2012)

Wollstonecraft, Mary, *Of the Importance of Religious Opinions. Translated from the French of Mr. Necker* (Dublin: M. Mills, 1789)

Wollstonecraft, Mary, *Posthumous Works of Mary Wollstonecraft Godwin*, ed. William Godwin, 4 vols (London: J. Johnson, 1798)

Wollstonecraft, Mary, *Thoughts on the Education of Daughters* (Oxford and New York: Woodstock Books, 1994; facsimile of London: J. Johnson, 1787)

Wollstonecraft, Mary, *A Vindication of the Rights of Men, in a Letter to the Right Honourable Edmund Burke* (London: Joseph Johnson, 1790), pp. 1–68, in Mary Wollstonecraft, *A Vindication of the Rights of Woman & A Vindication of the Rights of Men*, ed. Janet Todd (Oxford: Oxford World's Classics, 1993)

Wollstonecraft, Mary, *A Vindication of the Rights of Woman*, 2nd edition (London: Johnson, 1792), pp. 63–282, in Mary Wollstonecraft, *A Vindication of the Rights of Woman & A Vindication of the Rights of Men*, ed. Janet Todd (Oxford: Oxford World's Classics, 1993)

Wollstonecraft, Mary, *A Vindication of the Rights of Woman & A Vindication of the Rights of Men*, ed. Janet Todd (Oxford: Oxford World's Classics, 1993)

Wollstonecraft, Mary, *The Works of Mary Wollstonecraft*, ed. Janet Todd and Marilyn Butler, 7 vols (London: Pickering & Chatto, 1989)

Woodward, G. M. and Isaac Cruikshank, *A Long String of Resolutions for a New Year* (London: S. W. Fores, 1792)

Wordsworth, William, and Samuel Taylor Coleridge, *Lyrical Ballads*, ed. R. L. Brett and A. R. Jones (London and New York: Routledge, 2005)

Wordsworth, William, *The Excursion*, ed. Sally Bushell, James A. Butler, and Michael C. Jaye (Ithaca and London: Cornell University Press, 2007)

Wordsworth, William, *The Prelude, 1799, 1805, 1850*, ed. M. H. Abrams (New York: Norton, 1979)

World Health Organization, *Preventing Suicide: A Global Imperative* (2014), www.who.int/mental_health/suicide-prevention/world_report_2014/en/ (accessed 25 November 2016)

Wright, John, *A Revealed Knowledge of Some Things That Will Speedily be Fulfilled in the World* (London: 1794)

Yarrington, Alison, and Kelvin Everest, eds, *Reflections of Revolution: Images of Romanticism* (London and New York: Routledge, 1993)

Yousef, Nancy, 'Savage or Solitary?: The Wild Child and Rousseau's Man of Nature', *Journal of the History of Ideas*, 62 (2), (April 2001), 245–63

ACKNOWLEDGEMENTS

This book first originated in two conversations in 2009: one with my agent, Tracy Bohan, after having read Richard Holmes' *Age of Wonder*, about the potential for a history of projects that failed; and the second, with Isla Rowland, about disappointment – who feels it most often, and why. It is an emotion that has become even more politically relevant in Britain and America in the intervening eight years.

In the course of researching and writing this study of disappointment, its trajectory and effects, I am first and foremost grateful to the institutions and funding bodies on whose formal support it has depended. The Leverhulme Trust funded my three-year Early Career Fellowship at Queen Mary, University of London, and at Wolfson College, University of Oxford; and the Fellowship's generous research grants enabled me to carry out many of the library and archive visits essential to the book's research. I am indebted to colleagues at Queen Mary – especially Anne Janowitz, Markman Ellis and Christopher Reid – for supporting my research. At Oxford, I am extremely grateful to the Dorset Foundation, who funded my Weinrebe Research Fellowship at the Oxford Centre for Life-Writing, where I learned so much about the theory and practice of biography from the best in the business: Hermione Lee, Elleke Boemer, the Centre's Advisory Committee, and the Centre's researchers, including Lyndsey Jenkins and Olivia Smith. I am especially grateful to Hermione for her generosity, kindness, and professional and personal support. For helping me to shape my early ideas for *A Revolution of Feeling* into the ambitious book proposal that was hiding within my rough, fragmentary notes, I owe a great deal to Tracy Bohan at the Wylie Agency. And, at the other end of the process, this book would have looked very different without the insightful and thought-provoking comments, questions and suggestions, particularly about the book's architecture, from my editor at Granta, Bella Lacey; and I am so grateful to copyeditor Daphne Tagg for her attentive eye to detail, and to the whole production team. I also owe thanks to Sara Holloway, the editor of my first book, whose voice I still hear in my head at the end of each paragraph, encouragingly probing me to 'say a little more'.

The subject of this book – the history of emotion in 1790s Britain – has been an enormous departure from my first book on the history of the Ordnance Survey, Britain's mapping agency. I conducted much of my research in the British Library in London, and in its outpost at Boston Spa, and owe enormous thanks to its staff. I am also grateful to the custodians of the various archives I consulted, especially the Abinger Collection at the Bodleian Library, Oxford; the archives of the Davies Gilbert family at the Cornwall Record Office; the Edgeworth Papers at the National Library of Ireland; the Pforzheimer Collection at the New York Public Library; and the National Archives. As well as the British Library, York University Library, Cambridge University Library, Wolfson College (Oxford) library and the Bodleian Library provided hospitable environments in which to conduct my reading.

I am so very grateful to every individual scholar, text, library, archive and conference that has helped me to get to grips with the complexities of eighteenth-century moral philosophy, the history of the French Revolution, the history of British radicalism, biographies of the key figures in this book, and psychoanalytical, neuroscientific, historical and cultural accounts of emotion and its history. In terms of thinking about the history and biology of emotion and desire, I have been particularly influenced by the work of Thomas Dixon, William M. Reddy, Barbara Rosenwein, Lynn Hunt, Antonio Damasio, Adam Phillips, Jon Mee, Tiffany Watt-Smith, Emma Donoghue, and the great German social psychologist Erich Fromm. The 1790s in Britain – and the broader transitional period between the eighteenth and nineteenth centuries – has been brought to life in the works of multiple historians and literary critics, but especially resonant for me have been the works of Albert Goodwin, Mark Philp, Iain Hampsher-Monk, Marilyn Butler, John Barrell, Clive Emsley, E. P. Thompson, Clarke Garrett, Marsha Schuchard, Kenneth R. Johnston, Leonore Davidoff and Catherine Hall, and Boyd Hilton. I have found the work of Ruth Scurr, Simon Schama and Gwynne Lewis especially helpful in understanding the history of 1790s France. I owe huge thanks to each scholar involved in excavating and narrating details of the lives of the principal figures in this book. The work of Victoria Myers, David O'Shaughnessy, William St Clair, Peter H. Marshall and especially Mark Philp and Pamela Clemit has been indispensable in helping me to form an image of William Godwin. The editorial, biographical, historical and critical researches of Janet Todd, Barbara Taylor, Claire Tomalin, Lyndall Gordon and Laura Kirkley have vividly brought Mary Wollstonecraft to life. Trevor Levere, Roy Porter, Dorothy S. Stansfield and Mike Jay have conducted painstaking work into Thomas Beddoes' life and career. It would not have been possible to have written about Coleridge, Southey and pantisocracy without the labours of Richard Holmes, Mary C. Park, Nicholas Roe, Earl Leslie Griggs, William Arthur Speck, Mark Storey, Lynda Pratt, Kenneth Curry, Adam Sisman, David V. Erdman, and Lewis Patton and Peter Mann. I would also like to offer profuse thanks to the contributors and editors of the *Oxford Dictionary of National Biography*.

Numerous conversations about the politics of emotion have shaped the research and writing of this book. I am very grateful to Barbara Rosenwein, who, during the course of her Humanitas Visiting Professorship in Historiography at Oxford, took time to discuss my intentions for the book, and offered invaluable suggestions. I am indebted to Laura Kirkley for reading over early drafts of the manuscript and offering constructive and encouraging comments, with very short notice! I owe thanks to William McCarthy for his idea about the identity of the elusive 'Mr. W.', the temporary object of Anna Beddoes' affections; and I am grateful to Sharon Ruston for pointing me in the direction of further exciting work about Anna; and to John Beddoes, who is in the midst of conducting that work himself. Deborah Cameron provided instrumental recommendations for reading on gender, emotion, language and the idea of it being 'good to talk'. Jackie Scott suggested sociological articles on the cultural construction of female desire. Molly Crockett clarified the effects of nitrous oxide on the brain, and Carol Bolton helped me to think about Southey and the sexual politics of pantisocracy. I am grateful to Caroline Criado-Perez for her enthusiasm about the subject of emotion and feminist politics, and for pointing me in the direction of articles that have been invaluable in the course of writing this book. And I owe thanks to Marina Strinkovsky for conversations about 'untranslatable emotions' and the nature of Russian *tocka*; and to Ruth Hanley for thought-provoking comments on attachment and regulation.

I want to offer heartfelt thanks to all the feminist friends who have provided support, analysis and insight during the course of writing this book, profoundly shaping my approach to feminism, class, politics and emotion. I am particularly indebted to Sarah Ditum, not only for valiantly reading the entire manuscript, but for her own wonderful writing: a model to which to aspire. Friends including Isla Rowland, Rebecca Linden, Andrew Spencer, Dominic Lash and much-loved and much-missed Josie

Camus provided welcome respite and support. And I am grateful to those who have caused their own revolution of feeling: my three children, Molly, Martha and Esme, to whom this book is dedicated. The experience of birthing and helping to raise them has precipitated in me not just an emotional revolution, but a political awakening, and revealed to me the entwined, inseparable nature of emotion and politics. So I must offer thanks, too, to everyone who has helped in the care of our children, enabling me to carve out space for research and writing: their grandparents, their carers at school and nursery, including Louisa Reinhardt, but most of all, to Pete Newbon, who has done more than his fair share of laundry, early mornings and bedtimes, and has offered love, support and emergency chicken curry.

ILLUSTRATION CREDITS

Attr. Jacques-Louis David, *The Tennis Court Oath*, 1790–1794,
   © Granger Historical Picture Archive/ Alamy Stock Photo
John Opie, *Mary Wollstonecraft*, oil paint on canvas, *c*.1790–91, © Tate
   Gallery, London
Sir Thomas Lawrence, *Thomas Holcroft and William Godwin*, pencil with
   black and red chalk, 1794, © National Portrait Gallery, London
John Opie, *Henry Fuseli*, oil on canvas, 1794, © National Portrait
   Gallery, London
Ellen Sharples, *Joseph Priestley*, pastel, *c*.1797, © National Portrait
   Gallery, London
Luigi Galvani, Experiments on the Sciatic Nerve of Frogs; First
   Detection of Galvanic Currents, from *Memorie sulla elettricita
   animale*, 1797, © Wellcome Library, London
Angelica Kauffman, *Monk from Calais*, oil on canvas, 1766–1781 (*c*.1780),
   © The State Hermitage Museum, St Petersburg
Sampson Towgood Roche, *Thomas Beddoes*, watercolour and
   bodycolour on ivory, 1794, © National Portrait Gallery, London
Artist unknown, *Tom Wedgwood*, from a chalk drawing belonging
   to Miss Wedgwood, of Leith Hill Place, frontispiece to R.B.
   Litchfield, *Tom Wedgwood: The First Photographer* (London:
   Duckworth and Co., 1903), p. ii. Image © Rachel Hewitt
Unattributed, *Burning of Dr. Priestley's House at Fairhill*, from Samuel
   Smiles, *Lives of the Engineers* (London: John Murray, 1861–62).
   Image © Mary Evans Picture Library
Horace Hone, *Richard Lovell Edgeworth*, watercolour and bodycolour
   on ivory, 1785, © National Portrait Gallery, London
Artist unknown, *Anna Maria Beddoes*, miniature, 1807. Image © John
   Beddoes. I am very grateful to John Beddoes for providing me
   with an image of this portrait, and permission to reproduce.

Adolphe and Émile Rouargue, *Tower of the Temple Prison during the French Revolution*, steel engraving, *c.*1845, © Roger-Viollet/ Topfoto

Robert Hancock, *Samuel Taylor Coleridge*, black, red and brown chalk and pencil, 1796, © National Portrait Gallery, London

Robert Hancock, *Robert Southey*, black, red and brown chalk and pencil, 1796, © National Portrait Gallery, London

Lieutenant Smith, *George Young and his Wife (Hannah Adams) of Pitcairns [sic] Island*, frontispiece to John Barrow, *Eventful History of the Mutiny and Piratical Seizure of HMS Bounty* (London: John Murray, 1831), © Reproduced by kind permission of the Syndics of Cambridge University Library (Hanson.e.10)

Thomas Beddoes and James Watt, Apparatus for Procuring Air, 1794–1796, from *Considerations on the Medical Use of Factitious Airs and on the Manner of Obtaining them in Large Quantities* (London: Johnson, 1794), part 2, facing page 32, © Wellcome Library, London

James Gillray, *The Prophet of the Hebrews*, hand–coloured etching, 5 March 1795, © The Trustees of the British Museum

James Gillray, *Copenhagen House*, hand-coloured etching, 16 November 1795, © National Portrait Gallery, London

Attr. George Cruikshank, *Talk of an Ostrich!*, hand-coloured etching, 13 December 1795, © The Trustees of the British Museum

James Gillray, *Scientific Researches!*, hand-coloured etching, 23 May 1802, © The Trustees of the British Museum

Bernard Picart, after Charles Le Brun, 'La Joie', from *Caracteres des Passions Gravés par Bernard Picart sur les Desseins de Mr. le Brun* (Amsterdam: 1713), p. 35, © Wellcome Library, London

Bernard Picart, after Charles Le Brun, 'L'esperence', from *Caracteres des Passions Gravés par Bernard Picart sur les Desseins de Mr. le Brun* (Amsterdam: 1713), p. 23, © Wellcome Library, London

Bernard Picart, after Charles Le Brun, 'Tristesse', from *Caracteres des Passions Gravés par Bernard Picart sur les Desseins de Mr. le Brun* (Amsterdam: 1713), p. 31, © Wellcome Library, London

Bernard Picart, after Charles Le Brun, 'Le Pleurer', from *Caracteres des Passions Gravés par Bernard Picart sur les Desseins de Mr. le Brun* (Amsterdam: 1713), p. 39, © Wellcome Library, London

Thomas Willis, Diagram showing the Brain and its Nerves, from *Cerebri Anatome: Cui Accessit Nervorum Descriptio et Usus* (Amsterdam: 1666), p. 222 © Wellcome Library, London

INDEX